D1609915

THE GENERAL LAW OF E.C. EXTERNAL RELATIONS

AUSTRALIA
LBC Information Services – Sydney

CANADA AND USA
Carswell – Toronto

NEW ZEALAND
Brooker's – Auckland

SINGAPORE AND MALAYSIA
Sweet & Maxwell Asia
Singapore and Kuala Lumpur

CENTRE FOR EUROPEAN LEGAL STUDIES (CELS) CAMBRIDGE

THE GENERAL LAW OF E.C. EXTERNAL RELATIONS

EDITED BY

Alan Dashwood

Professor of European Law, University of Cambridge
Fellow, Sidney Sussex College
of the Inner Temple, Barrister

AND

Christophe Hillion

Deputy Director, Centre for European Legal Studies, Cambridge

LONDON
SWEET & MAXWELL
2000

Published in 2000 by
Sweet & Maxwell Limited of
100 Avenue Road
London NW3 3PF
(http://www.sweetandmaxwell.co.uk)
Typeset by MFK Information Services Ltd, Stevenage, Herts.
Printed and bound in Great Britain by
MPG Books Ltd, Bodmin, Cornwall.

No natural forests were destroyed to make this product, only farmed timber was used
and replanted.

ISBN 0 421 590 70 X

A CIP catalogue record for this book is available from
the British Library

©
Sweet & Maxwell
2000

INTRODUCTION

The aim of this volume is to provide a re-examination in depth of the structural doctrines and principles of the law governing the European Community's external relations, and of relevant aspects of Community and Member State practice. The focus is on the powers expressly or implicitly conferred by the E.C. Treaty, allowing or requiring action to be taken in the international sphere through the Community institutions; and on the interplay between those powers and the external powers of the Member States, which remain subjects of international law in the fullest sense. The Common Foreign and Security Policy is touched upon only in so far may impinge on the theory and practice of E.C. external relations law.

The systematic elements of this branch of Community law are entirely judge-made. Therein lies the explanation of the division of the book into two Parts, the first entitled "Analysis" and the second "Synthesis". In Part I, the leading judicial authorities are examined individually and in detail. In our perception, Opinion 1/94 of the Court of Justice on the WTO Agreement constitutes a watershed between the "classic" case law, mainly of the 1970s, which was the subject of extravagant over-interpretation in some of the academic literature, and the more recent authorities which re-assert the applicability of the general principle of conferred powers, and clarify the subtle relationship between Community and Member State competence, in the external relations field. The reassessment of the older cases involves peeling away the accretion of sometimes fantastical commentary, to arrive at a clearer understanding of what the Court actually decided, and its reasons for doing so: while analysis of the cases from the 1990s is directed towards establishing whether they confirm the earlier ones (which, on a sober view of the latter, they generally do); or, if they represent a departure, why this should be happening. Part II attempts a restatement of E.C. external relations law under a series of broad themes. The aim here is to paint as complete a picture as possible of the general law as it stands, in light of the interaction between the Court's developing jurisprudence and successive amendments to the E.C. Treaty.

Underlying our approach, as reflected in the structure of chapters, are some fundamental distinctions. We distinguish, first and foremost, between two great questions of principle, which we designate, respectively, "the existence question" and "the exclusivity question". The *existence* question asks how the E.C. comes to be competent as an international actor, particularly in matters where the language of the Treaty suggests that authorisation is only being given to legislate internally: this is a question about the attribution of powers to the Community. The *exclusivity* question, which makes sense only once it has been acknowledged that the Community enjoys external relations competence in a certain matter, asks whether it follows from the existence of such competence that the Member States have lost the right to act autonomously: it is a question about the interplay between the powers of the E.C. and those of individual States. The two questions are logically distinct but are often hard to disentangle in the case law. Another important distinction is that between the *substantive* attribution of external relations competence (authorisation of the Community to do specified things), and the *procedural* attribution of such competence (the requirement that, in doing the things authorised, the Community act by specified legal means). We also distinguish *dedicated* external relations provisions, like Article 133 (ex. Article 113) on the common commercial policy, which concern specifically and primarily matters that bring the Community into a relationship with other international actors, and *extension* provisions, like Article 174 (4) (ex. Article 130r (4) on the environment, which authorise the Community to engage in international cooperation in areas where the main thrust of policy is towards internal activity. Those various distinctions are more fully discussed in Chapter 8, below.

It is our hope that, by imposing a tight conceptual structure, and by the clear editorial standpoint we have sketched out, sufficient coherence has been preserved, in spite of the collective nature of this work. The advantage of collective authorship is that it allows differing views to be presented on topics that remain fiercely controversial in both the academic and the political worlds.

Some of the papers that we include were originally given at a conference organised by the Centre for European Legal Studies (CELS) at Cambridge in December 1995, though they have since been revised. Other papers have been specifically commissioned. Papers which reflect the development of E.C. external relations law at a certain moment during the past decade are presented in the collection for their historical interest.

In common with other publications, we have been plagued by the change in the numbering of Articles of the E.C. Treaty and the TEU. Our normal convention is to give the amended numbering, followed by the "ex" numbering in brackets: *e.g.* Article 310 EC (ex. Article 238). However, in some instances where historical developments are being discussed, it seemed more logical to give the old numbering, with an indication as to how it has now altered. We crave our readers' indulgence for the rather messy outcome of these pragmatic decisions.

The present volume belongs to the series of publications reflecting the research activity of CELS. Our warm thanks are due to Diane Abraham, the Secretary/Administrator of CELS, for her expert help in the task of editing.

Alan Dashwood   Cambridge
Christophe Hillion   July 2000

TABLE OF CONTENTS

Introduction   v
Table of Cases   ix
Table of Abbreviations   xiv

PART I: ANALYSIS

Chapter 1   *The classic authorities revisited*
             By Alan Dashwood and Joni Heliskoski   3

Chapter 2   *Haegeman, Demirel and their progeny*
             By Ilona Cheyne   20

Chapter 3   *The Bangladesh and EDF Judgments*
             By Angela Ward   42

Chapter 4   *The WTO and OECD Opinions*
             By Takis Tridimas   48

Chapter 5   *Left to its own devices? Opinion 2/94 and the protection of
             Fundamental Rights in the European Union*
             By Anthony Arnull   61

Chapter 6   *Internal struggle for international presence: the exercise of
             voting rights within the FAO*
             By Joni Heliskoski   79

Chapter 7   *Fragmentation or evasion in the Community's development
             policy? The impact of* Portugal v. Council
             By Steve Peers   100

PART II: SYNTHESIS

A.   *E.C. External Competence*

Chapter 8   *The attribution of external relations competence*
             By Alan Dashwood   115

Chapter 9   *The WTO Opinion and implied external powers of the Com-
             munity: a hidden agenda?*
             By Nanette Neuwahl   139

Chapter 10   *The scope of the Common Commercial Policy post-Opinion
             1/94: clouds and silver linings*
             By Alec Burnside   152

Chapter 11   *E.C. frameworks of international relations: cooperation, part-
              nership, association*
              By Steve Peers   160

B.   **Community Competence and Member State Competence**

Chapter 12   *Exclusive, concurrent and shared competence*
              By David O'Keeffe   179

Chapter 13   *The European Union and mixed agreements*
              By Allan Rosas   200

Chapter 14   *The fourth pillar of the European Union after the Amsterdam
              Treaty*
              By Ramon Torrent   221

C.   **Implementation of International Agreements**

Chapter 15   *Organising joint participation of E.C. and Member States*
              By Christiaan Timmermans   239

Chapter 16   *The duty of cooperation: a flexible concept*
              By Stephen Hyett   248

Chapter 17   *International instruments as a source of Community Law*
              By Ilona Cheyne   254

D.   **E.C. External Relations in the Era of the Amsterdam Treaty**

Chapter 18   *E.C. External Relations Provisions Post-Amsterdam*
              By Alan Dashwood   279

Chapter 19   *Common strategies and the interface between E.C. external
              relations and the CFSP: lessons of the Partnership between the
              E.U. and Russia*
              By Christophe Hillion   287

Index   303

TABLE OF CASES

Acme Industry v. Council (Case T-48/96) October 12, 1999 . . . .   17.18
ADBHU (Case 240/83) [1985] E.C.R. 531. . . . .   7.09
Affish v. Rijksdienst voor de Keuring van Vee en Vlees (Case C-183/95) [1997] E.C.R.
    I-4315. . . . .   2.22, 17.10, 17.14, 17.15, 17.16
Ahlstrom v. Commission (Woodpulp I) (Joined Cases 89, 104, 114, 116, 117, 125–29/
    85) [1988] E.C.R. 5193. . . . .   11.17
Amministrazione delle Finanze dello Stato Chiquita Italia (Case 469/93) [1995] E.C.R.
    I-4533. . . . .   2.20, 2.25, 17.04, 17.07, 17.15
Antonissen (Case C-292/89) [1991] E.C.R. I-745 . . . .   6.09
Atlanta AG and Others v. Council and Commission (Case C-104/97P) October 14,
    1999 . . . .   17.18

Bosphorus Hava Yollari AS v. Minister for Transport, Energy and Communications
    (Case C-84/95) [1996] 1 E.C.R. 2253; [1996] 3 C.M.L.R. 257. . . . .   2.21, 17.12
Bozkurt v. Staatssecretaris Van Justitie (Case C-434/93) [1995] E.C.R. I-1475. . . . . . .   2.15
Bresciani (Case 87/75) [1976] E.C.R. 129; [1976] 2 C.M.L.R. 62. . . . . .   2.06, 2.07, 2.20, 2.25,
    13.09, 17.07, 17.15
Brother Industries Ltd v. Council (Case 56/85) [1990] 1 C.M.L.R. 792 . . . .   17.15
Bulk Oil (Zug) v. Sun International (Case C-174/84) [1986] E.C.R. 559 . . . .   17.06
Burgoa (Case 812/79) [1980] E.C.R. 2787; [1981] 2 C.M.L.R. 193 . . . .   17.01

Canon v. Council (Cases 277 and 300/85) [1989] 1 C.M.L.R. 915 . . . .   17.15
Chappell Series A, No. 152, (1990) 12 E.H.R.R. 1 . . . .   5.07
Commission v. BASF (Case C-137/92P) [1994] E.C.R. I-2555 . . . .   17.14
Commission v. Council (Case 16/88) [1989] E.C.R. 3457 . . . .   18.06
Commission v. Council (Case 22/70) [1971] E.C.R. 263. . . .   1.01, 1.02, 1.05, 1.06, 1.07, 1.08,
    1.10, 1.11, 1.13, 1.14, 1.15, 1.18, 1.19,
    1.20, 1.21, 3.03, 4.08, 4.11, 6.01, 6.07,
    6.08, 6.09, 6.12, 8.01, 8.03, 8.06, 8.13,
    8.14, 8.15, 8.17, 8.19, 8.20, 8.21, 8.22,
    9.03, 9.07, 9.10, 11.05, 12.02, 12.03,
    12.05, 12.06, 12.07, 12.08, 12.09, 12.13,
    12.16, 12.17, 12.19, 12.20, 12.21, 13.02,
    13.04, 13.14, 14.08, 15.01, 18.02
Commission v. Council (Case C-25/94) [1996] E.C.R. I-1469. . . .   4.12, 6.02, 6.03, 6.05, 6.07,
    12.19, 13.02, 13.08, 13.13, 15.04, 15.09
Commission v. Council (Case 45/86) [1987] E.C.R. 1493; (1988) 2 C.M.L. Rev.. .   5.10, 7.02,
    8.04, 9.07, 11.10
Commission v. Council (Commodity Coding) (Case 165/87) [1988] E.C.R. 5545;
    (1990) 1 C.M.L. Rev.. . . . .   9.07
Commission v. Council (Case C-170/96) [1998] E.C.R. I-2763. .   3.02, 3.05, 3.06, 7.10, 17.02,
    19.11
Commission v. Council (Case 242/87) [1989] E.C.R. 1425 . . . .   5.10
Commission v. Council (Case 275/87) [1989] E.C.R. 259 . . . .   9.07
Commission v. Germany (Re International Dairy Agreement) (Case C-61/94) [1996] 1
    E.C.R. 3603; [1997] 1 C.M.L.R. 281. . . . .   2.20, 17.09, 17.10, 17.11, 17.12
Commission v. Germany (Case C-431/92) [1995] E.C.R. I-2189 . . . .   9.02
Commission v. Greece (FYROM Sanctions) (Case C-120/94) [1996] E.C.R. I-1513. .   7.04
Commission v. Ireland (Case 61/77) [1978] E.C.R. 417. . . . .   6.01
Commission v. Italy (Case 10/61) [1962] E.C.R. 1; [1962] C.M.L.R. 187 . . . .   17.01

ix

Commission v. U.K. (Case 804/79) [1981] E.C.R. 1045. . 1.11, 6.01, 12.03, 12.04, 12.16, 12.19
Costa v. ENEL (Case 6/64) [1964] E.C.R. 585. . . . . 6.01, 12.02

Delimitis v. Henniger Brau AG (Case C-234/89) [1991] E.C.R. I-935; [1992] 5
    C.M.L.R. 210 . . . . 6.12
Demirel v. Stadt Schwäbisch Gmünd (Case 12/86) [1987] E.C.R. 3719; 1 C.M.L.R.
    421. . . . . 2.01, 2.11, 2.12, 2.14, 2.15, 2.16,
                                                        2.17, 2.21, 2.24, 2.25, 11.09, 11.11,
                                                        11.12, 13.01, 13.02, 13.09, 13.10, 13.11,
                                                        17.02, 17.04, 17.06, 18.06, 19.02
Dürbeck (Case-112/80) [1981] E.C.R. 1095, [1982] 3 C.M.L.R. 314. . . . . 2.11
Deutsche Shell v. HZA Hamburg-Harburg (Case C-188/91) [1993] E.C.R. I-363. . . . . 2.17,
                                                        2.24, 17.04, 18.05

Ebony Maritime SA v. Prefetto della Provincia di Brindisi (Case C-177/95) [1997] 2
    C.M.L.R. 24 . . . . 17.12
Eker v. Land Baden-Württemberg ny (Case C-386/95) unreported 2.15
Epicheiriseon Metalleftikon Viomichanikon Kai Naftiliakon v. Council (Case
    C-121/86) [1989] E.C.R. 3919 . . . . 17.06
Eroglu v. Land Baden Württemberg (Case C-355/93) [1994] E.C.R. I-5113. . . . . 2.15, 18.05
ERT (Case C-290/89) [1991] E.C.R. I-2925. . . . . 5.02, 5.11
European Parliament v. Council (Case C-316/91) [1994] E.C.R. I-625. . . . . 3.01, 3.05, 3.06,
                                                        14.04, 15.07
European Parliament v. Council (Case C-360/93) [1996] E.C.R. I-1195. . . . . 10.11
European Parliament v. Council and Commission, (Joined Cases C-181/91 and C-248/
    91) [1993] E.C.R. I-3685. . . . . 3.01, 3.02, 3.03, 3.04, 3.05, 3.06, 12.10

Factortame and Others (Case C-221/89) [1991] E.C.R. I-3905 . . . . 6.02
Fediol v. Commission (Case 70/87) [1989] E.C.R. 1781; [1991] 2 C.M.L.R. 489. . . 2.13, 2.14,
                                                        2.16, 2.17, 2.18, 2.19, 17.07,
                                                        17.10, 17.18
Fediol v. Commission (Case 187/85) [1988] E.C.R. 4155 . . . . 2.21
Fediol v. Commission (Case 191/82) [1983] E.C.R. 2913 . . . . 17.06
Fediol v. Commission (Case 188/85) [1988] E.C.R. 4193 . . . . 17.13
Ferchimex v. Council (Case T-164/94) [1995] E.C.R. II-2681 . . . . 17.06
France v. Commission (Case C-327/91) [1994] E.C.R. I-3641. . . . . 6.07, 6.09, 17.03
France v. Commission (Joined Cases 15 and 16/76) [1979] E.C.R. 321 . . . . 5.11
Funke v. France Series A, No. 256 (1993) 1 C.M.L. Rev. 5.08

Germany v. Commission (Case 24/62) [1963] E.C.R. 63; (1963) C.M.L. Rev. 347. . . . 9.07
Germany v. Council (Case C-122/95) [1998] E.C.R. I-973 . . . . 17.13
Germany v. Council (Case 280/93) [1994] E.C.R. I-4973. . 2.18, 2.19, 2.20, 7.02, 7.08, 17.06,
                                                        17.10, 17.13, 17.16, 17.17
Goldstar v. Council (Case C-105/90) [1992] 1 C.M.L.R. 996 . . . . 2.21
Grant v. South West Trains Ltd (Case C-249/96) [1998] 1 C.M.L.R. 5.13
Greece v. Commission (Case-30/88) [1989] E.C.R. 3711; [1991] 2 C.M.L.R. 169. . 2.14, 2.15,
                                                        2.24, 2.25, 17.04, 18.05
Günaydin v. Freistaat Bayern (Case C-36/96) [1998] 1 C.M.L.R. 871 . . . . 2.15

Haegeman (Case 181/73) [1974] E.C.R. 449; [1975] 1 C.M.L.R. 515. . . 2.04, 2.05, 2.06, 2.07,
                                                        2.09, 2.11, 2.12, 2.15, 2.18,
                                                        2.20, 2.21, 2.24, 13.09,
                                                        17.02, 17.03, 17.04, 17.06,
                                                        17.10, 18.06
Hallouzi Choho v. Bestuur van direct effect Sociale Verzekeringsbank ny (Case
    C-126/95) unreported 2.16
Handyside v. United Kingdom Series A, No. 24, 1 E.H.R.R. 737 . . . . 5.12
Hauer (Case 44/79) [1979] E.C.R. 3727; [1982] C.M.L.R. 42. . . . . 2.01

Hermes International v. FHT Marketing Choice (Case C-53/96) [1998] E.C.R.
    I-3603. . . . .   2.22, 2.23, 11.08, 13.02, 13.10, 13.11,
                            17.09, 17.10, 17.12, 17.14, 17.15, 17.18, 18.02
Hoesch AG v. Bergrohr GmbH (Case 142/88) [1989] E.C.R. 3413; [1991] 1 C.M.L.R.
    383. . . . . 2.17, 17.11
Hoechst v. Commission (Joined Cases 46/87 and 227/88) [1989] E.C.R. 2859. . . .   5.03, 5.07

Interfood v. Hauptzollamt Hamburg (Case-92/71) [1972] E.C.R. 231. . . . . 2.21, 17.12
International Fruit Company v. Produktschap voor Groenten en Fruit (Joined Cases
    21 to 24/72) [1972] E.C.R. 1219; [1975] 2 C.M.L.R. 1. . . . .   2.01, 2.02, 2.03, 2.04, 2.05,
                                2.06, 2.10, 2.11, 2.13, 2.14, 2.19,
                      2.25, 5.11, 17.02, 17.03, 17.07, 17.12, 17.18
Internationale Handelsgesellschaft (Case 11/70) [1970] E.C.R. 1125, [1972] C.M.L.R.
    255 . . . . 2.01
Irish Cement v. Commission (Joined Cases 166 & 200/86) [1988] E.C.R. 6473. . . . . .   6.07
Italy v. Council (Case 166/78) [1979] 2575. . . . .   6.09

Kadiman v. Freistaat Bayern (Case C-351/95) unreported 2.15
Kol v. Land Berlin (Case C-285/95) [1997] 3 C.M.L.R. 1175. . . . .   2.15
Kramer (Joined Cases 3, 4 and 6/76) Kramer [1976] E.C.R. 1279.   1.01, 1.08, 1.09, 1.10, 1.11,
                                1.12, 1.13, 1.14, 1.17, 4.11,
                                6.01, 6.11, 8.02, 8.17, 8.21,
                                8.22, 12.02, 12.13, 12.14,
                              12.16, 12.17, 12.20, 13.02,
                                13.04, 17.02, 17.03
Kupferberg (Case 104/81) [1982] E.C.R. 3641; [1983] 1 C.M.L.R. 1. . .   2.08, 2.09, 2.10, 2.11,
                                2.12, 2.13, 2.15, 2.17, 2.20,
                                2.23, 2.25, 17.04, 17.06,
                              17.09, 17.10, 17.11, 17.15,
                                      17.18
Kus v. Landeshauptstadt Wiesbaden (Case C-237/91) [1992] E.C.R. I-6781; [1993] 2
    C.M.L.R. 887. . . . . 2.15, 17.06, 18.05
Kziber (Case C-18/90) [1991] E.C.R. I-199. . . . . 2.16, 17.06

Legros (Case C-163/90) [1992] E.C.R. I-4625 . . . .   2.25
Leifer (Case C-83/94) [1995] E.C.R. I-3231. . . . .   2.21, 7.10, 11.10, 13.13, 17.02, 17.12
Luisi and Carbone v. Ministero del Tesora (Joined Cases 286/82 & 26/83) [1984]
    E.C.R. 377; (1985) 3 C.M.L. Rev. 52. . . . . 10.07
Luxembourg v. Parliament (Case 230/81) [1983] E.C.R. 255. . . . .   6.12, 16.04

Maclaine Watson v. Council and Commission (Case C-241/87) [1990] E.C.R. I-1797.   17.05
Matsushita v. Council (Case C-175/87) [1992] 3 C.M.L.R. 137. . . . . 2.21, 17.12
Medici Grim v. Council (Case T-7/99) June 29, 2000 . . . . 17.18
Meilicke v. ADV/ORGA (Case C-83/91) [1992] E.C.R. I-4871 . . . .   5.09
Metalsa (Case 312/91) [1994] 2 C.M.L.R. 121. . . . . 2.18, 2.25, 17.06
Ministero Delle Finanze v. Foods Import (Case C-38/95) [1997] 1 C.M.L.R. 1067 . . .   2.21
Mondiet v. Islais (Case C-405/92) [1993] E.C.R. I-6133 . . . .   6.11

Nakajima v. Council (Case C-69/89) [1991] E.C.R. I-2069. . . . .   2.16, 2.17, 2.18, 2.19, 17.06,
                                  17.07, 17.10, 17.18
Nashua Corp. v. Commission and Council (Case C-150/87) [1990] 2 C.M.L.R. 6 . . . .   17.15
Nederlandse Spoorwegen (Case 38/75) [1975] E.C.R. 1439, [1976] 1 C.M.L.R. 167 . .   2.05
Netherlands v. Council (Case C-58/94) [1996] E.C.R. I-2169; [1996] 2 C.M.L.R. 996 .   6.11
Niemietz v. Germany Series A, No. 251, (1993) 16 E.H.R.R. 97 . . . .   5.07
NMB (Deutschland) v. Commission (Case C-216/91) [1992] C.M.L.R. 80. . . . . . . 2.21, 17.12
NMB France Sarl v. Commission (Case T-162/94) [1997] 3 C.M.L.R. 164.   2.21, 17.06, 17.12
Nold v. Commission (Case 4/73) [1974] E.C.R. 491. . . . . 5.03, 5.11

O'Dwyer and Others v. EU Council (Cases T-466/93, T-469/93, T-473/93, T-474/93 &
    T-477/93) [1996] 2 C.M.L.R. 148. . . . . 17.06

Old (Case 4/73) [1974] E.C.R. 491, [1974] 2 C.M.L.R. 338 . . . .   2.01
Oleifici Italiani SpA v. EC Commission (Case T-267/94) [1998] 1 C.M.L.R. 692 . . . .   17.06
Opel Austria v. Council (Case T-115/94) [1997] 1 C.M.L.R. 733. . . . .   2.21, 2.24, 2.25, 17.04,
                                                                              17.06, 17.11
Open Door and Dublin Well Woman v. Ireland Series A, No. 246 (1993) 15 E.H.R.R.
    244 . . . .   5.08
Orkem v. Commission (Case 374/87) [1989] E.C.R. 3283 . . . .   5.08

Pabst & Richarz (Case 17/81) [1982] E.C.R. 1331; [1983] 3 C.M.L.R. 11. . .   2.01, 2.07, 2.11,
                                                                              2.16, 17.06
Parliament v. Council (Case C-271/94) [1996] E.C.R. I-1689 . . . .   5.10
Parliament v. Council (Case C-316/91 [1994] E.C.R. I-625. . . .   4.03, 6.09, 7.02, 12.12, 13.02,
                                                                              15.02, 17.07
Parliament v. Council (Case C-360/93) [1996] E.C.R. I-1195. . . . .   4.05, 12.19, 13.02
Parliament v. Council and Commission (Joined Cases C-181/91 & C-248/91) [1993]
    E.C.R. I-3685. . . . .   6.08, 12.18, 12.19, 12.21, 15.02, 19.04
Partie Ecologiste "Les Verts" v. Parliament (Case 294/83) [1986] E.C.R. 1339; [1987] 2
    C.M.L.R. 343. . . . .   17.02, 17.14
Polydor v. Harlequin Record Shops (Case 270/80) [1982] E.C.R. 329; [1982] 1
    C.M.L.R. 677. . . . .   2.01, 2.08, 2.25
Portugal v. Council (India Agreement) (Case C-268/94) [1996] E.C.R. I-6177. . .   5.12, 7.01,
                                                                 7.03, 7.04, 7.05, 7.06, 7.07, 7.08,
                                                                 7.09, 7.11, 11.06, 11.09, 11.10, 11.13,
                                                                 11.14, 11.15, 12.02, 12.18, 12.21, 13.02,
                                                                              13.04, 13.12, 13.13
Procureur de la Republique v. Bouhelier (Case C-225/78) [1979] E.R.C. 3151. .   2.25, 17.06

R. v. H.M. Treasury and Bank of England, ex p. Centro Com (Case C-124/95) [1997]
    E.C.R. I-81; [1997] 1 C.M.L.R. 555. . . . .   7.10, 10.11, 11.10, 11.14, 11.17, 13.02,
                                                                              13.13, 17.02
R. v. MAFF, ex p. Anastasiou (Case C-432/92) [1995] 1 C.M.L.R. 569 . . . .   17.06
Racke (Case C-162/96) [1998] E.C.R. I-3655. . . . .   7.04, 13.02, 13.06
Razanatsimba (Case 76/77) [1977] E.C.R. 2229 . . . .   13.09
Razanatsimba (Case C-65/77) [1977] E.C.R. 2229 . . . .   2.25
Rima Eletrometalurgia v. Council (Case C-216/91) *The Times*, January 27, 1994 . . .   2.21
Rush Portuguesa v. Office National d'immigration (Case C-113/89) [1990] E.C.R.
    I-1417; (1991) 3 C.M.L. Rev. 818 . . . .   10.08

Salamander AG and Others v. Parliament Council (Joined Cases T-172/98 & T-175/
    98) June 27, 2000. . . . .   5.16
Sat Fluggesellschaft mbH v. Eurocontrol (Case C-364/92) [1994] 5 C.M.L.R. 208 . . .   17.08
Schlüter (Case 9/73) [1973] E.C.R. 1135. . . . .   2.02, 2.03, 2.13
Sevince v. Staatssecretaris van Justitie (Case C-192/89) [1990] E.C.R. I-3461. . . .   2.14, 2.15,
                                                                 2.17, 2.24, 17.04, 17.06, 18.05
SFEI and Others v. Commission (Case T-77/95) [1997] E.C.R. 11-1 . . . .   5.11
Sharp v. Council (Case C-179/87) [1992] E.C.R. I-1635; [1992] 2 C.M.L.R. 415. .   2.21, 17.06,
                                                                              17.12
Simmenthal (Case 106/77) [1978] E.C.R. 1-629 . . . .   12.10
Singer (Case 290, 291/81) [1983] E.C.R. 847 . . . .   2.11
SIOT (Case 266/81) [1983] E.C.R. 731; [1984] 2 C.M.L.R. 231. . . . . .   2.11, 2.13, 2.17, 17.11
SNCF and B.R. v. Commission (Joined Cases T-79 and T-80/95) [1996] E.C.R. 11-1491   5.11
Society for the Protection of Unborn Children Ireland v. Grogan and Others (Case
    C-159/90) [1991] E.C.R. I-4685. . . . .   5.08
SPI and SAMI (Cases 267–9/81) [1983] E.C.R. 801; [1984] 1 C.M.L.R. 354.   2.11, 2.13, 2.15,
                                                                              17.09
Stanley Adams v. Commission (Case 53/84) [1985] E.C.R. 3651 . . . .   17.05
Stauder v. Ulm (Case 29/69) [1969] E.C.R. 419 . . . .   5.02

Timex v. Council and Commission (Case 264/82) [1985] E.C.R. 849 . . . .   17.06

T. Port GMBH v. Hauptzollamt Hamburg-Jonas (Cases 364–365/95) [1998] E.C.R.
     I-1023. . . . . 2.22, 17.10, 17.14, 17.15, 17.16

United Kingdom v. Council (Joined Cases C-51/89, C-90/89 & C-94/89) [1991] E.C.R.
     I-2757. . . . . 9.07, 12.15

Van Duyn (Case 41/74) [1974] E.C.R. 1337; [1975] 1 C.M.L.R. 1 . . . . 17.01
Van Gend en Loos (Case 26/62) [1963] E.C.R. 1; [1963] C.M.L.R. 105 . . . . 17.01
Vander Elst v. Office des Migrations Internationales (Case C-43/93) [1994] E.C.R.
     I-3803; (1995) 1 C.M.L. Rev. 513 . . . . 10.07

Wachauf v. Germany (Case 5/88) [1989] E.C.R. 2609 . . . . 5.03
Werner (Case C-70/94) [1995] E.C.R. I-3189. . . . . 2.21, 7.10, 11.10, 13.13, 17.02, 17.12

Zoubir Yousfi v. Belgium (Case C-58/93) [1994] E.C.R. I-1353. . . . . 2.16, 17.06
Zoulika Krid v. CNAVTS (Case C-103/94) [1995] E.C.R. I-719 . . . . 2.16
Zwartveld and Others (Case C-2/88) [1990] E.C.R. I-3365 . . . . 6.12

ABBREVIATIONS

ACP	:	Africa-Caribbean-Pacific
AETR	:	Accord Européen relatif au travail des équipages des véhicules effectuant des transports internationaux par route (also ERTA)
AG	:	Advocate-General
AJIL	:	American Journal of International Law
APEC	:	Asian-Pacific Economic Co-operation
ASEAN	:	Association of South-East Asia Nations
BISD	:	Basic Instruments and Selected Documents (GATT)
Bull EU	:	Bulletin of the European Union
CCP	:	Common Commercial Policy
CCT	:	Common Customs Tariff
CDE	:	Cahiers de Droit Européen
CEECs	:	Central and Eastern European Countries
CELS	:	Centre for European Legal Studies
CFI	:	Court of First Instance
CFSP	:	Common Foreign and Security Policy
COREPER	:	Comité des Représentants Permanents
CMLR	:	Common Market Law Reports
CMLRev	:	Common Market Law Review
CS	:	Common Strategy
CSCE	:	Conference on Security and Cooperation in Europe
EAs	:	Europe Agreements
EAEC	:	European Atomic Energy Community (also EURATOM)
EC	:	European Community
ECB	:	European Central Bank
ECHR	:	European Convention on Human Rights
ECJ	:	Court of Justice of the European Communities
ECR	:	European Court Reports
ECSC	:	European Coal and Steel Community
EDF	:	European Development Fund
EEA	:	European Economic Area
EEC	:	European Economic Community
EFA Rev	:	European Foreign Affairs Review
EFTA	:	European Free Trade Association
EHRR	:	European Human Rights Reports
EIIL	:	European Journal of International Law
ELI	:	European Law Journal
ELRev	:	European Law Review
EMAs	:	Euro-Mediterranean Agreements
EMU	:	Economic and Monetary Union
EP	:	European Parliament
EPC	:	European Political Co-operation

EU	:	European Union
FAO	:	Food and Agriculture organisation
FTA	:	Free Trade Area
FYROM	:	Former Yugoslav Republic of Macedonia
GATS	:	General Agreement on Trade in Services
GATT	:	General Agreement on Tariffs and Trade
GSP	:	Generalised System of Preferences
HL	:	House of Lords
ICLQ	:	International and Comparative Law Quarterly
IGC	:	Intergovernmental Conference
ILO	:	International Labour Organisation
IMF	:	International Monetary Fund
JHA	:	Co-operation in the fields of Justice and Home Affairs
LIEI	:	Legal Issues of European Integration
Mercosur	:	Mercado Común del Sur (Southern Common Market)
MFN	:	Most-favoured-nation treatment (GATT)
MJ	:	Maastricht Journal of European and Comparative Law
MLR	:	Modern Law Review
OECD	:	Organisation for Economic Cooperation and Development
OJLS	:	Oxford Journal of Legal Studies
OMC	:	Organisation Mondiale du Commerce (WTO)
OSCE	:	Organisation for Security and Co-operation in Europe
PCA	:	Partnership and Cooperation Agreement
PJCCM	:	Police and Judicial Cooperation in Criminal Matters
QMV	:	Qualified majority voting
RBDI	:	Revue Belge de Droit International
RMUE	:	Revue du Marché Unique Européen
RTDE	:	Revue Trimestrielle de Droit Européen
SEA	:	Single European Act
TEU	:	Treaty on European Union
TACIS	:	Technical Assistance for the Commonwealth of Independent States
TRIPS	:	Agreement on Trade-Related Aspects of Intellectual Property Rights
UNCED	:	United Nations Conference on Environment and Development
WTO	:	World Trade Organisation
YEL	:	Yearbook of European Law

PART I: ANALYSIS

PART 1: ANALYSIS

CHAPTER 1
The Classic Authorities Revisited

by

*Alan Dashwood and Joni Heliskoski**

SCOPE AND PURPOSES

1.01 This chapter offers a reappraisal of the classic authorities of the 1970s on the Community's implied external competence and on the circumstances in which the Community enjoys exclusive external comptence—*AETR*,[1] *Kramer*[2] and Opinion 1/76.[3] It also covers Opinion 2/91[4] which provided an opportunity for the Court of Justice to clarify a number of points much canvassed in the literature but on which the earlier authorities were, at best, equivocal. Between them, the four cases constitute the principal source of the rules governing this branch of Community law prior to the watershed, as it is commonly regarded, of the *WTO* Opinion of November 15, 1994.[5]

What, it may be asked, is there to gain, at this time of day, from once more going over such familiar ground, energetically mined by commentators for a good quarter of a century? Part of the answer lies in the sheer familiarity of the four cases—liable to breed, not contempt exactly, but a certain complacency as to our understanding of them. Very famous cases are liable to be read as if they were significant only for the few specific points on which they are repeatedly cited: *AETR*, for instance, is an even more interesting, and in some ways more puzzling, judgment than is usually recognised. Also, through repetition in the literature, which may even find an echo in jurisprudence, cases may come to be regarded as authorities on points which, on a close re-reading, they do not clearly decide: that is true of *Kramer*, and still more so of Opinion 1/76, on the issue of exclusive Community competence.

A further justification can be found in the mainly critical reaction to the way in which the issue of the EC's implied external competence was handled by the Court of Justice in the *WTO* Opinion. A widely held view is that, in ruling that the Community was not exclusively competent in the matters covered by the GATS and the TRIPS, thus opening the way for the conclusion of the WTO package as a mixed agreement, the Court retreated from previously held positions. The implication is that a more robust application of the existing case law would have brought a different result.[6] The present writers do not share that view. In our submission, the conceptual framework of EC

---

* Dr Joni Heliskoski is an official of the Ministry of Justice, Finland.
[1] Case 22/70, *Commission* v. *Council* [1971] E.C.R. 263.
[2] Joined Cases 3, 4 and 6/76, *Kramer* [1976] E.C.R. 1279.
[3] [1977] E.C.R. 741.
[4] [1993] E.C.R. I–1061.
[5] Opinion 1/94 [1994] E.C.R. I–5267.
[6] See, *e.g.* Bourgeois, "The EC in the WTO and Advisory Opinion 1/94: an Echternach Procession", 32 C.M.L.Rev. (1995) p. 763; De la Rochère, "L'ère des compétences partagées - à propos de l'étendue des compétences extérieures de la Communauté européenne", R.M.C.U.E. (1995) p. 461 and Geiger, "Der Vertragsschlußkompetenzen der Europäischen Gemeinschaft und auswärtige Gewalt der Mitgliedstaaten", 50 Juristen Zeitung (1995) p. 973.

external relations law, erected by the Court in the 1970s to organise and complement the meagre provisions of the original EEC Treaty, endures in its essentials: *WTO* and subsequent decisions have merely confirmed lessons which ought to have been learned earlier. Revisiting the classic authorities will provide a basis for judging who is right.

AETR: TWO PRINCIPLES OF IMPLICATION

Background and issues

1.02   The background to the *AETR* judgment is too well known to require much elaboration. The dispute was over arrangements for negotiating and concluding a revised version of the European Agreement concerning the work of crews of vehicles engaged in international road transport.[7] The subject-matter of the AETR fell within the scope of Council Regulation 543/69 on the harmonisation of certain social legislation relating to road transport, which had come into force on March 25, 1969.[8] Article 3 of the Regulation provided: "The Community shall enter into any negotiations with third countries which may prove necessary for the purpose of implementing this regulation". Nevertheless, the arrangements agreed by the Council on March 20, 1970 were on the footing that the revision of the AETR would be negotiated and concluded by the Member States. The legality of the Council's proceedings was attacked by the Commission before the Court of Justice, on the ground that competence in respect of the AETR now belonged exclusively to the Community.

The dispute raised a variety of important legal issues and the judgment of the Court is a rich source of jurisprudence. The present discussion is limited to the initial section of the judgment, where the Court was faced for the first time with the issue as to whether the Community could enter into international agreements without having been explicitly authorised by the Treaty to do so. The Commission had argued that treaty-making power in the field of transport came directly from the wording of Article 71 EC (ex Article 75) and that, while that competence was not, in itself, exclusive, it became so once it was exercised by the Community, through the enactment of common rules. On its side, the Council put forward what it evidently considered a knock-down argument: that "since the Community has only such powers as have been conferred on it, authority to enter into agreements with third countries cannot be assumed in the absence of an express provision in the Treaty"; and "Article [71] relates only to measures internal to the Community, and cannot be interpreted as authorising the conclusion of international agreements" (paragraphs 9–10). A pattern was thus set for future cases, the Commission's claim of exclusive competence for the Community putting in issue the logically prior matter of the existence of such competence.

Everyone knows the outcome: the Court of Justice upheld the Commission's view that, at the time of the contested Council proceedings, in principle the Community alone was competent to negotiate and conclude the AETR. However, the Court showed the flexibility which, Tridimas and Eeckhout have argued,[9] it not infrequently does, where the issue is one of respective Community and Member State competences not affecting the rights of individuals. It was held that, since the other parties to the revision of the AETR would have been disconcerted by the substitution, at a late stage in the negotiations, of the Community as sole party in place of individual Member States, the latter, in following the procedure laid down at the Council meeting of

---

[7] Hereinafter, "AETR". The Agreement, and hence the case, is best known by its French acronym.
[8] [1969] O.J. L77/49.
[9] Tridimas & Eeckhout, "The External Competence of the Community and the Case-Law of the Court of Justice: Principle versus Pragmatism", 14 Y.E.L. (1994) p. 143.

March 20, 1970, "acted, and continue to act, in the interest and on behalf of the Community in accordance with their obligations under Article [10][10] of the Treaty" (paragraph 90).

The AETR principle

1.03 The principle traditionally associated with the name of the *AETR* case appears in two versions, a few paragraphs apart, in the section of the judgment here under review. The first, and more frequently quoted, formulation is found in paragraphs 17–19:

> "In particular, each time the Community, with a view to implementing a common policy envisaged by the Treaty, adopts provisions laying down common rules, whatever form these may take, the Member States no longer have the right, acting individually or even collectively, to undertake obligations with third countries which affect those rules.
>
> As and when such common rules come into being, the Community alone is in a position to assume and carry out contractual obligations towards third countries affecting the whole sphere of application of the Community legal system.
>
> With regard to the implementation of the provisions of the Treaty the system of internal Community measures may not therefore be separated from that of external relations."

The other formulation, in paragraph 22, is in these terms:

> "... it follows that to the extent to which Community rules are promulgated for the attainment of the objectives of the Treaty, the Member States cannot, outside the framework of the Community institutions, assume obligations which might affect those rules or alter their scope".

The thrust of the two formulations is the same: treaty-making power becomes the sole prerogative of the Community, once measures have been adopted by the institutions pursuant to an objective authorised by the Treaty, in so far as the acceptance of international commitments by the Member States might interfere with the operation of those measures. There is, though, a significant difference of drafting: in paragraph 22 the phrase "Community rules" replaces "common rules" in paragraph 17, and there is no mention of "implementing a common policy". The impression that might have been given by the earlier paragraph, that the *AETR* principle is limited to cases where internal legislation has been enacted for the purposes of a common policy in the technical sense of the Treaty, was thus corrected by the judgment itself. On the other hand, there is no obvious reason for the phrase, "or alter their scope", at the end of paragraph 22, since this adds nothing to the notion of affecting enacted measures.

1.04 There are two points about the *AETR* principle, as originally stated and applied by the Court of Justice, it is important to underline, in order to aid understanding of the more recent case law.

First, the principle was treated by the Court as having a dual function. It may seem, on its face, to be about the circumstances that deprive the Member States of competence they previously enjoyed to act internationally in a certain matter, thereby rendering Community competence in the matter in question exclusive; and, indeed, the principle is so used in drawing out the consequences of the adoption of Regulation

---

[10] Ex Art. 5 EC.

543/69. However, that is only its secondary (almost incidental) function: as presented in the judgment, the principle serves, first and foremost, as a way of establishing the *existence* of Community competence. Logically, for that purpose it operates as a corollary of the primacy of Community law: if the Member States' competence is excluded, then the Community must be able to step into the breach.

The point is brought home by the position of paragraphs 17–19 in the judgment: they represent the final step in the Court's general justification of external Community competence in the absence of express attribution. The *AETR* principle is offered as a paradigm as to how "in a particular case the Community's authority to enter into international agreements" may be gathered from "the whole scheme of the Treaty". Similarly, in paragraph 22 the principle is used to establish the existence of treaty-making power for the Community in the particular field of transport.[11]

Secondly, the reasoning in *AETR* provides no warrant for extravagant theories to the effect that, once a given field of activity has been "occupied" by the enactment of a certain volume of internal legislation, external competence in respect of the whole field vests exclusively in the Community.[12] The reference in paragraph 17 to the possible effect, on *"those rules"*, of international commitments assumed by the Member States, which is repeated in paragraph 22, shows that the rationale of the principle is to avoid any adverse impact on the particular measures which have been adopted, and on them only. To be sure, paragraph 18 speaks of the Community's exclusive competence, following the adoption of common rules, as "affecting the whole sphere of application of the Community legal system": however, we take that merely as a rather obscure way of making the point that, in whatever field common rules may be enacted, corresponding external relations competence will arise.

Capacity distinguished from authority (competence)

1.05 The Court of Justice has received little credit for one of the major feats of the *AETR* judgment, namely the reconciliation, achieved in a few short paragraphs, between the constitutional principle of the attribution of powers and the availability to the Community of treaty-making power in cases where nothing is said about this by the Treaty provision constituting the legal basis for action in the policy area in question.

The starting point for the Court is its interpretation of Article 281 EC (ex Article 210) as a provision acknowledging the international legal capacity of the Community. All the Article actually says is: "The Community shall have legal personality". It seems, prima facie, to be about the status of the Community within the legal order created by the Treaty, not least because the following Article provides: "*In each of the Member States*, the Community shall enjoy the most extensive legal capacity accorded to legal persons under their laws ..." Nevertheless, owing to its being "placed at the head of Part Six of the Treaty, devoted to 'General and Final Provisions'", Article 281 EC was interpreted by the Court as meaning "that in its external relations the Community enjoys the capacity to establish contractual links with third countries over the whole field of objectives defined in Part One of the Treaty, which part Six supplements" (paragraph 14). The judgment is saying, in effect, that the Article must be read in a similar way to Article 6, second paragraph ECSC[13] and Article 101, first paragraph

---

[11] See also Dashwood, "Implied External Competence of the EC", in Koskenniemi, (ed.), *International Law Aspects of the European Union* (Kluwer Law International, The Hague 1998) p. 113 at p. 118.

[12] *cf.* the position adopted by the Commission in the Opinion 1/94 proceedings [1994] E.C.R. I–5267 at 5323–5324 (regarding GATS) and 5336–5337 (regarding TRIPS).

[13] Art. 6(2) ECSC reads: "In international relations, the Community shall enjoy the legal capacity it requires to perform its functions and attain its objectives."

EURATOM,[14] as a general acknowledgement that the Community may act internationally within the limits of the objectives set (and, it should be added in view of what follows, the powers conferred) by the Treaty.

1.06 Capacity, however, it is made clear, is not the same thing as "authority" (or competence) to enter into an international agreement in given circumstances. Article 281 EC does not, in other words, constitute, in itself, a general legal basis for international action by the Community. As interpreted by the Court, the Article merely provides a signal (of which the Community's international partners are entitled to take note) that the specific conferment of treaty-making powers may be looked for in power-conferring provisions throughout the Treaty.

That leads on to the reconciliation with the attribution principle. The Court does not dispute the contention of the Council that the Community may not act internationally without being specifically authorised to do so. Where it differs from the Council is in holding that "[S]uch authority arises not only from an express conferment by the Treaty—as is the case with Articles [133] and [former] 114[15] for tariff and trade agreements and with Article [310][16] for association agreements—but may equally flow from other provisions of the Treaty and from measures adopted, within the framework of those provisions, by the Community institutions" (paragraph 16). Some 25 years later, in Opinion 2/94, the Court would say that the principle of conferred powers (now enshrined in Article 5 (ex Article 3 b), first paragraph of the EC Treaty) "must be respected in both the internal and the international action of the Community"; but that "specific powers ... are not necessarily the express consequence of specific provisions of the Treaty but may also be implied from them".[17]

Both statements acknowledge that the attribution principle has to be complied with. The only difference between them is that in *AETR*, as distinct from Opinion 2/94, the existence of external competence is not explained as a function of the doctrine of implied powers.

The *effet utile* principle

1.07 A clear lesson of the *AETR* judgment is that external Community competence may arise, despite the lack of express conferment, in more than one way. The words "in particular", which introduce paragraph 17, are already an indication that the famous principle, based on the prior enactment of internal measures, is being provided by way of illustration, and there may be other possibilities.

That is confirmed, when the Court turns to the concrete issue of competence to conclude the AETR. A remarkable feature of this part of the judgment is that it reads as if separate versions had been written and then patched together rather untidily. That the apparent incoherence may perhaps have been due to a difference of opinion between the judges is a tempting, but for lawyers as opposed to political scientists, finally not a very interesting, speculation. What is genuinely interesting is that, intertwined with the strand of reasoning based on the *AETR* principle (and more particularly on the existence of internal legislation in the form of Regulation 543/69) there is a strand of reasoning based on the quite different principle of the *effet utile* of Article 71 EC (ex Article 75), which is more usually associated with Opinion 1/76.

1.08 The first strand of reasoning runs through paragraph 21, recalling the duty of

---

[14] Art. 101(1) EURATOM provides: "The Community may, within the limits of its powers and jurisdiction, enter into obligations by concluding agreements or contracts with a third State, an international organisation or a national of a third State."

[15] Ex Art. 113 EC; Art. 114 EC was repealed by the Maastricht Treaty.

[16] Ex Art. 238 EC.

[17] Opinion 2/94 [1996] E.C.R. I–1759 *regarding the accession by the Communities to the Convention for the Protection of Human Rights and Fundamental Freedoms*, paras. 24–25.

loyal cooperation which is laid on the Member States by Article 10, EC (ex Article 5), and through paragraph 22, which restates with the modifications noted above, the *AETR* principle as formulated in paragraph 17. In paragraphs 25 to 27 the second strand of reasoning becomes briefly dominant; but it then disappears again behind the first strand in paragraphs 28 to 30, where the invocation of Regulation 543/69 and its Article 3 leads to the conclusion, in paragraph 31, that:

> "These Community powers exclude the possibility of concurrent powers on the part of Member States, since any steps taken outside the framework of the Community institutions would be incompatible with the unity of the Common Market and the uniform application of Community law".

It is worth citing paragraphs 25–27 in full (together with the introductory paragraphs 23 and 24, which seem equally relevant to both strands of reasoning):

> "23. According to Article [70],[18] the objectives of the Treaty in matters of transport are to be pursued within the framework of a common policy.
> 24. With this in view, Article [71](1)[19] directs the Council to lay down common rules and, in addition, 'any other appropriate provisions'.
> 25. By the terms of subparagraph (a) of the same provision, those common rules are applicable 'to international transport to or from the territory of a Member State or passing across the territory of one or more Member States'.
> 26. This provision is equally concerned with transport from or to third countries, as regards that part of the journey which takes place on Community territory.
> 27. It thus assumes that the powers of the Community extend to relationships arising from international law, and hence involve the need in the sphere in question for agreements with the third countries concerned."

The approach being taken here has nothing to do with the previously adopted internal legislation: the existence of external competence is inferred from the language of Article 71 EC (ex Article 75) itself. The logic underlying the inference is that, in order to be effective, provisions of the kind contemplated by the Article may have to have an international, as well as a purely internal, aspect. If the objective is to regulate the parts of journeys taking place in third countries, then the Community must be authorised to enter into international agreements, as and when it may be useful to do so.

Why, having found unequivocally that Article 71, properly interpreted in the light of its *effet utile*, confers treaty-making power, should the Court have reverted so abruptly, in paragraph 28, to the argument that Regulation 543/69 "necessarily vested in the Community power to enter into any agreements with third countries relating to the subject-matter governed by that regulation"? Historically, the answer may be perfectly simple. In this first case on the international competence of the Community, the Court may have wished to take its stand on the surest possible ground, which was that provided by the Regulation: this was also an economical solution, explaining at the same time the existence of Community competence and its exclusivity. However, look-

---

[18] Ex Art. 74 EC.
[19] Ex Art. 75(1) EC.

ing ahead to future disputes in situations where no common rules had yet been adopted, the Court may also have wished to give an indication that competence could also arise in other ways.

At all events, the Court itself would now appear to regard the *AETR* case as authority for an interpretation of Article 71 EC that recognises the existence of international Community competence in the transport field, independently of the enactment of internal measures.[20] In the writers' submission, the case thus constitutes the original source not only of the principle that bears its name but also of the different principle of inference from the objectives for which powers have been conferred, which was subsequently applied in *Kramer*, though arguably in narrower terms, and was then authoritatively formulated in Opinion 1/76.

KRAMER: APPLICATION OF THE "COMPLEMENTARITY PRINCIPLE"

Background and issues

1.09   That, in the absence of express conferment, treaty-making power may be enjoyed by the Community in matters not covered by internal legislation may seem an obvious conclusion from paragraphs 25–27 of the *AETR* judgment read with the benefit of hindsight. It did not seem so at the time, and the point was in issue in the *Kramer* cases, which were decided by the Court in July 1976.

To cut the facts of *Kramer* to the barest essentials, the cases concerned the compatibility with Community law of provisions adopted in the Netherlands to implement recommendations on quotas and certain other fisheries conservation measures, which had been issued pursuant to the North-East Atlantic Fisheries Convention. References had been made to the Court of Justice under Article 234 (ex Article 177) of the EC Treaty by Dutch District Courts in criminal proceedings brought against fishermen who were accused of having infringed the rules enacted by the Netherlands. The defendants had argued that only the Community was competent to adopt measures in the field of fisheries conservation and that the national measures were incompatible with the Community's rules on the fishing industry. By their questions to the Court of Justice, the national courts accordingly asked, in the first place, whether the Community alone had authority to enter into commitments such as those resulting from the Convention.

In responding to that question, the Court separated (as it had not done in *AETR*) the issue of the existence of Community competence to conclude the Convention from that of the exclusivity of such competence.

"Complementary" external competence

1.10   The Court reiterated, in paragraphs 17–20 of its judgment, the general arguments in paragraphs 13–16 of *AETR* providing a justification for the recognition of external Community competence in the absence of express conferment. One difference is that treaty-making power is said, for the first time, to flow *implicitly* from other provisions of the EC Treaty, from the 1972 Act of Accession[21] (mentioned because of its provisions on fisheries) and from acts of the institutions.

There follows a review by the Court of the variety of Community provisions, contained in Treaties or in legislation, that relate directly or indirectly to fisheries conservation. The Court noted, finally, Article 102 of the 1972 Act of Accession requiring the

---

[20]   See Opinion 1/94 [1994] E.C.R. I–5267, para. 76.
[21]   [1972] O.J. Spec. Ed. 14.

Council to determine, from the sixth year after accession at the latest, "conditions for fishing with a view to ensuring protection of the fishing grounds and conservation of the biological resources of the sea" (paragraph 29).

On the issue of the existence of international Community competence for fisheries conservation, the kernel of the judgment is in paragraphs 30–33. The main steps in the reasoning of the Court are as follows: "the Community has at its disposal, on the internal level, the power to take any measures for the conservation of the biological resources of the sea …"; its legislative competence must be understood to cover fishing on the high seas (this, it is said, follows not only from the relevant texts but "from the very nature of things"); conservation can only be effectively and equitably ensured "through a system of rules binding on all the States concerned, including non-member countries"; thus "… it follows from the very duties and powers which Community law has established and assigned to the institutions of the Community *on the internal level* that the Community has authority to enter into international commitments for the conservation of the resources of the sea" (emphasis added).

Here, as in paragraphs 25 to 27 of the *AETR* judgment, the logic is that of the *effet utile* of the texts authorising action by the Community. There is, however, a subtle difference between the two passages. The paragraphs from *AETR* do not put any particular emphasis on the Community's *internal* competence. The impression given is that the "common rules" and "other appropriate provisions" mentioned in Article 71 (1) EC (ex Article 75 (1)) can be laid down, as required, either by Community legislation or through the conclusion of international agreements. Article 71 (ex Article 75) is not, in other words, treated as a provision which refers expressly to internal measures, and to international measures only by implication. By contrast, in *Kramer*, the reasoning is that texts explicitly conferring competence "on the internal level" must, on grounds of equity and effectiveness, be read as impliedly conferring treaty-making power. The external competence of the Community is seen merely as a necessary complement of its internal competence. This "principle of complementarity", as we propose to call it, would be spelt out as an easily quotable formula some eight months later in Opinion 1/76.

Member States' transitional competence

1.11 The *Kramer* judgment is also commonly regarded as a leading authority on the exclusivity of the Community's external competence, arising from the very nature of the activity in question, independently of the exercise of the corresponding internal competence (and thus of the *AETR* principle).

That is, indeed, the view the Court of Justice takes of competence in the matter of fisheries conservation: as it subsequently explained in Opinion 1/94: " … the restriction, by means of internal legislative measures, of fishing on the high seas by vessels flying the flag of a Member State would hardly be effective if the same restrictions were not to apply to vessels flying the flag of a non-member country bordering on the same seas". The underlying principle was there expressed by the Court, perhaps rather crudely, as being that "internal powers can only be effectively exercised at the same time as external powers": the two sorts of competence are "inextricably linked".[22] However, the relevant authorities belong to a later period than *Kramer*, after the end of the six-year transition allowed by Article 102 of the Act of Accession.[23]

What the Court held in the *Kramer* case itself was that, at the time when the matters before the national courts arose, a system of fisheries conservation at Community level

---

[22] [1994] E.C.R. I–5267, paras. 85–86.
[23] See Case 804/79 *Commission* v. *United Kingdom* [1981] E.C.R. 1045, paras. 17 *et seq.*

was not yet in place, and the Member States, therefore, remained competent to assume commitments within the framework of the NEAFC. This was not a straightforward application of the *AETR* principle, however. The Court made clear that the powers of the Member States in the conservation field were "of a transitional nature": they would come to an end six years after the 1973 Accession, by which time the Council was required to have enacted the relevant legislation. Meanwhile, the Member States participating in the Convention were not free agents: they were under a duty not to enter into any commitments which could bind the Community in carrying out the tasks entrusted to it by Article 102; and they were also bound to proceed, within the Fisheries Commission established under the Convention, "by common action" (paragraphs 39–45).

OPINION 1/76: COMPLEMENTARITY AS A GENERAL PRINCIPLE

Background and issues

1.12 Even after the *Kramer* judgments, doubts seemed to linger as to whether the Community would enjoy international competence in the absence of either express conferment or the adoption of common rules that were liable to be affected: fisheries conservation was, after all, a somewhat special case. In finally quenching such doubts, and doing so in terms that implied a general principle was being laid down, Opinion 1/76 marked a decisive step in the development of the Community's external relations law.

The subject of the request for an Opinion under Article 300(6) EC (then Article 228(1) EEC) was a draft Agreement establishing a European laying-up fund for inland waterway vessels. The proposed scheme was designed to eliminate disturbances arising from surplus carrying capacity for goods by inland waterway in the Rhine and Moselle basins. It would not have been possible fully to attain that objective through autonomous Community rules, because of the traditional participation in the trade of barges from Switzerland. The scheme was thus to be based on an international agreement, with Switzerland as a party.

The main reason for the request to the Court of Justice was to test the compatibility with the EEC Treaty of various detailed arrangements under the draft Agreement, which would have entailed, in particular, the creation of organs with far-reaching executive and judicial powers. In the event, the Court found in those arrangements elements which could not be reconciled with the system of the Treaty.

However, for our purposes, the interest of the Opinion lies in the few paragraphs that deal with issues going to the competence of the Community to conclude the draft Agreement, and to the lawfulness of the participation alongside the Community of six of the Member States, in their individual capacities.

A general principle of implication

1.13 The legal basis for action by the Community in matters of transport by inland waterway is Article 71 EC (ex Article 75) which, *AETR* had shown, could be used for the conclusion of international agreements.[24] The Court of Justice was asked, however, to confirm that it was open to the Community to conclude the draft Agreement, without having first laid down internal measures relating to the proposed scheme.

Unlike in the *AETR* and *Kramer* cases, there was no dispute as to the competence of

---

[24] The fact that both *AETR* and Opinion 1/76 concern the same legal basis, *i.e.* Art. 71 EC (ex Art. 75), seems often to go unnoticed.

the Community to undertake international commitments in the field covered by the draft Agreement. However, the respective submissions of the Commission and the Council revealed yet again the two competing principles present in the *AETR* judgment: whereas the Commission argued that Article 71 as such confers on the Community power to enter into agreements in the sphere of common transport policy, the Council raised the issue whether the conclusion of the Agreement should be considered a measure taken in direct implementation of that Article (interpretation in the light of its *effet utile*) or pursuant to exclusive international competence resulting from the existence of hypothetical common rules laid down in application of the Treaty ("virtual" application of the *AETR* principle).

The Court's response, in paragraphs 3 and 4 of the Opinion, is couched in terms of a statement of general principle:

> "The power of the Community to conclude such an agreement is not expressly laid down in the Treaty. However, the Court has already had occasion to state … that authority to enter into international commitments may not only arise from an express attribution by the Treaty, but equally may flow implicitly from its provisions. The Court has concluded *inter alia* that whenever Community law has created for the institutions of the Community powers within its internal system for the purpose of attaining a specific objective, the Community has authority to enter into the international commitments necessary for the attainment of that objective even in the absence of an express provision in that connexion.
>
> This is particularly so in all cases in which internal power has already been used in order to adopt measures which come within the attainment of common policies. It is, however, not limited to that eventuality. Although the internal Community measures are only adopted when the international agreement is concluded and made enforceable, as is envisaged in the present case by the proposal for a regulation to be submitted to the Council by the Commission, the power to bind the Community *vis-à-vis* third countries nevertheless flows by implication from the provisions of the Treaty creating the internal power and in so far as the participation of the Community in the international agreement is, as here, necessary for the attainment of one of the objectives of the Community".

1.14   The principle encapsulated in those paragraphs is the one applied by the court in *Kramer*. Treaty-making power, it is said, "flows by implication from the provisions of the Treaty creating the internal power". The implication can be drawn because the possibility of entering into international agreements is seen as necessary for the attainment of the particular objective for the purposes of which "Community law has created for the institutions of the Community powers within its internal system". The Court is not saying, as it seemed to be in *AETR*, that Article 71 EC authorises the use of all appropriate means, including acceptance of international commitments, in pursuing the action which is contemplated. The external competence implicitly conferred by the legal basis in question is here treated as being in a real sense *ancillary to the expressly conferred internal competence*: it is recognised only in so far as the latter may appear insufficient to achieve the specified objective in an optimal way.[25]

To call this, as most commentators do, the principle of "parallelism" or of "parallel competence"[26] seems misleading. Things which are parallel, it has been pointed out,

---

[25] The difference in the operation of implication in *AETR* on the one hand and in *Kramer* and Opinion 1/76 on the other will be discussed more extensively in chapter 8.

[26] See *e.g.* Groux, "Le parallélisme des compétences internes et externes de la Communauté économique européenne", 32(2) C.D.E. (1978) p. 1.

run alongside each other without ever meeting: manifestly that does not convey the relationship between express internal and implied external competence, as explained in the quoted passage. The logic of that relationship is more accurately indicated by the name, "principle of complementarity", suggested in our discussion of the *Kramer* judgment.

As to the scope of the principle formulated in Opinion 1/76, two points are worth making. First, the words "*inter alia*" show that the Court is not foreclosing on other possibilities (*e.g.* acquisition of external competence pursuant to the *AETR* principle). Secondly, however, the formulation is sufficiently general to be taken as an expression of the normal basis on which the Community may be found to have external competence in the absence of explicit conferment. There is no language in paragraphs 3 or 4 tending to limit the implication of external competence to exceptional situations like that which gave rise to Opinion 1/76, where the particular measures it was proposed to take on the internal level would not work effectively unless they were combined with measures on the international level. As we shall see, in Opinion 2/91 the Court of Justice cited paragraph 3 as a passage containing a statement of general principle; and it did so again more recently, in Opinion 2/94.[27]

The exclusivity issue

1.15 The widely held view,[28] apparently shared by the Court of Justice, that Community competence in the matter of establishing a laying-up fund was exclusive, seems puzzling to us. As others have observed,[29] such a view sits uncomfortably with the notion that the competence conferred on the Community by Article 71 EC (ex Article 75) is non-exclusive. In Opinion 1/94 the Court stated, in the plainest terms possible, that "even in the field of transport, the Community's exclusive external competence does not automatically flow from its power to lay down rules at internal level".[30] Citing *AETR*, the Court went on: "the Member States, whether acting individually or collectively, only lose their right to assume obligations with non-member countries as and when common rules which could be affected by those obligations come into being". Since it is axiomatic that, in the circumstances of Opinion 1/76, common rules capable of being "affected" were not yet in existence, there is no clear reason why the problem of over-capacity could not have been the subject of an agreement between the Member States concerned and Switzerland. The fact that internal and external measures were "inextricably linked"[31] fails to carry conviction here, as a justification of exclusivity: measures of both kinds could surely have been taken at the national level.

The source of the misconception is, presumably, the discussion in paragraphs 6 and 7 of the Opinion relating to the individual participation in the draft Agreement of the six Member States that were parties to either the revised Convention of Mannheim for the Navigation of the Rhine or the Convention of Luxembourg on the Canalisation of the Moselle. This arrangement, the Court said, was explained and justified by the undertaking given by the six Member States, in Article 3 of the draft Agreement, to make any amendments to the earlier Conventions necessitated by the proposed scheme. The Court continued:

"...The participation of these States in the Agreement must be considered as

---

27 [1996] E.C.R. I–1759, para. 26 and see also Dashwood, *loc. cit.*, p. 120.
28 See, *e.g.*, Pescatore, "External Relations in the Case Law of the Court of Justice of the European Communities", 16 C.M.L.Rev. (1979) p. 615 at p. 623.
29 Tridimas & Eeckhout, *loc. cit.*, p. 167.
30 [1994] E.C.R. I–5267, para. 77.
31 *ibid.*, para. 86.

being solely for this purpose and not as necessary for the attainment of other features of the system. In fact, under Article 4 of the Agreement, the enforceability of this measure and of the Statute extends to the territories of all the Member States including those who are not party to the agreement; it may therefore be said that, except for the special undertaking mentioned above, the legal effects of the agreement with regard to the Member States result, in accordance with Article 228(2) of the [EEC] Treaty, exclusively from the conclusion of the latter by the Community. In these circumstances, the participation of the six Member States as contracting parties to the Agreement is not such as to encroach on the external power of the Community. There is therefore no occasion to conclude that this aspect of the draft Agreement is incompatible with the Treaty."

Does the Court's reasoning in that passage imply that competence to conclude the draft Agreement belonged, in principle, exclusively to the Community? The writers think not, because the possibility of acting under Member State powers rather than under Community powers was simply not in issue. The decision had been taken, and was uncontested, that the draft Agreement would be concluded, and internal implementing measures be subsequently taken, by the Community itself acting pursuant to Article 71 (ex Article 75). The issue considered by the Court in the quoted passage is whether having the six Member States as individual parties to the draft Agreement *together with the Community* would encroach on the latter's external competence; and the answer given by the Court clearly indicates that there would be such encroachment, were it not for the special justification provided by the undertaking to amend certain provisions of the Mannheim and Luxembourg Conventions.

The position of the Court expressed in the quoted passage can, perhaps, best be explained as a reverse application of the *AETR* principle. For the Member States, the actual exercise of the Community's external competence has the same implications as the exercise of its internal competence: they are precluded from acting autonomously under their own external (or, indeed, internal) powers, where this could affect the common rules introduced into the Community order through the conclusion of an international agreement. So understood, Opinion 1/76 would be an authority as to the circumstances in which the simultaneous exercise of Community and Member State powers for the purpose of concluding an international agreement is impermissible; but not as to the circumstances which preclude external action by the Member States *as an alternative* to action by the Community.[32]

OPINION 2/91: RESTATEMENT AND REFINEMENT OF GENERAL PRINCIPLES

Background and issues

1.16   After Opinion 1/76, the implied external competence of the Community was

---

[32] On the other hand, Opinion 1/76 provides no authority for the view of Tridimas and Eeckhout (*loc. cit.*, pp. 174–177) that Member States' participation in an international agreement should be ruled out if the agreement comes within the Community's competence and the Community decides to conclude it. In our submission, a distinction should in this respect be made between the Community's exclusive and non-exclusive external competence. If an agreement falls only in part within the Community's exclusive competence, the Community institutions (in practice, the Council) are perfectly entitled to refrain from using the Community's non-exclusive competence with regard to the other parts of the agreement, which will then have to be concluded under national powers. In that case, the agreement would be a mixed one.

only to be in issue again before the Court of Justice in Opinion 2/91 on the Convention covering safety in the use of chemicals at work, which had been drawn up within the framework of the International Labour Organisation (hereinafter, "Convention No. 170").

In its request under Article 300(6) EC (then Article 228(1) EEC), the Commission sought a ruling by the Court on the competence of the Community to conclude Convention No. 170 and on the consequences this would have for the Member States. A peculiar feature of the proceedings was that the Convention was open only to ratification by the Members of the ILO, whereas the Community had merely been granted observer status in the Organisation. However, procedures had been created to allow the exercise of Community competences within the ILO. As regards Convention No. 170, the Commission considered that the Community's competence was exclusive, a view contested by the Council and by several national delegations.

Doubts as to the admissibility of the request for an opinion had been raised by the German and Netherlands Governments, on the ground that the procedure provided for by Article 228(1) EEC was only available in cases where the Community itself could be a party to the envisaged agreement. The objection was dismissed by the Court of Justice, which recalled that it was possible under the procedure "to consider all questions concerning the compatibility with the provisions of the Treaty of an agreement envisaged and in particular the question whether the Community has the power to enter into that agreement" (paragraph 3). The Commission's request was solely concerned with the respective competences of the Community and the Member States within the area covered by Convention No. 170. It was not for the Court to assess any obstacles the Community might encounter in exercising its competence because of the constitutional rules of the ILO.

On the substance of the request, the Court concluded that the subject matter of Convention No. 170 fell in its entirety within the competence of the Community; however, except in certain matters covered by internal legislation of such a nature as to produce an *AETR* effect, that competence was shared with the Member States. In such cases, there was an obligation on the Community and national authorities to cooperate closely in negotiating and concluding the agreement in question, as well as in implementing the resulting commitments.

A particular virtue of Opinion 2/91 is the sharp separation in the Court's reasoning between the issue of the existence of Community competence and that of the exclusivity or otherwise of such competence. The relevant rules of law are set out almost in textbook fashion. The Opinion leaves no room for doubt that external competence arising by implication under the principle we are calling "the principle of complementarity" may very well co-exist with Member State competence in the same matter. Indeed, a pattern is here set, in which the Court's rather liberal approach to the criteria of implied attribution is matched by considerable reluctance to recognise the exclusivity of competence thus established.

Issues going to the existence of competence

1.17   Illumination is provided by the Opinion more particularly on two points.

First, as to the generality of the principle of complementarity formulated in paragraph 3 of Opinion 1/76. The principle is cited in a context which shows the intention of the Court to disconnect it from the unusual circumstances of both Opinion 1/76 and, previously, *Kramer*. Paragraph 3 is evidently to be taken as an expression of the normal (though not necessarily the only) way in which external competence may arise for the Community in the absence of explicit attribution.

Secondly, as to the meaning of the "necessity" criterion in the principle. The object of Convention No. 170 (to prevent or reduce the incidence of chemically induced illnesses and injuries at work) was found to lie within the Community's "internal legislative competence in the area of social policy" (more precisely, the power of the Council, pursuant to Article 138 EC (ex Article 118a), to lay down minimum health and safety requirements for workers); and that was taken as sufficient to enable the Community to be a party to the Convention (paragraphs 16–17). The Court, it seems, does not understand "necessary" as meaning "indispensable" to attain the objective for which competence to legislate internally has been granted. Health and safety standards such as those prescribed by Convention No. 170 could just as well have been introduced through autonomous Community measures enacted under Article 138 EC or some other relevant legal basis (as, indeed, they largely had been). On the other hand, it may be argued, possession of treaty-making power by the Community facilitates the adoption of such measures: for instance, the raising of minimum standards for Community workers may prove more easily acceptable if the possibility exists of negotiating a similar improvement in third countries, thereby countering so-called "social dumping". The test applied in practice by the Court may, we suggest, be formulated thus: does the Community need treaty-making power to ensure the optimal use, over time, of its expressly conferred internal competence?

However, it is important to be clear that external competence can only arise under the principle of complementarity in respect of the precise objective the internal competence is designed to serve: in the case of Article 138, that would be the improvement of the working environment, especially as regards health and safety, for workers in the Community. In the Opinion 1/94 proceedings the Commission made the mistake of claiming competence for the Community to conclude the GATS under the Articles of the EC Treaty relating to establishment and the provision of services. That, as the Court held, was plainly wrong, because the legal bases relied upon are ones with specifically internal market objectives. No implication could be drawn, from provisions about facilitating freedom of movement between the Member States, as to competence to conclude an international agreement on the liberalisation of establishment and services between the Community and third countries.[33]

Issues going to exclusivity

1.18   The Court identified two possible grounds on which the competence of the Community in a certain matter falls to be regarded as exclusive (paragraphs 8–9).

One such ground is that the Treaty provision endowing the Community with the competence in question itself excludes any concurrent Member State competence, whether internal or external. The only examples mentioned are Article 133 EC (ex Article 113) on external trade and Article 102 of the 1972 Act of Accession on fisheries conservation, indicating the exceptional character of such "pre-emptive exclusivity". Neither of those provisions, it may be noted, refers in so many words to the exclusivity

---

[33] [1994] E.C.R. I–5267, para. 81. See however, paras. 90 *et seq.* where the Court first explains that "it does not follow that the Community institutions are prohibited from using the powers conferred on them in [the field of establishment and provision of services] in order to specify the treatment which is to be accorded to nationals of non-member countries" and then goes on to mention numerous acts of the Council in that regard. The Court concludes that "[w]henever the Community has included in its internal legislative acts provisions relating to nationals of non-member countries or expressly conferred on its institutions powers to negotiate with non-member countries, it acquires exclusive external competence in the sphere of those acts" (para. 95). One possible explanation may be found in the ancillary nature of the external clauses incorporated in the internal legislative acts, see Dashwood, *loc. cit.*, p. 122: the provisions in question are always linked to rules applicable to the nationals of the Member States. See further Chap. 8.

of the competence conferred: this must be an inference drawn by the Court from the very nature of the envisaged activity.

The other ground is that the Community institutions have adopted "measures of such a kind as to deprive the Member States of an area of competence which they were able to exercise previously on a transitional basis". This, of course, is the *AETR* effect. Interestingly, the Court cites paragraph 22 of the judgment, rather than the more familiar paragraph 17.

It follows from what is said in the Opinion about those two grounds that, in cases where neither of them applies, the Member States remain competent to act internationally, despite the availability of Community competence relating to the same subject-matter. In such fields of "shared" competence, if it is envisaged to enter into an international agreement, there will be a political choice to be made (ultimately by the Council) between acting under the powers of the Member States or under those of the Community.

1.19 Another point clarified by Opinion 2/91 (though, as we have seen, it could have been gathered from a careful reading of *AETR*) was that the *AETR* principle cannot be restricted to instances where Community rules have been adopted within the framework of a "common policy". As the Court explained: "The Community's tasks and the objectives of the Treaty would also be compromised if Member States were able to enter into international commitments containing rules capable of affecting rules already adopted in areas falling outside common policies or of altering their scope" (paragraph 11).

Last but not least, Opinion 2/91 provided the earliest example of a situation where previously adopted internal legislation did not have the effect of rendering Community competence exclusive in respect of provisions of an international agreement covering the same ground. This was the case, in so far as the relevant EC rules and those embodied in Convention No. 170 were designed to impose only minimum standards: logically, there could be no conflict between the two sets of rules, hence no "effect" within the meaning of the *AETR* judgment. In the words of the Court:

> "If, on the one hand, the Community decides to adopt rules which are less stringent than those set out in an ILO convention, Member States may, in accordance with Article [138](3), adopt more stringent measures for the protection of working conditions or apply for that purpose the provisions of the relevant ILO convention. If, on the other hand, the Community decides to adopt more stringent measures than those provided for under an ILO convention, there is nothing to prevent the full application of Community law by the Member States under Article 19(8) of the ILO Constitution, which allows Members to adopt more stringent measures than those provided for in conventions or recommendations adopted by that organization" (paragraph 18).

In such a situation, where international commitments undertaken by the Member States may happily co-exist with Community rules, the *AETR* principle will not be available to serve either of its functions, as a source of implied competence or of exclusivity. In the absence of express conferment, competence can only then arise, as here, through the operation of the principle of complementarity.

CONCLUSION

1.20 The main points of law, as to the implied external competence of the Community and the circumstances where the Community enjoys exclusive competence, which result, in our view, from the four leading cases reviewed in this chapter, are summarised below.

(a) *The Community has general international capacity within the limits of the objectives set for it, and of the powers conferred on it, by the Treaty.*

That is the effect of Article 281 EC (ex Article 210), as interpreted by the Court of Justice. The Article does not, however, constitute a legal basis for international action in particular circumstances.

(b) *The Community may act in the sphere of external relations, more particularly by entering into international agreements, only where it has been authorised to do so. Such authorisation, however, need not be given expressly: it may arise by implication from the system of the EC Treaty, or from provisions prima facie creating competence to act by way of internal legislation.*

The Court apparently concedes that the principle of the attribution of powers has a double aspect: authorisation must be given both to pursue a given objective (substantive attribution) and to do so by specified means (procedural attribution).[34] However, the latter requirement can be satisfied through recourse to the doctrine of implied powers.

(c) *There are two possible grounds on which, in the absence of express conferment, external Community competence may arise:*

　(i) **either,** *pursuant to the AETR principle, where Community rules have been enacted and their operation might be affected if the Member States were free to accept international commitments in relation to the same subject-matter;*

　(ii) **or,** *pursuant to the complementarity principle as formulated in Opinion 1/76 and further clarified in Opinion 2/91, where external competence is needed to maximise chances of attaining the objective for which competence, exercisable within the Community order, has been explicitly created.*

Though the logic of implication differs under the two principles, in both cases the Community's internal competence in the matter in question is treated as primary and its external competence as ancillary: the latter arises in order either to prevent interference with measures already taken pursuant to the former, or to ensure its fully effective exercise in the future. That relationship between expressly conferred internal competence and implied external competence was less evident in *AETR*, where the Court seemed simply to interpret Article 71 EC (ex Article 75) as authorising whatever kind of action might be appropriate.

(d) *There are two possible grounds on which Community competence, where it exists, must be regarded as exclusive:*

　(i) **either,** *the activity authorised by the relevant legal basis is one which, by its very nature, precludes concurrent action by the Member States, if it is to be successfully undertaken;*

---

[34] On the distinction between "substantive" and "procedural" attribution, see further chapter 8.

(ii) **or,** *pursuant to the AETR principle.*

The first case, which we call "pre-emptive exclusivity" is very much the exception. To the examples given by the Court in Opinion 2/91 (external trade and fisheries conservation) should, presumably, be added monetary policy so far as concerns participants in the single currency. Normally, however, it is the *AETR* principle that brings exclusivity. Member States continue to enjoy concurrent competence, unless and until the Community has acted in the matter in question; and they may not forfeit competence even then, if their acceptance of international commitments would carry no real risk of conflict with the measures taken under Community powers.

(e) Where the Community's exclusive competence extends to only part of an envisaged agreement, and it is decided that the Member States will conclude, under their own powers, the part of the agreement in respect of which competence is shared, there must be close cooperation, at every stage, between the national and the Community authorities.

This represents the Court's answer to commentators who take an exaggerated view of the problems created by "mixed" agreements. It is clear from what the Court said in Opinion 2/91 that there is no obligation to act internationally on the basis of non-exclusive Community powers, where these exist. The only requirement is to take sensible steps in presenting a united front to international partners.

It will be for readers of the succeeding chapters to assess to what extent the more recent authorities may have modified the law as stated here.

CHAPTER 2

Haegeman, Demirel and their Progeny

by

Ilona Cheyne*

INTRODUCTION

2.01   In 1972, the European Court of Justice indicated that an international agreement could prevail over Community acts or secondary legislation.[1] Since that date, there has been a growing body of case law in which the relationship between international agreements and Community law has been gradually explored against a background of intense academic commentary.[2] While some questions have been answered in the course of this case law, others remain open. That this should be the case reflects the complexity of the problems that inevitably arise from awarding legal status to external agreements, both in specific disputes and in the broader constitutional context.

Once the fundamental principle was established that international agreements were capable of being interpreted and applied in Community law, the appropriateness of judicial review over the executive institutions' actions in the field of external relations and the constitutional basis of the Court's jurisdiction might not have been seriously questioned. However, the debate over the Court's persistent denial of direct applica-

---

*   Senior Lecturer, Newcastle Law School. I would like to thank Ian Mabbut and David Milroy for their assistance in the preparation of this chapter, and Alison Dunn for her helpful comments on an earlier draft.
[1]   Cases 21–24/72 *International Fruit Company* [1972] E.C.R. 1219, [1975] 2 C.M.L.R. 1, para. 28.
[2]   See, for example, Bebr, "Agreements Concluded by the Community and Their Possible Direct Effect" (1983) 20 C.M.L.Rev. 35; Bourgeois, "Effects of International Agreements in European Community Law: Are the Dice Cast?" (1984) 82 Michigan Law Review 1250; Castillo de la Torre, "The Status of GATT in EEC Law" [1992] 26 J.W.T. 53; Castillo de la Torre, "The Status of GATT in EC Law, Revisited" [1995] 29 J.W.T. 53; Cheyne, "International Agreements and the European Community Legal System" (1994) 19 E.L.Rev. 581; Eeckhout, "The Domestic Legal Status of the WTO Agreement: Interconnecting Legal Systems" (1997) 34 C.M.L.Rev. 11; Ehlermann, "Application of GATT Rules in the European Community" in Hilf, Jacobs and Petersmann, *The European Community and GATT* (1986), p. 127; Everling, "The Law of the External Economic Relations of the European Community" in Hilf, Jacobs and Petersmann, *The European Community and GATT* (1986), p. 85; Lee and Kennedy, "The Potential Direct Effect of GATT 1994 in European Community Law" (1996) 30 J.W.T. 67; Maresceau, "The GATT in the Case-Law of the European Court of Justice" in Hilf, Jacobs and Petersmann, *The European Community and GATT* (1986), p. 107; Meessen, "The Application of Rules of Public International Law Within Community Law" (1976) C.M.L.Rev. 335; Pescatore, "External Relations in the Case-law of the Court of Justice of the European Communities" (1979) 16 C.M.L.Rev. 615; Petersmann, "Application of GATT by the Court of Justice of the European Communities" (1983) 20 C.M.L.Rev. 397; Petersmann, "The EEC as a GATT Member— Legal Conflicts Between GATT Law and European Community Law" in Hilf, Jacobs and Petersmann, *The European Community and GATT* (1986), p. 23; Schermers, "The Direct Application of Treaties with Third States: Note Concerning the *Polydor* and *Pabst* Cases" (1982) 19 C.M.L.Rev. 563; Völker, "The Direct Effect of International Agreements in the Community's Legal Order" (1983) 1 L.I.E.I. 131; Waelbroeck, "Effect of GATT within the Legal Order of the EEC" [1974] 8 J.W.T.L 614.

bility to the GATT has raised important questions as to where the boundaries lie between Community law proper, international law, and the political institutions' power to conduct external relations. Like Sherlock Holmes' dog that did not bark, the non-applicability of the GATT has given us the greatest clues. The increasing legalisation and institutionalisation of the GATT principles within the framework of the World Trade Organisation (WTO) will also challenge the Court to clarify the basis on which it distinguishes between international agreements which have direct applicability and those that do not.

The purpose of this chapter is to review the development of the Court's approach to the applicability of international agreements in Community law.[3] In a group of cases stretching from *International Fruit*[4] in 1972 to *Demirel*[5] in 1987, which will be referred to as the "early cases", the Court developed a relatively settled jurisprudence. These early cases will be examined first; the later case law will then be examined in order to determine how the jurisprudence has developed and what issues remain to be solved.

THE EARLY CASES

2.02 In *International Fruit*, the Court was asked to determine, *inter alia*, whether the Court's jurisdiction to consider the validity of Community legislation under Article 234 EC (ex Article 177) extended to international law, and whether Community regulations concerning the import of apples were invalid because they were contrary to Article XI of the GATT. The Court stated that the wording of Article 234 required that no limits be placed on the Court's jurisdiction to consider the validity of acts of the institutions of the Community.[6] Rather, it should consider all grounds relevant to validity and these necessarily included the possible effects of international agreements.[7] The Court therefore asserted its jurisdiction to consider international agreements on the grounds that they bind the Community,[8] and it was expressed in the broadest possible form. It was also apparent that a conflict between an international agreement and a Community act or piece of secondary legislation would be resolved in favour of the former.[9]

The Court did not consider precisely whether the provisions of the GATT were generally applicable as a matter of Community law but, as might be expected where the matter had been referred to it under Article 177, went directly to consider whether the

---

[3] Emphasis will be laid on international agreements related to commercial policy. The large number of cases concerned with human rights will not be considered because they derive their inspiration from national and Community laws as well as from international law. See, for example, Case 11/70 *Internationale Handelsgesellschaft* [1970] E.C.R. 1125, [1972] C.M.L.R. 255; Case 44/79 *Hauer* [1979] E.C.R. 3727; [1982] C.M.L.R. 42; Case 4/73 *Old* [1974] E.C.R. 491, [1974] 2 C.M.L.R. 338.
[4] Above p. 20, n. 1
[5] Case 12/86 [1987] E.C.R. 3719, [1989] 1 C.M.L.R. 421.
[6] Cases 21–4/72 [1972] E.C.R. 1219, [1975] C.M.L.R. 1, para. 5.
[7] *ibid.*, para. 6.
[8] The Community had become a *de facto* party to the GATT by virtue of the institutions' assumption of the relevant functions, the conferral of powers to the Community by the Member States, Community practice and the recognition of the other parties, see *ibid.*, paras. 14–18.
[9] *ibid.*, para. 28. This was implicit in the Court's judgment, but stated clearly by Advocate General Mayras in his opinion. And see Meessen, above, p. 20, n. 2, at pp. 498–500.

GATT could be invoked by individuals.[10] In order to answer that question, the Court examined "the spirit, the general scheme and the terms" of the GATT.[11] In a phrase which the Court has consistently used throughout its case law on the applicability of GATT provisions in Community law, it referred to its "great flexibility of provisions", particularly in relation to its emphasis on negotiation and consultation in the settlement of disputes, and the right of parties to act unilaterally in cases of disagreement or economic difficulty.[12] The Court's examination of the spirit, scheme and terms of the GATT was therefore focused on the question of its degree of legal formalism, and the emphasis on political interpretation and application of its provisions was sufficient to prevent its judicial application. As a consequence, the Court considered that the GATT did not, and was not intended to, confer rights upon individuals which they could invoke before a court of law.[13] It repeated this reasoning in *Schlüter*[14] in order to deny direct effect to Article II of the GATT although, in that case, the duty in question was still given effect because it had been incorporated into Community law in the Common Customs Tariff.[15]

2.03   It can be noted here, in the light of more recent cases, that the Court's rather general examination of "the spirit, general scheme and terms" had in fact elided two tests: first, whether the nature of the international agreement as a whole meant that it was capable of being directly applied and second, whether the provision in question was sufficiently clear and unconditional for it to be judicially applicable.[16] In *International Fruit* and *Schlüter*, the Court emphasised the former test by identifying the lack of legal formalism in which specific provisions of the GATT were to be implemented and disputes over their interpretation and application resolved. It did not comment on the precision or unconditionality of the specific provision in question.[17] Thus, it was clear that the precision and unconditionality of a particular provision was not the only, or indeed the key, issue and that the nature of the agreement itself could be sufficient to exclude direct applicability.

This reasoning was met by considerable academic criticism both because it appeared to impugn the legal nature of the GATT and because it was an unsatisfactory legal test, being both broad and uncertain.[18] The term "flexibility" was particularly problematic. Most international agreements have their own dispute settlement procedures which,

---

[10] The term *direct applicability* will be used separately from *direct effect*. The former refers to the general question of whether an agreement can be applied as a matter of Community law, while the latter refers only to the right of an individual to rely before a national court, *i.e.* under Article 234. For a discussion of the distinction between these two concepts and the importance of that distinction in the application of international agreements, see Bebr, above, p. 20, n. 2 at p. 46; Bourgeois, above, p. 20, n. 2 at p. 1261; Castillo de la Torre (1992), above, p. 20, n. 2 at p. 36; Cheyne, above, p. 20, n. 2 at p. 590; Maresceau, above, p. 20, n. 2 at p. 116; Meessen, above, p. 20, n. 2, at pp. 495–496. The Court of Justice itself tends to use the terms interchangeably and in Community law there is very little difference in their meaning, see Hartley, *The Foundations of European Community Law* (3rd ed. 1994), at pp. 205–7.

[11] Cases 21–4/72 [1972] E.C.R. 1219, [1975] C.M.L.R. 1, para. 20.

[12] *ibid.*, para. 21.

[13] *ibid.*, para. 27. Bebr supports this finding on the grounds that different rules should apply to the question of direct effect with regard to international agreements than in Community law. Above, p. 20, n. 2 at pp. 36–8. Other writers have been critical of this reasoning, for example, Petersmann (1986), above, p. 20, n. 2 at pp. 58–9; Waelbroeck, above, p. 20, n. 2.

[14] Case 9/73 [1973] E.C.R. 1135.

[15] The question of incorporation has become a crucial factor in determining the applicability of the GATT, see below.

[16] The existence of two separate tests was for some time disguised by emphasis on the question of direct effect, *i.e.* whether the agreement could be said to have conferred rights upon individuals. See above, p. xx, n. 13, and Cheyne, above, p. 20, n. 2.

[17] The provisions in both cases, namely Articles XI and II, are as clear and unconditional as one might wish for.

[18] See, for example, Petersmann (1986), above, p. 20, n. 2 at pp. 58–9; Maresceau, above, p. 20, n. 2 at pp. 120–1; Petersmann (1983), above, p. 20, n. 2 at pp. 424–437; Cheyne, above, p. 20, n. 2 at pp. 591–2.

inevitably in the context of international law, include negotiations and consultations. Safeguard provisions and rights of derogation are also common. Thus, unless the Court of Justice was in practice going to exclude the direct applicability of all international agreements, the "flexibility" test was necessarily one of degree. The question was how that degree was to be measured and where the line was to be drawn.

2.04 The approach of the Court in *International Fruit* was therefore not conclusive. However, the approach employed in the next case, while apparently more precise, also gave rise to difficulties. In *Haegeman*,[19] the Court was asked to apply the provisions of an association agreement between the EEC and Greece (the Athens Agreement). It began by stating that international agreements concluded under Articles 300 and 310 EC (then Articles 228 and 238 EEC) formed "an integral part of Community law".[20] Thus, they not only fell within the Court's jurisdiction to consider, but the substantive provisions contained within those agreements also became a matter of Community law. This approach appeared to extend the legal effect of international agreements in Community law. In *International Fruit*, they could be used as a background against which legality or validity of general measures might be judged. *Haegeman*, on the other hand, made it clear that they could be interpreted and applied as if they were enacted as Community law.

The *Haegeman* dictum appeared to be extremely sweeping. It avoided using the test that the Court had previously applied in the case of the GATT, namely an examination of "the spirit, general scheme and terms" of the agreement. Interpretation of the international agreement in question was accordingly conducted on the basis that it now constituted Community law *qua* Community law, and the nature and purpose of the agreement appeared to be irrelevant to the question of whether it had acquired this status. To the extent that the Court did consider the purpose of the agreement, it did so in order to interpret the provision in context and not to consider whether it was the kind of international agreement to which it was appropriate to grant direct effect.[21]

2.05 Thus it appeared that the GATT, which had been adopted informally by the Community, attracted a different approach from that to be applied to treaties formally concluded under Article 300 and 310. This impression was at least partly reinforced by the fact that in *Nederlandse Spoorwegen*,[22] a case heard after *Haegeman*, the Court merely said that the Community had replaced the Member States with regard to commitments under the GATT and therefore it was up to the Community authorities to decide how to implement the GATT, no longer the Member States.[23] In other words, it was made clear that compliance with the GATT was a matter of Community law, but without any reference to it becoming an integral part of Community law which might have implied the possibility of detailed application.

At this point, it appeared that the tests applied to the GATT in *International Fruit* and to the Athens Agreement in *Haegeman* were different, and that the latter test appeared to be only a matter of whether the agreement had been formally adopted.[24]

---

[19] Case 181/73 [1974] E.C.R. 449, [1975] 1 C.M.L.R. 515.

[20] *ibid.*, para. 5.

[21] Case 181/73 [1974] E.C.R. 449, [1975] I.C.M.L.R. 515, paras. 10–21.

[22] Case 38/75 [1975] E.C.R. 1439, [1976] 1 C.M.L.R. 167.

[23] *ibid.*, paras 15–16. The Court had previously found that the GATT was binding on the Community to the extent that the Community had assumed the relevant powers previously exercised by the Member States, see *International Fruit*. Cases 21–24/72 [1972] E.C.R. 1219, [1975] 2 C.M.L.R. 1 para.18.

[24] Commentators have been divided on this point. Bebr argues that the form of conclusion is not important, above, p. 20, n. 2 at pp. 39–41; Völker believes that it is, thus denying that the GATT is an integral part of Community law, above, p. 20, n. 2 at pp. 133–4, 142–3. For a critical view of the Court's approach, see Hartley, "The European Court, Judicial Objectivity and the Constitution of the European Union" (1996) 112 L.Q.R. 95, and see, against, Arnull, "The European Court and Judicial Objectivity: A Reply to Professor Hartley", 112 L.Q.R. (1996) p. 411.

The question thus arose as to whether an agreement with the degree of flexibility and negotiability of the GATT, but which was formally adopted by the Community, would also become an integral part of Community law. In other words, could the method of adoption become crucial to the question of direct applicability or would the Court still avoid giving direct applicability to a formally concluded agreement which it considered was inappropriate for judicial application? To put it yet another way, did the phrase "an integral part of Community law" mean that the test of the spirit or nature of the agreement had been satisfied, or avoided, by the act of formal conclusion and a provision which was clear and unconditional would necessarily be directly applicable?

2.06 This question was partially answered in *Bresciani*,[25] which concerned the possible application of an international agreement concluded under Article 300 EC (ex Article 228), namely the Yaoundé Convention. In this case, the Court indicated that mere formal adoption under the *Haegeman* dictum would not be enough to lead to direct applicability and that the nature of the agreement itself would still be relevant. It employed the same test as in *International Fruit*, namely an examination of the spirit, general scheme and wording of the treaty and of the provision.[26] The Court found that the agreement was capable of direct applicability, and had no difficulty in finding that the provision in question was clear and not subject to any reservations. As a result, it was capable of conferring rights on individuals within the Community which they could invoke before the courts.[27]

However, in examining the agreement as a whole, the Court did not make it clear what criteria it was looking for. It simply stated that the Yaoundé Convention provided for third countries to be given trading privileges with the Community in order to promote their development.[28] The Court in *Bresciani* therefore did little to elucidate its previous case law in this respect. It was evident that the purpose of the Convention was important in order to discover whether it was capable of having direct applicability but, beyond stating the fact that it was designed to promote the development of countries which had historically close ties with some of the Community Member States, no reasoned link was drawn.

2.07 No more explicit reasoning was given in *Pabst & Richarz*,[29] although the two elements of the test were clearly applied. The Court identified the purpose of the Athens Agreement[30] as preparing Greece for entry into the Community by, *inter alia*, establishing a customs union, harmonising agricultural policies and introducing free movement of workers.[31] No mention was made of the degree of legal formalism shown by the Athens Agreement, the Court appearing to assume that there was no problem that would block applicability as it had done in the case of the GATT. The contents of its objectives were apparently important for direct applicability but, as in *Bresciani*, no explicit reasoning was given as to the nature of the link. As to the clarity and unconditionality test, it found that the provision in question was one which contained "a clear and precise obligation which is not subject, in its implementation or effects, to the adoption of any subsequent measure".[32] It could therefore be given direct effect.

2.08 The Court took the opportunity to clarify its reasoning in the next case,

---

[25] Case 87/75 [1976] E.C.R. 129, [1976] 2 C.M.L.R. 62.
[26] *ibid.*, para. 16.
[27] *ibid.*, para. 25.
[28] *ibid.*, paras. 17, 18 and 22. The Court took the view that an imbalance in the parties' obligations did not prevent it from being directly applicable. Although this was clearly stated, the question has never entirely been resolved. See below.
[29] Case 17/81 [1982] E.C.R. 1331, [1983] 3 C.M.L.R. 11.
[30] This was the association agreement between the EEC and Greece which had previously been considered in *Haegeman*. Case 181/73 [1974] E.C.R. 449, [1975] 1 C.M.L.R. 515.
[31] Case 17/81 [1982] E.C.R. 1331, [1983] 3 C.M.L.R. 11, para. 26.
[32] *ibid.*, para. 27.

Kupferberg,[33] which involved another association agreement, the Brussels Agreement between the EEC and Portugal. It found that the Agreement was capable of direct applicability and that the provision was sufficiently unconditional to have direct effect.[34]

The Court made several pronouncements as to why international agreements fell within the ambit of Community law. First, it pointed out that international agreements concluded with third countries were binding upon the Community and upon the Member States under Article 300 (ex Article 228).[35] Consequently, the Court stated, "it is incumbent upon the Community institutions, as well as upon the Member States to ensure compliance with the obligations arising from such agreements".[36] That duty to ensure compliance might fall upon either the Community institutions or the Member States, depending on the state of relevant Community law at the time.[37] In addition, the Court classified the duty resting on Member States as being held not just to third countries, but as an obligation to the Community itself "also and above all".[38] The Community had assumed responsibility for the fulfilment of the international agreement with the third country, and this was the reason why the agreement formed "an integral part of the Community legal system".[39] Since the provisions of an international agreement binding upon the Community were an integral part of Community legal system, their effect within Community law could not be allowed to vary according to whether the responsibility for fulfilling them lay with the Community institutions or the Member States.[40] In particular, if responsibility lay with the Member States, it could not depend on the individual rules of each national legal system as to what effect the provisions of the international agreement would have. It was up to the Court of Justice to ensure uniform application throughout the Community, "within the framework of its jurisdiction in interpreting the provisions of agreements".[41]

2.09   Although, on the face of it, the Court's remarks might suggest that the Community itself had an obligation under Community law to comply with international law, the better interpretation appears to be that the Court was referring only to an obligation of Community law under which Member States were required to ensure that the Community was able to fulfil its legal obligations to third States. Thus the fact that international agreements were an integral part of Community law gave rise to a range of possible legal consequences. On the one hand, it was certainly possible that an agreement could constitute Community law and create rights that could be invoked by Member States and individuals. It was apparent from the GATT cases, however, that this would only occur when both parts of the two-stage test were satisfied. Whether Member States (or individuals) gained enforceable rights would depend, not on whether the agreement was binding upon the Community or whether it was formally or informally adopted, but on whether the nature of the agreement and the provisions in question were capable of conferring those rights. On the other hand, being an integral part of Community law would mean that Member States would always have a duty under Community law to enable the Community to fulfil its external obligations under   international   law   without   Member   States   necessarily   gaining   a

---

[33]   Case 104/81 [1982] E.C.R. 3641, [1983] 1 C.M.L.R. 1.
[34]   *ibid.*, para. 23.
[35]   *ibid.*, para. 11, referring to Art. 228(2), changed to Art. 228(7) by TEU and to Art. 300(7) by the Treaty of Amsterdam. The same point had been made in an earlier case, Case 270/80, *Polydor* [1982] E.C.R. 329, [1982] 1 C.M.L.R. 677, at para. 9.
[36]   Case 104/81 [1982] E.C.R. 3641, [1983] 1 C.M.L.R. 1, para. 11.
[37]   *ibid.*, para. 12.
[38]   *ibid.*, para. 13.
[39]   *ibid.* Note, this is a more general phrase than "Community law" as used in *Haegeman*.
[40]   Case 104/81 [1982] E.C.R. 3641, [1983] 1 C.M.L.R. 1, para. 14.
[41]   *ibid.*

substantive set of rights under international agreements which they were entitled to enforce against the Community. In this regard, it is noticeable that the Court made no mention of any reciprocal obligation to Member States on the part of the Community to comply with international agreements.

Thus, being "an integral part of the Community legal system" would mean that legal consequences would follow from the adoption of an international agreement, but that it would not necessarily be applicable as if it were a substantive piece of Community law. This is arguably reflected in the use of the phrase "Community legal system" in *Kupferberg* rather than "Community law" as in *Haegeman*, connoting a broader range of legal effects than simply being applied as if enacted Community law. This reading would mean that the effect of the *Haegeman* dictum would be much narrower than it had first appeared. For an international agreement to have a greater legal effect than merely ensuring that the Community was free to comply with it externally, the agreement would also have to satisfy a test of direct applicability in order to assess whether it was justiciable before the Court.

However, the Court acknowledged in *Kupferberg* that there would be some circumstances in which the question of direct applicability could be pre-empted by the executive institutions and that only if they were to fail to use this power would the Court be in a position to determine whether the agreement should be enforceable through judicial review.[42] Thus a specific intention expressed in the agreement itself would be decisive, and the primary right to decide would lie with the Community institutions negotiating and concluding the international agreement.[43] Although the Court did not say so, this power would necessarily be limited in so far as they attempted to exclude the Court's jurisdiction as provided for under the EC Treaty.[44]

2.10 The Court's reasoning in *Kupferberg* helped to clarify the significance of the nature and purpose of an agreement. It was evident that the clarity and unconditionality of the provision would be irrelevant if the agreement as a whole was found not to be appropriate for direct applicability.[45] It identified the criteria to be examined as, briefly, the distribution of powers in external relations, reciprocity governing free trade international agreements, the institutional framework for dispute settlement established by such agreements, and powers to derogate under those agreements.[46]

The Court was required to explore the question of what degree of "flexibility" would be sufficient to exclude direct applicability because the Brussels Agreement shared many of these characteristics with the GATT, but it did so cautiously and inconclusively. On the question of reciprocity, the Court of Justice stated that the mere fact that one party permitted direct application of the Agreement within their own legal system while the other did not was not "in itself" sufficient to constitute a lack of reciprocity in the implementation of the Agreement.[47] As to the existence of separate

---

[42] *ibid.*, para. 17. The Court acknowledged, and implicitly accepted, the argument put forward by the participating governments that the criteria for determining whether a provision of ordinary Community law should have direct effect should not apply *mutatis mutandis* to international agreements which had become part of Community law. See, for example, Bebr, above, p. 20, n. 2 at pp. 36–8; Bourgeois, above, p. 20, n. 2 at p. 1261; Cheyne, above, p. 20, n. 2 at pp. 593–4.

[43] Bourgeois points out that this approach has the policy advantage of putting the burden on the executive institutions to prevent direct applicability if they think it would be inappropriate, above, p. 20, n. 2 at pp. 1264–1265. Meessen suggests the question of direct applicability is a matter of international law under Article 228, which would also support emphasising the intention of the parties to the treaty, above, p. 20, n. 2 at pp. 493–497.

[44] See, for example, Opinion 1/91 [1991] E.C.R. I–6079.

[45] This reasoning was compatible with, and helped to clarify, the Court's findings in *International Fruit*, above, p. 20, n. 1, and has been applied consistently in subsequent cases concerned with the GATT.

[46] Case 104/81 [1982] E.C.R. 3641, [1983] 1 C.M.L.R. 1, para. 16.

[47] *ibid.*, para. 18. Bourgeois suggests that this issue might be relevant in the future, above, p. 20, n. 2 at p. 1265–6, and it has recently become a key argument concerning the potential direct applicability of the WTO Agreement, see discussion below.

institutions set up by the Agreement, a joint committee had the power to make recommendations on the interpretation and application of the Agreement and, where
specified, had powers to make decisions on those matters. The Court found that the
mere existence of such decision-making and dispute settlement institutions did not
preclude direct applicability, apparently because it did not prevent interpretation of
the international agreement *qua* Community law.[48] The Court also found that the
power to derogate from the Brussels Agreement did not automatically exclude its
direct application in Community law. In this case, the power only occurred in specific
circumstances and usually only after consideration by the joint committee; the Court
suggested that in this case it would only affect the question of direct applicability
within Community law in matters where the power to derogate specifically existed.[49]
Since none of these elements disqualified the Agreement as they had the GATT, it was
therefore capable of having direct applicability.

It should be noted that all the reasons put forward by the Court were intended to
counter arguments that were based on its earlier reasoning in *International Fruit*. As a
result, the reasoning in *Kupferberg* is essentially negative and does not provide positive
justifications for direct applicability. This could suggest that the Court was acting on
the presumption that international agreements are capable of direct applicability
unless that presumption could be rebutted by showing an unacceptable degree of flexibility and lack of legal formalism. As to the degree of flexibility required to exclude
direct applicability, the line appeared to have been drawn between an agreement in
which general powers to negotiate, consult and derogate were embedded in the structure as a whole, and an agreement where the same powers might exist but were clearly
restricted to specific situations and particular provisions. The latter type of agreement
is more formally legalistic and thus more justiciable. This would also explain why lack
of reciprocal provisions for direct applicability in the parties' domestic legal systems
would be irrelevant in such a case. In the case of clear and non-negotiable provisions,
there would be less discretion in the hands of the parties, in particular the executive
institutions in the exercise of their external relations powers. There would therefore be
no question of policy as to whether the Court should constrain the executive institutions in their conduct of external relations, and it would have a more appropriate
role in interpreting and applying specific obligations already negotiated and concluded. However, it cannot be said that this was a hard and fast distinction.

2.11 As far as the GATT was concerned, however, the Court reaffirmed in a series
of three cases handed down on the same day that it did not have direct effect within
Community law for the same reasons it had given in *International Fruit*.[50] In *SIOT*,[51]
the Court took the opportunity to remind the Community that lack of direct effect did
not affect its obligation to ensure that it complied with the provisions of the GATT
with regard to third parties.[52] In the light of its remarks in *Kupferberg*, however, this
presumably meant no more than that Member States could still be called to account to
ensure that the Community was in a position to comply with the GATT. The cases of
SPI and SAMI[53] and *Singer*[54] were concerned with very specific agreements under the
GATT, namely the Tariff Protocols, and raised other issues. The Court asserted its
jurisdiction over both types of agreements on the grounds that uni-

---

[48] Case 104/81 [1982] E.C.R. 3641, [1983] 1 C.M.L.R. 1, paras. 19–20.
[49] *ibid.*, para. 21.
[50] In one case the Court does appear to have assumed the direct applicability of the GATT, namely, Case
112/80 *Dürbeck* [1981] E.C.R. 1095, [1982] 3 C.M.L.R. 314. However, this may have been an inadver-
tance, see Maresceau, above, p. 20, n. 2 at p. 121; Castillo de la Torre (1992), above, p. 20, n. 2 at p. 38.
[51] Case 266/81 [1983] E.C.R. 731, [1984] 2 C.M.L.R. 231.
[52] *ibid.*, para. 28.
[53] Cases 267–9/81 [1983] E.C.R. 801, [1984] 1 C.M.L.R. 354.
[54] Cases 290, 291/81 [1983] E.C.R. 847. This judgment was identical to that in *SPI and SAMI*.

form application of their provisions throughout the Community was necessary to prevent trade distortions.[55] There could be no question about the Tariff Protocols being clear and unconditional, but the Court found that they were not directly applicable by virtue of the same arguments used against the GATT itself, namely its great degree of flexibility.[56] This line of argument was partly justified by the Court on the grounds that the Tariff Protocols could only be effective through the operation of the customs tariffs of the parties. However, the main thrust of this approach appeared to suggest that the Protocols, notwithstanding their formal adoption and clarity of provisions, were "tainted" by the lack of legal formalism of the GATT as a whole.

The final case in this early group was *Demirel*,[57] in which the Court presented a more integrated approach to the question of direct applicability of international agreements without, however, giving a conclusive answer to the many questions to which the previous case law had given rise. The case concerned an association agreement between the EEC and Turkey (the "Ankara Agreement") which, like the agreements in *Haegeman* and *Kupferberg*, was designed to promote the strengthening of trade and economic relations between the two parties, and to encourage the progressive establishment of a joint customs union and progressive harmonisation of commercial policies. It also opened up the possibility of accession by Turkey to the Community.

In *Demirel*, the Court reaffirmed its jurisdiction over agreements concluded under Articles 300 and 310 (ex Articles 228 and 238), citing its dictum in *Haegeman* but using the broader phrase "Community legal system".[58] In particular, it noted the special nature of an association agreement in that it created "special, privileged links with a non-member country which must, at least to a certain extent, take part in the Community system".[59] This observation was made in the context of asserting the Court's jurisdiction, but appears also to have been relevant in the Court's finding that the agreement was capable of direct applicability in that it identified a link with the internal operation and substantive rules of Community law.

The Court offered an integrated formulation of the direct applicability test. The test would be satisfied when a provision in an agreement contained "a clear and precise obligation which is not subject, in its implementation or effects, to the adoption of any subsequent measure" considered in the context of the agreement's "wording and the purpose and nature of the agreement itself".[60] In this case, no examination of the nature of the agreement was necessary, given that the Court found that the provision in question was merely programmatic and was therefore not sufficiently precise and unconditional to be directly implemented.

2.12 By the time of *Demirel*, therefore, the Court had refined its approach to international agreements by using the *Haegeman* dictum to justify its procedural jurisdiction, while the questions of direct applicability and direct effect were decided by the two-stage test. The formulation used in *Demirel* incorporated the question of whether an agreement was capable of direct applicability in the phrase "wording, purpose and nature", and the question of whether it was judicially applicable in the requirement that provisions contain clear and precise obligations which do not require further acts in order to be implemented. Failure to satisfy either of these questions would be conclusive in excluding direct applicability.

At this point, the Court's jurisprudence had established a reasonably consistent

---

[55] *ibid.*, paras. 14–15.
[56] *ibid.*, para. 23.
[57] Case 12/86 [1987] E.C.R. 3719, [1989] 1 C.M.L.R. 421.
[58] *ibid.*, para. 7.
[59] *ibid.*, para. 9. This echoes the Court's approach in Case 17/81 *Pabst & Richarz* [1982] E.C.R. 1331, [1983] 3 C.M.L.R. 11.
[60] Case 12/86 [1987] E.C.R. 3719, [1989] 1 C.M.L.R. 421, para. 14.

basis, but it was not without its difficulties. The clearest element derivable from these cases was that the Court felt entitled to assert jurisdiction over international agreements in cases referred to it under Article 234 EC (ex Article 177). In the case of formally concluded agreements, this was based on an apparently literal reading of the article—"acts of the institutions". An additional ground, especially in the case of an informally concluded agreement such as the GATT, was a functional need to ensure uniform application throughout the Community legal system. This appeared to be based on a general understanding that the Community was required to comply with legal obligations vis-à-vis third States, even if they were not necessarily enforceable against the Community by Member States or individuals. At this stage it was only clear that the Community could enforce international agreements against Member States in so far as was required to ensure that the Community as a whole could comply with them.

It had also become clear that the *Haegeman* dictum was confined to a mere assertion of jurisdiction by the Court, and that it should be taken only to mean that international agreements which were an integral part of Community law or the Community legal system were *potentially* justiciable. The test for deciding whether an international agreement was justiciable was the two-stage test which reached its final formulation in *Demirel*. *Kupferberg* had shown that the stages were separate, and the range of early cases established that non-justiciability could arise either from uncertainty as to the provision in question or from doubts as to the nature of the agreement as a whole.[61] Fundamentally, what was left unanswered was a constitutional question of whether the exercise of external relations was to be subject to judicial review at all and, if so, under what circumstances. Some, though not all, of these questions have been answered in recent case law.

THE RECENT CASES

2.13 Even though it had consistently denied the direct effect of the GATT, the Court had nonetheless made it clear that the Community as a whole was under an obligation to comply with international agreements.[62] It was therefore possible that the GATT could still be relied upon in an action under Article 230 (ex Article 173) EC,[63] and this possibility was explored in *Fediol III*.[64] The applicants appealed against a decision by the Commission to reject a request for an investigation into their complaint that Argentina was carrying out an illicit commercial practice with regard to the export of soya cake. This complaint was made under the "new instrument of commercial policy" which extended the Community's remit to deal with trade practices of third countries which were "incompatible with international law or with the generally accepted rules".[65]

---

[61] The two overlap in so far as lack of clarity or conditionality in a particular provision reserves future decisions on detailed implementation to the political institutions and the other parties to the international agreement.

[62] See, for example, *Kupferberg*, Case 104/81 [1982] E.C.R. 3641, [1983] 1 C.M.L.R. 1, para. 11, and *SIOT*, Case 266/81 [1983] E.C.R. 731, [1984] 2 C.M.L.R. 231, para. 28.

[63] Commentators have been divided as to this question. Some have argued that the test should be different for Arts. 234 and 230 (ex Arts. 177 and 173). See, for example, Ehlermann, above, p. 20, n. 2 at pp. 138–139; Maresceau, above, p. 20, n. 2 at pp. 116–117; Schermers, above, p. 20, n. 2 at p. 86; Cheyne, above, p. 20, n. 2 at p. 597. Others have suggested that it would equally extend to Art. 173, see for example, Waelbroeck, above, p. 20, n. 2 at pp. 621–622. The point now appears to have been settled by the Court's judgment in the *Banana* case, discussed below.

[64] Case 70/87 [1989] E.C.R. 1781, [1991] 2 C.M.L.R. 489.

[65] Regulation 2641/84, O.J. 1984, L252/1, Art. 2(1). Now the Trade Barriers Regulation, No. 3286/94, O.J. 1994, L349/1.

The Commission argued, *inter alia*, that the applicant could not rely upon the Regulation because the Court could only review the Commission's interpretation of the term "illicit commercial practice" and the relevant rules of international law rules if it infringed rights held by individuals under Community law, and the GATT had been held not to be capable of conferring such rights.[66]

The Court reaffirmed its finding that the GATT itself was not capable of being relied upon by individuals, but pointed out that its rules had been incorporated into the Regulation.[67] Since the Regulation entitled individuals to rely on the GATT to show that the practice about which they were complaining was illicit, it followed that they were entitled to request the Court to review the legality of the Commission's decisions in applying the Regulation by reference to the GATT. The existence of a separate dispute settlement procedure was not sufficient to exclude direct applicability of provisions which were sufficiently precise and unconditional and had been incorporated by legislative act. Thus the question of incorporation became crucial to the applicability of GATT provisions, and avoided the test of justiciability of whether it was appropriate to give judicial consideration to the agreement itself.

2.14 With respect to the question of whether the provision itself was capable of direct applicability, the Court agreed that it had not previously applied the GATT because of the extreme flexibility of its provisions. However, this did not mean that its provisions were not justiciable—they had "an independent meaning" which could be interpreted in order to decide if certain specific practices were incompatible with them. This is perfectly consistent with the distinction between the nature of the agreement as a whole in the sense of its legal formalism, and the question of whether individual provisions themselves satisfy the test of being sufficiently clear, precise and unconditional to be applicable in a legal sense. Although the Court did not express it in these terms, its reasoning fell neatly into the two-stage test as formulated in its early case law. Thus the "flexibility" of the GATT's provisions was purely a problem relating to the nature of the agreement and institution itself and not to its substantive obligations.

The reasoning of *International Fruit* and other cases in which the GATT had been denied direct applicability appeared to be left untouched. The crucial distinction between those cases and *Fediol III* rested on the question of direct incorporation into Community law. If an international agreement which the Court considered to be non-applicable as it stood was incorporated through legislative enactment, the political institutions could be assumed to have accepted judicial control over its interpretation and application in Community law.

In *Greece* v. *Commission*[68] and *Sevince*,[69] the Court had to consider the stage of the direct applicability test concerned with legal certainty. More specifically, it had to determine whether failure of a provision to satisfy the test of clarity and unconditionality could be cured by measures taken by the parties to implement the agreement, and whether those measures would also have an effect within the Community legal system. The cases were concerned with the Ankara Agreement between the EEC and Turkey, which had been found in *Demirel* to be capable of direct applicability.

2.15 In *Greece* v. *Commission*, the Court dismissed a challenge to the validity of

---

[66] See *International Fruit*, Cases 21–4/72 [1972] E.C.R. 1219, [1975] 2 C.M.L.R. 1, *Schlüter*, Case 9/73 [1973] E.C.R. 1135, *SIOT*, Case 266/81 [1983] E.C.R. 731, [1984] 2 C.M.L.R. 231, *SPI and SAMI*, Cases 267–9/81 [1983] E.C.R. 801, [1984] 1 C.M.L.R. 354.

[67] Case 70/87 [1989] E.C.R. 1781, [1991] 2 C.M.L.R. 489, para. 19. Incorporation was effected by Art. 2(1) and the preamble, read together. Note that an earlier version of this reasoning was given in *Schlüter* where Art. II of the GATT was denied direct effect but the relevant duty could be applied because it had been incorporated into Community law by the CCT, Case 9/73 [1973] E.C.R. 1135.

[68] Case 30/88 [1989] E.C.R. 3711, [1991] 2 C.M.L.R. 169.

[69] Case C–192/89 [1990] E.C.R. I–3461.

the Commission's acts in implementing a decision of the Association Agreement Council. The Court reaffirmed its finding from *Haegeman* that provisions of an agreement concluded by the Community under Articles 300 and 310 (ex Articles 228 and 238) of the Treaty form "an integral part of the Community legal system".[70] The Association Council had been given powers of decision in order to attain the objectives of the Agreement and since the decision in question provided for cooperation within the institutional framework of the Association Agreement, the Court found that it was "directly connected" with the Association Agreement. As a result, therefore, it also formed "an integral part of the Community legal system" and the Court accordingly had jurisdiction to consider the decision.[71] The wording of the decision was sufficiently precise and unconditional to allow implementation without the need to adopt supplementary measures in Community law.

In *Sevince*, the Court reaffirmed that provisions of an agreement concluded under Articles 300 and 310 EC (ex Articles 228 and 238) formed "an integral part of the Community legal system" from the date of its coming into force,[72] and that decisions of the Association Council were likewise an integral part.[73] It therefore had jurisdiction and went on to find that a decision relating to the rights of Turkish workers in the Community was directly effective on the basis of the two-stage test as formulated in *Demirel*.[74] The Court looked first at whether the relevant provisions were sufficiently precise and unconditional and had no difficulty in so finding.[75] Once this stage had been satisfied, it then examined the purpose of the agreement.[76] However, it was not clear whether this still related to the question of clarity and amenability to judicial application, or whether it was intended to confirm that the nature of the agreement as a whole made it appropriate for the Court to consider.

It was clear, however, that the programmatic nature of the Agreement itself would not permanently exclude direct effect; it could be achieved through decisions giving it more concrete and specific implementation provided the nature of the agreement made it capable of direct applicability.[77] As in *Kupferberg*, the Court found that the existence of a safeguard provision did not necessarily exclude direct applicability, since it applied only in specific situations and could not, outside those specific circumstances,

---

[70] Case 30/88 [1989] E.C.R. 3711, [1991] 2 C.M.L.R. 169, para. 12. Again, note that this is a more general formulation than that used originally in *Haegeman*.

[71] *ibid.*, para. 13.

[72] Case C–192/89 [1990] E.C.R. I–3461, para. 8. Again, note that this is a more general formulation than that used originally in *Haegeman*.

[73] *ibid.*, para. 9. This was clearly directed at the question of jurisdiction which the Court immediately went on to assert by reference to Art. 234 (ex Art. 177) and the need to ensure uniform application throughout the Community of all provisions forming part of the "Community legal system". The Court cited *Haegeman, Kupferberg, SPI and SAMI*. Note that this decision has been severely criticised by Hartley on the grounds, *inter alia*, that a decision of an international body cannot be called an act of the Community institutions. Above, p. 23, n. 24 at pp. 99–100. See, *contra*, Arnull, above, p. 23, n. 24, at pp. 417–420.

[74] Case 12/86 [1987] E.C.R. 3719, [1989] 1 C.M.L.R. 421, para. 14. This finding has now been followed with regard to the same decision in Case C–237/91 *Kus* v. *Landeshauptstadt Wiesbaden* [1993] 2 C.M.L.R. 887; Case C–355/93 *Eroglu* v. *Land Baden-Württemberg* (unreported); Case C–434/93 *Bozkurt* v. *Staatssecretaris Van Justitie* [1995] E.C.R. I–1475; Case C–285/95 *Kol* v. *Land Berlin* [1997] 3 C.M.L.R. 1175; Case C–351/95 *Kadiman* v. *Freistaat Bayern* (unreported); Case C–386/95 *Eker* v. *Land Baden-Württemberg* (unreported); and Case C–36/96 *Günaydin* v. *Freistaat Bayern* [1998] 1 C.M.L.R. 871.

[75] Case C–192/89 [1990] E.C.R. I–3461, paras. 17–18.

[76] *ibid.*, para. 20, namely "to promote the continuous and balanced strengthening of trade and economic relations between the parties" and to establish an association between the EEC and Turkey "to strengthen its economy with aid from the Community, a transitional stage for the progressive establishment of a customs union and for the alignment of economic policies, and a final stage based on the customs union and entailing close co-ordination of economic policies".

[77] *ibid.*, para. 21.

affect the direct applicability of the relevant provisions.[78] Other than these negative findings, however, the Court gave no positive reason for finding justiciability.

2.16   The next case, *Kziber*,[79] gave the Court a straightforward opportunity to apply the *Demirel* formulation. The agreement in question was the EEC-Morocco Cooperation Agreement, and the Court found first that the relevant provision was clear, precise and unconditional.[80] It then examined the nature of the Agreement, which was designed to promote cooperation between the parties and the economic development of Morocco. There was no provision concerning the possibility of accession by Morocco as had been directly provided for in *Pabst*[81] or, more remotely, in *Demirel*.[82] Nonetheless, the Court was prepared to accept the appropriateness of direct applicability for this Agreement although, again, no explicit reasoning was given for this finding.[83]

In *Nakajima*,[84] the applicants challenged the legality of the Community's antidumping regulation[85] on the grounds that it was incompatible with the GATT Anti-Dumping Code to which the Community was a party. They argued that, even though individuals might not be entitled to rely directly on particular provisions of the Code or of the GATT, they could still request the Court to examine whether an implementing regulation was lawful in the light of those provisions when applying for its annulment or objecting to its applicability to them. In other words, they argued for a direct application of Article 230 EC (ex Article 173) on the grounds of the illegality of the implementing measure, rather than an application of the substantive GATT rules within the framework of the implementing legislation.[86] The Council argued that the Code, as was the case with the GATT, could not be relied upon by individuals for any purpose.

The Court did not reply directly to this argument, but pointed out instead that Nakajima were not relying on direct effect but simply questioning "in an incidental manner under [former] Article 184" the applicability of the regulation on one of the grounds provided for under Article 230.[87] However, it is not clear whether this was intended to mean that individuals might be allowed to rely indirectly on the GATT and its codes under Article 241 (ex Article 184) even though they might not rely directly on them under Article 230.[88]

2.17   The doubt as to the meaning of this part of the judgment is exacerbated because the Court went on immediately to point out that both the GATT and the Anti-Dumping Code were binding on the Community.[89] It did not elaborate on this point, but left it hanging in the air as a possible hint that either or both of these agreements might potentially be used to review the legality of Community legislation. In this

---

[78] *ibid.*, para. 25.
[79] Case C–18/90 [1991] E.C.R. I–199.
[80] *ibid.*, para. 17.
[81] Case 17/81 [1982] E.C.R. 1331, [1983] 3 C.M.L.R. 11.
[82] Case 12/86 [1987] E.C.R. 3719, [1989] 1 C.M.L.R. 421.
[83] This case has been followed with regard to the same agreement in Case C–58/93, *Zoubir Yousfi* v. *Belgium* [1994] E.C.R. I–1353 and Case C–126/95, *Hallouzi-Choho* v. *Bestuur van direct effect Sociale Verzekeringsbank* (unreported). The same reasoning was also applied in Case C–103/94, *Zoulika Krid* v. *CNAVTS* [1995] E.C.R. I–719 with regard to the EEC-Algeria Cooperation Agreement.
[84] Case C–69/89 [1991] E.C.R. I–2069.
[85] Regulation 2423/88, [1988] O.J. L209.
[86] Castillo de la Torre (1992) suggests the distinction between *Fediol* and *Nakajima* is that, in the former, the Court deals with the GATT rules *qua* international law, and in the latter it deals with them *qua* Community law. *Fediol* would therefore be analogous to a conflicts of law case. See above, p. 20, n. 2 at p. 40.
[87] Case C–69/89 [1991] E.C.R. I–2069, para. 28.
[88] Castillo de la Torre (1992), argues that the grounds in Article 241 (ex Art. 184) should not be different from those used under Article 230 (ex Art. 173), above, p. 20, n. 2 at pp. 39–40.
[89] Case C–69/89 [1991] E.C.R. I–2069, para. 29.

case, however, the Court chose to deal with the issue by giving the Code direct applicability on the grounds that it was incorporated into Community law by the implementing regulation. Since the regulation was adopted to comply with the Community's
international legal obligations, in particular with these provisions, and the Court had
previously held that the Community was required to ensure compliance with its international legal obligations,[90] it followed that it was necessary for the Court to examine
whether the Council had acted within the provisions of the Code.[91]

Unlike *Fediol*, the incorporation in *Nakajima* was derived from the Regulation's
stated intention to implement the Code. The most obvious difficulty that arises from
this reasoning is the question of how clear the intention to implement must be. May it
be inferred where there is no express reference to the international legal obligations?
Can the mere fact that an international law rule governs the same subject matter as a
piece of Community legislation be sufficient? Does the same reasoning extend to international legal obligations that arise subsequently to enactment of the relevant Community legislation? The answers to these questions depend on whether the basis of
direct applicability relies on the executive institutions' decision to incorporate and
therefore their decision to permit judicial involvement. In the light of the Court's
refusal otherwise to apply the GATT, this would appear to be the correct
interpretation.

In *Deutsche Shell* v. *Hauptzollamt Hamburg-Harburg*,[92] the Court extended its
finding in *Sevince* that a decision taken by a treaty body could itself be part of Community law by giving legal effect to a non-mandatory implementing measure.[93] It was
"directly linked" to the agreement which it implemented and was therefore part of
Community law.[94] Such a measure could not be directly effective, in that it could not
confer legally enforceable rights upon individuals. Nonetheless, national courts were
required to take them into consideration when resolving disputes.[95]

2.18   Although it had become clear from the early cases that individuals would
be unable to rely on the GATT under Article 234 (ex Article 177) and *Fediol III* and
Nakajima had suggested that the same would be true under Article 230 (ex Article
173),[96] it was still possible that Member States would have the right to invoke the
GATT.[97] In *Germany* v. *Council* (the *Banana* case),[98] Germany made a complaint challenging the validity of Council Regulation 404/93 on the common organisation of the
banana market, which attempted to consolidate and unify the different import policies
of the Member States and, at the same time, protect the interests of Community and
existing ACP producers. One of the grounds of Germany's challenge was that the regulation conflicted with the Community's obligations under international law, namely

[90] See *Kupferberg*, Case 104/81 [1982] E.C.R. 3641, [1983] 1 C.M.L.R., para. 11, *SIOT*, Case 266/81
[1983] E.C.R. 731, [1984] 2 C.M.L.R. 231, para. 28, and Case 142/88 *Hoesch AG* v. *Bergrohr GmbH*
[1989] E.C.R. 3413, [1991] 1 C.M.L.R. 383, at para. 30.
[91] Case C–69/89 [1991] E.C.R. I–2069, paras 30–31. The Court found in favour of the Council in this case.
It is notable that the Court appeared to make no distinction between the GATT as a whole and the Anti-
dumping Code, notwithstanding the fact that the latter was precise and unconditional and had been formally concluded under Art. 300 (ex Art. 228) See Castillo de la Torre (1992), above, p. 20, n. 2 at pp. 39–40.
[92] Case C–188/91 [1993] E.C.R. I–363.
[93] It was concerned with a Common EEC/EFTA Transit Procedure, a measure taken by the Joint Committee
of the Convention.
[94] Case C–188/91 [1993] E.C.R. I–363, para. 17. This is a return to the phrase used in *Haegeman* although,
in the previous paragraph, the Court had also used the phrase "Community legal order".
[95] *ibid.*, para. 18.
[96] *Fediol*, Case 70/87 [1989] E.C.R. 1781, [1991] 2 C.M.L.R. 489, and *Nakajima*, Case C–69/89 [1991]
E.C.R. I–2069, were both decided on the basis of incorporation into Community law therefore it could be
said that the question was never directly addressed.
[97] Cheyne, above, p. 20, n. 2; Ehlermann, above, p. 20, n. 2 at pp. 138–9.
[98] Case C–280/93 [1994] E.C.R. I–4973.

the Lomé Convention (Lomé IV) and the GATT. The Regulation had already been the subject of a GATT dispute settlement panel report which had found against the EC.[99]

The Court treated these two agreements differently. It appeared to assume that Lomé IV was directly applicable, finding merely that the Community Regulation was consistent with the relevant provisions.[1] The GATT, however, was more problematic. Germany argued that the applicability of GATT under Article 230 (ex Article 173) as a basis of review of the validity of Community acts was separate from the question of direct effect and therefore the previous GATT cases did not preclude reliance on it in this case. The Commission and Council, on the other hand, argued that the special nature of the GATT precluded it from being used as a basis of review except where the relevant Community provisions were adopted in order to implement obligations under the GATT, as had been the case in *Fediol* and *Nakajima*.

On the face of it, Germany's argument was based on the clear wording of Article 230, that the Court may review the lawfulness of Community acts on the basis of infringement of the EC Treaty "or of any rule of law relating to its application". The Court of Justice had consistently claimed jurisdiction over the interpretation of international agreements in Community law, and had stated that the Community was required to fulfil its obligations under international agreements, including the GATT.[2] It would seem eminently logical from the wording of Article 230, therefore, to treat any international agreement binding on the Community as relating to the application of the EC Treaty since all actions by the Community institutions are based on Treaty powers.[3]

However, the Commission based its arguments on the question of whether the GATT was an appropriate international agreement for the purposes of justiciability, in the light of its general scheme, spirit and terms. It argued that the GATT was enforced through diplomatic action rather than by legal means; it did not represent a set of legal rights and obligations but rather a system for negotiating a balance of advantages and disadvantages.[4] In effect, the Commission was arguing that an exercise of jurisdiction by the Court would be inappropriate for two reasons. First, the nature of the GATT system was such that its provisions were not amenable to judicial review. Secondly, intervention by the Court would curtail the freedom of action that the Commission needed (or wanted) in its conduct of affairs within the GATT.[5] The first was akin to the

---

[99] *European Economic Community—Import Regime for Bananas*, DS38/R, January 18, 1994, reproduced at 34 I.L.M. 177 (1995). The panel found that the banana regime was inconsistent with Art. I concerning non-discrimination between importing countries, Art. II concerning the level of permissible tariffs, and Art. III concerning discrimination between domestic and importing producers. The EC was able to block adoption of the report, but a new complaint was brought under the new WTO dispute settlement procedure which provides for automatic adoption unless there is unanimous consensus to reject. In *European Communities—Regime for the Importation, Sale and Distribution of Bananas, (complaints by Ecuador, Guatemala, Honduras, Mexico and the United States)* (WT/DS27, May 22, 1997), and *Report of the Appellate Body*, (WT/DS27/AB/R, September 9, 1997), both the Panel and the Appellate Body found that the EC's licensing procedures were inconsistent with, *inter alia*, Arts I, III:4 and X of the GATT 1994. The original finding that the preferential arrangements under the Lomé Convention were inconsistent with the GATT has now been overtaken by a waiver granted to the arrangement by the WTO.
[1] Case C–280/93 [1994] E.C.R. I–4973, paras. 100–102.
[2] See p. 33, n. 90, and see Case 312/91, *Metalsa* [1994] 2 C.M.L.R. 121.
[3] See Hartley (*Foundations*), above, p. 22, n. 10 at p. 187.
[4] Some commentators would argue that this is an incorrect view of the GATT and that it has instead a distinctly legal nature. See, in particular, Petersmann (1983), above, p. 20, n. 2 at pp. 429–434.
[5] Advocate General Gulmann shared the same concerns as the Commission. He pointed out that any exercise of jurisdiction by the Court of Justice with respect to the GATT might have the effect of changing the obligations of the Community within the GATT and, although he did not say so explicitly, it might curtail the options available to the Community institutions in their relations with other GATT parties. He took the view that the Court could exercise jurisdiction, but only if there were special grounds for subjecting institutionally adopted acts to judicial review, as in *Fediol* and *Nakajima*. *Germany v. Council* Case C–280/93 [1994] E.C.R. I–4973, para. 131.

Court's reasoning in its previous case law, the second was a policy issue that the Court had not directly addressed.

2.19 Despite the fundamental importance of these arguments, the Court did not explicitly consider these issues. It effectively adopted the Commission's view of the nature of the agreement by referring to its previous reasoning in *International Fruit* and later cases to the effect that the GATT was not capable of direct effect, and stated merely that the same reasons precluded direct applicability in an action under Article 230.[6] Thus Member States were no more able than individuals to invoke the GATT in Community law.

Since no obligation to make the GATT directly applicable could be derived from the international agreement itself, it would evidently depend entirely on whether the Community legislation had expressly referred to GATT provisions or had intended to implement a particular GATT obligation, as in the cases of *Fediol* and *Nakajima*. The Court in the *Banana* case therefore consolidated its position on the GATT and reaffirmed the pre-emptive rights of the executive institutions to determine whether its provisions should be given direct applicability. Its reasoning adequately met the argument of the Commission that it should be permitted to exercise its role in the GATT without being hindered by the Court's judicial supervision, but relied heavily on the lack of legal formalism of the GATT.[7] Now that the WTO Agreement has significantly increased the legal effectiveness of the GATT both substantively and procedurally, and assuming that the Court intends to continue its policy of non-interference in the conduct of international trade relations by the political institutions, the reasoning employed in the *Banana* case raises the question of how the Court will explain judicial self-restraint in the future.[8]

2.20 The Court was not required to change its approach in two subsequent cases concerning the GATT before the WTO Agreement came into force. In the first, *Amministrazione delle Finanze dello Stato Chiquita Italia*,[9] the plaintiff challenged a tax introduced by the Italian government on bananas, on the grounds that it violated provisions of the GATT and the Lomé Convention. The Court reiterated its previous findings on the applicability of the GATT and, in particular, its lack of direct effect.[10] With regard to the Lomé Convention, the Court drew a comparison with the Yaoundé Convention which it had already found capable of direct applicability in *Bresciani*. Thus the fact that the Lomé Convention was intended to promote the development of the other parties with a resulting imbalance of obligation between the parties, and the existence of separate dispute settlement procedures, would not necessarily preclude its direct applicability.[11] In addition, the Court found that the Lomé Convention was "an extension of the association arrangements which had originally been established unilaterally by the EEC Treaty".[12] On this basis, the Court found that the Lomé Convention was capable of having direct applicability.[13] The Court also asserted its

---

[6] Case C–280/93 [1994] E.C.R. I–4973, para. 109.
[7] Petersmann criticises these findings largely on the grounds that the relevant GATT provisions satisfy the clarity and unconditionality test and the jurisdiction test under Article 300. He does, however, meet the Court's reasoning more squarely by criticising the use of "the political question doctrine", *i.e.* a non-justiciability test, see "Proposals for a New Constitution for the European Union: Building-Blocks for a Constitutional Theory and Constitutional Law of the EU", 32 C.M.L.Rev. (1995) p. 1123, at pp. 1164–1172.
[8] Note that the Court made no reference to the changes due to come about under the WTO Agreement.
[9] Case 469/93 [1995] E.C.R. I–4533.
[10] *ibid.*, paras. 26–29.
[11] *ibid.*, para. 36. See also *Kupferberg*, Case 104/81 [1982] E.C.R. 3641, [1983] 1 C.M.L.R. 1, paras. 18–20.
[12] Case 469/93 [1995] E.C.R. I–4533, para. 33.
[13] Note that this had apparently been assumed by the Court in the *Banana* case, Case C–280/93 [1994] E.C.R. I–4973, paras. 100–102.

jurisdiction over the Lomé Convention when it stated that its provisions were "an integral part of the Community's legal order" since they had come into force.[14] The legal certainty test was satisfied by Article 1 of Protocol No. 5 to the Lomé Convention, on the grounds that it was "worded in clear, precise and unconditional terms".[15]

In the second case, *Commission v. Germany (Re International Dairy Agreement)*[16] the Commission challenged the legality of the application by a Member State of an international agreement binding on the Community, namely the International Dairy Agreement concluded under the auspices of the GATT.[17] There was no challenge to the applicability of the Agreement and its Protocols and the Court applied its provisions without comment, other than to assert its jurisdiction to interpret agreements concluded by the Community in order to ensure their uniform application throughout its territory.[18] Significantly, however, the Court made it clear that the primacy of international agreements over Community secondary legislation meant that, where there was room for interpretation of legislative provisions, they should be interpreted so as to conform with any relevant international agreement.[19]

2.21   In *Opel Austria v. Council*,[20] the Court had to consider whether a provision of the European Economic Area Agreement (EEA) was capable of direct effect. It did so by reasserting the *Haegeman* formulation to show that the Agreement was an integral part of the Community legal order, and that a provision might have direct effect if it was sufficiently unconditional and precise.[21] No mention was made of the *Demirel* formulation, and the question of the nature and purpose of the agreement was simply passed over. The Court appears to have assumed that it would be appropriate to interpret and apply the EEA as part of Community law, so no further assistance was given with regard to that part of the test.

It did, however, take the opportunity to reassert that the principle of good faith was binding on the Community.[22] The Court went on to identify the principle of legitimate expectations as a corollary in Community law of the principle of good faith in international law.[23] It was not clear, therefore, if the Court was suggesting that it could only

---

[14] Case 469/93 [1995] E.C.R. I–4533, para. 40. Note that again this is a more general phrase than that used in *Haegeman*.

[15] *ibid.*, para. 57.

[16] Case C–61/94 [1997] 1 C.M.L.R. 281.

[17] Essentially, Germany had allowed imports of dairy goods from countries that were not party to the Agreement at prices lower than the minimum set by the Agreement.

[18] Case C–61/94 [1997] 1 C.M.L.R. 281, para. 16, following *Kupferberg*, Case 104/81 [1982] E.C.R. 3641, [1983] 1 C.M.L.R. 1, para.14.

[19] Case C–61/94 [1997] 1 C.M.L.R. 281, para. 52. This reflects earlier case law, for example, Case 92/71 *Interfood v. Hauptzollamt Hamburg* [1972] E.C.R. 231 (GATT principles used to interpret CCT) and a series of antidumping cases in which the GATT Anti-Dumping Code has been used as a guide to interpretation and review of the Community's antidumping legislation, for example, Case 187/85 *Fediol v. Commission* [1988] E.C.R. 4155, Case 188/85 *Fediol v. Commission* [1988] E.C.R. 4193, Case C–105/90 *Goldstar v. Council* [1992] 1 C.M.L.R. 996, Case C–175/87 *Matsushita v. Council* [1992] 3 C.M.L.R. 137, Case 178/87 *Minolta v. Council* (Lexis: transcript), Case C–179/87 *Sharp v. Council* [1992] E.C.R. I–1635, [1992] 2 C.M.L.R. 415, Case C–188/88 *NMB (Deutschland) v. Commission* [1992] 3 C.M.L.R. 80, Case C–216/91 *Rima Eletrometalurgia v. Council*; *The Times*, January 27, 1994, and Case T–162/94 *NMB France Sarl v. Commission* [1997] 3 C.M.L.R. 164. See also Case C–70/94 *Werner* [1995] E.C.R. I–3189, para. 23 and Case C–83/94 *Leifer* [1995] E.C.R. I–3231, para. 24 (GATT is relevant for purpose of interpreting a Community instrument governing international trade), and Case C–84/95 *Bosphorus v. Hava Yollari* [1996] E.C.R. I–3953, [1996] 3 C.M.L.R. 257 (interpreting regulation in order to fulfil objectives of UN sanctions against Federal Republic of Yugoslavia). Recently, Advocate General Fennelly in Case C–38/95 *Ministero Delle Finanze v. Foods Import* [1997] 1 C.M.L.R. 1067, para. 24 note 26, put forward the view that paras. 19–21 of the judgment in *Fediol III* might be interpreted as meaning that there is a general principle under which Community law should be interpreted in harmony with the Community's obligations under international agreements.

[20] Case T–115/94 [1997] 1 C.M.L.R. 733.

[21] *ibid.*, para. 101. Note again that this is broader than the phrase originally used in *Haegeman*.

[22] *ibid.*, para. 90.

[23] *ibid.*, para. 93.

review the legality of the Council's acts because of a principle of Community law and if the reference to international law binding on the Community was merely a passing contextual reference.

2.22   Finally, some recent cases brought after the conclusion of the WTO Agreement have been decided but with inconclusive results as far as the question of its direct implementation is concerned. The question of whether different parts of the WTO Agreement should be given direct effect was discussed by the Advocate General in each case, but the issue was largely ignored by the Court.

In *Affish* v. *Rijksdienst voor de Keuring van Vee en Vlees*,[24] the Court was asked to rule on the validity of a Commission decision to prohibit the import of fish products from Japan on the grounds of risks to public health. Affish argued, *inter alia*, that this decision was incompatible with the Sanitary and Phytosanitary Agreement (SPS Agreement) concluded as part of the WTO Agreement.[25] Advocate General Cosmas took the view that the reasoning of the Court as it applied to GATT 1947 was equally applicable to the WTO Agreement, including GATT 1994.[26] His support for this view is expressed, oddly, in the form of a footnote which merely identifies those aspects of the WTO Agreement which show signs of flexibility. There is no serious attempt to consider other aspects of the argument, and thus his view loses some of its authority. He does, however, give rather more attention to the question of whether the SPS Agreement is capable of direct applicability, and in this respect puts forward convincing arguments that its provisions are not sufficiently clear or unconditional to be applied judicially.[27] The Court simply stated that, since the national Court had not asked it to consider the contested decision in the light of the SPS Agreement, it was not necessary to do so.[28]

The Court similarly avoided the question in *T. Port GmbH* v. *Hauptzollamt Hamburg-Jonas*[29] on the grounds that, on the facts of the case,[30] neither GATT 1947 nor GATT 1994 could be relied upon. Advocate General Elmer's reasoning was not helpful with regard to the implications of granting or denying direct applicability to the WTO Agreement in Community law. He was of the view that the Court should continue to apply its reasoning for denying direct applicability of the GATT to the new regime of the WTO Agreement, but gave no argued reasons for this view.[31]

In *Hermès International* v. *FHT Marketing Choice BVT*,[32] the Court was asked to interpret a provision of the TRIPs Agreement.[33] It was argued by three Member States that the Court had no jurisdiction to consider the TRIPs Agreement in the light of its previous opinion that intellectual property rights fall essentially within the competence of the Member States.[34] The Court, however, took the view that it was required to have jurisdiction because the Agreement governed matters that could fall within the scope of Community law and it would therefore be necessary in order to prevent future lack of uniformity of interpretation.[35]

---

[24] Case C–183/95 [1997] E.C.R. I–4315.
[25] Agreement on the application of sanitary and phytosanitary measures, Annex 1A to the WTO Agreement.
[26] Case C–183/95 [1997] E.C.R. I–4315, para. 119.
[27] *ibid.*, paras. 120–126.
[28] *ibid.*, para. 28.
[29] Cases 364–365/95 [1998] E.C.R. I–1023.
[30] Namely that the third state, Ecuador, to whom Germany would have owed international legal obligations had not been a party to GATT 1947 and did not become a party to the WTO Agreement until after the date of the contested measure.
[31] Cases 364–365/95 [1998] E.C.R. I–1023, paras. 27–29.
[32] Case C–53/96 [1998] E.C.R. I–3603.
[33] Agreement on Trade-Related Aspects of Intellectual Property Rights, Annex 1A to the WTO Agreement.
[34] Opinion 1/94 [1994] E.C.R. I–5267.
[35] Case C–53/96 [1998] E.C.R. I–3603, para. 32.

The Court acknowledged that the Community legislation should be interpreted consistently with the TRIPs Agreement as far as possible,[36] but declined to answer the question of direct effect on the grounds that it was only required to assist the national Court in interpreting its procedural rules. Interestingly, however, the Court indirectly acknowledged the intense interest generated by the possibility that it would have to rule on direct effect with regard to the new WTO Agreement; it "stressed from the outset" that it would not do so.[37]

Just as in the previous two cases, the Court did not accept the Advocate General's invitation to rule on whether the provision at hand was directly effective. This might be an indication of the difficulty there is experiencing in finding a coherent approach to the question. Even the Advocate General, although he thought the Court should deal directly with the issue, was tentative in his recommendations.[38] He pointed out that direct effect could not be denied to the Agreement on the grounds of the clarity and unconditionality of its provisions since they were no less clear than those of agreements to which the Court had already given direct effect.[39] Instead, the crucial part of the test was the nature of the WTO Agreement itself and, in this regard, he was of the opinion that there was a critical shift in the nature of the regulatory system from that of GATT 1947. Whereas GATT 1947 had been largely characterised by exceptions, the WTO Agreement was characterised by rules. This was particularly evident in the fact that GATT panel reports could easily be blocked, whereas this was not true under the WTO dispute settlement procedures. The result of this analysis was that, logically at least, the Court could, or should, change its approach to the question of direct applicability of the GATT rules.[40]

2.23 The basis on which the Court's approach should be changed, however, was a more difficult question to answer. The Advocate General acknowledged that non-reciprocal enforcement of the Agreement would disadvantage Community operators in relation to their competitors from other contracting parties which did not give direct applicability to the GATT rules, but argued that, as a matter of principle, this point would only be relevant if it were to be crucial for the question of direct applicability.[41] His interpretation of the Court's reasoning in *Kupferberg*[42] was that the key issue was the reciprocal implementation of an international agreement and whether reciprocal domestic enforceability was required in order to achieve that implementation.[43] He invited the Court to consider the important implications that would arise from a lack of reciprocal judicial enforcement but, at the same time, acknowledged that were particular difficulties in using the reciprocity argument in the context of a multilateral agreement.[44] His conclusion was that it would be better, if the Court wished to continue to allow the political institutions to take their own decisions about the GATT provisions, to justify their approach by reference to non-reciprocity rather than continue with reasoning that was so difficult to justify in the light of the development of the WTO, that it could increasingly be challenged as a political rather than a judicial view.[45]

---

[36] *ibid.*, para. 28.
[37] *ibid.*, para. 35.
[38] At the time of writing, this opinion was only available in French. My thanks to Jean-François Pepin for his assistance in translating the relevant passages. Any misunderstandings of the argument are solely attributable to the author.
[39] Case C–53/96 [1998] E.C.R. I–3603, para. 27.
[40] *ibid.*, paras. 28–30.
[41] *ibid.*, paras. 31–32.
[42] Case 104/81 [1982] E.C.R. 3641, [1983] 1 C.M.L.R. 1.
[43] Case C–53/96 [1998] E.C.R. I–3603, para. 33.
[44] See on this point, Petersmann (1983), above, p. 20, n. 2 at pp. 427–428.
[45] Case C–53/96 [1998] E.C.R. I–3603, para. 35.

These latter cases suggest that the Court is poised at the brink of an important new stage in its jurisprudence. It cannot forever decline to decide the question of whether the WTO Agreement, or parts of it, should have direct applicability in Community law. Its apparent reluctance to do so, however, indicates how difficult it is for the Court to present a coherent, principled approach to an increasingly complex judicial problem.[46]

CONCLUSIONS

2.24   The Court has succeeded in building up a relatively consistent jurisprudence in dealing with the effect of international agreements in Community law. However, consistency is not the same thing as certainty, and there are significant questions still to be answered.

The Court's finding that international legal obligations would prevail over secondary Community acts and legislation inevitably gave rise to questions of what kind of international agreements would be applicable, under what circumstances they would become part of Community law, and what the exact legal effects of such a status would be. Despite the caution with which the Court has dealt with the questions brought before it, some conclusions and inferences can reasonably be drawn.

First, the Court has jurisdiction to consider any international agreement binding on the Community. This is sometimes expressed as following from the wording of Article 234 (ex Article 177), leading to international agreements having the status of "an integral part of Community law" as it was put in *Haegeman*. On other occasions, particularly in the case of the GATT 1947 which became binding on the Community informally, the Court's jurisdiction is expressed as a functional need to ensure uniform application throughout the Community. These assertions of jurisdiction have been open to different interpretations, but it is now apparent that the *Haegeman* statement does not automatically lead to the direct implementation of an international agreement, a fact reflected in the general shift in the Court's terminology from "Community law"[47] to "Community legal system"[48] or "Community legal order".[49] The need for uniform interpretation is also more than a policy-based justification of jurisdiction, and is consistent with an understanding that the Court will ensure that Member States will enable the Community to comply with an international agreement. Whether the Court will also be prepared to ensure that the Community *does* comply is a different question.

Secondly, the fact that international legal obligations will prevail over secondary Community law is not relevant unless there is a conflict between them. Such a conflict can only occur when the international agreement has actually become a judicially applicable part of Community law. The general direction of the Court's jurisprudence,

---

[46] Since the writing of this chapter, the Court of Justice has applied its reasoning in *International Fruit* to the WTO agreements which thus do not have direct applicability in Community law. See Case C–149/96, *Portugal* v. *Council*, (unreported), discussed in addendum to Chapter 17.
[47] For example, *Haegeman*, Case 181/73 [1974] E.C.R. 449, [1975] 1 C.M.L.R. 515, para. 5, and used along with the phrase "Community legal order" in *Deutsche Shell*, Case C–188/91 [1993] E.C.R. I–363, paras. 16–17 and *Opel Austria* v. *Council*, Case T–115/94 [1997] 1 C.M.L.R. 733, paras. 49 and 79.
[48] For example, *Kupferberg*, Case 104/81 [1982] E.C.R. 3641, [1983] 1 C.M.L.R. 1, para. 13, *Demirel*, Case 12/86 [1987] E.C.R. 3719, [1989] 1 C.M.L.R. 421, para. 7, *Greece* v. *Commission*, Case 30/88 [1989] E.C.R. 3711, [1991] 2 C.M.L.R. 169, paras. 12 and 13, *Sevince*, Case C–192/89 [1990] E.C.R. I–3461, para. 8.
[49] For example, *Deutsche Shell*, Case C–188/91 [1993] E.C.R. I–363, para. 16, *Chiquita*, Case 469/93 [1995] E.C.R. I–4533, para. 40, *Opel Austria* v. *Council*, Case T–115/94 [1997] 1 C.M.L.R. 733, para. 79.

therefore, is concerned with international law *qua* Community law. Stating it thus does not answer the question of what is Community law proper, but it acknowledges that there may be legal matters in which the Community is involved but which fall outside the remit of the Court to supervise. Assertion of jurisdiction, as pointed out above, is merely a step towards potential justiciability. The question of justiciability needs more detailed discussion than is possible here,[50] but some issues may be dealt with briefly.

2.25   The test of justiciability, or direct applicability as the Court normally calls it, is to be found in the two-stage test discussed above. The stage which considers whether the provision at issue is sufficiently clear and unconditional, and does not require further implementing acts, is essentially a test of justiciability on the grounds of legal certainty. As such it is relatively unproblematic in so far as it involves a test of semantic interpretation and a determination that no significant discretionary powers remain in the hands of the political institutions. It is a test of judicially applicable standards common in most legal systems.[51]

However, it does have a particularly controversial aspect, namely its application by the Court of Justice to decisions made by international treaty bodies.[52] This apparently straightforward extension has been criticised on the basis that decisions taken in an international forum cannot properly be called "acts of the institutions" for the purposes of Article 234.[53] However that may be, it is an obvious development in so far as implementing decisions are a type of subsequent amendment or refinement of the treaty itself. If a decision were made in the form of a protocol to the treaty, for example, there would be little cause for controversy. But the nature of the procedure by which such decisions are taken does have important implications for the constitutional effects of giving them direct applicability in Community law because of the difference between that procedure and those used to approve the conclusion or amendment of an international agreement.

The other part of the two-stage test, concerning the nature and purpose of an international agreement, incorporates a number of complex issues.[54] The test has been variously described by the Court as an examination of "the spirit, the general scheme and the terms"[55] or the "purpose and nature"[56] of the treaty. Several elements may be discerned here. The Court may refer firstly to the contents and purpose of an international agreement or, secondly, to its legal nature in the sense of the formalism of its pro-

---

[50] It will be discussed more fully in a later chapter.

[51] In the case of Community law, however, there may also be a question of whether a provision which is directly applicable is also directly effective.

[52] *Greece* v. *Commission* Case 30/88 [1989] E.C.R. 3711, [1991] 2 C.M.L.R. 169 and *Sevince* Case C–192/89 [1990] E.C.R. I–3461.

[53] See above, p. 23, n. 24.

[54] It should be noted that the Court often makes reference to the nature and purpose of an agreement for purposes other than the question of its direct applicability, most frequently with regard to interpreting a provision of the agreement and ensuring that it is, within the context of the agreement, clear and unconditional. See, for example, *Kupferberg*, Case 104//81 [1982] E.C.R. 3641, [1983] 1 C.M.L.R. 1, paras. 23–27. This is true also of those cases where the Court has been asked to give direct applicability to a provision on the grounds that it is similar or identical to a provision in the EC Treaty itself. See, for example, Case C–65/77, *Razanatsimba* [1977] E.C.R. 2229, Case C–225/78, *Procureur de la Republique* v. *Bouhelier* [1979] E.C.R. 3151, Case 270/80, *Polydor* v. *Harlequin Record Shops* [1982] E.C.R. 329, Case C–163/90, *Legros* [1992] E.C.R. I–4625; *Metalsa*, Case 312/91 [1994] 2 C.M.L.R. 121, *Chiquita*, Case 469/93 [1995] E.C.R. I–4533,*Opel Austria* v. *Council*, Case T–115/94 [1997] 1 C.M.L.R. 733. In such cases, the existence of common objectives may be relevant to interpretation but this reasoning should be distinguished from the question of whether the agreement itself is capable of direct applicability as a matter of Community law. See also Opinion 1/91 [1991] E.C.R. I–6079.

[55] *International Fruit*, Cases 21–24/72 [1972] E.C.R. 1219, [1975] 2 C.M.L.R. 1, para. 20, *Bresciani*, Case 87/75 [1976] E.C.R. 129, [1976] 2 C.M.L.R. 62, para. 16.

[56] *Demirel*, Case 12/86 [1987] E.C.R. 3719, [1989] 1 C.M.L.R. 421, para.14.

cedures. A third element, which the Court has not made explicit, is the extent to which the Community has control over the implementation of the agreement, including the making of decisions.[57] Finally, the Court's case law acknowledges that the political institutions have the power to pre-empt the question of direct applicability, both to grant it by express incorporation in legislation and to withhold it by an express provision of the treaty.

So far, the debate has been largely expressed as a question of direct applicability and the circumstances in which an international agreement can be relied upon before the Community's courts. The fundamental issues which have been highlighted by the cases where direct applicability has not been given, namely those concerned with the GATT, show that the key questions are constitutional and relate to the limits of the Court's judicial function as the key issue for deciding direct applicability. It is above all else a constitutional question whether the Court should have a principle of non-justiciability which favours the political institutions' wish to exercise discretion and, if so, how such a test should be formulated. The Court has built a consistent basis for its refusal to grant direct applicability to the GATT which acknowledges that significant political discretion in the hands of the institutions should exclude judicial review. A clearer policy of non-justiciability over these matters is likely to be revealed in future cases concerned with the legalised structure of the GATT 1994 under the WTO Agreement.

---

[57] Each of these elements is discussed in more detail in a later chapter.

CHAPTER 3

Community Development Aid and the Evolution of the Inter-institutional Law of the European Union

by

Angela Ward*

3.01   The *Bangladesh*[1] and *EDF*[2] cases were substantively concerned with European Community development cooperation policy, and more particularly arrangements for the financing and distribution of development aid. Yet the rulings developed principles that went beyond these subject areas, carrying ramifications in the broader field of EU constitutional law. They made important contributions to the inter-institutional law of the European Union, and clarified the institutional arrangements that may be made when competence is shared by the Community and the Member States. They addressed whether or not there are circumstances in which the EC Treaty prevents the Member States from taking independent, collective action in coming to decisions concerning the donation of aid, and binds them instead to recourse to Community institutional structure. The cases also made it clear that Member States are entitled to second the services of the EU institutions in formulating and implementing decisions that are made in intergovernmental fora.

In addition, the rulings discuss the entitlement of the Court of Justice to review the legality of Council acts that are taken outside the EC institutional framework. It will be illustrated that, despite the supposed exclusion, under Article 46 TEU (ex Article L), of the Court of Justice from reviewing measures taken pursuant to the Common Foreign and Security Policy, and the Justice and Home Affairs pillars of the TEU,[3] the *Bangladesh* and *EDF* cases, and in particular the latter, laid the foundations for a restricted role for the Court to assess second and third pillar initiatives.[4]

3.02   The facts of the *Bangladesh* case were as follows. On May 14, 1991, the Member States of the EC decided to make a substantial donation of emergency aid to

---

* Reader in Law, University of Essex; former Deputy Director, Centre for European Legal Studies, Cambridge.
[1] Joined Cases C–181/91 and C–248/91 *European Parliament* v. *Council and Commission* [1993] E.C.R. 3685.
[2] Case C–316/91 *European Parliament* v. *Council* [1994] E.C.R. 625.
[3] Note that, under the Treaty of Amsterdam, the Justice and Home Affairs Pillar has been deconstructed. Visa, asylum, and immigration policy now forms part of the EC Treaty, and the remnants of the pillar have been retitled "Police and Judicial Cooperation in Criminal Matters". See Monar "Justice and Home Affairs in the Treaty of Amsterdam: Reform at the Price of Fragmentation", [1998] 23 E.L.Rev. 230.
[4] Case C–170/96 *Commission* v. *Council* [1998] E.C.R. I–2763. For a case commentary see Barents, (1995) 32 C.M.L.Rev. 249, in particular at p. 254. For post-Amsterdam developments and the ECJ see A. Albors-Lorens, *Changes in the Jurisdiction of the European Court of Justice Under the Treaty of Amsterdam* (1998), 35 C.M.L.Rev. 1273.

Bangladesh, as it had suffered terrible damage in April of that year as a result of a violent cyclone. It was agreed to grant special aid of ECU 60 million to Bangladesh, to be financed *bilaterally,* by each Member State. This decision was reached at a working lunch attended by Ministers of Foreign Affairs of the Member States, and by a member of the Commission. It was described as "a decision of the Member States meeting in Council". It was not reached, however, entirely in the absence of recourse to the EC institutional machinery. The Commission had submitted a plan for special action to the Ministers of Finance meeting informally in Luxembourg on May 11, and the plan was examined by the General Affairs Council on May 13 and 14. In addition, the task of coordinating the aid was entrusted to the Commission.

The General Secretariat of the Council of the EU issued a press release laying out the terms of the aid, the text of which appeared in the draft minute of the 1487th session of the Council of May 13 and 14, 1991 under item 12 "Other business – Aid to Bangladesh". The press release was entitled "Aid for Bangladesh – Council conclusions", and provided as follows:

> "The Member States meeting in the Council have decided, on the basis of a Commission proposal, to grant special aid of ECU 60 million to Bangladesh under a Community action. The distribution among the Member States will be based on GNP. The aid will be integrated into the Community's general action for Bangladesh. It will be provided either directly by the Member States or by means of an account administered by the Commission. The Commission will co-ordinate the whole of the special aid of ECU 60 million."

Almost all Member States chose to administer their own payments, with only the Greek Government electing to transfer their share of the package for administration by the Commission. Upon receipt of ECU 716 775.45 from the Greek Government, the Directorate General for budgets in the EU Commission made two entries, one of which recorded the receipt of these sums, the other of which authorised its expenditure.

The European Parliament brought two separate actions for annulment, under Article 230 (ex Article 173) of the EC Treaty which were joined at the Court registry. The first sought the annulment of the act adopted at the 1487th session of the Council held on May 13 and 14, 1991 which were referred to in the press release "Aid for Bangladesh, Council Conclusions". The second sought the same with respect to the above-mentioned budget entries made pursuant to this measure.

3.03   The crux of the Parliament's objections lay in recourse to intergovernmental consultation in deciding to grant aid to Bangladesh, rather than the machinery provided under the EC Treaty. The Parliament had argued that the act in question could only be properly adopted by the Council, and claimed that, in reality, it had indeed been the Council of the EU which had acted.[5] If that were so, then the above mentioned budget entries taken in implementing the aid were unlawful, because (i) they were taken pursuant to an illegal measure,[6] and (ii) the Parliament's powers had been infringed.[7] This was so because the Commission had failed to present to the Parliament an amending and supplementing budget to reflect the entries concerning the donation of aid by the Greek Government. In the alternative, if the Court were to rule

---

[5] Opinion of AG Jacobs, *European Parliament* v. *Council and Commission*, Joined Cases C–181/91 and C–248/91 [1993] E.C.R. 3685, para. 24.

[6] The Parliament expressly raised the plea of illegality under Art. 241 EC (ex Art. 184).

[7] Under Art. 272 (5) to (7) (ex Art. 203(5) to (7)) of the EC Treaty. The Parliament also argued that Art. 274 EC (ex Art. 205) and Art. 20 (1) and 22 of the Financial Regulation had been breached.

that the act in question was not an act of the Council that was reviewable under Article 230 EC (ex Article 173), the Commission had, in any case, acted unlawfully, because it had no authority to execute an act, which was not a Community act, within the framework and management of the Community budget.

The case turned centrally, however, on the issue of whether or not the act forming the principle part of the challenge, namely the decision to make a donation of aid referred to in the press release, was an act intended to have legal effects[8] that was amenable to judicial review. This question was bound up with the assessment of the Parliament's substantive complaints. The approach taken by the Court was purposive. In accordance with its past case law, it went beyond the designation of the measure as a "decision of the Member States"[9] and looked instead to its content, and all the circumstances in which it was adopted, to determine whether it was, in reality, a decision of the Commission.[10] Even then, however, the Court ultimately concluded that the measure was not an act of an EU institution, and declared the Parliament's application inadmissible.

It is submitted that one of the most significant aspects of the Court's ruling, and of the concurring opinion of Advocate General Jacobs, was the view taken of the role of the Commission in the adoption and implementation of the contested measure in determining its true nature. Neither the Court nor the Advocate General considered that the "proposal" made by the Commission to the Finance Ministers of May 11, concerning aid for Bangladesh, was necessarily a "proposal" within the meaning of Article 250 EC.[11] The Court held that Commission proposals of this kind "may just as well constitute mere initiatives taken in the form of informal proposals"[12] while the Advocate General reminded the Court that it was "normal practice for the Commission to be involved in the preparation of the decisions of the representatives of Member States meeting in Council".[13] Further, even though the fourth indent of Article 211 (ex Article 155) of the EC Treaty provides that the Commission only exercises "powers conferred on it by the Council for the implementation of rules laid down by the latter", the fact that the Commission was to have a role in administering the aid was not taken to be conclusive. The Court of Justice held that Article 211 (ex Article 155) did not preclude the Member States from entrusting the Commission with the task of coordinating collective action, and Advocate General Jacobs concluded that, provided that the activity in question is compatible with the Commission's duties under the Community treaties, there could be "no objection" to the Commission "accepting tasks outside the framework of the Community Treaties, commensurate with the political responsibilities of the Community."[14] He was also of the view that it was in the discretion of the Commission to decide whether to take on work of this kind.[15]

3.04 Weight was also placed on the fact that, in the field of humanitarian aid, the Community competence was not exclusive, and that the Member States could not be excluded *per se* from taking collective action in this field, either acting inside the Coun-

---

[8] Case 22/70 *Commission* v. *Council* [1971] ECR 263.
[9] *European Parliament* v. *Council and Commission,* Joined Cases C–181/91 and C–248/91 [1993] E.C.R. 3685, para. 15.
[10] *ibid.*
[11] At the relevant time, Art. 149 EEC. This became Art. 189a EC pursuant to the TEU, before being renumbered Art. 250 by the Treaty of Amsterdam.
[12] *European Parliament* v. *Council and Commission,* Joined Cases C–181/91 and C–248/91 [1993] E.C.R. 3685, para. 18.
[13] *ibid.*, at para. 23 of the AG's opinion.
[14] *ibid.*, at para. 27 of the AG's opinion.
[15] *ibid.*

cil or outside it.[16] The fact that the Member States had made recourse to GNP, a yard-stick that is typically used within the Community decision making, did not necessarily indicate that the measure in question was an act for the purposes of Article 230 EC (ex Article 173).[17] The treatment of the aid within the Commission's budget was also considered to be irrelevant for the purposes of classifying the act. It was held as follows:

> " (. . .) the contested decision leaves it to the Member States to choose whether to pay their contribution by way of bilateral aid or through an account administered by the Commission. Since the contested act does not require use of the Community budget for the part of the aid to be administered by the Commission, the budget entry made by the latter cannot have any bearing on how the act is categorised."[18]

Finally with regard to the legality, or otherwise of the Commission's budget entries, the Court ruled that they were not capable of infringing the Parliament's prerogatives under Article 272 (ex Article 203) of the EC Treaty. This was so because the contributions made by Greece were not items of Community revenue under Article 268 EC (ex Article 199), and nor were they outgoing expenditure within the meaning of that article, as the measure had been taken at an intergovernmental level and not within the framework of the Council. That being the case, the entry into the budget of the Greek contribution of special aid were not capable of amending the Community budget, and thereby infringing the Parliament's prerogatives.[19] Advocate General Jacobs went slightly further. He was of the view that, while the Commission was not entitled to make the budget entries because they did not relate to Community income and expenditure,[20] and that even though the decision to do so had been "improper",[21] no infringement of the Parliament's prerogatives had been thereby entailed.[22]

The case, therefore, left a potentially dangerous gap with respect to judicial review in the Community legal order. It indicated, that when the Member States act in a field in which competence is shared between the Member States and the Community, and the Member States elect to take a decision *via* intergovernmental agreement rather than through the EC institutional machinery, it would not be amenable to scrutiny by the Court of Justice. This was so because the initiative could not be considered an "act" for the purposes of Article 230 EC (ex Article 173). Advocate General Jacobs made reference to this problem and suggested that if Member States took collective action that was in breach of Community law, it would be open to the Commission to bring enforcement proceedings under Article 226 EC (ex Article 169).[23] He pointed out, however, that this remedy would not suffice in circumstances such as those before him, in which the Commission was in agreement with the measures that had been taken, and the problem concerned complaint by the Parliament of infringement of its prerogatives by recourse to the incorrect procedure for decision making.[24]

---

[16] *ibid.*, at para. 16 of the judgment. See also para. 25 of the Opinion of the AG. For a detailed discussion of Community and Member State competence in the field of humanitarian aid and development cooperation see O'Keeffe "Community and Member State Competence in External Agreements of the EU" 4 EFARev. (1999) 7, pp. 29–32.
[17] *European Parliament* v. *Council and Commission,* Joined Cases C–181/91 and C–248/91 [1993] E.C.R. 3685, paras. 21 and 22 of the judgment.
[18] *ibid.*, at para. 24.
[19] *ibid.*, at paras. 30 and 31.
[20] *ibid.*, at para. 41 of the AG's opinion.
[21] *ibid.*, at para. 45 of the AG's opinion.
[22] *ibid.*, at paras. 44 and 45 of the AG's opinion.
[23] *ibid.*, at para. 22 of the AG's opinion.
[24] *ibid.*

3.05   This lacuna was partly closed in the *EDF* case. It essentially concerned the method utilised by the Member States for the establishment of the European Development Fund for the donation of aid to third state parties to the fourth Lomé Convention. In another action in which the Parliament complained of breach of its prerogatives, the Court of Justice interpreted the relevant provisions of the Lomé Convention[25] as imposing a joint obligation on the Community and its Member States, considered together, to grant "the Community's financial assistance". Given that Community competence in the field of development aid was not exclusive, it was for the Community and the Member States to choose the source and method of financing. That being so, a structure in which the EDF was established by an inter-governmental Internal Agreement,[26] with implementation of the agreement to be entrusted to a Council regulation that was not made within the EC institutional structure (but made pursuant to an Internal Agreement)[27] in no way infringed the Parliament's prerogatives over the budget. The expenditure in question was not Community expenditure to which Article 279 EC (ex Article 209) applied.[28] In addition, the Court reiterated its conclusions in the *Bangladesh* case. That is, the Member States, when acting outside of the EC institutional framework, were not prevented from using procedural steps drawing on rules applicable to Community expenditure, and from associating Community institutions with that procedure. That did not mean, however, that any financial regulation had to be based on Article 279 EC (ex Article 209).

The case was more important for its conclusions on the question of the admissibility of the Parliament's action. The *EDF* case differed markedly from the ruling in *Bangladesh*, in that the Parliament lost its claim, not at the threshold of admissibility, but on the merits. The Court of Justice rejected submissions to effect that the impugned regulation was not a measure having legal effect, and in so doing formulated a general principle with important ramifications. It held as follows:

> "(...) an action taken by the Parliament against an act of an institution intended to have legal effects is admissible *irrespective of whether the act was adopted by the institution pursuant to Treaty provisions*".[29]

The consequences of this ruling, from the perspective of inter-institutional law, have been further developed in *Commission* v. *Council*.[30] The decision concerned the role of the Court of Justice in reviewing measures elaborated within the two intergovernmental pillars of the EU. In the context of challenge by the Commission to a Council Joint Action regarding airport transit visas,[31] (taken pursuant to Article 31 TEU (ex Article K (3)) in Title VI on Cooperation in the field of Justice and Home Affairs as it then was) Advocate General Fennelly concluded, on the basis of the *EDF* and *Bangladesh* rulings, that it was not enough for an act to be purportedly adopted under Title VI, TEU for Article 46 TEU (ex Article L) to operate,[32] and for the measure to be immune from Court of Justice review.[33] This would, according to the Advocate General, be contrary to the reasoning of the Court in Case 22/70, *Commission* v.

---

[25] Arts. 223, 231, 338, and 367 of the Convention and Art. 1 of the Financial Protocol.
[26] Internal Agreement 91/401/EEC on the financing and administration of Community aid under the Fourth ACP – EEC Convention, [1991] O.J. L229/288.
[27] [1991] O.J. L266/1.
[28] *European Parliament* v. *Council*, Case C–316/91 [1994] E.C.R. 625, paras. 24 to 39.
[29] *ibid*., at para. 9 (emphasis added).
[30] *Commission* v. *Council*, Case C–170/96 [1998] E.C.R. I–2763.
[31] [1996] O.J. L63/8.
[32] Note that Art. 46 TEU (ex Art. L) was amended by the Treaty of Amsterdam. See Monar, above, p. 42, n. 3.
[33] *Commission* v. *Council*, Case C–170/96 [1998] E.C.R.I.–2763, para. 15 of the AG's opinion.

Council (ERTA),[34] *Bangladesh* and *EDF*, and would deprive Article 47 TEU (ex Article M) of its utility.[35] Article 47 preserves the *acquis* developed under the treaties establishing the European Communities. In other words, the Court of Justice had jurisdiction to determine whether the measure should rightly have been adopted within the EC legal structure. He concluded as follows:

> "In providing that the 'Court shall review the legality of (...) acts of the Council', Article 173 clearly intended to confer on the Court jurisdiction only in respect of Council acts adopted within the scope of the Treaty. However, in order to exercise this jurisdiction, the Court is, in my view, not merely empowered but obliged, in accordance with Article 164 of the Treaty, to rule on whether a contested act is within the scope of the Treaty or not."[36]

Advocate General Fennelly therefore took the view that the Court had jurisdiction to review Council Joint Action taken pursuant to Title VI on Cooperation in the field of Justice and Home Affairs, and that the admissibility of the Commission's action could only be assessed in the light of the merits of the case.[37] The Court of Justice agreed with this approach, even though it made no express reference to the *EDF* and *Bangladesh* cases. It held that the combined effects of Article 46 and 47 (ex Articles L and M) of the TEU vested the Court of Justice with the task of ensuring that acts which "fall within the scope of Article K.3(2) of the Treaty on European Union do not encroach upon the powers conferred by the EC Treaty on the Community."[38]

3.06   The *Bangladesh* and *EDF* cases therefore made substantial contributions to the evolution of legal principles governing the administration of development aid, and cleared a path for the delimitation of Member States' competence with respect to the Union's two intergovernmental pillars. In the context of the former, they confirmed that Member States maintain a broad discretion in selecting the appropriate channels for the donation of development aid, and that "recruitment" of EC institutions in its distribution will in no way colour the choice of the "intergovernmental" route. With respect to the latter, the broad interpretation of the term "acts (...) intended to produce legal effects" which appeared in the *EDF* case, at the very least assisted the Court of Justice to ultimately rule, in *Commission* v. *Council*[39] that the exclusion of Court of Justice jurisdiction enshrined in Article 46 TEU (ex Article L) was not absolute.

---

[34] [1971] E.C.R. 263.
[35] Art. 47 TEU (ex Art. M) provides as follows: "Subject to the provisions amending the Treaty establishing the European Economic Community with a view to establishing the European Community, the Treaty establishing the European Coal and Steel Community and the Treaty establishing the European Atomic Energy Community, and to these final provisions, nothing in this Treaty shall effect the Treaties establishing the European Communities or subsequent Treaties and Acts modifying or supplementing them".
[36] *Commission* v. *Council*, Case C–170/96 [1998] E.C.R. I–2763, para. 16 of the AG's opinion.
[37] *ibid.*, at para. 18 of the AG's opinion. The Advocate General took the view that the measure fell outside the parameters of the EC Treaty, and more particularly (Art. 100c(1)) EC, and that the Commission's actions should be dismissed. Note that Art. 100 (c) was repealed under the Amsterdam Treaty.
[38] *Commission* v. *Council*, Case C–170/96 [1998] E.C.R. I–2763, para. 16. The Court of Justice also concluded, at para. 32, that the act fell outside the parameters of Art. 100(c) of the EC Treaty (repealed by the Amsterdam Treaty) and dismissed the application.
[39] Case C–170/96 [1998] E.C.R. I–2763.

CHAPTER 4
The WTO And OECD Opinions

by

*Takis Tridimas**

4.01 The external competence of the Community gives rise to some of the most intractable problems of Community law.[1] The founding Treaties offer no guidance with regard to the scope and nature of external competence. Also, the case law in this area appears to be less structured than in other areas.[2] In Opinion 1/94, *on the Agreement establishing the WTO,*[3] the Court addressed some fundamental issues pertaining to the external competence of the Community and revisited its previous case law. In particular, the Court had the opportunity to pronounce on the scope of the common commercial policy, the implied competence of the Community, and the duty of cooperation between the Community institutions and the Member States in the conclusion and implementation of international agreements. Issues of competence were also examined in Opinion 2/92, *on the Third Revised Decision of the OECD on National Treatment.*[4] This chapter examines the salient aspects of the Court's rulings and their ramifications for Community competence.

THE BACKGROUND TO THE WTO OPINION

4.02 The Final Act embodying the results of the Uruguay Round of Multilateral Trade Negotiations was formally signed in Marrakesh on April 15, 1994 thus ending "the most complex negotiations in world history".[5] Those negotiations, which had commenced with the Punta del Este Ministerial declaration of September 20, 1986, lasted for seven years. They were unprecedented in scope and complexity, and resulted in the signing of 22 agreements, a host of ministerial decisions and declarations, and no less than 26,000 pages of national tariff and services schedules.[6] The Final Act contains

---

* Professor of European Law, University of Southampton.
[1] For general works on the subject, see *inter alia*, McGoldrick, *International Relations Law of the European Union* (Longman, 1997), Macleod, Hendry and Hyett, *The External Relations of the European Communities* (OUP, 1996), P. Eeckhout, *The European Internal Market and International Trade: A Legal Analysis* (OUP, 1994). See also for an attempt to restate the law, *CELS EC Treaty Project*, (1997) 22 E.L.Rev. 395 at pp. 504 *et seq.*
[2] See Tridimas and Eeckhout, "The External Competence of the Community and the Case-law of the Court of Justice: Principle versus Pragmatism", (1994) 14 Y.E.L. 143.
[3] [1994] E.C.R. I–5267. Comments on the Opinion include: Tridimas and Eeckhout, *op. cit.*; Simon, "La compétence de la Communauté pour conclure l'accord OMC: l'avis 1/94 de la Cour de justice", *Europe* (1994) chronique 9; Louis, "Les relations extérieures de l'Union européenne: unité ou complémentarité", RMUE (1995), p. 8; Bourgeois, The EC in the WTO and Advisory Opinion 1/94: An Echternach Procession, (1995) C.M.L.Rev. p. 763; Emiliou, The Death of Exclusive Competence? (1996) 21 E.L.Rev. 294.
[4] Opinion 2/92 [1995] E.C.R. I–521.
[5] This is how the negotiations were described by the Council of the European Union. See Opinion 1/94 [1994] E.C.R. I–5267 at 5279. The Agreement came into force on January 1, 1995.
[6] See Van den Bossche, "The Establishment of the World Trade Organisation: The Dawn of a New Era in International Trade?", (1994) 1 M.J. 396 at p. 396.

an agreement establishing the World Trade Organisation (WTO) which lays down an institutional and procedural framework for the conduct of trade relations among its Members. The establishment of an institutional structure, which ironically was not one of the initial objectives of the Uruguay Round, was one of its most important achievements. The WTO agreement does not contain any substantive provisions. Such provisions are contained in its annexes which form an integral part of it. They include the following:

(a) the Multilateral Agreements on Trade in Goods, including GATT 1994 (Annex 1A);

(b) the General Agreement on Trade in Services (GATS) (Annex 1B);

(c) the Agreement on Trade-Related Aspects of Intellectual Property Rights (TRIPS) (Annex 1C);

(d) an understanding on Rules and Procedures governing the settlement of disputes ("the Disputes Settlement Understanding") (Annex 2); and

(e) a trade policy review mechanism (Annex 3).[7]

Although from the beginning of the Uruguay Round there was uncertainty as to scope of the Community's competence, it was agreed that, in the interests of consistency, negotiations on behalf of both the Community and the Member States would be conducted by the Commission. Upon the conclusion of negotiations, the WTO Agreement was signed by the Council and Commissioner Sir Leon Brittan, on behalf of the Council, and the representatives of the Member States, on behalf of their respective governments. On April 6, 1994, shortly before the date when the Agreement was to be signed in Marrakesh but after its crucial approval by the Trade Negotiations Committee, the Commission sought the Opinion of the Court pursuant to Article 300 EC (ex Article 228(6)) as to whether the Community had exclusive competence to conclude the Agreement and its annexes.

The late stage at which the Opinion of the Court was sought raised serious doubts as to the admissibility of the request. Spain launched a formal objection of inadmissibility. It argued that the procedure of Article 300(6) can only be initiated where the Community has not yet entered into any international obligations. The signature of the Final Act at Marrakesh authenticated the texts resulting from the negotiations and entailed an obligation on the part of the signatories to submit them for the approval of their respective authorities. The Court dismissed the plea of inadmissibility stating that, pursuant to Article 300(6), the Opinion of the Court can be sought "at any time before the Community's consent to be bound by the agreement is finally expressed".[8] Although that seems to stretch to the maximum the concept of an agreement which is "envisaged" under the terms of Article 300(6), it is in fact correct. Under Article 2 of the Final Act embodying the results of the Uruguay Round, by signing it, the contracting parties agreed to submit the WTO agreement for the considerations of their respective competent authorities with a view to seeking, as appropriate, approval in accordance with the procedures applicable in each State. It follows that the WTO

---

[7] In addition, Annex 4 contains four plurilateral agreements relating respectively to government procurement, trade in civil aircraft, dairy products, and bovine meat. Those agreements apply only to those WTO members who accept to be bound by them.

[8] Opinion 1/94 [1994] E.C.R. I–5267, para. 12. *Cf.* Opinion 3/94, *Framework Agreement on Bananas* [1995] E.C.R. I–4577 where the Court dismissed the request for an opinion as inadmissible.

Agreement would become binding only once it was concluded by the Community and ratified by the participating States. At the time of the request, therefore, the agreement was still "envisaged". The late stage when the request was made, however, in combination with the tight schedule for final conclusion, put the Court under intense pressure to submit its Opinion within a short period.

THE ISSUES RAISED

4.03   The crucial issues raised in the opinion were whether the Community had exclusive competence to conclude GATS and TRIPS. The Commission argued that both GATS and TRIPS fell within the exclusive competence of the Community by virtue of Article 133 EC (ex Article 113) EC or, alternatively, by virtue of the Community's implied powers. That view was vehemently disputed by the Council, the Parliament, and a number of Member States. It will be noted that the solution to the dispute was not only of theoretical but also of enormous practical importance. This is because the agreements in issue are framework agreements providing for the general rules on the basis of which trade is to be conducted and liberalised. The Court's ruling therefore would provide authority for the conduct of trade policy and the representation of the Community in the WTO in the future.[9]

Before discussing the main issues raised, it is appropriate to recall some other findings made in the ruling. First, the Court confirmed that the Member States were competent to conclude the WTO agreement in relation to their overseas countries and territories in so far as they remained outside the ambit of the EC Treaty.[10] Also, the Court held that, since the WTO only had an operating budget and was not intended to be a financial policy instrument, the fact that the Member States would bear some of its expenses could not of itself justify their participation in the conclusion of the WTO Agreement.[11] Finally, the Multilateral Agreements on Trade in Goods were held to come within the scope of Article 133 EC (ex Article 113). The Court interpreted the scope of application of the ECSC Treaty restrictively so as not to affect the exclusivity of the common commercial policy. It held that the Community has the power to conclude under Article 133 EC (ex Article 113) an international agreement which applies in general to all types of goods, even where such goods include ECSC products. The ECSC Treaty, read in the light of Article 133 EC (ex Article 113) has the effect of reserving competence to the Member States only with regard to agreements which apply specifically to ECSC products.[12]

GATS, TRIPS AND THE COMMON COMMERCIAL POLICY

4.04   The Commission's main submission was that GATS fell within the scope of Article 133 EC (ex Article 113). Traditionally, the case law has endorsed a dynamic and evolutionary notion of trade policy interpreting Article 133 EC (ex Article 113) in the light of developments in the international economic environment.

Thus in the *Natural Rubber Agreement* it was held that the common commercial policy does not include only liberalisation measures but also instruments to regulate international trade.[13] In *WTO*, the Court referred to the emerging pattern of world

---

[9] See Tridimas and Eeckhout, *op. cit.*, p. 160.
[10] [1994] E.C.R. I–5267, para. 17.
[11] *ibid.*, para. 21; *Cf.* Opinion 1/78, *Natural Rubber Agreement* [1979] E.C.R. 2871, Case C–316/91 *Parliament* v. *Council* [1994] E.C.R. I–625.
[12] [1994] E.C.R. I–5267, para. 27 and see Opinion 1/75, *Export Credits* [1975] E.C.R. 1355.
[13] See Opinion 1/78, *Natural Rubber Agreement* [1979] E.C.R. 2871.

trade, according to which basic industry is increasingly transferred to developing economies, whilst developed economies have tended to become mainly exporters of services and of goods with high value-added content. In the light of that trend and the open-ended nature of the common commercial policy, the Court concluded that trade in services could not necessarily be excluded from the scope of Article 133 EC (ex Article 113). That finding, however, was not the end of the enquiry. The Court looked at the definition of services given in GATS with a view to ascertaining to what extent services may be said to fall within Article 133 EC (ex Article 113), given the overall scheme of the Treaty. GATS distinguishes four modes of supply of services:

(a) cross-frontier supplies, which do not involve any movement of persons;

(b) consumption abroad, which entails the movement of the consumer in the territory of the WTO member country in which the supplier is established;

(c) commercial presence, namely the presence of a subsidiary or branch in the territory of the WTO member country in which the service is to be rendered;

(d) the presence of natural persons from a WTO member country, enabling a supplier from one member country to supply services within the territory of any other member country.

It is clear that GATS understands the provision of services broadly. It encompasses forms of trade some of which would be governed by the provisions of the EC Treaty on the right of establishment rather than the freedom to provide services.

4.05   The Court found that only the cross-frontier mode of supply falls within the scope of Article 133 EC (ex Article 113). This is because in the case of cross-frontier supplies, the service itself travels and there is no inter-state movement either on the part of the service provider or the part of the recipient. That situation therefore is not unlike trade in goods and there is no reason why it should not fall within the concept of the common commercial policy.[14] The Court found that, in the light of the scheme of the Treaty, the other three modes of supply did not come within the ambit of the common commercial policy. It reasoned as follows. Article 3 EC (ex Article 3) distinguishes between the common commercial policy, on the one hand, and measures concerning the entry and movement of persons in the internal market, on the other hand.[15] It follows that the treatment of nationals of non-member countries on crossing the external frontiers of Member States cannot be regarded as falling within the common commercial policy. The Court held that, more generally, the existence in the Treaty of specific chapters on the free movement of natural and legal persons shows that those matters do not fall within the common commercial policy.[16] It could be argued that neither argument is conclusive.[17] The Court however was understandably reluctant to extend the scope of the common commercial policy, and therefore establish exclusivity, across the whole range of services, including aspects of the right of establishment, given that the movement of third country nationals to and from Member States is still largely governed by national law and not by Community law.

The economic rationale underlying the Court's reasoning appears to be the following. Exclusive Community competence in relation to external trade in goods is justified mainly by the need to avoid deflections of trade. The provisions of the Treaty on the free movement of goods applies not only to goods originating in Member States but

---

[14] Opinion 1/94, [1994] E.C.R. I–5267, para. 44.
[15] See Articles 3(b) and 3(d) EC.
[16] Opinion 1/94, [1994] E.C.R. I–5267, para. 46.
[17] See further for this argument, Tridimas and Eeckhout, *op. cit.*, 161–162.

also to goods imported from third countries which are in free circulation in the Community. If Member States were able to conduct independently their own commercial policies, an internal market would not be possible. A restrictive regime imposed in one Member State would be undermined by a liberal regime established in another and deflections of trade would occur. The danger of deflections of trade is not present in the same way in relation to services, as in contrast to goods, production and consumption takes place simultaneously. Here the distinction between the various modes of supply becomes material. Services which can be provided on a cross-border basis (tradeable services) are in general more susceptible to deflections of trade than the other modes of supply, precisely because the first do not require mobility of labour. It may therefore seem reasonable to equate the cross-border form of supply of services with goods.

It may be argued, however, that it makes little sense to divide competence on the basis of the mode of supply since in most cases the subject matter of regulation will be a given service rather than a given mode of supply. Few services can be provided only on a cross-border basis. The issue became material in *Parliament* v. *Council (Public procurement)*.[18] The case concerned two decisions adopted on the basis of Article 133 EC (ex Article 113) by which the Council approved on behalf of the Community an Agreement with the United States on public procurement entered into in the context of the GATT Multilateral Agreement on Government Procurement. The Parliament argued that the decisions should have been adopted not only on the basis of Article 133 EC (ex Article 113) but also on the basis of Articles 47(2), 55 and 95 EC (ex Articles 57(2), 66 and 110a) which, unlike Article 133 EC (ex Article 113), provided at the time for the cooperation procedure. The Court pointed out that the Agreement was concerned not only with goods but also, on an independent basis, with the provision of services. Then, referring to *WTO*, it stated that, in the present state of Community law, only services which are supplied across frontiers fall within the scope of Article 133 EC (ex Article 113). The Court held, however, that the modes of supply of services covered by the two decisions could not be reduced to the sole hypothesis of a trans-frontier supply involving no movement of persons. They related also to supplies made thanks to a commercial presence or the presence of natural persons in the territory of the other contracting party. On that basis, it held that the decisions should not have been adopted solely on the basis of Article 133 EC (ex Article 113) and annulled them, whilst maintaining in force their effects pursuant to Article 231(2) EC (ex Article 174 (2)) EC.

4.06   The above case illustrates that in most cases it will not be possible to separate between different modes of supply. The effect of the Court's ruling in *WTO* is that, since they share competence, the Commission and Member States are locked in a relationship of cooperation. Also, the ruling gives the green light to the Commission to address in the future regulatory issues arising from technological advances which increasingly make possible the cross-supply of services, *e.g.* tele-medicine. All in all, the ruling ensures that the Commission is an important factor in the international regulation of services but alongside, and not in lieu of, the Member States.

In *WTO* the Court examined separately transport services. It held that such services do not fall within the scope of Article 133 EC (ex Article 113) since transport is subject to a specific title of the Treaty (Title IV) which is distinct from the Title on the common commercial policy. The Court applied in effect the rule *lex specialis derogat legi generali* and rejected the Commission's argument that the Title on Transport governs only rules on safety whereas Article 133 EC (ex Article 113) covers rules of a commercial

---

[18]   See, *e.g.* Case C–360/93 *Parliament* v. *Commission (Government Procurement)* [1996] E.C.R. I–1195, paras. 29–30.

nature.[19] It is notable that the pronouncement on transport contrasts with that on agriculture. The Court rejected the argument that the Agreement on Agriculture, which is part of the WTO Multilateral Agreements on Trade in Goods, should have been adopted not only on the basis of Article 133 EC (ex Article 113) but also on the basis of Article 37 EC (ex Article 43). It held that the Agreement on Agriculture was not intended to achieve the objectives of the common agricultural policy but rather to establish, on a worldwide basis, a fair and market-oriented agricultural trading system. The fact that commitments undertaken pursuant to the agreement required internal measures to be adopted under Article 37 EC (ex Article 43) did not prevent the international commitments themselves from being entered into pursuant to Article 133 EC (ex Article 113) alone.[20] Thus agriculture is treated differently from transport as regards its relations with the common commercial policy: agreements on the former may fall within its scope whereas agreements on the latter may not.[21]

Unsurprisingly, the Court rejected the Commission's view that the Community had exclusive competence to conclude TRIPS. The Commission essentially argued that the rules concerning intellectual property rights are closely linked to trade in goods and services to which they apply.

The Court held that such link was not sufficient to bring them within the scope of Article 133 EC (ex Article 113) as intellectual property rights do not relate specifically to international trade. They affect internal as much as, if not more than, international trade.[22]

The Court also pointed out that the primary objective of TRIPS was to strengthen and harmonise protection of intellectual property rights on a worldwide basis. Since TRIPS lays down rules in fields in which there are no Community harmonisation measures, its conclusion would make it possible at the same time to achieve harmonisation of the laws of the Member States. In the internal sphere, however, the Community is competent to harmonise national laws in the field of intellectual property on the basis of Treaty articles (*i.e.* Articles 94, 95 and 308 EC (ex Articles 100, 100a and 235)) which provide for different voting rules and procedures from those applicable under Article 133 EC (ex Article 113). Thus, if the Community were recognised as having exclusive competence in relation to TRIPS, it would be able to achieve internal harmonisation evading the procedures and safeguards provided for in the Treaty. The only aspect of TRIPS which was held to be within the scope of Article 133 EC (ex Article 113) was the rules seeking to prohibit the release into free circulation of counterfeit goods. Those rules provided for measures to be taken at the external frontiers of the Community and found their counterpart in internal Community legislation.[23] In conclusion, the Court held that TRIPS could not be concluded only on the basis of Article 133 EC (ex Article 113).

THE COMMUNITY'S IMPLIED POWERS

4.07 In *WTO* the Commission submitted as a subsidiary argument that, even if the Community did not have exclusive competence to conclude GATS and TRIPS under

---

[19] Opinion 1/94, [1994] E.C.R. I–5267, paras. 49–50. In the *OECD* Opinion the Court reiterated that international agreements on transport fell within the scope of the common transport policy and not within the scope of the common commercial policy. See Opinion 2/92, [1995] E.C.R. I–521, para. 27.
[20] Opinion 1/94, [1994] E.C.R. I–5267, para. 29.
[21] See further, Tridimas and Eeckhout, *op. cit.*, pp. 162–163.
[22] Opinion 1/94, [1994] E.C.R. I–5267, para. 57.
[23] See Council Regulation 3842/86 laying down measures to prohibit the release for free circulation of counterfeit goods, [1986] O.J. L357/1.

Article 133 EC (ex Article 113), such exclusive competence flowed implicitly from the provisions of the Treaty establishing its internal competence. In the Commission's view, exclusive competence to conclude GATS flowed from the Treaty provisions on the right of establishment and the freedom to provide services. The Court dismissed that argument by stating as follows:[24]

> "Unlike the chapter on transport, the chapters on the right of establishment and on freedom to provide services do not contain any provision expressly extending the competence of the Community to "relationships arising from international law"... [T]he sole objective of those chapters is to secure the right of establishment and freedom to provide services for nationals of Member States. They contain no provisions on the problem of the first establishment of nationals of non-member countries and the rules governing their access to self-employed activities. One cannot therefore infer from those chapters that the Community has exclusive competence to conclude an agreement with non-member countries to liberalise first establishment and access to service markets ...".

It is important to ascertain the meaning of that passage. The Court did not state that the institutions may not, on the basis of the powers conferred upon them by the chapters on the right of establishment and the freedom to provide services, regulate relations with third states. In fact, the institutions have done so on occasion, as the Court recalled at a later part of its ruling. Rather, the meaning of the above dicta is that the aforementioned chapters of the Treaty do not confer on the Community exclusive competence in the external sphere. The Court rejected the Commission's submission that the Member States' freedom to conduct external policy in relation to trade in services was liable to undermine the internal market. It stated in response that there is nothing to prevent the institutions from arranging, in laying down common rules, concerted action in relation to third countries or from prescribing the approach to be taken by the Member States in their external dealings.[25]

The Commission sought support for its arguments in Opinion 1/76 on *Inland Waterway Vessels*[26] which concerned a draft agreement on the regulation of vessels in the Rhine-Moselle waterway system. There, the Court held that the draft agreement, which aimed at establishing a European laying-up Fund, was incompatible with the Treaty because it granted to the Member States the power to determine the operation of the Fund. The ruling in Opinion 1/76 could be interpreted as meaning that, where it is necessary for the Community to enter into an international agreement in order to attain its objectives, the Community has exclusive competence to do so in so far as it has competence in the internal sphere.[27] In other words, exclusivity is not dependent on the exercise of internal powers by the adoption of Community legislation. In *WTO* the Court rejected that view. It distinguished Opinion 1/76 on the ground that the agreement in issue in that case sought to rationalise the navigation in the inland waterways sector of the Rhine and Moselle basins. That objective could not be attained by the adoption of internal Community rules owing to the traditional participation of Swiss vessels. The need to bind Switzerland made it necessary to act by way of an international agreement. It was therefore justifiable for the Community to have exclusive external competence even though internal legislation had not been adopted. By contrast, the situation was different in the field of services. Attainment of the freedom of

---

[24] Opinion 1/94, [1994] E.C.R. I–5267, para. 81.
[25] *ibid.*, para. 79.
[26] Opinion 1/76, *draft Agreement establishing a European laying-up fund for inland waterway vessels* [1977] E.C.R. 741.
[27] *ibid.*, especially paras. 3 and 4.

establishment and the freedom to provide services for nationals of the Member States is not inextricably linked to the treatment to be afforded in the Community to nationals of third States or in third States to Community nationals.[28]

4.08   The distinction drawn in *WTO* seems correct. It is true that in Opinion 1/76 the Court appeared to take a strict view of exclusivity. It held that the agreement in issue fell within the exclusive competence of the Community despite the fact that transport is a policy where, unlike the common commercial policy, the competence of the Community has not been held by the case law to be *a priori* exclusive. The pronouncements of the Court on exclusivity, however, should not be read in the abstract but in the context of the case. The draft agreement was held to be incompatible with the Treaty not because it infringed some abstract notion of exclusivity but because it gave too much power to the Member States. It substituted Member State action for a Community policy and relegated the institutions to secondary actors in the decision-making.[29] The Court was particularly concerned to avoid those arrangements forming a precedent, thus enabling Member States to conduct their own external relations independently in the future.[30]

In *WTO*, the Court confirmed the finding in *ERTA*[31] that, in principle, the mere existence of powers in the internal sphere does not give rise to exclusive external competence. The external competence of the Community becomes exclusive only in so far as common rules have been established at the internal level.[32] In short, internal competence can give rise to exclusive external competence only if it is exercised. That applies not only to the provisions on the right of establishment and the freedom to provide services but also to internal powers arising from Article 95 (ex Article 100a) and the residual provision of Article 308 EC (ex Article 235).[33] The same reasoning was applied in relation to TRIPS. Harmonisation of the laws of the Member States on intellectual property rights did not necessarily have to be accompanied by agreements with non-member countries in order to be effective. The Community therefore did not have exclusive competence in relation to TRIPS. In effect, the case law subordinates exclusive external competence to the exercise of internal powers. This derives from the model of the EC Treaty which makes establishment of the internal market the central goal of the Community.

An issue which is left open by the *WTO* Opinion is whether, under any circumstances, exclusivity may arise from Article 308 EC (ex Article 235) or whether such possibility is precluded. The Court stated that Article 308 EC (ex Article 308) cannot in itself vest exclusive competence in the Community at international level. Referring to Opinion 1/76, it pointed out that "save where internal powers can only be effectively exercised at the same time as external powers", internal competence can give rise to exclusive external competence only if it exercised. That applied *a fortiori* to Article 308 EC (ex Article 235).[34] It is arguable that those dicta do not foreclose the possibility that, in exceptional circumstances, the Community may derive exclusive external competence from Article 308 EC (ex Article 235). That would be the case where it is necessary for the institutions to act for the attainment of the Community objectives, the Treaty provides no specific legal basis for such action, and such action to be effective can only take the form of an international agreement.

---

[28]   Opinion 1/94 [1994] E.C.R. I–5267, para. 86.
[29]   Opinion 1/76 [1977] E.C.R. 741, paras. 9–14.
[30]   *ibid.*, para. 14.
[31]   Case 22/70 *Commission* v. *Council* [1971] E.C.R. 263.
[32]   Opinion 1/94 [1994] E.C.R. I–5267, paras. 77, 89.
[33]   Opinion 1/94 [1994] E.C.R. I–5267, paras. 88–89.
[34]   *ibid.*, para. 89. This finding was reiterated in the *OECD* Opinion. See Opinion 2/92 [1995] E.C.R. I–521, para. 36.

THE OECD OPINION

4.09   In the *OECD* Opinion[35] the Belgian Government sought the Court's Opinion as to whether the Community had exclusive or joint competence to participate in the Third Revised Decision of the OECD on national treatment. The Third Decision itself concerned matters of procedure but formed part of the so-called OECD national treatment rule. Under it, contracting States express their intention to grant to undertakings, which are owned or controlled by nationals of another contracting State and operate in the national territory, treatment which is no less favourable than the treatment accorded to domestic undertakings. The Commission proposed that the Third Decision should be concluded on the basis of Articles 47 and 133 EC (ex Articles 57 and 113).

In its request for an Opinion, the Belgian Government asked, in particular, (a) whether the dual legal basis proposed by the Commission was justified, (b) if not, what was the correct legal basis, and (c) whether the Community had exclusive or joint competence to participate in the decision. The Council and some governments questioned whether the Court had jurisdiction under Article 300(6) EC (ex Article 228(6)) to rule on the choice of legal basis of a measure to be adopted in order to conclude an agreement. The Court pointed out that, pursuant to Article 300(6) EC, an opinion may be sought on questions concerning the division of powers between the Community and Member States. Since the request for an Opinion raised such issues, it was admissible. The Court also held that, the fact that certain questions may be dealt with by means of other remedies, such as an action under Article 230 EC (ex Article 173), did not preclude the Court from being asked to decide on them pursuant to the procedure provided for by Article 300(6) (ex Article 228(6)).

The Court's approach on admissibility seems correct. Since the determination of the scope of Community competence will normally involve the interpretation of Treaty articles, issues pertaining to legal bases may be inextricably linked to the division of competences. Even if it is accepted that the determination of the correct legal basis may not be part of the operative part of the Court's ruling, it may well be an integral part of the Court's reasoning.

4.10   Belgium argued that the Third Decision fell fully within the scope of Article 133 EC (ex Article 113) EC. The same view was supported by the Commission despite its initial proposal that the Community's participation should be based on Articles 47 and 133 EC (ex Articles 57 and 113). The Court held that since the Decision dealt purely with procedural issues, its subject-matter should be determined by reference to the substantive rule to which it related, namely the rule of national treatment.[36] The Court held that that rule concerned mainly the conditions for the participation of foreign-controlled undertakings in the internal life of the Member States in which they operated. It also concerned the conditions for their participation in trade between Member States and third countries but it affected internal trade to the same extent, if not more than, international trade.[37] That is undoubtedly correct: the thrust of the Decision lies with internal trade rather than international, although to a secondary degree it also affects the latter, *e.g.* by governing access of OECD undertakings to

---

[35] Opinion 2/92, *on the Third Revised Decision of the OECD on National Treatment* [1995] E.C.R. I–521.
[36] According to the Report of the Committee on International Investment and Multinational Enterprises, the rule of national treatment applies in particular in relation to measures concerning the following: (1) government procurement; (2) official aids and subsidies; (3) access to local finance; (4) tax obligations; and (5) rules applying to investments other than direct investment operations and investment by "direct branches", *i.e.* branches whose parent company is a non-resident. The Revised Declaration did not seek to regulate the entry of foreign investment or the conditions of establishment of foreign companies.
[37] Opinion 2/92 [1995] E.C.R. I–521, paras. 4, 26.

import quotas from third countries. The connection with the common commercial policy, however, seems tenuous and on the basis of *WTO* it would be difficult to conclude that the national treatment rule fell solely within the scope of Article 133 EC (ex Article 113).

In *OECD* the Court reiterated that, in principle, the mere existence of powers in the internal sphere does not automatically give rise to exclusive external competence. Then, with a view to establishing whether the Community had exclusive competence in relation to the national treatment rule, it proceeded to examine whether the matters covered by the Third Decision were already the subject of internal legislation containing provisions on the treatment to be accorded to foreign-controlled undertakings, or empowering the institutions to negotiate with non-member countries, or effecting complete harmonisation of the rules governing the right to take up an activity as a self-employed person. The Court accepted that the Community has adopted measures capable of serving as a basis for an exclusive external competence. Such measures fell within the scope of Articles 47(2), 71, 80 and 95 EC (ex Articles 57(2), 75, 84 and 100a). They did not however cover all the fields of activity to which the Third Decision related.[38] On that basis, the Court concluded that the Community was competent to participate in the Third Decision but that such competence was shared with the Member States.

A RESTATEMENT OF THE LAW

4.11   It may be useful at this juncture to summarise the rules governing the external competence of the Community following *WTO*. Those rules may be stated as follows:[39]

(a)   The competence of the Community to enter into international agreements may arise expressly from a provision of the Treaty or may flow by implication. Where Community law has bestowed the institutions with power to legislate in the internal sphere in order to attain a specific objective, the Community has competence to enter into international commitments in order to attain that objective even in the absence of an express provision to that effect (*in foro interno in foro externo*).[40]

(b)   In principle, the external competence of the Community is not exclusive but concurrent with that of the Member States.

(c)   The external competence of the Community is exclusive in the following cases:

   (i)   where exclusivity arises by virtue of a Treaty provision;[41]
   (ii)   where the Community institutions have exercised their powers in the internal sphere;[42]

---

[38] *ibid.*, para. 34.
[39] See further Tridimas and Eeckhout, *op. cit.*, 154 *et seq.*
[40] See Opinion 1/76 [1977] E.C.R. 741, paras. 3–4; Opinion 2/91, *Convention No 170 of the ILO concerning safety in the use of chemicals at work* [1993] E.C.R. I–1061, para. 7; Joined Cases 3, 4 and 6/76 *Kramer and Others* [1976] E.C.R. 1279.
[41] According to the case law as it stands, exclusive competence arises by virtue of two provisions: Article 133 EC (ex Article 113) and Article 102 of the First Act of Accession (conservation of sea resources); see Opinion 2/91, [1993] E.C.R. I–1061, para. 8.
[42] *ERTA, Commission* v. *Council*, Case 22/70 [1971] E.C.R. 263; Opinion 2/91 [1993] E.C.R. I–1061, paras. 8–9.

(iii) where the adoption of internal rules by the institutions is not sufficient to attain a Community objective and the only way of attaining that objective is the conclusion by the Community of an international agreement. In such a case, in derogation from (ii) above, the Community has exclusive external competence even if internal rules in the sphere in question have not been adopted.[43] For exclusivity to arise under this rule, the external aspects of the activity must be inextricably linked to the internal ones.[44] That occurs where the participation of third States for the effective regulation of an economic activity is *a sine qua non*.

The rule laid down in paragraph (c)(ii) above requires some further explanation. In *ERTA*, the Court stated:[45]

"... each time the Community, with a view to implementing a common policy envisaged by the Treaty, adopts provisions laying down common rules, whatever form these may take, the Member States no longer have the right, acting individually or even collectively, to undertake obligations with third countries which affect those rules.
... to the extent to which Community rules are promulgated for the attainment of the objectives of the Treaty, the Member States cannot, outside the framework of the Community institutions, assume obligations which might affect those rules or alter their scope."

In *ILO* it was held that the blocking effect of Community law ensues not only where the institutions have adopted rules within the framework of a common policy, as stated in *ERTA*, but any type of rules.[46] Further, in *WTO* the Court stated that the Community acquires exclusive external competence in a certain field not only where Community legislation covers the internal aspects of that field but also where legislation has expressly conferred on the institutions power to negotiate with non-member countries.[47] As we saw above, that extension of blocking effect was confirmed in *OECD*.

It seems that exclusivity arising as a result of a Treaty provision is different from exclusivity arising as a result of the exercise by the institutions of their internal powers. In the first case, at least in theory, the Community occupies the field and pre-empts State action. Save in exceptional cases, Member States may not legislate even in the absence of Community legislation. In the second case, Community legislation has a blocking effect. Member States may not adopt inconsistent measures, *i.e.* legislation which "affects the Community rules or alters their scope". In general, the case law suggests that the notion of inconsistency is not very broad. In *WTO* the Court held that TRIPS was not liable to affect existing Community legislation in the field of intellectual property rights within the meaning of *ERTA*. In certain areas covered by TRIPS, such as trademarks, the Community had only achieved partial harmonisation and in others, such as industrial designs and patents, no harmonisation legislation had been adopted. Those findings are fully compatible with the earlier ruling in the *ILO* Opinion. On the basis of *WTO* and *OECD*, it seems that the Community does not acquire exclusive competence to conclude an international agreement unless existing Community legis-

---

[43] Opinion 1/76 [1977] E.C.R. 741.
[44] Opinion 1/94 [1994] E.C.R. I–5267, para. 86.
[45] *Ibid.*, paras. 17, 22.
[46] Opinion 2/91 [1993] E.C.R. I–1061.
[47] Opinion 1/94 [1994] E.C.R. I–5267, para. 95.

lation covers all the main aspects of that agreement or confers on the institutions power to regulate relations with third States.

THE DUTY OF CO-OPERATION

4.12 Since the Commission failed in its arguments that GATS and TRIPS fell within the exclusive competence of the Community, in its ruling in *WTO* the Court concluded that the Community and the Member States were jointly competent to conclude both agreements.[48] An important aspect of the *WTO* Opinion is the duty of cooperation laid down by the Court. It held:[49]

> "... where it is apparent that the subject-matter of an agreement or convention falls in part within the competence of the Community and in part within that of the Member States, it is essential to ensure close cooperation between the Member States and the Community institutions, both in the process of negotiation and conclusion and in the fulfilment of the commitments entered into. That obligation to cooperate flows from the requirement of unity in the international representation of the Community..."

The Court went on to state that the duty of cooperation was all the more imperative in the case of the WTO agreements, as a result of their close inter-connection and also as a result of the cross-retaliation measures established by the Dispute Settlement Undertaking. In the absence of close cooperation, the Community and the Member States would be unable to retaliate effectively since they could retaliate individually only in those areas which fell within their competence.[50]

The duty of co-operation makes in effect the Community and the Member States "each other's prisoner".[51] Although the Court did not give any specific guidelines, it is arguably further reaching that the duty imposed by the former Article 116 EC and seeks to exploit the collective bargaining power of the Community and the Member States in international relations.[52] It is a duty from which concrete legal obligations flow. Thus, subsequently, in the *FAO* case[53] the Court invoked breach of the duty of co-operation, as embodied in a binding "arrangement" between the Council and the Commission regarding participation and voting in meetings of the Food and Agriculture Organisation of the UN, to annul a decision by which the Council decided that the Member States and not the Commission would vote for the adoption of an agreement concerning the conservation of sea resources.

CONCLUSION

4.13 The *WTO* Opinion reiterates that, where it comes to defining the competence of the Community in the external sphere, the Court follows a pragmatic approach. To use a solecism, it is generous in acknowledging competence but mean in granting exclusivity. Thus the duty of co-operation between the Community and the Member

---

[48] By contrast, the Court rules that the Community had sole competence, pursuant to Art. 133 EC (ex Art. 113), to conclude the Multilateral Agreements on Trade in Goods.

[49] Opinion 1/94 [1994] E.C.R. I–5267, para. 108; See also Opinion 1/78 [1979] E.C.R. 2871, paras. 34–36; Opinion 2/91 [1993] E.C.R. I–1061, para. 36.

[50] [1994] E.C.R. I–5267, para. 109.

[51] See Editorial (1995) 32 C.M.L.Rev. 385, p. 387.

[52] *Ibid.* Article 116 EC was repealed by the TEU.

[53] Case C–25/94 *Commission* v. *Council* [1996] E.C.R. I–1469.

States in conducting external policy becomes of paramount importance. Overall, the case law seems to suggest that the competence of the Community in the external sphere is exclusive only where exclusivity is necessary in order to safeguard effective and co-herent regulation of inter-Community relations. The concept of exclusivity, however, is a relative one. It should not be approached in the abstract but in relation to the final issue which the Court is called upon to determine.

In *WTO* the Court clarified previous authorities. It interpreted Opinion 1/76 restric-tively and laid to rest the argument that external exclusivity arises automatically from the mere existence of powers in the internal field. One wonders whether instead of battling with exclusivity, it might be more helpful to determine the issue whether a trade agreement falls in its entirety within the scope of Community competence, whether exclusive or concurrent, in which case mixity may serve no purpose.[54]

It would be incorrect to conclude that in *WTO* the Court interpreted narrowly the scope of the common commercial policy. The Commission's argument that GATS and TRIPS fell within the ambit of Article 133 EC (ex Article 113) was far fetched. The WTO Agreement encompasses a wide and diverse range of areas covering sectors which are governed largely by rules and policies of the Member States. The opinion leaves the door open to further broadening of the common commercial policy. Also, given that the interests of the Community and the Member States are closely inter-twined, it is difficult to see how the Member States can operate and negotiate effec-tively outside the common umbrella of the Community institutions. This is acknowledged by the duty of cooperation imposed by the Court and, most import-antly, by new Article 133 EC, (ex Article 113) as amended by the Treaty of Amster-dam. A fifth subparagraph added to Article 133 provides that "The Council, acting unanimously on a proposal from the Commission and after consulting the Parliament, may extent the application of the previous paragraphs to international negotiations and agreements on services and intellectual property insofar as they are not covered by these paragraphs". All in all, the signs are that the Community will increasingly replace the Member States in the conduct of trade policy not only in relation to goods but also in relation to services.

---

[54] See further Tridimas and Eeckhout, *op. cit.*, pp. 174–175.

CHAPTER 5

Left To Its Own Devices? Opinion 2/94 and the Protection of Fundamental Rights in the European Union

by

Anthony Arnull*

5.01   In Opinion 2/94[1] the European Court of Justice ruled that, "[a]s Community law now stands, the Community has no competence to accede to the European Convention for the Protection of Human Rights and Fundamental Freedoms." That ruling, delivered on the eve of the intergovernmental conference (IGC) which opened in 1996, raised a number of important issues. One is the scope of the Community's powers to act in the fundamental rights field, both internally and on the international plane. A related issue is whether there is a gap in the Community system for the protection of fundamental rights which accession to the European Convention might usefully fill. A more technical question posed by the Opinion concerns the stage at which it is appropriate for the Court to rule on the compatibility with the Treaty of international agreements which may be envisaged. Each of those issues will be addressed in this chapter. An attempt will also be made to assess the potential effect in the fundamental rights field of the product of the 1996 IGC, the Treaty of Amsterdam.[2]

THE PROTECTION OF FUNDAMENTAL RIGHTS IN THE COMMUNITY LEGAL ORDER

5.02   It is appropriate to begin with a short account of the place of fundamental rights in the legal order of the Community. Although the EC Treaty has always contained provisions prohibiting discrimination on grounds of nationality and requiring equal pay for men and women, it did not originally refer to fundamental rights in a general sense. However, the Court of Justice began in due course to acknowledge that such rights might constitute general principles of law which it had a duty to uphold.[3] One of the most comprehensive summaries of the effect of the Court's case law is to be found in the *ERT* case,[4] where the Court was asked for a preliminary ruling on the effect of, *inter alia*, Article 10 of the European Convention for the Protection of

---

*   Professor of European Law, University of Birmingham.
[1]   [1996] E.C.R. I–1759.
[2]   The Treaty entered into force on May 1, 1999.
[3]   This was first recognised in Case 29/69 *Stauder* v. *Ulm* [1969] E.C.R. 419, para. 7.
[4]   Case C–290/89 [1991] E.C.R. I–2925.

Human Rights and Fundamental Freedoms to help the referring court determine the legality of a national system of exclusive television rights. The Court declared:[5]

> "... it must first be pointed out that, as the Court has consistently held, fundamental rights form an integral part of the general principles of law, the observance of which it ensures. For that purpose the Court draws inspiration from the constitutional traditions common to the Member States and from the guidelines supplied by international treaties for the protection of human rights on which the Member States have collaborated or of which they are signatories ... The European Convention on Human Rights has special significance in that respect ... It follows that ... the Community cannot accept measures which are incompatible with observance of the human rights thus recognized and guaranteed.
>
> As the Court has held ... it has no power to examine the compatibility with the European Convention on Human Rights of national rules which do not fall within the scope of Community law. On the other hand, where such rules do fall within the scope of Community law, and reference is made to the Court for a preliminary ruling, it must provide all the criteria of interpretation needed by the national court to determine whether those rules are compatible with the fundamental rights the observance of which the Court ensures and which derive in particular from the European Convention on Human Rights."

5.03   Thus, the fundamental rights upheld by the Court as general principles of law condition the way in which Community provisions are interpreted.[6] As rules of law relating to the application of the Treaty, their infringement may also provide a ground for the annulment of Community acts.[7] Moreover, the Court of Justice seeks to ensure that those rights are respected not just by the institutions of the Community but also by the Member States when they act within the scope of the Treaty.[8]

The developing case law of the Court of Justice in due course prompted steps by the other institutions and the Member States to underline the Community's political commitment to respect for fundamental rights. In 1977, the European Parliament, the Council and the Commission issued a Joint Declaration stressing "the prime importance" they attached to the protection of fundamental rights and referring expressly to the European Convention. In their Declaration on Democracy made in Copenhagen in 1978, the Heads of Government of the Member States associated themselves with the Joint Declaration of the previous year and solemnly declared "that respect for and maintenance of representative democracy and human rights in each Member State are essential elements of membership of the European Communities."[9]

With the signature of the Single European Act in 1986 came the first reference in a Community Treaty to fundamental rights, the Preamble referring to the fundamental rights recognised in the constitutions and laws of the Member States, the European Convention and the European Social Charter. A stronger commitment was given in the Treaty on European Union signed in Maastricht, Article F(2) of which stated that "[t]he Union shall respect fundamental rights, as guaranteed by the European Convention for the Protection of Human Rights and Fundamental Freedoms signed in Rome on November 4, 1950 and as they result from the constitutional traditions common to

---

[5] *ibid.*, paras. 41 and 42.
[6] See, *e.g.* Joined Cases 46/87 and 227/88 *Hoechst* v. *Commission* [1989] E.C.R. 2859, para. 12. That decision is discussed below.
[7] See, *e.g.* Case 4/73 *Nold* v. *Commission* [1974] E.C.R. 491.
[8] See, *e.g.* Case 5/88 *Wachauf* v. *Germany* [1989] E.C.R. 2609; Case C–2/92 *Bostock* [1994] E.C.R. I–955.
[9] Both the Joint Declaration and the Declaration on Democracy are published in an appendix to the report of the House of Lords Select Committee on the European Communities, see p. 64, n. 16 below.

the Member States, as general principles of Community law." That provision purported to extend to the Union as a whole part of the law applicable under the first pillar. However, Article L of the TEU signed in Maastricht excluded Article F(2) from the jurisdiction of the Court of Justice, so the Union Treaties contained no judicial mechanism for enforcing the obligation it sought to lay down.[10] Nonetheless, the provision reflected an increased awareness at the political level of the need for the Union to demonstrate the importance it attached to fundamental rights. That awareness was reflected in other provisions agreed at Maastricht: Article 130u EC provided, in paragraph 2, that Community policy in the area of development cooperation was to "contribute to the general objective of developing and consolidating democracy and the rule of law, and to that of respecting human rights and fundamental freedoms"; Article J.1(2), fifth indent, provided that developing and consolidating respect for human rights and fundamental freedoms was to be one of the objectives of the common foreign and security policy established by Title V;[11] and Article K.2(1) stated that matters falling within the scope of Title VI must be dealt with in compliance with the European Convention. It should not be forgotten, however, that, by virtue of Article L, Titles V and VI also fell outside the jurisdiction of the Court of Justice, unless (in the case of Title VI) jurisdiction was conferred on it by conventions drawn up under Article K.3(2)(c).

Since the EC Treaty was signed, there had therefore been a steady expansion in the extent to which the Court of Justice would intervene to ensure protection for fundamental rights. Whatever the weaknesses of the TEU, there had undoubtedly also been a corresponding increase in political awareness of the importance of acting—and being seen to act—in accordance with such rights. However, those developments could not disguise the fact that the transfer of competence involved in acceding to the Community—and now the Union—causes a corresponding diminution in the jurisdiction of the organs of the European Convention, in the sense that matters which were previously resolved at national level are dealt with after accession by the institutions of an entity which is not subject to the control mechanisms established by the Convention. This came to be seen in some quarters as incompatible with the oft-proclaimed commitment of the Community and the Union to respecting fundamental rights.

5.04   Accordingly the Commission, with the support of the European Parliament, began to float the idea of accession to the European Convention by the Community itself, so that its institutions would be subject to the review mechanisms set up under the Convention in the same way as the Member States. In 1979 the Commission published a memorandum[12] advocating accession in which it suggested that a legal basis for taking that step might be found in Article 308 EC (ex Article 235).[13] That article provides:

> "If action by the Community should prove necessary to attain, in the course of the operation of the common market, one of the objectives of the Community and this Treaty has not provided the necessary powers, the Council shall, acting unanimously on a proposal from the Commission and after consulting the European Parliament, take the necessary measures."

---

[10] This changes with the Treaty of Amsterdam. See further below.
[11] Evidence of the impact of that provision, and of former Art. F(2), may be found in Council Decision 94/776/EC appointing an ombudsman for Mostar for the duration of the European Union administration of Mostar, [1994] O.J. L312/34.
[12] "Memorandum on the accession of the European Communities to the Convention for the Protection of Human Rights and Fundamental Freedoms", Bulletin of the European Communities, Supplement 2/79.
[13] And, in the case of the Coal and Steel Community and Euratom, Arts. 95 ECSC and 203 EAEC respectively.

The Commission's memorandum was the subject of a report by the House of Lords Select Committee on the European Communities, which took the view that "[t]he immediate practical gains of accession are likely to be limited, the benefits being largely indirect and to some extent symbolic".[14] It pointed out that the use of Article 308 as the legal basis for accession was contested and thought that amendments to the Treaty would be necessary to enable accession to take place.[15] The Select Committee concluded that there were more pressing demands on the Community's resources. That negative response to the Commission's memorandum was echoed in the Council and no concrete steps ensued.

However, the Commission remained convinced that accession would be beneficial and in 1990 it re-ignited the debate by issuing a Communication in which it asked the Council for authority to begin negotiations. The Commission observed that "no matter how closely the Luxembourg Court monitors human rights, it is not the same as scrutiny by the Strasbourg Court, which is outside the Community legal system and to which the constitutional courts and supreme courts of the Member States are subject." The Commission maintained that the ramifications of accession would be limited to matters which fell within the Community's field of competence: the legal systems of the Member States would be affected only as regards the scope of a Community legal act and accession would have no bearing on the effects of the Convention in other areas. Thus, accession would not result in any new obligations for the Member States of the Community. It would simply give their citizens better protection against Community measures which might infringe their fundamental rights. The Commission envisaged Community accession not only to the Convention itself but also to each of the Protocols which had been added to it in so far as they were relevant to the field of application of Community law. Although some of the Protocols had not been accepted by all the Member States, the Commission's view was that any Member State which had not accepted a particular Protocol would be unaffected by Community accession as far as national law was concerned. With regard to the legal basis for accession, the Commission repeated its view that recourse to Article 308 (and the corresponding provisions of the other Treaties) would be justified.

The Commission's Communication was the subject of a further report by the House of Lords Select Committee, which remained of the view that the benefits of accession would be limited and that the Community had more pressing tasks.[16] However, influenced by the references to fundamental rights and to the European Convention in both the Single European Act and the TEU (which had been signed but had yet to enter into force), the Select Committee was now "inclined to the view that the Council could make use of the powers in Article [308] so far as EEC accession is concerned."[17]

The Commission's request for negotiating directives led the Council in 1994 to ask the Court of Justice under Article 300(6) EC (ex Article 228(6)) whether accession by the Community to the European Convention on Human Rights would be compatible with the EC Treaty.

---

[14] "Human Rights" (Session 1979–80, 71st Report, HL 362), p. xvi, para. 32.

[15] *ibid.*, p. xv, paras. 31(i)(a) and p. xxviii, para. 29.

[16] See "Human Rights Re-examined" (Session 1992–93, 3rd Report, HL Paper 10), p. 41, paras. 104 and 105. The Commission's Communication is published as an appendix to the report.

[17] *ibid.*, p. 37, para. 87. The Committee agreed with the Commission that the accession of Euratom could be effected under Art. 203, EAEC but thought that Art. 95 ECSC could not be used as the basis for accession by the Coal and Steel Community.

THE COURT'S OPINION

The admissibility of the request

5.05 The Court began by examining the admissibility of the Council's request. Article 300(6) enables the Court to be asked for an opinion only where an agreement is "envisaged" and several Governments argued that the Council's request was premature. There was consensus that the only possible legal basis for accession was Article 308, which required the Council to act unanimously, but the Member States were not agreed on the desirability of accession. Even if such agreement were in principle to be reached, various approaches to the extent of any accession by the Community and to the institutional difficulties which would be raised might be contemplated. No agreement could therefore be described as "envisaged" within the meaning of Article 300(6).

In response to those objections, the Court observed that Article 300(6) was intended "to forestall complications which would result from legal disputes concerning the compatibility with the Treaty of international agreements binding on the Community."[18] It was to avoid the complications that might arise if the Court found an agreement incompatible with the Treaty after it had been concluded that Article 300 (6) made provision for a prior reference to the Court. In order to establish whether the lack of firm information about the precise terms of any accession agreement affected the admissibility of the present request, the Court distinguished between two problems that would be raised by accession. These were (a) the competence of the Community to conclude an agreement to accede; and (b) the compatibility of any such agreement with the EC Treaty, in particular with its provisions relating to the jurisdiction of the Court.

With regard to the question of competence, the Court reiterated[19] that it was in the interests of the Community institutions and of all the States concerned, both members and non-members, to have that question clarified from the outset. All that was necessary was that the purpose of the agreement envisaged should be known before negotiations commenced. In this particular case, the Court said that "the general purpose and subject-matter of the Convention and the institutional significance of such accession for the Community are perfectly well known."[20] It did not matter that the Council had not yet adopted a decision to open negotiations. The question of accession was "on the Council's agenda"[21] and it envisaged the possibility of negotiating and concluding an agreement. Its request for an Opinion appeared to have been prompted, the Court said, "by the Council's legitimate concern to know the exact extent of its powers before taking any decision on the opening of negotiations."[22] The Court concluded that the request was therefore admissible in so far as it concerned the question of the Community's competence to conclude an agreement of the type envisaged.

As regards the compatibility of any accession agreement with the Treaty, the European Parliament and a number of the Governments which submitted observations drew attention to the Court's first Opinion on the EEA Agreement. There the Court held that "[t]he Community's competence in the field of international relations and its capacity to conclude international agreements necessarily entails the power to submit

---

[18] Opinion 2/94 [1996] E.C.R. I–1759, para. 3. The Court referred to Opinion 3/94, *concerning the Framework Agreement on Bananas* [1995] E.C.R. I–4577. There the Court declined to rule on the compatibility with the Treaty of the agreement in question since it had been concluded by the time its Opinion was delivered.
[19] See Opinion 1/78 [1979] E.C.R. 2871.
[20] Opinion 2/94 [1996] E.C.R. I–1759, para. 12.
[21] *Ibid.*, para. 14.
[22] *Ibid.*

to the decisions of a court which is created or designated by such an agreement as regards the interpretation and application of its provisions."[23] However, in order to rule on whether accession to the Convention would be compatible with the rules contained in the Treaty, particularly Articles 220 EC (ex Article 164)[24] and 292 EC (ex Article 219)[25] concerning the jurisdiction of the Court, the Court said it would need sufficient information on "the arrangements by which the Community envisages submitting to the present and future judicial control machinery established by the Convention."[26] Since no detailed information had been provided as to *how* the Community was to be subjected to the jurisdiction of an international court, the Court said it was not in a position to give an opinion on the compatibility of Community accession to the Convention with the rules of the Treaty.

The Community's competence to accede to the European Convention

5.06   In examining the Community's competence to accede, the Court drew attention to the first paragraph of Article 5 EC (ex Article 3b), according to which the Community is to act "within the limits of the powers conferred upon it by this Treaty and of the objectives assigned to it therein." The Court said that it followed from that provision that the Community was based on the principle of conferred powers, a principle which applied in both the internal and the external spheres. This meant that the Community only had those powers which had been conferred on it, either expressly or by implication. The Court reiterated that, wherever the institutions of the Community enjoyed internal powers for the purpose of achieving a given objective, "the Community is empowered to enter into the international commitments necessary for attainment of that objective even in the absence of an express provision to that effect".[27] However, no provision of the Treaty gave the institutions any general power to enact rules on human rights or to conclude international conventions in that field.

The Commission had been supported by the Parliament and a number of Governments in arguing that a legal basis for accession to the European Convention could be found in Article 308 of the Treaty. They maintained that the protection of fundamental rights was a "transverse" or "horizontal" objective to be pursued by the Community in the exercise of all its activities and that such protection was essential for the proper functioning of the common market. However, several other Governments disputed the legitimacy of recourse to Article 308 as the legal basis for accession and their doubts were shared by the Court of Justice.

The Court made some general observations about Article 308 before considering whether it could be used as a basis for accession by the Community to the Convention. It declared that the article, "being an integral part of an institutional system based on the principle of conferred powers, cannot serve as a basis for widening the scope of Community powers beyond the general framework created by the provisions of the Treaty as a whole and, in particular, by those that define the tasks and the activities of the Community."[28] In particular, the article could not be used as a basis for the adoption of provisions whose effect would in substance be to amend the Treaty.

The Court went on to note that respect for fundamental rights had been emphasised

---

[23] Opinion 1/91 [1991] E.C.R. I–6079, para. 40.
[24] "The Court of Justice shall ensure that in the interpretation and application of this Treaty the law is observed."
[25] "Member States undertake not to submit a dispute concerning the interpretation or application of this Treaty to any method of settlement other than those provided for therein."
[26] Opinion 2/94 [1996] E.C.R. I–1759, para. 20.
[27] Opinion 2/94 [1996] E.C.R. I–1759, para. 26. The Court referred to Opinion 2/91, *on ILO Convention No 170 concerning safety in the use of chemicals at work* [1993] E.C.R. I–1061, para. 7.
[28] Opinion 2/94 [1996] E.C.R. I–1759, para. 30.

in a variety of declarations made by the Member States and the Community institutions, in the Single European Act and in the TEU. Fundamental rights also formed an integral part of the general principles of law upheld by the Court. It continued:[29]

> "Respect for human rights is therefore a condition of the lawfulness of Community acts. Accession to the Convention would, however, entail a substantial change in the present Community system for the protection of human rights in that it would entail the entry of the Community into a distinct institutional system as well as the integration of all the provisions of the Convention into the Community legal order.
>
> Such a modification of the system for the protection of human rights in the Community, with equally fundamental institutional implications for the Community and the Member States, would be of constitutional significance and would therefore be such as to go beyond the scope of Article [308]. It could be brought about only by way of Treaty amendment."

The Court therefore came to the conclusion with which this chapter began.

THE IMPLICATIONS OF THE COURT'S OPINION

The protection of fundamental rights in the Community

5.07   Opinion 2/94 placed the ball firmly back in the court of the Member States: if they really thought accession by the Community to the European Convention was desirable, they had an ideal opportunity at the 1996 IGC to make the necessary amendments to the Treaty. However, accession would also mean negotiating changes to the Convention itself, which is at present open only to Members of the Council of Europe[30] and whose institutions and procedures would have to be adapted to accommodate the Community. In addition, further consideration of the *extent* to which the Community should bind itself, and the consequences of any disparities between the obligations of the Community and those of individual Member States, would be required.[31] It seems doubtful whether the effort which would be needed to resolve those issues would produce any substantial reinforcement of fundamental rights in the Community. If there is a serious lacuna in the system for the protection of fundamental rights in the European Union, it arises not under the first but under the second and, particularly, the third pillars. However, since those pillars fall outside the scope of the EC Treaty, they would not be affected by accession of the Community to the Convention. Moreover, there can be no question of accession by the Union itself, since it lacks legal personality.[32] The simplest way of filling that lacuna would be to bring the second and third pillars within the jurisdiction of the Court of Justice, as the Court itself proposed in its report on the application of the TEU. The extent to which the Treaty of Amsterdam gives effect to that proposal is considered below.

As far as the first pillar is concerned, the protection of fundamental rights would be significantly enhanced if the standing rules which private applicants must satisfy under Article 230 EC (ex Article 173) in order to seek the annulment of Community acts

---

[29] *ibid.*, paras. 34 and 35.
[30] Art. 66(1) of the Convention. Membership of the Council of Europe is in turn open only to European States: Art. 4, Statute of the Council of Europe.
[31] See the House of Lords Select Committee's 1992 Report, above, p. 164, n. 16, paras. 63–68 and 101–103.
[32] The idea of conferring legal personality on the Union featured in draft treaty texts produced during the 1996 IGC by both the Irish and the Dutch Presidencies but was dropped at the last minute.

were relaxed. As the House of Lords Select Committee pointed out in its 1992 Report[33] and the Court of Justice reiterated in its own report on the application of the Maastricht Treaty, those rules are at present too strict to guarantee that someone who claims his fundamental rights have been infringed by a Community institution can have recourse to the Community Courts.[34] The difficulty of distinguishing fundamental rights cases from other actions for annulment is one reason why any such relaxation should be general in scope.[35] Indeed, the right to seek judicial review of government action where the applicant is adversely affected might itself be regarded as a fundamental one.[36]

Lest it be objected that the Court of Justice is an inadequate guardian of the rights enshrined in the European Convention,[37] it should be emphasised that it has never knowingly disregarded a relevant provision of the Convention or refused to follow the case law of the Strasbourg Court.[38] Cases where that Court has subsequently adopted a view of the Convention's scope which differs from that taken by the Court of Justice are rare. An example which is sometimes cited in this context is *Hoechst* v. *Commission*,[39] a competition case concerning the scope of the Commission's investigatory powers under Regulation 17.[40] In that case, the Court of Justice held that Article 8(1) of the Convention, which provides that everyone has the right to respect for his private and family life, his home and his correspondence, did not extend to business premises, noting that there was no case law of the Strasbourg Court on the subject.[41] In *Niemietz* v. *Germany*,[42] the Court of Human Rights subsequently ruled that Article 8(1) did actually extend to professional or business premises and found that it had been infringed by a search of a lawyer's office. None the less, in *Hoechst* the Court of Justice went on to recognise that protection against arbitrary or disproportionate intervention constituted a general principle of Community law and to set out various conditions which the Commission had to meet when carrying out investigations under Regulation 17. Given the derogation laid down in Article 8(2) of the Convention,[43] it

---

[33] Above, p. 164, n. 16, para. 78.
[34] See also the observations of the Belgian and French Governments in Opinion 2/94. Annulment proceedings brought by private applicants now commence in the Court of First Instance.
[35] See further Arnull, "Private applicants and the action for annulment under Article 173 of the EC Treaty", (1995) 32 C.M.L.Rev. 7; Waelbroeck and Verheyden, "Les conditions de recevabilité des recours en annulation des particuliers contre les actes normatifs communautaires", (1995) 31 C.D.E. 399; Vandersanden, "Pour un élargissement du droit des particuliers d'agir en annulation contre des actes autres que les décisions qui leur sont adressées", (1995) 31 C.D.E. 535; Editorial Comments, (1996) 33 C.M.L.Rev. 215, p. 220.
[36] See Bradley, "Administrative Justice: a Developing Human Right?", (1995) 1 European Public Law 347.
[37] See Coppel and O'Neill, "The European Court of Justice: taking rights seriously?", (1992) 29 C.M.L.Rev. 669. For a detailed rebuttal of their case, see Weiler and Lockhart, " 'Taking rights seriously' seriously: the European Court and its fundamental rights jurisprudence", Part I (1995) 32 C.M.L.Rev. 51 and Part II (1995) 32 C.M.L.Rev. 579. It may be noted that, in the notorious *Brunner* case, (1994) 1 C.M.L.Rev. 57, the German Bundesverfassungsgericht accepted that protection for fundamental rights under the first pillar was adequate.
[38] See further Arnull, "Opinion 2/94 and its implications for the future constitution of the Union"(CELS Occasional Paper No. 1, Cambridge, 1996), p. 1 at pp. 10–13.
[39] Joined Cases 46/87 and 227/88 [1989] E.C.R. 2859.
[40] See further Wils, "La compatibilité des procédures communautaires en matière de concurrence avec la Convention européenne des droits de l'homme", (1996) 32 C.D.E. 329, p. 352; Waelbroeck and Fosselard, "Should the decision-making power in EC antitrust procedures be left to an independent judge? The impact of the European Convention on Human Rights on EC antitrust procedures", (1994) 14 Y.E.L. 111.
[41] The Court of Justice has been criticised for failing to refer to the judgement of the Strasbourg Court delivered earlier the same year in the *Chappell* case, Series A, No. 152, (1990) 12 E.H.R.R. 1: see Clapham, "A human rights policy for the European Community", (1990) 10 Y.E.L. 309, pp. 337–338.
[42] Series A, No. 251, (1993) 16 E.H.R.R. 97.
[43] "There shall be no interference by a public authority with the exercise of this right except such as is in accordance with the law and is necessary in a democratic society in the interests of national security, public safety or the economic well-being of the country, for the prevention of disorder or crime, for the protection of health or morals, or for the protection of the rights and freedoms of others."

may be doubted whether the practical result would have been much different had the Court accepted that Article 8(1) was applicable.

5.08 The scope of the Commission's investigatory powers under Regulation 17 was also challenged in *Orkem* v. *Commission*,[44] where the question arose whether an undertaking under investigation had the right to remain silent. The applicant sought to rely on Article 6 of the Convention, which embodies the right to a fair trial, but the Court of Justice said that "neither the wording of that article nor the decisions of the European Court of Human Rights indicate that it upholds the right not to give evidence against oneself."[45] In *Funke* v. *France*,[46] the Court of Human Rights held that Article 6 did indeed embody a right to remain silent and not to incriminate oneself. However, the Court of Justice went on in *Orkem* to hold that the rights of the defence, which it described[47] as "a fundamental principle of the Community legal order", prevented the Commission from compelling an undertaking "to provide it with answers which might involve an admission on its part of the existence of an infringement [of the Treaty competition rules] which it is incumbent upon the Commission to prove."[48] There may admittedly be room for argument over whether the rights of the defence under EC law have precisely the same scope as the right not to incriminate oneself under Article 6 of the Convention, but any discrepancy is likely to be marginal.

A final example worth mentioning is the *Grogan* case,[49] where the Court of Justice was asked about the compatibility with the Treaty rules on services of a national restriction on the publication of information concerning the availability of abortion facilities lawfully provided in another Member State. The Court held that such a restriction fell outside the scope of the relevant provisions of the Treaty where those performing the abortions were not involved in distributing the information. Since the relevant national legislation did not come within the ambit of Community law, the Court said it had no jurisdiction to assess its compatibility with fundamental rights. In *Open Door and Dublin Well Woman* v. *Ireland*,[50] the Court of Human Rights subsequently held that an injunction granted by the Irish Supreme Court in similar circumstances restraining the applicants from imparting or receiving information about abortion facilities available abroad amounted to a breach of Article 10 of the Convention concerning freedom of expression.

These cases were cited by the then President of the Court of Human Rights to illustrate an alleged difference in the approach taken by the two Courts and what he called the inherent weaknesses of *la solution prétorienne*.[51] It is submitted that the criticism implicit in those remarks is misplaced. Because the circumstances of the *Grogan* case fell outside the scope of the Treaty, the Court of Justice lacked jurisdiction to apply the Convention. It did not therefore express any view about the effect of Article 10. The restrictive view taken by the Court of Justice of the scope of the Treaty rules on services

---

[44] Case 374/87 [1989] E.C.R. 3283. See Wils, *op cit*, p. 345.
[45] *ibid.*, para. 30.
[46] Series A, No. 256, (1993) 1 C.M.L.Rev. 897. *Cf. Saunders* v. *United Kingdom*, judgment of December 17, 1996, Reports of Judgments and Decisions 1996–VI, [1997] 23 E.H.R.R. 313.
[47] Case 374/87 [1989] E.C.R. 3283, para. 32.
[48] *ibid.*, para. 35.
[49] Case C–159/90 *Society for the Protection of Unborn Children Ireland* v. *Grogan and Others* [1991] E.C.R. I–4685. See generally de Búrca, "Fundamental human rights and the reach of EC law", (1993) 13 O.J.L.S. 283; Phelan, "Right to life of the unborn v promotion of trade in services: the European Court of Justice and the normative shaping of the European Union", (1992) 55 M.L.R. 670; O'Leary, "The Court of Justice as a reluctant constitutional adjudicator: an examination of the abortion case", (1992) 16 E.L.Rev. 138.
[50] Series A, No. 246, (1993) 15 E.H.R.R. 244.
[51] See Ryssdal, "Human Rights in the European Union"in *The Developing Role of the European Court of Justice* (European Policy Forum/Frankfurter Institut, August 1995), p. 9, at pp. 11–12.

might well have been motivated by a desire to avoid considering a question on the effect of the Convention which was pending before the Court of Human Rights.[52] But there is no overlap, and consequently no inconsistency, between the rulings of the two Courts.

The procedure laid down in Article 300(6)

5.09　Even if the Court had found in Opinion 2/94 that the Community was competent to accede to the European Convention and that accession might be compatible with the Treaty, there does not seem to have been any realistic prospect that negotiations would begin. The Court's willingness to entertain the Council's request for an Opinion therefore seems somewhat surprising. In challenging the admissibility of the request, the United Kingdom drew an analogy with the preliminary rulings procedure under Article 234 EC (ex Article 177).[53] In that context, the Court has repeatedly emphasised that its function is "not to deliver advisory opinions on general or hypothetical questions".[54] The "complications" which the Court said it was the purpose of Article 300(6) to avoid cannot arise where the only possible legal basis for concluding an agreement requires the Council to act unanimously and the requisite unanimity is lacking. Moreover, in those circumstances it cannot convincingly be said that an agreement is "envisaged" by the Council.[55] Even if it is enough for an agreement to be "envisaged" by the Commission or by a Member State, the question of its compatibility with the Treaty in a situation such as this is merely "general or hypothetical". It seems odd that a Court which is concerned about its ever-increasing workload should agree to deal with such a question.

Moreover, there appears to be an inconsistency in the reasoning which led the Court to confine its examination of the Council's request to the question of the Community's competence. On that question, the Court regarded it as important that "the institutional significance" of accession for the Community was "perfectly well known".[56] However, on the question of the compatibility of accession with the Treaty, the Court said that it had "been given no detailed information as to the solutions that are envisaged" in order to submit the Community "to the jurisdiction of an international court".[57] Evidently the full "institutional significance" of accession was not clear after all. The Court should simply have said that, since the Community was not competent to accede to the Convention, the question of the compatibility of accession with the Treaty did not need to be addressed.

The scope of Article 308

5.10　The principle of conferred powers reflected in the first paragraph of Article 5 EC (ex Article 3b)[58] is not new: the Community has always been based on that principle. Thus, Article 7(1) EC (ex Article 4(1)) provides that "[e]ach institution shall act within the limits of the powers conferred upon it by this Treaty" and corresponding provisions may be found in the ECSC and Euratom Treaties.[59] The principle begs the

---

[52] *Cf.* the Report for the Hearing in *Grogan* at p. I–4687 and the Opinion of AG Van Gerven at p. I–4727.
[53] The Court used the analogy itself, albeit in a slightly different context, in Opinion 1/91 [1991] E.C.R. I–6079, paras. 58–61. For further discussion, see de Schutter and Lejeune, "L'adhésion de la Communauté à la Convention Européenne des Droits de L'Homme: à propos de l'avis 2/94 de la Cour de Justice des Communautés", (1996) C.D.E. 555, pp. 560–563.
[54] Case C–83/91 *Meilicke* v. *ADV/ORGA* [1992] E.C.R. I–4871, para. 25.
[55] See the remarks of Dashwood in CELS Occasional Paper No. 1, above, p. 168, n. 38, pp. 19–20.
[56] Opinion 2/94 [1996] E.C.R. I–1759, para. 12.
[57] *ibid.*, para. 21.
[58] See also Art. 5 TEU (ex Art. E).
[59] See Arts. 3 and 3(1) respectively.

question: what are the limits of the powers conferred on the Community by the Treaty? The approach to be taken in answering that question has changed since the entry into force of the TEU, whose authors evidently wished to set clearer limits to the Community's capacity to encroach on the prerogatives of the Member States by defining the Community's own powers with greater precision.[60] That wish was acknowledged by the Court in Opinion 2/94 and provided the starting point for its analysis of the scope of the Community's powers to act in the field of fundamental rights.

The Court pointed out that the Treaty did not expressly confer on the Community any general power to enact rules on fundamental rights or to conclude international conventions on the subject. The Court also made it clear that no such power could be inferred from any of the specific powers to act which the Treaty confers on the Community. Thus, if the Community has a general power to adopt provisions for the protection of fundamental rights, it can only be based on Article 308. Leaving aside procedural matters, there are three substantive conditions which must be satisfied in order for recourse to that article to be permissible: (a) Community action must be necessary to attain "one of the objectives of the Community"; (b) the need for the Community to act must arise "in the course of the operation of the common market"; and (c) there must not be another provision of the Treaty giving the Community the necessary powers to act. The Court has insisted on rigorous compliance with the third condition[61] and the emphasis placed in Opinion 2/94 on the principle of conferred powers suggests that it is likely in future to take an equally strict view of the first and second conditions, notwithstanding the tendency of the political institutions in the past to treat them with a degree of flexibility.[62]

It is therefore significant that, while the Court deals in its Opinion with the question whether the Community enjoys express or implied powers to act in the field of fundamental rights under other provisions of the Treaty, it does not address the other conditions which must be satisfied if the use of Article 308 is to be justified. Since failure to meet either of those conditions would have reinforced, or provided an alternative ground for, the Court's conclusion that accession to the European Convention could not be based on Article 308, it may be inferred that the Court accepted that the protection of fundamental rights is one of the Community's objectives which it is necessary to attain in the course of the operation of the common market. That view is entirely consistent with the Court's description of respect for human rights as "a condition of the lawfulness of Community acts".

The Court's conclusion that Article 308 could not be used as the basis for accession was based, not on the language of the article itself, but on its place in the scheme of the Treaty. As the Court pointed out:[63] "On any view, Article 308 cannot be used as a basis for the adoption of provisions whose effect would, in substance, be to amend the Treaty without following the procedure which it provides for that purpose". Accession to the Convention would be of "constitutional significance" because it would "entail a substantial change in the present Community system for the protection of human rights". It therefore went beyond the scope of Article 308 and could only be effected by way of amendment to the Treaty. Thus, the Court seems to have taken the view that the constitutional implications of Community accession would

---

[60] See generally Dashwood, "The limits of European Community powers", (1996) 21 E.L.Rev. 113.

[61] See, *e.g.* Case 45/86, *Commission* v. *Council* [1987] E.C.R. 1493 (recourse to Art. 308 not justified since contested measures fell within scope of common commercial policy and could have been adopted under Art. 133 EC (ex Art. 113)); Case 242/87, *Commission* v. *Council* [1989] E.C.R. 1425 (contested measure exceeded scope of former Art. 128 EEC (which was repealed by the TEU), so use of Art. 308 as well justified); Case C–271/94, *Parliament* v. *Council* [1996] E.C.R. I–1689 (contested measure should have been adopted under third para. of Art. 156 EC (ex Art.129d), so use of Art. 308 inappropriate).

[62] See Dashwood, *op. cit.*, pp. 123–124.

[63] Opinion 2/94 [1996] E.C.R. I–1759, para. 30.

have resulted from the application to the Community of the machinery set up by the Convention to safeguard the rights it enshrines rather than the substantive content of those rights, which the Court seeks to observe in any event as general principles of law.[64] It would consequently be a mistake to conclude that Article 308 is completely devoid of potential in the field of fundamental rights.

5.11   The possibility that the Court might treat the European Convention in the same way as GATT[65] and regard the Community as having assumed the obligations of the Member States[66] cannot therefore be excluded *a priori* as far as the Convention's substantive guarantees are concerned. However, that approach was not open to the Court when, in *Nold* v. *Commission*,[67] it first acknowledged that international treaties for the protection of human rights constituted a guide to the general principles of law, because at the time the act disputed in that case was adopted the Convention had not been ratified by all the Member States.[68] This appears to be the explanation for the Court's reference in *Nold*[69] to "international treaties for the protection of human rights on which the Member States have collaborated or of which they are signatories". Moreover, the "GATT approach" might have been taken to suggest that there was a distinction between fundamental rights protected under international treaties and those recognised by the constitutional traditions of the Member States, which was evidently not the Court's intention. The solution preferred by the Court is now so well established that a change of approach seems unlikely. It may in any event be doubted whether such a change would have much practical effect.

More significantly, Opinion 2/94 does not exclude the possibility that Article 308 might be used as the basis for a horizontal Council measure on fundamental rights applicable to all activities carried out within the scope of the Treaty, such as a regulation laying down a Community catalogue of such rights. Such a catalogue might be designed specifically with the needs of the Community in mind, as has been suggested by the Commission,[70] or might simply reproduce the substantive provisions of the Convention, perhaps requiring the Court of Justice to take account of the principles laid down by the Strasbourg Court.[71] At the international level, Article 308 might in principle be used as the basis for Community accession to international treaties for the protection of fundamental rights which have a less developed supervisory mechanism than the European Convention (for example, an obligation to report periodically on

---

[64]   For a different interpretation of the Court's Opinion, see Dashwood in CELS Occasional Paper No. 1, above, p. 168, n. 38, pp. 24–27. The Court's use of the term "constitutional significance"is criticised by de Schutter and Lejeune, above, p. 170, n. 53, pp. 572 *et seq.*

[65]   See Joined Cases 21 to 24/72, *International Fruit Company* v. *Produktschap voor Groenten en Fruit* [1972] E.C.R. 1219, para. 18. The 1947 version of GATT has now been superseded by the Agreement establishing the World Trade Organisation, of which the Community is a member. See Opinion 1/94 [1994] E.C.R. I–5267.

[66]   See Schermers and Waelbroeck, *Judicial Protection in the European Communities* (5th ed., 1992) pp. 103–105; *cf. contra* Dashwood in CELS Occasional Paper No. 1, above, p. 168, n. 38, p. 26.

[67]   Case 4/73 [1974] E.C.R. 491.

[68]   The applicant was seeking the annulment of a Commission decision adopted on December 21, 1972. France did not ratify the Convention until May 3, 1974, 11 days before the Court's judgment. The lawfulness of a decision is to be determined by reference to the circumstances prevailing at the time of its adoption: Joined Cases 15 and 16/76, *France* v. *Commission* [1979] E.C.R. 321, para. 7; Joined Cases T–79 and T–80/95, *SNCF and BR* v. *Commission* [1996] E.C.R. II–1491, para. 48; Case T–77/95, *SFEI and Others* v. *Commission* [1997] E.C.R. II–1, para. 74.

[69]   [1974] E.C.R. 491, para. 13. The formula was repeated in the *ERT* case, Case C–290/89 [1991] E.C.R. I–2925. See Schermers and Waelbroeck, *op. cit.*, p. 172, n. 66, p. 39.

[70]   See its 1979 Memorandum and its 1990 Communication.

[71]   A provision of that nature was included in the draft EEA Agreement considered by the Court in Opinion 1/91, [1991] E.C.R. I–6079: see para. 9. Although the Court did not object to the provision in itself, it was not included in the amended version which secured the approval of the Court in Opinion 1/92 [1992] E.C.R. I–2821: see p. I–2833. *Cf.* Art. 3(2) of the Agreement between the EFTA States on the Establishment of a Surveillance Authority and a Court of Justice, [1994] O.J. L344/1.

implementation[72]). The article might also provide the foundation for an agreement with the Contracting Parties to the Convention establishing a formal system for the exchange of information concerning judgments of the Luxembourg and Strasbourg Courts along the lines of the EEA Agreement.[73]

5.12   None of these steps would be of constitutional significance within the meaning of Opinion 2/94 because they would not entail any substantial modification of the existing mechanism for protecting fundamental rights in the Community. However, it seems doubtful whether any would command unanimous agreement in the Council. At least one of them, the adoption of a Community catalogue of fundamental rights, has been seen as undesirable as matter of principle: even if agreement could be reached on its content, such a catalogue might well have the effect of undermining the Convention.[74] One innovation, suggested by some of the Governments which submitted observations to the Court in Opinion 2/94, which might be of value would be an agreement permitting the Luxembourg and Strasbourg Courts to ask each other for preliminary rulings. However, it should be remembered that, unlike the Community system in which the uniform application of the law is of the utmost importance, primary responsibility for protecting the rights and freedoms enshrined in the Convention lies with the Contracting States: the machinery of protection established by the Convention is a subsidiary one.[75] In any event, such an agreement could only be concluded pursuant to an amendment to the Treaty since it would clearly have constitutional implications, at least if the rulings were to be binding on the referring court.[76]

What are the implications of the Court's Opinion for other provisions of the Treaty which confer legislative powers on the Community institutions? It may be noted that the Court did not say that the Community has no express or implied powers to adopt rules on fundamental rights,[77] but merely that it has no *general* power to enact such rules. Taken together with the Court's acknowledgement that Community acts must respect human rights as a condition of their lawfulness, the implication would seem to be, not only that Community acts adopted under specific powers must avoid infringing such rights, but that such powers can be used as the basis for provisions which are specifically designed to protect them. If this is correct, Articles 18(2) (ex Article 8a(2)) and 22 (ex Article 8e), second paragraph, of the Treaty might be used as the basis for measures concerning fundamental rights in connection with citizenship of the Union; similarly, Article 40 (ex Article 49) of the Treaty might be used as the basis for such measures in the field of freedom of movement for workers. That conclusion would

---

[72] See *e.g.* the European Social Charter; the International Covenant on Economic, Social and Cultural Rights; the International Covenant on Civil and Political Rights; the Convention against Torture and Other Cruel, Inhuman or Degrading Treatment or Punishment. In 1984, the European Parliament proposed that the Union should consider acceding to the first three of those instruments as well as to the European Convention: see Art. 4(3) of its draft Treaty establishing the European Union, [1984] O.J. C 77/33; Capotorti, Hilf, Jacobs and Jacqué, *The European Union Treaty* (1986), pp. 39–44.

[73] See Art. 106. Similar systems were established in relation to the Brussels and Lugano Conventions on jurisdiction and the enforcement of judgments (see [1988] O.J. L319/31) and the Rome Convention on the law applicable to contractual obligations (see [1989] O.J. L48/8).

[74] See the House of Lords Select Committee's 1980 report, paras. 21–23 and 33, and its 1992 report, paras. 39 and 76. Toth observes that the adoption of a Community catalogue of fundamental rights "would probably be the worst possible scenario", but argues that, in the light of Opinion 2/94, the Community lacks competence to enact such a catalogue without a Treaty amendment: "The European Union and human rights: the way forward", (1997) 34 C.M.L.Rev. 491, pp. 501–502.

[75] See, *e.g. Handyside* v. *United Kingdom*, Series A, No. 24, 1 E.H.R.R. 737, para. 48.

[76] This would be necessary as far as the rulings of the Court of Justice are concerned: see Opinion 1/91 [1991] E.C.R. I–6079, para. 61, where the Court said its function as conceived by the Treaty was "that of a court whose judgments are binding."

[77] Indeed, the Court has accepted that cooperation agreements concluded under Art. 181 EC (ex Art. 130y) may, by virtue of Art. 177(2) (ex Art. 130u(2)), contain provisions concerning respect for human rights: see Case C–268/94 *Portuguese Republic* v. *Council* [1996] E.C.R. I–6177.

seem to be reinforced by the difficulty of drawing a bright line between protecting fundamental rights and avoiding their infringement.

THE TREATY OF AMSTERDAM AND BEYOND

5.13   Opinion 2/94 undoubtedly disappointed some observers, who believe that accession to the Convention would both reinforce the protection of fundamental rights in the Community and have symbolic value.[78] However, an attempt has been made above to show that the Opinion does not exclude various other means, short of accession, by which those objectives could be achieved. The Court is the principal architect of the existing Community system for safeguarding fundamental rights, but on this occasion was more concerned with upholding the basic organising principle of conferred powers. Whatever the benefits of accession, the constitutional implications would clearly be profound. It is submitted that the Court was right to rule out Article 308 as the appropriate basis for taking such a step.

The lack of consensus among the Member States about the desirability of Community accession which emerged so clearly during the proceedings before the Court was also evident in the report of the Reflection Group, set up to prepare the ground for the 1996 IGC, which was published in December 1995.[79] That report made it clear that, from the beginning of the IGC, a majority of Member States favoured Community (or Union)[80] accession to the European Convention. From a legal point of view, the ruling of the Court amounted to no more than a small fly in the ointment, since it could have been reversed by a simple provision expressly giving the Community competence to accede. Although the Court did not rule on the question whether Community accession would be compatible with the Treaty, such a provision would have resolved that question by implication. From a political point of view, however, the Court's Opinion served to underline the potentially far-reaching consequences of accession and to reinforce the position of those Member States who opposed taking that step. In the event, the Treaty of Amsterdam which emerged from the IGC failed to reverse the Court's Opinion. Moreover, several provisions of the Treaty reflected the inability of the Member States to agree on either the desirability of reinforcing the protection of fundamental rights in the Union or the best way of achieving that objective.

On the credit side is a new Article 13 EC (ex Article 6a), which enables the Council, within the limits of the powers conferred by the Treaty on the Community, to "take appropriate action to combat discrimination based on sex, racial or ethnic origin, religion or belief, disability, age or sexual orientation." Unlike Article 12, which prohibits discrimination on the grounds of nationality within the scope of the Treaty, Article 13 does not itself prohibit any of the forms of discrimination to which it refers. It therefore seems incapable of producing direct effect, but it may be expected to affect the Court's approach to the interpretation of other provisions.[81] The article also gives the Council clear authority to act in areas where such authority was previously lacking.

Also, Article 46 TEU (ex Article L) gives the Court power to apply Article 6(2) TEU (ex Article F(2)) in cases which fall within its jurisdiction by virtue of other provisions

---

[78]   See JUSTICE, "Judging the European Union: Judicial Accountability and Human Rights"(1996) pp. 13–14; Gaja, (1996) 33 C.M.L.Rev. p. 973; Waelbroeck, (1996) C.D.E. 549; Burrows, (1997) 22 E.L.Rev. 58.
[79]   SEC(95)2163, para. 34.
[80]   This would have required the Union to be endowed with legal personality. See p. 167, n. 32, above.
[81]   See, *e.g.* Case C–249/96 *Grant* v. *South-West Trains Ltd*, [1998] 1 C.M.L.R 993.

of the Treaties. This makes little difference so far as the three Communities are concerned since Article 6(2) merely codifies the Court's existing case law, but it provides useful clarification with regard to Title VI of the TEU, in relation to which the Court has been granted new powers.[82] Although the Court's right to apply Article 6(2) is confined to cases involving "action of the institutions" that is not a restriction of any substance because the article is in any event addressed only to the Union (and not, for example, to the Member States).

5.14 More dramatic are the amendments which were made to Title I of the TEU. Article 6(1) (Article F(1)) now reads: "The Union is founded on the principles of liberty, democracy, respect for human rights and fundamental freedoms, and the rule of law, principles which are common to the Member States." This elevates to the body of the TEU a number of principles which were previously mentioned in its Preamble and may give them a constitutional status superior to that of other principles, in particular those relating to the functioning of the common market. The consequences might prove particularly significant in the field of competition, where the Court has encountered difficulty in reconciling Community law with the requirements of the European Convention.

The importance of the principles referred to in Article 6(1) is underlined in two ways. First, Article 49 TEU (ex Article O) restricts the right to apply for membership of the Union to "[a]ny European State which respects the principles set out in Article 6(1)". Secondly, provisions are inserted in the TEU[83] and the ECSC,[84] EC[85] and Euratom[86] Treaties permitting some or all of the rights of any Member State found to be in "serious and persistent breach" of those principles to be suspended. There is no equivalent provision in either the EC or the Euratom Treaties covering breaches of the economic and social principles on which those Treaties are based. Only in Article 88 ECSC do comparable powers exist where a Member State fails to comply with its obligations in the economic field. Those powers have never been exercised, but it seems useful to remind both existing and future Member States that membership of the Union requires constant vigilance to ensure that the principles mentioned in Article 6(1) are respected, not just at the moment of accession but on a permanent basis. If, like Article 88 ECSC, Article 6(1) TEU and its counterparts in the other Treaties fall into disuse, that will provide some measure of its success.

However, the heaviness of the procedure prescribed by these provisions and the potentially damaging consequences of invoking them make them weapons of last resort. They do little to reinforce the protection afforded to individuals in concrete cases. Moreover, Article 6(1) is not mentioned in Article 46 (ex Article L) among the provisions which the Court of Justice has jurisdiction to apply. That omission is paradoxical for at least three reasons. First, it casts doubt on the commitment of the Member States to the principles on which we are told the Union is to be regarded as founded. Secondly, where a decision is taken to suspend a Member State's rights under one or more of the Community Treaties, that decision is subject to review by the Court in accordance with the mechanisms which those Treaties provide. Unless such a challenge is brought on purely procedural grounds, it is hard to see how the Court could deal with it without considering the extent to which the principles set out in Article 6(1) had been breached. Thirdly, those principles undoubtedly constitute general principles of law in any event: the very text of Article 6(1) describes them as "principles

---

[82] See below. Title VI (under the conditions provided for by Art. 35 TEU) is expressly included in Art. 46 among the provisions which the Court has power to apply. The Court remains excluded from Title V.
[83] Art 7.
[84] Art. 96.
[85] Art. 309 (ex Art. 236).
[86] Art. 204.

which are common to the Member States". It therefore seems unlikely that the failure of Article 46 to mention Article 6(1) expressly will prevent the Court from applying the principles it lays down in cases where it has jurisdiction under the Treaties.

The lukewarm attachment of some Member States to the principles mentioned in Article 6(1) is also evident in a battery of new provisions designed to establish a somewhat piously entitled "area of freedom, security and justice". The relevant provisions are split between the first and third pillars. Title IV (ex Title IIIa) in the EC Treaty, entitled "Visas, asylum, immigration and other policies related to free movement of persons", confers on the Council new powers to act in a range of areas,[87] some of which previously fell within the scope of Title VI of the TEU. However, although Title IV is located in the first pillar, Article 68 EC (ex Article 73p) limits the extent to which it is subject to oversight by the Court of Justice. National courts of last resort are required to seek preliminary rulings on the interpretation of Title IV and the validity and interpretation of acts of the institutions based on it where these matters need to be resolved before judgment can be given. Moreover, the Council, the Commission and the Member States are entitled to ask the Court for a ruling on how the new Title and acts adopted under it should be interpreted.[88] However, lower national courts have no power to ask the Court for preliminary rulings in cases covered by the new Title. Moreover, by virtue of Article 68(2), the Court does not have jurisdiction to rule on measures connected with the removal of controls on the movement of persons across internal borders "relating to the maintenance of law and order and the safeguarding of internal security." The number of cases before national courts that are likely to fall within the scope of Title IV probably made some limit on the right of such courts to make references to Luxembourg inevitable.[89] However, restricting the Court's jurisdiction in cases concerned with law and order and internal security seems thoroughly undesirable from the point of view of fundamental rights, because it is in cases of precisely that nature that such rights are likely to be most at risk. So much for freedom, security and justice.

5.15   Similar objections may be levelled at Article 35 (ex Article K.7), which forms part of the amended Title VI of the TEU, renamed "Provisions on police and judicial cooperation in criminal matters." Article 35(1) gives the Court of Justice a preliminary rulings jurisdiction in relation to a range of measures adopted under the Title, although only at the request of national courts situated in Member States which have declared that they accept the involvement of the Court.[90] Since the TEU, in its Maastricht version, did not itself give the Court any preliminary rulings jurisdiction at all in relation to Title VI,[91] the new Article 35 may be considered progress. However, even where a reference is made from a Member State which has accepted the jurisdiction of the Court, Article 35(5) limits that jurisdiction in the following terms:

> "The Court of Justice shall have no jurisdiction to review the validity or proportionality of operations carried out by the police or other law enforcement services of a Member State or the exercise of the responsibilities incumbent upon

---

[87] Title IV does not apply to the United Kingdom, Ireland or Denmark except in the circumstances specified in protocols annexed to the TEU and the EC Treaty.

[88] Rulings given by the Court in response to such requests do not affect judgments of national courts which have become *res judicata*: Art. 68 (3) (ex Art. 73p(3)).

[89] See JUSTICE, "The jurisdiction of the European Court of Justice in respect of asylum and immigration matters"(May, 1997).

[90] See Art. 35(2). Member States may either confine the right to refer to courts and tribunals of last resort or extend it to any court or tribunal: Art. 35(3). In neither case does the Treaty impose an obligation to refer on courts of last resort, but a declaration (no. 10) adopted by the IGC notes that Member States may impose such an obligation as a matter of national law.

[91] But see Art. 31(2)(c) (Art. K3(2)(c)).

Member States with regard to the maintenance of law and order and the safe-guarding of internal security."

Although, like Article 68(2) EC,[92] it is for the Court to define its precise scope, Article 35(5) seems iniquitous: it is designed to limit the right of national courts asked to consider the legality of such operations or responsibilities, carried out or exercised pursuant to measures taken by the Council, to ask the Court of Justice for guidance. The result is to weaken the level of judicial scrutiny to which such activities are subject and to jeopardise the uniform application of the law in what, according to Article 29 (ex Article K.1), is meant to be "an area of freedom, security and justice" based on "common action among the Member States". That outcome is hard to reconcile with the founding principles set out in Article 6(1). It seems perverse to limit in this way the jurisdiction of the institution which is best placed to ensure that those principles are respected.

The balance is partly redressed by the last two paragraphs of Article 35. Article 35(6) is reminiscent of Article 230 EC (ex Article 173). It gives the Court jurisdiction to review the legality of "framework decisions and decisions" adopted under Title VI, but only in actions brought by a Member State or the Commission. The failure to confer standing on individuals to bring proceedings may, in the case of framework decisions, be thought justified by the nature of that type of act. Article 34(2)(b) (ex Article K.6(2)(b)) provides that framework decisions, which are to be used to approximate the laws and regulations of the Member States, "shall be binding upon the Member States as to the result to be achieved but shall leave to the national authorities the choice of form and methods." Such acts therefore resemble EC directives, except that it is expressly provided that framework decisions "shall not entail direct effect." Since individuals only exceptionally have standing to challenge (true) directives under Article 230 EC,[93] it might have been considered inconsistent to give them the right to challenge framework decisions. The failure to grant individuals standing to challenge decisions adopted under Title VI is harder to justify. Article 34(2)(c) empowers the Council to adopt such acts for *any purpose* consistent with the objectives of the Title other than that of approximating national laws. Decisions of this type are binding, although it is again provided that they "shall not entail direct effects". Nothing is said about the potential addressees of such decisions, although it may probably be inferred that they can only be addressed to the Member States. The Council is empowered to "adopt measures necessary to implement those decisions at the level of the Union". The manifest potential of such decisions, and of measures implementing them, to affect the rights and obligations of individuals makes the failure of Article 35(6) to confer on individuals standing to challenge their legality hard to reconcile with Article 6(1). One thing that can be said in favour of Article 35(6) is that it is consistent with Article 230 EC which, so far as the standing of natural and legal persons to bring annulment proceedings is concerned, remains unchanged.

5.16 Article 35(7) is more satisfactory, if only slightly. This provision, subject to certain conditions, gives the Court jurisdiction in disputes between Member States concerning the interpretation or application of acts adopted by the Council under Article 34(2). It also confers on the Court jurisdiction, subject to certain conditions, in disputes between Member States and the Commission over the scope of conventions established under Article 34(2)(d). This consolidates to some extent the rule of law by

---

[92] See also Art. 2(1) of the Protocol integrating the Schengen acquis into the framework of the European Union.
[93] See Joined Cases T–172/98 and T–175/98 to T–177/98 *Salamander AG and Others* v. *Parliament Council*, judgment of June 27, 2000.

providing a judicial mechanism for the resolution of disputes which might otherwise have to be settled at the political level. The right which the Commission enjoys to ask the Court to rule on the interpretation or application of conventions established under Article 34(2)(d) is particularly valuable when the Member State with which it is in dispute has not accepted the jurisdiction of the Court to give preliminary rulings. It is not clear, however, why the Commission's right to ask the Court to intervene does not extend to other acts adopted by the Council under Article 34(2), even where they are the result of a Commission initiative.[94] It is rather as if Article 226 EC (ex Article 169) were more limited in scope than Article 227 (ex Article 170).

In the area of fundamental rights as in so many others, it is hard to sum up the effect of the Treaty of Amsterdam in a few sentences. If one general point may be made in the present context, it is perhaps this. The academic debate about the desirability of Community or Union accession to the European Convention tends to take it for granted that fundamental rights should be protected and to focus on whether accession would be the best way of achieving that objective. The outcome of the 1996 IGC suggested that the Member States lack even this limited degree of consensus. The Treaty agreed at Amsterdam underlines the tension between States which regard the protection of fundamental rights as an important policy objective and States which attach greater importance to minimising legal constraints on government action. That tension is also evident in the conclusions of the Cologne European Council of June 1999, where it was agreed that an EU Charter of Fundamental Rights should be drawn up but the question of its legal status was left unresolved. Should the Charter become legally binding the case for Union accession to the European Convention would become overwhelming. Without it, the risk of inconsistency between the Luxembourg and the Strasbourg Courts would become intolerable.[95]

---

[94] Art. 34(2) enables the Council to act "on the initiative of any Member State or of the Commission".
[95] See further the House of Lords Select Committee on the European Union, "EU Charter of Fundamental Rights" (Session 1999–2000, 8th Report, HL Paper 67), para. 154.

CHAPTER 6

Internal Struggle for International Presence: The Exercise of Voting Rights Within the FAO

by

*Joni Heliskoski**

INTRODUCTION

6.01   Much of the traditional thought in international relations has been founded on the idea that membership of the international community is limited. It is limited to entities which fulfil a given set of criteria, determined each time by the community itself. Members *par excellence* have been the so-called sovereign States, and statehood the key organising concept of the community. Membership has, among other things, entitled members to participation in diplomatic conferences and other forms of inter-governmental organisation, which has then, in turn, served the precious purpose of manifesting and consolidating the very membership itself. Participation and presence have been vested with an intrinsic value of a kind capable of transcending any immediate policy objectives or other concerns discussed at such gatherings. The fact of being present has become a thing in itself, a recognised sign of status and privilege—something one is only supposed to give up with great reluctance.

Such ideas still seem to persist. This, it seems, can be demonstrated by the attempts of the European Community to take the place of its Member States in some of the traditional fora for international organisation. For *that Community* was essentially based on the idea of limiting some of the so-called sovereign rights of the Member States—pooling their resources, as the founding Treaty articulates it[1]—in favour of those of the Community, in pursuance of a common interest of the Community which was both distinct from and at a higher level than the particular interests of the Member States.[2] Efforts to that end could not, however, be limited to ones purely internal to the Community: the Community also had to enjoy a measure of *international* capacity, even in cases where this had not been expressly provided for in the Treaty.[3] In some instances, the Member States were deemed to lose their right to act on the international

---

* Dr Joni Heliskoski, Ministry of Justice, Finland.
[1] See the preamble of the Treaty establishing the European Economic Community of March 25, 1957 (title amended by Article G(1) of the Treaty on European Union of February 7, 1992, [1992] O.J. C224/1).
[2] See, *e.g.* Simon, *Le système juridique communautaire* (Paris 1997) pp. 47–50, and Case 6/64, *Costa* v. *ENEL* [1964] E.C.R. 585 at pp. 593–594 where the Court refers to national unilateral acts as being "... incompatible with the *concept of the Community*" (p. 594, penultimate para., emphasis added).
[3] The classic authority is the *AETR*, Case 22/70, *Commission* v. *Council* [1971] E.C.R. 263 at p. 274, paras. 13 *et seq. Cf.* also Opinion 1/76 (*Draft Agreement establishing a European laying-up fund for inland water-way vessels*) [1977] E.C.R. 741 at p. 755, paras. 3–4.

79

plane altogether: the requisite competence only belonged to the Community, and any concurrent action by the Member States would be, by definition, impossible.[4]

One of the areas falling within the exclusive competence of the Community is fisheries conservation. Fishery products are subject to Title II of the EC Treaty concerning agriculture, and ensuring the rational development of production as well as assuring the availability of supplies among the objectives laid down for the common policy Articles 32–33 EC (ex Articles 38–39). It was not, however, until the accession of Denmark, Ireland and the United Kingdom that an *overall Community solution* to the problem of conservation was contemplated: by virtue of Article 102 of the 1972 Act of Accession the Council was required to determine, from the sixth year after the accession at the latest, the conditions of fishing with a view to ensuring protection of the fishing grounds and the biological resources of the sea.[5] By the coming to an end of this transitional period on January 1, 1979, the initial obligations of abstention and common action of the Member States[6] had evolved into an exclusive rule-making authority of the Community: competence to adopt new measures of conservation henceforth belonged, to borrow the unequivocal expression of the Court, "fully and definitely to the Community".[7]

Neither the provisions of Title II of the Treaty nor Article 102 of the 1972 Act of Accession expressly provided that the Community's competence on fisheries conservation was also to have an external projection. However, an effective system of conservation can only be achieved by concerted action by all entities whose fleets engage in fishing activities in a given maritime area or waters adjacent to it. It therefore followed, as the Court explained, "from the very nature of things" that the rule-making authority *ratione materiae* of the Community also extended—in so far as the Member States had similar authority under public international law—to fishing on the high seas.[8]

In addition to the general framework of the United Nations, such concerted action has indeed been taken both within a number of regional fisheries organisations and through an even greater number of bilateral agreements. As it has become an established practice of coastal States to declare exclusive economic zones of 200 nautical miles from the baselines, the focus of internationally agreed conservation measures has shifted on to the high seas, where all States enjoy freedom of fishing—subject to their treaty obligations and the rules of customary international law.[9] In line with its internal constitutional development it has increasingly been the Community in its own right which has taken part in the adoption of such measures in the numerous international fora for fisheries conservation.[10]

6.02   However, the Community's path to the negotiating table has not always been

---

[4] See Case 22/70, *Commission* v. *Council*, [1971] E.C.R. 263 at p. 274, paras. 17–18. The exclusive nature of the Community's Common Commercial Policy under Article 133 EC (ex Article 113) was first recognised in Opinion 1/75 (*OECD Local Cost Standard*) [1975] E.C.R. 1355 at pp. 1363–1364.

[5] O.J. Spec. Ed. of March 27, 1972 p. 14 at p. 35.

[6] *Cf.* Joined Cases 3, 4 and 6/76 *Kramer* [1976] E.C.R. 1279 at p. 1311, paras. 42–45 and Case 61/77, *Commission* v. *Ireland* [1978] E.C.R. 417 at p. 449, paras. 65–66.

[7] Case 804/79, *Commission* v. *United Kingdom* [1981] E.C.R. 1045 at pp. 1072–1073, para. 17.

[8] Joined Cases 3, 4 and 6/76, *Kramer*, [1976] E.C.R. 1279 at p. 1309, paras. 30–33. The *rationale* was again explained by the Court in Opinion 1/94 (*Competence of the Community to conclude international agreements concerning services and the protection of intellectual property*) [1994] E.C.R. I–5267 at p. 5413–14, para. 85.

[9] *Cf.* Articles 87.1(e) and 116–119 of the United Nations Convention of the Law of the Sea of December 10, 1982, (1982) 21 I.L.M. 1261 (hereinafter "UNCLOS").

[10] For a comprehensive account of the practice, see European Parliament, *European Community Fisheries Agreements with Third Countries and Participation in International Fisheries Agreements* (Luxembourg 1993).

smooth. Fisheries conservation generally,[11] and specifically when dealt with at large international conferences,[12] has proved sensitive for the Member States. On the other hand, the EC Commission has sought to pursue a policy informed by the wider interests of the Community as a whole and not necessarily reflecting any particular interests of the Member States. Conflicting interests and aspirations have then turned into legal disputes concerning the scope and content of the Common Fisheries Policy, one recent example of which forms the object of the present analysis.[13] The dispute in question arose during the negotiations on an Agreement to promote compliance with international conservation and management measures by fishing vessels on the high seas, drawn up within the Food and Agriculture Organization of the United Nations (hereinafter "FAO").[14]

The Agreement concerned is designed to provide a response to a growing practice liable to undermine the effectiveness of fisheries conservation measures on the high seas: as efforts of high seas conservation have intensified, it has become common to transfer fishing vessels to flags of countries which neither participate in international conservation efforts nor take any unilateral measures to cooperate to that end.[15] Since *pacta tertiis nec nocent nec prosunt*, such countries are not bound by conservation standards or measures adopted by others. On the other hand, as flag States they are the only ones entitled to exercise jurisdiction on the high seas over vessels transferred to their flags.[16]

The initial approach within the FAO to combat this practice of flagging was to seek to agree on the conditions concerning registration and flagging of fishing vessels as well as their authorisation to fish on the high seas, with a view to ensuring compliance with

---

[11] Due to persisting disagreement in the Council, the Community's (internal) system for the conservation and management of fishery resources was only adopted in January 1983, more than four years after the time-limit envisaged in Article 102 of the 1972 Act of Accession. See Regulation 170/83 [1983] O.J. L24/1, replaced by Regulation 3760/92 [1992] O.J. L389/1.

[12] On the difficulties of agreeing on the scope of Community action at the Third United Nations Conference on the Law of the Sea, see, *e.g.* Ederer, *Die Europäische Wirtschaftsgemeinschaft und die Seerechtskonvention der Vereinten Nationen von 1982* (München 1988) pp. 84–89 and Simmonds, "The European Economic Community and the New Law of the Sea", 218 *Hague Recueil* 1989/VI p. 9 at pp. 112–115. Similar scenes could again be witnessed at the negotiations on the Agreement for the Implementation of the Provisions of the United Nations Convention on the Law of the Sea of December 10, 1982 relating to the Conservation and Management of Straddling Fish Stocks and Highly Migratory Fish Stocks of August 4, 1995 (1995) 34 I.L.M. 1542. It proved difficult for the Commission and the Member States to agree on whether or not the Agreement should fall within the exclusive competence of the Community. In the end, the Commission had to accept the Member States' participation alongside the Community. The communication of November 22, 1995 from the Commission to the Council on the signature of the Agreement (COM(95) 591 final) was still based on the Community's exclusive competence for all matters covered by the Agreement but this proved unacceptable to the Member States. The declaration on competence submitted by the Community on signature, on July 27, 1996, was already founded on the idea that certain measures of enforcement fell within the exclusive (*a contrario* para. 8 of the declaration) competence of the Member States (para. 7) whereas with regard to some other matters the competence was shared (para. 8). The Commission's proposal of October 4, 1996 for a Council Decision on the ratification by the Community of the Agreement (COM(96) 472 final)) as well as the Council's Decision (98/414/E.C.) of June 8, 1998 ([1998] O.J. L189/14) were both based on this latter conception (see Annex B hereto). The Community and all Member States are signatories but none of them had deposited the instrument of ratification by October 18, 2000.

[13] Case C–25/94, *Commission* v. *Council* [1996] E.C.R. I–1469.

[14] For the text of the Agreement as finally adopted by the FAO Conference on November 24, 1993, see [1996] O.J. L177/26.

[15] See the *Report of the Council of FAO*, Hundred and Second Session, November 9–20, 1992 (FAO, Rome 1992) para. 56, and for the decision to initiate negotiations on the Agreement, para. 58.

[16] *Cf.* Article 92 of the UNCLOS and see further Churchill & Lowe, *The Law of the Sea*, (revised ed., (Manchester, 1988) pp. 168–176.

internationally agreed conservation and management measures.[17] As between the European Community and its Member States, however, the FAO's opting for such a strategy was bound to revive the discussion on the scope of the Community's Common Fisheries Policy and the respective positions of the Community and the Member States with regard to the Agreement: even if the Community's exclusive competence on fisheries conservation was not disputed, the conditions of registration and flagging of vessels—some of the Member States were to argue—would in any event be something for the Member States to determine.[18]

6.03   It was the latter conception that prevailed at the Committee of Permanent Representatives of the Member States (hereinafter "COREPER") on March 16, 1993 when it first decided on the Community and the Member States' participation in the FAO Committee on Fisheries, where the formal discussions on the initial draft Agreement began.[19] The EC Commission was, however, persistent in its own interpretation of the situation. So much so that the dispute over the Community and the Member States' position at the negotiating table went on through the whole of negotiations, only to be settled by the Court of Justice some three years after the talks on the initial draft had commenced.

It is the Court's decision in the said dispute which will form the principal object of the present exposition. Before engaging, however, in any greater depth in the dispute and its handling by the Court a brief overview of the rules and principles governing the Community and the Member States' participation in the FAO appears necessary. They lay down the general framework for the Community and the Member States' position within the Organisation, and their understanding can therefore be regarded as a prerequisite for dealing with any specific questions arising within that context. Recognition of this can indeed be found in the structure and composition of the Court's decision itself: besides the Community and the Member States' competence on fisheries conservation, institutional aspects of their participation in the FAO received much attention.

EVENTS LEADING TO THE COURT: THE DISPUTE ON THE EXERCISE OF VOTING RIGHTS

6.04   The European Community is a *Member* of the FAO, alongside all of the Member States of the Community (*cf*. Art. II:3 FAO Constitution).[20] Leaving aside the

---

[17] See Arts. III–V of the "Draft Agreement on the Flagging of Vessels Fishing on the High Seas to Promote Compliance with Internationally Agreed Conservation and Management Measures", reproduced in the *Report of the Twentieth Session of the Committee on Fisheries*, 15–19 March 1993 (FAO, Rome, 1993) Appendix F.

[18] *Cf*. the Court's judgment of July 25, 1991 in Case C–221/89, *Factortame and others* [1991] E.C.R. I–3905 at p. 3970.

[19] Case C–25/94, *Commission* v. *Council*, [1996] E.C.R. I–1469 at p. 1502, para. 11. The facts in para. 11 are erroneously presented, however: notice of the COREPER decision was transmitted to the FAO for the Twentieth Session of the Committee of Fisheries (March 15–19, 1993), not for the Hundred and Third Session of the Council of the FAO (June 14–25, 1993) as the Court seems to suppose.

[20] Following the bringing to a conclusion of the negotiations on the Community's accession and the adoption by the FAO Conference of the necessary amendments to the Constitution and General Rules of the organisation permitting "regional economic integration organisations" (Article II:3; virtually, the EEC) to become Members (Resolution 7/91 of the Conference) the EC Council decided on November 25, 1991 to present a formal request for accession. The following day the Conference admitted the Community as a Member. See the *Report of the Conference of the FAO*, Twenty-sixth Session, November 9–27, 1991 (FAO, Rome 1991), esp. paras. 302, 376–379. On the amendments to the Constitution and the General Rules as well as the Community's accession and membership in the organization, see Schwob, "L'amendement à l'Acte constitutif de la FAO visant à permettre l'admission en qualité de membre d'organisations d'intégration économique régionale et la Communauté économique européenne", (1993) 29 (1) R.T.D eur 1; Tavares

particular aspects of the Community's position within the FAO which bear no relevance for the present purposes, the Community and the Member States' participation is governed by the principle of *alternative exercise of membership rights* (*cf.* Art. II:8 FAO Constitution).

In other words, the Community or its Member States are required to indicate before any FAO meeting, first, which of them has competence in respect of any specific question to be considered at the meeting[21] and—as they may both be competent—secondly, which will exercise the right to vote in respect of each particular agenda item.[22] The Community may cast, on matters within its competence, a number of votes equal to the number of its Member States entitled to vote in such a meeting; whenever the Community exercises its right to vote, the Member States may not exercise theirs, and conversely (Art. II:10 FAO Constitution).

So as to fulfil the above-mentioned obligations and to ensure effective participation in the FAO meetings, the Council and the Commission have reached an Arrangement concerning preparation for the meetings of the FAO as well as interventions and voting (hereinafter "Arrangement").[23] The Arrangement provides, *inter alia*, that the Commission shall, in advance of the Community co-ordination meetings, inform the Member States of its proposals regarding the statements and exercise of responsibilities on a particular topic within the FAO (Section 1.11). The Commission's proposals, as well as any subsequent decisions on the matter, should be guided by the following principles which the Arrangement lays down for statements and voting:

> "2.1 Where an agenda item deals with matters of exclusive Community competence, the Commission shall speak and vote for the Community.
>
> 2.2 Where an agenda item deals with matters of national competence, Member States shall speak and vote.
>
> 2.3 Where an agenda item deals with matters containing elements of both national and of Community competence, the aim will be to achieve a common position by consensus. If a common position can be achieved:
>
>> — the Presidency shall express the common position when the thrust of the issue lies in an area outside the exclusive competence of the Community. Member States and the Commission may speak to support and/or add to the Presidency statement. Member States will vote in accordance with the common position;
>> — the Commission shall express the common position when the thrust of the issue lies within the exclusive competence of the Community. Member States may speak to support and/or add to the Commission's

---

de Pinho, "L'admission de la Communauté économique européenne comme membre de l'Organisation des Nations Unies pour l'alimentation et l'agriculture (FAO)", (1993) R.M.C.U.E. 656 and Frid, *The Relations Between the EC and International Organizations—Legal Theory and Practice* (The Hague, 1995) pp. 243–279. The amended texts of the Constitution and the General Rules are reproduced in *Basic Texts of the Food and Agriculture Organisation of the United Nations*, vols. I-II (FAO, Rome, 1994).

[21] For the general declaration of competence submitted by the Community on application for membership (*cf.* Article II:5 FAO Constitution), see Annex II to the Commission's proposal for a Council decision on the accession, [1991] O.J. C292/8. According to the declaration "[t]he European Community has exclusive competence [*inter alia*] in ... all matters concerning fisheries which are aimed at protecting the fishing grounds and conserving the biological resources of the sea, in accordance with Article 102 of the 1972 Treaty of Accession." (Pt. II:(b)).

[22] Rule XLI:2 of the General Rules of the FAO.

[23] The text of the unpublished Arrangement is reproduced in Frid, *op. cit.*, Annex VI.

statement. The Commission will vote in accordance with the common position.

2.4 Should it prove impossible to reach a common position, Member States shall speak and vote. In accordance with the FAO rules of procedure, the Commission would be able to participate in the discussion."

In the first place, the aim will therefore be to establish either a Community (Section 2.1) or a *common* (Section 2.3) *position* on the basis of the Commission's proposals. In the latter case, it will also have to be decided who is to *express the common position and cast the vote*. This of course poses no difficulties if the Commission's proposals are accepted by all Member States. Should that not be the case, however, the Arrangement provides little further guidance; it merely states that the matter will be decided according to the procedure provided for in the EC Treaty and the agreed practice. In the absence of an agreement on this basis, the matter will be referred to COREPER (Section 1.12).

6.05   The text of the Arrangement thus seems to leave the interpreter with a number of open questions. It is not evident, for example, whether "common position by consensus" (Section 2.3) means a common position of the delegations of the Member States or whether the Commission also has to be involved. Section 1.12 seems to support the former interpretation: in the absence of an agreement between the Commission and the Member States, the matter will be referred to COREPER, the Committee of Permanent Representatives of the *Member States*. Once the common position has been established, it will further have to be determined where the "thrust of the issue" lies. But what procedural rule should apply to such a decision? Should recourse be had to the Treaty provision applying to the elements of *Community* competence[24] or should the matter be decided by consensus, given that elements of *national* competence are in any case involved? Since one Member State can always block the common position and thereby keep the vote for the Member States in the first place (*cf.* Section 2.4), the question of where the "thrust of the issue" lies in cases of shared competence could probably only be decided by consensus. And finally, is the COREPER decision to be considered final or should there always be a recourse to the Council, even if this has not been expressly provided for in the text of the Arrangement? On these and many other questions the Arrangement simply does not reveal the intentions of its drafters. The implications of their omissions were left to be worked out by subsequent practice.[25]

With little such practice behind it, this is basically the framework within which the facts of the present dispute between the Commission and the Council (and the Member States) ought to be placed.[26] Just as it had done for the March 1993 Session of the FAO Committee on Fisheries, the Commission again proposed that the declaration on competence and voting for the Hundred and Third Session of the FAO Council in June 1993—where the draft Agreement was again to be considered—should read "competence: mixed—vote: Community". At that stage of the negotiations there were already signs that the provisions on flagging were not going to be included in the

[24] In theory, one might even be inclined to think of the general rule in Article 205(1) EC (ex Article 148(1)): if no other provision in the Treaty were to apply, the decision could be taken by a majority of the delegations.
[25] Nor do commentators seem to have sought to address the many questions posed by the Arrangement with any considerable analytical rigour. See Frid, *op. cit.*, at pp. 255–258 and Sack, "The European Community's Membership of International Organisations", (1995) 32 C.M.L.Rev. 1227 at pp. 1254–1256.
[26] Unless otherwise stated, the description of the facts is based on the summaries appearing in the opinion of Advocate-General Jacobs and in the judgment itself. See Case C–25/94, *Commission* v. *Council*, [1996] E.C.R. I–1469 at pp. 1478–1479, paras. 17–22, and at pp. 1502–1504, paras. 11–20.

Agreement which would instead focus on the conditions concerning *authorisation to fish* on the high seas.[27] But COREPER nevertheless decided that the Member States should vote. The same was repeated in the COREPER of October 21, 1993: the Commission having proposed the right to vote for the Community at the Hundred and Fourth Session of FAO Council (November 2–5, 1993) and at the Twenty-seventh Session of the Conference of the FAO (November 6–24,) the COREPER once again modified the proposal to read "competence: mixed—vote: Member States". The Commission did not accept this, but nevertheless agreed to transmit the indication of competence for the two sessions in question.

6.06   In the "Fisheries" Council of November 22, 1993, the Commission then suggested that the Council adopt the following declaration:

> "The Council notes that the draft Agreement submitted to the [FAO] Conference for the adoption covers the conservation and management of fishery resources on the high seas by means of a licensing system and no longer through rules on the attribution or changing of flags as originally envisaged.
>
> In the circumstances, the draft Agreement, which also contains a number of provisions to aid developing countries is essentially, if not wholly, a matter of the exclusive Community competence and should normally have been approved on the Community's behalf by a Commission vote.
>
> In future, and depending upon each case, matters of this nature should be dealt with in accordance with section 2.1 or 2.3, second indent, of the FAO Arrangement ..."

By vote, the Council confirmed the decision of the COREPER (*i.e.* "competence: mixed—vote: Member States") and refused to adopt the suggested declaration. The Commission in turn took note of the Council's decision, reaffirmed its opinion on the question of competence, noted that the decision was taken contrary to the Arrangement and stated that it might bring the dispute before the Court of Justice. The Council for its part took note of the Commission's statements and considered that the questions of competence and voting rights had not been settled and invited the COREPER to re-examine the question of voting in due course. Two days later the Agreement to promote compliance with international conservation and management measures by fishing vessels on the high seas was adopted by the Conference of the FAO with all 12 Community Member States voting in favour. On January 24, 1994, an action was brought against the Council before the Court of Justice by the Commission, claiming that the Court should annul the Council's decision of November 22, 1993 confirming the previous COREPER decision to give the voting rights to the Member States.[28] By order of July 7, 1994 the United Kingdom was allowed to intervene in support of the defendant.

---

[27] At the beginning of the Hundred and Third Session of the FAO Council an open Technical Committee was established to review the initial draft Agreement considered by the Committee of Fisheries in its Twentieth Session (see above, p. 82, n. 17). The revised draft included in the report of the Technical Committee to the Council no longer contained any provisions on the conditions concerning registration (*cf.* Article III:3–4 of the initial draft) and those on the allocation of flag had been deleted and the Article in question (Article IV of the initial draft) placed in square brackets. See *Report of the Council of the FAO*, Hundred and Third Session, June 14–25, 1993 (FAO, Rome 1993) paras. 66–68 and Appendix E. As has been observed, "[d]ès le début des négociations ..., il apparut clairement qu'aucun consensus ne pourrait être obtenu sur un accord qui contiendrait des dispositions relatives à l'enregistrement national des navires de pêche ou à l'attribution d'un pavillon." Moore, "Un nouvel accord de la FAO pour contrôler la pêche en haute mer", *Espaces et ressources maritimes* (1993) No. 7, p. 62 at p. 64.
[28] [1994] O.J. C90/6.

As will emerge, the Court finally ruled in favour of the Commission and annulled the Council's decision of November 22, 1993. The objective of the following is to provide an analysis of the Court's judgment and to work out its implications for the system of the Community and the Member States' external relations in general, and for the state and functioning of their membership in the FAO in particular.

ADMISSIBILITY OF THE REQUEST: THE FUNCTIONAL APPROACH ENABLES JURISDICTION

6.07   In its application the Commission argued that the draft Agreement as submitted to the competent bodies of the FAO fell essentially, if not wholly, within the exclusive competence of the Community. More particularly, the key provisions setting up a system of authorisation for fishing on the high seas based on compliance with international conservation and management measures through flag State responsibility (Art. III) on the one hand, and providing for the maintenance of records of fishing vessels (Art. IV) on the other, did not fall within national competence. The Council had therefore not been entitled to attribute the right to vote on the adoption of the Agreement to Member States.[29]

The Council for its part made a preliminary objection of admissibility[30]: the contested Council decision was not, the Council argued, an act producing legal effects and therefore not open to annulment under Article 230 (ex Article 173) of the EC Treaty (AG, para. 33). The decision taken by COREPER on October 21, 1993 had been definitive, and confirmation of that decision by the Council was both unnecessary and impossible; no appeal to the Council was provided for by the Arrangement (AG, para. 36). The debate in the Council on November 22, had thus been purely political. If however the Court were to regard the Council vote as a "deliberation", it had merely confirmed the decision of the COREPER and, the Council argued, the Commission should have brought the action against that decision (AG, para. 38).[31] In any case, *any decision* that may have been taken was a matter purely of procedure or protocol and incapable of affecting the rights of the Commission or the allocation of competence as between the Community and the Member States (para. 30). The United Kingdom supported the Council's submissions: the decision of the Council had not produced any legal effects whatsoever (AG, para. 39).

The Commission replied that the legal effects of the Council's decision were undeniable (AG, para. 41): it had definitely deprived the Community of its right to vote for the adoption of the Agreement, affected the exercise of the Community's competence within the FAO and, finally, together with the fact that the Member States had voted, misled other States as to the competence of the Community (para. 31). On the other hand, decisions by the COREPER only became definitive when they were approved by the Council; the two-month period for bringing the action had thus only started to run when the Council had taken its decision (AG, para. 42).

---

[29] *ibid.*
[30] See the opinion of Advocate General Jacobs of October 26, 1995, Case C–25/94, *Commission* v. *Council* [1996] E.C.R. I–1469 at p. 1472, para. 3. In the following, abbreviation "AG" refers to the respective paragraphs of the Advocate General's opinion. All other references are to the judgment of the Court.
[31] In this context reference was made to Joined Cases 166 and 200/86, *Irish Cement* v. *Commission* [1988] E.C.R. 6473, where the Court had held that an action for the annulment of a decision which merely confirmed a previous decision which had not been contested within the time limit for bringing proceedings was inadmissible. Article 230, fifth subpara., EC sets a two-month time limit for the instituting of the proceedings. To this effect, *cf.* also Case 22/70, *Commission* v. *Council* [1971] E.C.R. 263 at p. 279, paras. 65–66.

Faced with the objection of admissibility, the Court first had to examine whether the contested decision amounted to a measure against which an action for annulment under Article 230 EC was available.[32] As it had done on a number of previous occasions,[33] the Court noted that the action should stand available in the case of all measures adopted by the institutions, whatever their nature or form, which are intended to have legal effects (para. 29).

This time, however, the application of the said criteria proved somewhat more difficult as far as the *identification of the author* of the contested act was concerned: the problem facing the Court was whether the recognition of the Member States' right to vote should indeed be attributable to the Council or whether, as the Council and the United Kingdom had argued, the issue had been settled definitely by the COREPER at its meeting of October 21, 1993.[34] The question appeared decisive, since the Commission's action had only been directed against the decision of the Council, not against that of the COREPER.

6.08 The Court found it appropriate to approach the problem by examining the position and functions of the respective bodies under the Treaty. In the light of Articles 202 and 207(1) EC (ex Articles 145 and 151(1)), the Court noted, it was clear that the COREPER was not an institution of the Community upon which the Treaty confers powers of its own, but an auxiliary body of the Council for which it carries out preparation and implementation work (paras. 24–26). Since the latter functions either could not give to the COREPER the decision-making powers which under the Treaty belong to the Council (para. 27), the COREPER *could not have adopted* a decision on the right to vote. Nor could the Council's vote be regarded as a confirmation of a previous COREPER decision (para. 28); logically, a decision which has not been taken cannot be subsequently *confirmed*. The Court therefore upheld the view of the Commission that the decision by the COREPER only had become definitive when it had been approved by the Council.

The Court's conclusion on the problem of attribution corresponds with the "functional approach" it has followed in defining the concept of reviewable act for the purposes of Article 230.[35] For the Court, the approach is functional in a sense that it enables judicial review in a wider set of circumstances (*cf.* Article 220 EC (ex Article 164)). On the other hand, to describe something as "functional" immediately leads to suspicion: "function" is potentially capable of dominating everything that may cross its path. At least as far as the present case is concerned, the Court's approach does not appear entirely unproblematic.

In the present context, the General Rules of the FAO (Rule XLI:2) expressly provide that the indication of competence and exercise of voting rights shall be made *before* any meeting of the Organisation, a proviso which must be presumed to serve an inter-

---

[32] Article 230 EC, first subpara., provides that "[t]he Court shall review the legality of acts adopted jointly by the European Parliament and the Council, of acts of the Council, of the Commission and of the ECB, other than recommendations and opinions, and of acts of the European Parliament intended to produce legal effects *vis-à-vis* third parties."

[33] *Cf.* Case 22/70, *Commission* v. *Council*, [1971] E.C.R. 263 at p. 277, para. 42, confirmed more recently in, *e.g.* Case C–327/91, *France* v. *Commission* [1994] E.C.R. I–3641 at p. 3672, para. 14.

[34] *Cf.* Joined Cases C–181/91 and C–248/91 *Parliament* v. *Council and Commission* [1993] E.C.R. I–3685, where the Council had raised an objection as to the admissibility of the action, contending that an act adopted at a Council session with a view of granting special aid to Bangladesh had not been adopted by the Council as an institution of the Community but by the twelve Member States meeting within the Council.

[35] Opinion of Advocate General Jacobs in *ibid.*, at p. 3705, para. 21.

est of some kind of the FAO and its other Members.[36] However, any arguments—endorsed by the United Kingdom, in particular—to establish on that ground that it *could not have been the Council* who actually decided on the voting rights were not even dealt with by the Court. In fact, the Court's treatment of the remaining aspects of the question of admissibility shows that they were silently rejected.[37]

The Court's handling of the problem of attribution also begs the question of what the legal situation would have been had the Commission never brought the matter to the Council or had the latter never proceeded to a vote on the declaration suggested on November 22, 1993.[38] In that case, there could obviously not have been any decision of the Council reviewable under Article 230, of the EC Treaty. On the other hand, the proceedings of the COREPER could not have constituted—if the logic of the Court were to be followed—a reviewable act either: if the COREPER could not have adopted a decision on the exercise of the right to vote (para. 28), there would not by definition have been any act to be quashed under Article 230 EC. Therefore, a request for the annulment of such a COREPER "decision" ought to have been declared *inadmissible.*[39]

If all this is accepted, the question then arises whether any remedy at all should stand available to control the conduct of the COREPER or—in the case of a refusal to proceed to a vote on a proposal or suggestion—the Council which seems to go against the spirit of the Treaty. In the latter case, proceedings could probably be brought against the Council under Article 232 (ex Article 175) of the EC Treaty for a failure to act. However, as far as decisions relating to international agreements to be concluded by the Community are concerned, there seems to be another, perhaps more appropriate procedure: Article 300(6) EC (ex Article 228(6)) provides that the Council, the Commission or a Member State may obtain the opinion of the Court of Justice as to whether an agreement to be concluded "... is compatible with the provisions of [the] Treaty". In spite of its wording, the provision enables an opinion to be sought on all questions

---

[36] Indeed, due to delayed submissions of the indications of competence and voting by the Community and the Member States and the inconveniencies caused thereby the FAO Council at its Hundred and Second Session "... *agreed* that in future the Declaration of Competences and the Right to Vote presented by the EEC and its Member States should be submitted to the Director-General well in advance for it to be translated, reproduced and circulated to Council members before the opening of the Council session concerned. The same principle should apply to other meetings of the Organization." *Report of the Council of the FAO*, Hundred and Second Session, November 9–20, 1992 (FAO, Rome, 1992), para. 7 (emphasis in original).

[37] Admittedly, the argument that the indication of competence and/or exercise of vote may not, due to the rules of the FAO, be changed once a meeting has started appears somewhat formalistic in the present case. It is difficult to see what the adverse effect upon the FAO and its Members could have been had the Council decided to give the right to vote to the Community on November 22, 1993. The Council's decision could then have been transmitted to the FAO for the vote on November 24. It had been most likely that the other FAO Members would have readily accepted any solution adopted by the Community and the Member States provided that they had not voted cumulatively, see Neuwahl, "Shared Powers or Combined Incompetence? More on Mixity", (1996) 33 C.M.L.Rev. 667 at p. 681. Another matter is that *in the course of actual negotiations* shifts on the Community side may be detrimental to the interests of the other participating entities and, indeed, to the negotiating process itself. *Cf.* Case 22/70, *Commission v. Council*, [1971] E.C.R. 263 at p. 285, paras. 85–86 and the "agreement" reached at the Hundred and Second Session of the FAO Council, see n. 36, above.

[38] Even though the Presidency, a member of the Council or the Commission may request a vote on those agenda items in respect of which this has been indicated (with an *) on the provisional agenda, the latter may never insist on a vote: the Council only votes on the initiative of either the Presidency or, provided that a majority of the Council's members so decides, the Council or the Commission. See Arts. 2(2) and 9(1) of the Council's Rules of Procedure, [1999] O.J. L147/13.

[39] If an act has been made by an authority which could not possibly have had the power to make it, the act may be regarded as being void. Since such a "non-existent" act can have no legal effects and is therefore not a reviewable act, the Court would lack jurisdiction under Article 230 EC. See Hartley, *The Foundations of European Community Law*, (4th. ed., Oxford, 1998) pp. 341–342.

concerning the compatibility with the provisions of the Treaty of an agreement envisaged and in particular on questions which concern the *division of competence* between the Community and the Member States.[40] Moreover, a request under Article 300(6) may be made any time before the Community's consent to be bound by an agreement is finally expressed.[41]

6.09 Against that background, it is difficult to see why the dispute forming the object of the present proceedings could not have been brought before the Court under Article 300(6) of the Treaty (*cf.* AG, para. 51). One might even feel inclined to think that the Court could have, by giving the "functional approach" a somewhat different application, *treated* the Commission's action as a request for an opinion under Article 300(6) EC.[42] Even though the provision in question does not authorise the Court to come up with any declaration of invalidity, it might nevertheless enable the Court to exercise some control over the legality of the conduct of Community institutions and the Member States, even at a time when negotiations are still in progress.[43] More importantly, such an approach would help to avoid the whole question of attribution of an act to one of the Community institutions, the handling of which by the Court sometimes seems to acquire a somewhat artificial stance. Likewise, it would also help to avoid all discussion on whether a given act was intended to have legal effects, a necessary precondition for judicial review under Article 230 of the Treaty.

In the present case, however, the question of legal effects[44] had to be addressed. And this was the other principal aspect of the issue of admissibility and, generally speaking, the point where the Court and the Advocate General parted company. The Advocate General had taken the view that any such effects were "entirely hypothetical" (AG, para. 51): the Council's decision, which had been of a procedural nature only, had not in fact been contested by the Commission at the time and, moreover, had no bearing on any issue of substance between the parties. It therefore seemed clear that the case dis-

---

[40] See Opinion 1/75, [1975] E.C.R. 1355 at p. 1360 and, *e.g.* Opinion 2/92 (*Competence of the Community or one of its institutions to participate in the Third Revised Decision of the OECD on national treatment*) [1995] E.C.R. I–521 at pp. 554–555, paras. 13–14.

[41] Opinion 1/94, [1994] E.C.R. I–5267 at p. 5392, para. 12.

[42] *Cf.* Case C–327/91, *France* v. *Commission*, [1994] E.C.R. 3641 at p. 3672, paras. 13–17 where the Court took the view that the action by France, even if directed against an agreement (between the Commission and the US regarding the application of their competition laws) itself, *must be understood as having been directed against the act* whereby the EC Commission had sought to conclude the Agreement and, consequently, regarded as admissible. See also the opinion of Advocate General Tesauro of December 16, 1993, p. 3643 at p. 3651, para. 16. For a critical review of the Court's handling of the question of admissibility, see Kaddous, "L'arrêt *France* c. *Commission* de 1994 (accord concurrence) et le contrôle de la 'légalité' des accords externes en vertu de l'Article [230] CE: la difficile réconciliation de l'orthodoxie communautaire avec l'orthodoxie internationale", (1996) 32 (5–6) C.D.E. p. 613.

[43] The Court has said it to be in the interests of all those concerned to have the question of competence clarified as soon as any negotiations have commenced. See Opinion 1/78 (*International Agreement on Natural Rubber*) [1979] E.C.R. 2871 at p. 2909, para. 35 and Opinion 2/94 (*Accession by the Communities to the European Convention for the Protection of Human Rights and Fundamental Freedoms*) [1996] E.C.R. I–1759 at pp. 1784–1785, para. 10.

[44] In general, Community law does not include any helpful positive definition of "legal effect" for the purposes of Article 230 EC. Of course, it might be said that to have legal effects an act must produce a change in somebody's rights and obligations, but this may not always be very helpful. See Hartley, *op. cit.*, at pp. 331–332. The Court's case law only provides guidance for working out a *negative* definition: an account of instances where judicial review is excluded because there is no legal effect. For a concise account, see Manin, *Les Communautés européennes, l'Union européenne—droit institutionnel*, (3ème éd., Paris, 1997) pp. 370–373; Isaac, *Droit communautaire général*, (5ème éd., Paris, 1996) p. 247 and Hartley, *op. cit.*, at pp. 332–341.

closed *no genuine dispute* and the Court should thus have dismissed the application (AG, para. 59).[45]

The Court however took a different view. It found that the Council's vote had legal effects in several regards. First, the decision had recognised the Member States as having the right to participate in the definitive adoption of the Agreement, an essential stage in the procedure for concluding an international treaty, and thereby affected the Community's rights attaching to its membership of the FAO (para. 33).[46] The Community as such had thus been prevented from having any effective say in the deliberations which would precede the final decision on the text,[47] the content of which could still have been changed.[48] Moreover, the Council's vote had prevented the Commission from expressing the common position arrived at in accordance with Section 2.3 of the Arrangement (para. 34).[49] And finally, the fact that the Member States had voted had given the other States and the FAO the impression that the thrust of the Agreement did not fall within the exclusive competence of the Community (para. 35) and had thus had effects as regards competence to implement the agreement and to conclude subsequent agreements on the same question (para. 36).[50] Therefore, the Council's vote had had legal effects as regards relations between the Community and the Member States, between the institutions of the Community and, finally, between the Community and its Member States on the one hand and other subjects of international law on the other (para. 37). On the other hand, the statement in the Council minutes (to the effect that the substantive questions of competence and exercise of voting rights had not been settled) could not be used for the purpose of interpreting the decision when no reference had been made to the content of that statement in the actual wording of the decision (para. 38).[51]

---

[45] For its action to have been admissible, the Commission—the Advocate General argued—would have had to show some real, direct interest in the outcome of the proceedings. This did not mean, however, that the Commission would have had to establish a particular interest of its own, something only required from the applicants mentioned in the fourth subpara. of Article 230 EC. What the Advocate General had in mind was the *general procedural principle* that courts do not normally adjudicate in the absence of a dispute. Actions may not be brought for the sole purpose of obtaining a decision which might be relevant for other, future cases; some genuine illegality with some actual consequences would have to be established by the applicant. Since the Commission had failed to do so in the present proceedings, the application—the Advocate General concluded—ought to have been rejected as inadmissible (see AG, paras. 51–59).

[46] *Cf.* the Advocate General who emphasised that the Council's decision had related "only to a particlar vote" (AG, para. 59) and that the act of voting was often "merely procedural" (AG, para. 74).

[47] See Rule XLI:3 of the FAO General Rules and Section 2.3, first indent, of the Arrangement.

[48] The Advocate General seemed to think that neither the voting on the Agreement nor the text itself would have undergone any change if the Council had adopted the declaration proposed by the Commission or even if it had decided—something which the Commission had not in his view proposed (see AG, para. 55)—that the Commission was to cast the vote (AG, para. 52). To the Court, however, the Council's decision had legal effects by sole virtue of the fact that the Community had been prevented from effectively taking part in the adoption of the text, the content of which *could* still have been changed.

[49] In his opinion the Advocate General had essentially sought to establish that the Commission had in fact never contested the conferment of the vote to the Member States and there had therefore been no genuine dispute between the parties (esp. AG, paras. 55 and 59). *Cf.* Case 22/70, *Commission* v. *Council*, [1971] E.C.R. 263 at p. 279 where the Court had held that when "... the questions put before the Court ... are concerned with the institutional structure of the Community, the admissibility of the action cannot depend on prior omissions or errors on the part of the applicant ..." (para. 63) and Case 166/78, *Italy* v. *Council* [1979] E.C.R. 2575 at p. 2596, para. 6 which concerned the annulment of a Council Regulation adopted by unanimity. Neither a lack of protest nor an express consent on the part of the applicant does seem to preclude judicial review.

[50] The Advocate General rejected that argument of the Commission: the other Members of the FAO "... can ... be presumed to be aware of the fact that the Arrangement [between the Council and the Commission] and its application are without prejudice to the question who should become party to the Agreement, and thus to the issue of competence." (AG, para. 58).

[51] The Court referred to Case C–292/89, *Antonissen* [1991] E.C.R. I–745. The Advocate General regarded the statement in the minutes as evidence of the fact that the Council's decision had been without prejudice of the issue of competence (*cf.* AG., para 51 to the last sentence of para. 21).

Evidently, both the Advocate General and the Court had set out the conceivable legal effects of the Council decision for the purposes of Article 230 of the Treaty. Their respective trails of reasoning tend, however, to bear witness of a different conception in this respect. While the Advocate General had emphasised the actual consequences of the Council's vote for the outcome of the negotiations as well as for the casting of the vote (*e.g.* AG, para. 52), the Court clearly stressed the effects upon the Community's membership *rights* within the FAO (para. 33) as well as its *competence* within the field covered by the Agreement (para. 36). While for the Advocate General any legal effects would have been in the first place actual, for the Court they were potential.[52]

The Court's approach thus laid particular emphasis on the effects *for the future* of the Council's vote, especially as regards those taking place on the international plane (see paras. 35–36). The Court seems to be saying that the FAO and its Members might somehow be entitled—by virtue of the General Rules of the Organisation (*cf.* Rule XLI:2)—to *vest the fact of casting the vote* by either the Community or the Member States *with legal significance* as to the attribution of competence between them, irrespective of what might (come to) be the correct position in Community law. In other words, the Community and the Member States might, for their part, be *precluded* from subsequently adopting different positions on the issue of competence, even if the rules and principles of Community law did require them to do so.[53] As regards the present case, one may however doubt whether the casting of the vote at the FAO Conference, let alone the contested decision of the Council as such, could have entailed any serious difficulties for the exercise of the Community's competence once the Agreement enters into force.[54] True, the vote by the Member States might have misled the FAO and its other Members but no rule or principle of international law should preclude the Community and the Member States from providing them with a correct account of the competence later on.[55]

---

[52] *Cf.* in this respect the Court's handling of the issue of admissibility in Case C–316/91, *Parliament* v. *Council* [1994] E.C.R. I–625 at p. 659 where it was held that "[a]dopting an act on a legal basis which does not provide for ... consultation [of the Parliament] is liable to infringe that prerogative, even if there has been optional consultation." (para. 16).

[53] The argument is of course reminiscent of the operation of the *estoppel* principle in international law: such an effect of preclusion may in principle arise by virtue of clear and consistent behaviour which causes the entity invoking the principle, in reliance on such behaviour, detrimentally to change position or suffer some prejudice. See *North Sea Continental Shelf, Judgment*, [1969] I.C.J. Rep. 3 at p. 26. In respect to the present problem, *cf.* the Separate Opinion of Judge Fitzmaurice in *Certain expenses of the United Nations (Article 17, paragraph 2 of the Charter), Advisory Opinion of 20 July 1962*, [1962] I.C.J. Rep. 151 at p. 210 where it is suggested that "... a Member State [of the United Nations] which does not vote *against* a given resolution [which only has a recommendatory intention and effect], can scarcely object if it is called upon to pay its share of the resultant expenses." (emphasis in original).

[54] As the *North Sea Continental Shelf Cases* (see n. 53 above) indicate, the conditions of estoppel are rather strict. On the other hand, the concept's relationship to some of the neighbouring principles, notably to that of acquiescence, is somewhat unsettled, see *Delimitation of the Maritime Boundary in the Gulf of Maine Area, Judgment*, [1984] I.C.J.Rep. 246 at pp. 304–305, paras. 129–130. This may have led some authors to exercise considerable caution in positing estoppel as a general principle of international law. See, *e.g.* Brownlie, *Principles of Public International Law*, (4th ed., Oxford, 1990) pp. 640–642.

[55] In fact, Article X:4 of the Agreement provides that "[w]hen a regional economic integration organisation becomes a party to this Agreement, such regional economic integration organisation shall, in accordance with the provisions of Article II.7 of the FAO Constitution, as appropriate, notify such *modifications or clarifications* to its declaration of competence submitted under Article XI.5 of the FAO Constitution as may be necessary in the light of its acceptance of this Agreement." (emphasis added).

SUBSTANCE: THE FAO ARRANGEMENT AS A SOURCE OF BINDING COMMITMENTS

6.10   After having established that the Council's decision of November 22, 1993 was a reviewable act under Article 230 EC the Court could proceed to the merits. In other words, it had to examine whether any of the grounds of review mentioned in the second sub-paragraph of Article 230 was present.[56] Even though the Commission had not based its application on any one particular ground listed in the provision, it seems evident that it had contemplated the third and the most general one rather than any of the three more specific ones. It was therefore for the Court next to establish whether the Council's vote had amounted to an "... infringement of [the] Treaty or of any rule of law relating to its application ...".[57] The Court's findings on admissibility might already have anticipated what was about to come; issues of admissibility and substance were closely linked and seemed to follow a similar logic (*cf*. AG, para. 3), as indeed often is the case with actions brought under Article 230 of the Treaty.

As explained, the Commission's contention had been that the draft agreement fell essentially if not wholly within the exclusive competence of the Community: the proposals for statements of competence it had submitted during the negotiations had only been inspired, first, by the awareness of the sensitivity of the competence question (as regards registration of vessel and allocation of flag, in particular) and, second, by the prospect that the issue of flagging could re-emerge at the final stage of the negotiations (AG, paras. 17 and 20). The Council, supported by the United Kingdom, had firmly contested that the thrust of the issue lay in an area within the exclusive competence of the Community: the functions of licences to fish on the high seas (Art. III of the Agreement), issued by Member States subject to compliance with conservation and management measures, the Council had argued, were comparable to those of authorisations to fly a particular flag.[58] The Commission for its part had taken the view that the two instruments differ fundamentally from each other (para. 46). Finally, the Council had pointed out that the provisions relating to the possibility of imposing penal sanctions (Art. III:8) or to cooperation with developing countries (Art. VII) fell within the competence of the Member States (para. 47).

It had nevertheless been common ground at the time of conclusion of the negotiations that the subject-matter of the Agreement fell in part within the competence of the Community and in part within that of the Member States; no-one had formally disputed that competence was shared by the Community and the Member States (para. 40).[59] The Community notion of shared competence does not, however, sit comfortably with the rules and principles governing the Community and the Member States' membership in the FAO. As explained, one of the fundamentals of the latter is that no

---

[56] Article 230 EC, second subpara., provides: "[The Court of Justice] shall for this purpose [of reviewing of the legality of the acts mentioned in the first subpara.] have jurisdiction in actions brought by a Member State, the Council or the Commission on grounds of lack of competence, infringement of an essential procedural requirement, infringement of this Treaty or of any rule of law relating to its application, or misuse of powers."

[57] On the broad interpretation given to this ground of review by the Court, see Hartley, *op. cit.*, at pp. 414–415; Isaac, *op. cit.*, at pp. 248–249 and Manin, *op. cit.*, at p. 382.

[58] *Cf.* Article IV of the initial draft, *Report of the Twentieth Session of the Committee on Fisheries*, see above p. 82, n. 12, Appendix F.

[59] Whatever views the Commission might have taken on competence at the time of the negotiations (*cf.* AG, paras. 17 and 20), it had nevertheless suggested on November 22, 1993 that the Council adopt a statement noting that "... the draft Agreement [was] essentially, if not wholly, a matter of the exclusive Community competence ...", see above, para. 6.06. *Cf.* also the Commission's proposal of July 22, 1994 for a Council Decision on accession of the EC to the Agreement (COM(94) 331 final) where it is explained that the Agreement falls *entirely* within the exclusive competence of the Community (para. 8 of the explanatory memorandum).

cumulative vote on the part of the Community and the Member States is possible. There *has to* be a decision as to who is to vote on a particular agenda item. But the notion of shared competence is by definition unable to provide any guidance as to how that issue ought to be resolved. If the problem was at all to be regarded as falling within the purview of the Community *legal* order in the first place, some additional rules or principles, transcending those concerning the mere allocation of competence, would be needed.

Applied to the dispute in issue, the problem in question presents itself as follows: who should have voted when the draft agreement was submitted for adoption by the FAO Conference on November 24, 1993? In its application the Commission had contended that the Council had not been entitled to attribute the vote to the Member States while the Council, supported by the United Kingdom, had argued to the contrary. So as to be able to review the legality of the Council's actions, the Court would of course first have to establish the rules which might govern the attribution of voting rights when the competence is shared. Without examining either the general system of the Treaty or any particular provisions thereof, the Court turned straight to the Arrangement between the Council and the Commission (*cf.* para. 40 to para. 7) which in its Section 2.3 provides for situations where an agenda item deals with matters containing elements of both national and Community competence. The attribution of vote is there linked to the question of whether or not the thrust of the issue lies in an area within the exclusive competence of the Community. If the answer is in the affirmative, the Commission is to cast the vote within the FAO—if not, the Member States are to vote in accordance with a common position. The question of where the thrust of the issue lay thus seemed to have become the crux of the litigation (*cf.* para. 40).

6.11   It did not require any particular effort from the Court—in the form of new interpretative maxims, for example—to establish that the draft agreement had concerned an issue the thrust of which at least lay within the exclusive competence of the Community (*cf.* para. 50). The Court was content first to confirm its established case law on the Community's competence in the field of fisheries conservation (paras. 41–44)[60] and then to ascertain that the *essential objective* of the Agreement was compliance with international conservation and management measures by fishing vessels on the high seas (para. 45). In response to the Council's submissions concerning the provisions relating to the imposition of penal sanctions (Art. III:8) or to assistance for developing countries (Art. VII) the Court said that they did not, in any event, appear to occupy a prominent position in the draft.[61] On the other hand, nowhere does the Court say that the Agreement falls (entirely) within the exclusive competence of the Community.[62]

However, a finding that an institution has not acted in accordance with the terms of

---

[60] Joined Cases 3, 4 and 6/76, *Kramer*, [1976] E.C.R. 1279 and Case C–405/92, *Mondiet v. Islais* [1993] E.C.R. I–6133 were referred to.

[61] The approach is consistent with that taken by the Court in Opinion 1/78, [1979] E.C.R. 2871 at p. 2917 where it was held that "... the fact that the agreement may cover [specific] subjects ... cannot modify the description of the agreement which must be assessed having regard to its *essential objective* rather than in terms of individual clauses of an altogether subsidiary or ancillary nature. This is the more true because the clauses under consideration are in fact closely connected with the object of the agreement .... The negotiation and execution of these clauses must therefore follow the system applicable to the agreement considered as a whole." (para. 56, emphasis added). This does of course not justify a conclusion that the logic of the Common Fisheries Policy would be the same in all respects as that of the Common Commercial Policy under Article 133 EC.

[62] *Cf.* Neuwahl, *loc. cit.*, at p. 682. The Court skilfully says that the Agreement did not concern an issue whose thrust did not lie in an area within the exclusive competence of the Community (para. 50). On the other hand, in para. 48 the Court refers to a situation "... where it is apparent that the subject-matter of an agreement or convention falls partly within the competence of the Community and partly within that of the Member States ...."

the Arrangement cannot as such be regarded as a ground for declaring a contested measure void, with all legal consequences (*cf.* Article 233 EC (ex Article 176)) that would entail. It must further be established that the provision which had not been observed had imposed a binding legal obligation upon the author of the contested act. If the body in question was *only* subject to obligations of some moral, political or even legal order other than Community law, there cannot be an infringement in the sense of Article 230 EC. On the other hand, the FAO Arrangement seemed to fall into the general category of inter-institutional arrangements aiming at cohesion and unity between the Community and the Member States as they act in the international scene.[63] Such *codes of conduct* have usually been regarded as non-binding "gentlemen's agreements", informal manifestations of the pragmatic attitude and therefore as acts incapable of creating enforceable obligations of Community law.[64] In keeping with that traditional approach, the present proceedings did not fall short of attempts to vest the FAO Arrangement with all such extra-legal qualities.[65]

The Court however adopted a different conception. The Arrangement between the Council and the Commission was regarded as a binding commitment between the two institutions, something they were obliged to abide to under Community law. The Court was—for the first time—prepared to regard an inter-institutional agreement as a source of rules of law relating to the application of the Treaty, as part of the *bloc de la légalité communautaire*,[66] the infringement of which could be contested under Article 230.

The Court broke the ground by first recalling its previous case law relating to situations where it was apparent that the subject-matter of an agreement fell partly within the competence of the Community and partly within that of the Member States.[67] Under such circumstances, the Court went on, it was essential to ensure close co-operation between the Member States and the Community institutions, both in the process negotiation and conclusion and in the fulfilment of the commitments entered into. That obligation to co-operate flowed from the requirement of unity in the international representation of the Community (para. 48). Second—and this is significant—the Court went on to make a deduction: in the present case, the Court said, *Section 2.3 of the Arrangement* represented *fulfilment*[68] *of that duty of co-operation* between the Community and the Member States within the FAO (para. 49). This was the decisive step to bring the Arrangement within the realm of Community law. And as soon as the said rule of law had been established, there could also be the infringement: consequently, the Court continued, by concluding that the draft agreement concerned an issue whose thrust did not lie in an area within the exclusive competence of the Community and accordingly giving the Member States the right to vote, the Council had acted in breach of Section 2.3 of the Arrangement which it had been required to

---

[63] *Cf.* in this respect esp., the Arrangement between the Council and the Commission concerning participation in international negotiations on raw materials ('PROBA 20') of March 27, 1981 (unpublished), reproduced in Völker & Steenbergen, *Leading Cases and Materials on the External Relations Law of the European Community, with emphasis on the common commercial policy* (Deventer, 1985) p. 48.

[64] See, *e.g.* Sack, *loc. cit.*, at pp. 1253 and 1256 and Heliskoski, "The 'Duty of Cooperation' between the European Community and Its Member States within the World Trade Organisation", (1969) VII *Finnish Yearbook of International Law* 59 at pp. 117–118.

[65] Such views had been endorsed not only by the Council (AG, paras. 34–37) but also by the Advocate General who had regarded the Arrangement as "pragmatic" (AG, para. 61).

[66] Isaac, *op. cit.*, at p. 249.

[67] Ruling 1/78 (*Draft Convention of the International Atomic Energy Agency on the Physical Protection of Nuclear Materials, Facilities and Transports*) [1978] E.C.R. 2151; Opinion 2/91 (*Convention concerning Safety in the Use of Chemicals at Work (ILO 170)*) [1993] E.C.R. I–1061 and Opinion 1/94, [1994] E.C.R. I–5267, were referred to.

[68] Expression "*mise en oeuvre*" in the French text may further clarify the Court's intentions.

observe (para. 50). Therefore, the Council's decision of November 22, 1993 had to be annulled (para. 51).

The Court did not engage in any extensive reasoning on *why* Section 2.3 of the Arrangement ought to be regarded as a source of a binding commitment between the Council and the Commission. The Court merely said that it was clear from the *terms* of the Arrangement that the two institutions had intended to enter into a binding commitment towards each other (para. 49). This statement might conceivably be interpreted to refer to the mandatory strain of language in Section 2.3 ("... the Presidency *shall* express the common position, when ...") on the one hand, and to the general nature of the Arrangement as a device designed to establish—by means of relatively detailed provisions—an internal procedure to enable the Community and the Member States to meet in practice the conditions set out for their participation in the work of the FAO by the Constitution and the General Rules of the Organisation, on the other. In that sense, the Arrangement must probably be distinguished from those codes of conducts which lay down general principles that will be given effect only subsequently by means of more detailed rules; the latter may then give rise to binding commitments, whereas the code itself has no legal effects.[69] Finally, nowhere in the Arrangement is it made explicit that the intention of the parties had been to create a device devoid of all normativity under Community law.[70] An express provision to that effect could well have made it more difficult to regard the Arrangement as a source of obligation in Community law.

6.12 On the other hand, significance should probably also be attached to what the Court did *not* say in the present context. As in the case of the three advisory opinions where it had outlined a duty of co-operation between the Member States and the Community institutions for the conduct of their external relations,[71] the Court again refrained from making any reference to Article 10 (ex Article 5) of the EC Treaty, a provision nevertheless sometimes mentioned as a *legal basis* for this obligation to cooperate.[72] One might therefore be inclined to ask whether this silence should be interpreted as carrying with it some specific normative meaning as to the place and function of that provision in the system of Community law.

On its face, Article 10 EC only seems to lay down obligations for the Member States. Should the wording of the provision prove decisive for determining its "organic" scope of application, no act of the Community institutions could of course be challenged on the ground that it infringed Article 10 of the Treaty. However, the Court has on some occasions resorted to language capable of suggesting that Article 10 might nevertheless impose obligations not only on the Member States but also on the institutions of the Community.[73] But, the—at times somewhat ambiguous—language

---

[69] See Case C–58/94, *Netherlands* v. *Council* [1996] E.C.R. I–2169 at pp. 2195–2196 where a Code of Conduct concerning public access to Council and Commission documents was not regarded as a reviewable act for the purposes of Article 230 EC (para. 27). The Court had said that the Code reflected the agreement reached between the Commission and the Council on the principles governing access to the documents of the two institutions, while inviting the institutions to implement those principles by means of specific regulations (para. 25). In those circumstances, the Code merely overshadowed subsequent decisions intended—unlike the Code itself—to have legal effects (para. 26).
[70] *Cf.* Pt. A of "PROBA 20", see above n. 63, which states that "[t]he essential element upon which the 'deal' ... is based consists in leaving aside any legal or institutional considerations with regard to the respective powers of the Community and the Member States."
[71] See above n. 67.
[72] See, *e.g.* Frid, *op. cit.*, at p. 149: "[The duty of cooperation] can be legally based on Article [10] EC and, complementary [sic!], on Article [3] Union Treaty."
[73] See esp. Case C–2/88, *Zwartveld and others* [1990] E.C.R. I–3365 at p. 3372, para. 17 and Case C–234/89, *Delimitis* [1991] E.C.R. I–935 at p. 994 where the Court said that "[u]nder Article [10] of the Treaty, the Commission is bound by a duty of sincere co-operation ..." (para. 53).

availed of by the Court need not necessarily be conclusive, and one might come up with a different, more coherent interpretation: it has been argued, quite convincingly, that the mutual duties of loyal co-operation should not be regarded as being imposed on the Community institutions by virtue of Article 10 but rather by virtue of a more general rule, one particular illustration or, if you like, a source of inspiration of which is Article 10, the scope of application of the Treaty provision nevertheless being limited to the Member States only.[74] On that premise, Article 10 could not have vested Section 2.3 of the Arrangement with a binding content in Community law as far as the Council was concerned. As regards the Member States, it could probably have been considered capable of doing so, albeit mainly as a particular expression or illustration of the more fundamental principle of co-operation outlined in the case law of the Court.[75] However, once it was the conduct of the Council as a Community institution which formed the object of the present dispute, the Court may not have felt entitled to apply Article 10. And even if it had done so, all controversy surrounding the proper "organic" scope of application of that provision could perhaps be better avoided by arguing from the general principle, *i.e.* that of the duty of co-operation between the Member States and the Community institutions.

Finally, it is significant that any actual or potential changes in the scope of the draft in the course of the negotiations did not suffice to justify the Council's vote on November 22, 1993. It will be noted that the Advocate General seemed to have been inclined to take into consideration both the fact that until the end of the Hundred and Third Session of the FAO Council in June 1993 the draft *had included* provisions on registration and flagging[76] and the possibility that the flagging issue *could re-emerge* at a later stage of the negotiations.[77] Although the Court did not expressly deal with that argument, the judgment nevertheless shows that it was rejected: the Court did not accept the Council's contention that the thrust of the Agreement had not lain in an area within the exclusive competence of the Community since *by the time* the Council had adopted the contested decision it had no longer contained the provisions on flagging, on which the Council had based its submissions (para. 45).[78]

---

[74] Blanquet, *L'article 5 du Traité C.E.E.—Recherche sur les obligations de fidélité des Etats Membres de la Communauté* (Paris, 1994) p. 291. His interpretation follows from Case 230/81, *Luxembourg* v. *Parliament* [1983] E.C.R. 255 at p. 287 where the Court refers to a "... rule imposing on the Member States and the Community institutions mutual duties of sincere cooperation, as embodied *in particular* in Article 5 of the EEC Treaty ..." (para. 37, itals added). Even Case C–2/88, *Zwartveld*, [1990] E.C.R. I–3365, has been interpreted to mean that the Commission's obligation to give confidential documents to the national court was deduced *from the principle of reciprocal duty of co-operation* which the Commission and the Member States have in the Community sphere. See Temple Lang, "Community Constitutional Law: Article 5 EEC Treaty", (1990) 27 C.M.L.Rev. 645 at pp. 677–678.

[75] *Cf.* also Simon, *op. cit.*, where "... le principe de coopération loyale *exprimé notamment* par l'artice [10] CE, à la fois entre institutions et entre institutions et États membres ..." is regarded as one of the "structural principles" of Community law (p. 231, emphasis added).

[76] He had referred to "the impossibility ... of changing the indication of competence in midstream" (AG, para. 58).

[77] The Advocate General thus concluded that "[a]t the time of deciding on the indication of competence [in November 1993] it [had been] legitimate to take account of the flagging dimension of the negotiation." (AG, para. 69).

[78] In this respect, the facts of the present case are different from that of the *AETR* Case where the actual negotiations had still been under way when the Council had decided that the Member States should continue to negotiate. The Court said that "[a]t that stage of the negotiations, to have suggested to the third countries concerned that there was now a new distribution of powers within the Community might well have jeopardised the successful outcome of the negotiations ...", Case 22/70, *Commission* v. *Council*, [1971] E.C.R. 263 at p. 282, para. 86.

Implications of the Dispute and the Judgment: Some Further Reflections

6.13 The implications and consequences of the Court's judgment could obviously be discussed from many different perspectives and with a whole gamut of relevant legal and other related issues in mind. Some of these questions have already been dealt with above, while many others will necessarily have to fall outside the scope of the present analysis. In the following, the emphasis will lie on issues relating more specifically to the Community and the Member States' membership in the FAO. However, at least some of the Court's findings may well lend themselves to extrapolation into other areas of the Community's external relations, too; for in principle, no Court case should ever be viewed in isolation, but rather as part of the totality of [t]ongoing law-creating and law-determining processes taking place within the Community, and involving some more fundamental ideas of those involved concerning the system as a whole. If the latter may often tend to be covered by a layer of technicalities and legal argument, one objective of the analysis should precisely be to seek to uncover some of these general systemic ideas.

The Court's judgment clarifies at least part of the ambiguity in the FAO Arrangement relating to the respective positions of the institutions and other bodies of the Community. The Court makes it clear that the COREPER has no decision-making powers of its own (*cf.* Section 1.12 of the Arrangement). It follows that if it in the end proved impossible to reach consensus on the Commission's proposals concerning the exercise of responsibilities at FAO meetings, the matter would *always have to be referred to the Council* (through written procedure or as an "A point" or otherwise) so as for the decision to create legal effects vis-à-vis the dissenting Member States or Community institutions (including the Commission (arg., Section 1.12)).[79] However, a number of other important questions remain unanswered. For example, what is the role of the Commission in the establishment of a common position under Section 2.3? And what is the relationship of the Arrangement itself to the provisions of the Treaty? In the case of exclusive Community competence, can the Commission (and, say, a qualified majority in the Council) decide to leave aside the Arrangement altogether—thus escaping the detailed provisions it lays down for the preparation of FAO meetings—and then proceed with the matter through the Treaty channel?

In addition to the said procedural ambiguities the Arrangement makes—for cases where an agenda item deals with matters containing elements within both national and Community competence—the choice as to who should exercise the responsibilities at FAO meetings dependent on the equally ambiguous criterion of where the "thrust of the issue" lies (Section 2.3). As has been observed, this may not be easy to determine[80] and can easily—with the "precious" assistance of the above-mentioned procedural ambiguities—be made subject to abuse. As far as the present case is concerned, it did not prove difficult for the Court to establish that at least the thrust of the issue lay in an area within the exclusive competence of the Community. But there might well be "harder" cases; even the present one might have proved more tricky, had the provisions on registration and flagging not been removed from the draft in June 1993 (arg., para. 46).

6.14 What might, however, to some extent lessen the worries for conscious abuse of the defects of the Arrangement in future is the Court's obvious willingness to exercise its jurisdiction under Article 230 (and conceivably under Article 226 EC (ex

---

[79] *Cf.* in this respect new Article 207(1) EC (ex Article 151(1)) provides that "[t]he [COREPER] may adopt procedural decisions in cases provided for in the Council's Rules of Procedure."
[80] Sack, *loc. cit.*, p. 1256 and Neuwahl, *loc. cit.*, pp. 680–681.

Article 169)). Not only has the Court developed and maintained a "functional" approach to the question of admissibility but it has also made it clear that it is determined to integrate some standards for the exercise of joint competences to the Community legal order. This is probably the principal advance to be found in the judgment. For the first time an inter-institutional agreement is brought within the purview of Article 230 EC and the duty of cooperation—hitherto, as far as external relations are concerned, only subject to some broad formulae in three advisory opinions—given some real teeth in the form of the binding force of Section 2.3 of the FAO Arrangement. Even if that has only been done within the specific context of the FAO, there is no reason why the Court should hesitate to resort to the same argument in other fields, such as the World Trade Organisation (hereinafter "WTO") as well. For if there once was to be a duty of co-operation it was to be for real; if the Community once was living in an era of shared or joint or otherwise divided competences,[81] there would surely need to be some rules for that, too.

Indeed, it is not easy to escape the thought that the Court's judgment carries with it traces of a counter-reaction to the Opinion 1/94 jurisprudence. It is too early to tell whether the Court will eventually succeed in toning down the criticism made towards the splitting up of competences for the WTO[82]. Any signs of willingness by the Court to give binding force to inter-institutional agreements such as the FAO Arrangement may even lead to a still greater disinterest among the Member States in entering into such arrangements: what has proved unacceptable to them in the form of a Treaty amendment[83] or formal Council decisions[84] could hardly be achieved through any informal instruments either, if the effects of the latter were to be at end of the day more or less the same as those of the former.[85]

The Agreement to promote compliance with international conservation and management measures by fishing vessels on the high seas will not be concluded by the Member States. This may sound surprising in the light of the fact that the Court never actually said that the Agreement fell within the exclusive competence of the Community, something so fiercely disputed by the Member States at the time of negotiations. In any case, the Commission's proposal on the Community's accession to the Agreement was based on the sole participation by the Community[86] and neither the

---

[81] *Cf.* Dutheil de la Rochère, "L'ère des compétences partagées. À propos de l'étendue des compétences extérieures de la Communauté européenne", (1995) R.M.C.U.E. 461.
[82] *Cf.* most notably Bourgeois, "The EC in the WTO and Advisory Opinion 1/94: an Echternach Procession", (1995) 32 C.M.L.Rev. 763 and Gilsdorf, "Die Außenkompetenzen der EG im Wandel—Eine kritische Auseinandersetzung mit Praxis und Rechtsprechung", (1996) EuR 145. But see Dashwood, "The Limits of European Community Powers", (1996) 21 E.L.Rev. 113 at p. 119.
[83] *Cf.* the *Presidency Introductory Note* of 16 July 1996 to the Intergovernmental Conference (Doc. CONF/3870/96 CAB) where the Irish Presidency had outlined a draft article designed to lay down an obligation for the Community and the Member States to speak with one voice in international fora. However, no such provision was any longer included in the Presidency's *General Outline for a Draft Revision of the Treaties* of 5 December 1996 ("Dublin II"), Doc. CONF 2500/96.
[84] *E.g.* Commission proposal for a Council Decision on the exercise of the Community's external competence at international labour conferences in cases falling within the joint competence of the Community and its Member States, COM(94) 2 final, which has not been adopted by the Council. *But see* Article 4 of and Annex III to Council Decision 97/836/EC of November 27, 1997 with a view to the accession by the European Community to the Agreement of the United Nations Economic Commission of Europe concerning the adoption of uniform technical prescriptions for wheeled vehicles, equipment and parts which can be fitted to and/or be used on wheeled vehicles and the conditions for reciprocal recognition of approvals granted on the basis of these prescriptions ('Revised 1958 Agreement'), which lay down the practical arrangements with regard to the involvement of the Community and the Member States in the Agreement, OJ 1997 L346/78.
[85] In spite of proposals from a number different Presidencies, no comprehensive code of conduct for the WTO has been adopted so far. See Heliskoski, *loc. cit.*, at pp. 120–122.
[86] See above, p. 92 n. 59.

Parliament[87] nor the Council[88] apparently wished to see any changes to this basic conception. The Community's instrument of acceptance was deposited with the FAO Director-General on August 6, 1996, before any EC Member State had deposited hers.[89]

This seeming lack of further individual conviction on the part of the Member States will probably become more understandable if viewed against their behaviour in the course of substantive negotiations on the draft Agreement. It seems that the negotiating objectives of the Member States had been well in conformity with the ones set by the Commission, or at least there was no apparent contradiction between the Community and the various national positions. An expert from the Commission had taken part in the informal Group of Experts which had been convened to "... ensure that the major issues and interests were covered ..." in the drafting[90] and which had assisted the FAO Secretariat in drawing up the initial draft Agreement to form the basis of the formal negotiations within the FAO.[91] No one from the EC Member States had, however, attended the meetings of the Group. In the actual negotiations, differences of opinion between the Commission and the Member States on policy had not seemed too paramount, or could at least be ironed out by means of internal coordination procedures. There had always been—as the Advocate General repeatedly pointed out in his opinion—a common position under Section 2.3 of the FAO Arrangement. The removal of the provisions on flagging from the draft had reportedly constituted a major victory for both the Community and the Member States. Finally, all twelve Member States had voted in favour of the adoption of the Agreement at the FAO Conference, in accordance with the common position.

Where does all this then leave the persisting dispute on the exercise of voting rights? Why, after all, did the Member States so unyieldingly continue to insist on individual votes? What was the true nature of their concern, the *leitmotiv* of all the armoury of legal arguments put forward to justify their behaviour? One may wonder whether it in fact was about whom is entitled to take care of the fish; the Member States' wishes to secure individual input in the project did not seem to be at the heart of the dispute. One can barely help thinking it was more about who was entitled to *be there* when the fish were decided to be taken care of, a struggle for international presence and prestige.

---

[87] Opinion of December 16, 1994, [1995] O.J. C18/438.
[88] Council decision 96/428/EC of June 25, 1996, [1996] O.J. L177/24.
[89] The deposit by Sweden had taken place on October 25, 1994, *i.e.* before the country joined the EU.
[90] *Report of the Council of FAO*, Hundred and Second Session, see above p. 81, n. 15 p. 10, para. 58.
[91] *Report of the Twentieth Session of the Committee on Fisheries*, see above, p. 82, n. 17 p. 13, para. 77.

CHAPTER 7

Fragmentation or Evasion in the Community's Development Policy?
The Impact of Portugal v. Council

by

*Steve Peers**

INTRODUCTION

7.01   In December 1996, the Court of Justice finally had an opportunity to define the scope of the Community's development policy.[1] The Portuguese government challenged the first development treaty agreed under the new development Title of the EC Treaty, on three grounds. Firstly, Portugal argued that the Community was not entitled to adopt a development policy independent from that of the Member States. Secondly, it argued that even if the Community could adopt its own development policy, certain provisions of the agreement with India (which in fact are standard clauses in the EC's development policy agreements) fell outside the scope of Article 130y, the legal basis for development treaties inserted by the Maastricht Treaty, and could only be included in such a treaty with the additional use of Article 235 EC, the 'subsidiary powers' clause which requires a unanimous vote.[2] Thirdly, it argued that some provisions in the agreement (again, standard provisions) fell entirely outside Community competence, requiring the joint participation of the Member States and the Community in order to conclude the agreement.

These three arguments were entirely dismissed by the Court, but in reaching its judgment it gave considerable indications as to what could, could not, and indeed must be included in development policy agreements. This chapter does not attempt to assess the reasoning of the parties to the case, the Advocate-General or the Court.[3] Rather it attempts to assess the impact of the case upon the Community's development policy.

COMMUNITY PRACTICE

7.02   Since 1991, the Community has replaced its remaining "first-generation"

---

* Reader in Law, University of Essex.
[1] Case C–268/94, *Portugal* v. *Council (India Agreement)* [1996] E.C.R. I–6177.
[2] This chapter refers to EC Treaty Articles before their renumbering by the Amsterdam Treaty ([1997] O.J. C340). Arts. 43, 57, 66, 73c, 109, 109e, 109k, 113, 130s, 130u, 130w, 130y, 228 and 235 EC will be renumbered respectively 37, 47, 55, 57, 111, 116, 122, 133, 175, 177, 179, 181, 300 and 308 by the Amsterdam Treaty.
[3] For notes on the judgment, see Burrows, 'Development Cooperation Defined', (1997) 22 E.L.Rev. 594; Peers, (1998) 35 C.M.L.Rev. 539–555.

agreements with developing countries (dealing only with trade) and its "second-generation" agreements (dealing with trade and limited areas of economic cooperation)
with a series of "third-generation" agreements.[4] After the Maastricht Treaty entered
into force in 1993, the Community based conclusion of the "third-generation" agreements on Articles 113 and 130y, rather than 113 and 235, but there was no substantial
alteration in content.[5] None of these agreements were mixed, but more recently, the
Community has signed or ratified some mixed agreements based in part on the development policy provisions.[6] These have included provisions for political dialogue and
also (in the cases of Mexico and Mercosur) provided explicitly for a framework for
future trade negotiations.

The Community's development policy legislation underwent a broader transformation as a result of the Maastricht Treaty. Before, the Community had adopted only a
limited number of regulations to govern its development spending. These included the
procedure for granting food aid and emergency humanitarian funding, as well as
mechanisms for agreeing on financial and technical aid to all non-associated developing countries, replaced by more specific regulations governing regional aid spending in
Asia/Latin America and in the Mediterranean.[7] Since the development policy title
entered into force, the Commission has taken the opportunity to propose development
policy regulations governing a number of very specific topic areas, many of which have
been agreed by the Council. Earlier regulations cover aid for South Africa and the West
Bank and Gaza Strip; environment and development; the fight against HIV and AIDS;
funding for a programme for co-operation with the private sector, EC Investment Partners; North-South co-operation against drugs; assistance to uprooted people; rehabilitation; humanitarian aid; and support for population policies.[8] The earlier regulation
on food aid and security has been revised.[9] Later regulations cover co-operation
with development non-governmental organisations (NGOs); decentralised co-
operation; the integration of gender issues into development policy; and a measure

[4] For comparison with other types of Community agreements, see Peers, 'EC Frameworks of International
Relations', in this volume.
[5] Before entry into force of the Maastricht Treaty, "third-generation" agreements were concluded with
Chile ([1991] O.J. L79/2); Mexico ([1991] O.J. L340/2); Paraguay ([1992] O.J. L313/72); Uruguay ([1992]
O.J. L94/2); Macao ([1992] O.J. L404/2). Since entry into force of Maastricht, they have been concluded
with India ([1994] O.J. L223); Sri Lanka ([1995] O.J. L85/33); Vietnam ([1996] O.J. L136/29); Brazil
([1995] O.J. L262/54); Nepal ([1996] O.J. L137/15); Laos ([1997] O.J. L334/15); the PLO for the benefit of
the Palestinian authority (Interim Euro-Med agreement, [1997] O.J. L147/1); Cambodia ([1999] O.J.
L269); and Yemen ([1998] O.J. L72). A treaty with South Africa ([1994] O.J. L341/62) was adopted as a
development treaty but is too brief to be considered a "third-generation" agreement. Several earlier development treaties were ratified after a long delay: those with the Andean states (COM (92) 463, November 25,
1992; [1993] O.J. C25/31); Central American states (COM (93) 52, February 12, 1993; [1993] O.J. C77/
31); now in force [1998] O.J. L127/10; [1999] O.J. L63/38.
[6] Agreements concluded with Mercosur ([1999] O.J. L175); Chile (now completely in force), and agreed
with Mexico, but not yet in force ([1999] O.J. L42/46 (Chile); COM (97) 527, October 24, 1997; [1997]
O.J. C350/6 (main agreement with Mexico); COM (97) 525, October 22, 1997; [1997] O.J. C356/28
(interim agreement with Mexico, not including a development policy base)). The Mercosur and Chile agreements were concluded based "on the Treaty" without specifying legal bases, but the Commission had proposed their conclusion on the joint legal basis of Articles 113 and 130y (proposal with Chile, COM (96) 259,
June 12, 1996; [1996] O.J. C258/5; proposal with Mercosur, COM (95) 504, October 23, 1995; [1996] O.J.
C14/3).
[7] Reg. 3381/82 [1982] O.J. L352/1 (food aid, based on Arts. 43 and 235); Reg. 1993/83 [1983] O.J. L196/6
(special program to combat hunger, based on "the Treaty'); Reg. 442/81 [1981] O.J. L48 (general financial
and technical co-operation, based on Art. 235); Reg. 443/92 [1992] O.J. L52/1 (Asia and Latin America
funding); Reg. 1763/92 [1992] O.J. L181/5 (Mediterranean funding).
[8] Reg. 2259/96 [1996] O.J. L306/5 (South Africa); Reg. 1734/94 [1994] O.J. L182/4 (West Bank/Gaza
strip); Reg. 722/97 [1997] O.J. L108/1 (environment); Reg. 550/97 [1997] O.J. L87/1 (HIV and AIDS); Reg.
213/96 [1996] O.J. L28/2 ('EC Investment Partners'); Reg. 2046/97 [1997] O.J. L287/1 (drugs); Reg.
443/97 [1997] O.J. L68/1 (uprooted people); Reg. 2258/96 [1996] O.J. L306/1 (rehabilitation); Reg.
1257/96 [1996] O.J. L163/1 (humanitarian aid); Reg. 1484/97 [1997] O.J. L202/1 (population policies).
[9] Reg. 1292/96 [1996] O.J. L166/1 (food aid and security).

to fund specific projects designed explicitly to support human rights and democracy.[10] In most cases, the Community had been spending money to support these goals any-way, but without the benefit of specific legislation governing its spending.[11] All of these measures have been adopted solely with the legal base of Article 130w, except for the environmental measure which was adopted jointly with Article 130s.[12] However, the EC has adopted regulations providing for Mediterranean and ex-Soviet regional fund-ing on the basis of Article 235, rather than as development policy. [13]

Legally, development policy was constrained by the Court's case law delineating development policy from commercial policy. Tariff reductions to aid developing coun-tries were classified as measures of commercial policy, not development policy, as were commodity funds established by international organisations.[14] Shortly before and then shortly after the Maastricht Treaty entered into force, the Court delivered judgments confirming that Community and national development policies were concurrent. The Member States were free to co-ordinate national policies during Council meetings, or, in the case of the European Development Fund, to entrust the management of a policy to the Commission, without having to use full Community procedures.[15] The Court also confirmed that legislation establishing an agricultural market organisation could be based on Article 43 EC even where one of its main objectives was to assist certain developing countries.[16]

THE EFFECT OF PORTUGAL V. COUNCIL

7.03   In its judgment, the Court had no difficulty confirming that the Community was entitled to pursue its own distinct development policy, in addition to that of the Member States, as the text of the new Title in the EC Treaty clearly suggested. The Court then confirmed the legality of including a human rights suspension clause in a development policy agreement, without having to use Article 235 EC also. Finally, the Court assessed Portugal's argument that references to drugs, intellectual property, and energy, tourism and culture required either the joint use of Article 235 or the con-clusion of a "mixed agreement" with the participation of the Member States.

The Court dismissed the arguments against inclusion of the last group of provisions by establishing a two-step analysis of development treaties. First, the legality of the clauses must be assessed by determining whether their subject-matter was such that co-operation of that sort could actually contribute to development of disadvantaged countries. Second, if the first threshold was reached, the clauses had to be assessed again to determine whether they were so detailed that the agreement actually included specific obligations in a particular field. If the clauses were not specific but only pro-

---

[10]   Reg. 1658/98 [1998] O.J. L213/1 (NGOs); Reg. 1659/98 [1998] O.J. L213/6 (decentralised cooper-ation); Reg. 2836/98 [1998] O.J. L354/5 (gender); Reg. 976/1999 [1999] L120/8 (human rights). See also Regs 2824/98 and 2840/98 on the West Bank/Gaza Strip ([1998] O.J. L351/13 and L354/14). Reg. 1728/2000 on South Africa ([2000] O.J. L198/1) and Reg 1880/2000 on uprooted people ([2000] O.J. L227/1).
[11]   See generally report on assistance to Asia and Latin America (COM (1998) 40, January 29, 1998).
[12]   Such a joint legal base does not create any practical problem, since both bases previously called for quali-fied majority voting and co-operation with the European Parliament. Since entry into force of the Amster-dam Treaty, they both provide for co-decision with the European Parliament.
[13]   Reg. 1488/96 [1996] O.J. L189 (Mediterranean); Reg. 1279/96 [1996] O.J. L165 (former Soviet Union).
[14]   Case 45/86, Commission v. Council (GSP) [1986] E.C.R. 1493; Opinion 1/78 (Re: Natural Rubber Agreement) [1979] E.C.R. 2871. The latter case did hold that Member States had to participate along with the Community in such fund agreements, despite the Community's exclusive competence over the Common Commercial Policy, as long as the Member States were contributing financially to the fund in question.
[15]   Case C–316/91, Parliament v. Council (EDF) [1994] E.C.R. I–653; Joined Cases C–181/91 and 248/91, Parliament v. Council (Bangladesh) [1993] E.C.R. I–3685.
[16]   Case C–280/93, Germany v. Council (banana market) [1994] E.C.R. I–4973.

vided a framework for future co-operation, then an agreement including them was validly adopted as development policy, and did not require the use of either Article 235 EC or joint ratification by the Member States.

The Court, quite appropriately, made no comment on the legality of development policy legislation adopted by the Community. To date, no legislation in the field has been challenged. But in light of potential future challenges, it is appropriate to consider here what approach should be used to judge the legality of development policy regulations, and to apply it to adopted and proposed measures.

The *Portugal* v. *Council* judgment inevitably cannot be transposed in its entirety to development policy legislation. However, the judgment's core findings *can* be transposed: the Community's development policy legislation must be valid if it is subject to protection for human rights and if it primarily contributes to the objectives of development policy, without involving external obligations for the EC beyond overseeing appropriate control over spending.[17]

Since the Court of Justice addressed Portugal's objections to the validity of the agreement with India by topic, it is easier to assess the impact of the judgment by following a similar approach.

Human Rights

7.04   In *Portugal* v. *Council*, the Court transformed the Treaty objective of ensuring that development policy *contributed* to human rights protection into an obligation to make development policy *subject to* the protection of human rights. In some ways, the impact of this development is limited, since this had been the stated policy of the Member States and the Community since the Declaration on human rights and development in 1991.[18] However, it has now become a constitutional obligation, rather than a policy choice.

It must follow from *Portugal* v. *Council* that each development treaty agreed by the Community *must* be made subject to human rights protection, and furthermore that development policy spending measures must also be so subject. Indeed, it might be argued that failure by the Community to take action in the event of serious human rights violations in a state linked by an agreement is a breach of the EC Treaty, as interpreted by the Court. However, it is difficult to see how such a case could reach the Court of Justice. If it did, the Community institutions could make a reasonable argument that they must retain substantial discretion in such cases, because a move to sever ties might in some cases reduce the Community's influence over the situation and increase the risk of human rights abuses. Many human rights groups would criticise the merits of such an argument, but it is inevitably difficult for a court to second-guess political judgment in such a situation.[19]

Conversely, could the Community's decision to suspend some or all aid to a country, or an entire agreement with that country, be subject to judicial review by the Court? Such a case could reach the Court of First Instance if a company or an NGO applied for funding but received a refusal because of the human rights situation in the relevant country, or the Court of Justice if a Member State were outvoted when the Community decided to suspend the application of an agreement. It is not yet established whether suspension of an agreement follows the same rules as conclusion of the agreement,

---

[17]   Presuming, of course, that the legislative procedure is correctly followed.

[18]   [1991] E.C. Bull. Nov., point 1.3.67.

[19]   See by analogy Advocate-General Jacobs' Opinion in Case C–120/94, *Commission* v. *Greece (FYROM sanctions)* [1996] E.C.R. I–1513; and analysis of the justiciability of different types of national security issues in S. Peers, 'National Security and European Law', (1996) 16 Y.E.L. 363 at pp. 398–403.

although the Amsterdam Treaty would seem to settle the matter.[20] Given the Courts' usual deferential standard of review of the Community institutions' acts, an attack on the *merits* of their decision is unlikely to succeed,[21] and it seems improbable in any event that the Community institutions would suspend aid unless the human rights situation were quite serious.[22] However, a claim might have greater chance of success if the Community institutions have failed to observe any procedures laid down in the relevant treaty and/or internal Community procedures.[23] Since the relevant agreements all provide for their suspension if one party breaches human rights principles, there can be no objection in public international law to their suspension *per se*, unless there were a procedural breach.[24]

Could a specific grant of funds under a development funding regulation be challenged for failure to observe human rights? It likely could have been challenged even before *Portugal* v. *Council*, on the basis of the pre-existing case law holding that Community acts which breach human rights principles protected by Community law are invalid. Where a development policy regulation specifically provides for observance of human rights principles, such a grant would be procedurally invalid without even having to call upon general principles of Community law or the development policy title in the EC Treaty. However, it is hard to see how an outraged NGO, or indeed any plaintiff except a Member State, would have standing to challenge such a Commission decision. Indeed, NGOs objecting to such a grant would lack not only the standing for a direct challenge, but also the forum for an indirect one. A Commission decision to grant funds to a non-Member State would have no effect in a Member State, and would not subsequently be administered by Member State authorities, unlike EC agricultural or trade policy law, the most frequent targets of indirect challenges.

The next question is whether the present Community development policy lives up to the obligation that it must be dependent on support for human rights. All development policy treaties agreed since 1991 indeed have clauses to some extent making their continued execution dependent on the observation of human rights principles by both parties.[25] However, the Community's approach to its legislation is more variable. Some regulations pay no attention at all to human rights concerns: for example, those on environment and development or on EC Investment partners.[26] On the other hand, in most cases, human rights concerns are integrated into the legislation. The regulation on population planning explicitly provides that funding cannot be used for forced abortions or forced sterilisation, for improper testing of contraception, or for any measure which would conflict with fundamental human rights.[27] The adopted regulation

---

[20]   Article 300(2) EC (ex Article 228(2)) now provides explicitly that "a decision to suspend the application of an agreement" must follow the same rules as the decision to agree it, bar only the procedure for consultation or assent of the Parliament. On Article 228(2), see discussion in Hendry, McLeod and Hyett, *The External Relations of the European Communities* (Oxford University Press, 1996), pp. 119–120.

[21]   See by analogy Case C–84/95, *Bosphorus* [1996] E.C.R. I–3953, in which the Court of Justice readily found that the human rights situation in the former Yugoslavia justified a restriction of a company's property rights by Community law.

[22]   This is borne out by recent EC policy on suspending aid: see answer to EP question [1996] O.J. C322/101.

[23]   See proposed internal EC procedure for suspending parts of the Lomé Convention on human rights grounds (COM (96) 69, February 21, 1996).

[24]   See *Portugal* v. *Council* judgment para. 27. For an attack on the validity of suspending a treaty without a clause allowing for suspension, see Case C–162/96, *Racke* [1998] E.C.R. I–3655. However, the Community purported to suspend the treaty with Yugoslavia at issue in *Racke* on grounds of "fundamental change in circumstances", rather than breaches in human rights. Suspension on grounds of fundamental change is explicitly permitted in the 1969 Vienna Convention on the Law of Treaties.

[25]   See COM (95) 216, May 23, 1995; M. Cremona, 'Human Rights and Democracy Clauses in the EC's Trade Agreements', in Emiliou and O'Keeffe, *The European Union and World Trade Law* (Wiley, 1996) p. 62.

[26]   See above, p. 101, n. 8.

[27]   See above, p. 101, n. 8, recital 10 and Art. 6.

on gender issues requires that "particular attention" be paid to human rights and democracy and sexual and reproductive health and rights.[28] Under the regulation on drugs co-operation, the Community can only contribute funding to projects where human rights have been guaranteed.[29] The HIV/AIDS regulation includes combating discrimination as one of its priorities; respect for individual rights is a principle; and measures under the Regulation may include projects encouraging non-discrimination and promoting respect for individual rights (especially reproductive rights).[30] Funding under the rehabilitation regulation can only be granted where a planned post-war or post-disaster recovery programme respects human rights and fundamental freedoms.[31] The regional funding measures also require respect for human rights.[32] The regulation on uprooted persons refers to a number of international human rights treaties in its recitals and provides for funding for combating sexual violence and for funding judicial settlement of cases relating to the violation of human rights.[33] Finally, the humanitarian aid regulation makes no reference to human rights protection, but as the recital points out expressly, the whole point of the legislation is to implement obligations under international humanitarian law.[34]

7.05   However, while the *Portugal* v. *Council* judgment made Community development policy subject to human rights concerns, it did not specify whether human rights could be a specific field of co-operation in a development policy agreement, noting merely that in the India agreement, it was not.[35] Denmark had argued that if human rights were ever the *main* field of co-operation in a given agreement, then that treaty would have to be adopted with Article 235 as a legal base.[36] It is not clear what view Denmark or the parties and other interveners took of the legal position if human rights were one of *several* fields of co-operation in a framework agreement.

The only development agreement to date with human rights as a specific topic of co-operation is the one initialled with Mexico in 1997, and in that case the Commission has proposed the inclusion of the human rights provisions in the main agreement to be adopted as a mixed agreement, not the interim agreement to be adopted by the Community alone.[37] Several agreements (although not the agreement with India) include as a specific field of co-operation the development of democracy, but the legality of such clauses is discussed below since the Court did not really address the issue in *Portugal* v. *Council*.[38] There can be no doubt that the specific human rights co-operation in the proposed treaty with Mexico is valid, since it is not included in a treaty to be concluded with the Community alone. But could it have been? And could the Community sign a treaty, or adopt development legislation, addressing solely human rights issues?

First, it is submitted that the promotion of human rights can form a specific field of

---

[28] See above, p. 102, n. 10, Art. 2(3).
[29] See above, p. 101 n. 8, Art. 4.
[30] *ibid.*, Arts. 1(1), 1(2)(c), 2(5) and 2(6).
[31] *ibid.*, Art. 2(1).
[32] Priorities in Regs. 1734/94 and 2259/96 (see above, p. 101, n. 8).
[33] See above, p. 101, n. 8, Art. 2.
[34] See above, p. 101, n. 8.
[35] [1996] E.C.R. I–6177, para. 28.
[36] *ibid.*, para. 20.
[37] See above, p. 101, n. 6, Art. 39 of main agreement (human rights as a specific field of co-operation). Art. 60(2) of the agreement suspends the entry into force of the entire Title VI on co-operation, including the human rights co-operation, until various liberalisation agreements have been adopted by the EC-Mexico Joint Council.
[38] The 'essential elements' clause impugned by Portugal dealt with 'human rights and democratic principles', but in its judgment the Court referred almost entirely to the role of human rights in Community law. Furthermore, Opinion 2/94 *(ECHR)* [1996] E.C.R. I–1759, addressed only the issue of the Community's external relations powers over human rights, not over fostering democracy.

co-operation in a development policy treaty agreed by the Community alone, without any need to have recourse to Article 235 or the participation of the Member States. It is true that Opinion 2/94 held that the Community had no express or implied external relations powers in the field of human rights under a specific provision of the EC Treaty, and that Article 235 could not provide powers for the Community to accede to the European Convention on Human Rights (ECHR).[39] But the inclusion of human rights in a framework development policy agreement would be subject to the general rules for assessment of such agreements set out in *Portugal* v. *Council*. Some would argue that applying the first criterion could be difficult in principle, on the grounds that human rights are a 'Western' concept that hinders development, rather than contributes to it. However, given the importance of human rights in the Community legal order and the subjection of the Community's development policy to human rights concerns, it seems unlikely that the Court of Justice would accept such an argument. Indeed, it would be politically difficult for a Member State to make it. Applying the second criterion, if the human rights co-operation provided for in an agreement did not impose specific commitments upon the Community, it could therefore be included in that agreement, just like energy, tourism and culture, without the need for additional legal bases.

As for a specific treaty, or specific legislative act, dealing *solely* with human rights and development policy, the issue is currently under dispute. The proposed regulation providing purely for funding human rights and democracy programmes must have met with legal objections, for the Council Legal Service provided an opinion on it in late 1997, presumably at the request of at least one Member State.[40] For the reasons set out above, the legislation as later adopted meets these tests, since it addresses a specific feature hampering development and would not impose specific external obligations upon the Community.

Intellectual property

7.06 The Court's judgment did not make it clear whether the intellectual property provisions of the treaty with India fell within the scope of development policy, commercial policy, or both. The wording of the judgment suggests that the provisions could definitely fall within the scope of development policy, since they contributed to the specific objective set out in the EC Treaty of assisting developing countries' integration into the world economy, without providing for specific commitments.[41] Alternatively, the Court suggested more phlegmatically that the provisions did not fall outside the scope of commercial policy, as it had already held in Opinion 1/94 that dual Community and Member State competence over intellectual property did not preclude the inclusion of clauses in commercial policy agreements organising consultation procedures or calling on the other party to increase the protection which it provided for intellectual property.[42] It extended that ruling modestly here by finding that clauses expressing general support for high levels of intellectual property protection fall within the scope of development policy.[43] This finding will have no impact on current

---

[39] *ibid.*, paras. 23–36. The Opinion did not rule out the possibility of the Community ever agreeing *any* external human rights treaties, only the ECHR on the grounds that acceding to it would 'entail a substantial change in the present Community system for the protection of human rights' (para. 34). This will not always be the case.

[40] However, the opinion concerned the legality of human rights funding for *developed* states.

[41] [1996] E.C.R. I–6177, paras. 73–76.

[42] *ibid.*, para. 77, referring to Opinion 1/94 *(WTO)* [1994] E.C.R. I–5273, para. 68.

[43] [1996] E.C.R. I–6177, para. 74.

Community practice, which is merely to include exhortation clauses in its development policy agreements.

Similarly, if the Community were to conclude an agreement on protection of intellectual property rights with a developing country, it would have to fall within the joint competence of the Community and the Member States, unless it related solely to a Community measure harmonising intellectual property rights.[44] However, the legal position has since changed. Since entry into force of the Amsterdam Treaty, the common commercial policy has become "two-tiered", with an inner tier comprising the current policy, within exclusive Community competence, and an outer tier allowing the Community to conclude intellectual property agreements without participation of the Member States.[45]

Finally, the Commission has not proposed any development policy measure which would assist developing countries to adopt and implement intellectual property legislation. It is submitted that such a measure would fall within the scope of development policy as defined by the Court in *Portugal* v. *Council*, since it would assist developing states' integration into the global economy. However, the measure would fall outside the scope of development policy if it harmonised intellectual property law within the Community or obliged the Community to make specific external commitments regarding the protection of intellectual property.

Drug abuse

7.07 The Court used the rare words, "restrictive interpretation", when describing the Community's competence to include drug abuse provisions in the agreement with India.[46] However, it did not suggest that all the drug abuse provisions in the agreement had to be interpreted restrictively — only those in Article 19(2)(d), referring to exchange of information, including on money laundering. First, the Court began by accepting that controlling drug abuse fell within the objectives of development policy explained in Article 130u EC, since "production of narcotics, drug abuse and related activities can constitute serious impediments to economic and social development".[47] The second step was to assess whether the measures in the treaty with India constituted specific commitments going beyond the structure of a framework agreement. They did not, since they consisted of statements of intent on drug policy or measures (like training and rehabilitation) which were "linked to the social and economic objectives pursued by development co-operation".[48] The Court also classed assistance in monitoring trade with precursors as development policy, although the Community's separate specific agreements on precursors' trade have been adopted as commercial policy.[49] Finally, the exchange of information provision mentioned above only fell within the field of development co-operation if it was closely linked to the other forms of co-operation against drug abuse.

Have the Community's development policy treaties met these criteria? Many of them have even vaguer references to the fight against drugs than found in the treaty with India, so those provisions are clearly within the criteria. Other treaties contain

---

[44] For an example of this exception, see Opinion 1/94 *WTO* [1994] E.C.R. I–5273, para. 70.
[45] For implications, see Peers, 'EC Frameworks of International Relations', in this volume.
[46] [1996] E.C.R. I–6177, para. 66.
[47] *ibid.*, para. 60.
[48] *ibid.*, para. 63.
[49] See for example, EC-Mexico precursors agreement ([1997] O.J. L77).

slightly more definitive language, but none appear to commit the Community to specific measures that would constitute acts going further than the criteria.[50]

The drugs legislation adopted by the Council also appears to stay within the boundaries set by *Portugal* v. *Council*. It focuses co-operation on states which have ratified the relevant UN Conventions and implemented money-laundering legislation, and one of its goals is the development of institutional capacity to ensure that obligations under such agreements are met.[51] But this does not commit the Community to specific external actions.

Other areas

7.08   In some ways, Portugal was unlucky that the first development policy agreement concluded after the Maastricht Treaty entered into force was the treaty with India. This is because the latter treaty only gave Portugal three additional targets beyond the three discussed above: energy, tourism and culture. Many other development policy agreements include provisions on a number of items with specific heads in the EC Treaty or not presently covered in the EC Treaty at all. In addition, as noted above, the Community institutions have adopted or proposed development policy legislation on a wide variety of specific subjects.

In some cases, there is little doubt about the validity of development policy provisions. Portugal did not raise an argument against the provision for assisting human resources development in India, as it obviously fell within the objectives of development policy as defined in the EC Treaty, and there was no other possible legal base that it could have fallen under.[52] Most "third-generation" development treaties also include co-operation on agriculture, fisheries, mining, transport, scientific and technical matters and the environment. Co-operation on agriculture obviously meets the Court's criteria unless the Community commits itself in a development treaty to amending its common market organisations.[53] By analogy, fishing co-operation meets the criteria if it falls short of committing the Community to an agreement on trade in fish or on fishing rights. Provisions on transport, mining and scientific and technical co-operation also easily meet the tests. On the former, references to transport in EC development agreements are vague and at best refer to the possibility of a separate agreement. On the others, assistance with mining and technical development are clearly development policy in the classic sense. Rebuilding physical infrastructure also manifestly falls within the scope of development policy.[54]

The environment and development regulation is unchallengeable, since it includes a dual legal base; and as noted above, there is no procedural difference between environment and development measures. EC development treaties usually include support for resolving various environmental problems hindering development in the non-Member State and have never come close to committing the Community to specific obligations.[55]

---

[50] For an example of a drugs clause in a mixed agreement, see the EC-Mexico main agreement (see above, p. 101, n. 6,), Art. 28(2)(d), which refers to combating precursors and narcotic chemicals in implementation of a 1996 UN Agreement. For a more definitive commitment, stretching Community powers to their limit, see Art. 11, EC-Laos agreement (see above, p. 101, n. 5), according to which the parties shall "consider special measures" to combat cultivation, production and trafficking. Admittedly this is only an exhortation clause, but the Community lacks any powers over drug trafficking.

[51] Reg. 2046/97 [1997] O.J. L287/1, Arts. 1 and 4.

[52] EC-India agreement [1994] O.J. L223, Art. 18.

[53] *Germany* v. *Council*, Case C–280/93 [1994] E.C.R. I–4973.

[54] EC-Cambodia agreement [1999] O.J. L269, Art. 12.

[55] For instance, see Art. 4 of the EC-Chile 1991 treaty [1991] O.J. L79/2, regarding support to combat soil erosion, draft environmental legislation, establish environmental protection structures and arrange relevant research and training.

In contrast, development treaty provisions on subject-matter normally at the edge or entirely outside the scope of EC competence are more contestable. Several such subjects of co-operation will be addressed: the role of women; population policy; health policy; investment; taxation; financial services; monetary policy; vocational training; humanitarian aid; government (or public administration); democracy; regional peace consolidation; and support for refugees and displaced persons.

The Court's analysis in *Portugal* v. *Council* made it clear that energy, tourism and culture could fall within a framework development agreement if they met the two-step test described above. In the agreement with India, they did. The equivalent clauses in other EC agreements seem to meet the criteria also—although in the agreement with the PLO, the level of detail in the cultural clause must be close to the limit of what may be included.[56] As for the other specific issues addressed in development policy agreements or Community legislation, it is submitted that in each case they also fall within the relevant tests.

7.09   The proposed regulation on the role of women in development policy lays out clearly the reasons that assistance directed toward women is particularly appropriate for developing countries. Moreover, there is substantial evidence of the acceptance of this principle by international development institutions and at relevant conferences.[57] The Commission admits that the proposal is part of its plan to make women's' issues mainstream in all Community policies. This has become a requirement under the Amsterdam Treaty,[58] but it is likely that if the issue arose, the Court of Justice would find that it is already present as a principle guiding Community law.[59]

The regulations on demographic policies and HIV/AIDS also make particular mention of the role of women in developing countries.[60] The Community has no explicit power over population policy and can only "foster co-operation" with third countries in the public health field (see Article 129 EC). But both subjects also qualify squarely as part of development policy: both address "serious impediments to economic and social development" in the population and health fields, as did the drug abuse provisions of the EC-India agreement. Neither of them imposes obligations beyond administering funding in accordance with specified criteria.[61] References to population policies do not appear at all in agreements with third countries, and the occasional reference to combating HIV or AIDS is very general.[62] Broader clauses on health co-operation are sometimes included, but population and health co-operation obviously contribute to development and the clauses do not commit the Community to specific measures.[63]

A number of development policy treaties refer to the possibility of the EC *Member*

---

[56] EC-PLO agreement [1997] O.J. L147/1, Art. 57. See also Regulation on NGO funding (n.10, p.102 above), Art. 2, on targeting aid to threatened cultures (especially threatened indigenous cultures).

[57] The recitals refer to relevant clauses in the Convention on Elimination of all forms of Discrimination Against Women and the UN Declaration on the right to development.

[58] New Art. 2 of the EC Treaty provides that promoting "equality between men and women" is one of the Community's tasks, while new Art. 3(2) provides that "[i]n all the [EC's] activities" listed in Art. 3(1) including development policy, the Community must "aim to eliminate inequalities, and to promote equality, between men and women".

[59] Compare with the Court's approach to environmental issues before specific amendments to the EC Treaty (Case 240/83, *ADBHU* [1985] E.C.R. 531).

[60] Reg. 1484/97 [1997] O.J. L202/1, Recital 7 and Art. 4(1), population regulation; Reg. 550/97 [1997] O.J. L87/1, Arts. 1(2)(b) and 2(1)(e), HIV/AIDS regulation.

[61] See the priorities in the HIV/AIDS regulation (Reg. 550/97 [1997] O.J. L87/1, Art. 1(1)) which include developing scientific understanding—but *not* basic research.

[62] See, for instance, EC-Nepal agreement [1996] O.J. L137/15, Art. 13.

[63] See, for example, EC-Central America treaty [1999] O.J. L63/38, Art. 23 covering health care management and administration; health care policies; training health workers; combating cholera; and mother and child health care.

States and the signatory third state agreeing measures on either investment protection or double taxation.[64] It is clear from Opinion 2/92 that the former is within the mixed competence of the Community and the Member States, but it is doubtful whether the Community has any external competence at all in the field of direct taxation.[65] Despite this limited competence it is submitted that the relevant agreements do not exceed the Community's powers, as they only refer to the Member States' powers in the field and do not entail any commitment at all by the Community. Indeed, they do not even contain any "soft law" recommendations to the Community or consultation procedures—elements that by analogy with the case law on intellectual property, should fall within EC competence when included within a development policy agreement.

The agreement with the PLO is another matter. It requires the parties to refrain from creating any obstacles to direct investment on the West Bank or Gaza Strip, or liquidation or repatriation of yield or related profit.[66] While in practice the clause may be directed at the PLO, its wording creates obligations for the Community. In the absence of joint use of Article 73c(2) EC to conclude the agreement, such a specific commitment regarding capital goes beyond the powers which the Community can exercise when concluding a development policy agreement.

The relationship between development policy and tax, investment and financial services can be separated from the relationship between development policy and monetary policy. This is because the latter is an express external competence of the Community—but an unusual one. The power for the Community to agree to an international exchange rate system, to treaties "concerning monetary or foreign exchange régime matters" or to define a position "at international level" for "issues of particular relevance to economic and monetary union" cannot be exercised until January 1, 1999; might be subject to different negotiating arrangements; and shall not bind Member States with a derogation or opt-out from monetary union.[67] Of these, external competence concerning "monetary...matters" will require only a qualified majority vote to exercise, but quite apart from the particular features of this power, it is not clear what external monetary powers the EC possesses prior to the adoption of the single currency. Certain of the EC's development policy agreements refer to exchanges of information on monetary matters and co-operation within Bretton Woods institutions.[68] It would seem by analogy with the *Portugal* v. *Council* rulings on drugs and intellectual property that such limited clauses can fall within development policy co-operation; but any step outside them would be legally questionable.

Vocational training is included in many agreements, but would appear to fulfil the tests also. The relevant clauses sometimes go into detail on the extent of the clauses but never into quite enough detail to alter the basis of the agreement.[69] In any event, the Community has exercised its powers to "foster co-operation" with third countries in the field of vocational training and education to sign agreements with them; and exercising such powers entail the same procedure as the adoption of development agreements.[70]

[64] For instance, see EC-Vietnam agreement [1996] O.J. L136/29, Art. 5 (investment); EC-Chile 1991 agreement [1991] O.J. L79/2, Art. 2(3) (double taxation).
[65] Opinion 2/92 (*OECD Investment measures*) [1995] E.C.R. I–521.
[66] EC-PLO agreement [1997] O.J. L147/1, Art. 28.
[67] Art. 109 EC (external competence); Art. 109e(3) EC (entry into force); Art. 109k EC (derogating Member States); TEU Protocols on monetary union and Denmark and the UK. See conclusions of Luxembourg European Council, [1997] E.U. Bull. Dec.
[68] EC-Mexico 1991 agreement [1991] O.J. L340/2, Art. 2(2)(j); EC-Laos agreement [1997] O.J. L334/15, Art. 3.
[69] For example, see EC-Vietnam agreement [1996] O.J. L136/29, Art. 13(2)(d); 1991 EC-Mexico agreement [1991] O.J. L340/2, Art. 36.
[70] EC-US education agreement ([1995] O.J. L279); EC-Canada education agreement ([1995] O.J. L300).

7.10 The various clauses in development policy treaties on government or public administration, democratic development, and regional peace agreements should be considered together with the regulation on humanitarian aid, as each address essentially "political" matters for which the Community does not have express internal or external powers.[71] Combating "obstacles posed by unexploded objects" is a comparable field of co-operation.[72] At first sight, these are all "second pillar" matters and indeed each of them has been the subject of formal Common Foreign and Security Policy (CFSP) measures.[73] But there is a close parallel with the case law on the relationship between trade policy and foreign policy: the existence of foreign policy objectives does not prevent a measure from falling within the EC's commercial policy, as long as the *content* is of a commercial policy nature.[74]

The same would apply here by analogy: if a measure meets the two-step test for qualification as a development policy measure, it should be considered as such regardless of the foreign policy objectives that gave rise to it. Only a foreign policy decision *per se*, such as a decision to back a peace plan, appear at a peace conference or support a particular cause, should be treated as a CFSP measure. Several items of adopted or proposed legislation apply this distinction explicitly, providing that aid must be given regardless of political distinctions.[75] However, Council practice has been on occasion to impose first-pillar obligations in second-pillar measures.[76]

Parallel issues arise with the development policy measures affecting refugees and other displaced persons, although as yet there is no case law on the boundary between the first and third pillars.[77] The regulation on assisting uprooted people defends its categorisation as a measure of development policy on the grounds that "this type of aid is a prerequisite for development", thus contributing to the objectives set out in Article 130u EC.[78] The beneficiaries include refugees as defined in the Geneva Convention, displaced persons, returnees and demobilised soldiers, along with host countries.[79] The legislation is at the very edge of Community competence, but it is submitted that the relevant measures do contribute to development and that they do not oblige the Community to accept specific international commitments in international humanitarian law or take a particular foreign policy view. Refugees in a *developed* country could receive assistance "in duly justified, exceptional cases". However, refugees and displaced persons in the Community have received support under third-pillar Joint Actions.[80] This should not pose a problem, since Community and national development policies are concurrent and so it should not matter that co-ordinated Member State policies overlap with the Community's as long as there is no conflict.

Certain individual development agreements also make a brief reference to the sup-

---

[71] For the aid regulation see Reg. 1257/96 [1996] O.J. L163/1; for government co-operation, see [1999] O.J. L63/38, 1993, Central America agreement Art 29 and [1991] O.J. L79/2, Chile agreement Art. 12; for democracy co-operation, see [1991] O.J. L340/2, Paraguay agreement Art 12; for regional peace co-operation, see [1999] O.J. L63/38, Central America agreement Art 27.

[72] EC-Laos agreement [1997] O.J. L334/15, , Art. 3.

[73] See the discussion of CFSP practice by Edwards for 1994 ((1994) 14 Y.E.L. 541) and Peers for 1995–96 ((1996) 16 Y.E.L. 611) 1997 (1997) 17 Y.E.L. 539 and 1998 (1998) 18 Y.E.L. 659.

[74] Case C–124/95, *Centro-com,* [1997] E.C.R. I–81; Case C–70/94 *Werner* [1995] E.C.R. I–3189; Case C–83/94, *Leifer* [1995] E.C.R. I–3231.

[75] See recitals, proposed human rights regulation [1997] O.J. C282/14 and humanitarian aid regulation Reg. 1257/96 [1996] O.J. L163/1.

[76] For detailed analysis, see Timmermans, 'The Uneasy Relationship Between the Communities and the Second Union Pillar: Back to the "Plan Fouchet"?', (1996/1) L.I.E.I. 61.

[77] See Case C–170/96, *Commission* v. *Council (airport transit visas)* [1998] E.C.R. I–2763.

[78] Reg. 443/97 [1997] O.J. L68/1, recital 9.

[79] *ibid.,* Arts. 2 and 4. There is no reference to the EU Joint Position on the definition of "refugee" ([1996] O.J. L63). In some of the relevant countries, the Convention may not have been ratified or may receive a different interpretation.

[80] [1997] O.J. L205/3 and 205/5.

port of refugees as a distinct field of co-operation. The legality of such measures should not be called into question since their coverage is even less specific than that of the Regulation.[81] However, the provision in the 1991 EC-Chile agreement calling for assistance with voluntary repatriation of scientists is more problematic.[82] It almost obliges Member States to harmonise their immigration policies but falls narrowly short.[83] Various declarations to agreements recalling that the Community's *Member States* place great importance on readmission of illegal immigrants do not commit the Community in any way, so pose no problem.

CONCLUSION

7.11   It is a trite observation that any policy to assist developing countries must attempt to address as many of the individual factors hindering development as possible. A new dam might well be useful in encouraging industrial development, but if it leads to or adds to severe environmental problems, it will be counter-productive. Furthermore, if the infrastructure to take advantage of the new power supply does not exist, the new dam is useless; and if a focus on such megaprojects draws time, energy and attention away from other serious development problems in that country, it is *worse* than useless.

The Community's development policy, as practised in its agreements and its internal legislation, ostensibly tries to take a broad approach, addressing causes as well as symptoms, planning prevention as well as attempting cures. Its success at achieving these broad goals is a question for policy analysts which lies beyond the scope of this paper. But an unduly restrictive legal definition of development policy, failing to take account of the necessity for a broad approach, could end up hindering the organisation and development of such a policy. On the other hand, a casual acceptance of the breadth of such a policy would allow the Community institutions to avoid the more restrictive rules for adopting external relations measures which have been established for other areas of Community law.[84]

Will the *Portugal* v. *Council* case allow the Community to avoid fragmentation of its development policy on the one hand, and evasion of its internal rules for agreeing other treaties on the other? It seems likely that it will. The Community institutions are free to agree framework agreements with developing countries, but are on notice that a specific, detailed agreement in a particular field will probably have to be adopted under another, potentially more restrictive, legal base. Similarly, as argued above, the institutions are free to continue the present approach to funding legislation, as long as the legislation does not result in specific external commitments. The result should allow the Community to continue with its modern and flexible development policy and to focus its attention on the merits of the policy, rather than its legality.

---

[81] See COM (93) 52, February 12, 1993, EC-Central America agreement Art. 26.

[82] [1991] O.J. L79/2, Art. 6(2)(e); see also Art. 2(2) of EC-Paraguay agreement [1992] O.J. L313/72.

[83] See third-pillar Decision on voluntary repatriation policies ([1997] O.J. L147). Assistance for repatriation within third countries or between other third countries should not present a problem, since it does not affect persons entering or residing in the EU (see Reg. 1257/96 [1996] O.J. L163/1, humanitarian aid regulation Art. 2(f)).

[84] On the latter concern, see Opinion 1/94 (*WTO*) [1994] E.C.R. I–5273, para. 60.

PART II: SYNTHESIS

A. EC EXTERNAL COMPETENCE

CHAPTER 8

The Attribution of External Relations Competence

by

Alan Dashwood

INTRODUCTORY SURVEY

8.01 It was suggested in the Introduction to this volume that both the case law and the academic literature on the external relations competence of the European Community have been dominated by two great questions of principle, which were designated "the existence question" and "the exclusivity question".[1] The logically prior of those, "the existence question", is the subject of the present chapter.[2] It may be formulated (adapting language that was first used in the *AETR* judgment) as follows: how do the powers of the Community come to extend to relationships arising from international law, and hence involve the need in the sphere in question for agreements with the third countries concerned?[3] The exclusivity question becomes relevant only once it is clear that the Community enjoys external relations competence in a certain matter, and asks whether that competence is shared with the Member States (which is the usual situation), or whether they no longer have the right to act autonomously in that matter. That question is considered by Professor O'Keeffe in chapter 12, below.

---

[1] The distinction was first drawn by the author in his contribution on "Implied External Competence of the EC" to Koskenniemi (ed.), *International Law Aspects of the European Union* (hereinafter, "Koskenniemi, *Aspects*"), p. 113. Following the *AETR* judgment, Case 22/70, *Commission* v. *Council* [1971] E.C.R. 263, and the other authorities of the 1970s which are reviewed in Chapter 1, above, there was a proliferation of academic literature on the subject of the Community's external relations competence. Much of this literature, which sought to draw out the implications of the 1970s authorities, has been superseded by the clarification of the Court's position in Opinion 1/94, *WTO* [1994] E.C.R. I–5267, and the further confirmation provided in Opinion 2/94 *ECHR* [1996] E.C.R. I–1759. Among the treatments of the subject belonging to the pre-Opinion 1/94 era which are of enduring importance, mention may be made of: Pescatore, "External Relations in the Case Law of the Court of Justice", (1979) 16 C.M.L. Rev. 615; Temple Lang, "The ERTA Judgement and the Court's Case Law on Competence and Conflict", (1986) 6 Y.E.L. 182; Stein, "External Relations of the EC: Structure and Progress" in *Collected Courses of the Academy of European Law* (1990) Vol. I–1, p. 115; Weiler "The External Legal Relations of Non-Unitary Actors" in Timmermans and Völcker (eds.), *Division of Powers between the European Communities and their Member States in the Field of External Relations*, p. 35, esp. pp. 67 to 80. For a balanced appreciation of the position post-Opinion 1/94, see Tridimas and Eeckhout, "The External Competence of the Community: Principle versus Pragmatism", (1994) 14 Y.E.L. 143. See also the general account in Macleod, Hendry and Hyett, *The External Relations of the European Communities* (Clarendon Press, 1996), ch. 3. The remarkable analysis of Opinion 1/94 by Pescatore, "Opinion 1/94 on 'conclusion' of the WTO Agreement: is there an escape from a programme disaster?", (1999) 36 C.M.L.Rev. 387 is mainly focused on the issue of the scope of Community competence under Art. 133.

[2] The existence question is here considered from the point of view of Community law. How far the Community is endowed with legal personality and capacity as a matter of international law is for the latter to determine. The leading authority is the Advisory Opinion of the International Court of Justice on *Reparation for Injuries Suffered in the Service of the United Nations*, [1949] I.C.J. Rep. 174.

[3] See [1971] E.C.R. 263, para. 27.

The existence question arises because the limited and specific conferment of powers under the EC Treaty is one of the defining features of the relationship between the Community and its Member States.[4] The principle of the attribution of powers has been expressed, from the beginning, as applying to the main institutions of the European Community;[5] and it was erected into an organising principle of the constitutional order through the insertion into the EC Treaty of the provision which has become Article 5 (ex Article 3b), and which includes a first paragraph stating: "The Community shall act within the limits of the powers conferred upon it by this Treaty and of the objectives assigned to it therein".[6] The new paragraph made explicit what previously had been immanent in the system of the Treaty, that the Community order is not a self-authenticating one: powers cannot be generated within the order itself above and beyond those conferred by the constitution-making authority, as provided for by Article 48 (ex Article N) of the TEU. As the Court of Justice put it bluntly in Opinion 2/94, the Community "has only those powers which have been conferred upon it".[7]

The abiding interest of the existence question is due to the fact that, even in the latest version of the EC Treaty, the provisions on the external relations competence of the Community are scattered and incomplete; and the text remains silent as to the possibility of pursuing some of the Community's central objectives by action taken within the international legal order. It has, therefore, fallen to the Court of Justice, as usual, to supply the deficiencies of Community constitution-makers and legislators, by developing the doctrine of implied external relations competence. The challenge was to explain how, in an order based on the attribution of powers, the Community could be recognised as competent to enter into international agreements in circumstances where this could be seen as necessary for the attainment of one or more of the objectives set by the Treaty, but authorisation had not been explicitly given by a provision identifiable as the legal basis for the contemplated action. The principal steps in meeting that challenge were taken by the Court in the "classic authorities" analysed in Chapter 1 of this volume, which must now be read together with the more recent Opinion 1/94 (WTO),[8] Opinion 2/92 (OECD)[9] and Opinion 2/94 (ECHR).[10]

In Opinion 2/94, the Court gave an authoritative restatement of the general principles governing the attribution of competence to the Community in the field of external relations:

> "23. It follows from Article 3b of the Treaty, which states that the Community is to act within the limits of the powers conferred upon it by the Treaty and of the objectives assigned to it therein, that it has only those powers which have been conferred upon it.
>
> 24. That principle of conferred powers must be respected in both the internal action and the international action of the Community.
>
> 25. The Community acts ordinarily on the basis of specific powers which, as the Court has held, are not necessarily the express consequence of specific provisions of the Treaty but may also be implied from them.

---

[4] For a detailed examination of the constitutional significance of the attribution principle, and of the techniques of attribution in the EC Treaty, see Dashwood, "The Limits of European Community Powers", (1996) 21 E.L.Rev. 113.
[5] See Art. 7 (1) (ex Art. 4 (1)), second sub-para.
[6] Described by the Court of Justice in Opinion 2/94 as the "principle of conferred powers". See [1996] E.C.R. I–1759, para. 24.
[7] *ibid.*, para. 23.
[8] [1994] E.C.R. I–5267.
[9] [1995] E.C.R. I–525.
[10] [1996] E.C.R. I–1759.

26. Thus, in the field of international relations, at issue in this request for an Opinion, it is settled case-law that the competence of the Community to enter into international commitments may not only flow from express provisions of the Treaty but also be implied from those provisions. The Court has held, in particular, that whenever Community law has created for the institutions of the Community powers within its internal system for the purpose of attaining a specific objective, the Community is empowered to enter into the international commitments necessary for attainment of that objective even in the absence of an express provision to that effect ...".

8.02   The principles there recalled by the Court of Justice may be summarised as follows:

(a) *The principle of the attribution of powers (or of "conferred powers") applies as much to action by the Community in the sphere of international law as it does to action taken within the internal legal order.*

That has to be so, because it has been held by the Court that provisions contained in international agreements become part of Community law without any formality being required other than the conclusion of the agreement; and, where appropriate, such provisions may even have direct effect. If the Community enjoyed general power to enter into international agreements in furtherance of any objectives whatever, the attribution principle would be undermined.

(b) *The Community acts ordinarily on the basis of specific powers (including in external relations matters).*

In principle, action by the Community must be specifically authorised by a provision of the Treaty or of primary legislation which constitutes its legal basis. The qualification "ordinarily" in paragraph 25 refers, presumably, to the limited scope provided by Article 308 EC (ex Article 235) for creating subsidiary powers. Because the procedural requirements that have to be satisfied by the institutions differ from one power-conferring provision to another (more particularly as regards the Council's voting rules and the degree of involvement of the European Parliament), it is constitutionally vital to identify the correct legal basis for a given act. If the wrong provision is chosen, this can result in the annulment of the act by the Court of Justice.

(c) *However, the requisite authorisation for the acceptance of international commitments by the Community need not be expressly given by the specific provision relied on as the legal basis: it may be implied from that provision.*

This is the crucial step in reconciling the doctrine of implied external competence with the attribution principle. The latter is taken to be satisfied, provided that it is possible to point to a legal basis in the Treaty (or in primary legislation) specifically authorising the Community to enter into international commitments of the kind in question, though doing so by implication and not in so many words. That competence in matters of external relations may arise in such a way, is said by the Court in paragraph 26 of Opinion 2/94 to be "settled case law".

(d) *Such an implication will be drawn, where the Community institutions have been given powers within the internal order to pursue a specific objective, as to the possibility of entering into the international commitments necessary for the attainment of that specific objective.*

The Court of Justice here reiterates the principle of complementarity, as it was christened in Chapter 1 of this volume. The principle, first discernible in the reasoning employed by the Court in its *Kramer* judgment,[11] was famously articulated in paragraphs 3 and 4 of Opinion 1/76;[12] and it was then reformulated in Opinion 2/91[13] in terms substantially reproduced in paragraph 26 of Opinion 2/94. The logic of implication encapsulated in the principle is that of ensuring, if necessary by action on the international plane, the effectiveness (*effet utile*) of the expressly conferred power to legislate internally. The phrase "in particular" in paragraph 26 presumably indicates that, in highlighting the complementarity principle, the Court does not wish to exclude the possibility that implied external competence may arise in other ways (*e.g.* under the *AETR* principle).

Two comments on the Court's brief but illuminating résumé in Opinion 2/94 of the law on the attribution of external relations competence are offered at this juncture, to pave the way for the discussion in the last section of the present chapter.

8.03   First, no reference was made in the quoted passage to Article 281 EC (ex Article 210); which is odd, because, in its original exposition in *AETR* as to how external relations competence may arise in the absence of express authorisation, the Court took the Article as its starting point.[14] The interpretation of Article 281 as a provision recognising the Community's general international capacity was treated by the Court as clear evidence that, in addition to the meagre number of legal bases expressly authorising the Community to enter into international agreements, there must be other provisions from which "[s]uch authority ... may equally flow ...".[15]

Secondly, the doctrine as expounded by the Court is based on a strong double dichotomy—between express and implied conferment and between internal and external competence: *implied external* competence arises under legal bases conferring *express internal* competence, the former providing a means of ensuring the greater efficacy of the latter. Again, there is a contrast with the position originally taken in the *AETR* judgment. There, the fact that authority to enter into international agreements may flow from provisions other than ones that confer it expressly, is not explained by the logic of implication. Nor, in interpreting Article 71(1)(a) (ex Article 75(1)(a)) of the Treaty in the light of its *effet utile*, did the Court attach any priority to the objectives to be achieved by internal legislation.

In the section of the present chapter that follows this introductory survey, the focus is on the provisions of the EC Treaty that have a particular bearing on the attribution of external relations competence to the Community. It will be seen that the technique of attribution has evolved in the course of successive revisions of the Treaty. The next section will be devoted to some issues going to the Community's implied external competence, which have been highlighted by the more recent case law. In the final section, an alternative account is offered of the attribution of external relations competence, building on elements of the *AETR* judgment which have been overlooked in subsequent cases, and softening the dichotomies of the restatement in Opinion 2/94.

---

[11] Joined cases 3, 4 and 6/76 [1976] E.C.R. 1279.
[12] [1977] E.C.R. 741.
[13] [1993] E.C.R. I–1061.
[14] [1971] E.C.R., para. 14.
[15] *ibid.*, at paras. 15 and 16.

EXTERNAL RELATIONS PROVISIONS OF THE EC TREATY

The original EEC Treaty[16]

8.04   In the original version of the EC Treaty, express references to the external relations competence of the Community were rare.

There was, first and foremost, the legal basis provided by the Article which, as amended, has become Article 133, for implementing the common commercial policy. The texts of Article 113, as it then was, and Article 114 (now repealed) are of sufficient interest in the history of the Treaty provisions on external relations to be worth quoting in full:

Article 113

"1. After the transitional period has ended, the common commercial policy shall be based on uniform principles, particularly in regard to changes in tariff rates, the conclusion of tariff and trade agreements, the achievement of uniformity in measures of liberalisation, export policy and measures to protect trade such as those to be taken in case of dumping or subsidies.

2. The Commission shall submit proposals to the Council for implementing the common commercial policy.

3. Where agreements with third countries need to be negotiated, the Commission shall make recommendations to the Council, which shall authorise the Commission to open the necessary negotiations.

   The Commission shall conduct these negotiations in consultation with a special committee appointed by the Council to assist the Commission in this task and within the framework of such directives as the Council may issue to it.

4. In exercising the powers conferred upon it by this Article, the Council shall act by a qualified majority.

Article 114

The agreements referred to in Article 111 (2) and in Article 113 shall be concluded by the Council on behalf of the Community, acting unanimously during the first two stages and by a qualified majority thereafter."

The legal basis for Community action in the regulation of external trade resulting from those provisions was almost completely self-contained. The scope of the objectives that may be pursued is broadly defined by the notion of "implementing the common commercial policy", to be interpreted in the light of paragraph (1) of the Article and of the general objectives laid down by Article 131 (ex Article 110).[17] The Community, it is made clear, is being authorised both to take unilateral internal measures[18]

---

[16] The name of the European Economic Community (EEC) was changed to "European Community" (EC) by Art. G1 of the TEU as signed in Maastricht.
[17] For instance, the Court of Justice noted in the *GSP* case that "Article [131] lists among the objectives of commercial policy the aim of contributing 'to the harmonious development of world trade' ", which presupposes that commercial policy will be adjusted in order to take account of any changes of outlook in international relations: Case 45/86, *Commission* v. *Council* [1987] E.C.R. 1493, para. 19. That made it possible for the Community to adapt its common commercial policy to take account of the particular situation of developing countries as trading partners.
[18] Art. 133 (2) and (4).

and to negotiate and conclude international agreements.[19] As to the former, the pre-scribed procedure is that the Council shall act by a qualified majority on a proposal from the Commission. As to the latter, it falls to the Council acting on a Commission recommendation, and again by a qualified majority, to decide whether negotiations should be opened; responsibility for conducting the negotiations is given to the Com-mission, which must consult with a committee appointed for the purpose by the Coun-cil, and observe any directives the Council may have issued to it; while power to conclude agreements belongs to the Council, which acts, since the end of the tran-sitional period, by a qualified majority.

The drafting of Article 133 provides a reminder that the effective pursuit of external relations objectives may be no less dependent on the availability of internal legislative competence as on the capacity of the Community to act within the international order. Anti-dumping policy, for instance, has its international dimension in the GATT Code, and its internal dimension in the rules and procedures established by Council regu-lations,[20] and in the practice of the Commission. Internal legislative and administrative competence and external relations competence belong naturally together, their rela-tive practical significance in a given context being a function of the activity which is authorised.

8.05   Outside the field of the common commercial policy, the only legal basis in the primordial Treaty explicitly authorising the Community to enter into international agreements was the present Article 310 (ex Article 238) relating to the particularly intimate form of relationship with a third country which is known as "association". The first paragraph of the Article, which remains unchanged, provides: "The Com-munity may conclude … agreements establishing an association involving reciprocal rights and obligations, common action and special procedures". Originally, there was also a second paragraph (deleted by the TEU), stating: "These agreements shall be concluded by the Council, acting unanimously after consulting the Assembly". The Article was, however, less complete than Article 133 in two respects: it was silent as to the possibility of enacting internal legislation (which may be necessary to implement effectively a complex association such as that created by the EEA Agreement)[21]; and, while referring to the procedure for the conclusion of an association agreement, it said nothing about the initiation and conduct of negotiations.

Besides those express legal bases, the Treaty included three provisions authorising international co-operation for various purposes, without specifically alluding to the possibility of making this the subject of international agreements. The provisions have survived intact as, respectively, Article 302 (ex Article 229) on the duty of the Com-mission to maintain appropriate relations with the organs of the United Nations, of its specialised agencies and of the GATT, as well as with all international organisations; and Articles 303 and 304 (ex Articles 230 and 231) on co-operation between the Com-munity and, respectively, the Council of Europe and the OECD. Article 304, it may be noted, speaks of determining the details of arrangements with the OECD "by common accord". Apart, however, from that rather gnomic statement (which may, perhaps, refer to common accord within the Council, as well as between the EC and the OECD), the three Articles contain no indication of the decision-making procedures to be fol-lowed in pursuing co-operation.

The only other provision of the original Treaty which referred explicitly to the Com-

---

[19] Art. 133 (3) and (former) Art. 114.
[20] Currently, the structural measure on the Community's anti-dumping system is Reg. 384/95 of December 22, 1995, as amended, [1996] O.J. L56/1.
[21] See, *e.g.* Reg. 2894/94 of November 28, 1994 concerning arrangements for implementing the Agreement on the European Economic Area, [1994] O.J. L305/6. This has Art. 310 as its substantive legal basis, an instance of implied *internal* competence.

munity's external relations competence was the one that has become, after substantial amendment, the present Article 300 (ex Article 228). The portion of the original Article relevant for present purposes is the first subparagraph of paragraph (1), which read:

> "Where this Treaty provides for the conclusion of agreements between the Community and one or more States or an international organisation, such agreements shall be negotiated by the Commission. Subject to the powers vested in the Commission in this field, such agreements shall be concluded by the Council, after consulting the Assembly where required by this Treaty".

The introductory phrase makes clear that Article 300 applies only where some other provision of the Treaty specifically authorises the action contemplated by the international agreement it is proposed to enter into. Paragraph (1) of the Article merely designates the Commission as the institution empowered to negotiate such agreements, and the Council as the institution with power to conclude them, after consulting the European Parliament.

8.06   All of those Articles from the original EEC Treaty may be described as "dedicated external relations provisions". They are, in other words, provisions concerned specifically and primarily with matters that bring the Community into a relationship with other international actors: Article 133 is about trade; Article 310 about establishing associations; Articles 302 to 304 are about relations with international organisations; and Article 300 is about the procedure for negotiating and concluding international agreements.

Dedicated external relations provisions may be distinguished, for analytical purposes, from the category here called "extension provisions" because they expressly authorise the Community to engage in international co-operation in areas where the main thrust of policy is directed towards activity on the internal plane. The Treaty as originally drafted contained no provisions of the latter kind: the first examples were introduced by the SEA. Thus the legal bases for action in the policy areas at the heart of the common market project—Article 37 (ex Article 43) on agriculture and fisheries, Article 71 (ex Article 75) on transport, Article 83 (ex Article 87) on competition, Article 93 (ex Article 99) on the harmonisation of indirect taxation and Article 94 (ex Article 100) on the general approximation of legislation and administrative practices in the Member States—included no explicit allusion to the possibility of pursuing the objectives they authorise, by entering into international agreements. Nor have those legal bases been amended, in the course of successive revisions of the Treaty, explicitly to authorise such action.

Another distinction it is useful to introduce at this point is that between the *substantive attribution* of powers, and their *procedural attribution*. By "substantive attribution" is meant the empowerment (legal authorisation) of the Community to do specified things, *i.e.* to act in certain fields or in furtherance of certain objectives, as identified in the power-conferring provision (legal basis). By *procedural attribution*, is meant the requirement that, in doing the things authorised, the Community act, through its institutions, by specified legal means, *i.e.* following a certain procedure or using certain kinds of instrument, as identified in the power-conferring provision. Both aspects of attribution may be covered within a single legal basis. Or there may be separate substantive and procedural legal bases for a given course of action by the Community.

The two provisions of the original EEC Treaty expressly authorising the Community to enter into international agreements both contained procedural as well as substantive attributions, though, as we have seen, Article 133 was more complete in that respect than Article 310. At the same time, in Article 300, first paragraph there was a general procedural legal basis available "[w]here this Treaty provides for the conclusion of agreements between the Community and one or more States or an international organisation". Such a provision would have been almost wholly redundant if the Community's international capacity were confined to the field of trade and to the establishment of associations. The inclusion of Article 300 in the Treaty was a very strong indication (though, oddly, not one highlighted by the Court of Justice in *AETR*) that the substantive attribution of power to act by way of international agreements was intended to result, for the Community, from legal bases other than Article 133 and Article 310.

Nevertheless, as a procedural legal basis the primitive Article 300 was seriously deficient. It said nothing about the need for the Council to authorise the opening of negotiations nor about the issuing of negotiating directives. On those matters, prior to the amendment of Article 300 by the TEU, the practice was to apply paragraph (3) of Article 133 by analogy, whatever the object of the agreement being negotiated. Nor did the Article contain any voting rules for the conclusion of international agreements by the Council. Until special rules were introduced by the TEU, the Council procedure was assumed to be that prescribed by the substantive legal basis.

New legal bases

8.07   So far as concerns the external relations competence of the Community, the text of the EC Treaty, as developed through progressive revisions by the SEA, the TEU and the Treaty of Amsterdam, shows two main kinds of change. There has, first, been a distinct tendency, in cases where specific legal bases for Community action have been introduced into the Treaty, for it to be made explicitly clear that the new powers may be exercised, where appropriate, through international co-operation.

The Treaty now contains, besides Articles 133 and 310, four provisions explicitly conferring power to enter into agreements for the purpose of organising international co-operation in furtherance of Community policy in the fields in question. Two such provisions, Article 170 (ex Article 130m) on co-operation in Community research, technological development and demonstration, and Article 174(4) (ex Article 130r(4)) on co-operation in environmental matters, were added to the Treaty by the SEA. The other two provisions, Article 111 (ex Article 109) on external aspects of monetary policy and Article 181 (ex Article 130y) on development co-operation, were added by the TEU. No direct addition was made by the Treaty of Amsterdam. However, the power given to the Council under the new paragraph (5) of Article 133, to extend the application of that Article to international negotiations and agreements on services and intellectual property, in so far as those matters are not already within its scope, would, if ever exercised, bring a very important extension of the Community's external relations competence.[22]

In addition, the legal bases conferring narrowly circumscribed powers in the fields of education, vocational training, culture and public health, which were brought into the EC Treaty by the TEU, impose on the Community a standard requirement to "foster co-operation with third countries and the competent international organisations".[23] Similarly, under the Treaty Title on the development of trans-European networks, it is provided that "[t]he Community may decide to co-operate with third countries to

---

[22] For a detailed analysis of Art. 133 (5), see chapter 18, below.
[23] See, respectively, Art. 149(3) (ex Art. 126(3)), Art. 150(3) (ex Art. 127(3)), Art. 151(3) (ex Art. 128(3)) and Art. 152(3) (ex Art. 129(3)).

promote projects of mutual interest and to ensure the inter-operability of networks".[24] As in Articles 302 to 304, however, there is no express stipulation that co-operation for those various purposes may take the form of concluding international agreements.

Two of the new crop of legal bases, Article 133(5) and Article 181, can be classed as dedicated external relations provisions. As to the former provision, its potential for enlarging the scope of the common commercial policy is unlikely to be realised in the foreseeable future.[25] The latter provision is part of the Title organising the activity of the Community in the field of development co-operation, which is considered to include the furnishing of humanitarian aid and food aid.[26] Prior to the TEU, such activity (unless it fell to be regarded as an aspect of trade policy, or took place within the framework of an association) could only be founded on Article 308 (ex Article 235). Like Article 133, the Title on Development Co-operation includes a legal basis for the enactment of internal legislation, Article 179 (ex Article 130w), as well as Article 181 on the possible conclusion of international agreements.

Unfortunately, the dedicated external relations provisions of the EC Treaty remain a fragmentary collection that does not reflect the range, and the political and economic importance, of the Community's present activities. There is, for instance, no authorisation in the Treaty for the furnishing of balance of payments aid or technical assistance to countries other than developing countries. The failure by the constitutional authority thus far to provide dedicated legal bases for such actions means that recourse must normally be had to Article 308 (ex Article 235).[27] The solution is of doubtful legality, however, since the necessity of creating external relations powers of the kind in question can hardly be said to arise "in the course of the operation of the common market".

8.08   Apart from Article 133(5) and Article 181, the amendments to the EC Treaty which are noted above belong to the category of "extension provisions". They make explicit, what the authors of the original Treaty chose not to spell out: that the powers being conferred in a given field of activity such as the protection of the environment, though designed to enable the Community to develop its own internal policies, may, where appropriate, be exercised through international co-operation. The gain in clarity brought by this change of drafting style is welcome.

However, not all of the legal bases which have been created by amendments to the EC Treaty and the objects of which, experience has shown, may be furthered, if only occasionally, by international co-operation, have been equipped with extension provisions. An important example is Article 95 (ex Article 100a), the general legal basis for approximation measures having as their object the establishment and functioning of the internal market; another is Article 137, the legal basis for measures in the field of social policy, into which the old Article 118a has been subsumed. The silence of Article 137 on the subject of international co-operation might seem surprising, since the possibility of entering into such co-operation (though, not as we have seen, of concluding international agreements) is expressly mentioned in the Chapter on Education, Vocational Training and Youth, which is found in the same Title of the Treaty as the Social Provisions Chapter. However, the difference can be explained historically.

---

[24] Title XV (ex Title XII) of Part Three of the Treaty, Art. 155(3) (ex Art. 129c(3)).
[25] The unanimity which was lacking among the delegations negotiating the Amsterdam Treaty, for the direct conferment on the Community of new external relations competences in respect of services and intellectual property, will not easily be found within the Council.
[26] See Reg. 1257/96 of June 20, 1996 concerning humanitarian aid, [1996] O.J. L163/1; Reg. 1292/96 on food aid policy and food aid management and special operations in support of food security, [1996] O.J. L166/1. As internal legislative measures, the Regulations have as their legal basis Art. 179 (ex Art. 130w).
[27] See, e.g. Reg. 1279/96 of June 25, 1996 concerning the provision of assistance to economic reform and recovery in the New Independent States and Mongolia, [1996] O.J. L165/1.

Article 118a was brought into the Treaty by the SEA. By the time Chapter 3 on Education, etc, was added by the TEU, the Community's external relations competence in the matters covered by Article 118a had been recognised by the Court of Justice in Opinion 2/91[28]: to have inserted an international co-operation clause into the Article would have been superfluous, and might have been interpreted as an attempt to restrict that competence. More surprising is the absence of an extension provision from the new Title IV which has been introduced into Part Three of the Treaty, in view of the subject-matter of the Title, "Visas, Asylum, Immigration and Other Policies Related to Free Movement of Persons".

Taking provisions like those, together with the legal bases dating from the original Treaty which remain similarly inexplicit, it can be seen that, despite the development of the text of the EC Treaty as described above, there remains considerable scope for the doctrine of implied external competence which has been developed by the Court of Justice.

Procedural attribution separated from substantive attribution

8.09   The other main change to the text of the Treaty which is of present concern has been a more rigorous and systematic separation of the procedural attribution of external relations competence from its substantive attribution. Article 300 has been transformed into a procedural code covering the essential aspects of the negotiation and conclusion of international agreements, and some aspects of their implementation; and the substantive legal bases expressly authorising the Community to enter into such agreements have been adapted to this development.

The text of Article 300, as consolidated following the Treaty of Amsterdam, now reads, so far as here relevant:

> "1.   Where this Treaty provides for the conclusion of agreements between the Community and one or more States or international organisations, the Commission shall make recommendations to the Council, which shall authorise the Commission to open the necessary negotiations. The Commission shall conduct these negotiations in consultation with special committees appointed by the Council to assist it in this task and within the framework of such directives as the Council may issue to it.
>
>   In exercising the powers conferred upon it by this paragraph, the Council shall act by a qualified majority, except in the cases where the first subparagraph of paragraph 2 provides that the Council shall act unanimously.
>
> 2.   Subject to the powers vested in the Commission in this field, the signing, which may be accompanied by a decision on provisional application before entry into force, and the conclusion of the agreements shall be decided on by the Council, acting by a qualified majority on a proposal from the Commission. The Council shall act unanimously when the agreement covers a field for which unanimity is required for the adoption of internal rules and for the agreements referred to in Article 310.
>
>   By way of derogation from the rules laid down in paragraph 3, the same procedures shall apply for a decision to suspend the application of an agreement, and for the purpose of establishing the positions to be adopted on behalf of the Community in a body set up by an agreement based on Article 310, when that body is called upon to adopt decisions having legal

---

[28] [1993] E.C.R. I–1061.

effects, with the exception of decisions supplementing or amending the institutional framework of the agreement.

The European Parliament shall be immediately and fully informed on any decision under this paragraph concerning the provisional application or the suspension of agreements, or the establishment of the Community position in a body set up by an agreement based on Article 310.

3. The Council shall conclude agreements after consulting the European Parliament, except for the agreements referred to in Article 133(3), including cases where the agreement covers a field for which the procedure referred to in Article 251 or that referred to in Article 252 is required for the adoption of internal rules. The European Parliament shall deliver its opinion within a time-limit which the Council may lay down according to the urgency of the matter. In the absence of an opinion within that time-limit, the Council may act.

By way of derogation from the previous sub-paragraph, agreements referred to in Article 310, other agreements establishing a specific institutional framework by organising co-operation procedures, agreements having important budgetary implications for the Community and agreements entailing amendment of an act adopted under the procedure referred to in Article 251 shall be concluded after the assent of the European Parliament has been obtained.

The Council and the European Parliament may, in an urgent situation, agree upon a time-limit for the assent.

...".

The contrast with the meagre procedural paragraph of the original Article 228 is striking. The bulk of the amendments date from the TEU; additions by the Treaty of Amsterdam were the references to signing and to provisional application in the first subparagraph, and the whole of the second and third sub-paragraphs, of paragraph (2).[29]

The first paragraph of the Article, laying down the procedure for the initiation and the conduct of negotiations, reproduces, almost word for word, the language of Article 133(3). Procedural provisions which, prior to the TEU, used to be applied by analogy outside the field of the common commercial policy, have thus been formally extended to international agreements of all kinds.

Paragraph (2), first sub-paragraph and paragraph (3) of the Article establish standard procedures for the conclusion of international agreements. The voting rule of the Council is normally a qualified majority; however, the Council must act unanimously where the agreement covers a field in which unanimity is required for the adoption of internal rules, or when concluding association agreements. As to the involvement of the European Parliament, this is limited to consultation, even in fields where the co-decision procedure or the co-operation procedure are prescribed for enacting internal rules. There are, however, two exceptional cases; for trade agreements, conclusion of which is often a matter of urgency, the rule of the former Article 114 has been preserved, that the Parliament does not have to be consulted; whereas, for the various categories of important agreements mentioned in Article 300(3), second sub-paragraph, including association agreements, mere consultation was not deemed sufficient, and the Parliament must give its assent.

8.10 The need for standard, relatively simple procedures for the conclusion of

---

[29] For a detailed analysis of the amendments, see chapter 18, below.

international agreements became apparent after the entry into force of the SEA, which established the co-operation procedure as the first step towards enhancing the role of the European Parliament in the legislative process. As we have seen, until the reinforcement of Article 300 by the TEU, it was necessary to complete the procedural attribution in the Article with elements drawn from the (legislative) procedure prescribed by the Treaty provision constituting the substantive legal basis for activity of the kind contemplated. If that procedure was co-operation (because, *e.g.* the agreement related to a matter which had been the subject of a piece of internal market legislation based on Article 95), the conclusion of the agreement would entail two readings before the Parliament, and an opportunity for the latter to propose amendments—almost certainly a waste of time and effort, since any changes to the text negotiated by the Commission would have to be accepted by the third country (or countries) concerned. Under the amended Article 300, the only *renvoi* to the substantive legal basis is to establish the Council's voting rule.

A further measure of simplification was provided by the Treaty of Amsterdam, through the insertion into Article 300(2) of a second sub-paragraph derogating from the requirements of paragraph (3) in two cases of urgency: a decision to suspend an international agreement, *e.g.* because the other party is in breach of a human rights clause; and the establishment of the position to be put forward by the Community side in a body set up under an association agreement, which has power to take decisions having legal effects. In both those cases, the Council acts on a proposal from the Commission, without having to consult, or obtain the assent of, the European Parliament[30]; however, the third sub-paragraph of Article 300(2) provides that the Parliament must be "immediately and fully informed" whenever such action is taken.

The completion of Article 300 as a general procedural legal basis has been reflected in the drafting of the individual provisions containing the substantive attribution of competence for the Community to enter into international agreements in specified fields. In Article 170 (research), Article 174(4) (environment) and Article 181 (development co-operation), the procedural attribution consists of a simple cross-reference: the authorised co-operation is to be "the subject of agreements between the Community and the third parties concerned, which shall be negotiated and concluded in accordance with Article 300". Article 310 (association agreements), now shorn of its second paragraph, contains no procedural attribution at all. Article 133 retains—superfluously—in its paragraph (3) the provisions now found in Article 300(1), though with the addition of a third sub-paragraph stating: "The relevant provisions of Article 300 shall apply": that replaces the former Article 114 on the procedure for concluding trade agreements, which was repealed by the TEU. Finally, Article 111 is the exception which proves the rule, by providing its own elaborate procedural attribution, adapted to the specific institutional framework of economic and monetary union, while declaring that this operates "[b]y way of derogation from Article 300".[31]

8.11   The strong differentiation between substantive and procedural attribution which has been achieved in the external relations field is reflected in the practice (generally though not systematically observed) of citing both kinds of legal basis in decisions authorising the conclusion of international agreements. For instance, the first "visa" of the Council Decision of January 26, 1990 concerning the conclusion of the Agreement on international humane trapping standards between the EC, Canada and Russia, reads: "Having regard to the Treaty establishing the European Community, and in

---

[30] Without the new provision, the procedure applicable would, in the first case, be that required for the conclusion of the agreement in question; and, in the second case, either that procedure or the procedure required for the enactment of internal legislation: see chapter 18, below.

[31] On the competence of the Community pursuant to Art. 111, see Zilioli and Selmayr, "The External Relations of the Euro Area: Legal Aspects", (1999) 36 C.M.L.Rev. 273.

particular Articles 113 and 100a in conjunction with the first sentence of Article 228 (2) and the first sub-paragraph of Article 228(3) thereof ...".[32] The citation of dual substantive legal bases indicates that the Community is drawing on both its power to regulate international trade and its power to take internal market approximation measures. The procedural citation indicates that the Council acted by a qualified majority on a proposal from the Commission and after consultation of the European Parliament. The practice in this matter is, however, not entirely consistent.[33]

A change has also taken place in the procedural attribution of internal legislative competence. In the original Treaty, every legal basis specified the procedure to be followed by the institutions when acting for the purposes there authorised. Nor did the introduction of the co-operation procedure by the SEA lead immediately to the adoption of the technique of cross-referring to the provision laying down the procedure (then Article 149(2), now Article 152). For instance, Article 95, in its original manifestation as Article 100a, provided: "... The Council shall, acting by a qualified majority on a proposal from the Commission in co-operation with the European Parliament and after consulting the Economic and Social Committee, adopt ...". Since the TEU, however, provisions conferring powers to be exercised by either co-decision or co-operation have been incorporating the formula, "acting in accordance with the procedure referred to in Article 251" (or, as the case may be, "the procedure referred to in Article 252"). Nonetheless, a difference as compared with the attribution of external competence is that there is no provision equivalent to Article 300 which comprehensively regulates the attribution of the different kinds of procedure available under the Treaty for the enactment of internal legislation. It is thus indispensable for every legal basis authorising such legislation to identify the applicable procedure. By contrast, in the case of external relations competence, Article 300 can do its work even without any express cross-reference in the substantive legal basis.

THREE POINTS ON IMPLIED EXTERNAL COMPETENCE

8.12 The broad lines of the doctrine of implied external competence, as restated by the Court of Justice in the passage of Opinion 2/94 set out in the introductory survey, appear now to be settled and reasonably clear. There are, however, some points arising more particularly from the reasoning in Part VIII of Opinion 1/94 ("The Community's implied external powers, GATS and TRIPS")[34] that call for further discussion; either because old misunderstandings have finally been laid to rest and the importance of the clarification provided by the Court needs to be underlined; or because, given that the focus of the case was on the alleged exclusivity of Community competence to conclude the WTO Agreement, the full relevance of the Court's analysis to the existence question may not have been apparent, at any rate before it was further illuminated by Opinion 2/94.

Complementarity v. parallelism

8.13 The logic of the principle first enunciated in Opinion 1/76[35] and restated in

---

[32] Council Decision 98/142/EC of January 26, 1998, [1998] O.J. L42/40.

[33] See, *e.g.*, Council Decision 94/800/EC of December 22, 1994 concerning the conclusion on behalf of the European Community, as regards matters within its competence, of the agreements reached in the Uruguay Round multilateral negotiations (1986–1994), [1994] O.J. L336/1. A string of substantive legal bases, is cited "in conjunction with the second sub-paragraph of Article [300(3)]". This identifies the appropriate Parliamentary procedure (assent) but not the appropriate Council voting rule (unanimity, pursuant to the second sentence of Art. 300(2)).

[34] [1994] E.C.R. 5267, paras. 72 to 105.

[35] [1977] E.C.R. 741, paras. 3 and 4.

Opinion 2/91[36] and Opinion 2/94,[37] has been confirmed as that of complementarity. According to the principle, competence to enter into international agreements arises by implication, under legal bases that refer explicitly only to procedures and forms of instrument used for the enactment of internal legislation, where such competence is needed to advance the objectives for which the power to legislate has been expressly given. The scope of the resulting external relations competence is thus confined to the actions which the Community legislator is authorised to undertake. To make the point another way, the principle only affects the substantive attribution of powers to the Community so far as concerns the specification of the legal order within which action may be taken (not only the internal, but also the international, order): it does not add to the range of things that can be done.[38]

The rival logic to complementarity, that of "parallelism", received its quietus in Opinion 1/94, where it had been strongly urged on the Court by the Commission. According to that conception of the principle, every substantive attribution of powers of action on the internal Community plane implicitly entails the attribution of powers, in the same field of policy, on the international plane. So understood, the principle would not simply be about recognising the possibility of entering into international agreements in cases where power to do so had not been expressly conferred: it would provide a way of extending the substantive competence of the Community, by automatically giving every authorisation of internal action an external reach.

That conception of the principle did not chime well with the Court's famous formulation. However, it received a boost from the somewhat unguarded language in which, as we have seen, the Court expressed its conclusion, in Part III of Opinion 2/91, as to the external relations competence of the Community derived by implication from the then Article 118a:

> "The Community thus enjoys an internal legislative competence in the area of social policy. Consequently, Convention No. 170, whose subject-matter coincides, moreover, with that of several directives adopted under Article 118a, falls within the Community's area of competence".[39]

What the Court should have said, to avoid any misunderstanding, was that the specific objectives of Article 118a (encouraging improvements in the working environment, as regards the health and safety of workers) would be served by the Community's entering into ILO Convention No. 170. However, its words could be taken, on a superficial reading, as meaning that the conferment of internal legislative competence in the area of social policy had as its corollary the acquisition by the Community of general competence to carry on external relations in the whole of that policy area.

At all events, the Commission seems to have read Opinion 2/91 in that way. Part of its case in the WTO proceedings was that, irrespective of possible limitations on the scope of the common commercial policy, the Community had implied competence, which in the circumstances must be exclusive, to conclude, among other things, the GATS. As reported by the Court, the starting point for the Commission was "to identify the internal powers of the institutions from which the Community's international

---

[36] [1993] E.C.R. I–1061, para. 7.
[37] [1996] E.C.R. I–1759, para. 26.
[38] Tridimas and Eeckhout, op. cit., while accepting the terminology of "parallelism", are in agreement that the principle "is not to be understood as widening the external competence of the Community from a substantive point of view": (1994) 14 Y.E.L. 153. See also Koskenniemi, Aspects at pp. 120–121.
[39] [1993] E.C.R. I–1061, para. 17.

competence may be inferred".[40] Legal bases, the Commission argued, existed under the EC Treaty provisions on the right of establishment and freedom to supply services, covering for the purposes of internal free movement all four of the modes of supply referred to in the GATS (the cross-frontier supply of services, consumption abroad, commercial presence and the movement of persons).[41] The fact that the provisions in question related only to nationals of the Member States was claimed to be immaterial, since "it is a characteristic of the rule laid down in the *AETR* judgment that it falls to be applied in cases where the Treaty has provided expressly only for the establishment of internal rules".[42] Put shortly, the Commission's position was that, because the Community had been authorised to legislate so that nationals of the Member States might freely become established or provide services anywhere in the internal market, it followed that there must be corresponding power to take the steps (both legislative and by way of international agreements) necessary in order to liberalise establishment and the supply of services between the Community and third countries.

8.14   That position was roundly rejected by the Court of Justice in a passage of Opinion 1/94 where it drew a contrast between the Treaty provisions on transport and those on establishment and services.[43]

As to the former, recalling its *AETR* judgment, the Court pointed out that the Community was empowered, pursuant to Article 71(1)(a) (ex Article 75(1)(a)), to lay down "common rules applicable to international transport to or from the territory of a Member State or passing across the territory of one or more Member States". It followed that "the powers of the Community extend to relationships arising from international law, and hence involve the need in the sphere in question for agreements with the third countries concerned".[44] There was, in other words, power to legislate in respect of the parts of a journey taking place in third countries, as well as of the parts taking place within the Community.

The Commission's reported understanding of *AETR* was thus evidently mistaken: the actual subject-matter of the Agreement in question (working conditions of international transport crews) did fall within the scope of the competence which had been expressly conferred; all that was missing was a reference to the exercise of that competence by concluding an international agreement. The GATS provisions on international transport could be similarly analysed.

It was quite otherwise, the Court held, with regard to establishment and the provision of services:

> "Unlike the chapter on transport, the chapters on the right of establishment and on freedom to provide services do not contain any provision expressly extending the competence of the Community to 'relationships arising from international law'. As has rightly been observed by the Council and most of the Member States which have submitted observations, the sole objective of those chapters is to secure the right of establishment and freedom to provide services for nationals of Member States. They contain no provisions on the problem of the first establishment of nationals of non-member countries and the rules governing their access to self-employed activities. One cannot therefore infer from those chapters that the Community has exclusive competence to conclude an agreement with non-member countries to liberalise first establishment and access to service markets other

---

[40] [1994] E.C.R. I–5267 at I–5320.
[41] *ibid.*
[42] *ibid.*
[43] The author drew attention to this contrast in Koskenniemi, *Aspects*, at p. 121.
[44] [1994] E.C.R. I–5267, para. 76.

than those which are the subject of cross-border supplies within the meaning of GATS ...".[45]

The Chapters of the EC Treaty on the right of establishment and on services (respectively, Chapters 2 and 3 of Title III of Part Three) are thus essentially inward-looking. The objectives they authorise are directed towards opening up business opportunities throughout the Community for nationals of the Member States. (There is, indeed, a power for the provisions of the Chapter on services to be extended to nationals of third countries, but only those already established within the Community.[46]) No authorisation is given for the enactment of internal legislation specifically aimed at facilitating freedom of movement, with a view to establishment or the provision of services, between the Community and third countries.

The last sentence of the quoted passage expresses the Court's conclusion that the Community lacks *exclusive* competence to conclude an agreement like the GATS. However, that should not be taken as implying that there might be non-exclusive competence to do so. The plain drift of the passage is that no competence of any kind to conclude an agreement designed to facilitate the international provision of services can be derived by implication from legal bases wholly focused on liberalisation within the internal market.

There are two rather obvious lessons to draw from that passage of Opinion 1/94. First, the logic of parallelism contended for by the Commission cannot be right, otherwise the Community would have been competent to conclude the GATS. Secondly, implied competence to conclude the GATS under the Treaty Chapters on establishment and the provision of services did not arise through the operation of the principle of complementarity, because the objectives of the Agreement were not ones which the Community legislator was authorised by those Chapters to pursue.

8.15   A third lesson, which the Court of Justice seemed anxious to hammer home in Opinion 1/94, is that the legal bases contained in the establishment and services Chapters have frequently and, it seems, quite properly, been used for the enactment of Directives that include provisions either regulating the treatment of third country nationals within the Community or empowering the Commission to negotiate agreements on the treatment of Member State nationals in third countries.[47] Whence the competence to enact such measures? Since it cannot be conjured by the legislator out of thin air, it must somehow flow from the relevant provisions on establishment and services, despite their focus on the internal market.

The answer, it is submitted, lies in the fact that the "external provisions" referred to by the Court are an accessory and integral element of measures which, considered as a whole, are very firmly targeted on internal market objectives. Competence arises through straightforward application of the complementarity principle, because policy choices made by the legislator with a view to attaining those objectives are seen to require some measure of co-operation with international trading partners in order to be effectively implemented.

The point is well illustrated by one of the examples chosen by the Court of Justice, Council Directive 89/646,[48] which established a system of uniform authorisation of credit institutions, coupled with the requirement of mutual recognition of national

---

[45] *ibid.*, para. 81.
[46] See Art. 49(2) (ex Art. 59(2)).
[47] See [1994] E.C.R. I–5267, paras. 90 to 94.
[48] Second Council Directive of December 15, 1989 on the co-ordination of laws, regulations and administrative provisions relating to the taking up and pursuit of the business of credit institutions and amending Directive 77/780/EEC, O.J. 1989 L386/1. See Koskenniemi, *Aspects*, pp. 121 to 122.

controls: this obviates the need for a credit institution, once established in a Member State, to obtain fresh authorisation if it should wish to operate in another Member State, for instance by opening a branch there. The Directive is described in the first recital of its preamble as "the essential instrument for the achievement of the internal market . . ., from the point of view of both the freedom of establishment and the freedom to provide financial services, in the field of credit institutions". It is Title III of the Directive, with the heading "Relations with third countries", that concerns us. The Title provides machinery, including the possibility of negotiating international agreements, to help ensure that third countries whose credit institutions enjoy access to the whole of the internal market pursuant to the Directive, accord comparable market access to Community operators. As the twentieth recital explains, the machinery is needed because, now that authorisation by a single Member State has a Community-wide effect, reciprocal arrangements with third countries must be on a Community basis in order to be effective.

The Court's evocation of this new class of cases where implied external competence arises "from measures adopted, within the framework of [Treaty] provisions, by the Community institutions",[49] is one of the seminal insights of Opinion 1/94. It may not be too bold to conclude that legal bases in the Treaty which contain no express reference to international co-operation or to the possibility of entering into international agreements, fall, for the purposes of the application of the complementarity principle, broadly into two categories. The classification must be considered highly tentative, as long as relevant case law remains scarce.

8.16   On the one hand, there is the category of what may be termed "open provisions". Those either show on their face that they "extend to relationships arising from international law", like Article 71(1)(a) (ex Article 75(1)(a)); or they concern matters which in a developed legal order may naturally be regarded as having an external dimension (even though it may be only of secondary importance). External competence is available under such provisions when needed to further objectives for which legislative competence has been expressly given. Open provisions can be found in the fields of agriculture, fisheries, transport, capital and payments and social policy, as well as in the new Title IV of Part Three on aspects of the treatment of third country nationals.

On the other hand, there is the category of "internal provisions", specifically focused on matters which are in principle confined within the four walls of the Community legal order. External relations competence, it is thought, will normally arise under the provisions in this category only in the context of implementing action taken by the Community legislator, which establishes the need for such competence. The category would include the Chapters on establishment and services, and also, presumably, that on workers, as well as Part Two of the Treaty, "Citizenship of the Union". A more doubtful candidate is Article 95 (ex Article 100a). The notion of measures "which have as their object the establishment and functioning of the internal market" is certainly very wide. However, "approximation of the provisions laid down by law, regulation or administration by Member States" has the ring of strictly internal business, on which the Community legislator should have his say, before any power to act externally can arise.[50]

A fourth and entirely general lesson from Opinion 1/94 is that the application of the

---

[49] The quotation is from the *AETR* judgment, [1971] E.C.R. 263, para. 16.
[50] The only instance of which the writer is aware, where an international agreement has been concluded on the basis of Art. 95 in respect of matters not wholly covered by previously adopted legislation (and not within the scope of the second legal basis, Art. 133) is the Agreement on international humane trapping standards: Council Decision 94/800/EC of December 22, 1994 [1994] O.J. L336/1.

principle of complementarity requires close analysis of the provision it is proposed to rely on as the legal basis for the agreement in question. The objectives the Community has been authorised to pursue by enacting internal legislation must be determined with precision and an assessment made of the likely contribution of the contemplated agreement to the attainment of one or more of those particular objectives. The Community will be competent under the complementarity principle to conclude an agreement judged necessary for the attainment of one or more of the objectives specified by the legal basis.

To return, by way of example, to the field of social policy, where the legal basis is now Article 137. The scope of possible legislative action, and hence potentially of external relations competence, is much more widely defined than under the old Article 118a. Directives can now be adopted by co-decision not only on workers' health and safety but also on working conditions in general, on the information and consultation of workers, on the integration of persons excluded from the labour market and on equal treatment of men and women on the labour market and in employment.[51] In addition, on certain matters that are more sensitive politically, including social security and social protection of workers, there is power for the Council to act by unanimity under the consultation procedure.[52] However, the legislative competence conferred by Article 137 is limited to the adoption of "minimum requirements for gradual implementation, having regard to the conditions and technical rules obtaining in each of the Member States".[53] Moreover, Community directives must "avoid imposing administrative, financial and legal constraints in a way which would hold back the creation of small and medium-sized undertakings".[54] All of those constraints, it is submitted, would have to be taken into account in determining whether implied competence existed for concluding an international agreement on any of the aspects of social policy covered by the Article. For instance, since internal measures may only impose minimum requirements, it is not thought Article 137 could be the legal basis for an agreement imposing mandatory requirements.

Two meanings of "*necessary*"

8.17   The nature of the causal relationship entailed in the notion of an international agreement's being "necessary" for the attainment of given objectives, is the next point to be considered.

On a narrow view, the necessity criterion of implied external relations competence might be equated with indispensability: the implication that competence exists would be drawn in situations where internal action and international action were inextricably linked, so that authorisation of the former must be taken to extend to the latter, since otherwise it would have been futile. That was a possible reading of Opinion 1/76, despite the generality of the language of paragraphs 3 and 4, because the project of creating a laying-up fund for barges operating in the Rhine and Moselle basins, to provide temporary relief from over-capacity, would only work if Swiss carriers were included: an international agreement with Switzerland, complementing the measures to be taken by internal legislation, was thus indispensable. In *Kramer*, too, where the complementarity principle was applied by the Court of Justice for the first time, the link between the Community's internal and external activity in the field of fisheries conservation followed, as the judgment puts it, "from the very nature of things".[55]

---

[51] Art. 137(1) and (2).
[52] Art. 137(3).
[53] Art. 137(2), first sub-para.
[54] *ibid.*
[55] [1976] E.C.R. 1279, paras. 30/33.

However, we have seen in Chapter 1 that in Opinion 2/91 the Court of Justice presented a reformulation of paragraph 3 of Opinion 1/76 as expressing a general principle of implication, in terms that would not have been suitable if the principle of complementarity were applicable only in the peculiar circumstances of cases like *Kramer* and Opinion 1/76. Moreover, the Court went on to apply the principle as the basis for implied external relations competence in a field (that of the adoption of minimum health and safety standards for workers) where it was perfectly possible for the Community institutions to pursue the objectives of the Treaty by autonomous internal action. The suggestion made in Chapter 1 was that, in practice, the Court employs a test as to whether Treaty-making power is needed by the Community *to ensure the optimal use, over time, of its expressly conferred internal competence*. Such a test would be one of facilitation rather than of indispensability.

Doubt was rekindled because of language in the passage of Opinion 1/94 where the Court addresses the argument in favour of the Community's exclusive competence to conclude the WTO Agreement, which the Commission drew from Opinion 1/76.[56] According to the Commission, participation by the Community alone in the Agreement was "necessary" in the sense of Opinion 1/76 for both internal and external reasons: because the coherence of the internal market was liable otherwise to be impaired; and because the Community, as a player on the international stage, could not afford to hold aloof from the global approach to international trade (embracing services and intellectual property as well as goods) which was encapsulated in the Agreement and its annexes. The Court riposted by pointing out that in Opinion 1/76, and in the matter of fisheries conservation, it was impossible to attain the Community's objective by the establishment of autonomous common rules: "[I]t is understandable, therefore, that external powers may be exercised, and thus become exclusive, without any internal legislation having first been adopted".[57] The situation with regard to services was different: "attainment of freedom of establishment and freedom to provide services for nationals of the Member States is not inextricably linked to the treatment to be afforded in the Community to nationals of non-member countries or in non-member countries to nationals of Member States of the Community".[58]

Should that passage be understood as indicating that the Court of Justice, after all, takes a restrictive view of the principle of complementarity: that implied external competence arises under the principle only where the conclusion of an agreement is seen as indispensable to the effective exercise of the legislative power which has been expressly conferred on the Community, and not where the attainment of the objective(s) to be pursued by the legislator may simply be facilitated? In particular, where the Court says that "external powers may be exercised, and thus become exclusive, without any internal legislation having first been adopted", is it implying that, in the absence of any inextricable link, implied external competence is acquired only after the exercise of the internal power (*i.e.* under the *AETR* principle), including in respect of the category of "open provisions"?

8.18 There are three reasons why, it is submitted, that cannot have been the Court's meaning.

First, the issue for the Court was the alleged exclusivity of Community competence, in respect of the WTO Agreement, which the Commission sought to found on Opinion 1/76. In stressing the absence, in the case of the GATS, of special circumstances like those concerning the creation of a laying-up fund for Rhine barges or the conservation

---

[56] [1994] E.C.R. I–5267, paras. 82 *et seq.*
[57] *ibid.*, para. 85 *in fine*.
[58] *ibid.*, para. 86.

of marine resources, the Court was evidently seeking to distinguish Opinion 1/76 as an authority on the *exclusivity* of Community competence.[59]

Secondly, such a restrictive conception of the principle of complementarity would not be consistent with what the Court had to say, only a few paragraphs earlier in Opinion 1/94, about implied external competence under Article 71(1)(a) (ex Article 75 (1)(a)) of the Treaty. It is clear from paragraphs 76 and 77 of the Opinion that competence to conclude agreements on international transport matters exists independently of the enactment of internal legislation: the relevance of the latter event is that it renders exclusive a power previously enjoyed concurrently with the Member States. However, it cannot be said that, in the case of transport, internal and external powers are "inextricably linked". The Community would have been able to regulate the matters which were the subject of the AETR purely on the basis of autonomous common rules: this would simply have been less effective than co-operating with the third countries concerned.

Thirdly, the prominence given to the complementarity principle in Opinion 2/94, the general terms in which the principle was restated and the reference in the relevant paragraph of the Opinion to the corresponding paragraph of Opinion 2/91, would make no sense if the Court were conscious of having restricted implied exclusive competence, when the internal competence has not yet been exercised, to cases where an inextricable link can be demonstrated.

The problem, it is submitted, lies in the ambiguity of the word "necessary". In the answer to the existence question which the Court has provided in the form of the principle of complementarity, the word has the broader meaning of "tending to facilitate": implied external competence arises, where this will help ensure the optimal exercise of the expressly conferred internal competence. In dealing with the exclusivity question, on the other hand, the Court uses the word in its more restrictive sense of "indispensable": to exclude the possibility of action by the Member States, the external competence, and the as yet unused internal competence, must be inextricably linked. That the ambiguity should sometimes risk misunderstanding, as in Opinion 1/94, is not at all surprising.

One principle of implication or two?

8.19   In enunciating the principle of complementarity, the Court of Justice has been careful to include the qualifying phrase, "in particular".[60] As suggested above, the phrase must be intended to indicate that the Court is not excluding the possibility that implied external competence may arise in other ways. One such would be the *AETR* principle, regarded as an independent source of Community competence, and not merely as rendering such competence exclusive.

In the *AETR* judgment itself, it was noted in Chapter 1 of this volume, the *AETR* principle figures as the final step in the general justification of the recognition by the Court that the Community may be competent to conclude international agreements in cases where it has not been expressly authorised to do so.[61] The words, "In particular", which introduce paragraph 17 of the judgment, show that the Court considered the situation there referred to, where previously adopted common rules are liable to be affected by a contemplated agreement, as an especially telling example of how such competence may arise. It went on, in paragraph 21, to identify as the source of the

---

[59] See chapter 1, above, as to the exclusivity issue in Opinion 1/76, which arose only because it had already been decided in principle to regulate the internal aspect of the laying-up scheme by legislation at Community level.
[60] The phrase is found in para. 7 of Opinion 2/91 and in para. 26 of Opinion 2/94. In para. 3 of Opinion 1/76, the phrase used is "*inter alia*".
[61] See [1971] E.C.R. 263, paras. 12 to 19.

principle, the requirement imposed on the Member States by Article 10, EC (ex Article 5), "on the one hand to take all appropriate measures to ensure fulfilment of the obligations arising out of the Treaty or resulting from action taken by the institutions and, on the other hand, to abstain from any measure which might jeopardise the attainment of the objectives of the Treaty". The underlying logic is, accordingly, that of the primacy of Community law: Member States must abstain altogether from undertaking international commitments which might affect Community rules, because the usual remedy of disapplying incompatible national legislation would not be available in such cases. That creates a gap, which can only be filled by Community competence.

The principle of complementarity, based on the logic of ensuring the effective exercise of Community powers, was developed by the Court of Justice to explain how, in the absence of express conferment, external relations competence could arise without the corresponding legislative competence having first been exercised. There is language in Opinion 1/76 which suggests the Court may regard the *AETR* principle simply as an instance *a fortiori* of complementarity. Thus, following what has come to be accepted as the standard formulation of the complementarity principle in paragraph 3 of the Opinion, the first sentence of paragraph 4 goes on: "This is particularly so in all cases in which internal power has already been used in order to adopt measures which come within the attainment of common policies". The word "This" can only be taken as a reference to the operation of the principle just stated by the Court, which is said to be at work in *all cases* where external relations competence arises from the actual exercise of legislative powers. Subsequent judgments and Opinions contain no clear reference to the *AETR* principle as a source of external relations competence. In particular, Part VIII of Opinion 1/94 treats *AETR* as authority only for two things: external relations competence in the transport field, regarded as a consequence of the wording of Article 71(1)(a), and not of the prior enactment of Regulation 543/69[62]; and the exclusivity of the Community's external competence in matters covered by enacted legislation.[63]

8.20 Should the *AETR* principle still be regarded then, as expressing an independent basis on which implied external relations competence may arise? In the writer's submission, it should be.

To be sure, the acceptance by Member States of international obligations liable to affect the operation of enacted common rules, may impede the attainment of the objectives for which legislative competence has been given to the Community. The removal of that impediment, through the acquisition by the Community of (exclusive) external relations competence can thus be seen as "necessary" to enable the legislator to pursue the specified objectives effectively, and hence as a special case of complementarity.

However, the argument proves too much. If the logic of the *AETR* principle were that of complementarity, why should the principle be confined to the situation where internal Community competence has already been exercised? Continuing Member State competence in external relations may impede the attainment of Treaty objectives by constraining *future* legislative activity, just as it would do by affecting already enacted measures. That was part of the Commission's case for the exclusivity of Community competence to conclude the WTO Agreement, which the Court explicitly rejected.

The *AETR* principle should, therefore, continue to be recognised as a principle with its own distinctive logic. It is derived, not from the elusive notion of *l'effet utile*, but from the fundamental constitutional principle that Community rules prevail over national ones. That also makes the principle simple and straightforward to apply.

---

[62] [1994] E.C.R. I–5267, para. 76.
[63] *ibid.*, paras. 77 and 95 to 96.

At all events, it is treated as axiomatic in the day-to-day practice of EC external relations that the adoption of a piece of internal legislation has among its automatic consequences (and aside from any issue of complementarity) the acquisition by the Community of competence to undertake international commitments in all the matters covered by the measure, including ones in respect of which such competence had previously been lacking. That was why, for instance, the Council cited Articles 44, 47 and 55 (respectively, ex Articles 54, 57 and 66) among the substantive legal bases of the Decision on the conclusion of the WTO Agreement, despite having argued in the Opinion 1/94 proceedings (and having convinced the Court) that the sole objective of those provisions was to achieve internal liberalisation.[64] Nobody with experience of Council practice in the conclusion of international agreements could be in the slightest doubt that the *AETR* principle is alive and well, in both of its aspects.

AN ALTERNATIVE PRINCIPLE OF ATTRIBUTION

8.21   This final section represents, in effect, an invitation to the Court of Justice to reconsider the general rationale it has developed, in the cases from *Kramer* onwards, to explain how external relations competence can arise under legal bases that refer explicitly only to procedures and forms of instrument used for the enactment of internal legislation. The rationale—that authorisation to enter into international agreements is impliedly granted in so far as it may be needed in order to attain the objectives for which internal legislative competence has been expressly granted—is encapsulated in what has been designated "the principle of complementarity". The double dichotomy on which the principle is based (express/implied conferment and internal/external competence) was noted in the introductory survey.

The thrust of the invitation tendered to the Court, respectfully and with considerable diffidence, is that it abandon the logic of complementarity in favour of the straightforward principle that the existence of external relations competence in a given case depends on the true construction of the relevant power-conferring provision. The Court should not, as it did in *Kramer*,[65] for instance, first consider whether competence exists to adopt internal legislation on the matters that are the subject of a contemplated agreement, and go on to draw the inference that the Community has been implicitly authorised to conclude the agreement because this is necessary to ensure the effectiveness of such legislation. It should go straight to the question: is the external action which is envisaged a natural and expected way of attaining any of the objectives authorised by the proposed legal basis? This is here referred to as "the true construction principle".

Underlying the true construction principle is an idea the author has expressed elsewhere, that a legal basis in the Treaty which is silent as to the possibility of concluding international agreements, should not, therefore, be understood as conferring internal legislative powers only.[66] Thus, it is submitted, there should be no practical difference, so far as concerns their external relations application, between, say, Article 174(4) (ex Article 130r (4)) of the Treaty which falls into the category of extension provisions, since it refers explicitly to the possibility of the Community's acting in environmental matters by way of international agreements, and Article 37 (ex Article 43) on agricul-

---

[64]   The other substantive legal bases cited in the Decision are: Art. 37 (ex Art. 43); Art. 71 (ex Art. 75); Art. 80 (2) (ex Art. 84(2)); Art. 93 (ex Art. 99); Art. 94 (ex Art. 100); Art. 95 (ex Art. 100a); Art. 133 (ex Art. 113); and Art. 308 (ex Art. 235). The eighth recital of the preamble makes clear that, with the exception of Art. 133, all substantive legal bases are invoked under the *AETR* principle.
[65]   See the reasoning in paras. 19 to 33 of the judgment.
[66]   See "The Limits of European Community Powers", (1996) 21 E.L.Rev. at p. 125.

ture and fisheries, which is an open provision. Properly construed, both provisions, it is submitted, may be regarded as expressly attributing external relations competence to the Community.

No claim is made as to the originality of the true construction principle, because the source of it is the Court's own reasoning in paragraphs 23 to 27 of the *AETR* judgment. It was noted in Chapter 1, and recalled in the introductory survey of the present chapter, that no special emphasis is placed on the Community's internal legislative competence in those paragraphs, and nothing is said about external relations competence arising by implication.[67] The Court looks at the substance of what is authorised by Article 71(1)(a) (ex Article 75(1)(a)) of the Treaty, and comes to the conclusion that regulating journeys which may take place, in part at least, inside third countries, necessarily entails acting internationally as well as internally. That is a conclusion about the scope of the powers *expressly* conferred on the Community by Article 71.[68] Interestingly, in Opinion 1/94 also, the Court treated the external relations competence of the Community in transport matters as resulting from the express words of the Article. Indeed, to have done otherwise, and given logical priority to the conferment of legislative competence, would have seemed artificial; as it does in other fields where the possibility of acting in relation to third countries is of the essence of the authorised activity, such as fisheries conservation.

8.22 The main support for the true construction principle is to be found, once again, in the *AETR* judgment, this time in what the Court of Justice had to say about Article 281 (ex Article 210) as meaning that "in its external relations the Community enjoys the capacity to establish contractual links with third countries over the whole field of objectives defined in Part One of the Treaty ...".[69] As indicated in Chapter 1, the Court chose to interpret the laconic statement, "The Community shall have legal personality", as a general acknowledgement of the international capacity of the EC within the limits of the objectives set and the powers conferred by the Treaty, similar in effect to Article 6, second paragraph ECSC and Article 101, first paragraph Euratom. That is not to treat Article 281 as a legal basis in itself, as the Court made clear by the distinction it drew between "capacity" and "authority".[70] The Court must have meant (though by the time of *Kramer* it seems to have forgotten) that the Article be read together with each and every one of the legal bases in Part Three of the Treaty, which give concrete substance to the objectives stated in Part One.[71] If that is done, any counter-indication from the fact that a power-conferring provision refers to legislative but not to external relations competence, is automatically negated.

That reasoning has been reinforced by the evolution of Article 300 (ex Article 228) of the Treaty into a general procedural legal basis for actions in the field of external relations. The absence, from the substantive legal basis for a given category of international agreements, of a specific procedural attribution has become the normal state of affairs. Nor is it counter-indicative that cross-references to Article 300 may be lacking, since, as we have seen, the Article can function perfectly well without them. In fact, the cross-referencing of Article 300 in the Treaty is sporadic: for instance, though association agreements are specifically provided for in paragraphs (2) and (3) of Article 300, the latter Article is not mentioned in Article 310 (ex Article 238). Nor is there mention of it in the provisions on international co-operation in the fields of education, vocational training, culture, public health and the development of trans-Euro-

---

[67] See the analysis of the rationale of implied external competence in Koskenniemi, *Aspects*, at pp. 114 to 116.
[68] See [1994] E.C.R. I–5267, para. 76, which adopts the reasoning of *AETR* para. 27.
[69] [1971] E.C.R. 263, para. 14.
[70] *ibid.* and paras. 15 to 16.
[71] The Court cited Art. 281 in *Kramer*, but then ignored the Article in its reasoning.

pean networks, or under Articles 302 to 304 of the Treaty; though it must surely be intended that such co-operation may be organised, where appropriate, in the framework of binding agreements.

The suggested change of rationale has been made easier by the developments in the case law on the principle of complementarity which are discussed in the previous section of this chapter. Everything which is said there about the lessons to be drawn from Opinion 1/94—as to the relative scope of the Treaty Title on transport and the Chapters on establishment and services, the distinction between open and internal provisions and the need for close analysis of the proposed legal basis—would apply equally well if the true construction principle had already received the Court's official blessing. Nor, it is thought, would the acceptance of the principle lead to an appreciable extension, with constitutional implications, of the Community's external relations competence, now it is clear that the necessity criterion of complementarity is based on the broader notion of facilitating (rather than being indispensable to) the attainment of the objectives set by the legal basis. Only in the assessment of those objectives would any practical effect be likely, since under the true construction principle the constraint on interpretation that comes from having to treat the provision in question as one primarily conceived as a basis for internal legislation, would not be felt.

8.23   If the consequences of change would be so relatively modest, it may be asked: why not stick to the tried and trusted principle of complementarity? There are three considerations that make the true construction principle attractive.

First, its simplicity. There is no need to worry about the nature of the link between "express" internal and "implied" external competence. Nor, since the principle does not depend on the doctrine of implied powers, would the temptation be so great to indulge in the kind of extravagant speculation about "parallelism" that led the Commission astray in the *WTO* proceedings.

Secondly, full value would be given to ideas of the Court that date from its earliest consideration of the attribution of external relations competence, and which have never been repudiated; while, at the same time, the principle appears fully in tune with the most recent case law.

Thirdly, a principle of the attribution of external relations competence which assumes such competence to be available whenever it appears, on analysis, that conclusion of an envisaged international agreement is likely to advance objectives specifically authorised by a legal basis in the Treaty, would be better suited to the stage of development the Community has now reached. In a mature constitutional order, the natural way of interpreting an express grant of powers is that they are to apply as needed, internally or externally, in furtherance of the objectives specified.[72]

Whether the Court of Justice will embrace the true construction principle of attribution remains to be seen. It may be a long while before the accidents of litigation provide another opportunity, like Opinion 1/94, for investigating the deep structure of the Community's external relations competence. In the meantime, the law remains as it was restated by the Court in Opinion 2/94, and we must be grateful for the illumination there provided, as well as in Opinion 1/94.

---

[72] The principle developed here was advertised by the author in the Conclusion of his contribution to Koskenniemi, *Aspects* at pp. 122 to 123.

CHAPTER 9

The WTO Opinion and Implied External Powers of the Community—A Hidden Agenda?

by

*Nanette Neuwahl**

INTRODUCTION

9.01 The World Trade Organisation Opinion[1] is undoubtedly one of the most important judgments delivered by the Court of Justice in the last couple of years. The stakes were very high, as it concerned the exclusivity of Community powers to conclude agreements embodying the results of the Uruguay Round. In a nutshell, the outcome of the case was that the Commission was not allowed to "hijack", as some Member States would put it, the whole sphere of external economic relations, since the Court considered that the Community did not have exclusive power to conclude all Uruguay Round agreements. As a "consolation prize", however, the Commission obtained an expansion of the Common Commercial Policy to include the cross-frontier supply of services.

While the Opinion has been commented upon as "hardly a surprise", its wisdom has been questioned.[2] This is understandable given the breadth of the Community's (exclusive) powers within these very important agreements, the Community's reputable status in GATT, and the fact that unilateral Member State action can affect and damage the Community's interests. A case could therefore be made for transferring all powers in connection with these agreements to the Community. Without wishing to dwell on the merits of this broad issue, it is proposed here to deal rather with a matter which has received less attention so far, namely, the doctrine of implied powers.

Due to the all-or-nothing approach of the "parties" and the Court, the issue of implied powers has once again been neglected in this Opinion, although it was a major case on EC external relations. This assertion is based on the consideration that the European Court of Justice has never clearly ruled that the Community has non-exclusive treaty-making power. The existence and extent of such powers,

---

* Jean Monnet Professor of European Union Law, The University of Liverpool.
[1] Opinion 1/94, *Competence of the Community to conclude international agreements concerning services and the protection of intellectual property ("WTO")* [1994] E.C.R. I–5267; (1995) 1 C.M.L.Rev. 205.
[2] Hilf, "The ECJ's Opinion 1/94 on the WTO—No Surprise, but Wise?", (1995) 6 E.J.I.L. 245.

which have sometimes been referred to as "potential powers"[3] or "concurrent powers"[4] is not among the matters which the Court of Justice is usually called upon to resolve. The Community, rather than openly exercising such powers, has recourse to the conclusion of mixed agreements, *i.e.* Member States appear as contracting parties to an international treaty alongside the Community so that the competences of both the Community and the Member States can be seen to complement each other. The extent of the Community's treaty-making power is thus not discussed at law.

It is often assumed that the Community has non-exclusive treaty-making power, and indeed the fact that it undertakes formal commitments in these fields would indicate that the matter is not really in dispute. However, it is precisely because the question does not arise at law, that the Community and individual Member States are in a position to create their own conceptions about the existence and extent of such powers, and moreover to maintain, so to speak, their own hidden agenda on the subject. The *WTO* Opinion is an illustration of the fact that differences of opinion exist which are not openly addressed and that problems subsist which really ought to be confronted. In order to assist in this, what follows could be regarded as the perspective of the "devil's advocate".

THE ALL-OR-NOTHING APPROACH OF THE COMMISSION

9.02   In its request for an Opinion, the Commission concentrated on the question of exclusivity, in order to obtain from the Court of Justice a declaration that the Community should be a contracting party to the Uruguay Round agreements to the exclusion of the Member States. Its questions to the Court were as follows:

"As regards the results of the Uruguay Round GATT trade talks contained in the Final Act of 15 December 1993:

(1) Does the European Community have the competence to conclude all parts of the Agreement establishing the WTO concerning trade in services (GATS) and the trade-related aspects of intellectual property rights including trade in counterfeit goods (TRIPs) on the basis of the EC Treaty, more particularly on the basis of Article [133][5] EC alone, or in conformity with Article [95][6] EC and/or Article [308][7] EC?

(2) Does the European Community have the competence to conclude alone also the parts of the WTO Agreement which concern products and/or services falling exclusively within the scope of the ECSC and EAEC Treaties?

---

[3] The term "potential" seems to refer broadly to a state of affairs which may materialise sometime in the future, without prejudice to the question of how it could be brought about, *i.e.* whether by Treaty amendment, intergovernmental decision, Community legislation or judicial decision. This conception of "potential" is too broad for what the expression really seeks to convey. Indeed, the expression is commonly used in a more specific context, namely, to denote powers which the Community can use by having recourse to a decision-making process specified in the Treaty and which, if used, lead to pre-emption of Member State powers. This being so, they are real powers rather than potential ones. For this reason, the expression "non-exclusive powers" is to be preferred.
[4] This expression is not ideal because it implies that the exercise of powers by the Community pre-empts all Member State action only in the *same* field, which is not necessarily the case. The use of powers by the Community may also pre-empt Member State action in quite *different* fields if such an action affects the full effectiveness of the Community measure.
[5] Ex Art. 113 EC.
[6] Ex Art. 100a EC.
[7] Ex Art. 235 EC.

> 3) If the answer to the above two questions is in the affirmative, does this
> affect the ability of Member States to conclude the WTO Agreement, in the
> light of the agreement already reached that they will be original Members
> to the WTO?"[8]

The formulation of these questions was less than perfect because the Commission failed to make explicit reference to any treaty-making powers which the Community may have on the basis of a doctrine of parallelism between internal and external powers. Not only were the questions specifically[9] directed at an interpretation of Articles 133, 95 and 308 EC in the hope of establishing an exclusive Community power, but they also appeared to disregard a question which hitherto has not been conclusively dealt with by the European Court of Justice.

As the European Community is still deemed by some as not having any implicit treaty-making powers unless they are exclusive by virtue of pre-emption or necessity, this question needed to be addressed separately by the Commission in order to see whether the Community had any competence at all to conclude all of the Uruguay agreements.

Observations made by several Member States put into doubt not only the exclusive character of the Community's powers but also their extent, especially as regards the right of establishment and services.

For instance, after considering the different modes of supply of services covered by GATS, the Spanish Government concluded that three of them—consumption abroad, commercial presence and the movement of persons—should "fall within the competence of the Member States. Articles 39, 43 and 49 EC (ex Articles 48, 52 and 59) regulate the free movement of workers, the right of establishment and the freedom to provide services only in relation to nationals of the Member States of the Community".[10] The Netherlands' Government mentioned "the movement of natural persons (nationals of non-member countries) into the territory of a Member State"[11] as an example of when the Member States have exclusive competence. As an example of a sector in which the Community has "no competence whatsoever" the German Government pointed to the right of workers from non-member countries to enter, reside and work in connection with the provision of services, as well as the status of non-member country undertakings.[12]

If international agreements on such matters exist to which the Community is a party, they are mixed agreements in the sense that Member States are also parties to the agreement. Practice, as such, is not relevant for the interpretation of the division of powers between the Community and the Member States, and the Court has never been asked to clarify matters of practice in, for example, a challenge under Article 230 EC (ex Article 173) for lack of competence, or in the context of a preliminary reference. Neither has the Court volunteered an opinion on the matter.

Disputes regarding non-exclusive Community powers could have been addressed in the *WTO Opinion*. Nevertheless the Commission, in pursuit of greater goals, concentrated on questions of exclusivity. Why? One ought to rule out considerations of the pressure of time, at least as a primary explanation. Was the Commission so sure that the Community had exclusive powers that it considered the rest irrelevant? I think not.

---

[8] [1994] E.C.R. I–5267, at 5282–5283.
[9] On the Court's understanding of the adverbial phrase "in particular" which is frequently employed in Community acts, see Case C–431/92, *Commission* v. *Germany* [1995] E.C.R. I–2189 at para. 15.
[10] Opinion 1/94, [1994] E.C.R. I–5267, at 5309.
[11] *ibid.*, at 5310.
[12] *ibid.*, at 5311.

There are chiefly two ways in which the Commission's attitude can be explained: either the Commission was firmly convinced that the Community had at least non-exclusive external powers, in which case, as we shall see, it ought perhaps now to start to doubt this; or the Commission was unsure from the outset about non-exclusive external powers and did not want to risk an adverse decision from the Court. Whatever the reason behind the Commission's strategy, it now has to live with the consequences of not raising the matter explicitly.

In hindsight, given the fact that the Commission failed to convince the Court that the Community's treaty-making powers concluding agreements on the basis of Articles 133, 308 and/or 95 EC was an exclusive one, the price to be paid for neglecting to raise further questions explicitly is two-fold:

(a) continued lack of clarity concerning the Community legal basis for concluding this and other international agreements; and

(b) the necessary imposition of a mixed agreement formula for many future mixed agreements, even where this could be avoided.

THE APPROACH OF THE COURT

9.03   As if to emphasise that it was not called upon to solve the question of the non-exclusive, implied treaty-making powers of the Community, the Court made it clear from the outset that it would focus on the question of exclusivity:

> "The questions put to the Court by the Commission in its request for an Opinion ... seek to ascertain, first, whether or not the Community has exclusive competence to conclude the Multilateral Agreements on Trade in Goods, in so far as those Agreements concern ECSC products and Euratom products. Those questions further relate to the exclusive competence the Community may enjoy by virtue of either Article [133] of the EC Treaty, or the parallelism of internal and external competence, or Articles [95] or [308] of the EC Treaty, to conclude the General Agreement on Trade in Services ... and the Agreement on Trade-Related Aspects of Intellectual Property Rights, including trade in counterfeit goods."[13]

Even if the Commission had made clear where it believed the emphasis of the Opinion should be, the Court of Justice could have interpreted the questions posed more generously, in particular, whether the European Community can derive additional treaty-making power from provisions of the Treaty granting it an internal competence. Arguably, the Court should have introduced an *obiter dictum* of sorts in order to anticipate the difficulties alluded to earlier. Yet nowhere in the ruling does the Court address the question openly. Whenever the Court touches on the matter of implied external powers, it does so only in order to address the question of exclusivity.[14] Worse still, whatever it does say about implicit external powers is rather restrictive and offers ammunition to advocates of the most restrictive interpretation of these powers. For instance, in para. 76, where the Court appears to make the point that exclusive implied powers are the exception rather than the rule, it also chooses to describe the *ERTA* case[15] in words which seem to restrict the scope of such treaty-making powers:

---

[13] *ibid.* at para. 1.
[14] See also the approach of the Commission, *ibid.* at para. 74.
[15] Case 22/70, *Commission v. Council* ("*ERTA*" or "*AETR*") [1971] E.C.R. 262; (1971) C.M.L.Rev. 335.

> "It was on the basis of Article [71](1)(a)[16] which, as regards that part of a journey which takes place on Community territory, also concerns transport from or to non-member countries, that the Court held in the *AETR* judgment ... that "the powers of the Community extend to relationships arising from international law, and hence involve the need in the sphere in question for agreements with the third countries involved'."[17]

Here, the Court seems to imply that the Community has no competence to conclude the agreement as regards certain aspects of transport agreements, notably where transport on foreign territory is concerned. Furthermore, in reply to an argument of the Commission that Member State freedom in the area of transport may lead to the distortion of competition and undermine the Single Market, the Court states that nothing prevents the institutions from "arranging, in the common rules laid down by them, concerted action in relation to non-member countries or from prescribing the approach to be taken by the Member States in their external dealings."[18]

The Court is silent on the possibility of the Community itself concluding international agreements on non-exclusive aspects of transport policy. It may perhaps be thought that the power of the Community to conclude international agreements in the field of transport is not really doubted. However, other readings of the *ERTA* judgment are certainly possible, the more so as the circumstances surrounding the case were rather particular.

In the *WTO* Opinion, the Court goes on to observe that there is a difference between the chapter of the EC Treaty on transport and the chapters on establishment and the freedom to provide services: the latter do not contain any express provision for the extension of Community competence to "relationships under international law"; the only objective of those chapters is "to secure the right of establishment and freedom to provide services for nationals of Member States".[19]

The Court draws the conclusion that there is no exclusive competence:

> "They [the chapters on establishment and services] contain no provisions on the problem of the first establishment of nationals of non-member countries and the rules governing their access to self-employed activities. One cannot therefore infer ... that the Community has exclusive competence to conclude an agreement with non-member countries to liberalise first establishment and access to service markets, other than those which are the subject of cross-border supplies within the meaning of GATS, which are covered by Article [133]."[20]

Yet the Court, by pointing to the absence of express provisions granting competence, casts severe doubt on the authority of the Community to conclude treaties on these matters. The existence of such authority seems to be closely tied to the internal division of power. This is again reaffirmed and even reinforced as the Court of Justice comes to speak of Opinion 1/76.[21] Here the Court attaches much importance to the (intended) adoption of internal Community legislation.

---

[16] Ex Art. 75(1)(a) EC.
[17] Opinion 1/94, [1994] E.C.R. I–5267, at para. 76.
[18] *ibid.*, at para. 79.
[19] *ibid.*, at para. 81.
[20] *ibid.*
[21] Opinion 1/76, *Draft Agreement establishing a European laying-up fund for inland waterway vessels* [1977] E.C.R. 741; (1977) 2 C.M.L.Rev. 279, referred to by the Court in Opinion 1/94, [1994] E.C.R. I–5267, at paras. 82 *et seq.*

9.04   It will be recalled that in Opinion 1/76 the Court found that the Community had an exclusive power in a situation where legislation was envisaged and where the effectiveness of such measures depended on the conclusion in parallel of an international agreement with a third country. In that case it appeared to be impossible to achieve the objective of eliminating short-term overcapacity and rationalising the economic situation in the inland waterways section of the Rhine and Moselle basin without including Switzerland in the scheme.

> "Similarly, in the context of conservation of the resources of the seas, the restriction, by means of internal legislative measures, of fishing on the high seas by vessels flying the flag of a Member State would hardly be effective if the same restrictions were not to apply to vessels flying the flag of a non-member bordering on the same seas. It is understandable, therefore, that external powers may be exercised, and thus become exclusive, without any internal legislation having first been adopted."[22]

One could infer from these passages that if the restrictive conditions referred to, namely the need for the "simultaneous" exercise of internal and external powers as well as a strict requirement of necessity in light of the objective of the internal provisions, are not fulfilled, it would not be "understandable" how external powers might be exercised.

The Court follows on from here, observing, in a more general fashion, that attainment of the freedom of establishment and the freedom to provide services for nationals of the Member States is "not inextricably linked to the treatment to be afforded in the Community to nationals of non-member countries or in non-member countries to nationals of Member States of the Community".[23] It is to be noted that the same point is not raised in the case of agreements on goods or the cross-frontier supply of services, as these benefit from a provision of the Treaty which is traditionally held to be exclusive—Article 133 EC. On a theoretical level, one may well ask how the attainment of the internal free movement of goods and cross-frontier supply of services (which are moreover not subject to the same amount of "internal" scrutiny by the Court) is inextricably linked to the treatment of foreign goods or cross-frontier services or the treatment of Community produce abroad. In this connection, the argument is often raised that a common market, as opposed to a free trade area, requires a common external tariff and a common commercial policy. Moreover, the creation of the Community has to be seen in the light of the intention of the founding Member States to liberalise world trade. Whereas there is clearly no agreement to include the free movement of persons, the freedom of establishment and the general provision of services in that notion, the inclusion of the cross-frontier supply of goods[24] seems to be based on tendencies in international trade as well as on a certain resemblance of that type of services to goods. Because all this does not apply to persons, establishment and services in general (nor, presumably, to capital), these other freedoms are now subject to a totally different treaty-making regime, which is tied up very closely to the authority for and the intention to adopt internal Community measures rather than being subject to wholesale exclusivity.

---

[22] Opinion 1/94, [1994] E.C.R. I–5267, at para. 85.
[23] *ibid.*, at para. 86.
[24] *ibid.*, at para. 44.

"[I]t does not follow that the Community institutions are prohibited from using the powers conferred on them in that field in order to specify the treatment which is to be accorded to nationals of non-member countries. Numerous acts adopted by the Council on the basis of Articles [44][25] and [47](2)[26] of the Treaty . . . contain provisions in that regard. . . ."[27]

The Court does not refer here to the conclusion of international agreements. On the contrary, the next paragraph follows on in an unfortunate way: "It is evident from an examination of those acts that very different objectives may be pursued by incorporation of external provisions."[28]

9.05   As a result, uncertainty as regards the implied treaty-making power of the Community in cases other than those which come under Opinion 1/76 subsists. No attention is paid to the possibility of the Community becoming a party to an international agreement except where the Community adopts internal rules.

"Whenever the Community has included in its internal legislative acts provisions relating to the treatment of nationals of non-member countries or expressly conferred on its institutions powers to negotiate with non-member countries, it acquires exclusive external competence in the spheres covered by those acts.

The same applies in any event, even in the absence of any express provision authorising its institutions to negotiate with non-member countries, where the Community has achieved complete harmonisation of the rules governing access to self-employed activity."[29]

The emerging picture suggests that the Community may only act in the external sphere to the extent that it has exclusive powers by virtue of pre-emption or necessity. In any case, due to the fact that the Court does not sufficiently distinguish between mere competence and exclusive competence, the legality of the Community's concluding the entire GATS becomes clouded. The Court simply states categorically that "the competence to conclude GATS is shared between the Community and the Member States",[30] thus, neatly concealing to what extent the Community is (not) competent.

The argumentation regarding TRIPs is, for present purposes, not much different. In this section of the judgment it appears that the Court is perfectly capable of distinguishing between exclusive powers and competence in a broader sense. It is quite remarkable, though, that it does so only in relation to the arguments of some Member States that they are competent in respect of the provisions of TRIPs relating to the proposed measures to secure the effective protection of intellectual property rights.[31] This would appear to imply that the Community could not conclude a treaty requiring parties to adopt rules "ensuring a fair and just procedure, [or] rules regarding the submission of evidence, the right to be heard, the giving of reasons for decisions, the right of appeal, interim measures and the award of damages"[32] and so forth. The Court states that:

---

[25] Ex Art. 54 EC.
[26] Ex Art. 57(2) EC.
[27] [1994] E.C.R. I–5267, at para. 90.
[28] *ibid.*, at para. 91.
[29] *ibid.*, at paras 95–96.
[30] *ibid.*, at para. 98.
[31] *ibid.*, at para. 104.
[32] *ibid.*

"If that argument [*i.e.* that the above matters fall within the competence of the Member States] is to be understood as meaning that all those matters are within some sort of domain reserved to the Member States, it cannot be accepted. The Community is certainly competent to harmonise national rules on those matters ..."[33]

But when speaking about those Community competences, the Court is again nebulous:

"The Community is certainly competent to harmonise national rules on those matters, in so far as, in the words of Article [94][34] of the Treaty, they "directly affect the establishment or functioning of the common market'. But the fact remains that the Community institutions have not hitherto exercised their powers in the field of the "enforcement of intellectual property rights", except in Regulation No. 3842/86 ... laying down measures to prohibit the release for free circulation of counterfeit goods."[35]

It is striking again that the Court explicitly refers to the internal competence of the Community but not to any external one. If it implicitly recognises an external power, the end of the quote again seems to imply that the Community, in order to have an external competence, must have adopted internal rules.

9.06   In the subsequent and final section of the judgment, which deals with the duty of co-operation between Member States and Community institutions, there is substantial confusion between questions of competence and exclusivity. Indeed, the picture which emerges from this section of the Opinion is not promising. The Court recognises in so many words the "quite legitimate"[36] concern of the Commission that:

"... interminable discussions will ensue to determine whether a given matter falls within the competence of Community, so that the Community mechanisms laid down by the relevant provisions of the Treaty will apply, or whether it is within the competence of the Member States, in which case the consensus rule will operate."[37]

This is an awkward passage. Apparently, a matter can either fall within the competence of the Community or that of the Member States, there being no overlap between the two. In areas of Community competence, Community mechanisms apply; in areas of Member States' competence, there must be consensus. Community competence therefore seems equal to exclusive competence; if the reference to the "competence of the Community" covers non-exclusive competence, it makes no sense because, in practice, there is no guarantee in such areas that Community mechanisms will apply. Whereas it is therefore likely that the notion "Community competence" is being equated here with exclusive competence, the wording chosen in this paragraph does not necessarily imply that the Community cannot acquire additional (exclusive) competence.

Admittedly, if the Court means that the Community has a power beyond exclusivity, its contention that *consensus* must apply in fields of *Member States' competence* is difficult to understand, as one could also decide that Community

---

[33] *ibid.*
[34] Ex Art. 100 EC.
[35] [1994] E.C.R. I–5267, at para. 104.
[36] *ibid.*, at para. 107.
[37] *ibid.*, at para. 106

mechanisms apply. It can perhaps be explained with reference to the "political" compromise (*i.e.* without legal effect) which had been struck by the Commission that all decisions be taken by unanimity.[38]

In any case the terminology employed is unfortunate because again it seems to convey the idea that in practice or in law the Community only has competence where it is exclusive.

Lastly, the same is true for the following passage of the ruling, in which the Court comes very close indeed to saying that the competence of the Community is restricted to the free movement of goods and that it has no power of action under GATS or TRIPs:

> "[I]f [in the context of dispute settlement procedures] the Community were given the right to retaliate in the sector of goods but found itself incapable of exercising that right, it would, in the absence of close co-operation, find itself unable, *in law*, to retaliate in the areas covered by GATS or TRIPs, those being within the competence of the Member States."[39]

THE REQUIREMENT OF ADEQUATE REASONING AND THE LEGAL BASIS FOR THE CONCLUSION OF THE AGREEMENTS

9.07   As a result of these uncertainties, the Opinion leaves doubts as regards the proper legal basis for concluding the Uruguay Round agreements. Inasmuch as the Court did not address the latter question properly, it remains unclear which articles, other than Article 133 EC, might serve as a basis for the conclusion of the individual agreements. This cannot be justified simply with reference to time pressure. Nor can earlier statements of the Court to the effect that under a mixed agreement the division of power is an internal matter which does not concern third countries[40] be taken to mean that the division of power is immaterial for internal purposes. There are just too many cases now in which the Court has elaborated on the duty to state adequately the reasons on which a Community act is based.[41] This would serve a variety of different purposes: it would further a proper administration of justice, it would inform interested parties of the reasons underlying the decision, and it would inform Member States and the institutions of the procedural requirements which the decision was required to respect.[42] In the *Brennwein* case[43] the Court itself mentioned three reasons for adequate reasoning:

(a)   the parties involved must know their rights;

(b)   the Court of Justice must be able to exercise its judicial review; and

(c)   Member States, as well as those of its nationals who may be concerned, must know how the institutions concerned apply the Treaty.

---

[38] For the unconventional approach of the Commission during the negotiations see Kuijper, "The Conclusion and Implementation of the Uruguay Round Results by the European Community", (1995) 6 E.J.I.L. 222 at pp. 222–224.

[39] Opinion 1/94, [1994] E.C.R. I–5267, para. 109, emphasis added.

[40] Ruling 1/78, *Draft Convention of the International Atomic Energy Agency on the Physical Protection of Nuclear Materials, Facilities and Transports* [1978] E.C.R. 2151.

[41] Case 45/86; *Commission v. Council ("Generalised Tariff Preferences")* [1987] E.C.R. 1493; (1998) 2 C.M.L.Rev. 131 as well as Case 165/87, *Commission v. Council (Commodity Coding)* [1988] E.C.R. 5545; (1990) 1 C.M.L.Rev. 457, Case 275/87, *Commission v. Council* [1989] E.C.R. 259; and Cases C–51, 90 and 94/89, *United Kingdom and Others v. Council (COMETT II)* [1991] 1 E.C.R. 2757; (1992) 1 C.M.L.Rev. 40.

[42] Case 45/86 [1987] E.C.R. 1493, at paras. 7–9.

[43] Case 24/62, *Germany v. Commission* [1963] E.C.R. 63; (1963) C.M.L.Rev. 347

Whereas it may be conceded that it would perhaps have been difficult for the Court to make the appropriate detailed analysis within the limited time available, it is nevertheless regrettable that, given the remaining uncertainty surrounding the proper legal basis of the relevant Community measure, the stated objectives of adequate reasoning may not be met in the *WTO* Opinion.

Naturally, in the preamble to the Decision concluding the Uruguay Round Agreements[44] the Council gives its own views on the legal basis of the agreements.

The first thing to be noted is that the Decision makes explicit that the Community is only partly competent, *i.e.* that this is a mixed agreement. This is rather unique, although a prior Council Decision concluding the Energy Charter Treaty now contains similar provisions.[45]

The specific legal bases chosen, in addition to the (perhaps pertinent, but unhelpful) customary reference to the Treaty as a whole are then the equivalent of Articles 133 and 300(3) EC (ex Articles 113 and 228(3)), as well as Articles 37 (ex Article 43), 54 (ex Article 54), 47 (ex Article 57), 55 (ex Article 66), 71 (ex Article 75), 80(2) (ex Article 84(2)), 93 (ex Article 99), 94 (ex Article 100), 95 (ex Article 100a) and 308 (ex Article 235) EC.[46]

Can one infer from the Decision that the Council recognises the existence of a non-exclusive external power? The wording of the Council Decision is unclear in this respect. Whereas the choice of the above-mentioned articles of the Treaty appears to have been inspired by the fact that there existed common rules with the same legal basis which were affected by the agreements, in one paragraph the Council appears to adopt a broader view:

"... the competence of the Community to conclude international agreements does not derive only from explicit conferral by the Treaty but may also derive from other provisions of the Treaty and from acts adopted pursuant to those provisions by the Community institutions."[47]

Although this sweeping statement can be read as a confirmation of the existence of non-exclusive, "potential" powers, it can equally well be understood contextually, as containing an implicit reference to pre-emption or necessity. Indeed, the rest of the decision is devoted to "*ERTA* reasoning":

"... where Community rules have been adopted in order to achieve the aims of the Treaty, Member States may not, outside the framework of the common institutions, enter into commitments liable to affect those rules or alter their scope;
... a portion of the commitments contained in the Agreement establishing the World Trade Organisation, including the Annexes thereto, falls within the competence of the Community under Article [133] of the Treaty; ... furthermore, of the remainder of the said commitments some affect Community rules adopted on the basis of Articles [37], [44], [47], [55], [71], [80](2), [93], [94], [95] and [308] and may therefore only be concluded by the Community alone."[48]

The Decision then mentions, oddly enough, that no common rules have as yet been

---

[44] Council Decision 94/800/EC of December 22, 1994 concerning the conclusion on behalf of the European Community, as regards matters within its competence, of the agreements reached in the Uruguay Round multilateral negotiations (1986–1994), [1994] O.J. L336/1.
[45] Council Decision 94/998/EC of December 15, 1994 on the provisional application of the Energy Charter Treaty by the European Community, [1994] O.J. L380/1.
[46] Council Decision 94/800/EC, see above, n. 44, Recital 1.
[47] *ibid.*, Recital 10.
[48] *ibid.*, Recital 11–12.

adopted on the basis of what is now Article 57 EC (ex Article 73c),[49] an article which is not mentioned as a basis for the conclusion of the agreements, although it is manifestly considered relevant. (Perhaps this article would have been mentioned as a legal basis had internal measures been adopted.) One commentator takes the "negative ERTA justification" in relation to this article as a statement implying that there is no (exclusive) Community treaty-making power in the field.[50] He also suggests that this would be incorrect because the article "would seem to found both an autonomous and a contractual Community power to act in the field of free movement of capital to or from third countries involving direct investment, establishment, the provision of financial services or the admission of securities to capital markets".[51]

9.08   All this raises the question of how exactly to determine the legal basis for the conclusion of an international agreement, especially where this covers matters which do not come under the Common Commercial Policy. Is the Council to refer (and to refer only) to the legal basis of acts which have been adopted before the conclusion of the agreement and which are going to be affected by the agreement? To do this would obviously help to prevent such acts from being amended without observing the procedural guarantees inherent in the Treaty articles on the basis of which they were adopted. However, is it really necessary that the same procedures be observed? Arguably a measure adopted by unanimity should require unanimity also if it is included in an international treaty. But experience in the field of the Common Commercial Policy shows that parliamentary involvement in the conclusion of trade agreements is considered too cumbersome a requirement to be practical, even in respect of matters which would require such involvement in the internal plane.

Also, where an internal measure is based on more than one Article of the Treaty, the choice of legal basis for the conclusion of an agreement may be too approximate, as the part of the internal rule which is going to be affected may not warrant a reference to all the Articles serving as a basis for the measure as a whole. The conclusion must therefore be that the basis on which internal acts have been concluded, although it may indicate the existence of an exclusive power, cannot inform the basis for the conclusion of an international treaty.

When determining treaty-making authority, should one mention the bases of acts needed subsequently to implement the provisions of the agreement? First of all, this may involve a technical problem, because it cannot always be foreseen which acts may be concerned by the agreement in the future. A reference to all areas affected in future may not therefore be feasible, inviting at best an indiscriminate reference to the Treaty as a whole. Secondly, as regards the Common Commercial Policy, which the Court decided can subsume ancillary matters, implementation powers may be irrelevant and the mentioning of an additional basis would be inappropriate because then treaty-making procedures might have to be followed which are considered too cumbersome. This rule must not necessarily apply to other fields of policy, where the mention of implementing powers may serve to protect the decision-making power in the fields concerned. Further arguments in favour of mentioning those articles of the Treaty which give the Community an implementing power would be that it would give information about the existence of a "concurrent" treaty-making power, which would be required in any case where the Community becomes a party to an agreement without the Member States. In addition, it would show that the Community is capable of implementing the agreement by having recourse to Community procedures, bearing in mind that even if this were not the case its obligations may be perfectly valid under

---

[49] *ibid.*, Recital 14.
[50] Kuijper, *op. cit.*, at p. 235.
[51] *ibid.*

international law. On the other hand, one is inclined to believe that this information is not indispensable. Not only can it be omitted if the treaty-making procedure so requires, but the mixed agreement formula seems in practice to obviate any inquiries.

9.09   It therefore seems that the determination of the treaty-making authority of the Community has to be done on its own particular merits, rather than merely by reference to existing or future Community activity on the internal plane. The determination of the legal basis could depart from considerations relating to the essential aim of the Treaty and how this fits in with the (potential as well as exclusive) treaty-making powers of the Community. This, the Commission has sought to do, by arguing in the first place that given that the majority of the agreements constitute trade policy and related matters and the problem of cross-retaliation, the trade policy article should be used.

The fact that the Commission's views were not accepted (they required a flexibility which the Member States had already shown they did not possess in the broader context of Maastricht) did not, however, discharge the Council of the obligation to take the question of the legal basis most seriously. There are some indications that this has not been done.

In the present context it will suffice to point to several questionable considerations in the Council Decision. The concern is with the ancillary nature of some of the commitments, the confusion about the extent of the Community's powers for the conclusion of some of the so-called "plurilateral" agreements, and the applicability of the principle of subsidiarity.

In the opinion of Kuijper [52] the references to what are now Articles 37, 93 and 94 as legal bases are contrary to the Court's opinion, or superfluous, because the Court seems to have included the treaty provisions in question under the exclusive power of the Community for the Common Commercial Policy.

Confusion also exists as to the meaning of Article 2(1) of the Decision, approving the plurilateral agreements "with regard to that portion of them which falls within the competence of the European Community". This is a puzzle, as the Commission takes the view that both the Dairy and Bovine Meat Agreements as well as the Agreement on Civil Aircraft and the Government Procurement Agreement come within the exclusive power of the Community, the latter because the Community occupied the field through Directives, if not by virtue of (an analogous application of) Article 133.

Finally, it could be argued that, if the existence of exclusivity is not a determining factor in the choice of legal basis, the Council Decision should have devoted some attention to the question of subsidiarity, as in all those fields that principle would apply. The fact that no attention was paid to subsidiarity is yet again an indication that the Community is deemed to act only on the basis of its exclusive powers.

WOULD IT HAVE MADE ANY DIFFERENCE?

9.10   Would it have made any real difference had the Court acknowledged that the Community had treaty-making power in respect of all subject-matters for which it had internal competence? Arguably, the choice of legal basis and the practical consequence drawn from the ruling, *i.e.* mixity, would have been just the same. Admitting the existence of an implied external power over the whole area of the Treaty would not have changed the fact that the Treaty deals with freedom of establishment and the freedom to provide services only for nationals of Community Member States within the Com-

---

[52]   *ibid.*, at p. 234.

munity, and not for nationals of non-Community Member States or for Community nationals abroad.

Nevertheless, a confirmation of the existence of non-exclusive powers, even in the most general terms, would have counteracted a restrictive interpretation of the *ERTA* judgment and other cases dealing with the external relations powers of the Community.

The Member States would have had nothing to lose, since mixity is not ruled out by the recognition of an implied external competence. Mixity is not even ruled out in the case of an agreement coming within the exclusive power of the Community, such as in Opinion 1/78.[53] Yet for the Community it may make a noticeable difference. As long as there is doubt about the existence of a Community power to conclude certain provisions, mixity can be argued as a "must". There is in practice not even the possibility of arguing in a given case that participation exclusively by the Community would be preferable and that all Member States would be required to become contracting parties to any international treaty, outside the Common Commercial Policy for which the Community has competence without there being a complete occupation of the field. Moreover, mixity could be on the agenda as soon as even a procedural matter, like the issue of adequate remedies, is proposed for inclusion in an agreement.

Had the Court mentioned that the Community has implied external powers also where the conclusion of an international agreement is not "inextricably linked" with the adoption of internal measures, the Member States would, without losing anything, have been prevented from raising the issue of mixity as a matter of course.

---

[53] Opinion 1/78, *International Agreement on Natural Rubber* [1979] E.C.R. 2871; (1979) 3 C.M.L.Rev. 639.

CHAPTER 10

The Scope of the Common Commercial Policy Post Opinion 1/94: Clouds and Silver linings

by

Alec Burnside*

10.01   The Commission's great hope was that the ECJ in Opinion 1/94[1] would recognise Article 133 EC (ex Article 113) as the sole legal basis for the entire WTO and all its agreements. The idea has its attractions, not least in its simplicity in view of the complex web of issues arising from the Court's eventual Opinion. In earlier, more activist and integrationist days, the Court might have been attracted by this argument. However, the argument goes well beyond anything previously recognised by the Court. Also, the political spirit at the time of the Opinion and the vociferous opposition of the Council, eight Member States and indeed the European Parliament made it unlikely that the Court would authorise such a progressive argument. As such, it is no surprise that the Court took a more conservative line.

If the Opinion on the scope of the common commercial policy (CCP) can be reduced to a single (lengthy) soundbite, it is this: the CCP covers virtually all trade in goods but only limited aspects of both trade in services and treaty-making in the field of intellectual property. The "cloud" here is clearly the limited role in relation to services. Nevertheless, in relation to goods, the *WTO* Opinion has a silver lining, indeed in some ways it is gold-plated. In recognising exclusive competence for the Community under Article 133 EC (ex Article 113) in relation to GATT the Court resolved in the Commission's favour some long-standing issues of uncertainty, notably in relation to the ECSC Treaty. While the Opinion has its disappointments for the Commission in relation to services, there is much from which the Commission might draw some comfort.

ARGUMENTS DEPLOYED BY THE ECJ

10.02   A number of different arguments recur at various points in the Opinion.

(a) The Court employs in various contexts, the argument that an international agreement of a general character may be adopted under the CCP despite the inclusion in the agreement of elements that would in their own right belong under a different heading. In other words, where the agreement displays a pri-

---

* Partner at Linklaters & Alliance, Brussels.
[1] Opinion 1/94, *Competence of the community to conclude international agreements concerning services and the protection of intellectual property* (WTO) [1994] E.C.R. I–5267; (1995) 1 C.M.L.Rev. 205.

mary purpose, secondary purposes may be swept along under the same legislative basis.[2]

(b) By contrast, the Court in other instances looks to the general scheme ("économie") of the EC Treaty to justify the conclusion that the CCP cannot apply. By reference to the general scheme of the Treaty, one may decide whether a measure should fall to be dealt with under one Chapter of the Treaty or another. And yet within this second argument, and contrary it seems to the first argument, the Court is willing to recognise particular exceptions which can fall within the CCP.[3]

(c) Further, the Court was willing on occasion to recognise the use of Article 133 EC (ex Article 113) for adoption of an external measure, given the measure's particular characteristic, although any internal measures in the same field would have to be based on a distinct Treaty Article. The Court here places particular weight on the recitals to the relevant agreement as a demonstration of its significance for international trade.[4]

The result is a patchwork which, like certain pieces of modern art, may be a thing of beauty to some, but others may not be quite sure what it all means.

As an undergraduate reading law at Cambridge many years ago, I was taken aback by a particular House of Lords ruling in which it seemed to me that principles were plucked from the air, rather than based on precedent or established ideas. When I asked my supervisor when one can reason like that, he replied: when you are a Lord of Appeal in Ordinary. No doubt these words of wisdom about the latitude granted to Lords of Appeal in Ordinary, which have stayed with me all these years, could now equally be applied to the judges of the Court of Justice.

GOODS

10.03 The Court of Justice recognised the exclusive competence of the Community under the CCP to conclude GATT.[5] That the CCP applies to goods comes as no surprise. There were, however, hurdles to overcome in relation to goods under the ECSC and Euratom Treaties. Euratom did not occasion any significant discussion.[6] However, the Court addressed head-on the old issue of whether a measure under Article 133 EC (ex Article 113) can cover ECSC products, holding that it can where, as in this instance, the agreement in question is of general application and not specific to coal and steel products.[7] The Court thereby swept a secondary purpose within the ambit of a primary purpose, applying the first argument noted above. Such reasoning is questionable, since it would seem common practice, in internal legislation where a particular legal basis is insufficient for the intended purpose, to supplement it with another relevant legislative basis. For example, the Merger Regulation[8] was adopted on the basis of old Article 87 EEC, since Articles 85 and 86 EEC already applied to

---

[2] *ibid.*, at paras. 25–27 and 48–51.
[3] *ibid.*, at paras. 36–47.
[4] *ibid.*, at paras. 28–31.
[5] *ibid..* at paras. 22–34.
[6] See *ibid..* at para 24.
[7] *ibid.*, at para. 25.
[8] Regulation 4064/89 on the control of concentrations between undertakings, [1989] O.J. L395/1 (*Corrigendum*: [1990] O.J. L257/13).

certain aspects of mergers, but with Article 235 EEC to supplement and fill in the gaps.[9]

This is no doubt a convenient result, particularly given the imminent demise of the ECSC Treaty. It seems to represent a judicial means of transposing coal and steel from the ECSC Treaty into the EC Treaty, thus achieving progress where none has yet been made at the political level despite the impending expiry of the ECSC Treaty.[10] Yet the capital markets seem not to be concerned by the lack of decision on the future of the ECSC. It still commands the highest credit rating, even when borrowing for a maturity date when it will no longer exist! This shows a truly touching faith in the likelihood of political agreement in these highly-charged days.

It remains the case that a legal basis under the ECSC Treaty, namely Article 95 ECSC, the counterpart to Article 308 EC (ex Article 235), will need to be used for international treaties that are specific to ECSC products. That being so, one might enquire why the Court did not recognise a need to have GATT jointly concluded under separate EC and ECSC legal bases. No reason is offered to explain why a secondary aspect can be passed under the legal basis applicable to the main body of a measure, without any recourse to the legal base that would properly be required for the secondary aspect.

AGRICULTURE

10.04   The Court further held that agriculture could be dealt with under Article 133 EC (ex Article 113), despite the fact that Article 37 EC (ex Article 43) is the appropriate basis cited for internal EC legislation.[11] Here the Court employed the third of the arguments above, namely, reliance on the international purpose of the agreement. Thus the Agreement on Agriculture could be concluded by the Community under Article 133 EC (ex Article 113), since its objective "is to establish, on a worldwide basis, a fair and market-oriented agricultural trading system".[12] Similarly, the Agreement on the Application of Sanitary and Phytosanitary Measures could be adopted under Article 133 EC (ex Article 113) since, as reflected in its preamble, its goal is "the establishment of a multilateral framework of rules and disciplines to guide the development . . . of sanitary and phytosanitary measures in order to minimise their negative effects on trade".[13] It is worth adding that Article 37 EC (ex Article 43), like Article 133 EC, would require only a qualified majority vote in Council, and therefore no issue relating to distortion of the legislative process arises from the Court's reasoning on the Agreements on Agriculture.[14]

AUTONOMOUS MEASURES AND THE LEGAL BASIS ISSUE

10.05   An interesting issue discussed in Brussels is whether an internal Community

---

[9] Article 83 EC (then Art. 87 EEC) provides for the adoption of Community legislation to give effect to the principles set out in Arts 81 and 82 EC (ex Arts 85 and 86). Article 308 EC (then Art. 235 EEC) provides the legal basis for the adoption of measures to fulfil one of the objectives of the Community where the Treaty does not provide the power to do so.
[10] Article 97 ECSC provides that the Treaty is of a limited duration of fifty years, hence its impending expiry in 2001.
[11] Opinion 1/94, [1994] E.C.R. I–5267, at paras. 28–31.
[12] ibid., at para. 29, quoting the preamble to that Agreement.
[13] Quoted ibid., at para. 31.
[14] Indeed, this may have been a significant factor affecting the Court's reasoning. Cf. the Court's approach to the TRIPs Agreement, below.

measure, adopted pursuant to or to give effect to an international agreement such as GATT, may also be adopted under Article 133 EC (ex Article 113); or whether it requires recourse to an appropriate alternative legal basis such as, for example, the relevant ECSC Treaty Article. It is said that the view finding favour is that Article 133 EC alone may be used, but only if the autonomous Community measure is connected to the Treaty obligation and has the same general remit. It is questionable whether this is consistent with the principle which the Court used in relation to agriculture, *i.e.* that the purpose of a new agreement might justify treatment under Article 133 EC even though the corresponding domestic measures would all be under Article 37 EC (ex Article 43).

TECHNICAL BARRIERS

10.06 The Court held, without hesitation, that the Agreement on Technical Barriers to Trade fell within the ambit of Article 133 EC (ex Article 113).[15] Referring to the agreement's preamble, the Court noted that the Agreement on Technical Barriers is designed "to ensure that technical regulations and standards and procedures for assessment of conformity with technical regulations and standards do not create unnecessary obstacles to international trade." It discounted arguments put by the Netherlands that Member States should retain competence because of the optional nature of some Community Directives on technical standards and the fact that complete harmonisation had not been achieved, and indeed is not envisaged, in the relevant field.

SERVICES

10.07 The Court was willing to recognise that services "cannot immediately, and as a matter of principle, be excluded from the scope of [Article 133 EC (ex Article 113)]".[16] The Commission had asserted that in most developed countries the services sector has become the dominant sector of the economy. While basic industries still characterise developing countries, developed economies have tended to focus on the export of services and goods with a high value-added content. However, the Court was swayed from proceeding further down this path by an analysis of the overall scheme of the EC Treaty in relation to "services" as defined in GATS, thus applying the second argument identified above.[17]

GATS identifies four modes of supply of services:

(1) cross-border supplies not involving any movement of persons;

(2) consumption abroad, in which the recipient of the service travels to the country of the service provider;

(3) commercial presence, or what in traditional EC language we would call establishment, *i.e.* setting up a subsidiary or branch in a foreign country for the purpose of supplying services there;

---

[15] Opinion 1/94 [1994] E.C.R. I–5267, at paras. 32–33.
[16] *ibid.*, at para. 41.
[17] *ibid.*, at paras. 36–47.

(4) "the presence of natural persons", *i.e.* a service supplier in one country sending staff into another country to provide services locally to recipients there.

Here the Court began, unfortunately, to pick and choose. Cross-border supply of services was held to be sufficiently similar to cross-border supply of goods to be treated under the CCP. The services offered by providers in many sectors (for example transactions involving the provision of telecommunications, media services and financial services) are provided by electronic means and involve no cross-border movement of persons.

All the other modes of service provision, since they will generally involve the movement across border of third country nationals, were considered beyond the scope of the CCP and required separate treatment under Articles 39, 43, 48 and 49 EC (ex Articles 48, 52, 58 and 59). The Court referred here to Article 3 EC (ex Article 3) which lists the activities of the EC, and distinguished *inter alia* between a common commercial policy (Article 3(b) EC) and measures concerning the entry and movement of persons in the internal market (Article 3(d) EC).

It passed unmentioned that, for example, a locally incorporated subsidiary within the EC would count as an EC person (under Article 48 EC (ex Article 58))[18] or that the people staffing an EC branch of a non EC supplier might in fact be Community nationals; or that the freedom to provide services (Article 49 EC (ex Article 59)), includes the freedom for recipients of services to travel to another Member State in order to receive services there.[19] Indeed, the right to provide services includes the right of a service provider to bring employees from third countries into a Member State to provide a service.[20] Even if these had been recognised, though, it seems likely that the line of reasoning based on the general scheme of the Treaty would have taken precedence over the principle that an issue of secondary importance can be swept within the ambit of the Treaty basis needed for the issue of prime importance. This is all the more given the reasoning which the Court had in relation specifically to services in the transport sector.

TRANSPORT

10.08   In relation to transport, the Court focused on the existence of the specific title in the EC Treaty on transport services.[21] Here, however, it saw the need to explain away a series of previous international agreements based on Article 133 EC (ex Article 113), involving the suspension of transport services,[22] such as the embargoes against

---

[18] Article 48 EC (ex Article 58) guarantees the right of freedom of establishment for companies or firms established in a Member State to set up subsidiaries elsewhere in the EU.

[19] In Joined Cases 286/82 and 26/83, *Luisi and Carbone* v. *Ministero del Tesoro* [1984] E.C.R. 377; (1985) 3 C.M.L.Rev. 52; the Court held that the freedom to provide services guaranteed by Articles 49 and 50 EC (ex Articles 59 and 60) included the freedom for recipients of services to go to another Member State in order to receive services there without being obstructed by restrictions. "Recipients of services" was held to include tourists, persons receiving medical treatment and persons travelling for the purposes of education or business.

[20] For example, in Case C–43/93, *Vander Elst* v. *Office des Migrations Internationales* [1994] E.C.R. I–3803; (1995) 1 C.M.L.Rev. 513; and Case C–113/89, *Rush Portuguesa* v. *Office national d'immigration* [1990] E.C.R. I–1417; (1991) 3 C.M.L.Rev. 818; the Court held that Articles 49 and 50 EC (ex Articles 59 and 60) precluded Member States from requiring an undertaking established in another Member State to obtain work permits for third country nationals.

[21] Namely Title V (ex Title IV) of the EC Treaty, discussed at paras. 48–52 of Opinion 1/94 [1994] E.C.R. I–5267.

[22] Opinion 1/94 [1994] E.C.R. I–5267 at para. 51.

Iraq and Kuwait which had been based on Article 133 EC. The justification of such agreements was to be found, once again, by sweeping a secondary issue within the ambit of the Treaty basis used for the primary issue. Since those embargoes were aimed primarily at trade in goods, it was a "necessary adjunct" to embargo also the related transport services that would be needed for those goods.

The Court took the opportunity at this point in the Opinion to reiterate the point that the mere fact that a practice had been engaged in before did not prove that it had been done correctly, which should lend some hope to all those struggling against engrained administrative practices.

INTELLECTUAL PROPERTY

10.09   The Agreement on Trade-Related Aspects of Intellectual Property Rights (TRIPs) fell outside Article 133 EC (ex Article 113).[23] The Commission had argued forcefully that the rules concerning intellectual property are closely linked to trade in the products and services to which they apply and presented the Court with a catalogue of past international agreements concluded on the basis of Article 133 EC in which intellectual property rights had played a role.

In giving its Opinion the Court could have drawn on any of the tools of analysis previously discussed. However, it chose to base its Opinion on the perceived primary objective of TRIPs being "to strengthen and harmonise the protection of intellectual property on a worldwide scale".[24] This harmonisation was, however, of as much concern within the Community as externally, and therefore the "scheme of the Treaty" argument prevailed. Had the Court chosen to base its Opinion on the recitals to TRIPs, as it had done in relation to the recitals relating to agricultural matters, it would have reached the opposite result. One of the recitals to TRIPs gives as its objective the reduction of "distortions and impediments to international trade ... taking into account the need to promote effective and adequate protection of intellectual property rights",[25] *i.e.* reflecting the Court's third argument. The recognition that the purpose of the agreement on agriculture was "to establish ... a fair and market-oriented agricultural trading system" was sufficient to bring agricultural aspects within the scope of Article 133 EC (ex Article 113), even though Article 37 EC (ex Article 43) would be the proper legal basis for internal measures. Similarly, the Court's conclusion that the Agreement on Technical Barriers to Trade fell within the scope of Article 133 EC (ex Article 113) was based on its finding that the provisions of that agreement are designed simply to ensure that no unnecessary obstacles to international trade are created. The Court could have taken this avenue in relation to intellectual property.

That it did not may be explained by its recognition that the use of Article 133 EC (ex Article 113) would circumvent the proper internal constraints for internal legislation.[26] More precisely, since Article 133 EC functions on the basis of qualified majority voting, the unanimity requirement of certain Treaty Articles which are used for intellectual property harmonisation would be undermined. That is a cogent and important argument. Given the monist approach which prevails in Community law in relation to the direct effect of international agreements, *i.e.* that there is no need for internal measures to give effect to a particular international agreement, it is all the more important that international agreements are not used to circumvent proper internal procedures.

---

[23] *ibid.*, at paras. 54–71.
[24] *ibid.*, at para. 58.
[25] See the first recital of TRIPS.
[26] Opinion 1/94 [1994] E.C.J. I–5267, at para. 60.

In addition to all of this reasoning, however, the Court brought in two further principles. First, faced with the catalogue that had been cited to the Court of existing international agreements under Article 133 EC (ex Article 113) with intellectual property clauses, it resorted to the primary/secondary reasoning seen in relation to ECSC goods, which also reappeared as the "necessary adjunct" argument in relation to embargoes under Article 133 EC and transport services. Here the argument re-emerges under the simple guise of the intellectual property clauses in such agreements being "ancillary provisions" of extremely limited scope.[27] To complete the patchwork, the Court plucks one aspect out of TRIPs and recognises the application of Article 133 EC to it, namely the rules on counterfeit goods.[28] In this area the Community has previously legislated under Article 133 EC, in a measure addressed to the customs authorities at the external frontiers of the Community. It follows inexorably, but messily, that on this one point it was for the Community alone to conclude international agreements.

CONCLUSIONS

10.10   Reverting to the analogy of clouds and silver linings, it seems fair to suggest that there is stormy weather ahead. If it were a football game one might say "clouds 5, silver linings 2"—but at least rain did not, in the end, interrupt play.

The different tools of analysis and principles applied seem to lend great, and unfortunate, scope for gerrymandering in the future. Appropriate packaging or bundling of Treaty arrangements, to sweep secondary aspects in with supposedly overriding primary aspects, would be one technique. Self-serving and general recitals trying to set an agreement in the context of international trade and commercial policy, although the subject matter of the agreement might be more specific, would be another device. Even if such ruses might work in the main, counter attacks might always be launched by identifying, within the agreement, specific aspects requiring a different legal basis because of the scheme of the Treaty or because of particular areas necessarily falling within Article 133 EC (ex Article 113).

The Commission and the Member States will be no doubt well aware of the scope for invention given them by this Opinion. While the Opinion casts sunlight in some areas which were previously dark, such as the treatment of ECSC products, it leaves, on the whole, patchy fog and poor visibility. Detours have been sign-posted, but there is still a risk of nasty pile-ups.

ADDENDUM

The Common Commercial Policy : Developments Since Opinion 1/94

10.11   Developments since Opinion 1/94 was published in 1994, have largely affirmed the ECJ's decision in that case, with respect to the demarcation of EC competence under the Common Commercial Policy (Article 133) in the field of services, intellectual property and otherwise.

In *European Parliament* v. *Council*,[29] the ECJ, in annulling two Council decisions, affirmed the test laid down in Opinion 1/94.

In the *Centro-Com* Case,[30] the ECJ held that an export restriction was not deprived

---

[27] *ibid.*, at paras. 67–68.
[28] *ibid.*, at para. 55.
[29] Case C–360/93 [1996] E.C.R. I–1195, para. 29–30.
[30] Case C–124/95 [1997] E.C.R. I–81

of its character as a CCP measure (and, therefore, the EC was not deprived of its competence under Article 133) merely because it fulfilled a foreign policy objective. This follows the ruling in Opinion 1/94[31] that ancillary measures or secondary purposes do not deprive the EC of competence under the CCP.

Finally, the Treaty of Amsterdam inserted a sub-paragraph (5) into Article 133. This provides that the Council (acting on a Commission proposal and after consulting the European Parliament) may, acting *unanimously*, extend the treaty-making capacity under the CCP in individual contexts to cover those services and intellectual property excluded by Opinion 1/94. In reality, the difficulties in achieving the required unanimity has robbed this provision of most of its practical value.

---

[31] See point (a) of the three arguments of the Court cited at p. 152 above.

CHAPTER 11

EC Frameworks of International Relations: Co-operation, Partnership and Association

by

*Steve Peers**

INTRODUCTION

11. How does the Community determine whether a treaty with a third state, or a group of states, is to be a partnership, co-operation or association agreement? When the Community signs an agreement of each type, is it obeying the limits on its powers? Or conversely, is it failing to utilise all the powers available to it, as a result of a conservative interpretation of what they are? Clearly, the legal complexities of the Community's external relations are well illustrated by the institutions' ever-changing approach to the types of international agreement which the Community signs. Such approaches indicate the views, shifting over time, about both the legal constraints to the Community's external legal actions and the appropriateness of the exercise of its potential powers. However, it would seem that apart from aspects of the subject matter of EC agreements which have been subject to litigation (notably commercial and development policy), the *type* of agreement which the Community concludes with a given third state is determined by politics, not law.

COMMUNITY PRACTICE

11.02 The Community's practice falls broadly into three main periods, although in each period there was considerable gradual development.

Pre–1976: strict interpretation

11.03 It is well known that before the Single European Act entered into force in 1987, the Community had only two express external relations' powers—over the common commercial policy and association agreements.[1] Even after the Court of Justice ruled in 1971 that additional implied external powers existed, the Member States were initially reluctant for the Community to exercise them.[2] The practice regarding trade agreements is a good example.

---

* Reader in Law, University of Essex.
[1] See Hendry, McLeod and Hyett, *The External Relations of the European Communities* (Oxford, 1995), especially Chapter 3; Leopard, "External Relations Power of the EEC in Theory and Practice", (1977) 26 I.C.L.Q. 54.
[2] See Hendry, *et. al*, *op. cit.*, especially chapter 11; Leopard, *op. cit.*

The Community's power to adopt association agreements was not limited in time under the 1958 EEC Treaty. Article 238 EEC provided that it could negotiate such agreements from the first day the new Treaty entered into force. Therefore, it negotiated three important association agreements in its first few years—the treaties with Greece and Turkey and the first Yaounde Convention.[3] The Treaty provided no definition of what an "association agreement" might contain, but in the agreements with Greece and Turkey the EC institutions clearly took the view that they could insert measures covering the entire subject matter of the EC Treaty. Indeed, it is possible that at the time, the institutions believed that the agreements *had* to cover the Treaty's entire subject matter, on the assumption that a non-Member State could not legally be offered an association with only a part of the Community's policies. So both association agreements provided for a future customs union with the Community, as well as: future free movement of goods, services and workers; limited free movement of capital; the adoption of the common agricultural policy; freedom of establishment; and competition and state aids rules based on those in the EEC Treaty.[4] Indeed, both agreements provide for potential future membership of the associated state. The effect of most of the substantive provisions was delayed, and in many cases awaited subsequent negotiation, but the wide extent of the future legal obligations was clear. However, Member States did insist that the agreements with Greece and Turkey be concluded as mixed agreements—the first use of this unique creation of Community law.[5]

The Yaounde Convention, replacing a Convention annexed to the original EEC Treaty which expired after five years, did not aim at future membership of the associated African states.[6] However, it did insist upon reciprocity from the associates, as Article 238 EEC would seem to require, with its reference to "reciprocal rights and obligations". The Convention, a mixed agreement, provided for free trade in most goods and equality in establishment, along with substantial aid.

Yaounde was followed, during the transitional period, by a second Yaounde Convention, the two Arusha Agreements with Kenya, Uganda and Tanzania, and an agreement with Nigeria (although the first Arusha Agreement and the Agreement with Nigeria never entered into force).[7] Each of these was also a mixed agreement using Article 238, EEC as a legal base, and was based closely on the Yaounde Convention. The Community also adopted other association agreements late in the transitional period, with Morocco and Tunisia.[8] These agreements, concluded by the Community alone, indicated that the Community was shifting its view of what an association agreement had to entail: the relevant treaties provided only for freer movement of goods, not any other aspect of Community integration.

After the transitional period ended, Community practice on the contents of association agreements relaxed even further. The two agreements with Malta and Cyprus were initially substantively a very limited form of free trade agreement, with the parties awarding each other modest preferences on certain goods and envisioning a future customs union, but not attempting integration in any other area.[9] Indeed there was not even a mention of competition issues. Even today the scope of these agreements has

---

[3] [1963] O.J. L26/296 (Greece); [1964] O.J. L27/3685 (Turkey); [1964] O.J. L93/1430 (Yaounde I).

[4] The extent of free movement of capital had to be limited because it was also a limited goal under the EEC Treaty, Art. 73b–73g, inserted by the Treaty on European Union, which took effect on January 1, 1994 (now renumbered Art. 56–60 EC).

[5] See generally O'Keeffe and Schermers (eds.) *Mixed Agreements* (Kluwer, 1983).

[6] See generally Grilli, *The European Community and the Developing Countries* (Cambridge, 1993).

[7] [1970] O.J. L282/54 (Arusha II); Arusha I and the EC-Nigeria agreement were not published in the Official Journal.

[8] [1969] O.J. L197/1 (Morocco); [1969] O.J. L198/2 (Tunisia).

[9] [1971] O.J. L61 (Malta); [1973] O.J. L133 (Cyprus).

barely been widened, with protocols on financial co-operation and inclusion in EC programmes, and a protocol on the first stage of Cypriot adoption of a customs union, but no further developments.[10] Indeed, the initial association agreements and most subsequent Protocols have all been concluded with the EC alone, with no participation of the Member States.

11.04 Once the Community gained full competence over commercial policy under Article 113, EEC at the end of the transitional period in 1970, it used the power to adopt two types of agreements. One group of treaties consisted of free trade agreements (FTAs) with the European Free Trade Association (EFTA) states and Israel.[11] These liberalised all trade in goods between the parties, with subsidiary provisions on competition, state aids, and payments. A second group of treaties based on Article 113 EEC were non-preferential agreements with developing countries in Asia and Latin America. In this period, Argentina, Uruguay, India, Brazil, Sri Lanka, Mexico, Pakistan, Bangladesh and China agreed such treaties with the Community.[12] Unlike the Yaounde (and later the Lome) associates in Africa, the Caribbean and the Pacific, these states gained neither association status or trade preferences from their agreements with the EC—although the EC has granted most of them tariff reductions under its autonomous General System of Preferences (GSP) since 1971.[13] The agreements were strictly limited to trade issues, covering only the mutual grant of most-favoured nation (MFN) status and the aspiration to co-operate in stepping up links which would foster increased trade between the parties. In light of subsequent EC policies, they would later become known as "first-generation" development agreements.

The Community also signed association agreements (preferential, but non-reciprocal) with all the Southern Mediterranean states in 1976, although the relevant treaties were styled "Co-operation Agreements" and did not enter into force until 1978.[14] All these agreements were mixed and fell well short of the ambitious early association agreements with Greece and Turkey. Most only added financial and technical co-operation to trade preferences, although the Maghreb agreements also added social provisions which have since become the subject of important litigation.[15] The trade provisions in each agreement were also implemented in advance by an Interim Agreement. These were based purely on Article 113 EEC and covered the same subject-matter as the FTAs with the EFTA states and Israel agreed slightly earlier.[16] The Community also decided to transform its relations with Portugal and Israel from free trade into association, in order to offer these countries technical and financial co-operation; but it did this not by means of new association agreements, but by mixed Protocols,

---

[10] [1987] O.J. L393/1 (Protocol on first stage of customs union with Cyprus). The Protocol scheduled completion of the first stage at January 1, 1998, with a second stage to be negotiated; in the absence of such negotiations it can be presumed that the parties have subsumed such issues into the accession negotiations which began in March 1998.
[11] FTAs with Switzerland ([1972] O.J. L300/189); Sweden ([1972] O.J. L300/97); Norway ([1973] O.J. L171/1); Iceland ([1972] O.J. L301/1); Finland ([1973] O.J. L328/1); Portugal ([1972] O.J. L301/165); Austria ([1972] O.J. L300/2) and Israel ([1975] O.J. L136/2).
[12] See agreements with Argentina ([1971] O.J. L249/19); Uruguay ([1973] O.J. L333); India ([1974] O.J. L82); Brazil ([1974] O.J. L102/23); Sri Lanka ([1975] O.J. L247/2); Mexico ([1975] O.J. L247/11); Pakistan ([1976] O.J. L168/1); Bangladesh ([1976] O.J. L319/1) and China ([1978] O.J. L123).
[13] There was a long delay before granting the GSP to China.
[14] Agreements with Algeria ([1978] O.J. L263); Morocco ([1978] O.J. L264); Tunisia ([1978] O.J. L265); Egypt ([1978] O.J. L266); Lebanon ([1978] O.J. L267); Jordan ([1978] O.J. L268) and Syria ([1978] O.J. L269).
[15] For discussion, see Peers, "Towards Equality: Actual and Potential Rights of Third-Country Nationals in the European Union", (1996) 33 C.M.L.Rev. 7; Cremona, "Citizens of Third Countries: Movement and Employment of Migrant Workers in the European Union", (1995) 2 LIEI 87.
[16] Agreements with Algeria, Morocco and Tunisia ([1976] O.J. L141); Syria ([1977] O.J. L126); Egypt ([1977] O.J. L126); Jordan ([1977] O.J. L126) and Lebanon ([1977] O.J. L133). See earlier trade agreement based on Article 113 EEC alone with Egypt ([1973] O.J. L 251).

concluded using Article 238 EEC, attached to the agreements previously agreed with the Community alone.[17] In addition, it concluded the first Lome Convention as a mixed agreement based on Article 238 EEC, a legal base used to conclude all subsequent Lome Conventions.[18] Finally, the Community entered into a series of trade agreements based on Article 113 EEC with the Northern Mediterranean states of Spain and Yugoslavia.[19]

1976–91: The Era of Article 235 EEC

11.05 After pressure from Canada for a broad-ranging agreement, the Community decided to change its practice. It did not wish to sign an association agreement but agreed with Canada's desires for broader relations than those which a trade agreement based on Article 113 EEC alone could justify. The solution was to draw upon the existence of the implied external powers of the Community which the Court of Justice had recognised in the *ERTA* judgment.[20] But the Community decided that Article 235 EEC had to be used to conclude the agreement, in addition to Article 113 EEC, since the agreement covered economic co-operation (specifically industrial, technical, scientific and environmental co-operation) in addition to trade.[21]

The use of Article 235 EEC here opened the floodgates. By 1976, the Community had agreed all of the association agreements it desired for another fifteen years, bar that with Yugoslavia in 1980.[22] But it desired broader relationships with developing countries, and so used Articles 113 and 235 EEC in combination for a group of "second-generation agreements" with developing states, and later for most of its first agreements with the former Soviet bloc countries. The only use of Article 113 EEC by itself was for very limited agreements with states which were still essentially communist: Romania in 1980 and Czechoslovakia in 1989; and its use in such agreements was still clearly limited to trade alone.[23]

The "second-generation" co-operation agreements were concluded with: Yemen; the six states of the Gulf Co-operation Council; China; India; Pakistan; the five states of ASEAN (the Association of South-East Asian nations); the four Central American states (with Panama); the five states of the Andean bloc; Brazil; and Argentina.[24] They included references to energy, environmental, industrial, technical, scientific, agricultural, mining, forestry and transport co-operation. The agreements with the ex-communist states were concluded with: Hungary; Poland; Bulgaria; the Soviet Union; and Romania and Czechoslovakia after the Community wanted to expand relations with those states beyond trade.[25] They included economic co-operation in matters similar to those addressed by the "second-generation" development agreements.

---

[17] Additional Protocols to EC–Israel and EC–Portugal agreements ([1978] O.J. L270 and L274); and see EC-Portugal Interim Agreement ([1976] O.J. L266).
[18] Lome I ([1976] O.J. L25); Lome II ([1980] O.J. L347); Lome III ([1986] O.J. L86); Lome IV ([1991] O.J. L229); proposed Lome IV revisions (COM (95) 707).
[19] [1970] O.J. L182 (Spain); [1970] O.J. L58 (Yugoslavia); [1973] O.J. L224 (Yugoslavia).
[20] Case 22/70, *Commission* v. *Council* (ERTA) [1971] E.C.R. 263.
[21] [1976] O.J. L260/2.
[22] In force 1983 ([1983] O.J. L41); interim agreement based on Art. 113 EEC ([1980] O.J. L130).
[23] [1980] O.J. L352/5 (Romania); [1990] O.J. L88/2, (Czechoslovakia).
[24] [1985] O.J. L26/2 (Yemen); [1989] O.J. L54/3 (Gulf states); [1985] O.J. L250/1 (China); [1981] O.J. L328/5 (India); [1986] O.J. L108/2 (Pakistan); [1980] O.J. L144/1 (ASEAN); [1986] O.J. L172/1 (Central America); [1984] O.J. L153/2 (Andean bloc); [1982] O.J. L182/1 (Brazil) and [1990] O.J. L295/67 (Argentina). See also extension of EEC-ASEAN agreement to Brunei ([1985] O.J. L81).
[25] [1988] O.J. L327/1 (Hungary); [1989] O.J. L339/1 (Poland); [1989] O.J. L291/8 (Bulgaria); [1990] O.J. L68/1 (USSR); [1990] O.J. L291/29 (Czechoslovakia); [1991] O.J. L79 (Romania).

After 1991: Association, development and partnership agreements

11.06   Beginning in 1991, the Community took several decisions about its future external relationships that were to transform its approach to trade agreements again. First, it returned to the practice of signing association agreements with a vengeance. It agreed the EEA with the (then) seven EFTA states, ultimately less Switzerland;[26] it agreed ten Europe Agreements with states in Central and Eastern Europe, all of whom it later deemed suitable to apply for membership of the EC;[27] and it revised its Mediterranean policy substantially, agreeing new "Euro-Mediterranean Agreements" (EMAs) with Israel, Morocco, Tunisia and Jordan.[28] The content of these mixed agreements ranged substantially. The EEA obliged unprecedented integration into the Community legal system; the Europe Agreements included free trade areas, competition provisions, political dialogue, and a wide range of co-operation; and the EMAs followed the Europe Agreements closely but ultimately intend less integration. The Europe Agreements and the EMA with Israel were preceded by standard Interim Agreements based on Article 113 EEC.[29]

Secondly, the Community took to signing "third-generation" co-operation agreements with developing countries. Before the Maastricht Treaty entered into force, with its new provisions on development policy, these were still based on Articles 113 and 235 EEC; since that date they have almost all been based on Articles 113 and 130y of the EC Treaty (the latter providing a legal base for development policy agreements).[30]

Thirdly, the Community has taken to agreeing "transversal" partnership treaties which are not trade, co-operation or association agreements. The institutions have therefore taken the view, in light of Opinion 1/94 (*WTO*) that such agreements must be concluded with a variety of legal bases.[31] A peculiar exception to this new approach was the Partnership and Co-operation Agreement (PCA) with Russia, concluded with the joint legal bases of Article 113 and 235 EC.[32] Shortly before initialling this agreement, the Commission had initialled a PCA with Ukraine; the Commission went on to initial PCAs with Kazakhstan, Moldova, Belarus and Kyrgystan in 1994 and to propose the conclusion of all five based on Articles 113 and 235.[33] Opinion 1/94 forced a

---

[26] [1994] O.J. L1/1; [1995] O.J. L86/58 (extension to Liechtenstein).

[27] [1993] O.J. L347 (Poland); [1993] O.J. L348 (Hungary); [1994] O.J. L357 (Romania); [1994] O.J. L358 (Bulgaria); [1994] O.J. L358 (Czech Republic); [1994] O.J. L360 (Slovak Republic); [1998] O.J. L26 (Latvia); [1998] O.J. L51 (Lithuania); [1998] O.J. L68 (Estonia); [1999] O.J. L51 (Slovenia).

[28] [1998] O.J. L97 (Tunisia); [2000] O.J. L147 (Israel); [2000] O.J. L70 (Morocco); COM (97) 554, October 29, 1997 (Jordan). Negotiations for new agreements with Egypt, Lebanon, Algeria and Syria are ongoing. The Interim EMA with the PLO for the benefit of the Palestinian Authority ([1997] O.J. L187) is actually a trade and development agreement, not an association agreement, and was agreed with the Community alone.

[29] [1992] O.J. L114 (Poland); [1992] O.J. L115 (Czechoslovakia); [1992] O.J. L116 (Hungary); [1993] O.J. L81 (Romania); [1993] O.J. L323 (Bulgaria); [1993] O.J. L349 (Czech and Slovak Republics); [1994] O.J. L373 (Estonia); [1994] O.J. L374 (Latvia); [1994] O.J. L375 (Lithuania); [1996] O.J. L344 (Slovenia); [1996] O.J. L71/2 (Israel). Technically, the agreements with the Baltics were not Interim Agreements but fully-fledged Free Trade Agreements as the Community was some months from finishing negotiations for Europe Agreements with the three states.

[30] For a list of such treaties, see above, p. 101, n. 5. The EC has also concluded a final "second-generation" development agreement during this period, with Mongolia ([1993] O.J. L41/46), based like the "third-generation agreements" on Articles 113 and 235 EEC.

[31] Opinion 1/94, *WTO* [1994] E.C.R. I–5267.

[32] COM (94) 257, June 15, 1994; in force late 1997 ([1997] O.J. L327). See earlier Interim Agreement based on Article 113 alone ([1995] O.J. L247).

[33] PCAs in force with Ukraine ([1998] O.J. L49), and with Kazakhstan ([1999] O.J. L196), Kyrgystan ([1999] O.J. L196), Moldova ([1998] O.J. L181) and Belarus (COM (95) 44, February 22, 1995).

rethink, and the Commission duly proposed conclusion using a variety of different legal bases, namely Articles 54(2), 57(2), 73c(2), 75 and 84, EC along with 113 and 235.[34] In the meantime, standard Interim Agreements have been concluded or proposed on the basis of Article 113 EC.[35]

11.07 It was not long before Community practice adapted to Opinion 1/94, and the Commission began to propose partnership negotiations with third states that would be designed with conclusion on a variety of legal bases in mind. Such treaties have now been agreed with Mexico and Korea,[36] along with treaties on the "post-Soviet model" with Armenia, Azerbaijan, Georgia, Uzbekistan and Turkmenistan.[37] In addition, the Commission proposed adoption of treaties with Chile and Mercosur based on Articles 113 and 130y EC, albeit as mixed agreements due to their provisions for political dialogue; the Council did not refer to particular Treaty articles when agreeing to apply certain articles provisionally.[38]

The main treaty with Mexico is to be based on Articles 54(2), 57, 66, 73c(2), 75, 84(2), 113 and 130y EC, while the treaty with Korea is to be based on Articles 73c(2), 75, 84, 113 and 235 EC. In the case of Mexico, the Commission has even proposed, for the first time in EC history, conclusion of an Interim Agreement including more than just commercial policy legal bases. Because of the inclusion of procurement, the proposed Treaty bases for its conclusion are Articles 57(2), last sentence, 66 and 113.

Two final points should be noted. First, the use of Articles 113 and 235 EC together is not quite a thing of the past. In addition to the anomalous PCA with Russia, the EC's first treaties with the Baltic states and Slovenia, and its current treaties with San Marino, Albania and the former Yugoslav Republic of Macedonia (FYROM), have used these Treaty articles.[39] It seems that the Community is still willing to use this combination of Treaty articles when it believes a development, association or partnership treaty is inappropriate at that time; indeed Articles 113 and 235 EC are now being used for "entry-level" agreements.[40] Second, the EC has recently, for the first time, agreed a development policy treaty which provides for preferential trade relations.[41]

EFFECTS OF THE AMSTERDAM TREATY

11.08 Several features of the new Treaty can be noted at the outset. First, an early

---

[34] See COM (95) 137, May 8, 1995. The Commission indicated that it was basing its revised proposal on the legal bases for conclusion on the legal bases which the institutions agreed to use to conclude the Energy Charter Treaty ([1998] O.J. L69/5).
[35] Interim Agreements previously in force with Ukraine ([1995] O.J. L311), Kazakhstan ([1996] O.J. L147), Kyrgystan ([1997] O.J. L235) and Moldova ([1996] O.J. L40); and proposed with Belarus (COM (95) 245, February 28, 1995).
[36] Proposed treaties with Korea (COM (96) 141, March 27, 1996); and Mexico (COM (97) 527, October 24, 1997); proposed Interim Agreement with Mexico (COM (97) 525, October 22, 1997).
[37] PCAs with Armenia ([1999] O.J. L239); Azerbaijan ([1999] O.J. L246); Georgia ([1999] O.J. L205); Uzbekistan ([1999] O.J. L229); and Turkmenistan (COM (97) 693, February 6, 1998). Each of these, except Turkmenistan at time of writing, has been the subject of a concluded Interim Agreement: Armenia ([1997] O.J. L129/3); Azerbaijan ([1998] O.J. L285); Georgia ([1997] O.J. L129/23); and Uzbekistan ([1998] O.J. L43/2) proposed with Turkmenistan (COM (1998) 617, Dec. 2, 1998).
[38] [1996] O.J. L69 (Mercosur); [1996] O.J. L209 (Chile); see above p. 101, n. 6.
[39] [1992] O.J. L342 (Albania); [1992] O.J. L403 (Estonia, Latvia and Lithuania); [1993] O.J. L189 (Slovenia); [1997] O.J. L348 (FYROM); [1991] O.J. C302/12 (San Marino, not yet in force). See also customs union with Andorra, based on Arts. 99 and 113 EEC ([1990] O.J. L374/16).
[40] Both the Albania and FYROM treaties hint at future "upgrading" of relations, but a replacement for the latter treaty had not yet been agreed at the time of writing and the planned upgrading of the former has been forestalled by various difficulties in Albania.
[41] Agreement with the PLO, see above, p. 164, n. 28. Other treaties include or have included liberalised trade with developing countries; but they have all been association agreements.

proposal to add a new legal base to provide explicitly for the adoption of "transversal" treaties apparently gained little support, and so was not included in the final text. However, the Treaty has provided in the new Article 133(5) (ex Article 113(5)), for the possibility to transfer certain aspects of services and intellectual property which currently fall outside the common commercial policy (CCP) into the scope of that policy.[42] This transfer will have to be agreed by unanimity in the Council. This might mean that fewer treaties agreed by the Community will require participation of the Member States; or alternatively or additionally, it might mean that more Interim Agreements adopted by the Community while awaiting national ratification of the full treaty text will include provisions on services and intellectual property. It might also have an impact on the extent to which the Court of Justice can interpret the relevant agreements and determine their legal effects in the Community.[43] Finally, the new Title IV of Part 3 of the EC Treaty now gives the Community implied powers to enter into external commitments regarding immigration, asylum and civil co-operation matters; the extent to which the Community uses this power obviously remains to be seen.[44]

ASSESSING THE LEGALITY OF COMMUNITY PRACTICE

Human Rights

11.09   It is now standard practice for all EC agreements, whether development, association, partnership or interim trade agreements, to provide for possible partial or full suspension or denunciation in the event of serious human rights breaches.[45] The *Portugal* v. *Council* case addressed whether a development policy agreement could include such a clause without recourse to Article 308 EC (ex Article 235).[46] There is a separate issue, however: the legality of similar or identical human rights clauses in other types of agreements. Where a partnership agreement is partly based on the legal base of development policy among several others, as in the proposed agreement with Mexico, there should be no problem. After all, the agreement with India which was attacked in *Portugal* v. *Council* was partly based on Article 133 (ex Article 113) and the Court did not signal that this posed any difficulty for the inclusion of the human rights clause. Indeed, it would be awkward if the Community could only suspend the part of the agreement dealing with aid, although that is its current practice.[47]

Agreements having nothing to do with development policy are the real problem. These include not just association and partnership agreements, but the occasional agreements still based on Articles 133 (ex Article 113) and 308 EC (ex Article 235) and the common interim trade agreements based on Article 133 alone. In Opinion

---

[42] For the exact current dividing line, see Opinion 1/94, [1994] E.C.R. I–5267.

[43] Case C–53/96 *Hermes International* v. *FHT Marketing Choice* [1998] E.C.R. I–3603; now Opinion in Cases C300/98 and C392/98 Christian Dior and Layher (pending).

[44] Articles 61–69 EC (ex Articles 73i–73q). It should be noted that a number of association agreements already include provisions on immigration; that express external powers on services under Article 133(5), EC (ex Article 113(5)) will cover part of this area; and that implied external powers can also stem from Article 137, EC (ex Article 118b) giving the Community power to adopt rules on third-country nationals' working conditions. This does not affect voting rules in the Council or Parliament, but the point is relevant because only courts from which no appeal is possible can initially send references to the Court of Justice regarding the new Title or measures adopted under it (Article 68 EC (ex Article 73p)). *Quaere* whether if a future agreement is based in part on a clause in the new title and in part on clauses in other parts of the Treaty, all courts or tribunals could nonetheless refer questions on all provisions of the agreement to the Court?

[45] For full analysis, see Cremona, "Human Rights and Democracy Clauses in the EC's Trade Agreements", in Emiliou and O'Keeffe, *The European Union and World Trade Law* (Wiley, 1996); and for application to development agreements, see above, Chapter 7, para 7.04.

[46] Case C–268/94 [1996] E.C.R. I–6177.

[47] See answer to EP question on withdrawal of EC aid on human rights grounds ([1996] O.J. C322/101).

2/94, the Court of Justice ruled that the Community did not have the competence to ratify the European Convention on Human Rights (ECHR), because the Community lacked a specific legal base to agree human rights measures internally (and therefore externally) and because the alternative source of competence, Article 308, could not provide the Community with competence to conclude a treaty which altered the EC's methods of judicial protection of human rights.[48] The Opinion does not appear to preclude the Community entering into *any* external human rights commitment, as the *Portugal* v. *Council* judgment made clear. But the Community can (indeed, apparently *must*) include human rights clauses in its development agreements because of the wording of the development policy title in the Treaty. The other external relations provisions of the EC Treaty contain no reference whatsoever to human rights. Is the Community still empowered to conclude treaties with human rights clauses in the absence of such explicit wording in the Treaty?

The question should be answered by reference to each of the different types of EC external agreement. For association agreements, it is tempting to argue that there is no problem subjecting them to human rights clauses, because they are usually jointly concluded by the Community and its Member States. The human rights clauses are thus within Member State competence, not EC competence. But that is an unsatisfactory answer, because many measures adopted subsequently by Association Councils are wholly within EC competence; the Community may wish to respond to human rights problems in the third state by suspending aid or commercial policy benefits within EC competence, rather than by suspending co-operation by Member States within their competence. In *Demirel*, the Court of Justice made clear that most provisions of association agreements should be construed as falling within Community competence.[49] Therefore another answer should be found.[50]

11.10   Two alternative answers are possible. First, it is arguable that since association agreements may involve a third state in potentially almost the entirety of the EC Treaty, they simultaneously incorporate the Community legal system's respect for human rights and can therefore include human rights clauses without going beyond the scope of Community competence. Additionally or alternatively, it is arguable that if the Community can use Article 308 EC (ex Article 235) to provide it with competence to subject its treaties to human rights clauses, as the parties to *Portugal* v. *Council* all assumed, then an association agreement can include human rights clauses because Article 310 EC (ex Article 238) allows the Community to use all the competences which it enjoys in specific provisions of the EC Treaty, without having to call upon such competences expressly.

The advantage of the second argument is that it also provides justification for the use of human rights clauses in transversal partnership agreements, all of which to date (except that initialled with Mexico) have included the use of Article 308 EC (ex Article 235), as well as in the infrequent agreements based on Articles 133 and 308, EC (ex Articles 113 and 235). If the use of the old Article 235 EEC entitled the Community to include human rights clauses in its pre-TEU development policy agreements, surely it entitles the Community to include similar clauses in other types of treaties. Of course, it is not clear if the parties in *Portugal* v. *Council* were *correct* to assume that Article 308 EC (ex Article 235) entitles the Community to exercise such competence; after all, past practice is not definitive proof that the Community has certain powers.[51]

---

[48] Opinion 2/94 [1996] E.C.R. I–1759.
[49] Case 12/86 [1987] E.C.R. 3719, [1989] 1 C.M.L.R. 421.
[50] It may still be the case that where an agreement includes human rights as a specific field of co-operation, such co-operation falls within Member State competence: see comments on the EC-Mexico agreement in Chapter 7 of this volume.
[51] See, for instance, Opinion 1/94 [1994] E.C.R. I–5267.

Even if Article 308 EC (ex Article 235) does include such powers for the Community, it still leaves two problems. How can interim trade agreements based purely on Article 133 EC (ex Article 113) validly include human rights clauses; and how can the Community suspend only portions of its co-operation with third states on human rights grounds if such co-operation relates only to trade matters within the scope of Article 133 EC (ex Article 113)? An overall solution to the Community's competence to conclude *any* sort of treaty with a human rights clause can be found if the Court's finding in Opinion 2/94 (*ECHR*)[52] is appropriately interpreted in light of subsequent case law. In Opinion 2/94, the Court was concerned only with the Community's competence to conclude a potential act relating *solely* to the protection of human rights, not an act relating to another subject which was simply subject to the observance of human rights *principles*. It is clear from the consistent case law of the Court that a commercial policy act may have development policy or even foreign policy objectives, without such objectives altering the nature of the act as commercial policy.[53] Extending that logic, a commercial policy measure may be subject to human rights considerations without altering its nature as a commercial policy measure; and similarly removal of commercial policy benefits remains a commercial policy act even if the benefits are removed for reasons other than commercial policy. Similarly, other types of EC treaties can be subject to human rights considerations without altering their nature. The result is that the Community is free to subject any treaty it wishes to human rights clauses without any risk of exceeding its competence unless it wishes to agree a treaty solely about the protection of human rights.

Association Agreements

11.11   What must or can be included in an association agreement? The guidance from the Court here is limited. The only indication comes from the *Demirel* judgment: an association agreement indicates that, at least to some extent, the associated state has privileged links with the Community and participates in the Community system. Two questions arise here: first, how extensive do those links have to be? Secondly and conversely, what constitutes "too much integration" to be included in an association agreement?

As noted above, the agreements with Turkey, Greece, Cyprus and Malta envisage eventual membership of those states with the Community. All four agreements aimed to integrate the associated state into the EC customs union, and the first two foresaw extending all of the internal market freedoms and the agricultural policy. The EEA provided for the immediate integration of the "Full Monty" of the Community's internal market legislation.[54] In each case, it is submitted that the level of agreed or planned integration suffices for classification as an association agreement.

The remaining association agreements do not envisage membership or adoption of the customs union or the full internal market. Although all of the Europe Agreement states are now considered eligible for membership, the actual agreements with them do not expressly state that they were concluded in order to prepare the associate countries for membership. Also, although the agreements call generally for the harmonisation of laws between the parties, the elevation of these requirements into a proposed schedule for adoption of specific EC legislation was agreed outside the conclusion of the agree-

---

[52] Opinion 2/94 *ECHR* [1996] E.C.R. I–1759.
[53] Case 45/86 *Commission* v. *Council (GSP)* [1987] E.C.R. 1493; Case C–70/94 *Werner* [1995] E.C.R. I–3189; Case C–83/94 *Leifer* [1995] E.C.R. I–3231; Case C–124/95 *Centro-com* [1997] E.C.R. I–81.
[54] The common agricultural and fishing policies are not included, but otherwise there are relatively few derogations or exceptions.

ments themselves.[55] There is a legal debate over whether these developments count as subsequent practice between the parties which, in international law, would alter the interpretation of the original agreements.[56] In any event, the parties have agreed to co-operate on such a broad array of issues, and there are limited acknowledgements of freedom of establishment and freedom to provide services, so if there is a "level of integration" test that must be met for an agreement to be classified as an association agreement, it would seem that the Europe Agreements meet it.

Can more limited forms of integration into the Community system still justifiably be concluded as association agreements? Other association agreements have included the aid and non-reciprocal trade benefits provided under the Lome Conventions and their precursors; the more limited aid and non-reciprocal benefits under agreements with the Mediterranean states; and the more expansive co-operation and reciprocal trade benefits provided for under the recent Mediterranean treaties. As for the Lome Conventions, the Community's association with some of its Lome partners dates ultimately back to the Implementing Convention attached to the original EEC Treaty. This indicates that an association with developing countries with historical links with the Member States was always meant to be an important objective of the Community. The problem comes with the lack of reciprocity in these treaties: as noted above, Article 310 EC (ex Article 238) seems to require reciprocal rights and obligations to be included in each association agreement. It is arguable that a state can "take part" in the Community system, as per the *Demirel* judgment, by receiving benefits from the Community system, without necessarily having to give anything back; but the express requirement for reciprocity in the Treaty article has been quietly forgotten.

11.12 Even if the Community is entitled to adopt a non-reciprocal association agreement, might such agreements still fall below a "level of integration" threshold? It seems unlikely that the Lome Conventions and their predecessors could. Each has included a successively longer list of areas in which the partner states co-operate with the Community, and increasingly more complex institutional co-operation. True, the partner states are not eligible to join the Community, and they have no intention of establishing an internal market or customs union with the Community, but surely if the Community is entitled to adopt association agreements with developing countries, such agreements can have different goals from those adopted with nearby wealthy states.

It is the older agreements with Mediterranean states which arguably fall below the threshold. Indeed, most of them were called "Co-operation Agreements", not "Association Agreements". They were likely only adopted as association agreements because Member States had only just begun to relinquish their reluctance to use Article 235 EEC for external relations measures in 1976 and wished to ensure that agreements with these politically important non-member countries would be subject to approval in national parliaments. Apart from the social provisions in the treaties with the Maghreb states and Yugoslavia and the Additional Protocol with Portugal,[57] there is nothing in the treaties besides non-reciprocal trade provisions and the promise of aid on a limited number of grounds. Indeed, it is arguable that only the treaties with social provisions needed to be adopted as association agreements, since Article 235 EEC could have been used for the financial co-operation clauses as it was for many EC

---

[55] See White Paper on associates' legislative harmonisation with the EC (COM (95) 163, May 10, 1995), and analysis in Gaudissart and Sinnaeve, 'The Role of the White Paper', in Maresceau (ed.) *Enlarging the European Union* (Longmans, 1997), p. 41.
[56] See Muller-Graff, "Legal Framework for Relations between the European Union and Central and Eastern Europe", in Maresceau, *op. cit.*, p. 27 at pp. 33–34.
[57] See above, p. 162, n. 15.

agreements from 1976 to 1991. In light of *Demirel* and the case law on the EC-Maghreb agreements, finding that the social provisions in association agreements fall within Community competence, it is now arguable that none of the Mediterranean agreements needed to be mixed.

The more recent EMAs clearly do fall above a "level of integration" threshold. Not only do they include commitments to full free trade in industrial goods and limited liberalisation in agriculture, they expand co-operation on a wide range of items (some of which are outside EC competence), include provisions for political dialogue and aim for extended future regional integration into a "Euro-Mediterranean Free Trade Area".

The discussion above has focussed upon agreements which potentially might not have included enough integration to be considered association agreements. But there can also be association agreements which provide for "too much integration". The obvious example is the first version of the EEA which the Community and the EFTA states initialled, which the Court of Justice found incompatible with the EC Treaty on several grounds.[58] In certain respects, one can describe the Court's objections as opposition to "excessive integration". In particular, the level of judicial integration was impermissible. It is tempting to speculate whether there is a level of institutional integration which would similarly be impermissible, but since the EEA in its original and final forms eschewed votes for the EFTA states in the EC decision-making process, and the Community is never likely to agree to such involvement in any external agreement, the point is probably moot.[59]

Development policy

11.13   In addition to the recent *Portugal* v. *Council* judgment on the definition of development policy, there is a well-known division between commercial policy and development policy, as well as agricultural policy and development policy. Similarly, the Court has ruled that EC and national development policies are concurrent.[60] The effect of the former judgment is covered elsewhere in this volume.[61] As discussed in that chapter, the Community's development policy treaties have not diverged greatly from the EC-India agreement at issue in *Portugal* v. *Council*. A number of development agreements have clauses on issues outside or at the limit of Community competence, but the judgment established a two-step test for assessing the scope of EC development policy which the relevant treaties usually pass easily.

The potential problems come when the development policy clauses are combined with other EC Treaty clauses. Every treaty in each generation of development policy agreements has included the use of Article 133 EC (ex Article 113), initially by itself, then with Article 308 EC (ex Article 235), then with Article 181, EC (ex Article 130y). Over time, each generation of development agreement has focussed less and less on trade matters, and in any event with the exceptions of the EC-PLO, EC-Chile, EC-Mercosur and proposed EC-Mexico agreements, the EC's development agreements have always been non-preferential, requiring the parties only to grant each other Most-Favoured Nation (MFN) status. Of the four exceptions, only the EC-PLO agreement goes beyond MFN status itself, rather than provide a framework for future trade liberalisation. Since the treaty includes development policy clauses as well, it undoubt-

---

[58]   Opinion 1/91 *EEA* [1991] E.C.R. I–6079. See also Opinion 1/92 *EEA* [1992] E.C.R. I–2821.
[59]   See generally Reymond, "Decision-Making Procedure and Settlement of Disputes in the European Economic Area", (1993) 30 C.M.L.Rev. 449.
[60]   On both points, see Chapter 7 of this volume.
[61]   *ibid.*

edly had to be based on both Articles 133 and 181 EC (ex Articles 113 and 130y). What is more questionable is the inclusion of clauses requiring liberalisation of direct investment between the parties, without the additional use of Article 57(2) EC (ex Article 73c(2)) to conclude the agreement.[62] Liberalisation of trade between the EC and Chile and the EC and Mercosur takes place on the basis of separate agreements, concluded by the Community using legal bases relevant to each agreement. So will trade liberalisation between the EC and Mexico, but here the Community has already proposed the use of multiple legal bases besides those governing commercial and development policy to adopt the framework and interim agreements.

As for other treaties, the Court ruled in *Portugal* v. *Council* that it was not necessary to rule on whether Article 133 EC (ex Article 113) was correctly included in the EC-India agreement. Therefore the issue of whether Article 133 was correctly added in any non-preferential development agreement is moot.

An ongoing legal and political issue which has never come before the Court of Justice is the definition of "developing country" for the purpose of Community law. Since partnership or co-operation agreements with non-developing countries usually involve Article 308 EC (ex Article 235) as a joint legal base, they must be adopted unanimously, along with association agreements. Similarly, aid legislation to assist non-developing countries must be adopted on the basis of Article 308, in the absence of any other power in the EC Treaty. In contrast, development treaties and development policy legislation can be adopted by a qualified majority. It thus might matter crucially whether a state is classified as "developing" by the Community, for if it is, an individual Member State cannot veto a treaty with that state or a Community aid programme that could benefit it. Community practice does not seem to indicate any economic consistency: Singapore and other high or middle income states have been classified as "developing", while much poorer ex-Soviet states and somewhat poorer Central European, Middle Eastern and Mediterranean states have been classified as "non-developing", with the exception of the Palestinian authority. The practical result of this distinction has been particularly obvious in arguments over aid legislation, where proposals for assistance to Mediterranean and ex-Soviet states have been delayed by individual Member States and a proposed regulation on aid to Turkey has been blocked for nearly three years. But the politics of labelling a state as "developing" or "non-developing" have prevailed. The exception is the case of the GSP, where for political reasons many states receive preferential tariffs even though the EC does not consider them "developing" for other purposes, notably the ex-Soviet states, Albania and for several years, the rest of Central Europe except Yugoslavia. But legally the GSP is trade policy, rather than development policy, providing some justification for the anomalous practice.

Partnership agreements

11.14 In the absence of a "transversal" clause in the Amsterdam Treaty, the Community's practice of adopting agreements with multiple legal bases will continue, albeit perhaps with the additional inclusion of any services or intellectual property subjects transferred to the sphere of the Common Commercial Policy by use of Article 133(5) EC (ex Article 113(5)). The legality of the partnership agreements thus depends on checking each treaty to find a correspondence between the clauses used by the Community to conclude each treaty and the provisions contained within it.

---

[62] See *ibid.*, para 7.09; see also practice in the partnership agreements with ex-Soviet states and with Mexico, discussed below.

The EC Treaty provisions additional to Article 133 (ex Article 113) used in "transversal" treaties to date have been Articles 57(2), 71 and 80(2) EC (ex Articles 73c(2), 75 and 84(2)) (in all agreements); Articles 44(2) and 47(2) EC (ex Articles 54(2) and 57(2)) (in the PCAs and the treaty with Mexico); Article 308 EC (ex Article 235) (in the PCAs and the treaty with Korea); and Articles 55 and 181 EC (ex Articles 66 and 130y) (in the EC-Mexico agreement). To assess the need for the use of each individual EC Treaty clause, we can either use, or reason in parallel to, the two-step test established by the Court of Justice for development policy agreements in *Portugal* v. *Council*: does each clause in the agreement support the general objective of development policy, and does it contain only general obligations, rather than commit the Community to a specific obligation in a field? We need use the test itself only where the relevant agreement includes a development policy clause; the EC-Mexico agreement is the only transversal agreement to do so to date. When reasoning in parallel to the test, there is no need to repeat the test's first step, since the other legal bases in the EC Treaty are not as general in scope. But we still must apply the second part of the test. If a treaty does not contain a specific obligation in a particular field, but merely a general statement of principles, an obligation to negotiate later, or a consultation mechanism, there is no need to include the relevant EC Treaty article as a legal base to conclude the agreement. Similarly, there is no need to include Article 308 EC (ex Article 235) if the relevant treaty contains no obligations for the Community going beyond those addressed by the specific legal bases used.

Do the partnership agreements to date meet these criteria? First, it is certain that the use of Article 133 EC (ex Article 113) in each agreement is necessary. Although none of the relevant agreements create a free-trade zone between the parties, they do commit the parties to grant each other Most-Favoured Nation (MFN) status under the GATT (General Agreement on Tariffs and Trade), now subsumed by the WTO (World Trade Organisation). Although the point has never been litigated, an obligation to grant Most-Favoured Nation status is a substantive binding commitment that falls within the Community's common commercial policy. This is true even if the Community was already obliged to grant such status to its partner because the latter is a WTO member, because duplication of an identical legal commitment in multiple treaties does not diminish the separate binding obligation under each treaty. In any case, most of the states which have agreed partnership agreements with the Community are not yet WTO members, and so by concluding treaties granting MFN status to these states, the Community has assumed a contractual commitment to provide what it previously only provided autonomously.

As for Article 57(2) EC (ex Article 73c(2)), the 1997 judgment in *Centro-com* established that payments related to goods fall within the scope of the EC's common commercial policy, confirming the EC's long-held practice of including payments provisions within treaties based on Article 133 EC (ex Article 113) alone.[63] Therefore the mere inclusion of payments clauses cannot justify the inclusion of Article 57(2) EC (ex Article 73c(2)); the relevant agreement must also oblige the parties to undertake specific commitments to liberalise payments unrelated to the free movement of goods, and/or liberalise the free movement of capital. It should not be necessary for the obligations to extend to full liberalisation, as long as they extend beyond mere aspirations or exhortations. All the agreements with the ex-Soviet states meet this test, as they require the parties to provide for limited liberalisation of investments. Similarly, the treaty with Mexico requires future negotiations on a capital liberalisation agreement.

---

[63] [1997] E.C.R. I–81. It should also be noted that the GATT has always included balance-of-payments provisions related to trade in goods.

But there appears to be nothing to justify the use of this legal base in the agreement with Korea.

11.15   Article 71 EC (ex Article 75) covers rail, road and inland waterway transport, while Article 80(2) EC (ex Article 84(2)) covers air and sea transport. Again, their inclusion should not be necessary in a partnership agreement unless that agreement contains specific obligations in the relevant area of transport. In the case of all the PCAs with ex-Soviet states, this test is met for both Articles, since each agreement requires the liberalisation of inland waterways and obliges the parties to avoid certain types of shipping concentrations that are also restricted within the Community by internal Community legislation. For Mexico, the inclusion of both Articles as legal bases appears justified because the future services liberalisation agreement that must be negotiated will presumably include transport services. However, while the agreement with Korea contains specific obligations on shipping, there appears to be nothing to justify the use of Article 71 EC (ex Article 75).

Article 44(2) EC (ex Article 54(2)) is included because of the liberalisation of requirements to establish companies in the relevant agreements. Article 47(2) EC (ex Article 57(2)) is included because the relevant provisions affect the Community's legislation on financial services. In both cases, these legal bases clearly appear necessary.

Is there anything left for Article 308 EC (ex Article 235) to cover? In the agreements with the ex-Soviet states and Korea, there certainly is, because the parties have committed themselves to a broad array of economic co-operation measures and have not included a development co-operation clause. The proposal to conclude the agreement with Mexico rightly follows the judgment in *Portugal* v. *Council* and excludes the use of Article 308 EC (ex Article 235), since the agreement includes a legal base for development policy.

Two other legal issues remain. First, does the EC-Mexico agreement have to include a long list of different legal bases, given that it does not impose any current obligations, but merely establishes a framework for future negotiations? It is submitted that it does, because the treaty does not merely suggest that the parties might *wish* to conclude an agreement in specific fields, but *obliges* them to begin interconnected negotiations these fields. This distinguishes the agreement from the India agreement at issue in *Portugal* v. *Council*, where the Court held that the mere possibility in the India agreement for future negotiations on specific issues did not prejudice the character of the treaty as a framework development co-operation agreement. True, the EC-Mexico treaty is also a framework treaty, but the future negotiation of specific agreements is mandatory, rather than permissive.

Secondly, does the inclusion of the competition clauses in the ex-Soviet PCAs and the EC-Mexico main and interim agreements require the inclusion of legal bases specific to competition law? Although the issue has never been litigated, the presumption has always been that competition clauses in the EC's treaties were ancillary to trade matters. Indeed, no general agreement with a third state has ever been concluded with the joint legal base of Articles 83 and 89 EC (ex Articles 87 and/or 94), although treaties specifically addressing competition matters and the Community position in Association Councils adopting competition measures have been adopted with the use of such legal bases. It is arguable that the PCAs with ex-Soviet states, while imposing significant obligations on the parties, do not impose enough obligations to require a separate competition legal base. This view is harder to defend for the EC-Mexico main and interim agreements, both of which give the Joint Council established by the agreements the task of negotiating a detailed substantive competition agreement, similar to the first EC-US competition agreement. Since all other aspects of the EC-Mexico treaties which provide for future negotiations in the Joint Council have accompanying legal bases, why not competition law?

Co-operation Agreements: use of Articles 133 and 308

11.16   The legal restriction upon the use of Article 308 EC (ex Article 235) is well-known and applies whether the Community uses the clause internally or externally: the clause can only be used when no other provision of the EC Treaty provides the Community with power to act. Thus the "entry-level" co-operation agreements which the Community still occasionally adopts, and the PCA with Russia, must be able to meet the "no other provision" test.

The test appears to be met in all cases, with the significant exception of the EC-Russia PCA. The agreements with Albania, FYROM and San Marino oblige the Community to grant MFN status to Albanian goods, implement non-reciprocal trade liberalisation for FYROM goods, and establish a customs union with San Marino. The latter undoubtedly requires the use of Article 133 EC (ex Article 113), and so should the former, as argued above. But the remainder of these agreements do not provide for specific obligations on the part of the parties. Rather they provide only for areas for "co-operation", meaning in practice areas in which the Community will provide aid to assist its partner state. There is no provision of the Treaty allowing for such economic co-operation with non-developing countries, and so Article 308 EC (ex Article 235) has to be used.

The PCA with Russia is another matter. It would seem obvious that since this agreement is not only similar to those partnership agreements with other ex-Soviet states, but also provides for more specific obligations than those agreements do, it should have been adopted as a partnership agreement in more than its title. The parties are obliged to liberalise capital movements; to facilitate establishment by companies; to apply market access principles to maritime transport; to liberalise inland waterways; and to grant MFN status for trade in specified services. Certainly the inclusion of Article 308 EC (ex Article 235) is justified because the agreement also provides for economic co-operation in many fields without specific obligations. But it is not justified to the exclusion of the legal bases that should have been included to govern the specific commitments included in this treaty: Articles 44(2), 47, 57 and 80 EC (ex Articles 54(2), 57, 73c(2) and 84).

Interim agreements

11.17   So far, all interim agreements concluded by the EC have been on the basis of Article 133 EC (ex Article 113) alone, until the proposed EC-Mexico interim agreement (discussed in para 11.13 above). As noted above (para 11.14), the *Centro-com* judgment has now confirmed that the payments clauses in these agreements do indeed fall within the scope of Article 133. Obviously, the substantive clauses liberalising free movement of goods also fall within the scope of Article 133; there is no need for the EC to use Article 37 EC (ex Article 43) to adopt the agricultural concessions in these agreements, since the Court confirmed in Opinion 1/94 that an agreement governing trade in goods as a whole did not need the use of Article 37 in addition to Article 133.[64]

A potential problem is the use of competition clauses in these agreements. The early agreements with the EFTA states and Israel only contained general aspirations to ensure that the parties upheld the principles of free competition and avoided state subsidies which distorted trade. Such exhortations are arguably ancillary to the main object of liberalising trade in goods, and the Court of Justice later confirmed that these clauses did not create substantive obligations on the parties or rights for individuals.[65]

---

[64]   Opinion 1/94 *WTO* [1994] E.C.R. I–5267.
[65]   Joined Cases 89, 104, 114, 116, 117, 125–29/85 *Ahlstrom* v. *Commission* (Woodpulp I) [1988] E.C.R. 5193.

However, the competition clauses in several newer treaties are a different matter. These clauses do not just appear in the main text of the Europe Agreements and EMAs adopted on the basis of Article 310 EC (ex Article 238), but also appear in the Interim Agreements adopted on the basis of Article 133 EC (ex Article 113). They provide for later adoption of detailed rules on private competition and state aids by the Association Council set up by each agreement, which is not problematic. What is problematic is that they provide for detailed obligations in the meantime, which arguably go beyond a merely ancillary status.

CONCLUSION

11.18   The Community's classification of agreements is governed by politics, not law. An examination of the detailed provisions for economic co-operation in the EC-FYROM co-operation agreement, a "third-generation" development co-operation agreement, a partnership agreement, and a recent association agreement, will show that there are many areas in common. Developing countries and the Community sometimes co-operate in specific areas unique to developing countries, or to a particular developing country, but quite frequently co-operate in the same areas which the Community and industrial countries co-operate in. The apparent legal requirement in Article 310 EC (ex Article 238) that association agreements contain reciprocal obligations has been set aside for political convenience when the Community wished to conclude non-reciprocal treaties; a recent upswing in the number of association agreements with reciprocal obligations is due to the Community changing its political mind, not its legal interpretation. Similarly, it seems that association agreements contain as much or as little integration with a third state as the Community wishes to engage in, depending solely on its political will. A particular association agreement might even contain fewer integration obligations than a partnership or co-operation agreement. Partnership agreements and co-operation agreements are both *ad hoc* political creations with no formal existence in the EC Treaty, apart from post-TEU co-operation agreements with developing states. Finally, the EC's definition of "developing" countries for trade and aid purposes is not based on any economic criteria and is moreover internally inconsistent.

It is notable, however, that the institutions and Member States are rarely interested in "rocking the boat". Even though the Parliament has occasionally grumbled that certain treaties should have been submitted for its assent, rather than its consultation, since they establish important "co-operation procedures", it has never resorted to litigation to establish the exact contours of its assent powers pursuant to that provision. The Commission's preference for Community-only agreements and qualified majority voting have never led it to sue the Council to annul the conclusion of an EC trade, partnership, co-operation or association agreement. Before 1995, only one Member State sued to annul an agreement adopted by qualified majority, when it felt that an important feature of its foreign policy (avoiding new ties with Indonesia) might be threatened by Community practice. Third states have been interested largely in the substance of each individual agreement, although they doubtless welcome the political flexibility available to the Community in choosing between different types of agreement without having to worry about altering the substance which can be offered in each category of treaty.

Given this lack of litigation and absence of clear legal rules, the decision over the type and contents of agreement the Community adopts might almost just as well be a foreign policy matter decided under the second pillar. Certainly it is crucially relevant for enforcement of and for individual rights deriving from the agreements that they in fact become an integral part of Community law after their entry into force. But the great latitude the Community institutions and Member States enjoy in practice obviously suits all involved; even the Parliament and Commission can live with the disappointment of their legal hopes in the interest of presenting a unified face to the outside world. As long as most agreements are adopted by unanimity, and the Community institutions and Member States feel constrained to get along when in the company of third states, political discretion seems likely to triumph over legal rules.

B: COMMUNITY COMPETENCE AND MEMBER STATE COMPETENCE

CHAPTER 12

Exclusive, Concurrent and Shared Competence

by

*David O'Keeffe**

12.01 The respective powers of the Community and Member States to conclude international agreements is a story with several twists. The initial disputes between the Community and the Member States which were at the centre of the early case law concerned the question whether the Community had competence to conclude international agreements in certain areas. This was succeeded by a debate as to whether the Member States could continue to participate in international agreements in conjunction with the Community by way of shared competence. Given the affirmative answer to this question for some matters, the most recent case law concerns the exercise of a shared competence by the Community and the Member States. This progression is not linear; the problem of competence continues to be disputed in all its aspects.[1]

The terrain for this evolving controversy has been the source, nature and extent of Community competence.[2] The Court's role in the delineation or demarcation process is evidently crucial.[3] On the one hand, it will be influenced by its traditional purposive teleological interpretation of the Treaty and of the objectives of the Community, while on the other, it may demonstrate a concern for Member States' rights *vis-à-vis* the Community.[4] The Court's recent case law shows a concern not to grant exclusive competence unless this has been expressly sanctioned by the Member States, either in the Treaties or in internal legislation.[5] Where there is doubt, the Court appears to feel that

---

* Professor of European Law and Co-Director, Centre for the Law of the European Union, University College London. With the Editors' agreement, a version of this article was published in (1999) 4 *European Foreign Affairs Review*, under the Title "Community and Member State Competence in External Agreements of the EU".

[1] See the excellent analyses of competence by Macleod, Hendry and Hyett, *The External Relations of the European Communities* (Clarendon Press, 1996) and McGoldrick, *International Relations Law of the European Union* (Longman, 1997). I have largely followed their analytical structure. See also Emiliou, "The allocation of competences between the EC and its Member States in the sphere of external relations" in Emiliou and O'Keeffe (eds.), *The European Union and World Trade Law* (Wiley, 1996).

[2] The term competence is to some extent misleading. The Court itself appears to use the words competence and powers interchangeably. The test for competence should result from an analysis as to whether a proposed measure will attain the objectives of the Treaty, in conformity with the Treaty itself, its procedures and any other rule of Community law: see McGoldrick, *op. cit.* note 1 at p. 43.

[3] The Court appears to distinguish between the source of the Community's competence, express or implied, and the nature of the competence, whether it is exclusively for the Community, or shared between the Community and the Member States: Opinion 2/91 (*ILO*) [1993] E.C.R. I–1061, para. 7.

[4] It is surely not surprising that in the current state of the Community, where Member States remain the key actors, and nearly all Member States contested a total Community exclusive competence to ratify all WTO agreements in Opinion 1/94 (*WTO*) [1994] E.C.R. I–5267, and five Member States raised major internal objections, including those of a national constitutional nature in Opinion 2/94 (*ECHR*) [1996] E.C.R. I–1759, the Court took account of these political and legal realities in both Opinions.

[5] Dutheil de la Rochère, "L'ère des compétences partagées à propos de l'étendue des compétences extérieures de la Communauté européenne", (1995) R.M.C.U.E. 461 at p. 469.

---

the Member States, which have the Treaty-making power, should themselves draw the line between exclusive and shared competence, an approach which defers to the emphasis on conferment of powers in Article 5 (ex Article 3b) as inserted by the TEU.[6]

THE SOURCE OF COMMUNITY COMPETENCE

12.02   The Community acquires competence by the conferring of powers upon it.[7] The source of Community competence is the constitutive Treaties which decide the aims and objectives of the Communities and the procedures to be followed. The Member States have permanently transferred some of their powers to the Community, thereby limiting their sovereignty.[8] Unless powers have been conferred, the presumption is that the Member States are competent.[9]

The three Communities have competence to enter into international agreements and to act internationally. The powers of each Community differ.[10] The original EEC Treaty conferred specific powers in the external field in limited areas. Apart from the provisions on co-operation with international organisations,[11] the EEC had express power to enter into agreements only as regards the common commercial policy[12] and association agreements.[13] Following Treaty amendments, the Community additionally has had competence in monetary or foreign exchange regime matters,[14] research and development,[15] the environment[16] and development co-operation.[17] However, in the first three of these areas, the Community does not have exclusive competence; its competence is shared with that of the Member States. There are also certain powers concerning fostering co-operation at the international level which it has been contended give a Community power to enter into international agreements[18] in the areas of education, vocational training and youth,[19] culture[20] and public health.[21]

---

[6] Dashwood, "The limits of European Community Powers" (1996) 21 E.L.Rev. 113–128 remarks at p. 115 that Art. 5 (ex Art. 3b) as a whole marks a shift in the Community's deep structure of which the Court of Justice has duly taken note.

[7] Art. 5 EC (ex Art. 3b).

[8] Case 6/64 *Costa* v. *ENEL* [1964] E.C.R. 585.

[9] In Opinion 2/94 [1994] E.C.R. I–1759 at paras. 23–24 the Court held that it follows from Art. 5 EC (ex Art. 3b) that the Community only has those powers which have been conferred upon it: "that principle must be respected in both the internal action and the international action of the Community."

[10] Unlike the ECSC and EEC Treaties, the Euratom Treaty explicitly provided in Art. 101(1) that the Community may within the limits of its powers and jurisdiction, enter into obligations by concluding agreements or contracts with a third State, an international organisation or a national of a third State. The phrase "within the limits of its powers and jurisdiction" means within the limits of its external as well as internal powers. Commentators appear to agree that the provision is a statement of the doctrine of parallelism between internal and external competence implying that the Community's external competence applies to all issues covered by its internal competence: Kapteyn and VerLoren van Themaat, *Introduction to the Law of the European Communities* (Kluwer, 1990) (ed. L.W. Gormley), p. 771. As a result, a doctrine of implied powers is unnecessary. As regards the ECSC, the Treaty does not confer a specific Treaty-making power on the Community although it is often contended that such a power exists, and that the doctrine of parallelism applies.

[11] Arts. 302–304 EEC.

[12] Art. 113 EEC.

[13] Art. 238 EEC.

[14] Art. 111(3) EC (ex. Art. 109(3)).

[15] Art. 170 EC (ex Art. 130m).

[16] Art. 174(4) EC (ex Art. 130r(4)).

[17] Art. 181 EC (ex Art. 130y, EC). Art. 71(1)(a) EC (ex Art. 75(1)(a)) allows the adoption of common rules applicable to international transport.

[18] Macleod, Hendry and Hyett, *op. cit.* at p. 47. The question was raised in Case C–268/94 *Portugal* v. *Council* [1996] E.C.R. I–6177, but the Court did not rule on the issue.

[19] Arts. 149(3) and 150(3) EC (ex Arts. 126(3) and 127(3)).

[20] Art. 151(3) EC (ex Art. 128(3)).

[21] Art. 152(3) EC (ex Art. 129(3)). See also Art. 155(3) EC (ex Art. 129c(3)) concerning trans-European networks.

However, the Treaty provisions concerning external relations and in particular international treaty-making are not complete and a reliance on the unwritten authority for foreign relations has been inevitable although it sits uneasily with the thrust of Article 5 (ex Article 3b) of the Treaty. Indeed it may be this strain, together with political considerations, which has led the Court in recent case law to restrict the move to exclusive Community competence.[22]

In case law, the Court based the capacity of the Community to enter into binding agreements with other subjects of international law over the whole field of objectives set out in Part One of the Treaty, on Article 281 EC (ex Article 210) which confers legal personality on the Community.[23] To determine whether the Community has the competence to enter into an agreement depends on the question whether a Treaty provision expressly or impliedly confers this power, having regard to the whole scheme of the Treaty, no less than to its substantive provisions. The Court has held that authority to enter into international agreements may not only arise from an express conferment by the Treaty but may also flow implicitly from its provisions.[24] Such authority may also result from other provisions of the Treaty and measures adopted by the Community institutions within the framework of the Treaty provisions or the acts of accession.[25] The Court has found that whenever Community law has created powers within its internal system for the institutions of the Community for the purpose of achieving a specific objective, the Community has authority to enter into the international commitments necessary for the attainment of that objective, even in the absence of an express provision in that connection.[26]

EXCLUSIVE COMPETENCE

12.03 Once the existence of Community competence is established, the pivotal question concerns the nature of Community competence, that is whether it is exclusive or is shared with the Member States. Where competence has been transferred completely by the Member States, the Community competence is exclusive[27] and there is no residual continuing concurrent Member State competence.[28] Alternatively, shared competence describes the situation where both the Community and the Member States retain power to act and where the Community shares powers in a given area with the Member States and the external agreements of the Community need to take this into account.

Exclusive competence may be derived from (i) express provisions of the Treaty or the Acts of Accession, (ii) the scope of internal measures adopted by the Community institutions, (iii) express provisions in internal Community measures, and (iv) where internal powers could only be effectively exercised at the same time as external powers.[29]

---

[22] See Dashwood, *op. cit* at pp. 115–6.
[23] Case 22/70 *Commission* v. *Council (AETR)* [1971] E.C.R. 263 at 274.
[24] Opinion 1/76 (*European laying-up fund for inland waterway vessels*) [1977] E.C.R. 741 at para. 3. Implied powers arise principally where measures have been adopted by the Community on the basis of an internal power, where power to legislate exists but has not been exercised or where a power to act is implicit in an article of the Treaty conferring an internal power. There is also the competence based on general law-making provisions including Arts. 94, 95 or 308 EC (ex Arts 100, 100a or 235).
[25] Joined Cases 3, 4 and 6/76 *Kramer* [1976] E.C.R. 1279 at para. 20.
[26] Opinion 1/76 [1977] E.C.R. 741 at para. 3.
[27] See *AETR*, [1971] E.C.R. 263 at para. 17; Opinion 1/75 (*Local Cost Standard*) [1975] E.C.R. 1355 at 1364; Case 804/79 *Commission* v. *U.K.* [1981] E.C.R. 1045 at paras 17, 18, 20.
[28] Opinion 1/75 [1975] E.C.R. 1355 at p. 1364; Opinion 2/91 [1993] E.C.R. I–1061 at para. 8.
[29] I follow here the typology used by Macleod, Hendry and Hyett and by McGoldrick, *op. cit.* at p. 56 *et seq.* and p. 68 *et seq.* respectively.

Express provisions of the Treaty

12.04   The Community has exclusive competence derived from express provisions of the Treaty or the Acts of Accession. The Court has held that the Community has exclusive external competence in the areas of common commercial policy[30] and the common fisheries policy.[31] The extent of these fields is critical: if a particular issue is deemed to fall within the scope of the common commercial policy, there will be exclusive Community competence; conversely, where a topic falls outside that scope, then competence may remain shared with the Member States.[32]

The Court has justified the attribution of exclusive competence in relation to Article 133 EC (ex Article 113) by noting that the common commercial policy envisaged by that article was conceived in the context of the operation of the common market, for the defence of the common interests of the Community within which the particular interests of the Member States must endeavour to adapt to each other. Departing from this notion of common interests, the Member States were therefore no longer free to act concurrently to secure their own interests. The provisions of Article 133 EC (ex Article 113) and former Article 114 EC (repealed by the Treaty of Amsterdam) on the conclusion of international agreements clearly showed that the exercise of concurrent powers by the Member States and the Community was impossible. Community competence was therefore exclusive.[33]

The Court's view on the CCP was echoed in its judgment on the establishment of the common fisheries policy.[34] Internal legislation had been taken by the Community on the basis of a Treaty power. Effective and equitable conservation measures of the biological resources of the seas could only be taken at the international level.

Scope of internal meaures

12.05   The Community may also acquire exclusive competence as a result of the scope of internal measures adopted by the Community institutions but which do not confer an express power on the Community to enter into international agreements. Under the *AETR* doctrine,

> "each time the Community, with a view to implementing a common policy envisaged by the Treaty, adopts provisions laying down common rules, whatever form these may take, the Member States no longer have the right, acting individually or even collectively, to undertake obligations with third countries which affect those rules. As and when such common rules come into being, the Community alone is in a position to assume and carry out contractual obligations towards third countries affecting the whole sphere of application of the Community legal system."[35]

The rationale for the doctrine is to avoid unilateral or collective action by Member States which would conflict with internal Community measures. In that sense this judge-made principle is no more than an application of the principle of loyalty enshrined in Article 10 EC (ex Article 5). It is an extended reading of the principle of the supremacy of the Community legal order over national law, as it would be absurd if

---

[30] Opinion 1/75 [1975] E.C.R. 1355; Opinion 1/94 [1994] E.C.R. I–5267.
[31] Case 804/79 *Commission* v. *UK* [1981] E.C.R. 1045.
[32] See for example Opinion 1/94 [1994] E.C.R. I–5267, and Opinion 2/92 (*OECD*) [1995] E.C.R. I–525.
[33] Opinion 1/75 [1975] E.C.R. 1355 at p. 1364.
[34] Case 804/79 *Commission* v. *UK* [1981] E.C.R. 1045.
[35] *AETR* [1971] E.C.R. 263 at paras. 17–18.

the prohibition on the adoption of national measures which conflicted with Community law should apply only to internal national legislation and not also to international commitments entered into by Member States. As the Court held in *AETR*, "with regard to the implementation of the provisions of the Treaty the system of internal Community measures may not therefore be separated from that of external relations."[36] However the principle laid down in *AETR* does go very far. Not surprisingly the ruling was controversial at the time it was handed down.[37] The extent of the Court's ruling has never been clear and has been the subject of much debate. Subsequent case law has further delineated the doctrine which may be summarised as follows.

Internal rules exhaustive

12.06 Where internal Community rules completely or exhaustively regulate a particular area, the Member States are therefore precluded from legislating in the area. At the internal level, this is described as pre-emption; on the external level, the Community measures give rise to exclusive Community competence externally for that area. In Opinion 1/94, the Court held that:

> "even in the absence of any express provision authorising its institutions to negotiate with non-member countries, where the Community has achieved *complete harmonisation* of the rules governing access to a self-employed activity, because the common rules thus adopted could be affected within the meaning of the *AETR* judgment if the Member States retained freedom to negotiate with non-Member countries."[38]

However, the determination whether an area has been completely or exhaustively occupied by the Community is itself subject to interpretation. The definition of the relevant field is critical. Conventional analysis would suggest that regard must be had to the legal base of the internal Community measure or measures, the reasons for adoption as set out in the preamble, and the subject-matter and scope of the measures themselves. Comparison with the international commitment sought to be adopted then follows. Thus in Opinion 2/92 *(OECD)*, the Court found that internal Community measures had been adopted on the basis of Articles 47(2), 71, 80 and 95 EC (ex Art. 57(2), 75, 84 and 100a) and this could in principle serve as a basis for an exclusive external competence. However, the Court noted that it was undisputed that those measures do not cover all the fields of activity to which the OECD decision at issue related. Thus whereas the Community was competent to participate in the OECD Decision, that competence did not cover *all* the matters to which the Decision related. Thus it did not have exclusive competence in the areas where internal common rules had not been adopted.[39]

---

[36] *ibid.*, at para. 19.
[37] Stein, "External relations of the European Community: Structure and process", vol. 1, *Academy of European Law* (1990), pp. 115–188 at p. 160.
[38] Opinion 1/94 [1994] E.C.R. I–5267 at para. 96 (emphasis added). Presumably this statement was not designed to exclude the *AETR* test of an alteration of scope, reiterated in Opinion 2/91 [1993] E.C.R. I–1061.
[39] It will be noted in the above analysis that the *AETR* Court (and the Court in Opinion 1/94) referred to the adoption of "common rules". This expression appears occasionally in the Treaty (Arts. 34(2)(a), 71(1)(a) (ex Arts. 40(2)(a), 75(1)(a)), but it does not appear to have a specific meaning. In the wake of the *AETR* judgment, it has been suggested that the phrase common rules has been given a substantive meaning: McGoldrick, *op. cit.* at p. 73. On common rules, see Kapteyn and Verloren van Themaat, *op. cit.* at p. 774. In Opinion 2/91, the Court used the expression "Community rules".

Internal rules not complete or exhaustive

12.07   The *AETR* doctrine also applies where Community legislation is not complete or exhaustive. In Opinion 2/91, the Court found that the Community enjoyed an internal legislative competence in the area of social policy. Consequently, the ILO Convention at issue in the Opinion, whose subject-matter coincided moreover with that of several directives adopted under Article 137 (ex Article 118a) of the Treaty, fell within the Community's area of competence. In order to determine whether this competence was exclusive in nature, the Court first pointed out that the provisions of the Convention were not of such a kind as to affect rules adopted pursuant to Article 137. The Court found that Part III of the Convention was concerned with an area which:

> "is already covered *to a large extent* by Community rules progressively adopted since 1967 with a view to achieving an ever greater degree of harmonisation and designed, on the one hand to remove barriers to trade resulting from differences in legislation from one Member State to another and, on the other hand, to provide, at the same time, protection for human health and the environment."[40]

The Court cited directives based on Articles 94 and 95 (ex Articles 100 and 100a). The Court concluded that the commitments arising from Part III of the Convention, falling within the area of the directives mentioned, were "of such a kind as to affect the Community rules laid down in those directives and that consequently Member States cannot undertake such commitments outside the framework of the Community institutions".[41]

From Opinion 2/91, one can thus deduce that the test to be applied in determining whether the Community's competence is exclusive is first to ascertain whether there are Community rules intended to establish common standards and, in the affirmative, second, to determine whether the extent of those rules is such that action by the Member States would affect them or alter their scope. It should be noted that in Opinion 2/91, the Court accepted that although the provisions of Part III of the Convention which it cited were wider than those of the directives, and the directives contained some provisions which were more extensive than those of the Convention, there was no contradiction between these provisions of the Convention and the directives. What appeared to count for the Court was the evidence of a long-standing Community effort going back for nearly a quarter of a century to establish common rules and the *extent* of those rules. It would seem to follow that the possibility of exclusive Community competence will increase if Community internal legislation is extensive in a given area, thus reducing the leeway for Member State action.

However, the extent of the Community action required to lead to exclusive external competence is not clear. In dealing with GATS in Opinion 1/94, the Court noted that the Community could acquire exclusive external competence in the spheres covered by internal legislative acts where the Community has achieved *complete harmonisation* of the rules governing access to a self-employed activity because the common rules thus adopted could be affected within the meaning of the *AETR* judgment if the Member States retained freedom to negotiate with non-Member countries.[42] This was not, however, the case in all service sectors and the Court concluded that the competence to conclude GATS was shared between the Community and the Member States. Gaja points out that this reference in Opinion 1/94 to complete harmonisation is a more

---

[40] Opinion 2/91 [1993] E.C.R. I–1061 at para. 25 (emphasis added).
[41] *ibid.*, at para. 26.
[42] Opinion 1/94 [1994] E.C.R. I–5267 at para. 96.

rigorous requirement for the existence of an exclusive competence than as regards the Court's statement in Opinion 2/91.[43]

Moreover, in dealing with TRIPs in Opinion 1/94, the Court considered whether the subordinate legislative acts adopted in the Community context could be affected within the meaning of the *AETR* judgment if the Member States were to participate in the conclusion of TRIPs. The Court noted here that the harmonisation achieved within the Community in certain areas covered by TRIPs was *only partial* and that in other areas no harmonisation had been envisaged, and the Community had exercised its powers in the field of the enforcement of intellectual property rights in only one area. Thus whereas when dealing with GATS the Court referred to the absence of a complete harmonisation, in dealing with TRIPs it referred to "only partial harmonisation". However it is clear from the Opinion that at any rate the mere existence of Community legislation will not necessarily lead to exclusive Community external competence; the Member States only lose their right to enter into obligations with non-member countries as and when common rules which could be affected by these obligations come into being. The apparent insistence on exhaustive coverage in Opinion 1/94 seems to find some confirmation in Opinion 2/92, but contrasts with the test set out in Opinion 2/91. As the first two Opinions are subsequent to Opinion 2/91, it may be that the test contained therein has now been implicitly over-ruled.

Internal rules set minimum standards

12.08 Where Community legislation sets minimum standards or requirements, Member States may conclude international agreements which set higher standards. This would seem to follow from Opinion 2/91.[44] The fact that it is sometimes difficult to determine whether a specific international convention or internal Community act establishes a higher standard, with consequent legislative difficulties, is also not a reason to attribute exclusive Community competence.[45]

The question of minimum standards or requirements is of particular difficulty, all the more given the Community trend towards harmonisation on the basis of minimum standards, allowing higher standards to be adopted by Member States in some cases, as in the case of Article 138(3) EC (ex Article 118a(3)).[46] In Opinion 2/91 (*ILO*), the Court had to deal *inter alia* with certain health and safety directives adopted under Article 138 EC (ex Article 118a). As noted above, the Court took the view that the field covered by the ILO Convention at issue, the subject-matter of which coincided with that of several directives adopted under Article 138, fell within the Community's area of competence. However the Court decided that there was no exclusive Community external competence on this ground as the provisions of the Convention were not of such a kind as to affect rules adopted pursuant to Article 138 EC. The Court explained in the Opinion that if the Community adopted rules which were *less stringent* than those set out in an ILO Convention, the Member States could rely on Article 138(3) to adopt more stringent measures for the protection of working conditions or apply for that purpose the provisions of the relevant ILO convention. If on the other hand, the Community decided to adopt *more stringent* measures than those provided for under an ILO Convention, there was nothing to prevent the full application of the more stringent Community rules as the ILO Constitution specifically allowed states to

---

[43] Gaja, *Introduzione al diritto comunitario* (Edizioni Laterza, 1996) at p. 144.
[44] Opinion 2/91 [1993] E.C.R. I–1061 at paras. 18–21.
[45] *ibid.*, at para. 20
[46] For example, in the field of consumer protection under Art. 153 EC (ex Art. 129a) or in the environmental field under Art. 176 EC (Art. 130t).

adopt more stringent measures than those provided under ILO conventions or recommendations.

Given the increasing trend in Community policy to set minimum standards, the issues faced in Opinion 2/91 are likely to recur. To ensure shared competence, Member States would appear to have to show that any international convention they enter into should contain a clause such as that found in the ILO Constitution which allowed for higher standards and a specific recognition that the international convention is setting only minimum requirements. Failing that, under the reasoning adopted by the Court in Opinion 2/91, it would appear likely that the provisions of the international convention might be held by the Court to affect the Community rules within the meaning of the *AETR* principle as otherwise it might be found that Member States would have no room for manoeuvre in the event that the Community decided to adopt higher standards. Moreover, adhesion to an international convention of this type would only appear to be possible where the introduction of higher standards by Member States is specifically envisaged by Community law as was the case under Article 138(3).

The result reached by the Court in Opinion 2/91 reflected the internal allocation of competences within the Community legal order. Where common rules are in fact minimum requirements or standards, and recognise this explicitly, leaving to Member States the possibility to maintain or introduce more stringent measures, there appears to be no reason why the existence of the common rules should give rise to an exclusive external Community competence at the expense of the Member States who otherwise have a certain freedom to act internally. The only question, from the point of view of the Community interest, is that Member States' international commitments to certain standards should not be an obstacle to the adoption of more stringent measures by the Community.

Rules adopted with a view to implementing a common policy

12.09   The *AETR* principle appeared to be confined to rules adopted with a view to implementing a common policy. However, the Court has expanded the reach of the ruling by holding in Opinion 2/91 that the *AETR* doctrine is not confined to instances where the Community has adopted rules within the framework of a common policy. The obligation of loyalty under Article 10 EC (ex Article 5) applies to all the areas corresponding to the objectives of the Treaty and the Community's tasks and the objectives of the Treaty would also be compromised if Member States were able to enter into international commitments containing rules capable of affecting Community rules already adopted in areas falling outside common policies or of altering their scope.[47] This extremely broad statement applies therefore to all areas of Community activity where there are Community rules within the meaning of Opinion 2/91, subject obviously to the exceptions set out in Opinion 1/94 concerning GATS and TRIPs but which must be of general application.

Contradiction between Community rules and proposed international convention

12.10   The Court's approach to exclusive Community competence does not appear to require a contradiction between the Community rules and a proposed international convention to be signed by the Member States. As mentioned above in relation to Opinion 2/91, the Court did not find any contradiction as such between the

---

[47] Opinion 2/91 [1993] E.C.R. I–1061 at paras. 11–12.

provisions of the Convention at issue there and the directives to which it referred. Nevertheless it seems from its Opinion that it considered that the mere fact of the existence of the Community rules at issue was sufficient to prevent the adoption of the Convention by the Member States (without prejudice to the eventual ruling). The Court simply found that the commitments arising from the Convention were "of such a kind as to affect the Community rules" at issue and that consequently Member States could not undertake such commitments outside the framework of the Community institutions.[48] Thus, no contradiction between the Convention and the Community rules was necessary to found exclusive Community competence.

The justification for this approach appears to be a very faithful reading of *AETR* in that the Court evidently considers that the mere conclusion of an international agreement by Member States could "affect" the Community rules or alter their scope. This absolutist position which is founded on highly theoretical bases could be justified by the desire not to see barriers being erected towards the gradual evolution of Community rules. It precludes Member State competence in such areas. In this sense, this approach is very similar to that used by the Court in *Simmenthal* concerning the adoption of national legislation, where it held that the principle of the precedence of Community law precluded the valid adoption of new national legislative measures to the extent that they would be incompatible with Community provisions.[49]

One presumes that it is still theoretically possible for the Court to hold in the future that there may be some instances where certain international commitments would not affect common Community rules or alter their scope.[50] This may be a key to understanding the Court's approach in the *Bangladesh*[51] and *EDF*[52] cases. However, the Court's ruling in Opinion 2/91 *(ILO)* appears to assume that an effect on common rules is well-nigh inevitable.

Internal rules repealed

12.11 One point which remains to be clarified is whether the *AETR* doctrine carries over even in the event of Community internal rules being repealed. One could argue that the power to regulate remains with the Community and Member States should not be able to regulate in the field concerned as this might affect potential Community action in the field. However, the better view appears to be that Member States may re-acquire competence where Community rules no longer regulate an area. This would seem to be inevitable to prevent a legal vacuum, and also in accordance with the underlying reasons which may have led to repeal.

Express provisions in internal Community measures

12.12 Community acts frequently confer power on the Community to enter into

[48] *ibid.*, at para. 26.
[49] Case 106/77 *Simmenthal* [1978] E.C.R. 629 at para. 17.
[50] McGoldrick, *op. cit.* at p. 75 gives two examples where this may occur: where Member States purported to extend the territorial application of the EC rules or where the international obligations assumed by them would affect the common rules in a beneficial way. It is not necessarily the case that the Court would take this view; in the first example, the territorial scope of Community law is itself a matter for Community law which cannot be altered unilaterally by the Member States, and in the second, any effect on Community rules, benign or not, seems to be outlawed by the Court in Opinion 2/91. However his point is taken to the extent that there may in the future be examples of a benign effect on common rules which may lead the Court to relax its position in very special cases.
[51] Joined Cases C–181/91 and C–249/91, *European Parliament* v. *Council and Commission* [1993] E.C.R. I–3685.
[52] Case C–316/91 *Parliament* v. *Council* [1994] E.C.R. I–625.

agreements with third countries. In Opinion 1/94, the Court held that "whenever the Community has included in its internal legislative acts provisions relating to the treatment of nationals of non-member countries or expressly conferred on its institutions powers to negotiate with non-member countries, it acquires exclusive external competence in the spheres covered by those acts".[53] Clearly any Community act must respect and be subordinate to the terms of the Treaty. Thus, this express conferment of competence may not interfere with the power otherwise reserved to the Member States by the Treaty. Moreover, it does not immediately follow that all competence conferred on the Community in this way is exclusive; the Community act must be examined to determined whether this is effectively the case.

Internal and external powers exercised together

12.13   The Community may have exclusive external competence even if no common rules have been adopted and where the power being exercised does not, as such, give rise to exclusive Community competence. Thus the external competence based on the Community's internal powers may be exercised, and thereby become exclusive, without any internal legislation having first been adopted. However, this will relate to a situation where the conclusion of an international agreement is necessary in order to achieve Treaty objectives which cannot be obtained by the adoption of autonomous rules.[54]

This particular and difficult circumstance is well illustrated by Opinion 1/76 concerning the Community's participation in an agreement for the control of river traffic on the Rhine and Moselle. The Community had internal competence to regulate inland waterway traffic by virtue of its Treaty powers concerning transport, but had not exercised this competence. As a non-Member State, Switzerland, also participated in the arrangement, a Community measure would not have been sufficient or appropriate and it was thus necessary to bring it into the scheme by means of an international agreement. The question which arose was whether the Community could conclude the agreement on the basis of its internal powers concerning transport without, however, having exercised those powers internally. In Opinion 1/76, the Court referred to the principle established in *Kramer*[55] whereby "authority to enter into international commitments may not only arise from an express attribution by the Treaty but equally may flow implicitly from its provisions". The Court held that this authority was not limited to cases in which internal power had already been used in order to adopt measures which come within the attainment of common policies. It continued:

> "Although the internal Community measures are only adopted when the international agreement is concluded and made enforceable, as is envisaged in the present case by the proposal for a regulation to be submitted to the Council by the Commission, the power to bind the Community *vis-à-vis* third countries nevertheless flows by implication from the provisions of the Treaty creating the internal power and in so far as the participation of the Community in the international agreement is, as here, necessary for the attainment of one of the objectives of the Community."[56]

As a result of Opinion 1/76, the impression was given that there was a parallelism

---

[53] Opinion 1/94 [1994] E.C.R. I–5267 at para. 95.
[54] ibid., at para. 85; Opinion 2/92 [1995] E.C.R. I–525 at para. 32.
[55] [1976] E.C.R. 1279.
[56] Opinion 1/76 [1977] E.C.R. 741 at para. 4.

between the internal and external competence of the Community although the Court had not specifically so ruled. To observers familiar with the developments from *AETR* to *Kramer*, this seemed the logical consequence of Opinion 1/76. If in *AETR* the Court had held that the exercise of internal legislative power could bring about a transfer of treaty-making power from the Member States to the Community, in *Kramer* the Court appeared to have taken the position that the mere existence of internal power automatically gives rise to parallel external power, but only in wholly exceptional situations. Opinion 1/76 thus appeared the culmination in a series of cases aimed at enhancing the Community's external relations powers. Moreover, the parallelism that was discerned in Opinion 1/76 reflected the choice in the EURATOM Treaty and had an appealing logic for a Community which was an international actor with international legal personality.

In Opinion 1/94, however, the Court rejected this broad interpretation of Opinion 1/76. The Commission, relying on Opinion 1/76, argued that the Community's participation in GATS was necessary for the attainment of one of the objectives of the Community, *i.e.* to ensure the coherence of the internal market and because the Community could not be inactive as regards international trade and also, that the Community's exclusive external competence was not limited to cases in which use had already been made of internal powers to adopt measures for the attainment of common policies. The Court rejected the application of Opinion 1/76 to GATS. According to the Court, Opinion 1/76 concerned a situation where the objective of rationalisation of the inland waterways sector concerned could not be achieved by autonomous common rules as that objective could not be achieved without the participation of Switzerland through an international agreement. The Court gave an example of the need for exclusive Community competence in the case of conservation of resources of the seas. There similar considerations applied as regards the effectiveness of external measures over internal measures given the need to bind third countries. It was therefore understandable that external powers may be exercised and thus become exclusive without any internal legislation having first been adopted. This was not the case, however, as regards services. The attainment of freedom of establishment and freedom to provide services for nationals of the Member States was not inextricably linked to the treatment to be afforded in the Community to nationals of non-member countries or in non-member countries to nationals of Member States of the Community. The Commission's interpretation of Opinion 1/76 was thus rejected. The Court also rejected the application of Opinion 1/76 to TRIPs, based on similar arguments to those regarding services. According to the Court, "unification or harmonisation of intellectual property rights in the Community context does not necessarily have to be accompanied by agreements with non-member countries in order to be effective".[57]

12.14 The Court similarly held in Opinion 2/92 that although it was true that the external competence based on the Community's internal powers may be exercised and may thus become exclusive, without any internal legislation having been adopted (Opinion 1/76), "this relates to a situation where the conclusion of an international agreement is necessary in order to achieve Treaty objectives which cannot be attained by the adoption of autonomous rules (see Opinion 1/94, paragraph 86)."[58]

Thus whereas in Opinion 1/76, the Community could exercise external powers without internal common rules having been adopted, giving rise to exclusive competence, provided that the internal power existed, in both Opinion 1/94 and

---

[57] Opinion 1/94 [1994] E.C.R. I–5267 at para. 100.
[58] Opinion 2/92 [1995] E.C.R. I–525 at para. 32.

Opinion 2/92, the Court stressed that this will only arise where the conclusion of an international agreement is necessary if a Treaty objective cannot be achieved by the establishment of common autonomous rules (although in Opinion 2/91, the Court appeared to refine this somewhat by referring to Community law powers within its internal system created "for the purpose of achieving a *specific* objective").[59] As a result of the Court's case law in Opinion 1/94 and Opinion 2/92, one can conclude that the Community may acquire exclusive external competence on the basis of Opinion 1/76 where the participation of a non-member country or countries is "necessary" to enable the Community to fulfil one of its objectives and specific Treaty objectives cannot be achieved by internal Community legislation as they would not be binding on the non-member country or countries.[60] If an alternative exists to achieve the specific Treaty objective, then it is doubtful if the Community would have exclusive external competence.[61] In short, the scope of Opinion 1/76 would appear to have been reduced to instances which closely resemble the factual and legal situation in that case.[62]

If this interpretation is correct, Opinion 1/76 would no longer appear to be the basis for exclusive external competence in the far-reaching sense which had been attributed to it. If this is so, this could create some theoretical difficulty for the Community institutions, but having regard to the practice, it does not appear to have significant consequences.[63]

Competence based on general law-making provisions

12.15   Article 308 (ex Article 235) of the EC Treaty provides for a law-making power if action by the Community is necessary to attain, in the course of the operation of the common market, one of the objectives of the Treaty and the latter has not provided the necessary powers.[64] Specific harmonisation powers exist with respect to the common market and internal market respectively.[65]

The Court held in *AETR* that Article 308 also applies in the field of external relations. The decision to take measures under Article 308 is up to the discretion of the

---

[59]   Opinion 2/91 [1993] E.C.R. I–1061 at para. 7 (emphasis added).

[60]   The requirement of necessity can also be discerned in *Kramer* [1976] E.C.R. 1279 at paras. 30–33. Gaja, *op. cit.* at pp. 145–6, points out that the requirement of necessity to realise one of the objectives of the Community is not very clear as it seems to make the existence of the competence depend on an evaluation of the content of the agreement and a comparison of the effects deriving from the conclusion of the Agreement on the part of the Community and of the effects which would result instead from a failure to conclude or from an eventual conclusion on the part of the Member States.

[61]   Opinion 1/94 [1994] E.C.R. I–5267 at para. 85; Opinion 2/92 [1995] E.C.R. I–525 at para. 32.

[62]   McGoldrick *op. cit.* at p. 61, argues that an alternative reading of Opinion 1/94 is that the necessity of third State participation is relevant only to the question of exclusive Community competence. In this case, the general Opinion 1/76 doctrine would remain and the Community would have competence to conclude international agreements even in the absence of internal measures, if Community participation is necessary for the attainment of one of the specific objectives of the Community. This competence would not be exclusive; until the competence was exercised, the Member States would remain competent to enter into international agreements.

[63]   Gaja, *op. cit.* at p. 146, states that no such agreement has been adopted, not even the one which was the subject-matter of Opinion 1/76. He notes that the Member States have never openly contested the existence of this shared competence, but have never given the Community institutions the opportunity to exercise it. It is submitted that the result of the interpretation of Opinion 1/76 in Opinion 1/94 and Opinion 2/92 suggested in the text could in any event be tempered by the acquisition of external exclusive competence through the doctrine of implied powers in so far as internal measures are adopted which could be affected by Member State obligations with third countries, and by the conferment by Treaty amendments of express external powers.

[64]   Provisions similar to Art. 308 (ex Art. 235) exist for the ECSC and EURATOM: Art. 95 ECSC and Art. 203 EURATOM.

[65]   Arts. 94 and 95 EC (ex Arts. 100 and 100a).

Council. It is a tightly scrutinised power which may only be used in order to attain one of the objectives of the Community where no other provision of the Treaty gives the Community institutions the necessary powers to adopt the measure in question[66] and may not go beyond the scope of the Treaty.[67] Obviously measures taken under the general law-making power may not conflict with specific Treaty provisions as they relate to internal or external competence.

Exclusive external competence may arise under a general law-making power of this type as follows. If internal powers are effectively exercised and internal measures adopted on the basis of the general law-making power, this will give rise to exclusive external competence as discussed above. The position is more complex where no internal measures have been taken. In Opinion 1/94, reiterated in Opinion 2/92, the Court excluded that Article 308 could by itself vest exclusive competence in the Community at international level. Save with regard to the exception arising from Opinion 1/76 where internal powers can only be effectively exercised at the same time as external powers, "internal competence can give rise to exclusive external competence only if it is exercised."[68]

This narrow interpretation seems to be justified as internal legislation under Article 308 should be regarded as an extraordinary measure. At the external level, an uninhibited use of Article 308 to provide for exclusive external competence even where no effective internal measure was taken would be detrimental to the terms of the transfer of sovereignty by the Member States. Despite the strict scrutiny to which Article 308 is subject as regards necessity and the aims of the Community, it nevertheless has a very wide scope and its acceptance as the basis for exclusive Community competence in the absence of internal measures could give rise to an extensive exclusive Community competence of unpredictable range. It therefore seems appropriate that its use as a basis for exclusive Community competence should be tempered by the requirement that there must first be internal measures adopted on the basis of the law-making powers.

The Court's concern for a cautious use of Article 308 is evident in Opinion 2/94 *(ECHR)* where the Court held that the provision could not "serve as a basis for widening the scope of Community powers beyond the general framework created by the provisions of the Treaty as a whole and, in particular, by those that define the tasks and the activities of the Community."[69]

As regards the use of Article 95 EC (ex Article 100a), the Court in Opinion 1/94 held that it was undeniable that where harmonising measures have been exercised, the harmonisation measures thus adopted may limit, or even remove, the freedom for the Member States to negotiate with non-member countries. "However an internal power to harmonise which has not been exercised in a specific field cannot confer exclusive competence in that field on the Community."[70]

The general law-making articles have been used as the basis for the conclusion of agreements in areas in which there was a Community objective but where there were no internal measures as in the case of environmental protection prior to the adoption of the Single European Act and development co-operation prior to the adoption of the Treaty on European Union. It seems to follow from the Court's rulings in Opinion 1/94

---

[66] Joined Cases C–51/89, C–90/89 and C–94/89 *United Kingdom* v. *Council* [1991] E.C.R. I–2757, para. 6; Opinion 2/92 [1995] E.C.R. I–525 at para. 36.
[67] Opinion 2/94 *(ECHR)* [1996] E.C.R. I–1759.
[68] Opinion 1/94 [1994] E.C.R. I–5267 at para 89; Opinion 2/92 [1995] E.C.R. I–525 at para 36.
[69] Opinion 2/94 [1996] E.C.R. I–1759 at para. 30.
[70] Opinion 1/94 [1994] E.C.R. I–5267 at para. 88.

and Opinion 2/92 that this should no longer be the case. The Community's competence will be exclusive if the internal measures adopted constitute common rules.[71]

The effect of exclusive competence

12.16   Where the Community has exclusive competence for a given area, the Member States may no longer act in that area. Where there is express exclusive competence deriving from the Treaty or Act of Accession, the Court has recognised that the exercise of such competence excludes any concurrent competence on the part of the Member States, internally and internationally.[72] According to the Court in *AETR*, "to the extent to which Community rules are promulgated for the attainment of the objectives of the Treaty, the Member States cannot, outside the framework of the Community institutions, assume obligations which might affect those rules or alter their scope."[73] Moreover, in Opinion 1/75, the Court held that "it cannot . . . be accepted that in a field such as that governed by the Understanding in question . . . the Member States should exercise a power concurrent to that of the Community, in the Community sphere and in the international sphere . . . the exercise of concurrent powers by the Member States and the Community in this matter is impossible."[74]

The justification for this is that following the transfer of powers in specific areas to the Community by the Member States, the Member States should no longer remain free to enter into international agreements which would affect measures adopted by the Community or alter their scope. Where there is exclusive competence, the Member States may not in relations with third countries, adopt positions which differ from those which the Community intends to adopt. The Court has held that this "would thereby distort the institutional framework, call into question the mutual trust within the Community and prevent the latter from fulfilling its task in the defence of the common interest."[75]

A further consequence of exclusive consequence is that the Community is able to exercise its powers freely unconstrained by the Member States.[76] The Member States must use all means at their disposal in order to ensure the participation of the Community in such agreements.[77] However, there are cases where the Community has exclusive competence but nevertheless Member State action is possible both internally and externally. This has been accepted by the Court in certain cases where the Member States act on behalf of the Community in the Community interest.[78] Presumably even if the Community has exclusive competence but the international agreement at issue only provides for conclusion by states, the Community could conclude it through the medium of the Member States.

SHARED COMPETENCE

12.17   Community competence is not necessarily exclusive. Some Treaty pro-

---

[71] It should be noted, however, that according to the recent Council practice the Community normally participates in an international agreement only where there are internal rules covering the subject-matter of the agreement.
[72] Opinion 2/91 [1993] E.C.R. I–1061 at para. 8 referring to Art. 133 (ex Art. 113) (Opinion 1/75, *Donckerwolcke*) and Art. 102 of the Act of Accession (Case C–804/79 *Commission* v. *U.K.* [1981] E.C.R. 1045).
[73] *AETR* [1971] E.C.R. 263 at para. 22.
[74] Opinion 1/75 [1975] E.C.R. 1355 at p. 1364.
[75] *ibid.*
[76] Ruling 1/78 [1978] E.C.R. 2151 at para. 32.
[77] *Kramer* [1976] E.C.R. 1279 at paras 44–45.
[78] *Kramer* [1976] E.C.R. 1279 at paras 39–45; Case 804/79 *Commission* v. *U.K.* [1981] E.C.R. 1045. See Macleod, *op. cit.* at pp. 63, 236–7.

visions now provide expressly for shared competence. In other cases, the Member States generally have concurrent competence until Community competence is exercised and the exercise of parallel competence could affect the Community rules or alter their scope. The Member States clearly favour shared competence, and this has been the subject of the most recent case law. The Court's relatively relaxed approach has ensured that the complex balance between the Community and its Member States is ensured.

Under the Treaty on European Union, certain Treaty provisions specify that without prejudice to Community competence and Community agreements the Member States may negotiate in international bodies and conclude international agreements.[79] Examples come in Article 111(5) (ex Article 109(5)) on monetary matters, Article 174 (ex Article 130r(4)) in the case of the environment and Article 181 (ex Article 130y) concerning development co-operation. These provisions are presumably subject to the findings of the Court concerning the non-exclusive competence of the Community in *Bangladesh* and *EDF* and the other cases concerning development co-operation discussed below. However, according to a Declaration attached to the TEU, these provisions do not affect the principles laid down in *AETR*.[80] Thus, even where shared competence is so prescribed, the adoption of common rules internally will create exclusive competence externally as regards the relevant field.

Where competence is shared, Member States have the power to enter into agreements and to take action in the field in question, subject to their obligations under Community law. Shared external competence is the subject of particular concern to the Community's international partners. The Court has recognised that "when a question of powers is to be determined it is clearly in the interests of all the States concerned, including any non-member countries, for such a question to be clarified as soon as any particular negotiations are commenced."[81] Despite expectations to the contrary some years ago, it is an enduring feature of Community law.

In some agreements, Member States may have exclusive competence for some areas, while the Community may have exclusive competence in other areas.[82] In other instances, there may be a genuine sharing of competence between the Community and the Member States. It is unclear whether the presumption should be that shared competence is the general rule unless there is an indication to the contrary. In the *EDF* case, Advocate General Jacobs stated that in the absence of any indication to the contrary which would point to the conclusion that the Community's competence in development aid to the ACP states was exclusive, it could be accepted that the Community and the Member States share competence in that field.[83] This would seem to indicate that the general presumption is that competence is shared unless there is an indication to the contrary.[84] It would seem that there is a presumption that Member States have a

---

[79] This is the formula in Art. 111 (ex Art. 109(5)); it is reversed in Art. 174 (ex Art. 130r(4)) and Art. 181 (ex Art. 130y).

[80] Declaration on Arts. 109, 130r and 130y of the Treaty establishing the European Community, as signed in Maastricht. The Declaration was relied on by Portugal in Case C–268/94 *Portugal v. Council* [1996] E.C.R. I–6177, but it was not discussed by the Court; Advocate General La Pergola simply stated that the Declaration confirmed that Member States do not have the power to undertake obligations with third countries which affect common rules adopted by the Community or alter their scope.

[81] Opinion 1/78 (*International Agreement on Natural Rubber*) [1979] E.C.R. 2871 at para. 35. Contrast the Court's statement that "the exact nature of the division of powers is a domestic question in which third parties have no need to intervene": Ruling 1/78 [1978] E.C.R. 2151 at para 35.

[82] As in Ruling 1/78 [1978] E.C.R. 2151.

[83] Opinion of Advocate General Jacobs in *EDF* Case C–316/91 *Parliament v. Council* [1994] E.C.R. I–625 at para. 40.

[84] It is of course possible that this is confined to situations where there is an express external relations power as in the case of development co-operation but the nature of the Community competence is not delineated and the external relations power of the Member States is preserved.

concurrent competence until exclusive Community competence is ascertained or discerned. In Opinion 1/94, the Court held that the Community's external competence does not automatically flow from its power to lay down rules at internal level: "the Member States, whether acting individually or collectively, only lose their right to enter into obligations with non-member countries as and when common rules which could be affected by those obligations come into being".[85] In Opinion 1/94 the Court added, presumably to drive the point home, that "only in so far as common rules have been established at internal level does the external competence of the Community become exclusive."[86]

Humanitarian aid and development co-operation

12.18   Shared competence has arisen in a number of cases concerning humanitarian aid and development co-operation which it is convenient to treat together. Some were decided prior to the entry into force but after the conclusion of the TEU in Maastricht which specifically provides for shared competence in the field of development co-operation, whereas others were decided after the entry into force.

In the *Bangladesh* case, it was common ground that in the field of humanitarian aid the competence of the Community was not exclusive but concurrent with that of the Member States.[87] In a rather staccato statement, the Court held that "the Community does not have exclusive competence in the field of humanitarian aid, and that consequently the Member States are not precluded from exercising their competence in that regard collectively in the Council or outside it."[88] The TEU was not in force at the material time.

The *EDF* case was decided after the entry into force of the TEU but the latter was not binding at the material time. The Court considered the distribution of powers between the Community and its Member States in the field of development aid. It held that "The Community's competence is not exclusive. The Member States are accordingly entitled to enter into commitments themselves *vis-à-vis* non-Member States, either collectively or individually, or even jointly with the Community."[89] It held that this finding was supported by Article 130x, then newly inserted by the TEU, which provides for the Community and the Member States to co-ordinate their policies on development co-operation and to consult each other on their aid programmes and for the possibility of joint action. Oddly the Court did not analyse Article 130y. In the absence of derogations expressly laid down in the Lomé Convention, the Community and its Member States were jointly liable to the ACP States for the fulfilment of every obligation undertaken, including those relating to financial assistance. The obligation to grant the Community's financial assistance fell on the Community and its Member States, considered together. The Member States were entitled collectively to exercise their competence in that field with a view to bearing the financial assistance to be granted to the ACP States, and to choose the source and methods of financing, outside the Com-

---

[85] Opinion 1/94 [1994] E.C.R. I–5267 at para 77. The statement was repeated in Opinion 2/92 [1995] E.C.R. I–525, at para. 31 in almost identical terms: ". . . as and when there are common rules which could be affected by such obligations." The difference, which does not appear significant, derives from the French texts: the wording in Opinion 1/94 "qui pourraient être affectées" is changed in Opinion 2/92 to "susceptibles d'être affectées".

[86] Opinion 1/94 [1994] E.C.R. I–5267 at para. 77.

[87] Opinion of Advocate General Jacobs in Joined Cases C–181/91 and C–248/91 *Parliament* v. *Council and Commission* [1993] E.C.R. I–3685 at para. 25.

[88] *ibid.*, at para. 16.

[89] *EDF* [1994] E.C.R. I–625 at para. 26.

munity budget and in accordance with different procedures. It may be remarked that the Court did not consider the source of the Community's competence in *Bangladesh* and *EDF.*

In *Portugal* v. *Council*,[90] which fell under the scope of the TEU provisions, by then in force, the Court, after reviewing the Treaty provisions concerning development co-operation, held that the Community had specific competence to conclude agreements with non-Member countries in the sphere of development co-operation and that, on the other hand, that competence was not exclusive but is complementary to that of the Member States.[91] The fact that a development co-operation agreement contains clauses concerning various specific matters cannot alter the characterisation of the agreement, which must be determined having regard to its essential object and not in terms of individual clauses, provided that those clauses do not impose such extensive obligations concerning the specific matters referred to that those obligations in fact constitute objectives distinct from those of development co-operation.[92] The mere inclusion of provisions for co-operation in a specific field does not therefore necessarily imply a general power such as to lay down the basis of a competence to undertake any kind of co-operation action in that field. It does not, therefore, predetermine the allocation of spheres of competence between the Community and the Member States or the legal basis of Community acts for implementing co-operation in such a field.[93] This very broad approach to the content of the agreement recalls the wide-ranging interpretations of common commercial policy in Opinion 1/75 and Opinion 1/78 and contrasts with the stricter approach taken in Opinion 1/94 as regards intellectual property and services. The result reached is of course the converse to that reached in the earlier cases.

12.19 In the *FAO* case[94] the Court considered the "essential object" of the draft agreement at issue there; certain matters included in the agreement which fell within the competence of the Member States did not appear to occupy a "prominent position" in the agreement. This would seem to accord with the approach in *Portugal* v. *Council* in that both judgments focus on the content and the essential object of the agreements in question. On the other hand, it is not certain if this is a new trend: the Court's judgment on the US-EEC agreement on government procurement may suggest otherwise.[95] There the Court did not consider that the essential object of the agreement concerned trade in goods, which was almost certainly the case, but rather held that the agreement covered the provision of services going beyond trans-frontier supply involving no movement of persons. An approach in line with the almost contemporaneous *FAO* case (and the later *Portugal* v. *Council* case) would have suggested that the main thrust of the agreement concerned trade in goods rather than the supply of services.

The Court's approach to the TEU provisions seems to indicate that it viewed the parallel competence provided there as confirming the effective existing division of competence between the Community and the Member States prior to the entry into force of the TEU, the difference being that the Community now has an express complementary competence. In any event, the case law confirms that the Community and the Member States separately have competence to enter into international agreements and to adopt measures concerning development aid and humanitarian aid. The Court

---

[90] Case C–268/94 *Portugal* v. *Council* [1996] E.C.R. I–6177.
[91] *ibid.*, at para. 36.
[92] *ibid.*, at para. 39.
[93] *ibid.* at para. 47.
[94] Case C–25/94, *Commission* v. *Council* [1996] E.C.R. I–1469.
[95] Case C–360/93, *Parliament* v. *Council* [1996] E.C.R. I–1195.

confirmed in the *EDF* case that Member States retained the power to act individually or collectively.[96] The Member States may also act jointly with the Community given the nature of their competence.

This shared concurrent competence does not appear to be such as to deprive the Member States of their competence to act even where the Community acts in the same field, as they enjoy a parallel competence under Article 181(4) (ex Article 130y(4)). This point was examined by Advocate General Jacobs, though not by the Court, in the *EDF* case. He considered that the result of this reasoning would be that it would not be possible for the Community and the Member States to act jointly. He distinguished the *EDF* case from *Commission* v. *United Kingdom*[97] as the latter case concerned an area where the competence of the Community was "total and definitive" and not one where competence was shared between the Community and the Member States. There was nothing in that case to suggest that where the Community exercises its competence in an area which falls within the concurrent competence of the Community and the Member States, the Member States are necessarily prohibited from exercising their competence. Clearly this does not solve the problem of whether concurrent competence exists but it is assumed. Interestingly Advocate General Jacobs considered that *AETR* did not apply as "if the Member States undertook the obligation to provide development aid to the ACP States, that would not affect any internal rules adopted by the Community".[98] It may be that this statement concerning the consequence, or more precisely, the lack of consequence, of Member State action for internal rules is partly the key to an understanding of the Court's attitude to competence in the *Bangladesh* and *EDF* judgments. Indeed it has been suggested that in the area of development policy the likelihood of common rules in the *AETR* sense will be rare.[99]

There is an appealing logic to the idea inherent in *EDF* that once the Community and the Member States undertake obligations by entering into an international agreement, the Member States are not necessarily excluded from undertaking that obligation jointly with the Community. If the reverse were true, the inevitable consequence of Community action would be to preclude Member State action. Seen from a post-Maastricht perspective, this would nullify the clear intention of the Treaty-makers who sought to give the Community express competence while preserving the competence of the Member States in the field of development co-operation. It may be that this was borne in mind by the Court in both the *Bangladesh* and *EDF* cases; indeed in the latter case, it specifically referred to the new Treaty provisions even though they were not in force at the material time. Moreover, if the view stated were adopted, it would also nullify the possibility of joint action by the Member States with the Community; it is possible that the Court was anxious to preserve the possibility of joint action without the spectre for Member States that this would necessarily lead to exclusive Community competence.

Other examples of shared competence

12.20   The Member States may have shared competence where the Community has competence which it has not exercised. This occurred in *Kramer* where the Community had not, at the material time, exercised its exclusive competence in respect of the common fisheries policy. The Member States were therefore competent to assume international commitments in the area until the adoption of Community rules or at the

---

[96] Advocate General Jacobs had so held in the *Bangladesh* case, which concerned a collective act of the Member States: Opinion of Advocate General Jacobs, *Bangladesh* case [1993] E.C.R. I–3685 at para. 25.
[97] Case 804/79 [1981] E.C.R. I–1061.
[98] Opinion of Advocate General Jacobs in *EDF* [1994] E.C.R. I–625 at para 47.
[99] Macleod, Hendry and Hyett, *op. cit.*, at p. 343.

latest the end of the relevant transitional period by which time the Council was obliged to adopt measures for the conservation of the resources of the sea. The Court noted that the Member State competence was only of a transitional nature; it could only be exercised in respect of Community law, it could not hinder the Community interest and common action was necessary.[1]

There will also be shared or concurrent competence where the Community has power to adopt common rules but these are not exhaustive in that the Community rules adopted do not cover all the subject-matter of an international agreement. Thus in Opinion 2/92, where the internal measures adopted by the Community did not cover all the fields of activity to which the international agreement at issue there related, the Community and the Member States shared joint competence to participate therein.

Shared competence may also arise where an agreement includes provisions within Member State competence and Community competence. If an agreement concerns subject-matter which goes beyond the scope of the exclusive Community competence and provided that those clauses do not have merely accessory character in that they constitute objectives distinct from those in the field of exclusive Community competence, the Member States may participate in the negotiation and conclusion of the agreement for the part which exceeds the exclusive competence of the Community.[2] In Opinion 2/91, the Community had exclusive competence in certain areas but not in others where the Member States were exclusively competent, as in the case of responsibility for the international relations for overseas countries and territories. The Court's reasoning as to minimum standards has already been described above; presumably as regards the underlying measures for the protection of workers, Member States had a concurrent competence until the Community standards were raised.

In Opinion 1/78, on the other hand, although the agreement by its subject-matter fell within the scope of Article 133 (ex Article 113), the financing of the agreement was determinant for the question of whether the agreement fell within the exclusive competence of the Community. The Court concluded that it would so fall if the agreement were to be financed by the Community budget, but if it were to be financed by the Member States, the latter should participate in the agreement together with the Community and "the exclusive competence of the Community could not be envisaged in such a case."[3]

The effect of shared competence

12.21 The shared competence of the Member States does not, however, give them complete freedom of action. It would seem that once the Community enters into an international agreement the subject-matter of which falls within the concurrent competence of the Community and the Member States, the Member States are bound by the obligations of Article 10 EC (ex Article 5) to facilitate the obligations of the Community's obligations arising out of the agreement and may not act unilaterally in a way which would compromise their duty to proceed by common action within the framework of the agreement.[4] Likewise, it would seem to follow from the case law[5] that in such circumstances, the Member States are precluded from taking action which would

---

[1] See also Opinion 2/91 [1993] E.C.R. I–1061 at para. 12.

[2] Gaja, *op. cit.*, at p. 139.

[3] Opinion 1/78 [1979] E.C.R. 2871 at para. 60. It should be noted that in Opinion 1/94 [1994] E.C.R. I–5267, at para. 21 the Court held that the fact that the Member States would bear some of the expenses under the WTO Agreement "cannot, in any view, of itself justify participation of the Member States in the conclusion of the WTO Agreement".

[4] Opinion of Advocate General Jacobs, *EDF* [1994] E.C.R. I–625 at para. 48.

[5] *AETR*; Ruling 1/78 [1978] E.C.R. 2151 at paras. 33 to 36 ; Opinion 2/91 [1993] E.C.R. I–1061 at paras 36–8.

be capable of affecting that agreement or altering its scope. This would be the case even where the Treaty expressly provides for shared competence. In *EDF* Advocate General Jacobs noted that the exact limits of that duty could not be laid down in the abstract but depend on the agreement in question. He considered that in the field of development aid to third States, the risk that action undertaken by the Member States may have adverse consequences on action undertaken by the Community is much less than it is in other areas, such as that of social policy, presumably referring to the sort of situation presented in Opinion 2/91. As suggested above, this may be part of the key to understanding the approach adopted in the *Bangladesh* and *EDF* cases. The risk of conflict with the simultaneous exercise of Community competence was not discernible.

Moreover, the normal principles deriving from the *AETR* case apply in the case of shared competence; a *fortiori* where they are expressly preserved as was done by the Declaration referred to above. Therefore in so far as the Community has adopted common rules in a given field, the Member States are precluded from entering into agreements which would affect those rules or alter their scope.

The Court has laid down a duty of co-operation in Opinion 1/94 concerning agreements the subject-matter of which falls in part within the competence of the Community and in part within that of the Member States, both in the process of negotiation and conclusion and in the fulfilment of the commitments entered into. The obligation to co-operate flows from the requirement of unity in the international representation of the Community.[6]

As the Community generally is not able to exercise its competence to conclude agreements in matters which come within its field of competence until common rules have been adopted, there is the risk that the Member States may conclude agreements which make it more difficult for the Council to adopt a different rule. It may be possible to deduce from the obligations of Article 10 (ex Article 5) an obligation on them not to pose obstacles to the development of the Community order through the conclusion of agreements with third countries.[7] However, there are enforcement difficulties if such an obligation is not respected, hence the suggestion of a system whereby the Community could be informed of negotiations concerning agreements between Member States and third States in areas of concurrent competence and to give the Community institutions the opportunity to make a prior examination of the content of the proposed agreement.[8]

CONCLUSION

12.22 The Court's case law on external powers has largely focused on the need to delineate the boundary between concurrent and exclusive competence as this was what was asked of it. In recent years, it has showed considerable flexibility in allowing shared competence. However, the ability of the Member States to conclude international agreements in an unco-ordinated way where there is shared competence could eventually be damaging to the internal market. Hence, in the future, it is to be hoped that the Court will be able to develop further matters such as the requirement of unity in the international representation in the Community and the development of the

---

[6] See Ruling 1/78 [1978] E.C.R. 2151 at paras. 34–36, Opinion 2/91 [1993] E.C.R. I–1061 at paras. 36–38, Opinion 1/94, [1994] E.C.R. I–5627 at para. 106 *et seq*. and Case C–25/94 *Commission* v. *Council* (*FAO*) [1996] E.C.R. I–1469 at paras 48–49.
[7] See in this sense Opinion of Advocate General La Pergola in *Portugal* v. *Council* [1996] E.C.R. I–6177 at p. 6186, note 18.
[8] Gaja, *op. cit.*, at p. 146.

external posture of the Community. Its statement on the duty of co-operation in Opinion 1/94 is helpful in this respect but does not appear to be sufficient as the example of the FAO negotiations shows. The duty of co-operation is likely to be the next principal field of confrontation between the Community and the Member States.

CHAPTER 13

The European Union and Mixed Agreements

by

Allan Rosas*

THE CONCEPT OF MIXED AGREEMENTS

13.01 The problem of mixed Community agreements, that is, agreements which include among their Contracting Parties not only one or more of the European Communities but also one or more of their Member States, has already been with us for quite some time.[1] While it may be largely unknown to the general public, "mixity" has become part of the daily life of the external relations of the European Union (E.U.), more precisely, of the European Communities.[2] Mixity has attracted scholarly attention, too, although, perhaps, not to the extent one could have expected.[3]

---

* Doctor of Laws, Professor. While the author is a member of the Legal Service of the European Commission, the views expressed in this article do not necessarily express the position of the European Commission or its Legal Service.

[1] The possibility of mixed agreements is expressly recognised in Art. 102 of the Treaty establishing the European Atomic Energy Community (EURATOM). The expression "mixed agreements" has been used by the Court of Justice, *e.g.* in Case 12/86 *Demirel* [1987] E.C.R. 3719 at 3751 (para. 8). Early examples of bilateral E.E.C. (later to become the E.C.) treaties counting also the Member States as Contracting Parties are the 1961 Agreement establishing an Association between the European Economic Community and Greece (OJ 1963, p. 296) and the 1963 Agreement establishing an Association between the European Economic Community and Turkey (OJ 1964, p. 3687). For a list of the mixed agreements of the 1960s and 1970s see Feenstra, "A Survey of the Mixed Agreements and their Participation Clauses", in O'Keeffe and Schermers (eds.), *Mixed Agreements* (Kluwer, 1983), p. 207.

[2] The European Union is an umbrella concept covering the three Communities and the new Titles on Common Foreign and Security Policy and Co-operation in the Fields of Justice and Home Affairs (after the entry into force of the Treaty of Amsterdam on May 1, 1999: Police and Judicial Co-operation in Criminal Matters) introduced by the Treaty of Maastricht. The legal personality of that part of the E.U. which falls outside the three Communities is contested, see, *e.g.* Paasivirta, "The European Union: From an Aggregate of States to a Legal Person?", (1997) 2 *Hofstra Law & Policy Symposium*, 37–59; Neuwahl, "A Partner with a Troubled Personality: EU Treaty-Making in Matters of CFSP and JHA after Amsterdam", (1998) 3 E.F.A.Rev. 177–195.

[3] Most of the relevant contributions are in the more general context of the external relations of the EU, see, *e.g.* Timmermans and Völker, *Division of Powers between the Communities and their Member States in the Field of External Relations* (Kluwer, 1981); O'Keeffe and Schermers, *op. cit.*; Dolmans, *Problems of Mixed Agreements: Division of Powers within the E.E.C. and the Right of Third States* (Asser Instituut, 1985); Groux and Manin, *The European Communities, in the International Order* (Commission of the European Communities, 1985), pp. 57–88; A. Conze, *Die völkerrechtliche Haftung der Europäischen Gemeinschaft* (Nomos, 1987), pp. 73–87; Neuwahl, "Joint Participation in International Treaties and the Exercise of Powers by the E.E.C. and its Member States: Mixed Agreements" (1991) 28 C.M.L.Rev. 717–740; *idem*, "Shared Powers or Combined Incompetence? More on Mixity" (1996) 33 C.M.L.Rev., 667–687; Frid, *The Relations between the EC and International Organizations* (Kluwer, 1995), pp. 111–116; MacLeod, Hendry and Hyett, *The External Relations of the European Communities* (Oxford, 1996), pp. 142–164; M. Kaniel, *The Exclusive Treaty-Making Power of the European Community up to the Period of the Single European Act* (Kluwer, 1996), pp. 145–174; McGoldrick, *International Relations Law of the European Union* (Longman, 1997), pp. 78–88; Bourgeois, Dewost and Gaiffe (eds.), *La Communauté européenne et*

In this article we shall use the concept of mixity in a wide sense, to include in principle all agreements concluded at the same time by one or more of the Communities and one or more of their Member States. Mixity in this *formal* meaning is an outcome of the fact that some international agreements cover areas which are not deemed to belong to the so-called exclusive competences of the Communities and thus necessitate—or at least enable—Member States" participation. As we shall see below, this broad group of treaties encompasses several sub-categories, some of which are not always regarded as implying mixity in the true sense ("false" mixity, "incomplete" mixity, and so on). A closer look at legal realities will reveal a number of theoretical and practical problems, which have not yet been fully explored.

It will be noted that the article does not specifically deal with treaties which are entered into by the Member States alone (and which thus are not mixed in the formal sense) but which in substance cover matters of exclusive Community competence. If Community adherence to such treaties is not possible (for instance, because the treaty is open to States only), the competence of the E.C. may be exercised "through the medium of the Member States acting jointly in the Community's interest".[4] Nor does the article deal with treaties concluded in the framework of the Common Foreign and Security Policy (CFSP), where the E.U. has not enjoyed legal personality.[5] It is arguable that this situation has not fundamentally changed with the entry into force of the Treaty of Amsterdam, although Article 24 of the Treaty on European Union (TEU) refers to the conclusion of CFSP agreements "by the Council".[6]

THE PRACTICAL RELEVANCE OF MIXITY

13.02 According to a commentary on the Communities' external relations, the fact that mixity problems "have been more discussed in the learned writings than in the case law of the Court suggests that the problems are greater in theory than in practice".[7] This statement can be contrasted with another recent comment, according to which mixed agreements "are of enormous legal significance for the international relations of the E.C.".[8]

While both writers may have a point, it is an inescapable fact that the number of mixed agreements is steadily increasing and that they have become an established phenomenon in the context of bilateral association and partnership agreements (mainly with Central and Eastern European countries as well as with the Mediterranean countries) and in multilateral co-operation areas such as the environment.[9] The Member States, sometimes because of general considerations of visibility, prestige and defence of national competences, sometimes simply because they wish to preserve the

---

les accords mixtes. Quelles perspectives? (Collège d'Europe, 1997); Koskenniemi (ed), *International Law Aspects of the European Union* (Nijhoff, 1998), notably articles by Dashwood (pp. 113–123), Rosas (pp. 125–148) and Granvik (pp. 255–272).

[4] Opinion 2/91, *ILO Convention No. 170* [1993] E.C.R. I–1061, para. 5. See also McGoldrick, *op. cit.*, pp. 82–83.

[5] See, *e.g.* Eaton, "Common Foreign and Security Policy", in O'Keeffe and Twomey (eds.), *Legal Issues of the Maastricht Treaty* (Wiley Chancery, 1994), pp. 215–225 at p. 224.

[6] See Paasivirta, *loc. cit.*, see above, n. 2; Neuwahl, *loc. cit.*, see above, n. 2.

[7] MacLeod, Hendry and Hyett, *op. cit.*, p. 144.

[8] McGoldrick, *op. cit.*, p. 78.

[9] The number of mixed agreements according to statistics available at the Legal Service of the European Commission is in the area of 130, out of a total of more than 700 agreements to which one of the Communities is a contracting party or signatory. On mixed agreements in the environmental field, see L. Granvik, "Incomplete Mixed Environmental Agreements of the Community and the Principle of Bindingness", in Koskenniemi, *op. cit.*, pp. 255–272; *idem, The Treaty-Making Competence of the European Community in the Field of International Environmental Conventions* (Publications of the Finnish Society of Environmental Law No. 31, 1999).

need for unanimity and thus a veto power,[10] are often keen on obtaining the mixed character of a given agreement. Opinions 2/91, 1/94 and 2/92,[11] where the Court of Justice held that competences are shared, have added legal fuel to such aspirations.

The Treaty of Amsterdam has not brought about any significant changes as far as the Communities" exclusive competences are concerned. As the efforts at the Intergovernmental Conference of 1996–1997 to enlarge the scope of Article 133 (ex Article 113) of the E.C. Treaty (ECT) to include fully trade in services, trade-related intellectual property rights and investments were not successful,[12] it is likely that these areas will continue to be dealt with in mixed agreements.

With the increasing number of mixed agreements, it is probable that we will face an increasing number of theoretical and practical problems. It should be noted that many of the mixed agreements concluded during the 1990s have not yet entered into force or have entered into force only recently. Thus, many of the legal and practical problems that the application and implementation of mixed agreements gives rise to (see below), are only tarting to surface now.

Moreover, while it is true that the case law of the Court of Justice of the European Communities often addresses the division of (external) competence between the Communities and their Member States, and the proper legal bases of Community competences,[13] there are some judgments or opinions also dealing with the implications of mixity, including the question of the competence of the Court of Justice itself to interpret mixed agreements.[14] The latter aspect was fundamental in a request made in 1996 by a Dutch court for a preliminary ruling concerning the interpretation of a provision of a mixed agreement, the WTO Agreement on Trade-Related Aspects of Intellectual Property Rights (TRIPS) which, in the context of Opinion 1/94 on the new WTO agreements of 1994, had been held by many Member States to fall within their national competence.[15] Is the Court competent to give a preliminary ruling on such a provision, in other words, is that provision covered by the reference, in Article 234 EC (ex Article 177), to "acts of the institutions of the Community"?

This question relates to fundamental questions of the legal implications of mixity. To what extent are the Communities internationally responsible for the implemen-

---

[10] It should be underlined, however, that mixity does not in itself imply unanimity as far as the conclusion of the agreement *on behalf of the Communities* is concerned. The need for unanimity follows from the practice to let the E.C. adhere especially to bilateral agreements only when all the Member States have become Contracting Parties.

[11] See below, n. 13.

[12] But according to a new para. 5 of Art. 133, the Council, acting unanimously on a proposal from the Commission and after consulting the European Parliament, "may extend the application of paragraphs 1 to 4 to international negotiations and agreements on services and intellectual property insofar as they are not covered by these paragraphs".

[13] See, notably, Case 22/70, *Commission v. Council* (AETR) [1971] E.C.R. 263; Opinion 1/75 *OECD Local Cost Standard* [1975] E.C.R. 1355; Joined Cases 3, 4 and 7/76 *Kramer* [1976] E.C.R. 1279; Opinion 1/76 *Draft Agreement for the Laying-up Fund for Inland Waterway Vessels* [1977] E.C.R. 741; Opinion 1/78 *Draft International Agreement on Natural Rubber* [1979] E.C.R. 2871; Ruling 1/78 *Draft Convention on the Physical Protection of Nuclear Materials, Facilities and Transports* [1978] E.C.R. 2151; Opinion 2/91 *ILO Convention no. 170* [1993] E.C.R. I–1061; Opinion 2/92, *OECD National Treatment Instrument* [1995] E.C.R. I–521; Opinion 1/94 *WTO Agreement* [1994] E.C.R. I–5267; Case C–360/93 *Parliament v. Council* (common commercial policy and services) [1996] E.C.R. I–1195; Case C–25/94 *Commission v. Council* (FAO-case) [1996] E.C.R. I–1469; Opinion 2/94 *Accession by the Community to the European Convention on Human Rights* [1996] E.C.R. I–1759; Case C–268/1994 *Portugal v. Council* (co-operation agreement with India) [1996] E.C.R. I–6177; Case C–124/95 *Centro-Com* (trade embargo against ex-Yugoslavia) [1997] E.C.R. I–81; Case C–162/96 *Racke* (suspension of trade agreement with ex-Yugoslavia) [1998] E.C.R. I–3655.

[14] See, *e.g.* Ruling 1/78 and Opinion 1/78 referred to above, in n. 13, and Case 12/86 *Demirel* [1987] E.C.R. 3719; Case 316/91 *Parliament v. Council* (European Development Fund) [1994] E.C.R. I–653; Case C–25/94 *Commission v. Council* ("FAO"case) [1996] E.C.R. I–1469.

[15] Case C–53/96 *Hermès* [1998] E.C.R. I–3603.

tation of mixed agreements, and to what extent are such agreements part of Community law? To what extent a mixed agreement not concluded by a Member State, is nevertheless binding on the latter, given that under Article 300(7) EC, Community agreements are binding not only on the EU institutions but also on the Member States? Apart from such questions of fundamental importance, mixity also poses an increasing number of day-to-day problems concerning the conclusion and management of such agreements, including the often long delays in their entry into force.

The answers to these questions may vary depending on the content and nature of a given (mixed) agreement. In the following section, an attempt is made to present a brief typology of mixed agreements.

A TYPOLOGY OF MIXED AGREEMENTS[16]

13.03   A basic distinction should be made between what can be termed *parallel* and *shared* competence. Parallel competence in this case implies that the Communities may adhere to a treaty, with full rights and obligations as any other Contracting Party, this having no direct effect on the rights and obligations of Member States being parties to the same treaty.[17] An example could be an international convention, such as the Agreement establishing the European Bank for Reconstruction and Development,[18] open to States and the E.C. alike, and obliging each Contracting Party to provide financial resources as a loan or grant to a third State or international fund (assuming that the participation of the E.C. would be covered by the Community budget).[19] Another example, although not as clear-cut, could be Community adherence to the 1989 Protocol Relating to the Madrid Agreement Concerning the International Registration of Marks, prompted by the need to protect the Community trade mark.[20] One can also cite the possibility of Community adherence to international human rights conventions to which the Member States are already parties.[21]

Shared competences, again, imply some division, between the Community and the Member States, of the rights and obligations contained in the agreement. One can, following the *Dolmans* case,[22] distinguish between mixed agreements with "*coexistent*" competence and mixed agreements with "*concurrent*" competence. In the for-

---

[16] See Schermers, "A Typology of Mixed Agreements", in O'Keeffe and Schermers, *op. cit.*, pp. 23–33; Dolmans, *op. cit.*, pp. 25, 39–42; MacLeod, Hendry and Hyett, *op. cit.*, p. 143; A. Rosas, "Mixed Union – Mixed Agreements", in Koskenniemi, *op. cit.*, pp. 125–148 at pp. 128–133.

[17] The notion of parallel competence is used by Dolmans, *op. cit.*, pp. 40–42. Schermers, *loc. cit.*, p. 24, notes that such treaties, which are covered by a formal (as distinct from a substantial) definition of mixed agreements, are "inherently ... not of a mixed nature".

[18] [1990] O.J. L372/1; see also MacLeod, Hendry and Hyett, *op. cit.*, pp. 187–189.

[19] The situation may be more complex if, as is the case with the Lomé Convention, financial assistance does not come from the Community budget but from a separate fund (in the case of Lomé the European Development Fund) consisting of Member States" contributions and based on a separate internal agreement between the Member States, see Case C–316/91, *Parliament* v. *Council* [1994] E.C.R. I–653. See also Opinion 1/78 *Draft International Agreement on Natural Rubber* [1979] E.C.R. 2871.

[20] Commission Proposal for a Council decision approving the accession of the EC to the Protocol, COM(96) 367 final of July 22, 1996. According to Art. 10 of the Madrid Protocol, each Contracting Party, including the E.C., has one vote. This implies that the E.C. and its Member States may have altogether 16 votes, a principle contested by the United States, which have so far refused to adhere to the Protocol.

[21] But such adherence may pose problems of Community competence, in the light of Opinion 2/94 [1996] E.C.R. I–1759, where the Court concluded that "as Community law now stands, the Community has no competence to accede to the European Convention for the Protection of Human Rights and Fundamental Freedoms" (para. 36). Moreover, human rights conventions binding on the Community, especially if they have direct effect, could, in matters of Community law, affect national law; in such a situation, Community adherence would not appear as completely separate from that of the Member States.

[22] Dolmans, *op. cit.*, pp. 25, 39–42, 97.

mer case, because the agreement contains provisions which fall under the exclusive competence of the Community and/or the Member States respectively, it is in principle possible to divide it into two separate parts, for which *either* the Community *or* the Member States are responsible. An obvious example would be a treaty containing one chapter on trade in goods and another on military defence. The situation could, in fact, be seen as two different treaties presented in one and the same document.[23] Less obvious examples are offered by those international commodities agreements to which the Member States contribute financially.[24] In this context, one can also mention the 1982 UN Convention on the Law of the Sea (although the situation is here quite complex).[25]

With respect to the Law of the Sea Convention, there is a presumed *"horizontal"* (sectorial) distribution of competences (*e.g.* fisheries v. questions of territorial jurisdiction, navigation and passage). One can also envisage a more *"vertical"* distribution of competences, meaning that the Community would be competent to conclude the main substantive parts of the agreement, while Member State participation would be deemed necessary because of the nature of its obligations relating to the implementation and enforcement of those substantive parts. An example could be the (draft) agreement considered in Ruling 1/78 (*IAEA convention on the physical protection of nuclear material*), at least as far as its provisions on penal sanctions and extradition were to be considered as requiring Member States" participation.[26] Another example may be the 1995 UN Agreement Relating to the Conservation and Management of Straddling Fish Stocks and Highly Migratory Fish Stocks which, mainly because of its provisions on compliance and enforcement (Part VI), has been defined by the EU Council as a mixed agreement.[27]

13.04 It should be noted that in many such instances (including the UN Agreement on Straddling Fish Stocks), the provisions relating to possible "coexistent" Member States competences may be of such a limited relevance that they should be seen as "ancillary" (subsidiary) to the essential objectives of the agreement. If this is the case, Member States participation would not be necessary—or, in cases of exclusive Community competence, even legally admissible (unless construed as a Community authorisation for Member States to participate). There is some case law of the Court of Justice on "ancillary" provisions, often related to Article 133 EC (ex Article 113) on

---

[23] MacLeod, Hendry and Hyett, *op. cit.*, mention as an example the Physical Protection of Nuclear Material Convention discussed in Ruling 1/78 [1978] E.C.R. 2151. See also Allott, "Adherence To and Withdrawal from Mixed Agreements", in O'Keeffe and Schermers, *op. cit.*, pp. 97–121 at pp. 118–119, who notes that for such mixed agreements "in the weak sense", it should be possible "to separate completely" the Community and Member States parts of the agreement.

[24] See the *Natural Rubber* case, Opinion 1/78 [1979] E.C.R. 2871, and MacLeod, Hendry and Hyett, *op. cit.*, p. 65, 182–185.

[25] Annex IX of the Convention is based on the principle that competence either belongs to the Community ("in respect of matters relating to which competence has been transferred to it") or the Member States. As will be seen from Art. 5 of Annex IX, however, the system is marked by a certain fluidity. Moreover, some rights and obligations of the Law of the Sea Convention may be intertwined to such an extent that it is difficult to speak of "coexistent" competences, see Schermers, *loc. cit.*, pp. 26–27. The instrument of confirmation of the Law of the Sea Convention was deposited by the EC on April 1, 1998 and the Convention entered into force for the EC on May 1, 1998, [1998] O.J. L179/1.

[26] [1978] E.C.R. 2151, at 2180 (para. 36). See also above, n. 23.

[27] In an E.C. Declaration submitted upon signature in accordance with Art. 47, it is noted that, while the Community has exclusive competence with respect to the conservation and management of living marine resources, including the regulatory competence granted under international law to the flag State in this respect, measures such as refusal, withdrawal or suspension of authorisation to serve as masters and other officers of fishing vessels, as well as certain enforcement measures relating to the exercise of jurisdiction by the flag State over its vessels on the high seas, are within the competence of the Member States, (1996) *Law of the Sea Bulletin* No. 32, p. 26. The E.U. Council concluded this Convention on 8 June 1998 but the deposit of ratification was made dependent on the ratification of the Convention by all Member States, [1998] O.J. L189/14.

common commercial policy.[28] In this context, it should also be stressed that the mere fact that Member States will have some obligations relating to the execution of the agreement does not, legally speaking, render the agreement mixed.[29] If such agreements are nevertheless concluded jointly by the EC and the Member States, one can, especially if the EC competences are of an exclusive character, speak of "false" mixity.[30]

Even when there are real national competences involved which "coexist" with Community competences, the nature of the agreement, especially if there is a "vertical" rather than "horizontal" (sectorial) relation between national and Community competences, may make it difficult, if not impossible, to separate the agreement into two parts. The *Natural Rubber* Opinion may be a case in point, to the extent that it addressed a possible scheme where under a commodities agreement, otherwise falling under exclusive Community competences in accordance with Article 133 EC (ex Article 113), the Member States would have directly, through the national budgets, financed the agreement, with implications also for its decision-making procedures.[31]

Such cases come close to what has been described above as *concurrent* competences, implying that the agreement in question forms a whole which cannot be separated into two parts.[32] Such a situation of truly shared competences may arise particularly if there is a non-exclusive Community competence covering the whole agreement. Articles 111 (ex Article 109), paragraph 5 (agreements relating to economic and monetary policy), 174 (ex Article 130r), paragraph 4 (environmental agreements), and 181 (ex Article 130y), paragraph 2 (agreements relating to development co-operation) ECT expressly provide that not only the Community but also the Member States may negotiate in international bodies and conclude international agreements.[33] Also in other areas the Community may have a non-exclusive competence to conclude agreements, namely if it has a corresponding competence to establish internal rules, but this competence has not yet been utilised.[34] Even if the latter competence has been utilised, the external competence may rest at least partly non-exclusive if the common internal rules are considered as minimum rules only[35] or do not cover the whole area regulated in the international agreement.[36]

Where the competence of the Community is non-exclusive, but there are no competences reserved for Member States either, mixity becomes facultative. One can thus

---

[28] Opinion 1/78 *Draft International Agreement on Natural Rubber* [1979] E.C.R. 2871, at p. 1917 (para. 56); Opinion 1/94 *WTO Agreement* [1994] E.C.R. I–5278, at 5408 paras 66–68; Case C–268/94, *Portugal v. Council* [1996] E.C.R. I–6177, paras 75, 77. See also Kaniel, *op. cit.*, pp. 55–57.

[29] Neuwahl (1991), *op. cit.*, pp. 732–733. In Opinion 1/75 *Understanding on a Local Costs Standard*, the Court held that "it is of little importance that the obligations and the financial burdens inherent to the execution of the agreement envisaged are borne directly by the Member States", [1975] E.C.R. 1361 at 1364. See also Opinion 2/91 *ILO Convention No 170* [1993] E.C.R. I–1061 at 1082 (para. 34).

[30] Schermers, *op. cit.*, p. 27.

[31] [1979] E.C.R. 2871, at 2917–2918 (paras 57–60). See above, n. 24 and MacLeod, Hendry and Hyett, *op. cit.*, p. 65.

[32] Allott, *loc. cit.*, p. 118–119, speaks of mixed agreements "in the strong sense", meaning that Community and Member States participation is "inextricably confused".

[33] However, according to a Declaration on Art. 109, 130r and 130y ECT contained in the Final Act of the TEU as adopted at Maastricht, this (non-exclusive) competence is subject to the AETR (ERTA) judgment of the Court of Justice (Case 22/70 *Commission v. Council* [1971] E.C.R. 263), that is, the principle that the adoption by the Community of common rules may create exclusive Community competences also in the fields covered by the said Articles.

[34] Joined Cases 3, 4 and 6/76 *Kramer* [1976] E.C.R. 1303 at 1308–1309 (paras 19–34); Opinion 2/91 *ILO Convention No 170* [1993] E.C.R. I–1061 at 1076–1077 (paras 7, 12); Opinion 2/92 *OECD National Treatment Instrument* [1995] E.C.R. I–521 at 558–560. See also Dashwood, "Implied External Competence of the EC", in Koskenniemi, *op. cit.*, pp. 113–123. *Cf.* O'Keeffe, "Community and Member State Competence in External Relations Agreements of the EU", (1999) 4 E.F.A.Rev. 7–36 at pp. 20–23.

[35] Opinion 2/91 [1993] E.C.R. I–1061 at 1078–1080 and MacLeod, Hendry and Hyett, *op. cit.*, p. 66.

[36] See notably Opinion 1/94 *WTO Agreement* [1994] E.C.R. I–5267.

distinguish between *obligatory* (legally necessary) and *facultative* (optional) mixity. This distinction, which is not always recognised in practice,[37] may admittedly sometimes be difficult to apply to concrete cases, as shown by the uncertainties as to whether Opinion 1/94 implies that Member States participation in the WTO Agreements on services (GATS) and intellectual property rights (TRIPS) was legally necessary or simply legally possible.[38] And even if Member States participation was not legally necessary *ab initio*, the question arises as to whether the fact that the Council opted for mixity excludes Community competences from some part of these agreements.

The concepts outlined above leads to the following typology:

I.   *Parallel* competences   facultative mixity

II.   *Shared* competences

     II.1.   *Coexistent* competences   obligatory mixity

          II.1A.   Horizontally coexistent

          II.1B.   Vertically coexistent

     II.2.   *Concurrent* competences   facultative mixity[39]

13.05   Finally, one can distinguish between mixed agreements of a predominantly *bilateral*, and those of a *multilateral* character. The most clear-cut example of a bilateral agreement would be a trade and co-operation agreement, or an association agreement, between the Community and its Member States on the one hand, and a given third country on the other.[40] An example of a multilateral treaty would be one involving parallel competences (as defined above) between the Community and the Member States, meaning that the Community's adherence would not, in principle, be different from the separate participation of some or all of the Member States. Especially in the latter case, it is legally envisageable that not all Member States are Contracting Parties, in which case one can speak of "incomplete" mixity.[41]

---

[37] In the discussions in the framework of the E.U. Council (including Coreper and the Working Groups) on the Community v. mixed character of a given agreement, it is almost always taken for granted that the lack of exclusive Community competences of necessity requires mixity (personal observations by the present author). Neuwahl (1991), *op. cit.*, 717–718, rightly observes that mixity is often not required by the division of competences between the Community and the Member States but "is due to some kind of expediency".
[38] The Court was asked by the Commission to rule that the Community had *exclusive* competence to adhere to GATS and TRIPS, either under (the then) Art. 113, the AETR doctrine, implied powers in accordance with Opinion 1/76, or (the then) Arts. 100a and 235 ECT. In denying the existence of exclusive competences for the whole subject areas covered by these two treaties, the Court concluded that the Community and its Member States "are jointly competent" to conclude GATS and TRIPS. Some of the Member States had argued that those provisions of TRIPS which relate to procedural safeguards to secure the effective protection of intellectual property rights (such as those ensuring a fair and just procedure) fall within their competence. The Court's answer was that "if that argument is to be understood as meaning that all those matters are within some sort of domain reserved to the Member States, it cannot be accepted. The Community is certainly competent to harmonise national rules on those matters..." [1994] E.C.R. I–5418–5419 para. 104. See also Dashwood, "Why Continue to Have Mixed Agreements At All?", in Bourgeois, Dewost and Gaiffe, *op. cit.*, pp. 93–98 at pp. 94–95; *idem, loc. cit.*, see above, p. 205, n. 34, pp. 120–121, who argues that conclusion of GATS by the EC on its own would not have been legally possible.
[39] In cases of concurrent competences, mixity is facultative *ab initio*. But if the Council (and the Member States) insists on mixity for political reasons, the question arises as to whether parts of the agreement become reserved for the Member States (in which case they should all become Contracting Parties, see below, p. 206 n. 41 and p. 213, n. 80.
[40] In the case of the Lomé Convention, such a "bilateral" relationship has been expressed as to applying to the Communities and their Member States "of the one part", and the 70 African, Caribbean and Pacific (ACP) States "of the other part", see Agreement Amending the Fourth ACP-EC Convention of Lomé, signed in Mauritius on November 4, 1995, full text of Lomé IV as amended published in *The ACP-EU Courier* No. 155 (January–February 1996).
[41] Schermers, *op. cit.*, p. 26. See also Allott, *op. cit.*, p. 97, who speaks of "partial participation" (by the Member States) and Granvik, *op. cit.*.

It should be underlined that the mere fact that there are more than one third State involved, making the agreement formally speaking a multilateral one (even if the Community and its Member States are conceived as one party), does not prejudge the intrinsic legal nature of the Community participation and the division of competences and responsibilities between it and its Member States. It may well be that also in such multilateral contexts, the relation between the Community and its Member States on the one hand, and any given third State party to the agreement on the other hand, should be viewed primarily as a "concealed bilateral"[42] one.

On the whole, the typology set out above should be seen merely as a tool to assist in the structuring of the discussion on the legal nature and implications of mixed agreements. A given agreement may fall under several of these categories, as seems to be exemplified by ILO Convention No. 170 as interpreted by the Court of Justice in Opinion 2/91.[43] It should also be admitted that the answer to be given to a specific problem arising from mixity may vary depending on the subject matter (the jurisdiction of the Court of Justice in the field of mixed agreements, the responsibility and liability of the Community and its Member States *vis-à-vis* third States, and so on). It is to such specific problems arising from mixity that we shall now turn.

LEGAL AND PRACTICAL PROBLEMS RELATING TO MIXED AGREEMENTS

13.06 The legal and practical problems arising from mixity[44] can be roughly divided into two groups: (a) problems relating to the very *existence* (birth and termination) and *extension* of treaty rights and obligations; (b) problems relating to the *application and interpretation* of the rights and obligations which are deemed to be in force. The first dimension raises issues such as the conclusion, suspension and termination of, and withdrawal from, treaties as well as the question of reservations. The second dimension relates to the operation and "management" of the treaty and to questions of implementation, responsibility and judicial control.

Birth and Termination of Treaty Obligations

Within the first category of questions, there is first and foremost the issue of conclusion and entering into force of the treaty. If the agreement relates to parallel competences (category I above), conclusion by the Community and by the Member States does not necessarily have to go hand in hand. But if mixity is obligatory (coexistent competences, category II.1), or when in cases of concurrent competences (category II.2) the Council rules out full Community coverage, it is a sound principle to require—as is often done in practice—that Community conclusion comes only after all

---

[42] Allott, *op cit.*, p. 106, refers to the possibility of conceiving mixed agreements as "concealed bilaterals".
[43] [1993] E.C.R. I–1061. In this Opinion, the Court seemed to hold that Part III of the Convention belonged to exclusive Community competences, the other parts to non-exclusive Community competences (because the relevant Community directives set minimum standards only), whereas the representation of certain dependent territories belonged to the competence of (some) Member States (but this right of representation is, strictly speaking, not a question of mixity, as the Member States involved do not act in their capacity as E.U. Member States). See also MacLeod, Hendry and Hyett, *op. cit.*, pp. 65–66.
[44] *Cf.* C.D. Ehlermann, "Mixed Agreements: A List of Problems", in O'Keeffe and Schermers, *op. cit.*, pp. 3–21.

the Member States have ratified the agreement in question.[45] This obviously may imply problems of timing, as Member States may be slow in providing ratification. Thus, it may take many years before a signed agreement enters into force, causing concerns not only for actors within the E.U. but also for third parties, who may suspect that the delay is due to obstruction rather than technical difficulties.

The case of an Agreement on customs union and co-operation with San Marino is an extreme example but serves to illustrate the point. In November 1991 the European Commission submitted its proposal for a Council decision on the conclusion of the Agreement[46] and the Agreement was signed in December 1991. Whereas the trade parts of the Agreement were put into force through an Interim Agreement concluded as a pure Community agreement in November 1992,[47] the main Agreement was considered a mixed one (because of its provisions on social matters) and thus had to await the ratification of all the then 12 Member States. When the E.U. was enlarged to 15 Member States on January 1, 1995, France had not yet ratified the Agreement and consequently it had not been concluded by the Community either. In this situation it became necessary to provide for the participation of the three new Member States through an Enlargement Protocol.[48] But this Protocol, too, had to be ratified by all Parties concerned, that is, San Marino, the 15 Member States, and the Community. At the time of writing (September 1999), the Enlargement Protocol has not entered into force (three Member States still having not concluded the Protocol), even if more than eight years have lapsed since signature.

One possibility in such a situation would be to conclude the Agreement on behalf of the Community already before the Protocol has been ratified by all the parties concerned (which would mean that the "national" part of the Agreement would not immediately enter into force with respect to the three new Member States).[49] As this solution was not acceptable at Council level, it was decided to allow for the provisional application[50] of the Protocol awaiting its ratification. A similar solution was chosen for the Agreements on Partnership and Co-operation signed with Russia[51] and Ukraine[52] in June 1994.

---

[45] This is particularly noticeable with respect to agreements of a predominantly bilateral nature such as the Europe and other association agreements. This does not prevent the provisional conclusion of the agreement, or the conclusion of a separate interim agreement, limited to Community competences. For an example of a multilateral agreement for which the Council decision spells out the requirement of simultaneous ratification by the E.C. and the Member States, see the Council decision on the ratification of the 1995 UN Agreement Relating to the Conservation and Management of Straddling Fish Stocks and Highly Migratory Fish Stocks, [1998] O.J. L189/14.

[46] COM(91) final, [1991] O.J. C302/10.

[47] Council decision on the conclusion of an interim Agreement on trade and customs union between the European Economic Community and the Republic of San Marino, [1992] O.J. L 359/13.

[48] The situation is not covered by Art. 5, para. 2, of the 1994 Act concerning the conditions of accession of the three new Member States, which provides for their obligation to accede to the (mixed) agreements already concluded by the Community and its Member States with third parties, [1994] O.J. C241/22.

[49] This solution is proposed by the Commission in COM(97) 8 final of January 29, 1997.

[50] See Art. 25 of the Vienna Convention on the Law of Treaties and Art. 300 (2) EC (ex Art. 228(2)) as amended by the Treaty of Amsterdam.

[51] See the Commission proposal for the conclusion of the Agreement, COM(94) 257 final, of June 16, 1994. The trade parts of the Agreement were implemented through an Interim Agreement concluded in July 1995, [1995] O.J. L147/1. An Enlargement Protocol (providing for the addition of the three new Member States) was proposed by the Commission in April 1996 in COM(96) 150 final. The Partnership Agreement with Russia entered into force on December 1, 1997, [1997] O.J. L327/1.

[52] Commission proposal for the conclusion of the Agreement in COM(94) 226 final, modified by COM (95) 137 final (relating to an amendment of the Agreement of May 8, 1995), and for an Enlargement Protocol in COM (96) 133 final. An Interim Agreement on trade entered into force on February 1, 1996, [1995] O.J. L311/1. The Partnership Agreement with Ukraine entered into force on March 1, 1998, [1998] O.J. L49/1.

Another problem concerns *withdrawal* from,[53] as well as the *termination* and *suspension* of the operation of mixed agreements, notably suspension as a consequence of the breach of the agreement by the other side.[54] If it is a question of partial suspension, which affects the Community part of the agreement only, suspension can take place on the basis of a decision of the EU Council, without separate decisions by the Member States.[55] But if suspension affects the whole mixed agreement, or those parts of it which belong to Member States' competences, the participation of the latter is arguably required. An example is offered by the 1991 Decision of the Council, together with the Representatives of the Governments of the Member States, meeting within the Council, to suspend the application of the 1983 Agreements concluded with the Socialist Federal Republic of Yugoslavia.[56]

13.07   Article 366a of the revised Lomé Convention IV offers an example of an express suspension clause in a mixed context. The provision provides for the partial or full suspension of the Convention if a Party has failed to fulfil one of the essential elements referred to in Article 5, that is, basic obligations relating to respect for human rights, democratic principles and the rule of law. According to Article 366a, the term "Party" refers to the Community and the Member States of the European Union on the one side, and each ACP State, on the other.

As the procedural rules for the suspension of the Lomé Convention have been unclear, the Commission submitted in February 1996 a proposal for a Council decision on a framework procedure for implementing Article 366a.[57] The Council adopted the framework decision in March 1999, after the European Parliament had given its assent.[58] The new framework decision provides for a simplified procedure for the taking of appropriate measures by a Council decision, adopted either by qualified majority (partial suspension) or unanimity (total suspension). The eventuality of suspension affecting the national competences involved in the Lomé system[59] is tackled by an amendment to an Internal Agreement between the Member States on the measures

---

[53] See Ehlermann, *op. cit.*, p. 16, who refers to Art. 8 (c) (i) of Annex IX of the UN Convention on the Law of the Sea, according to which the Community will not be able to denounce the Convention if any of its Member States is still a Contracting Party and the Community continues to have competence over matters governed by the Convention.

[54] See Arts. 54–72 of the Vienna Convention on the Law of Treaties. Article 60 regulates the question of termination or suspension of the operation of a treaty "as a consequence of its breach". Art. 300 (2) EC (ex Art. 228(2)) EC, confirms that Community agreements may be suspended by a decision of the Council, on the proposal of the Commission. The question of suspension has acquired increased importance with the inclusion, since the early 1990s, of so-called human rights clauses in the bilateral agreements concluded by the Community alone or jointly with its Member States, see the Communication from the Commission on the Inclusion of Respect for Democratic Principles and Human Rights in Agreements between the Community and Third Countries, COM(95) 216 final of May 23, 1995 and Brandtner and Rosas, "Human Rights and the External Relations of the European Community: An Analysis of Doctrine and Practice", (1998) 9 E.J.I.L. 468–490 at pp. 473–477.

[55] An example of such partial suspension of a mixed treaty is provided by Regulation 3300/91 [1991] O.J. L315/1, suspending the trade concessions provided for by the Co-operation Agreement between the E.E.C. and the Socialist Federal Republic of Yugoslavia of 1983. The legal base for this Regulation was Art. 133 EC (ex Art. 133). See also Case C–162/96 *Racke* [1998] E.C.R. I–3655.

[56] [1991] O.J. L315/47. As was noted above, n. 55, a separate Regulation was adopted to suspend the trade concessions. This was apparently done in the interest of legal security (given the possible private interests involved). With respect to a separate Agreement between the Member States of the European Coal and Steel Community and the Socialist Federal Republic of Yugoslavia (which was thus not a Community agreement in the strict sense), suspension of trade concessions was based on a Decision of the Representatives of the Government of the Member States, meeting within the Council, [1991] O.J. L315/49.

[57] COM(96) 69 final of February 21, 1996.

[58] Council decision on the procedure for implementing Article 366a of the fourth ACP-EC Convention of March 11, 1999, [1999] O.J. L75/32. The assent of the Parliament was necessary as the legal basis of the decision is Art. 310 EC (ex Art. 238) which is also the legal basis of the Lomé Convention.

[59] See above, p. 203, n. 19.

to be taken and the procedures to be followed in applying the Fourth ACP-EC Convention,[60] according to which the Council, in deciding on suspension, is authorised to cover the field of national competences as well. Thus, the Council, applying the new framework decision and the accompanying amendment of the Internal Agreement, can always decide on partial suspension of the Convention by qualified majority, even if Member States competences are involved. There are already some cases of the application of the new framework decision.[61]

The very existence and extent of treaty obligations may also be affected by *reservations*.[62] It is beyond doubt that the Community may formulate reservations to agreements it concludes and may also object to reservations formulated by others, even if practice is scarce in this field.[63] In the case of mixed agreements, the matter becomes more complex. It would seem that Community reservations can be formulated to the whole agreement in the case of parallel competences, and in the case of co-existent and concurrent competences to those parts of the agreements which have not been reserved for the Member States.

It is not obvious that the latter limitation always applies to Community *objections* to reservations. An objecting party has to determine whether it accepts treaty relations with the reserving party, and it may also wish to make a pronouncement as to the permissibility of a reservation, in particular its relation to the object and purpose of the agreement. Even if a reservation relates to the "national" part of an agreement, there are arguments for allowing a Community objection determining that the reservation is incompatible with the object and purpose of the treaty, as such a reservation may affect the entire treaty régime.

An example of a reservation potentially affecting Community competences and interests is a reservation made by Lebanon in March 1996 to the 1988 UN Convention against Illicit Traffic in Narcotic Drugs and Psychotropic Substances. The reservation relates to provisions which do not fall under the declaration of Community competences made at the time of conclusion in October 1990 but which may later have

---

[60] 91/402/E.E.C., [1991] O.J. L229/301; Decision of the Representatives of the Governments of the Member States of the European Communities, meeting within the Council, of March 11, 1999 amending the internal agreement on the measures to be taken and the procedures to be followed in applying the fourth ACP-EC Convention, [1999] O.J. L75/30.

[61] While formal consultations under Art. 366a have been held with several countries, that is, *Togo*, Communication from the Commission to the Council of July 8, 1998, SEC (1998) 1189 final; *Nigér*, Communication from the Commission to the Council of April 26, 1999, COM(1999) 204 final; *Guinea-Bissau*, Communication from the Commission to the Council of July 9, 1999, COM(1999) 361 final; *The Comoros*, Communication from the Commission to the Council of June 15, 1999, COM(1999) 295 final, sanctions measures were taken against Nigér on July 29, 1999, Communication from the Commission to the Council of July 8, 1999, COM(1999) 350 final, Council Decision of July 29, 1999.

[62] Arts. 19–23 of the Vienna Convention on the Law of Treaties of 1969 and the same articles in the corresponding Convention relating to treaties concluded by international organisations of 1986.

[63] In 1994, the Commission submitted a modified proposal to the Council for the conclusion of Council of Europe Convention No. 123 (1985) for the Protection of Vertebrate Animals for Experimental and Other Scientific Purposes, signed by the Community in 1987. In this modified proposal (the original proposal was submitted in 1989), it was suggested to formulate a reservation to Art. 28 on the obligation to provide statistical information, COM(94) 366 final of September 9, 1994 (following amendments proposed by the European Parliament, a new modified proposal was made in 1996, COM(96) 293 final). The Convention was concluded by the Community on March 23, 1998, subject to the reservation, Council Decision 1999/575/EC, [1999] O.J. L222/29 (the text of the reservation is contained in Annex B of the Council Decision, which refers to the reservation in Arts. 1 and 2). See also MacLeod, Hendry and Hyett, *op. cit.*, pp. 117–118, 133, who refer to the possibility of reservations restricting the territorial application of an agreement and mention as an example the conclusion of the 1979 Convention on the Conservation of European Wildlife and Natural Habitats, which (as expressly allowed under Article 21 of the Convention) contained an exception for Greenland ([1982] O.J. L38/2).

become part of Community competences.[64] Is a Community objection dependent on an up-dating of the declaration of competence, and what is the relevance of the question whether the Lebanese reservation is compatible with the object and purpose of the UN Convention, or whether it constitutes a valid reservation at all?[65]

Reservations, and objections to reservations, formulated by Member States to mixed agreements would be highly problematic, if no Community co-ordination has taken place. It is obvious that Member States may not enter into reservations to provisions belonging to exclusive Community competences, or object to reservations affecting such provisions. But also with respect to other parts of a mixed agreement, individual Member States" reservations, or objections to reservations, may constitute violations of the duty of co-operation and the principle of unity of external representation, as formulated by the Court of Justice. For instance, an objection to a reservation may exclude treaty relations between the reserving and the objecting State, which in the case of a mixed agreement could lead to legal uncertainty and confusion, if such an objection has been made by one or more Member States but not by the Community. The Commission has recently initiated a discussion on the procedures to follow in the co-ordination of reservations, and objections to reservations, with respect to mixed agreements.[66]

Problems of Application and Implementation

13.08   It is not possible within the confines of this article to enter into a detailed discussion on the practical problems facing the Community and its Member States in the external representation of the E.U. in mixed contexts, including participation in the work of other international organisations.[67] It should be stressed that in some organisations, notably the World Trade Organisation, it is often possible in day-to-day work to avoid battles of competence between the Commission and the Member States and to secure some unity of representation through the former.[68]

More problems have been encountered in the Food and Agriculture Organisation (FAO), to which the Community is a member, as illustrated by the controversy over the right to vote in the FAO Conference on the adoption of an Agreement to Promote Compliance with International Conservation and Management Measures by Fishing Vessels on the High Seas. The 1993 decision of the E.U. Council to allocate the right to vote to the Member States, despite the predominant if not exclusive Community competences in the fields covered by the Agreement, was, in a case brought by the Com-

[64] Council Decision 90/611/E.E.C., [1990] O.J. L326/56. The declaration of competence (annexed to the Council decision) covers Art. 12 of the Convention only, while the Lebanese reservations relate to Arts 5, 7 and 32. Apart from the reservation to Art. 32 relating to the settlement of disputes, the reservations relate to provisions prohibiting parties to invoke banking secrecy laws in order to avoid obligations under the Convention relating to the production of documents in legal proceedings. After the conclusion of the Convention by the Community, the question of banking secrecy may have been affected by a money laundering directive adopted in 1991 (Directive 91/308, [1991] O.J. L166/77).
[65] The Lebanese Government simply stated that it "has reservations" regarding certain paragraphs in Arts 5 and 7. Is such a declaration precise enough to constitute a valid reservation?
[66] Commission Staff Working Paper, "Reservations and objections to reservations with regard to mixed agreements", SEC(1998) 2249 of December 23, 1998.
[67] See, e.g. Sack, "The European Community's Membership of International Organisations", (1995) 32 C.M.L.Rev. 1227–1256; Denza, "The Community as a Member of International Organisations", in Emiliou and O'Keeffe (eds.), The European Union and World Trade Law after the GATT Uruguay Round (John Wiley & Sons, 1996), pp. 3–15; Frid, op. cit., passim.
[68] The representation of the Community in the WTO does not seem to have been seriously hampered by the lack of a Code of Conduct. So far, the Commission and the Council have not been able to agree on such a Code. See Sack, loc. cit., 1248, 1253; Heliskoski, "The 'Duty of Co-operation' between the European Community and Its Member States Within the World Trade Organisation", in (1996) 7 Finnish Yearbook of International Law (Kluwer, 1997), pp. 59–133 at pp. 116–122.

mission against the Council, annulled by the Court of Justice, as "the thrust of the issue" lay in an area within the exclusive competence of the Community.[69]

In the *FAO* case, the Court held that an arrangement concluded between the Commission and the Council and setting up a co-ordination procedure between the Commission and the Member States represented fulfilment of the *duty of co-operation* which the Court has articulated for areas of mixed competence as following from the "requirement of unity in the international representation of the Community".[70] In many instances, including organisations of which the Community is not a member despite the existence of Community competences (*e.g.* the International Labour Organisation (ILO)[71] and the Organisation for Economic Co-operation and Development (OECD)[72]) the lack of similar arrangements providing for the co-ordination of mixed competences may make it even more difficult to implement the duty of co-operation.[73] It is an unfortunate fact that day-to-day Community work in the external field is riddled by disagreements between the Commission and the Member States on the division and exercise of competences.[74]

The WTO context has recently highlighted the question of how competence is to be exercised and the E.C. be represented in *dispute settlement* with third countries. In a case involving exclusive Community competence under Article 133 EC (ex Article 113), the United States took action both against the E.C. and two of its Member States, Ireland and the United Kingdom. The case, on behalf of the Community, was handled by the European Commission. In its report, the WTO Appellate Body, in refuting the assumption of the Panel that special importance should be given to the practice by the customs authorities of Ireland and the United Kingdom, observed that the export market for the United States "is the European Communities, not an individual Member State".[75]

13.09   While this case concerned trade in goods, in other words an area of exclusive Community competence, the situation is more complex with respect to trade in

---

[69] Case C–25/94 *Commission* v. *Council* [1996] E.C.R. I–1469. This was in application of an arrangement on the preparation for FAO meetings, statements and voting concluded between the Council and the Commission in December 1991. On this arrangement, see Sack, *loc. cit.*, 1254–1256; Frid, *op. cit.*, pp. 255–261. See further chapter 6 by Heliskoski.

[70] Paras. 48–49 of the *FAO* judgment. The Court referred to its earlier case law in Ruling 1/78 [1978] E.C.R. 2151, paras. 34–36; Opinion 2/91 [1993] E.C.R. I–1061, para. 36; Opinion 1/94 [1994] E.C.R. I–5267, para. 108.

[71] See Opinion 2/91 [1993] E.C.R. I–1061 and Frid, *op. cit.*, p. 281 et seq.

[72] See Art. 304 (ex Art. 231) of the E.C. Treaty; Opinion 2/92 [1995] E.C.R. I–521 (*cf.* Opinion 1/75 [1975] E.C.R. 1355, which concluded that a certain arrangement elaborated within the framework of the OECD belonged to the exclusive competence of the Community under Art. 133 of the E.C. Treaty); Denza, *op. cit.*, pp. 11–12.

[73] On December 22, 1986 the Council adopted a decision relating to Community participation in ILO negotiations but limited to cases of exclusive Community competence. In January 1994, after Opinion 2/91, the Commission submitted a proposal for a Council decision on the exercise of the Community's external competence in cases of joint competences (COM(94) 2 final), but this proposal has not been acted upon by the Council. See Frid, *op. cit.*, pp. 295, 312–313; Denza, *op. cit.*, pp. 10–11. In the OECD context, there is a Council decision of June 9, 1988 relating to the approval, on behalf of the Community, of binding OECD decisions covering Community competences, see Opinion 2/92 [1995] E.C.R. I–521 at 527.

[74] Sack, *loc. cit.*, 1256, notes that:

"Member States are often tempted to keep cases of exclusive EC competence to a minimum, and in cases of joint competence, to keep the main responsibility within their domain. In some respects this is understandable and sometimes leads to an overreaction on the part of the Commission, but its general result is a constant battle of wills which places an excessive burden on the machinery of the Council and the Commission and wastes precious energy that might be better directed against the outside world."

[75] *European Communities—Customs Classification of Certain Computer Equipment*, Report of the Appellate Body AB–1998–2 of June 5, 1998, para. 96. It will be noted that the name of the case refers to the European Communities only. The Panel (Report of February 5, 1998) declined a request by the United States to broaden the name of the case to include reference to the two EU Member States.

services (the GATS Agreement) and trade-related intellectual property rights (the TRIPS Agreement). The United States has recently initiated consultations with EU Member States rather than the Commission on a number of GATS and TRIPS cases.[76] The European Commission, representing the Communities, has insisted on becoming involved in these consultations and representatives of the Commission have participated alongside the delegation of the Member State concerned. In a TRIPS case initiated against Ireland, which was about to lead to the establishment of a Panel, it was agreed that the E.C., too, should be a defendant.[77] The dispute was subsequently settled out of court. The case may nevertheless constitute a precedent for a practice according to which the E.C. should always be a co-defendant in cases brought under GATS or TRIPS against one or more E.U. Member States. This is because the E.C. appears responsible for the implementation of these agreements in their entirety, given that no declaration of competence has been given.[78] In the same vein, offensive GATS and TRIPS cases initiated by the E.U. against third countries should be brought jointly by the E.C. and its Member States, as has also been the practice so far.[79] A case initiated by a Member State, without E.C. co-ordination, would pose a veritable threat to the principles of co-operation and unity of representation.

Further clarifications on such issues could, of course, be sought from the Court of Justice either under the Opinion procedure provided for in Article 300 (ex Article 228), paragraph 6, as actions of annulment under Article 230 (ex Article 173), or as infringement cases under Article 226 (ex Article 169) of the E.C. Treaty. The Article 234 (ex Article 177) institution of preliminary rulings, on the other hand, would not normally provide an opportunity to clarify the duty of co-operation.

The Article 234 procedure, however, raises the more general question of the *judicial control* of mixed agreements. To what extent are mixed agreements "acts of the institutions of the Community" which can be the object of a preliminary ruling according to Article 234? The fact that in such instances the Council and the Member States have insisted on mixity could be taken as an indication that they have wanted to reserve Community participation in the agreement to areas of exclusive Community competence.[80]

True, the fact that in such instances the Council and the Member States insist on mixity may be taken as an indication that they want to reserve Community participation to areas of exclusive Community competences. But can this presumed desire limit the jurisdiction of the Court of Justice, especially if it is not clearly expressed and/or the agreement itself forms a whole which is not easily broken down into two separate parts? The need for unity of interpretation, including on such a fundamental question as to whether the agreement has direct effect or not, would certainly speak in

---

[76] Cases DS80 (*Belgium—Measures Affecting Commercial Telephone Directory Services*), DS82 (*Ireland—Measures Affecting the Grant of Copyright and Neighbouring Rights*), DS83 (*Denmark—Measures Affecting the Enforcement of Intellectual Property Rights*), DS86 (*Sweden—Measures Affecting the Enforcement of Intellectual Property Rights*), DS125 (*Greece—Enforcement of Intellectual Property Rights for Motion Pictures and Television Programs*).

[77] Case WT/DS82/1 (see above, n. 76).

[78] See below, pp. 215 and 216, at n. 89 and 93–95.

[79] Cases DS38 (*United States—The Cuban Liberty and Democratic Solidarity Act*, Panel established but suspended in April 1997 and lapsed on April 21, 1998); DS79 (*India—Patent Protection for Pharmaceutical and Agricultural Chemical Products*, Panel reported adopted on September 22, 1998); DS114 (*Canada—Patent Protection of Pharmaceutical Products*); DS117 (*Canada—Measures Affecting Film Distribution Services*).

[80] In the Council Decision 94/800/E.C. of December 22, 1994 ([1994] O.J. L336/1) on the conclusion on behalf of the E.C. of the WTO Agreements emanating from the Uruguay Round, it is spelled out that the conclusion of these agreements on behalf of the E.C. is only "as regards matters within its competence". [1994] O.J. L336/1. See also Heliskoski, *op. cit.*, p. 90.

favour of the competence of the Court over the whole range of issues covered by the agreement.[81]

The Court of Justice has already in the past delivered some preliminary rulings on the interpretation of (mixed) association agreements.[82] This approach was reaffirmed and made more explicit in *Demirel*, where the Court, by reference to Article 310 EC (then Article 238) (the legal basis for the agreement in question), held that it could interpret the part of the 1963 Association Agreement with Turkey which related to freedom of movement of persons.[83] The Court noted that freedom of movement of persons is covered by the Treaty (without making a distinction between right of entry into the community and freedom of movement inside the Community) and comes, through the device of Article 238, under Community competences. It was thus not necessary to rule on whether the Court would also have competence to interpret provisions of mixed agreements which fall under national competences proper.

This judgment concerned an association agreement covered by Article 310 EC (ex Article 238). Such agreements are seen as pre-accession agreements or at least agreements which are based on "privileged and special links" between the E.C. and the third country concerned.[84] They require unanimity in the Council.

13.10   The *Hermès* case decided in 1998[85] concerned a provision (Article 50) of the TRIPS Agreement, which the E.C. had concluded in 1994 "with regard to that portion of [it] which falls within the competence of the European Community".[86] Three Member States (France, Netherlands, United Kingdom) submitted that the Court of Justice had no jurisdiction to answer the question put by the Dutch court, as the Community had not adopted any harmonising measures in the area covered by Article 50 (authority of national judicial authorities to adopt provisional measures to guarantee the enforcement of intellectual property rights) and thus this provision did not fall within the scope of application of Community law and the Court had accordingly no jurisdiction to interpret the provision.

The Advocate General (Mr Tesauro) held that the Court is competent to give a preliminary ruling on all provisions of TRIPS. He invoked, *inter alia*, the requirements of uniformity of interpretation (to avoid the possibility of 16 different interpretations of such a fundamental question as direct effect) and the responsibility of the E.C., in the absence of a declaration of competence, for the implementation of the entire agreement in relation to third countries.

The Court arrived at the same conclusion, but focused its attention on the existence of the Community trade mark, established by Regulation 40/94 of December 20, 1993 on the Community trade mark.[87] The Court noted that Article 50 of TRIPS applies to Community trade marks as well as national trade marks, and that it was thus in the Community interest to obtain a uniform interpretation of that provision, even if the dispute before the national Dutch court did not concern Community but Benelux trade marks. On this basis, the Court had "in any event" jurisdiction to interpret Article 50 of the TRIPS Agreement.[88] But this discussion is preceded by the following laconic

---

[81] See also Neuwahl, *op. cit.*, pp. 734–736, who notes that "the competence of the Court of Justice in matters regarding the application of mixed agreements is very broad".

[82] Case 181/73 *Haegeman* [1974] E.C.R. 449; Case 87/75 *Bresciani* [1976] E.C.R. 129; Case 76/77 *Razanatsimba* [1977] E.C.R. 2229.

[83] Case 12/86 *Demirel* [1987] E.C.R. 3749, at 3750–3751. See also Case C–192/89 *Sevince* [1990] E.C.R. 3461 at 3500–3501.

[84] Case 12/86 *Demirel* [1987] E.C.R. 3749, para. 9.

[85] Case C–53/96 *Hermès* [1998] E.C.R. I–3603.

[86] Council Decision 94/800/E.C. of December 22, 1994 (see above, p. 213, n. 80).

[87] [1993] O.J. L 11/1.

[88] Case C–53/96 *Hermès* [1998] E.C.R. I–3606, para. 29 of the judgment.

statement, which is a general comment to the argument on lack of jurisdiction put forward by three Member States:[89]

> "It should be pointed out, however, that the WTO Agreement was concluded by the Community and ratified by its Member States without any allocation between them of their respective obligations towards the other contracting parties."

This statement (note the word "however") could be seen as an (implicit) acceptance of the thesis put forward by the Advocate General, that is, the responsibility of the E.C. for the implementation of the whole agreement.

If a mixed agreement is an "act of the institutions of the Community", as provided in Article 234, it forms part of Community law and, in that capacity, also the law of Member States and could, if having direct effect, be invoked by individuals before national courts.[90] Thus "national" problems of implementation (notably in States with a dualist system) would not arise. While it is clear that this would apply to areas of exclusive Community competences with respect to agreement implying co-existent competences (category II.1 above), the situation is less clear with respect to cases of concurrent (II.2) competences. If in line what has been said above, it is accepted that mixed agreements such as the association agreements and the TRIPS Agreement constitute in their entirety Community law, then the question arises as to what are, if any, the legal implications of Member States participation in the agreement in question, given the supremacy of Community law over (other) national law. If there are in fact no parts of the agreement "reserved" for the Member States by a decision of the Council or otherwise, it would seem that their adherence to the agreement becomes mainly of a symbolic nature as far as the application of the agreement is concerned.[91]

13.11 If, on the other hand, there are areas clearly reserved for the Member States, defaults in the domestic implementation of the "national" part of the agreement (*e.g.* non-incorporation in a dualist system) may imply that that part of the agreement cannot be invoked before national courts and authorities. One can also envisage other problems of a constitutional nature, such as the question whether binding decisions of a joint body established under the agreement ("Association Council" or the like) belong to the area of national competences and would thus entail a new transfer of powers from the national to the Community level.[92]

As can be seen from the *Hermès* case, these problems are related to the question of the international *responsibility* of the Community for the implementation of a mixed agreement.[93] While in the case of parallel competences (category I above), each party alone bears the responsibility for the fulfilment of the entire agreement, the situation is

---

[89] *ibid.*, para. 24 of the judgment.

[90] In fact, this was one of the issues in Case 12/86 *Demirel* [1987] E.C.R. 3749 and Case C–53/96 *Hermès* [1998] E.C.R. I–3603. The Court in *Demirel* answered the question in the negative, while the Court in *Hermès* left the question open.

[91] Is this not the case at least with respect to association agreements and other agreements of concurrent (category II.2) competences, in view of *Demirel, Hermès* and other relevant case law (see above, p. 214, nn. 82–85)? The fact that the Council and the Member States have not foreseen participation in the mixed agreement of all the Member States ("incomplete" mixity) would also suggest that there is no area in the agreement reserved for Member States competences.

[92] Such problems are discussed in an Opinion (No. 20/1995) delivered on 30 November 1995 by the Constitutional Committee of the Finnish Parliament and concerning the conclusion of the 1995 Europe Agreement with Estonia (which is a mixed agreement).

[93] *Cf.* Case 12/86, *Demirel* [1987] E.C.R. 3749, para. 11, where the Court held that the Member States, in ensuring respect for commitments arising from an agreement concluded by the Community, fulfil an obligation in relation to the Community, "which has assumed responsibility for the due performance of the agreement".

more complex in the field of shared competences. If competences are co-existent (category II.1), the Community (or a Member State) may escape responsibility for violations of provisions falling outside its competence, provided it does not act *ultra vires* and if the third State is aware, or should be aware, of the lack of competence.[94] If competences are concurrent (category II.2), the Community and the Member States arguably entail joint responsibility for the implementation of the whole agreement, in other words, a case could be brought against them jointly; but the Community seems to have also several responsibility, that is, it is responsible alone for the implementation of the whole agreement.[95]

Mixed agreements also raise the question of the responsibility of the E.C. and the Member States towards each other for the fulfilment of the agreement.[96] In situations of parallel competence (category I above), and perhaps in situations of co-existent horizontal competence (II.1.A), the situation might be governed by public international law and such a responsibility could accordingly not be excluded. However, in situations of co-existent vertical competence (II.1.B), such as the Agreement on Straddling Fish Stocks,[97] as well as concurrent competence (II.2) such as the TRIPS Agreement,[98] the relation between the E.C. and the Member States, and the Member States among themselves, seems to be one of Community law, so that the rights and obligations apply between the Community and its Member States, on the one hand, and third States, on the other. Sometimes this is made explicit by the insertion of a so-called "disconnection clause" in the agreement itself.[99]

CONCLUDING OBSERVATIONS

13.12 With all these problems and open questions, it is not surprising that ways and means are sought to avoid mixity altogether. Pure Community agreements may be preferred not only by the Commission but sometimes also by some or all of the Member States, mainly in order to speed up the process and avoid complications of various sorts. There have been situations where third States, out of similar considerations, have expressed a preference for a pure Community agreement.[1] An alternative, which seems to have become more common during recent years, is to avoid cumbersome

---

[94] See, *e.g.* Dolmans, *op. cit.*, pp. 73 *et seq.*; Conze, *op. cit.*, pp. 73–92. *Cf.* C. Tomuschat, "Liability for Mixed Agreements", in O'Keeffe and Schermers, *op. cit.*, pp. 129 *et seq.* and Bleckman, "The Mixed Agreements of the E.E.C. in Public International Law", in O'Keeffe and Schermers, *op. cit.*, pp. 157 *et seq.*, who assert an assumption of the unity of the mixed agreement and ensuing joint responsibility of the Community and its Member States. Arts. 4 and 6 of Annex IX of the Convention on the Law of the Sea are based on the principle that an international organisation (or its Member State) has responsibility only for violations of provisions falling under its competence. But if a third State Party requests the Community for information as to who has responsibility in respect of any specific matter, failure to provide information or the provision of contradictory information "shall result in joint and several liability" (Art. 6, para. 2).

[95] See Case 12.86 *Demirel* [1987] E.C.R. 3749 and Advocate General Tesauro in Case C–53/96 *Hermès* [1998] E.C.R. I–3603. Mr Tesauro observed (apparently with respect to mixed agreements involving shared competences, at least (to use our terminology) agreements involving shared and concurrent competence), that "the fact that the Community is a party *vis-à-vis* the contracting non-member States and that, under Art. [300] of the Treaty, an international agreement (also) concluded by the Community is binding on the institutions of the Community and on the Member States, inevitably means that the Community is responsible *vis-à-vis* every party to the agreement in question", see [1998] E.C.R. I–3620 (para. 20).

[96] See Kuijper, "The Conclusion and Implementation of the Uruguay Round Results by the European Community", (1995) 6 E.J.I.L., 222–244 at 227–229.

[97] See above, p. 204, n. 27.

[98] See above, p. 214, n. 85 and n. 95 on this page.

[99] Kuijper, *op. cit.*, at 228.

[1] This observation is based on the experience of the present author in his capacity, since 1995, as a member of the Legal Service of the Commission.

procedures by adopting a "soft law" instrument in the form of a declaration or an action plan, which may be adopted by the Council and sometimes also signed by the Council Presidency and/or the Commission, but without the need for 15 national ratifications.[2]

As far as treaties, and notably bilateral agreements, are concerned, one obvious path is to try to devise the negotiation directives to be adopted by the Council,[3] and to conduct the actual negotiations, so as to avoid areas of national competence. It should be noted that Member States are often unwilling to authorise the Community alone to conclude bilateral agreements containing concurrent competences. An example, we would argue, would be the existence of substantive provisions relating to intellectual property rights. Such clauses (as well as clauses on services or direct investment) in a draft bilateral agreement would almost inevitably lead to an assertion of mixity, as at least some Member States seem to interpret Opinion 1/94 as establishing exclusive national competences in this field.[4]

To avoid such assertions of mixity, the Commission may try to avoid provisions on questions such as intellectual property rights, services, or investments. An alternative is to couch them in non-committal language or as unilateral commitments on the part of the third State, implying that they, in accordance with the case law of the Court of Justice, become ancillary (subsidiary) obligations falling under Article 133 (common commercial policy) of the E.C. Treaty and thus under exclusive Community competences.[5]

To take another example, the Opinion of the Court of Justice denying competence for the Community to adhere, on the basis of Article 308 (ex Article 235) of the E.C. Treaty, to the European Convention on Human Rights[6] has probably reinforced an effort on the part of the Commission to avoid, in connection with the human rights clause to be inserted in bilateral agreements of a general nature,[7] specific references to binding human rights conventions or the development of new standards in the field of human rights.[8] The idea is to keep the human rights clause as a mere reaffirmation of general principles which constitute customary international law or general principles of law recognised by civilised nations[9] already binding on the Community, so that the

---

[2] See, e.g. the Barcelona Declaration adopted at the Euro-Mediterranean Conference of 27–28 November 1995 and the New Transatlantic Agenda signed by President Clinton, Prime Minister Gonzales of Spain (representing the then Spanish Council Presidency) and President Santer of the European Commission, text published in (1996) 1 E.F.A. Rev. 125. See also the documents adopted at the E.U.-U.S. Summit in London on May 18, 1998 with a view to resolve the so-called Helms-Burton dispute (Understanding with Respect to Disciplines for the Strengthening of Investment Protection, Transatlantic Partnership on Political Co-operation, Understanding on Conflicting Requirements), see S. Smis and K. Van der Borght, "The E.U.-U.S. Compromise on the Helms-Burton and D'Amato Acts", (1999) 93 A.J.I.L. 227–236; idem, "The Cuban Liberty and Democratic Solidarity (Libertad) Act of 1996, Some Aspects from the Perspective of International Economic Law", Revue Belge de Droit International 1998/1, pp.217–258.

[3] See Art. 300(1) EC (ex Art. 228(1)).

[4] See above, p. 206, n. 38 and p. 214 n. 85, on the potential competence of the Community to conclude international agreements in the field of intellectual property rights.

[5] See above, p. 205, n. 28.

[6] Opinion 2/94 [1996] E.C.R. I–1759. See comments by Kokott and Hoffmeister in (1996) 90 A.J.I.L. 664–669; R. Errera in Gazette européenne—Gazette du Palais 1–3 décembre 1996, pp. 11–14.

[7] See above, p. 209, n. 54.

[8] The Court stated in Opinion 2/94 [1996] E.C.R. I–1759 that "no Treaty provision confers on the Community institutions any general power to enact rules on human rights or to conclude international conventions in this field" (para. 27). However, this does not necessarily imply that the Community is debarred from joining any human rights treaty. The paragraph quoted above was followed (paras 28–36) by a discussion on Art. 308, EC (then Art. 235), which was ruled out as a proper legal base, not necessarily because human rights would not constitute "an objective of the Community" (as Art. 308 requires), but because of the particular institutional and constitutional problems linked to adherence to the European Convention, with its elaborate control machinery.

[9] See Art. 38, para. 1 (b) and (c), of the Statute of the International Court of Justice.

main legal implication of the clause is to spell out a right of suspension in case of violation of such fundamental human rights.[10]

13.13 While, also after Opinion 2/94, the human rights clause couched in such general terms has not caused Community agreements to become mixed, there have been continuing differences of opinion between the Commission and the Council as to the legal implications of provisions in the trade and investment domain. In 1995–96, agreements with the Southern Common Market (Mercosur) and its Party States (Argentina, Brazil, Paraguay and Uruguay)[11] and South Korea[12], and in 1999, with South Africa, were at Council level held to be mixed, on grounds that could not be accepted by the Commission. A "legal compromise" was to insert a clause on political dialogue, which could be considered a "Second pillar" (Common Foreign and Security Policy) issue and thus be accepted by the Commission as a ground for mixity. In such a situation of "mixity at all costs", the Commission found itself in the strange role of insisting on a clause making mixity legally necessary (obligatory mixity).

On the other hand, the Commission has recently succeeded in negotiating a string of bilateral agreements which have been or will be concluded as pure Community agreements, without the participation of the Member States. Such agreements have been negotiated with Bangladesh, Cambodia, Laos, Macedonia, Pakistan, the Palestine Authority (represented by the Palestine Liberation Organisation), Vietnam and Yemen.[13] This may be seen as a result of a concerted effort on the part of the Commission, in order to avoid lengthy and cumbersome ratification procedures with respect to agreements for which there was no concrete need to include provisions belonging to Member States competences.

Such efforts are bolstered by the judgment of the Court of Justice in *Portugal* v. *Council* concerning the 1994 trade and co-operation agreement with India.[14] The Court held that general clauses on human rights, energy, tourism and culture, the fight against drugs and intellectual property rights fell within the ambit of Articles 177 EC (ex Article 130u) and 181 EC (ex Article 130y) on development co-operation. Thus, the agreement belonged to the sphere of Community competences and could be based on Articles 133 EC (ex Article 113) and 181. In this context, it is interesting to note that in the *FAO* case the Court, despite the fact that the Commission had agreed to mixity, may have hinted at the possibility that mixity in this case was not legally required, the provisions for which national competence had been argued by the Council being of an ancillary character.[15] Moreover, in the *Centro-Com* case the Court reaffirmed that political motives behind trade measures (in this case the trade embargo

---

[10] See Case C–268/94 *Portugal* v. *Council* [1996] E.C.R. I–6177; where the Court observed (para. 27) that an important function of the human rights clause may be to secure the right to suspend the agreement in case of human rights violations committed by the third State. See also Brandtner and Rosas, *op. cit.*, 474; Rosas, "The Role of the Universal Declaration of Human Rights in the Treaty Relations of the European Union", in Baehr, C. Flinterman, M. Senders (eds.), *Innovation and Inspiration: Fifty Years of the Universal Declaration of Human Rights* (Royal Netherlands Academy of Arts and Sciences, 1999), pp. 201–209 at p. 205–206.

[11] [1999] O.J. L112; [1999] O.J. L175. When the Agreement was not yet in force, parts of it were applied provisionally through a Council decision of November 20, 1995, [1996] O.J. L69/1.

[12] COM(96) 141 final of March 27, 1996. As conclusion of the agreement is subject to national ratifications, it has not yet entered into force.

[13] Co-operation agreement with Vietnam, [1996] O.J. L136/29; The Palestine Liberation Organisation, [1997] O.J. L187/1; Laos, [1997] O.J. L334/14; Macedonia, [1997] O.J. L348/1; Yemen, [1998] O.J. L72/17; Cambodia, [1999] O.J. L269. The agreement with Bangladesh was signed on May 22, 2000, but the Agreement with Pakistan has not yet been concluded at the time of writing.

[14] Case C–268/94 [1996] E.C.R. I–6177. See also above, n. 10 on this page.

[15] Case C–25/94 *Commission* v. *Council* [1996] E.C.R. I–1469. In para. 47 of the judgment, the Court noted the argument of the Council according to which the provisions in the FAO draft Agreement relating to penal sanctions and development co-operation belonged to the competence of the Member States but added that these provisions "do not, *in any event*, appear to occupy a prominent position in the draft Agreement" [1996] E.C.R. I–1510 (emphasis added).

against Ex-Yugoslavia) are not a sufficient reason to remove them from the ambit of Article 133 of the E.C. Treaty (in favour of Title V on Common Foreign and Security Policy).[16]

This case law seems to be based on the following two considerations: (a) The provisions of the E.C. Treaty, such as Articles 133 and 177, should not be interpreted narrowly; they may leave room for a number of measures which are not expressly provided for in the Treaty articles (this, of course, is no innovation but a mere reaffirmation of a traditional approach); (b) the fact that an area such as human rights, trade embargoes or the fight against drugs may be considered in the contexts of Titles V (common foreign and security policy) and/or VI (Police and Judicial Co-operation in Criminal Matters) of the TEU does not as such remove it from the sphere of the E.C. Treaty. On the contrary, the TEU seems to be based on the principle of preference for Community competence.[17]

13.14   There is thus still room for pure Community agreements. While many of them will continue to be based on Article 133 or other provisions conferring a competence of an exclusive nature (including the ERTA principle),[18] there seems to be a growing number of agreements belonging to the category of concurrent competences (category II.2 above). Development co-operation agreements and environmental agreements often belong to this category, as concurrent competences are spelled out in the E.C. Treaty,[19] but in accordance with what has been said above, a potential competence may exist in many other areas (such as intellectual property rights) covered by the E.C. Treaty as well. It remains to be seen to what extent the Council will agree to the Community becoming a party to such agreements and conventions, without insisting on Member States participation. In many instances this will presumably not be the case, and mixity will continue to be with us. The fact that the recent Intergovernmental Conference did not agree on a broadening of Article 133 EC (ex Article 113) so as to cover all questions of services, intellectual property rights and investment, is a telling sign of the unwillingness of Member States to give up mixity even in areas of commercial policy. During the spring of 1999, the Member States refused to accept a trade and co-operation agreement negotiated with South Africa as a pure Community agreement, even if it was obvious that there was no legal need to conclude the agreement as a mixed agreement.[20]

While mixity thus may be inevitable in some areas, it is also true that mixity often makes life more difficult for everybody involved. It is to be hoped that in the near future the Union will be able to tackle the following challenges:

---

[16]   Case C–124/95 [1997] E.C.R. I–81. The Court also concluded that payments in relation to trade in goods are covered by the then Art. 113 (the U.K. had frozen bank accounts belonging to a Yugoslav company thus preventing their use for payment of medical supplies sold by an Italian company). See also Cases 70/94 *Werner* [1995] E.C.R. I–3189 and C–83/94, *Leifer* [1995] E.C.R. I–3231, and A. Rosas, "Les relations internationales commerciales de l'Union européenne—Un apercu juridique et développements actuels", in M. Tupamäki (ed.), *Liber Amicorum Bengt Broms* (Finnish Branch of the International Law Association, 1999), pp. 399–416 at pp. 401–404.
[17]   This consideration stems from Art. 1 TEU (ex Art. A), according to which the Union shall be founded on the European Communities, "supplemented" by the policies and forms of co-operation introduced by the Treaty of Maastricht, and Art. 47 TEU (ex Art. M), according to which the provisions of Titles V and VI shall not affect the Community Treaties.
[18]   Case 22/70 [1971] E.C.R. 263. See also Rosas, *op. cit.*, p. 405–406.
[19]   Art. 174 EC (ex Art. 130r), para. 4, and Art. 181 (ex Art. 130y). It will be recalled that these concurrent competences are subject to the "AETR" (ERTA) principle on exclusive Community competence, see above, p. 205 n. 33, *supra*.
[20]   The proposal from the Commission to the Council to conclude an agreement on trade, development and co-operation between the Community and South Africa is contained in document COM(1999) 245 final of May 11, 1999. The agreement was signed on October 11, 1999. While the Commission preferred a Community agreement, the great majority of Member States wanted the agreement to become mixed. The author was involved in the negotiation and conclusion process.

(a) The need to extend, by Council decisions, the application of Article 133 on common commercial policy to all international agreements on services and/or intellectual property rights,[21] so as to enable the Community to apply its common commercial policy to areas which have become crucial elements of international trade (as compared to 1957, when trade in goods was still the predominant feature of world trade).

(b) The need to discuss the possibility of pure Community rather than mixed agreements in areas of concurrent competences. While Member States participation in such agreements may be legally permissible, practical reasons in many cases speak in favour of pure Community agreements. It should be recalled that Member States" participation in such agreements may often, from a strictly legal point of view, matter very little, as the agreement may be fully applicable as a Community agreement, binding in that capacity not only the E.C. institutions but also the Member States.[22]

(c) The need to respect and operationalise the duty of co-operation in areas of shared competences. In so far as the Member States—as they often do—insist on obligatory (legally required) mixity, with an explicit or implicit assertion that some parts of the agreement fall outside Community competences, they must also accept the implications of such an approach, notably a duty to accede themselves to the agreement without undue delay.

A combination of pragmatism and considerations of the common good, rather than battles of prestige, should be at the focus if these challenges are to be adequately met.

---

[21] According to para. 5 of Art. 133, added by the Treaty of Amsterdam, the Council, acting unanimously on a proposal from the Commission and after consulting the European Parliament, may extend the application of paras 1 to 4 to "international negotiations and agreements on services and intellectual property insofar as they are not covered by these paragraphs".

[22] According to Art. 300(7) Community agreements "shall be binding on the institutions of the Community and on Member States".

CHAPTER 14

The "Fourth Pillar" of the European Union After The Amsterdam Treaty

by

Ramon Torrent*

THE MAASTRICHT TREATY, THE UNION AND THE FOURTH PILLAR

14.01   The Treaty on European Union (TEU) made the language of "pillars" of the European Union fashionable. It is a pity. I believe that talking in this way gives rise to a very simplistic and essentially incorrect view of what the European Union actually is. But since everybody continues to speak of "pillars", I am virtually compelled to speak of the "fourth pillar" of the European Union.

If there are pillars, it must mean that there is a building to be constructed. Instead of constructing the conventional but misleading "Greek temple with three columns", I shall draw to your attention a very simple diagram I regard as much more meaningful:

The Union is the political and institutional framework within which the following competences are exercised:

The remaining competences of the Member States continue to be exercised outside the Union's institutional system.

↓

the competences of the European Community

certain of the Member States' competences
— CFSP and PJCCM
— FOURTH PILLAR

but when they are exercising their competences, Member States must comply with the obligations imposed on them by Community legislation (and by the TEU).

* Observatory of Globalisation, Universitat Autònoma de Barcelona, former director of external economic relations in the legal service of the Council of the European Union until 1998. The ideas contained in this paper were expressed for the first time at the Colloquium on the consequences of Opinion 1/94 of the Court of Justice, organised by the Centre for European Legal Studies of the Faculty of Law at Cambridge on December 9, 1995. They were then developed further at a seminar organised by the College of Europe, Bruges, as a result of which they were published in a collection entitled *La Communauté européenne et les accords mixtes* [The European Community and joint agreements], Bourgeois, Dewost et Gaiffe (eds.), (Presses interuniversitaires européennes, Brussels, 1997). With the permission of the College of Europe, this paper now supplements that publication and brings it up to date. All the ideas expressed are my own and do not necessarily represent the views of the institution in which I work.

In the diagram, you will find:

(a) the players endowed with competences and legal personality: the Community[1] and the Member States;

(b) the European Union, *i.e.* the political and institutional framework within which all Community competences (left-hand column) and certain of the Member States' competences (middle column) are exercised (see postscript); "certain" of their competences only, because their remaining competences continue to be exercised outside the Union framework (right-hand column); [2]

(c) you will also find in the diagram the two Treaty functions between which no distinction is usually made: the function of attributing competences to the Community and that of imposing obligations on Member States when they retain their competences. [3]

14.02   Before returning to this diagram with some examples, I should like to say something about Common Foreign and Security Policy (CFSP or the "second pillar"). If you were to read the TEU, you might understand CFSP as having a very wide scope and as covering, in particular, Member States' actions in the areas of external economic relations where they retain their competence. In fact:

(a) Article 12 TEU (ex Article J.2) refers to "any matter of foreign policy" and to "action in international organisations and at international conferences" with no exceptions (thus without excluding economic organisations and conferences);

(b) Article 13 TEU (ex Article J.3) is also general in its scope;

(c) moreover, and to conclude, Article 3 TEU (ex Article C) expressly establishes that "the Union shall ... ensure the consistency of its external activities as a whole in the context of its ... economic ... policies".

But nobody has interpreted CFSP as broadly as this. Why not? Because it was a narrow interpretation of CFSP that best served the corporatist interests of the officials who had to put it into practice.

---

[1] In this paper, the term "European Community" or "Community" naturally refers to the three Communities: the E.C., Euratom, the ECSC.

[2] At a time when the tendency to use Brussels as an alibi is becoming more widespread, it is salutary to recall that the majority of the policies most directly affecting citizens (not only education, health or public transport policies, but also work organisation and wages policies) are developed by our Member States outside the institutional framework of the Union.

[3] The subject of this paper does not permit me to go into more detail about the (essential !) distinction between the field of application of the Treaties and the scope of the Community's competences. So I shall restrict myself to one example : Arts. 149, 150, 151 and 152 EC (ex Arts. 126, 127, 128 and 129) limit the Community's competences: their scope excludes "any harmonisation of the laws and regulations of the Member States". However, this restriction does not mean that national legislation in the fields of culture, education or health is outside the field of application of the Treaties: quite the reverse, it is obliged to continue to respect the general principle of non-discrimination on the grounds of nationality and its specific translation in the field of the four freedoms.

(a) On the part of the ministries of foreign affairs, it was from the outset a question of "appropriating" CFSP, even if they did not particularly like it; it was not a question of "ceding" an element of CFSP to finance ministries or other ministries under the pretext that it also covered external economic relations.

(b) On the part of the Commission services, it was clear from the outset that "outside the Church—that is to say outside the Community—no salvation is to be found"; with regard to external economic relations in particular, there was only one strategy, namely to stretch the Community's exclusive competence *ad infinitum*; this strategy was incompatible with that of stimulating effective coordination of Member States' external economic policies in the context of CFSP.

Be that as it may, I fear that we are permanently condemned to an interpretation of CFSP which excludes from its scope external economic relations in the fields in which the Member States retain competence.[4]

Let us return for a moment to my diagram, with some examples:

Schengen. Where does it fit in? Originally, certainly in the right-hand column. There is no doubt that it could have been put in the middle column (which would have been a much better place for it); and the Accord itself acknowledges that certain of its rules may be replaced by a Community regulation in the left-hand column. (The introduction of Schengen into the Union system in this way is, in fact, the object of the relevant protocol in the Amsterdam Treaty.)

Action with regard to the former Yugoslavia. If we are talking about the sending in of armed forces, we are, at least for the moment, in the right-hand column. If we mention the "European administration" of the town of Mostar, we have moved into the middle column. If we look at the trade rules applicable to the republics created out of the former Yugoslavia, we are now in the left-hand column.

One last example may be helpful. What about the European Monetary System? It was always in the right-hand column—it should not be forgotten that those who drew up the Maastricht Treaty did not consider it a good idea to make the European monetary system part of the Community; from the institutional point of view, it was always akin to the Schengen Accord, being an agreement among the central banks of certain Member States. But after entry to the third stage of EMU, overnight monetary policy has fallen within the exclusive competence of the Community and has moved into the left-hand column. Nor should this be forgotten, at least if one wishes fully to understand the (very great) problem that EMU poses in terms of external relations: the problem is not one of ensuring that the states that are in adopt a "joint position",[5] but of

---

[4] The distinction introduced above in n. 3 between the field of application of the Community Treaties and the scope of the competences attributed to the Community is also essential, appropriately adapted, to an understanding of the scope of Common Foreign and Security Policy (CFSP). CFSP does not cover the whole of the foreign and security policy of Member States. The activities they develop in this field outside the Union's institutional system do not fall within CFSP, but equally, they do not necessarily fall outside the field of application of Title V of the TEU. They are, for example, subject to certain requirements in respect of reciprocal information and co-ordination (*cf.* Art. 12 TEU (ex Art. J.2), para. 1 and the first sentence of para. 3). Thus the field of application of the provisions of Title V of the TEU is wider than the scope of CFSP (that is to say, the scope of the competences that Member States exercise jointly within the institutional system of the Union).

[5] On that question, the reader can refer to the discussion between the author and Zilioli/Selmayr in the *Common Market Law Review* (1999) vol. 36, no. 2; (1999) vol. 36, no. 4; (2000) vol. 37, no. 3.

ensuring (which is not easy) that the Community can take over from the states that are in, since they will have lost their external competence in respect of monetary policy.

14.03   Let us consider another example which relates to our theme: "European" agreements, or "partnership" agreements with the republics of the former USSR. Where do they fit into our diagram? If you were to put this question to the majority of the departments in the foreign ministries of our Member States and to the majority of Community officials, you would receive the same answer, one which to them is obvious: these agreements are made up of two parts, the economic aspect, which comes under the left-hand column ("first pillar", "Community pillar"), and the political dialogue element, which comes under the middle column ("CFSP", "second pillar").[6] I am sure the reader is ahead of me when I say that this "obvious" answer is, to be blunt, wrong.

Why? Because one of the essential objects of these agreements (in the case of the partnership agreements, I would go so far as to say *the* essential object) comprises the rules applicable to the treatment of undertakings: investment/establishment and treatment post-establishment.[7] And at present, according to the Court's jurisprudence in its *WTO* and *OECD*[8] opinions, there is no longer any doubt that to a very great extent this question comes under Member States' competences in respect of economic matters. As a result, in accordance with my diagram, the object of these agreements is not completely covered by the "first pillar" and "second pillar" element; one last essential element remains, namely that which comes under Member States' competences in economic matters and, more particularly, in respect of external economic policy or relations.

But this last element does not, as one might expect, come under the right-hand column in my diagram: Member States' competences outside the institutional system of the Union. In fact, in the context of these agreements, Member State competences in respect of external economic relations are exercised "by their governments" (*i.e.* outside the Union's system) only at the time of national ratification procedures. Before this (in the negotiations) and after this (when the agreements are put into effect), national competences are exercised "in Brussels", in conjunction with national "CFSP" competences and Community competences.

Now we come to my Fourth Pillar: Member States' competences in respect of external economic relations (and, as we shall soon see, not only "economic" relations, and not even only "external" relations) exercised, *de facto*, within the institutional system of the union.

This is not the third pillar (Police and Judicial Co-operation in Criminal Matters—PJCCM), nor the second (CFSP) (even though this would be possible if its scope were to be interpreted more widely), nor the first (because it is Member State competences

---

[6] It should come as no surprise that they agree on this incorrect answer. It is this same agreement, based on different premises, that has given rise to a very narrow interpretation of CFSP.

[7] The agreement with Russia is aimed, above all, at preventing Russia from treating an investment by Exxon (American company) in Siberia more favourably than an investment by Shell (Anglo-Dutch company). This is the reason for the very curious wording of what is, in my opinion, the most important provision in the whole agreement: Article 28 on the "conditions relating to the establishment and activity of companies". It is established that, "without prejudice to the reservations listed in Annex 4, Russia shall grant to Russian subsidiaries of Community companies a treatment no less favourable than that granted to other Russian companies or to Russian companies which are subsidiaries of any third country companies whichever is the better, in respect of their operation".

[8] This Opinion, in which the Court confirms the jurisprudence in its Opinion 1/94, has not been sufficiently taken into account (this relates to Opinion 2/92, *on the competence of the Community or of one of its institutions as regards participating in the third revised decision of the OECD Council in respect of national treatment* [1995] E.C.R. I–521).

that are being exercised, and not Community competences)—therefore it can only be called the "fourth" pillar.

If I have succeeded in making you see my fourth pillar, it will be easy for you to find other examples.

In a multilateral context, the prime example is obviously that of participation in the World Trade Organisation (WTO). Once the agreements resulting from the Uruguay Round entered into force, they were put into effect in the same way as they had been negotiated: Member States' competences were exercised within the institutional system of the Union, together with and in conjunction with those of the Community.[9] Another example which is very important but is less well known is that of the negotiations within OECD with a view to a multilateral agreement on investment (MAI): here again, it was within the institutional system of the Union that Member States, in conjunction with the Community, defined the guidelines (approved by Council on November 27, 1995) that should be followed during the negotiations.

14.04   In terms of bilateral arrangements, the example of European agreements or partnership agreements can be widened to include all the "joint" or "mixed" agreements with non-member countries. The only difference lies in the greater or lesser weight of the national competences brought into play in the agreements.[10] In fact, one of the best examples of the bringing into play of the fourth pillar is that of a joint agreement almost as old as the Community itself: the Yaoundé/Lomé Conventions with the ACP countries. The financial element is one of the key elements of these Conventions, but it is not a Community matter: the financial contributions involving the EDF (European Development Fund) are still the responsibility of Member States. But these financial contributions are administered within the institutional system of the Union under conditions established in the "Internal Financial Agreement" (IFA) concluded among Member States. In fact, therefore, one could interpret this IFA as a formalisation of my fourth pillar.[11]

On the other hand, it may be useful to take a look at two other examples which I believe deserve attention:

(a) The first is that of the "action plans" with the United States and Canada. Are people aware that their "Building bridges across the Atlantic" element, relating to health, education, culture and youth policy, can be taken seriously only if Member States take responsibility for it, within the union? [12] However, if

---

[9] See the decisions (which were very important in terms of their substance) adopted by the Council, acting on behalf of the Community and the Member States, since the entry into force of the Uruguay Round agreements: the accession of new members to the WTO, the finalisation of negotiations pending on financial services and the movement of physical persons, prorogation and then finalisation of negotiations on basic telecommunications services, approval of the Ministerial Declaration of Singapore, prorogation of negotiations on measures providing safeguards in the context of GATS, introduction of the "panel" demand in respect of the United States, with regard to the Helms-Burton Act, etc.

[10] The only borderline case would be that of the agreement on the European Economic Area: in this case, the only provisions involving national competences are those concerning "political dialogue", which are thus covered by the second pillar. It is the only case I know of a "joint" agreement involving no fourth pillar.

[11] This is, in fact, the interpretation reached by the Court of Justice in Case C–316/91 *European Parliament* v. *Council* [1994] E.C.R. I–625. The Court rejected the appeal against the Council by the European Parliament, which submitted that the EFD had been "communautarised" by the IFA. The Court accepted the Council's argument that the IFA was only an instrument facilitating administration of the competences *of Member States* by linking Community institutions with them.

[12] For if one has even the slightest sense of the absurd, how could one conceive of a rational "partnership" in these spheres between the Community as such, with an available budget of a few dozen Euros, and the United States, with all its billions of dollars? Only an entity comprising all the Member States complete with their budgets and the range of activities these budgets finance is in a position to be an *equal* partner for the United States in these spheres.

that is the case, all these "action plans" do is to extend my "fourth pillar" to external relations in matters of health, education, culture and youth policy...

(b) The second example is that of the "pre-accession strategy" and accession negotiations with the Countries from Central and Eastern Europe (CCEE). I shall not comment on them politically, but shall consider the institutional context. In this context, the situation is clear: it is not the Community, exercising its competences, which negotiates the accession of these states to the European Union; it is Member States which will negotiate this accession. When one discusses the different "chapters" of accession with CCEE, all that is happening is that member states are jointly exercising national competences that will finally be put to the test on the occasion of the approval of the act of accession of these states. Does not this "joint exercising" constitute my "fourth pillar"?

An initial conclusion suggests itself: not only does the "fourth pillar" exist (even if it is an animal that is very often unaware of its own existence),[13] but it is developing further, inescapably and at a rapid rate. "Inescapably" not because the Court of Justice was in error in acknowledging that there are limits to the Community's exclusive external competence (as many commentators on Opinion 1/94 imply, even daring to accuse the Court of having yielded to pressure from I know not whom). "Inescapably" because in reality, international economic relations—and, in fact, international relations in general—are covering more and more sectors and becoming increasingly interdependent; consequently, it is becoming more and more impossible for each of our Member States to find its own "little niche"; it becomes necessary to take joint international action within the Union, and in conjunction with the action of the Community (and this need comes from outside—it is "the world" that imposes it on us). That is the reality of the situation; policies need to deal with this reality, and legal experts need to equip them with the legal means to do so. In order to stimulate thought on the subject, I shall go on to give you an idea of what I see as the essential—but embryonic—elements of the "law of the fourth pillar".

The Law of the Fourth Pillar before The Amsterdam Treaty

The legal framework of the fourth pillar

14.05 There is no one article in the Treaties specifically regulating the development of the fourth pillar. However, this does not mean that the fourth pillar is "outside the law". Far from it! The fourth pillar is developing (in good faith on the part of those promoting its development, if I may be allowed to say so) by virtue of the obligations in respect of loyal co-operation imposed by the Treaties (as interpreted by the Court) on Member States and on the Community institutions (Article 3 TEU (ex Article C), Article 10 EC (ex Article 5), ILO/Uruguay Round jurisprudence of the Court of Justice). The fourth pillar "unionises" the exercising of Member State competences; this "unionisation" takes place around the Community. Does this not define the orthodoxy in the system of the Treaties in their current form?

---

[13] Have readers considered the fact that the European Council on employment in Luxembourg in November 1997 simply represents application of the "fourth pillar" to internal policies?

The Council's role

14.06 The development of the fourth pillar demonstrates the extent to which it is incorrect to think that the essential problem inherent in "jointness" or "mixity" is that of the single spokesperson for the Community and the Member States. Obviously the problem does not lie in knowing "who will speak", but in knowing "who will decide" (who will decide what will then be communicated by the one who speaks). And it is also obvious that the only "centre of decision-making" capable of deciding jointly on behalf of the Community and the Member States is the Council, which is on the one hand a Community institution and, on the other, an institution capable of acting on behalf of the Member States, either in the context of CFSP or in the context of my fourth pillar.[14]

In this context, the tendencies still apparent to set out to "intergovernmentalise" the Council by reducing it to the "fifteen Member States" are deeply regrettable. Of course I understand that this mode of action may be an effective way of serving certain corporatist interests within the Commission: the more the Council effaces itself, the stronger the impression becomes that the Community *is* the Commission (a confusion that is all the more likely to arise in an age like the present one, where the language of signs and symbols is beginning to prevail: what is the "E.C."—the European "Community" or the European "Commission"?). I am also aware that this mode of action can be successful only with the complicity of national governments who see "Brussels" as something foreign, and consequently see the Council only as the place in which "the 15" more or less control what the Community (*i.e.* as they see it, the Commission) does.

However, these trends are enormously destructive, both in general and in terms of our specific problem. In fact, if one cannot understand the difference between "the Council" and "the 15", then it is not possible to understand that the only possible solution to the problems of "jointness" or "mixity" involves the Council acting "with two hats on"—as "Council/Community" and as "Council/15"—in order to prevent "the 15" from taking action outside the Council. Herein lies the basis for the proper administration of "mixity".

The Council's role in the administration of joint agreements, ensuring democratic control

14.07 And I imagine this also comes as a surprise. The Council, guarantor of democratic control? Yes. Let us not discuss this in abstract terms, but let us take a meaningful and important example: what was presented, in April 1996, as a "proro-

---

[14] In some cases, my fourth pillar has been put into effect by means of a decision adopted by representatives of Member State governments meeting within the Council at the same time as the decision taken by the Council acting on behalf of the Community. This is a legal formality: from the political and institutional point of view, it is really the Council that has decided on behalf of both the Community and all the Member States. It should, then, come as no surprise that, in the case of negotiations carried out within the WTO, members manage without this formality: in this case, it is the Council itself which decides, in a single decision on behalf of the Community and Member States.

Two legal points in this connection:

As I have just indicated earlier, these decisions by the Council "on behalf of Member States" are not "outside the law". On the one hand, they represent the best way of fulfilling the obligations imposed on the Member States in respect of coherence and co-operation. On the other hand, they could always be interpreted as (implicitly) constituting actions by the Council in application of the CFSP in the sphere of external economic relations.

When action is taken by the Council and by representatives of Member State governments meeting within the Council, the decision taken by the latter should not be analysed, as the majority of commentators wish, in terms of an international agreement *among them*, in simplified form. In reality, it is a "bundle" of decisions made up of 15 individual decisions by means of which the 15 Member States, acting in concert within the Council, enter into commitments *in respect of third countries*. This is why this "bundle" of decisions by representatives of Member State governments can usefully be replaced by a Council decision.

gation" of negotiations within the WTO on basic telecommunications services (I do not need to emphasise the huge economic stakes involved in these negotiations). This was not simply a prorogration: the important thing was that what had previously been only "offers to enter into commitments", simple negotiating tools, were transformed into "schedules", into lists of specific undertakings, submitted to the WTO in that form (although naturally with the option of withdrawing or modifying them before February 15, 1997).[15] What was the only decision by virtue of which the Community and the Member States accepted this prorogation/depositing of lists of undertakings? A decision taken by the Council, "wearing its two hats", *i.e.* representing the Community and Member States. What was the alternative to this Council decision? A *de facto* decision by the officials on the spot, from both the Commission and national governments. I stress that this would have been a *de facto* decision outside the scope of every statutory regulation and, because of this, at the point when one would have wanted to submit this decision to inspection, one would have discovered that it had no originator who would accept responsibility for it. Currently, at least, the decision has an originator which is accountable for it: the Council.

This example makes it clear that behind the tension between the Community and Member States, and between the Council and the Commission, there lurks the tension between politicians (in respect of whom one can exercise [more or less] a degree of democratic control) and officials in specialised departments. The example also makes clear the error consistently made by those who maintain that, in the context of multilateral organisations, the alternative to a Council decision is a Commission decision. This is not so: the alternative to a Council decision is a *de facto* and non-accountable decision by officials on the spot who will not wait for a decision by the Commission before they take action (naturally I am referring to the Commission as an institution, to the "college"), any more than they would wait for a decision from the Council.

The fourth pillar and the exercising of the Community's non-exclusive competences

14.08   The fourth pillar comprises the exercising of Member State competences (other than those covered by CFSP and PJCCM) within the institutional system of the Union. Consequently, the question arises of whether this could not be replaced by the exercising of the Community's non-exclusive competence at international level.

In the context of the legal options, the answer is definitely in the affirmative. The majority[16] of the matters covered by the fourth pillar are also covered by the Community's non-exclusive competence. And this non-exclusive competence may be

---

[15] However, in the case of the Community and its Member States, acting jointly, a withdrawal or modification of this kind requires a unanimous decision, which means that a single Member State can block it. This is why the Council, having approved the prorogation of negotiations, and once it had learned the true nature of the documents prepared by the experts in Geneva, was obliged to take a second decision on *April 30, 1996*: the apparently surreal decision to "withdraw the list of undertakings on *February 13, 1997*". This was the only way of preventing the undertakings from becoming, in practice, definitive commitments, which would actually have been the case, in practice, had the Council not taken this second decision.

[16] Perhaps one could even say all of them, with the exception of those where Community competence is explicitly excluded (*cf.* above, footnote 3)?

directly exercised at international level, even if it has not previously been exercised internally.[17]

But the fact that something is legally possible does not mean that there is any obligation to utilise this possibility. As long as the Community legislator does not wish to make use of this option (*i.e.* does not wish to exercise the Community's non-exclusive external competence), the Member States retain their competence, and "jointness" and my fourth pillar remain in place if this external competence of the Member States needs to be exercised in conjunction with that of the Community.

Why does the Community legislator not wish to exercise this non-exclusive external competence? In order that we may reflect on an answer to this question, it seems to me essential to go down the following track: in cases where the Community has exclusive external competence, this is exercised in accordance with internal regulations in existence before the external competence is exercised. If the Community is negotiating in the context of Article 133 EC (ex Article 113), what it is negotiating is, in fact, amendments to the existing rules of the customs union; the external action is rooted in internal regulations. By definition, the same applies in the event of an "*AETR* effect".

Completely the opposite applies if we analyse the possibility of the exercising of the Community's non-exclusive external competence. When the negotiations within the OECD on the MAI (multilateral agreement on investment), for example, included negotiating the rules applicable to privatisations, in what basis would external action by the Community have been rooted? What should its position have been, one strongly favouring privatisations and favouring opening them up to companies from non-member countries (which would have been typical of the governments of certain of our Member States), or a less favourable attitude (as would have been typical of other governments)?

There are countless examples: what is the Community to negotiate at international level in respect of patents, if national legislations continue not to be harmonized at Community level? And there is the question of foreign investments: are we aware that the Community does not possess a standardised regime applicable to foreign investments? What attitude should it take at international level—liberal or protectionist, interventionist or deregulatory? In other words, is it possible to act responsibly at international level if one does not know what one wants within the Community? Is it possible to develop, at international level, a policy that does not exist within the Community? This, is what external exercising of a non-exclusive competence not exercised within the Community would amount to.[18]

---

[17] *cf.* Opinion 1/76, *Inland waterways vessels* [1977] E.C.R. 741. In my opinion, there is no contradiction between the position adopted by the Court in this opinion and that adopted in Opinion 1/94, provided one makes a distinction between two questions. The second is that of the conditions under which a non-exclusive competence explicitly attributed by the Treaty can give rise, in an exceptional case, to an *exclusive* external competence; this exceptional case is that of the specific agreement that is the subject of Opinion 1/76 to which the Court draws attention in para. 85 of the legal grounds of Opinion 1/94. The first question, however, is the general one of whether a non-exclusive competence can be directly exercised at international level without first having been exercised within the Community. On this point, the clear and specific affirmative answer given by the Court in Opinion 1/76 remains valid, and is not invalidated by Opinion 1/94, which relates to the *existence* of *exclusive* competences and not the *exercising* of *non-exclusive* competences.

It is not the Court itself which has provided a restrictive interpretation of Opinion 1/94 in relation to Opinion 1/76, but some of the legal literature, which persists in believing that Opinion 1/94 constituted a "retrograde step" in relation to the preceding jurisprudence (and which still does not satisfactorily comprehend the distinction between exclusive and non-exclusive competences, since it wishes to go on believing that this *legal* distinction is obliterated when the Community finds itself confronted with the *[political]* need to take action at international level).

[18] Obviously, these questions relate to cases where the situation is not such that external action by the Community represents the only means of regulating a problem within the Community (*cf.* para. 86 of the legal grounds of Opinion 1/94).

It is thus completely normal, if at the current stage of construction of the Community a matter is (still) the object of 15 national policies, for it to be these 15 national policies that manifest themselves at international level. This means, of course, that they will reveal any differences existing between them. Nevertheless, the development of the fourth pillar proves that these differences can be managed *within a single framework*, so that the whole can present itself to the outside world as a Union (Community plus all the Member States) which, while it is certainly not uniform, is still coherent.

THE FOURTH PILLAR AND THE AMSTERDAM TREATY

14.09   From the viewpoint of the negotiations involved in the Amsterdam Treaty, Opinion 1/94 of the Court of Justice had played an extremely positive part: it had clarified what the Treaties said on the subject of the division of competences between the Community and the Member States in the sphere of external economic relations (which was obviously not the way in which a large number of "experts" wished to interpret them). This clarification enabled the debate on the reform of the Treaties to be based on strong foundations.

A debate of this kind should have followed *two* tracks: one relating to possible extension of the Community's competences, and one relating to the mechanisms facilitating coherent exercising of Community competences *and* those of the Member States when they are jointly participating in an international agreement or organisation.

The two tracks were not alternatives, and should have been followed "in parallel". In fact, it was obvious from the start of the negotiations that an increase in the Community's exclusive external competences, however extensive, would not remove the Member States' external competences; consequently, the problem of the "jointness" of agreements and of participation in international organisations would still remain, although the greater the increase in the Community's exclusive competences, the smaller its scope would be. In this context, the case of future participation in the Bretton Woods institutions, in particular the IMF, is a very significant one. If it is essential for the Community to participate[19], owing to its exclusive competence in matters of monetary policy and euro exchange rates, nobody could imagine that Member States would not continue to have competence in economic policy matters: for this reason, they will continue to participate in them as regards the spheres where they retain competence. Thus we have "jointness" now and for ever.

The route involving extension of Article 113 to include "new areas"

14.10   From the outset, the increase in the Community's exclusive external competences was presented in the form of an extension of former Article 113 EC to include services, direct investments and intellectual property (the "new areas"). This approach came up against two insurmountable problems.

The first problem was that this approach did not distinguish between external and internal competences. It failed to take into account that Article 113 EC confers on the Community not only an exclusive external competence in respect of negotiating and concluding international agreements, but also an *exclusive competence within the Community* to adopt autonomous measures and internal regulations on its subject matter (the system of international trade relating to goods).[20] This means that

---

[19] See the discussion referred to in footnote 5.
[20] And, following Opinion 1/94, of international cross-border supply of services.

if Article 113 were simply to be extended to cover services (the same applies to direct investments or intellectual property), the result would be that Member States would lose all their competences in respect of legislating *within* the Community in the field of services. If I may say so, this would not have been federalism, but Community ultra-Jacobinism.

This problem becomes all the more acute given the reality of international negotiations on the subject of services (and/or direct investments). There is a (very widespread) error consisting in the belief that these international negotiations follow the same logic as GATT—*i.e.* that they relate to the system of international trade. This is, quite simply, incorrect: GATT covers the rules applicable to imports into the Community of Ford cars manufactured in the United States, but does not cover the internal rules applicable to Ford U.K.[21] On the other hand, the key objective of the GATS (or of the negotiations within the OECD on a multilateral agreement on investment) is to impose obligations on the United Kingdom in respect of the internal rules applicable to the activities of Bank of America—*UK* (including, for example, the rules applicable to employees). The same argument applies to TRIPs, for example: this sets out to impose obligations on the United Kingdom in respect of patent applications submitted by IBM—*UK*.

The second problem was also linked to the failure to understand the reality of international negotiations in these "new areas". These negotiations are based on the concept of "treatment"; this concept is "universal" in character. GATS, for example, has a twofold universality[22]: it covers *all service sectors* (from hotel-keeping and cleaning of premises to telecommunications, via education and health care), and, even more importantly, it covers *all aspects* of the rules applicable to service undertakings and service providers (from the rules applicable to employees to those on expropriation or privatisation of public service enterprises). The same argument applies to TRIPs, *viz.* this covers all aspects of the "treatment" of intellectual property (thus including legal procedures and the criminal law applicable). How could one envisage simply "extending Article 113" to cover these "new areas", relieving Member States of all competences in the whole range of aspects covered by the concept of "treatment"?

The route involving integration of the administration of "jointness"

14.11 The second track to be followed with the aim of reforming the Treaties was to confront the problem of "jointness" head on (a problem which, as I have already said, was destined to continue, to a greater or lesser extent depending on the extent to which the Community's competences were extended). In order to do this, it was necessary to lay down in the Treaty the pre-existing obligation (then Article C TEU, Article 5 EC and Court jurisprudence) for coherence between the positions of the Community and Member States within international organisations, *in combination with an adequate procedure.*

The progress of the Amsterdam negotiations

14.12 The duty of discretion to which I, as a former official, am obliged to adhere, means that I am unable to go into detail about the progress of the negotiations. Nevertheless, I believe that some elements can be opened up to public consideration.

---

[21] With the exception of TRIMs (Trade-related investment measures, within the meaning of annex 1A of the WTO Agreement), whose scope is extremely limited and which are thus irrelevant to our discussion.
[22] In its Opinion 1/94, the Court made this analysis put forward by the Council in its written comments its own, *cf.* [1994] E.C.R. I–5291.

(a) The legal adviser of the Intergovernmental Conference produced from the out-set a legal analysis which made clear the existence of two distinct, but related, problems, which needed to be tackled by following the two tracks mentioned above in *parallel*. From the start, the Commission blocked pursuit of the second track, by persuading successive presidencies, the Irish and the Dutch, to pro-gress only the first track (extension of Article 113 to cover new areas).

(b) It was again the Conference's legal adviser who found technical solutions enabling as much progress as possible to be made down the track of extending Article 113, by offering two specific solutions to the two problems analysed above, which had proved insurmountable in the course of the negotiations:

   (i) separating external competences from internal competences (by restrict-ing the extension of Article 113 and of the Community's exclusive com-petence purely to "negotiation and conclusion of international agreements", while preserving the competence of Member States *within* the Community, provided the provisions of these agreements concluded by the Community were complied with); this was absolutely in tune with the objective pursued, which was none other than to strengthen the role and presence of the Community in international negotiations and bodies;

   (ii) reducing the scope of the extension of Article 113, either by limiting it to negotiations and agreements in the context of certain international organ-isations (notably the WTO), or, alternatively or additionally, by restrict-ing it to certain service sectors and/or certain aspects of the rules applicable to undertakings (by excluding, for example, the rules applicable to employees or to taxation).

(c) In the course of the final weeks of the negotiations, it became obvious that the route involving extension of Article 113 was as dead as a dodo, even in combi-nation with separation of external competences from internal competences and a reduction in the scope of such an extension.

(d) The definitive results of the Intergovernmental Conference are now known: the stubborn pursuit of a single route, that of extending Article 113, has led nowhere. Everything remains unchanged, except for the addition to Article 113 (now Article 133) of a paragraph 5, which is destined never to be applied.

The waste of the opportunity to integrate the administration of "jointness"

14.13   What kind of provision integrating the administration of "jointness" could have been introduced into the TUE via the Amsterdam Treaty? Here it is:

(a) When the Community and the Member States participate jointly in an inter-national economic organisation, the Council shall define the joint positions they must abide by and defend, including during negotiations on international agreements. The Council shall act unanimously on a proposal by the Com-mission or, in areas falling within Member State competences, on the initiative of one or more Member States. The Presidency of the Council and the Commission shall state these joint positions in accordance with modalities to be agreed between them. For subjects that do not fall within the Com-munity's exclusive competence, Member State representatives shall retain their right to take part in meetings within the organisation and to intervene in them subject to adherence to the joint positions defined by the Council.

(b) In the event that it is not possible to achieve unanimity within the Council, the Community shall be able at all times to define and implement its position in the context of the relevant provisions of the Treaties establishing the European Communities and in accordance with the procedures laid down therein.

In such a case, each Member State shall also be able to define and implement its position, unless the Council, acting on a qualified majority, has decided that individual action by one or more Member States would conflict with the general interests of the Union.

(c) Any international commitment resulting from implementation of the procedures laid down in the preceding paragraphs shall be accepted by the Community, by the Member States, or by the Community and the Member States, on the basis of their respective competences and in application of the relevant Community and national procedures.

Such a provision is virtually self-explanatory, in terms of both its political significance and its legal significance (in fact, the two coincide):

(i) paragraph (c) ensures compliance with the division of competences between the Community and the Member States, as laid down in the Treaties;

(ii) paragraph (a) formalises my "fourth pillar" and brings the Member States within the Union's institutional system;

(iii) the first sub-paragraph of paragraph (b) has two objectives: (1) it guarantees the Community's autonomy of decision-making; (2) in so doing, it acts as a lever to promote the unanimity envisaged in paragraph 1; in other words, if the necessary majority existed for action by the Community as such, would the governments of the Member States constituting the minority dare to present themselves as such at international level, faced with the Community and a majority of governments?

(iv) the second subparagraph of paragraph (b) is intended to prevent action by a single Member State (or a minority of Member States) from being able to call into question the higher interests of the Union (Community plus Member States) as a whole; its logic derives from the asymmetry between action and inaction: one cannot compel a Member State to act against its wishes in an area where it retains competence, but it is not offensive for it to be compelled to abstain from action if a majority of Member States consider that this action will put higher interests at risk.

Would such a provision have been able to achieve the necessary consensus during the negotiations? The only answer I can give is completely subjective. I know that this provision, put forward in a completely informal way and on my own account, aroused great sympathy among certain senior officials with responsibility for external economic relations who, in London, Madrid and Paris, had noted the failure of the route involving extension of Article 113. This being the case, I remain convinced that, had it received support from the Presidency and the Commission, it would have been included in the Amsterdam Treaty.

Conclusions

14.14   One final comment before I conclude.

We are so absorbed in the "problems" posed by "jointness" that we forget the risks we run when we assert that a Community with limited competences is evenly matched with very powerful partners, such as the United States, who always put down all their cards at the same time—risks that "jointness", on the other hand, helps to prevent.

I shall limit myself to two examples as genuine as life itself:

(a) the United States government begins by discussing with the Japanese government matters relating to disequilibria in their trade balance, and ends up reaching agreement on certain taxation policies aimed at stimulating economic growth (which could increase the demand for imports, among other effects);

(b) the United States government begins by discussing trade with the Russian government and ends up concluding an agreement aimed at creating a partial cartel in the world satellite launch market.[23]

Unless a decision is made to create a genuine federal state in Europe, it is obvious that the Community will never be in a position to play these games: it does not have (and will not have) either the competences and the necessary powers with regard to economic policy to play the game with Japan, or the necessary powers with regard to industrial policy and economic planning to play the game with Russia. Only if the Community and the Member States act in concert will the European Union be in a position to be a player in games of this kind.

Conclusion

14.15   One may now understand why I stated at the beginning that I do not like the language of "pillars". It is an impoverishing language that attempts to force into a rigid and compartmented mould a reality that shifts, and which constitutes a unique entity.

The "pillars" approach inevitably results in a static view of the Union (just as static as a Greek temple), which prevents it from being understood as a dynamic reality. If one still wanted to go on talking of pillars, one should speak of "*two* pillars" at most or, better still, of "two constituents" of the European Union: the Community on one hand, and on the other, the 15 Member States, acting jointly. The first constituent is very well consolidated, and the second is evolving. "Evolving", firstly, as regards its rules: better defined in the case of CFSP and JHA, less well defined in the case of my fourth pillar; it is also "evolving" in terms of its scope—*there is no precise demarcation line between (more or less joint) action by the Member States outside the institutional framework of the Union and the more or less joint action they develop within this framework*.

Politicians are responsible for ensuring unity and coherence in the action, which should as far as possible be indissociable, taken by the two constituents of the European Union. In fact, the rights and interests of citizens constitute a very complex whole, which even has contradictions within it, but which, whatever the state of things, is never divided into "pillars".

Legal experts are responsible for finding the means by which this action by-the-Community—and—by-the-Member-States-acting-jointly can evolve in conformity

---

[23] As readers can imagine, I did not invent this example.

with the law.[24] In order to fulfil this obligation, we need to be creative and to know how to transform risks into trump cards.

This is the approach we need to adopt towards the administration of the "jointness" or "mixity" of international agreements. If we approach it from the angle of the Community, there is, of course, a risk that the need for joint external action by the Community and by all the Member States—which, by definition, requires unanimity on the part of Council members—will not completely cancel out the Community's autonomy of action, which very often requires only a qualified majority within the Council. But we can transform this risk into a trump card. The lack of an article in the Amsterdam Treaty integrating "jointness" makes this task more difficult for us, but not impossible. In the context of the Treaties in their current form, the lack of specific rules applicable to the problem cannot be transformed into an excuse for a small minority to block action by the whole: if necessary, and even in a "mixed" context, the Community—if it is able to act on a qualified majority within the Council—and the Member States which constitute this qualified majority can forge ahead. As I suggested a little earlier, is any small minority of Member States likely to dare to contradict the point of view jointly put forward by the Community and the vast majority of Member States?[25] As always, would not the possibility of acting on a qualified majority be the best means of settling disagreements?

But we can only go down this route if we accept "mixity" wholeheartedly: as a fact of life that does not have to be concealed like a secret vice; as a fact wanted by 15 democratic states and which must, therefore, not only be accepted but also be championed.

POSTSCRIPT

Recent experience after the entry into force of the Amsterdam Treaty would advise further discussion of a particular point alluded to in the present chapter but not essential to the understanding of the "fourth pillar": how to interpret CFSP (and PJCCM)? As a joint exercise of Member States competences (as I suggest) or as the progressive development of a legal personality of a Union endowed with its own specific competences? Those who defend the second thesis should be able to explain how the Union can be differentiated "17th actor" while continuing to be the common framework of the other 16. Or should we interpret that the Community does not act within the framework of the Union but alongside it?

---

[24] Compliance with the law, which is always important, is even more so in a situation like that of action within the Union, which does not possess satisfactory democratic control mechanisms. In these circumstances, scrupulous compliance with the Treaties, which were democratically approved by our 15 Member States and their populations, constitutes the primary and fundamental guarantee of democracy. Naturally, when I refer to the Treaties, I mean the Treaties *as they are*, and not as one would wish them to be; I consider it essential to point this out in the context of our discussion.

[25] And if it were to dare to do so, would not non-member countries be capable of comparing the weight of this small minority with that of the Community and a majority of Member States?

C: IMPLEMENTATION OF INTERNATIONAL AGREEMENTS

CHAPTER 15

Organising Joint Participation of EC and Member States

by

*Christiaan Timmermans**

INTRODUCTORY REMARKS

15.01   Organising the joint participation of the E.C. and the Member States within an international organisation is a complex issue of great political sensitivity, in a number of respects. One set of problems relates to the admission of the E.C. by the other members as an active participant in an international organisation where such admission is justified by virtue of the scope of the Community's substantive powers (as a member, a special member, a full participant: World Trade Organisation (WTO), Food and Agriculture Organisation (FAO), Commission for Sustainable Development (CSD), Fishery Organisations).[1] Secondly, there are the equally formidable difficulties of how to organise the most generally joint participation of the Community and its Member States, once the Community has been so admitted, and how to apply satisfactorily the arrangements agreed to that effect between the Community and the Member States. This is a subject of continuous fierce and very time-consuming discussion between the Member States and the E.C. institutions. It is also a subject which justifies more attention in academic circles than it has received to date.

Of course, the present stage reached in the division of external powers between the Community(ies) and the Member States adds greatly to the complexity of the issue. Mixity, *i.e.* shared competences, is the rule, while a clear-cut exclusivity of competence either on the part of the Member States or on the part of the Community, is the rare exception. Things would have been easier, had the Member States shown more willingness to use the opportunities offered by the case law of the Court in favour of a *foro interno, foro externo* approach.[2] They have not done so. Sometimes one gets the

---

* Deputy Director-General Legal Service of the European Commission. Only personal views are expressed. The text is the slightly revised version of a lecture given at Cambridge on December 9, 1995.

[1] *Cf.* Sack, "The European Community's Membership of International Organisations" (1995) 32 C.M.L.Rev. 1227; Frid, *The Relations between the EC and International organisations* (Academisch Proefschrift, Amsterdam, 1995). See also Brinkhorst, "The European Community at UNCED: Lessons to be Drawn for the Future" in *Institutional Dynamics of European integration Essays in Honour of Henry C. Schermers* (Curtin and Heukels, eds., 1994) Vol. II, pp. 609–617.

[2] Opinion 1/76 *Draft Agreement establishing a European laying-upfund for inland waterway vessels* [1977] E.C.R. 741; (1977) 2 C.M.L.Rev. 279; Opinion 2/91 *Convention No. 170 of the International labour Organisation concerning safety in the use of chemicals at work ("ILO")* [1993] E.C.R. I–1061 at para. 17; (1993) 3 C.M.L.Rev. p. 800.

impression that in external affairs, Member States founded the Community to contest its competences rather than to exercise them. It makes one think of Paul Henry Spaak's farewell speech to the Parliamentary Assembly of the Council of Europe, having acted as its first president for two years, when he referred to the endless debates between federalists and intergovernmentalists: "J'ai été étonné par la somme des talents dépensés dans cette Assemblée pour expliquer pourquoi *il ne fallait pas* faire quelque chose".[3] This situation has prevailed for years and will most probably continue: Member States will accept external Community action only where the Community's external competence is considered to be exclusive. The question whether that is the case is often restrictively interpreted. Only rarely, mostly for reasons of urgency, are Member States prepared to exercise a non-exclusive external competence, as for example in the case of the Community's government procurement agreement with the U.S.A.[4] It is an anomaly for collective national action to be preferred in circumstances where the Community has the power to act. It shall be recalled that the *first* question put to the Court by the Commission in the WTO case was whether the Community was as such competent to conclude all parts of the WTO Agreement.[5] Only the last question raised the issue of exclusivity. It is regrettable that the Court did not answer the first question.[6] If it had done so in the affirmation, the aforementioned anomaly would have been made more manifest.[7]

This contribution will concentrate on the subject of Community participation in international organisations and on the situation of mixed competences. When discussing the various questions as to how to organise that participation, it shall focus primarily on questions regarding the relationship between the Community and the Member States. It is not proposed to discuss the complications which arise from the extremely diverse *structures d'accueil* for the Community in the various international organisations regarding its status as a participant (whether as an observer, a participant with special rights, or member). That is a subject for a separate paper, if not a separate book. Suffice to say that, in principle, Community law, with the help of the Court, has developed appropriate answers to the existing variety of practices within international organisations. One might cite as an example the arrangement whereby Member States act as trustees for the Community.[8]

FORMS OF MIXITY

15.02   Before entering into the substance of this paper, a few words must be said

---

[3] Emphasis added. Cited in Paul van de Meersche, *Europese integra tie en desintegra tie 1945–heden* (1978).
[4] Decision 92/215/E.C. of May 29, 1995 concerning the conclusion of an Agreement in the form of exchange of letters between the European Community and the United States of America on government procurement [1995] O.J. L134/25.
[5] Opinion 1/94 *Competence of the Community to conclude international agreements concerning services and the protection of intellectual property ("WTO")* [1994] E.C.R. I–5267; (1995) 1 C.M.L.Rev. 205.
[6] Nowhere does Opinion 1/94 answer the question whether the Community is as such empowered to conclude all the agreements involved. Only the thesis of an *exclusive* competence is explicitly denied. The interpretation given by the Court of Opinion 1/76 [1977] E.C.R. 741, tightening considerably the test of necessity, concerns the issue of exclusiveness, not the acceptance as such of a virtual competence. If the latter had been true, it would be hard to accept that a simple clause in a harmonisation Directive in the field of establishment or services referring to the treatment of third-country nationals or companies would be sufficient to warrant an exclusive external competence in that regard (Opinion 1/94 [1994] E.C.R. I–5267, at para. 95)—external competences cannot be created by secondary law alone. They can only be activated or brought to life by secondary law. For this to happen they must necessarily be implied by the legal bases for these rules of secondary law as virtual external competence. That is how the Council used them when concluding the agreement on government procurement with the United States (see above, n. 4).
[7] Although in its written submissions admittedly the Commission put all the emphasis on exclusivity.
[8] See Case 22/70 *Commission* v. *Council ("ERTA")* [1971] E.C.R. 263 at para. 90; (1971) C.M.L.Rev. 335; also see Opinion 2/91 [1993] E.C.R. I–1061, at para. 5.

about the various forms of mixity, *i.e.* of shared competences.[9] In my view at least two types of mixity can be distinguished according to the relationship between Community and national competence:

(a) *classic or real mixity*: the Community is only competent for part of the subject. The remainder falls within national competence and the Community has no competence at all in this respect *e.g.* participation by Member States in respect of their overseas territories[10]; or aspects of penal law and extradition[11];

(b) *quasi or sometimes even false mixity*: the Community has exclusive competence for part of the subject. For the remainder it could claim a virtual, or a parallel, competence with the Member States. So it is up to the Member States to decide whether to act through the Community or collectively outside the Community framework, *e.g.* ILO Conventions similar to Convention No. 170[12] and the WTO Agreement with regard to GATS and TRIPS.[13] A distinction should be drawn according to whether Community competence is virtual or parallel. Exercising virtual competence would, as a rule, have a pre-emptive effect and would thus oust national competence. That would not be the case with parallel competence, *e.g.* humanitarian aid[14] and development co-operation.[15]

Why make these distinctions? They seem to be relevant for at least two reasons. Where there is quasi-mixity, it will usually be the case that competences can only be exercised together because they are inextricably linked. On the other hand, solving co-ordination problems between Community and Member States might be easier where the Community has at least a virtual or a parallel competence for the whole subject matter. I shall come back to this.

How should the participation of the Community in international organisations for those situations of mixed competences be organised where the exercise of Community and national competences is inextricably linked, *i.e.* where the action in a particular case cannot be reserved either to the Community or to the Member States but where they are condemned to act together? The Court has stressed, in this type of case, the duty of Member States to co-operate where competence is mixed.[16] This obligation, which exists under Community law, is more specific than the general principle of loyalty or *Bundestreue*, under Article 10 EC (ex Article 5). It is also more specific, as it is directly linked by the Court to "the requirement of unity in the international representation of the Community".[17] The obvious idea is that Member States, when acting together with the Community, should present a common, coherent approach. Community action should not be hampered or undermined by countervailing action by Member States.

[9] See, on this subject, Neuwahl, "Joint Participation in International Treaties and the Exercise of Power by the EEC and its Member States Mixed Agreements", (1991) 28 C.M.L.Rev. 717.
[10] Opinion 1/94 [1994] E.C.R. I–5267, at para. 17.
[11] Ruling 1/78, *Draft Convention of the International Atomic Energy Agency on the Physical protection of Nuclear Materials, Facilities and Transports* [1978] E.C.R. 2151, at para. 31.
[12] *i.e.* the Convention in Opinion 2/91 [1993] E.C.R. I–1061.
[13] Opinion 1/94 [1994] E.C.R. I–5267.
[14] Joined Cases C–181 & 248/91 *Parliament* v. *Council and Commission ("Bangladesh")* [1993] E.C.R. I–3685.
[15] Case C–316/91 *Parliament* v. *Council ("EDF")* [1994] E.C.R. I–625.
[16] See Ruling 1/78 [1978] E.C.R. 2151; Opinion 2/91 [1993] E.C.R. I–1061; and Opinion 1/94 [1994] E.C.R. I–5267.
[17] Opinion 1/94 [1994] E.C.R. I–5267, at para. 108.

Three questions arise:

(a) What are the implications of this duty of co-operation?

(b) How should the exercise of this duty be organised where further decision-making is necessary to that effect?

(c) Are there possible sanctions if this duty is breached?

THE IMPLICATIONS OF THE DUTY OF CO-OPERATION

15.03   The Court has made it quite clear that the duty of co-operation must be observed in the three relevant stages of external action:

(a) negotiation;

(b) conclusion (*i.e.* the entering into international obligations either by concluding treaties or agreeing to decisions of organs of international organisations);

(c) execution (*i.e.* the adoption of the necessary implementing measures).

Negotiation

15.04   Co-operation here means to establish the Community's position according to the relevant Community procedures, to co-ordinate Member States' positions, and finally, to ensure co-ordination between the position of the Community and those of the Member States. Were co-ordination to fail so that a common position could not be achieved, there should be no action, in other words no participation in the negotiation. To allow the Member States to go their own way would be incompatible with the requirement of unity in the international representation of the Community. Indeed, where the shared competences at issue are inextricably linked, Member States acting alone would usurp Community powers or might even, by agreeing to international commitments in areas of Community competence, commit the Community, at least under international law. Accordingly, there should be either co-ordinated action or no action at all. This applies also to the co-ordination with regard to *who presents* the common position whether the Commission or the Presidency *or both* in co-ordination. In this respect, it is suggested that the FAO arrangement falls short of adhering to these principles. According to this arrangement, if a common position of Community and Member States is not reached, Member States shall speak and vote.[18] Proba 20, the arrangement regarding the negotiation and conclusion of Commodity agreements, is much more correct in this respect.

Conclusion

15.05   Here, too, the principle should be either joint action or no action. That logic has been followed by Article 102 of the Euratom Treaty. It would be incompatible with the duty of co-operation for a Member State, or Member States, but also for the

---

[18] Arrangement between the Council and the Commission regarding preparation for FAO meetings, statements and voting (internal arrangement of December 19, 1991, unpublished), s. 2.4. See also Case C–25/94 *Commission* v. *Council ("FAO")* [1996] E.C.R. I–1497.

Community, to enter into an international commitment in the absence of a common decision to that effect. So, to give an example, ratification of ILO Convention No. 170, the subject of Opinion 2/91, by Member States alone without Community co-ordination would be incompatible with the duty of co-operation.

Execution

15.06   It suffices to recall here the points established by the Court's case law: when implementing a mixed agreement, the Community and the Member States should act in conformity with the division of their internal powers.[19]

How to organise the exercise of the duty of co-operation?

15.07   In order to stop continuous squabbling, the Council, the Commission and the Member States have resorted to informal arrangements between themselves in practice. The European Parliament is excluded, however. The legal status of these arrangements is insecure. They are not formal decisions adopted according to normal procedures. They have not been published, although they are public. That is how transparency often works within the Community. A famous example is Proba 20, the arrangement regarding the negotiation of Commodity Agreements adopted in 1981 to translate into practice the findings of the Court in Opinion 1/78. The scope of these arrangements is not necessarily the same. At the very least, they regulate how to ensure a single or co-ordinated representation of the Community and the Member States in negotiations. They may also, but with varying degrees of detail, regulate how to organise co-ordination, in other words, how to achieve a common position.

It should be said that Proba 20, notwithstanding many negative comments in academic literature at the time, has apparently worked rather well. It has allowed co-operation without too much friction between the Community and the Member States. Experience thus far with the FAO Arrangement has been much less positive. In cases of mixed competence, the need to establish for each item on the agenda, where the thrust of the issue lies - within exclusive Community competence or within national competence -causes considerable problems.[20] To illustrate the level of sophistication which has been reached in this respect, take the General Rules of FAO, which have been amended to allow voting by the EC as a "Member Organisation". The rules deal explicitly with the situation where, for a given item of the agenda, both the Member Organisation and its Member States are competent. In such circumstances both are allowed, according to these rules, to speak; but the rules add that: "In such cases the meeting, in arriving at its decision, shall take into account only the intervention of the party which has the right to vote".[21] This becomes rather surrealistic.

In its judgment of March 19, 1996 in the FAO case, the Court has accepted the binding nature of the FAO arrangement, considering its wording, at least for Council and Commission, as parties to this arrangement.[22] The question was not raised in the FAO case itself, but it will be difficult to contest that Member States also are bound by

---

[19]   Ruling 1/78 [1978] E.C.R. 2151, at para. 36; Case 12/86 *Demirel* v. *Stadt Schwäbisch Cmünd* [1987] E.C.R. 3719 at para. 9.
[20]   See the FAO Arrangement, above, n. 18, at s. 2.3.
[21]   General Rules of the Organisation, Rule XLI (3), Resolution 7/91, Report of the Twenty-sixth session of the Conference of the FAO, Rome November 9–27, 1991, C 91/REP, point 302.
[22]   See above, n. 18, at para. 49.

this arrangement. The arrangement intends to execute the duty of co-operation between Member States and the Community in view of ensuring unity in the international representation of the Community; indeed, it defines clear obligations for the Member States for that purpose. It is interesting to note that Member States themselves are not party to the arrangement. The latter has been confirmed by a Council decision only, not by a "mixed" decision, that is to say a Council decision which is at the same time a decision taken by the representatives of the Member States within the framework of the Council. Apparently, the Council has acted in this case not only as the competent institution for exercising the relevant Community powers but also in view of the co-ordination of the exercise of Member States competences. However, no trace can be found of an authorisation of the Council to act on behalf of the Member States, as is the case for instance with regard to the management by the Community of the European Development Fund.[23] The question then arises whether the arrangement has been lawfully concluded. Was the Council empowered to act? In my view the Council was. The duty of co-operation, in view of which this arrangement has been concluded, constitutes a Community law obligation, also as far as the co-ordination with regard to national competences is concerned. The Council could also have formalised the arrangement by incorporating it in a decision based on Article 116 EEC, which was at that time still available, but has subsequently been deleted by the Treaty of Maastricht. This does not at all imply that the Community has now lost the necessary competence to take such a decision. Apparently, the Council shares that opinion because the arrangement continues to be applied, without any modifications, after the entry into force of the Maastricht Treaty. It would be legally acceptable in my view, always because of the Community law nature of Member States obligations to co-operate, to provide for the necessary procedural arrangements for that purpose in the Council decision to conclude the international agreement in question.[24]

It would also be possible to enact, later on a separate decision with the same legal base as the decision to conclude. The latter approach could be followed to formalise a possible code of conduct concerning the joint action of Community and Member States within the World Trade Organisation. A less formal solution would be to opt for a similar kind of interinstitutional arrangement as was used in the case of the FAO.

15.08   It is obvious that Member States are reluctant to agree such procedural arrangements. Drafts for a Code of Conduct concerning the WTO were the subject of intensive discussions from 1995 to mid-1996, but have been suspended since then. Similar discussions took place with regard to the Energy Charter. These failed also. Various drafts for a new Treaty provision (in fact a revival, in one form or another, of the former Article 116 EEC) to create a legal basis for Council decisions for these purposes have been discussed in the Intergovernmental Conference preparing the Amsterdam Treaty, but no agreement could be reached. The main arguments in favour of such arrangements are of course transparency, and more discipline, also because compliance to the extent that the arrangements are of a binding nature, is justiciable. But that might not be precisely to the liking of Member States. Until now Community and Member States have been able to ensure unity of representation in the WTO without major difficulties. Whether that will continue, remains to be seen. If not, the issue of a Code of Conduct might come back on the political agenda. An uncertain factor in this context concerns the position the European Parliament will take. The TEU has considerably reinforced the EP's rights in the field of external relations. To be concluded, the WTO Agreement required the approval of the European Parliament. It

---

[23]   *Cf.* Case C–316/91 *European Parliament* v. *Council* [1994] E.C.R. I–653.
[24]   Just as the simplified procedure provided for by Article 300(4), EC (ex Art. 228(4)) could be incorporated in that decision.

may be expected that the Parliament would like to have a say on the issue of a possible Code of Conduct.

Another question in this context relates to the decision-making procedures that are available to ensure, in cases of mixed competence, the establishment of a common position. The normal approach in that regard is to adopt the Community position, according to the relevant Community procedures (*i.e.* Article 300 EC (ex Article 228) together with the substantive legal base or, possibly, a simplified procedure),[25] to co-ordinate national positions and finally, to co-ordinate the latter with the Community position. This co-ordination is normally conducted rather informally, within the instances of the Council, in working groups, the "133 Committee" (ex "113 Committee") and COREPER and on the spot. If difficulties occur, the matter will be referred to Brussels to be discussed in COREPER or, if necessary, at Council level. These procedures, where working satisfactorily, need not be changed. The question is whether, where they do not, a more formal procedure should be followed, and if so, what procedure and on what legal base?

I refer particularly to those cases where the usual, informal procedures fail, or where there appears to be a need to formalise certain co-ordination decisions. An example might be decisions regarding joint notification by the Community and the Member States of the provisional application of international agreements within a given period. This used to be based, for Commodity Agreements, on Article 116 EEC.[26] That Article has been deleted by the TUE. Does that mean that such decisions, formerly based on Article 116 EEC, are now outside Community competence ? This would result in two separate decisions having to be taken, one for Community competence, the other for the national competences in the form of a *décision cadre* or possibly a common position or joint action under Article 12 (ex Article J.2), or Article 13 TEU (ex Article J.3) respectively. I have no objection to that approach where Community and Member States could act separately. However, where they must act together, because of the impossibility of cutting the subject into two parts, in other words in the case of inextricable linkage, which was mentioned earlier, then such co-ordination could in my view be based on the E.C. Treaty alone. Again, as with regard to a decision on procedural arrangements, what is at stake here is the exercise of a Community law obligation by Member States. To the extent that such co-ordination decisions are indispensable in allowing the exercise of Community competence, they might be based on the E.C. Treaty, *i.e.* the same legal base from which the relevant Community competence derives. I do not say they must; they might.

So, in my view, the past practice of applying Article 116 EEC, could be continued after the TUE on other legal bases. This would not take us very far, however, as such practice has remained of fairly limited scope. A good case for the approach I advocate here would be a retaliation decision allowed to the E.C. after a WTO dispute settlement, which would relate partly or even exclusively to issues under national control (GATS or TRIPS). I see no difficulty in using Community procedures to harmonise substance and details of this retaliation to be imposed by Member States, especially as the subject matter in itself is at least virtually covered by Community competence.[27] Moreover, such retaliation might easily affect the functioning of the internal market. In Opinion 1/94 the Court accepted[28] the mere insertion in a Council directive of a clause allowing for co-ordination of Member States' actions with regard to third countries or allowing for negotiations to be opened with third countries, as a sufficient basis

---

[25] *e.g.* the procedure provided for by Art. 300(4) EC.
[26] *e.g.* Council Decision 83/328/EEC of May 26, 1983 on the signature and notification of provisional application of the International Agreement on Jute Products (1982); [1983] O.J. L185/1.
[27] See above, n. 6.
[28] Opinion 1/94 [1994] E.C.R. I–5267, at paras. 79, 90, 95.

for an *exclusive* Community competence. If that is so, I have no difficulty in accepting a Community competence, with regard to the same issues, to co-ordinate *ad hoc,* where necessary because of the indivisibility of the subject, the exercise of what is still left, and must continue to be left, to national competences.

SANCTIONS

15.09   Of course, binding interinstitutional agreements on procedural arrangements for a co-ordinated exercise of mixed competences or formal Council decisions embodying such arrangements could be enforced through the Court of Justice, both against the institutions themselves and against the Member States (infringement procedures under Article 226 EC (ex Article 169)).[29] The infringement procedure would in any event be available where Member States breach their duty of co-operation either in the stage of negotiation or in that of conclusion, for instance by breaking Community solidarity and acting single-handedly in the negotiation or conclusion stage. Whether the infringement procedure is an appropriate instrument for those purposes is another question.

WTO CODE OF CONDUCT

15.10   A final word on the negotiation of such a Code. I am not in a position to discuss the numerous drafts which have been circulated. What I can do, however, is to give my personal view on the minimum requirements such a Code should satisfy. The most important objective would be to prevent a repetition of the unhappy experiences of the FAO, *i.e.* the need to spell out to the other partners, in respect of each item on the agenda of a meeting, how competence is divided between the Community and the Member States. That question should remain an internal issue between the Community and the Member States and should not become an issue at international fora themselves.[30] There, the Community and the Member States should present a common position and speak with a single voice. By presenting a common front it might be possible to avoid a situation where the other partners of the WTO will raise questions about who is going to act and for what subject, *i.e.* who is competent to do what. Only where there is unity of representation both as to presentation (who speaks) and substance (what is said), can FAO experiences be avoided. Of course, the starting position is excellent because that is precisely how the practice in GATT has been, and our partners in GATT have grown accustomed to it. Also, during the negotiations of the Uruguay round, the Community and the Member States were able to preserve unity, difficult as it sometimes might have been, *e.g.* the Blair House Agreement. The stakes in the discussions on a Code of Conduct are therefore high to allow for an adequate and efficient defence of the common commercial interests of the Community and the Member States or to sink into the bureaucratic swamp of declarations of competence and internal haggling about who is competent for what. Consequently, two basic minimum requirements for a WTO Code emerge:

(a) to provide for one negotiator within WTO for Community and Member States.

(b) to allow for action only on the basis of a common position of Community and Member States.

---

[29] *Cf.* Case C–25/94 *(FAO)* [1996] E.C.R. I–1497.
[30] As the Court has already held in Ruling 1/78 [1978] E.C.R. 2151, at para. 35.

Both principles should also apply to dispute settlement. Member States should not be allowed to initiate a dispute settlement procedure or to retaliate without Community co-ordination.

FINAL REMARK

15.11   To come back to Paul Henry Spaak and his remark on all that intellectual energy invested in arguing why something should *not* be done. In the light of Opinion 1/94, I am inclined to suggest that we stop sterile debates on the *nature* of competences. Let us try to get out of the false opposition between exclusive Community competences and exclusive national competence, with nothing in between. The questions should be: whether Community competence exists and what are the advantages of exercising it?[31] If these advantages are obvious, Member States should act through the Community. That is why the Community is there.

---

[31] *Cf.* also the concluding remarks of Tridimas and Eeckhout, "The External Competence of the Community and the Case-law of the Court of Justice Principle versus Pragmatism" (1994) 14 Y.E.L. 143 at 172–176.

CHAPTER 16

The Duty of Co-operation: A Flexible Concept

by

Stephen Hyett*

16.01   This chapter considers, from a legal perspective, the duty of co-operation governing the participation of the European Community[1] and its Member States in international organisations. It is important at the outset to distinguish between what the law requires and what the policy adopted by the institutions of the Community and the Member States may be in any particular case. This chapter seeks to show that the legal requirements of the duty of co-operation, as developed by the Court of Justice to date, most recently in Opinion 1/94,[2] result in a flexible legal concept which is capable of operating in different ways in various international organisations to meet the needs and objectives of the Community and the Member States.

An attempt is made in this chapter to show that the legal position governing the participation of the Community and the Member States in international organisations supports the following four propositions:

(1) in appropriate cases[3] both the Community and the Member States can have competence in international organisations;

(2) the Community and the Member States have the flexibility to adopt the most suitable model for any particular organisation or set of negotiations;

(3) the present Treaty provisions are capable of dealing with the matter and fundamental change is not needed now; and

(4) each international organisation needs to be individually considered and a single uniform model for participation by the Community and the Member States is unlikely to be appropriate.

BOTH THE COMMUNITY AND THE MEMBER STATES HAVE COMPETENCE

16.02   In Opinion 1/94 the Commission argued that the Community had exclusive

---

* Legal Director, Department of Trade and Industry.

[1] This chapter considers the matter from the point of view of the European Community (E.C.), although the position in respect of the European Coal and Steel Community (ECSC) and the European Atomic Energy Community (Euratom) is similar.

[2] Opinion 1/94, *Competence of the Community to conclude international agreements concerning services and the protection of intellectual property ("WTO")* [1994] E.C.R. I–5267; (1995) 1 C.M.L.Rev. 205.

[3] *i.e.* mixed agreements. For a discussion of mixed agreements, see MacLeod, Hendry and Hyett, *The External Relations of the European Communities* (1996), Chapter 6.

competence in respect of all matters covered by the agreements giving effect to the Uruguay Round, *i.e.* that it had exclusive competence regarding trade in goods, trade in services and intellectual property rights. Similarly, in Opinion 2/92[4] on the OECD National Treatment Instrument, the Commission argued that the Community had exclusive competence regarding trade in services and regarding the conditions for the participation of foreign controlled undertakings established in the Community engaged in the production of goods or the provisions of services. Taking these two cases together, the Commission was in effect arguing that the Community had exclusive competence in respect of the whole field of external economic relations.

The Court of Justice rejected this contention. In Opinion 1/94 it held that, whilst the Community had exclusive competence to conclude the multilateral agreement on trade in goods, the Community and the Member States were jointly competent to conclude the General Agreement on Trade in Services (GATS) and the Agreement on Trade-related Aspects of Intellectual Property (TRIPS). In Opinion 2/92 the Court held that the Community and the Member States were jointly competent to enter into the instrument in question.

The consequence of these Opinions is that the Court of Justice has recognised that, as a matter of E.C. law, both the Community and the Member States can be jointly competent in respect of an international agreement and that this was indeed the case in respect of certain of the agreements and measures in issue in the Opinions. This was and still remains an important issue for most of the Member States. It is important that, where the Member States have competence, that competence is given full recognition in the arrangements for the implementation of the agreements in question. Similarly, where new agreements are being negotiated, the competence of the Member States, and the rights which flow from it, are entitled to recognition.

In both Opinions, 1/94 and 2/92, the Court of Justice clarified the division of competences between the Community and the Member States in the areas of services, establishment and intellectual property. Now the institutions of the Community and the Member States have a workable means of ascertaining where competence lies in a particular case. However, its decision that the cross-border supply of services falls within Article 133 EC (ex Article 113) means that many international agreements in the field of services will be mixed; not many services sectors will fall wholly within Community or Member States' competence. This means that, in practice, the duty of co-operation and what it entails in any particular case, will assume great importance.

THE COMMUNITY AND THE MEMBER STATES MAY ADOPT THE MOST SUITABLE MODEL FOR ANY PARTICULAR ORGANISATION OR SET OF NEGOTIATIONS

16.03   In its observations in Opinion 1/94 the Commission argued that the Member States should be members of the World Trade Organisation (WTO) along with the Community for political reasons only. Community procedures would, according to the Commission's argument, apply. Thus the Commission would be the sole spokesman for the Community and the Member States, positions in the WTO would be taken only on the basis of Commission procedures. Member States would speak only to the extent that they were specifically authorised so to do. The Commission argued that this

---

[4] Opinion 2/92 *Competence of the Community or one of its institutions to participate in the Third Revised Decision of the OECD on national treatment* [1995] E.C.R. I–521.

was necessary to secure effective implementation of the WTO agreements. The Commission maintained that there would be problems if Member States were to express their own views where a lack of consensus existed. In its view, there would be interminable discussion on whether a matter fell within Community or Member State competence. The Commission concluded that the Commission's unity of action *vis-à-vis* the rest of the world would be undermined and its negotiating power greatly weakened.

The Court of Justice recognised these concerns but said that the allocation of competence cannot depend on problems which may possibly arise in the administration of the agreements. It said that where the subject matter of an agreement fell in part within the competence of the Community and in part within that of the Member States, it was essential to ensure close co-operation between the Member States and Community institutions, both in the process of negotiating and concluding the agreement and in the fulfilment of the commitments entered into. The Court stated that the "obligation to co-operate flows from the requirement of unity in the international representation of the Community,"[5] referring in support to Ruling 1/78[6] on the Draft Convention on the Physical Protection of Nuclear Materials and Opinion 2/91[7] on Convention No. 170 of the International Labour Organisation.

The section of Opinion 1/94 dealing with the duty of co-operation is relatively brief.[8] The Commission has argued that E.C. law requires that there must be a single spokesman on behalf of the Community and the Member States. Thus, for example, the Commission would be the sole spokesman in the negotiation of a mixed agreement and it would conduct a dispute settlement procedure even if the matter was not within the exclusive competence of the Community. It is submitted that this is not correct as a matter of law. The Court in Opinion 1/94 did not speak of a unity of representation of the Community and the Member States where competence was shared; instead it spoke of a duty of co-operation. These are clearly different concepts. For example, the relevant heading of Opinion 1/94 reads "The duty of co-operation between the Member States and the Community institutions". The Court referred to ensuring close co-operation. It used similar words in Opinion 2/91: "It is therefore for the Community institutions and the Member States to take all the measures necessary so as best to ensure such co-operation".[9]

16.04   The duty of co-operation is a duty of mutual co-operation. This is illustrated by the decision of the Court in *Luxembourg* v. *Parliament*.[10] The case was concerned with the geographic seat of the European Parliament. The Treaties establishing the European Communities provide for the seat of the institutions of the Communities to be determined by common accord of the Member States. This involves an intergovernmental act. The Member States had not taken a final decision; they had determined only provisional places of work for the European Parliament. The Parliament adopted a resolution to the effect that its plenary sessions would be held in Strasbourg, that as a general rule meetings of committees and political groups should be conducted in Brussels and that the operation of the secretarial and technical services of the Parliament would be revised. The resolution was challenged by Luxembourg. In the course of its judgment, the Court said:

[5] Opinion 1/94 [1994] E.C.R. I–5267, at para. 108.
[6] Ruling 1/78 *Draft Convention of the International Atomic Energy Agency on the Physical Protection of Nuclear materials, Facilities and Transports* [1978] E.C.R. 2151.
[7] Opinion 2/91 *Convention No. 170 of the International Labour Organisation concerning safety in the use of chemicals at work ("ILO")* [1993] E.C.R. I–1061; (1993) 3 C.M.L.Rev. 800.
[8] Opinion 1/94 [1994] E.C.R. I–5267, at paras. 106–110.
[9] Opinion 2/91 [1993] E.C.R. I–1061, at para. 38.
[10] Case 230/81 [1983] E.C.R. 255; (1983) 3 C.M.L.Rev. 726.

"It must nevertheless be emphasised that when the Governments of the Member States make provisional decisions they must in accordance with *the rule imposing on Member States and the Community institutions mutual duties of sincere co-operation*, as embodied in Article [10] of the EC Treaty,[11] have regard to the power of the Parliament to determine its internal organisation".[12]

A similar statement is made by Duran in *Commentaire Mégret*: "La Cour a toujours souligné que devoir *réciproquesé de co-opération loyale entre Etats membres et institutions*"[13]

The mutual nature of the obligation means that the Member States must co-operate with the Community institutions. But it also means that the latter must also co-operate with the Member States. The Court of Justice has recognised the validity of mixed agreements in Community law and consequently the competence that Member States have in their negotiation and implementation. The mutual duty of sincere co-operation means that there is an obligation on the Community institutions to recognise and give full force to the competence of the Member States. Thus, for example, it does not follow as a matter of law that, in respect of a matter where Member States retain competence, they no longer have the power to act if a common position cannot be agreed amongst all the Member States. The duty of co-operation is a flexible concept which allows the Community and the Member States to reach a practical solution tailored to the particular case.

FUNDAMENTAL CHANGE TO THE TREATIES IS NOT NEEDED NOW

16.05 It is submitted that major revision of the Treaties is not needed at the present time to deal with the participation of the Community and the Member States in international organisations. So far as the opening of negotiations and the conclusion of agreements is concerned, the Treaty provisions adequately provide for the situation where competence is shared between the Community and the Member States. Practice is still developing, but it is appropriate to look at the matter from the point of view of the Community and the Member States. So far as the position of the Community is concerned, the procedure in Article 300 EC (ex Article 228) will apply. That Article provides for the authorisation of negotiations, the issue of negotiating Directives and the conclusion of agreements. So far as the position of the Member States is concerned, there are well-established procedures for making decisions of an intergovernmental nature within the Council framework *i.e.* a Decision of the Representatives of the Governments of the Member States meeting within the Council. The Decision is taken by consensus. This was the procedure adopted by the Council on September 20, 1986 during the opening of the Uruguay Round negotiations and could have been used for the Decision on the modalities for negotiating the OECD Multilateral Agreement on Investment, a mixed agreement. Similarly, for the conclusion of agreements, a Decision of an intergovernmental nature adopted within the Council framework could be used.

It is therefore possible to bring the Community and intergovernmental procedures together. A problem is that qualified majority voting applies in certain areas within

---

[11] Ex Art. 5 EC.
[12] [1983] E.C.R. 255, at para. 37, emphasis added.
[13] See de Cockborne, *et al.* in Mégret, *Le Droit de la Communauté européenne: Preambule, Principes, Libre Circulation des Marchandises* (2nd ed., 1992) Vol. 1, p. 41.

Community competence[14] but consensus applies where the act is of an intergovernmental nature. This means that when the two procedures are brought together voting is, in effect, by consensus.

What is possibly more difficult in practice is the procedure for negotiating and implementing a mixed agreement. This raises the difficult question of who speaks on matters where both the Community and the Member States have competence, where the Member States alone have competence, and where the division of competence is unclear. Similarly, who is to attend meetings? Should there be a single representative or do all Member States have the right to be independently represented in meetings? What is the position so far as disputes are concerned, particularly where, in a body such as the WTO, there can be cross-retaliation in an area of Community competence for action by a Member State in an area within its competence? In this writer's view, the answers in practical terms will depend upon the particular organisation or mixed agreement in question. The legal position enables an answer to be found to the practical problems that arise in a particular context.

This is not to say all is well. There are problems. For example, the Commission does not always consult the Member States in full, or in a timely fashion, to enable them to give a considered opinion. However, this is a general problem applying equally where the matter falls within the exclusive competence of the Community, *e.g.* under the Common Commercial Policy. This is an important issue that the Commission should recognise; the Member States have interests that they achieve through the Community. It may be that, if there is to be a review of Article 300 EC (ex Article 228), the duties of the Commission to the Council and to Member States should be addressed.

EACH INTERNATIONAL ORGANISATION NEEDS TO BE INDIVIDUALLY CONSIDERED

16.06   The Member States and the institutions of the Community need to consider what arrangements will most effectively enable them to exercise fully their collective negotiating power in the international organisation concerned. They need to consider how their objectives can be best achieved and how their individual and common interests can be best defended. The writer does not accept that their negotiating power is necessarily stronger if all negotiations are concentrated into a single Community spokesman. In many cases, the Member States acting individually or collectively along with the institutions of the Community can be more effective.

Much will depend upon the institution or particular negotiations in issue. What suits the WTO may not suit the OECD or environmental organisations or even the World Intellectual Property Organisation. If one looks, for example, at the history of the WTO, its predecessor, the General Agreement on Tariffs and Trade (GATT), was originally concerned only with trade in goods. This fell in general within the exclusive competence of the Community. The Commission was traditionally the Community negotiator, and this practice was continued in the Uruguay Round although those negotiations included matters which, in the view of the Member States (a view upheld by the Court of Justice in Opinion 1/94), were within their competence. This role of the Commission is something that the other parties to the WTO are accustomed to. It may not, however, be appropriate outside the area of trade in goods, particularly if the WTO moves into new areas, such as trade and social issues, trade and the environment, and the effect of economic and monetary policy on trade.

---

[14] *e.g.* Arts. 133 and 300(2) EC (ex Arts. 113 and 228(2)).

Turning to the OECD, there is no tradition of the Community being the sole spokes-man. Furthermore, most issues considered in the OECD do not fall within the exclus-ive competence of the Community. Looking at the matter from a practical viewpoint, these are matters where the Member States have the expertise as a result of, for example, negotiating bilateral investment agreements and also because internal com-petence in respect of these matters remains with the Member States.

In agreeing any procedure it must be recognised that there will be cases where it is difficult to draw a dividing line between areas of Community and Member States com-petence. Although that dividing line has been significantly clarified in Opinion 1/94 and Opinion 2/92, there will be room for differing views at the margin and, indeed, the position will change over time as E.C. legislation is adopted. It is not in the interest of the Community and the Member States to squabble in public about the division of competence, and one of the purposes of the duty of co-operation is to avoid this.[15]

For these reasons the procedure adopted for the participation of the Member States and the Community in one organisation will not necessarily suit other organisations.

CONCLUSION

16.07   This paper has sought to show that the legal position governing the partici-pation of the Community and the Member States in international organisations is flex-ible and that it allows arrangements to be agreed which can suit the circumstances of the particular international organisation in question whilst recognising the positions of the Community and the Member States. It is submitted that with good will and common sense on all sides such arrangements can work. There *is* evidence that they can work, *e.g.* the successful outcome of the Uruguay Round itself and the conclusion of the financial services negotiations in the WTO in the summer of 1995. In the latter, the E.U. was able to take the lead as a result of the combined efforts of the Commission and the Member States. For example, the United Kingdom, given its position as a country with a major financial services industry, was better able to lobby in some parts of the world than the Commission.

Finally, it is important to remember that it is in the interests of the Community and the Member States to use their combined weight to the best effect. It is to their mutual advantage to do so and the practical application of the duty of co-operation must recognise this.

---

[15] See Ruling 1/78 [1978] E.C.R. 2151, at para. 35.

CHAPTER 17

International Instruments as a Source of Community Law

by

*Ilona Cheyne**

17.01   A systematic review of the Court's case law concerning the application of international agreements in Community law was undertaken in Chapter Two, where it was discovered that the Court had developed coherent, but not fully integrated, lines of reasoning. Some issues were left unresolved and it was argued that the Court would soon be required to reformulate its approach as the Community continued to develop its external policies and, most importantly, in the light of the formalisation of the GATT rules within the WTO legal structure. The present chapter will analyse the relevant case law and its problematic aspects in the light of some basic principles and theories of constitutional law and practice concerning the role of courts and judicial review. The purpose of the analysis is to clarify the legal and policy issues that underlie judicial implementation of international agreements in Community law.

Community law is equivalent to a domestic legal system in that it operates with its own laws and procedures separate from international law, notwithstanding the fact that its legal actors include sovereign states.[1] Where the Community legal order and international law overlap, therefore, the Court must, like most domestic courts, find an appropriate accommodation between the two. In order to determine whether an international instrument is a source of Community law for the purposes of the judicial review, the Court must ask two questions. The first is whether the international instrument in question has become part of Community law. To answer this question, a rule of recognition is required[2] and a finding that an international instrument has satisfied that rule will lead to the Court having jurisdiction over it. The second question is whether the issue before the Court is justiciable, which is an enquiry into whether judicial settlement of the dispute is feasible and, if so, whether it is appropriate.[3]

* Senior Lecturer, Newcastle Law School. I would like to thank Ian Mabbut and David Milroy for their assistance in the preparation of this chapter, and Alison Dunn for her helpful comments on an earlier draft.
[1] The Court has identified the Community legal order as separate and independent from international law. Case 26/62 *Van Gend en Loos* [1963] E.C.R. 1, [1963] C.M.L.R. 105. International law continues to regulate relations between the Member States, or between the Member States and non-member States which fall outside the E.C. Treaty. See Art. 307 EC (ex Art. 234); Case 812/79 *Burgoa* [1980] E.C.R. 2787, [1981] 2 C.M.L.R. 193; Case 41/74 *Van Duyn* [1974] E.C.R. 1337, [1975] 1 C.M.L.R. 1, Case 10/61 *Commission v. Italy* (*Radio Tubes* case) [1962] E.C.R. 1; [1962] C.M.L.R. 187. See also Mann, *The Function of Judicial Decision in European Economic Integration* (1972) pp. 4–25; Hartley, *The Foundations of European Community Law* (3rd ed., 1994), p. 95.
[2] The term "rule of recognition" is taken from Hart's analysis of legal systems as comprising a complex set of primary and secondary rules, see *The Concept of Law*, (Oxford University Press, 1961).
[3] It is recognised that the questions of jurisdiction and justiciability are not watertight and that some of the issues to be discussed could fall into one or either, or indeed both, categories. They are used here as convenient terms for the purpose of analysis.

What follows is an examination of the Court's case law in the light of these stages. It will be argued that they have become blurred in the terminology of the Court and that this has occurred, in part, because of the dynamic nature of the Community's external competence which has required a corresponding flexibility in the Court's approach. It will also be argued that circumstances, most notably the transformation of GATT 1947 into the WTO Agreement and GATT 1994, will require the Court to lay down a more explicit rule of non-justiciability and judicial restraint with regard to the Community's conduct of external relations.

RE-EXAMINING THE PRINCIPLES OF JURISDICTION AND JUSTICIABILITY IN COMMUNITY LAW

17.02   Examination of the Court's justifications for receiving and applying international agreements into Community law shows that they have not significantly changed since *International Fruit*,[4] *Haegeman*[5] and *Demirel*,[6] even in the face of a landmark challenge by a Member State in the *Banana* case.[7] This apparently static approach appears to suggest that there are fixed and well-understood rules of recognition and principles of justiciability, but this would ignore a qualitative shift in the executive institutions' involvement in external affairs. The wide reach of the Community's external relations powers which arose from the *ERTA* doctrine[8] has resulted in increasingly complex external policies, significantly different from the comparatively simple situation existing at the time of the *International Fruit* and *Haegeman* cases.[9]

Thus, as a matter of Community constitutional law,[10] the rule of recognition which governs the reception of international law into the Community legal system and the principles under which the Court determines its justiciability in disputes before it should be reconsidered. This enquiry requires a distinction to be made between the separate stages of reception and application of international agreements, and an examination of the constitutional and policy implications that surround the question of applying international instruments in Community law.

---

[4] Cases 21–24/72 *International Fruit Company* [1972] E.C.R. 1219, [1975] 2 C.M.L.R. 1.
[5] Case 181/73 [1974] E.C.R. 449, [1975] 1 C.M.L.R. 515.
[6] Case 12/86 [1987] E.C.R. 3719, [1989] 1 C.M.L.R. 421.
[7] Case C–280/93, *Germany* v. *Council* [1994] E.C.R. I–4973. The Court relied upon precisely the same reasoning to exclude application of the GATT under Art. 230 (ex Art. 173) as it had in *International Fruit* for the purposes of Art. 234 (ex Art. 177), see para. 109.
[8] Case 70/87 [1989] E.C.R. 1781, [1991] 2 C.M.L.R. 489. And see Cases 3, 4 and 6/76 *Kramer* [1976] E.C.R. 1279; Opinion 1/76 [1977] E.C.R. 741, para. 3.
[9] For example, the Community now plays an active part in its own right in international organisations and agreements which are concerned with broader questions than mere commercial policy, such as the Food and Agricultural Organisation and the UN Framework Convention on Climate Change. There is extensive literature on the extent and nature of the Community's external relations. See, for example, Brückner, "The European Community and the United Nations" (1990) 1 E.J.I.L. 174; Frid, "The European Economic Community. A Member of a Specialized Agency of the United Nations" (1993) 4 E.J.I.L. 239; Macleod, Hendry, and Hyett, *The External Relations of the European Communities* (1996); Okowa, "The European Community and International Environmental Agreements" (1995) 15 Y.E.L. 169. Another significant development of the Community's external affairs policy is the Common Foreign and Security Policy over which the Court's jurisdiction has been excluded under Art. 46 TEU (ex Art. L). Even here, however, the Court would still retain jurisdiction under Art. 47 TEU (ex Art. M) if matters under the E.C. Treaty were affected. See, for example, Case C–70/94 *Werner* [1995] E.C.R. I–3189 and Case C–83/94 *Leifer* [1995] E.C.R. I–3231; and C–124/95 *R* v. *HM Treasury and Bank of England, ex p. Centro-Com* [1997] 1 C.M.L.R. 555; Case C–170/96 *Commission* v. *Council* [1998] E.C.R. I–2763.
[10] This terminology follows from the Court's identification of the constitutional nature of the E.C. Treaty, see Case 294/83 *Partie Ecologiste "Les Verts"* v. *Parliament* [1986] E.C.R. 1339, [1987] 2 C.M.L.R. 343, para. 23; Opinion 1/91 [1991] E.C.R. I–6079, [1992] 1 C.M.L.R. 245.

Jurisdiction: reception of international agreements into Community law

17.03 In order for the Court to have jurisdiction over an international instrument, it must be satisfied that the instrument has been received into Community law.[11] A traditional method of analysing the relationship between international law and a domestic legal system is in terms of monism and dualism,[12] which seek to describe the types of rules of recognition that domestic legal systems employ. Monism would appear to be an attractive theoretical perspective from which to classify the Court's approach to international instruments, particularly after the Court's finding in *Haegeman* that the mere act of concluding an international agreement under Article 300 (ex Article 228) made it an "integral part of Community law".[13] Equally, the Court's finding in *Kramer*[14] that international law permeated Community law even in those areas over which the Community had competence tended to support this view. The Court's recognition in *International Fruit* of the primacy of international agreements over secondary acts or legislation is also a monist technique.[15] Furthermore, it might be supposed from the nature of the Community as an organisation comprising sovereign states that, notwithstanding the separate nature of Community law, international law would have a special status within its legal order.

In this regard, it is worth recalling that it is difficult for any legal system to avoid the need for some form of explicit rule of recognition which applies to law derived from outside its own law-making procedures, if that law is to have effect within the system.[16] Constitutional division of responsibilities for the conduct of external affairs and for the creation or determination of internal law makes the need for such a process inevitable. Because the legitimacy of rules is defined by a legal system's secondary rules of enactment and hierarchy, the domestic legal system has a choice: it may ignore any rules of international law, or it may incorporate or transform them into the internal system.[17] The legal consequences of international legal rules and obligations depend entirely on domestic constitutional law.

It follows from the above discussion that even those constitutions which take a monist approach by granting effect to international instruments without any legislative act of incorporation or adoption are simply employing a domestic rule of recognition. In principle, this rule is little different from one which requires a separate formal act of adoption to enable an international instrument to have domestic legal effect (as one might expect to find in a dualist system). In practice, lack of legislative consideration of each international agreement before it becomes part of the domestic legal system may result in more conflicts between the agreement and previously existing domestic law which will, in turn, require more frequent judicial settlement. If conflicts do occur, they are resolved by a rule of hierarchical recognition determining which is the superior

---

[11] This discussion will assume that the questions of competence and procedure are satisfied, since lack of space prevents their examination here. It should be noted, however, that the Court has recognised that international agreements which have been found to be invalid as a matter of competence or procedural irregularity in Community law will still be binding on the Community in international law. See Case C–327/91 *France* v. *Commission* [1994] E.C.R. I–3641, para. 25.

[12] Of course, theoretical approaches may not entirely explain state practice and this may be even more the case in a non-traditional legal construct such as the Community. In addition, even on a theoretical level, O'Connell suggested that neither monism nor dualism produces answers which are of relevance to the other because they start from different assumptions and ask different questions. O'Connell, *International Law* (2nd ed., 1970), Vol. 1, p. 43. Nonetheless, they are convenient terms with which to explore the development of the Court's jurisprudence on the use of international instruments as a source of Community law.

[13] [1974] E.C.R. 449, [1975] C.M.L.R. 515, para. 5.

[14] [1976] E.C.R. 1279.

[15] [1972] E.C.R. 1219, [1975] 2 C.M.L.R. 1, para. 28.

[16] See, for example, Meessen, "The Application of Rules of Public International Law Within Community Law", (1976) C.M.L.Rev. 335, at 492–3.

[17] *ibid.*

source of law. All of these aspects of a rule of recognition exist in the Court's case law but are not always clearly delineated.

The Court established basic rules of recognition and hierarchy in *International Fruit* and *Haegeman*. In *International Fruit*, international law was received into Community law by Article 234 (ex Article 177) as one of the possible grounds for finding acts of the institutions invalid.[18] This automatically gave international law superior status over secondary Community law, but arguably limited its effect to a ground of judicial review. This basis of jurisdiction appears to have been subsumed and extended by a different formulation in the later case of *Haegeman*, in which international agreements concluded under Article 300 (ex Article 228) were recognised as "an integral part of Community law".[19] This suggested that Article 300 was the mechanism by which this transformation had taken place and that the agreements were received as applicable Community law for all types of dispute settlement.

17.04   Part of the present uncertainty about the appropriate rule of recognition in Community law arises from the approach the Court adopted in *Haegeman*. The act of formal conclusion is not, as Hartley has pointed out, an act of incorporation as such but rather an act acknowledging that the Community is bound by the relevant agreement.[20] The extension of jurisdiction to international agreements under Article 234 is therefore at odds with the wording of that article because it assimilates the contents of the agreement with an act of the institutions.[21] The Court, however, has shown no signs of withdrawing from this basis of jurisdiction and has continued to give effect to formally concluded agreements. Indeed, it has gone further and extended the same reasoning to decisions made by international organisations[22] which, Hartley argues, are even more distant from the definition of "acts of the institutions".[23]

If these criticisms have validity,[24] it may be asked why the Court created a rule of recognition which did not require a legislative act. One possible reason would be that the purpose of Article 234 was for the Court to have jurisdiction not just over the literal acts of the institutions but also over their consequences. This would be consistent with the Court's identification in the *ERTA* case[25] of the essentially dynamic nature of the Community's external relations powers and their interpretation beyond a narrow and literal reading of the Treaty. If the Court had restricted itself to the mere question of whether the Community institutions had used the appropriate powers and procedures to conclude an agreement without having jurisdiction over the legal consequences, it would, in this view, have exercised an excessive level of self-restraint and prevented international agreements from enjoying their intended legal effectiveness. This interpretation would also be consistent with the Court's "activist" phase, during which much of the present jurisprudence was developed, particularly with the emphasis on the direct effect of Treaty provisions and the protection of the rights of private individuals.[26] Reluctance on the part of the Community institutions or Member States

---

[18] [1972] E.C.R. 1219, [1975] 2 C.M.L.R. 1, para. 6.
[19] [1974] E.C.R. 449, [1975] 1 C.M.L.R. 515, para. 5.
[20] Hartley, "International Agreements and the Community Legal System" (1983) 8 E.L.Rev. 383, at 390–391; Hartley, "The European Court, Judicial Objectivity and the Constitution of the European Union" (1996) 112 L.Q.R. 95, at 99.
[21] *ibid.*
[22] Case C–192/89 *Sevince* [1990] E.C.R. I–3461.
[23] Hartley (1996), *op. cit.* at 100.
[24] They are disputed, for example, in Arnull, "The European Court and Judicial Objectivity: A Reply to Professor Hartley" (1996) 112 L.Q.R. 411.
[25] Case 70/87 [1989] E.C.R. 1781, [1991] 2 C.M.L.R. 489.
[26] See Rasmussen, *On Law and Policy in the European Court of Justice* (1986). It should be noted, however, that a more sceptical view of the Court's activism is proposed in Tridimas, "The Court of Justice and Judicial Activism" (1996) 21 E.L.Rev. p. 199.

to give international agreements "teeth" by making them enforceable through Community legislation would not therefore have precluded such an interpretation. The Court's willingness to exercise jurisdiction over them is consistent with its expressed desire to "police" the operation of the Treaty and the exercise of the institutions' powers,[27] although it has shown more caution about the direct effect of international agreements than of the E.C. Treaty itself.[28]

The *Haegeman* approach was, at first, an apparently unqualified assertion of jurisdiction. It has now been put more guardedly, however, by generalised references to the Community "legal order"[29] or "legal system",[30] and it has become increasingly evident from the case law that a wide assertion of jurisdiction does not necessarily lead to justiciability.[31] The Court's case law has developed a more explicitly conditional approach, in which application of international agreements in Community law depends on whether they satisfy the two-stage test formulated in its final form in *Demirel*.[32] This is not a matter of reception of international agreements into Community law, but a matter of their application; not a matter of jurisdiction, but of justiciability.

Justiciability: application of international agreements in Community law

17.05 Although justiciability can be identified as a crucial issue for the Court's decision whether to apply an international agreement, it is not an easy concept to define. Most attempts result in identifying a set of overlapping and interconnecting elements leading up to a circular definition. Nonetheless, it is worthwhile making the effort to distinguish some of these elements in order to inform our analysis of the Court's case law and its possible future actions. There are two key questions to be asked under a justiciability principle to discover whether judicial action is appropriate in a given case: first, whether the issue at hand is inherently one of policy and, second, whether the court can discover judicially manageable standards with which to resolve the dispute.[33]

The policy aspect of justiciability is often described as a problem of separation of powers or as the "political question" doctrine, and is essentially a constitutional issue. Power in the hands of an authority other than the court may be explicitly created or it may be inferred from the circumstances. In the former case, for example, a treaty which expressly requires the government of a country to enact legislation will not, as a rule, be justiciable by that country's courts, because the responsibility for deciding

---

[27] See above, p. 255, n. 10.

[28] See Bebr, "Agreements Concluded by the Community and Their Possible Direct Effect" (1983) 20 C.M.L.Rev. 35 at 46; Bourgeois, "Effects of International Agreements in European Community Law: Are the Dice Cast?" (1984) 82 Michigan Law Review 1250 at 1261; Castillo de la Torre (1992), "The Status of GATT in E.E.C. Law" [1992] 26 J.W.T. 53 at 36; Cheyne, "International Agreements and the European Community Legal System" (1994) 19 E.L.R. 581 at 590; Maresceau, "The GATT in the Case Law of the European Court of Justice" in Hilf, Jacobs and Petersmann, *The European Community and GATT* (1986), p. 107 at p. 116; Meessen, *op. cit.* at pp. 495–496.

[29] See, for example, Case C–188/91 *Deutsche Shell* [1993] E.C.R. I–363 at para. 16; Case 469/93 *Chiquita* [1995] E.C.R. I–4533 at para. 40; Case T–115/94 *Opel Austria* v. *Council* [1997] 1 C.M.L.R. 733 at para. 79.

[30] See, for example, Case 104/81 *Kupferberg* [1982] E.C.R. 3641, [1983] 1 C.M.L.R. 1, at para. 13 *Demirel*; [1987] E.C.R. 3719, [1989] 1 C.M.L.R. 421, at para. 7; Case 30/88 *Greece* v. *Commission* [1989] E.C.R. 3711, [1991] 2 C.M.L.R. 169 at paras. 12 and 13; Case C–192/89 *Sevince* [1990] E.C.R. I–3461 at para. 8.

[31] See discussion in Chapter Two.

[32] [1987] E.C.R. 3719, [1989] 1 C.M.L.R. 421, para. 14. The development of this test is discussed in Chapter Two.

[33] For a discussion of these concepts within the context of U.S. constitutional law, see Tribe, *American Constitutional Law* (2nd ed., 1988) at pp. 67–72, 96–107; Vázquez, "Treaty-Based Rights and Remedies of Individuals" [1992] 92 Columbia L. Rev. 1082, at 1123–1133.

how to implement the treaty would have been assigned to the political institutions. The same non-justiciability principle would apply to a treaty which gave the government permission to act but did not require it to do so, making its power discretionary. In a case where power has not been explicitly delegated, the court may still judge that an issue is too heavily weighted with policy implications for it to be constitutionally suitable for judicial involvement, in effect using a sort of interpretative intuition about what would be appropriate for judicial review in the context of its political and cultural circumstances.[34] Questions that related to the allocation of resources, for example, or required knowledge or expertise that a court would be unlikely to possess, or which had a multiplicity of social, economic and political implications would be likely to fall into this category. In addition, courts will often exercise restraint to avoid unnecessarily embarrassing or hampering the political institutions in their conduct of external relations.

Although judicial decisions inevitably involve some or all of these characteristics, inappropriateness of judicial intervention will become increasingly likely as the questions move closer to the exercise of public policy choices.[35] Making such a judgment depends on an assessment of the constitutional traditions and the political dynamics within which the legal system is located. In the case of the Court of Justice, it not only has the powers and duties derived from the E.C. Treaty but must also identify and, in the absence of clear guidance, develop through its interpretation of the Treaty what the Community's constitutional traditions are and ought to be. It must also be particularly aware of the political realities of overextending its reach if it does not wish to provoke the hostility of the other institutions or the Member States.[36]

The second aspect of justiciability concerns the question of whether there exist standards of law which are sufficiently clear, precise and unconditional that a court can reasonably apply them. This overlaps substantially with the policy aspect of justiciability, since lack of clear legal provisions would indicate that a large area of discretion has been allocated to law-creating or administrative authorities, either because it had been explicitly delegated to them or because the issues were too complex to be resolved without the exercise of discretionary powers. Although the two separate aspects can be identified, therefore, they merge and overlap over a spectrum which extends from the question of whether judicial intervention is appropriate to the question of whether it is practicable.

17.06 One qualification should be added. A court can retain the right to review whether discretionary powers have been properly exercised under the terms of their grant, even though it has no power to review the merits of that exercise. Thus, in E.C. law, the Court will restrain itself from reviewing the substantive exercise of discretion by the political institutions, but has the duty to examine whether basic procedural requirements have been observed and that there is no evidence of manifest error or

---

[34] For a recent theoretical discussion of this concept, see Dworkin, *Freedom's law: the Moral Reading of the American Constitution* (1996). Vasquez also refers to "deeply held intuitions that certain types of issues are inherently not for judicial resolution", *op. cit.* at p. 1130.

[35] See, for example, Case 53/84 *Stanley Adams v. Commission* [1985] E.C.R. 3651, where the Court took the view that the decision to refer a matter to the Joint Committee could only be taken "for purposes which have to do exclusively with general interests of the Community, following an assessment which is essentially political and which cannot be challenged before the Court by an individual." (para. 15). For a general discussion of the extent of the Court's power to review the exercise of political discretion, see the opinion of Advocate General Darmon in Case C–241/87 *Maclaine Watson v. Council and Commission* [1990] E.C.R. I–1797 (case withdrawn).

[36] See, for example, Rasmussen, *op. cit.*

abuse.[37] This is true, for example, in cases of complex economic situations.[38] In the same way, the Court will apply general principles of law to limit the manner in which the political institutions implement their policies.[39]

It was stated above that the test for justiciability of international agreements in Community law is the two-stage test of direct applicability developed by the Court and finally formulated in *Demirel*.[40] One stage is concerned with legal certainty, which is a question of whether a provision provides judicially manageable standards or, in other words, whether it is amenable to judicial application. It is a test common to all judicial systems. However, it is possible for an international agreement to have provisions which are legally certain but still not qualify for direct applicability in Community law because it does not satisfy the other stage of the test.[41] This second stage relates to the nature and purposes of the agreement and is primarily concerned with the question of whether justiciability would be appropriate. Since it is this second stage which raises problems that are peculiar to the Community's appraisal of justiciability over international agreements, it will be the primary focus of the following discussion.

When examining the nature and purpose of international agreements, the Court has explicitly referred to two particularly relevant aspects. These are, first, the contents and purpose of an agreement and, second, the extent to which it creates and operates within a legally formal structure.

The Court has referred to the contents and purpose of an agreement frequently, although its reasons for doing so often remain opaque.[42] Where the Court has found direct applicability, it has rarely given explicit reasoning to explain the link between the two. Thus an idea of which characteristics of an international agreement are relevant can only be developed from inferences drawn from the Court's judgments.

First, and most obviously, a number of association agreements, ranging from those leading explicitly to accession to those aimed merely at closer economic ties, have been

---

[37] See, for example, Case C–121/86 *Epicheiriseon Metalleftikon Viomichanikon kai Naftiliakon* v. *Council* [1989] E.C.R. 3919, para.8: "... even though a discretion has been conferred on the Community institutions, the Court is required to verify whether or not they have observed the procedural guarantees contained in the basic regulation, and whether or not they have committed manifest errors in their assessment of the facts, have omitted to take any essential matters into consideration or have based the reasons for their decision on considerations amounting to a misuse of powers." See also, for example, Case 191/82 *Fediol* v. *Commission* [1983] E.C.R. 2913, para. 30; Case 264/82 *Timex* v. *Council and Commission* [1985] E.C.R. 849.
[38] See, for example, Case C–179/87 *Sharp* v. *Council* [1992] 2 C.M.L.R. 415, para. 58; Case C–69/89 *Nakajima* v. *Council* [1991] E.C.R. I–2069, para. 86; Case T–164/94 *Ferchimex* v. *Council* [1995] E.C.R. II–2681, paras. 111 and 131.
[39] See, for example, Case T–162/94 *NMB France Sarl* v. *Commission* [1997] 3 C.M.L.R. 164, para. 69; Cases T–466/93, T–469/93, T–473/93 T–474/93 & T–477/93 *O'Dwyer and others* v. *EU Council* [1996] 2 C.M.L.R. 148; Case T–267/94 *Oleifici Italiani SpA v EC Commission* [1998] 1 C.M.L.R. 692; Case C–280/93 *Germany* v. *Council* (the *Banana* case) [1994] E.C.R. I–4973 at paras. 90–91.
[40] Case 12/86 [1987] E.C.R. 3719, [1989] 1 C.M.L.R. 421, para. 14. This test is discussed in detail in Chapter Two.
[41] This was exemplified in the cases of *Fediol* and *Nakajima*, where GATT provisions were accepted as judicially applicable by the Court, even though justiciability over the agreement itself was considered to be inappropriate. See below, p. 263, n. 58.
[42] For a brief review of the types of international agreements to which direct applicability has been given, see Lee and Kennedy, "The Potential Direct Effect of GATT 1994 in European Community Law" (1996) J.W.T. 69, at pp. 82–84.

given direct applicability.[43] Co-operation agreements and free trade areas, including the European Economic Area, have also been granted this status.[44] All of these constitute an interlocking system with the Community in matters such as the free movement of goods or workers. Judicial supervision of the implementation of these agreements by the Community institutions would therefore seem appropriate given the involvement of individuals' interests and the importance of Member States' legislative acts. They are, in other words, not entirely external in effect or importance, but rather directly impinge on the day-to-day affairs of the Community.

17.07 The direct applicability of international agreements such as the Yaoundé and Lomé Conventions gives rise to slightly different questions.[45] They are analogous to association or co-operation agreements in that they involve provisions concerned with free movement of goods and non-discrimination, and they are designed to promote the economic development of the other parties. Indeed, the Court has pointed out that they are "an extension of association agreements" originally established by the E.E.C. Treaty.[46] At the same time, however, they share some similarities with the GATT, which is also multilateral and based on principles of free movement of goods and non-discrimination. A key difference, however, appears to be that these conventions are a project of the Community designed to further particular policy objectives of the Community and, more specifically, of Member States wishing to maintain historical trade links and who therefore have a particular interest in granting trade privileges. In addition, the bipolar nature of these Conventions means that the Community has retained power to control any future measures to implement them in a way which is essentially equivalent to being a party to a bilateral agreement.[47]

The primary characteristics of international agreements given direct applicability on the grounds of their contents and purpose therefore appear to arise from their closeness to the objectives of the Community and management of its affairs,[48] including agreements where the other parties' economic development has been adopted as a specific Community project. Such agreements are not likely to give rise to the possibility of Community violations, given their largely hortatory and open-ended character which allocates powers rather than obligations to the Community institutions. The Court is therefore unlikely to run the risk of conflict with the political institutions and potentially causing them embarrassment in their relations with third states by finding that they have acted unlawfully under the agreement. At the same time, the Court can feel reasonably confident that its involvement is likely to promote Community objec-

---

[43] See, for example, Case 104/81 *Kupferberg* [1982] E.C.R. 3641, [1983] 1 C.M.L.R. 1, Case 181/73 *Haegeman* [1974] E.C.R. 449, [1975] 1 C.M.L.R. 515, Case C–225/78, *Procureur de la Republique* v. *Bouhelier* [1979] E.C.R. 3151, Case 17/81, *Pabst & Richarz*, [1982] E.C.R. 1331, [1983] 3 C.M.L.R. 11, Case C–192/89 *Sevince* [1990] E.C.R. I–3461, C–237/91, *Kus* v. *Landeshauptstadt Wiesbaden* [1993] 2 C.M.L.R. 887. The direct applicability of association agreements is now firmly established. See, for example, Case C–432/92, *R* v. *MAFF, ex parte Anastasiou* [1995] 1 C.M.L.R. 569, where the Court applied the *Demirel* test straightforwardly to find direct effect of a Protocol to the E.E.C.-Cyprus Association Agreement.
[44] See, for example, Case C–174/84 *Bulk Oil (Zug)* v. *Sun International* [1986] E.C.R. 559, Case C–18/90 *Kziber* [1991] E.C.R. I–199, Case 312/91 *Metalsa* [1994] 2 C.M.L.R. 121, Case C–58/93 *Zoubir Yousfi* v. *Belgium* [1994] E.C.R. I–1353, *Opel Austria* v. *Council* [1997] 1 C.M.L.R. 733.
[45] See, for example, Case 87/75 *Bresciani* [1976] E.C.R. 129, [1976] 2 C.M.L.R. 62, Case 469/93 *Chiquita* [1995] E.C.R. I–4533.
[46] Case 469/93 *Chiquita* [1995] E.C.R. I–4533 at para.33.
[47] See Advocate General Jacobs" Opinion in Case C–316/91 *Re the European Development Fund: Parliament* v. *Council* [1994] E.C.R. I–625, at para. 69. A reference to this idea is made by Bourgeois, *op. cit.* at p. 1267, and by Montaña i Mora, "Equilibrium: A Rediscovered Basis for the Court of Justice of the European Communities to Refuse Direct Effect to the Uruguay Round Agreements?", (1996) J.W.T. 43 at 53.
[48] See Everling, "The Law of the External Economic Relations of the European Community" in Hilf, Jacobs and Petersmann, *The European Community and GATT* (1986), p. 85 at pp. 87, 97; Cheyne, *op. cit.* at pp. 592, 596–597; Lee and Kennedy, *op. cit.* at pp. 82–84.

tives and share in their achievement, and that it has implicit approval from the other institutions to exercise judicial review. All of these considerations are likely to be powerful factors in the question of whether such agreements are justiciable as part of the constitutional traditions of Community law.

Another element of the nature and purpose test concerns the level of legal formalism present in an international agreement and its operation, and is most explicitly discussed by the Court in the GATT cases. The Court's expressed reasons for denying direct applicability to the GATT are, of course, related to the "great flexibility of its provisions", in particular those concerned with derogations, safeguard measures and dispute settlement procedures.[49] It is clear from the cases of *Fediol*[50] and *Nakajima*[51] that the question of whether the substantive provisions were precise and unconditional was not the crucial obstacle to direct applicability.[52] The provisions that prevented the GATT from having direct applicability were those that allowed even clear and unconditional substantive obligations to be avoided or compromised. The Court adopted the position that the GATT 1947 was essentially a diplomatic organisation in which everything was negotiable and where members in practice always had the right of unilateral action. According to this view, judicial application of its provisions by the domestic courts of one of the parties would be inappropriate because the agreement would have clearly allocated responsibility for its interpretation and application to the political institutions of its parties, unless they voluntarily chose to assign a supervisory role to their domestic courts.

THE AREAS OF CONFUSION BETWEEN JURISDICTION AND JUSTICIABILITY

17.08 Although the distinction between jurisdiction and justiciability can be drawn reasonably clearly by reference to constitutional theory and the Court's own case law, there are a few areas of uncertainty arising from the cases about what is a question of jurisdiction and what is properly a question of justiciability.[53]

The Kupferberg problem

17.09 In *Kupferberg*,[54] the Court claimed jurisdiction over international agreements where it was necessary to ensure uniform application throughout the Community, at least to the extent of enforcement against the Member States.[55] However, this functional approach to jurisdiction implicitly assumes that the international agreement in question has already been received into Community law because its purpose is to ensure that it is applied uniformly, not that it is applied in the first place. It therefore locates the rule of recognition elsewhere. Since it appears to be rooted in the

---

[49] Case 21–4/72 *International Fruit* [1972] E.C.R. 1219, [1975] 2 C.M.L.R. 1.
[50] Case 70/87 [1989] E.C.R. 1781, [1991] 2 C.M.L.R. 489.
[51] Case C–69/89, *Nakajima* v. *Council* [1991] E.C.R. I–2069.
[52] See discussion in Chapter Two and below.
[53] The Court has sometimes made a very clear distinction between the two concepts. See, for example, Case C–364/92 *Sat Fluggesellschaft mbH* v. *Eurocontrol* [1994] 5 C.M.L.R. 208.
[54] Case 104/81 [1982] E.C.R. 3641, [1983] 1 C.M.L.R. 1.
[55] See, for example, *ibid.* at para. 14; Cases 267–9/81 *SPI and SAMI* [1983] E.C.R. 801, [1984] 1 C.M.L.R. 354, at paras 14–15; Case C–61/94 *Commission* v. *Germany (Re International Dairy Agreement)* [1997] 1 C.M.L.R. 281 at para. 16; Case C–53/96 *Hermès International* v. *FHT Marketing Choice* [1998] E.C.R. I–3603 at para. 32.

obligation of Member States to ensure that the Community is able to comply with its international obligations, the rule must be derived from a requirement that the Community be able to protect itself from liability for breaches of its obligations and to exercise its rights under international law. The ramifications of this interpretation can be surprising. On the one hand, it has not allowed Member States to bring actions against the institutions.[56] On the other, it has permitted international agreements to be considered in preliminary rulings for the purposes of settling disputes between individuals.[57]

The pre-emption problem: incorporation and exclusion

17.10 The Court has acknowledged that the political institutions have the power to pre-empt the question of direct applicability of international agreements, both to grant it by express incorporation in Community legislation[58] and to withhold it by an express provision in the agreement itself.[59]

In *Fediol*,[60] *Nakajima*[61] and the *Banana* case,[62] the Court accepted that some international agreements can only be applicable as Community law if they have been incorporated through a legislative act. In these cases, the legislative acts and their substantive contents literally constitute "acts of the institutions" and would therefore be compatible with Hartley's view of how Article 234 (ex Article 177) should be interpreted.[63] In other words, it has the appearance of a rule of recognition that applies to international agreements which do not satisfy the direct applicability test. But the direct applicability test itself cannot be a rule of recognition because, in the cases based on the *Haegeman* dictum, the direct applicability test is applied *after* the Court has already asserted jurisdiction. In other words, the direct applicability test must be a test of justiciability, not jurisdiction. Legislative incorporation as an alternative to satisfying the direct applicability test suggests that it has the same function, namely determining the justiciability of an agreement, while the issue of whether the Court has jurisdiction is decided separately. It should be seen, therefore, as a signal by the political institutions that a matter that was only potentially justiciable may now be judicially interpreted and applied.[64]

The Court's willingness to acknowledge that the political institutions have the power to exclude direct applicability is more problematic. The role of the Court as the arbiter of Community law as contained in the E.C. Treaty cannot be entirely excluded. In the case of an agreement which did not directly concern internal Community law or affect the rights of Member States or individuals, it might be possible to say that the Court would not necessarily have the right (or indeed the obligation) to adjudicate upon it. However, all powers of the institutions flow from the Treaty. It would be more accurate, therefore, to assume that the Court must always have jurisdiction over an agreement simply because it is an act of the institutions or a law governing the appli-

---

[56] Compare, for example, Case C–61/94 *Commission v. Germany (Re International Dairy Agreement)*, [1997] 1 C.M.L.R. 281, (Commission complaint against Member States for failure to comply with GATT-associated agreement), with Case C–280/93, *Germany v. Council* [1994] E.C.R. I–4973 (Member State complaint against Council for failure to comply with GATT not admissible).

[57] See, for example, Case C–53/96 *Hermès International v. FHT Marketing Choice* [1998] E.C.R. I–3603.

[58] Case 70/87 *Fediol* [1989] E.C.R. 1781, [1991] 2 C.M.L.R. 489; Case C–69/89 *Nakajima v. Council* [1991] E.C.R. I–2069. See also Eeckhout, "The Domestic Legal Status of the WTO Agreement: Interconnecting Legal Systems" (1997) 34 C.M.L.Rev. 11 at 41–48.

[59] Case 104/81 *Kupferberg* [1982] E.C.R. 3641, [1983] 1 C.M.L.R. 1 at para. 17.

[60] Case 70/87 [1989] E.C.R. 1781, [1991] 2 C.M.L.R. 489.

[61] Case C–69/89 [1991] E.C.R. I–2069.

[62] Case C–280/93 *Germany v. Council.* [1994] E.C.R. I–4973.

[63] Hartley (1996), *op. cit.*

[64] This point will be examined in more detail below.

cation of the E.C. Treaty,[65] but that it chooses to restrain itself from exercising that jurisdiction in certain cases. There may therefore be a presumption that judicial review would be excluded from an agreement in which the parties have agreed that there should be no domestic direct applicability, but this must be subject to the Court's primary role in overseeing the application of the E.C. Treaty and the protection of the rights for which it provides. The ultimate decision as to whether judicial review is appropriate or not must lie with the Court and not with the political institutions.[66]

In both cases, therefore, the Court's acknowledgment of the political institutions" power to pre-empt the issue is a matter of judicial restraint and the possibility remains that it will choose to exercise its jurisdiction in circumstances that appear to it to be appropriate.

The principle of good faith

17.11   The Court has stated that international agreements, including GATT 1947, are binding on the Community and its institutions.[67] To be binding on the Community may be the position in international law, but to be binding on the institutions which, as commentators have pointed out, have no international legal personality[68] must logically be a matter of Community law.

The refusal to give direct applicability to GATT 1947 and its associated agreements sits oddly with the wording of Article 300 (ex Article 228) and the Court's own jurisprudence in relation to the principle of good faith in international law.[69] This apparent contradiction is one of the reasons why it has been difficult to find a convincingly coherent justiciability principle. It has given the appearance of wanting to have it both ways, asserting a necessity of compliance with legal obligation and, at the same time, declining to require compliance as a matter of judicial review. If the Court transfers its non-justiciability approach to the WTO Agreement, it is difficult to see how it could continue to assert the need to comply with international obligations in the face of a

---

[65] This would certainly be the case in questions of competence and observance of treaty-making procedures. The issue here, however, is whether the Court would apply the substantive provisions of an international agreement.

[66] Note the clause that has been inserted in the preamble of the WTO implementing legislation which asserts that the WTO Agreement and its Annexes, including the GATS and its Protocols, are not susceptible to being directly invoked in Community or Member States courts. See Council Decision 94/800/E.C., [1994] O.J. L336/1, Council Decision 97/838/E.C., [1997] O.J. L347/45, and Proposal for a Council Decision 96/C 194/09, [1996] O.J. C194/12. Kuijper describes the clause as an expression of opinion by the political institutions, but acknowledges that the question of direct effect must ultimately lie with the Court. See "The Conclusion and Implementation of the Uruguay Round Results by the E.C." (1995) 6 E.J.I.L. 222, at 226–7, 236. Advocates General Cosmas and Tesauro are also of this view, see Case C–183/95 *Affish* [1996] E.C.R. I–4315, Opinion of December 10, 1996, at para. 127, and Case C–53/96 *Hermès* [1998] E.C.R. I–3603, Opinion of November 13, 1997, at para. 23, respectively. Advocate Elmer cited the clause in his Opinion in Cases 364–365/95 *T. Port GMBH* v. *Hauptzollamt Hamburg-Jonas* [1998] E.C.R. I–1023, at para. 28 but did not explain its relevance. See also Castillo de la Torre (1995), *op. cit.* at pp. 65–6; Lee and Kennedy, *op. cit.* at pp. 86–87; Eeckhout, *op. cit.* at pp. 37–40.

[67] See Case C–104/81 *Kupferberg* [1982] E.C.R. 3641, [1983] 1 C.M.L.R. 1 at para. 11, Case 266/81 *SIOT* [1983] E.C.R. 731, [1984] 2 C.M.L.R. 231 at para. 28; Case 142/88 *Hoesch AG* v. *Bergrohr GmbH* [1989] E.C.R. 3413, [1991] 1 C.M.L.R. 383 at para. 30; Case C–61/94 *Commission* v. *Germany (Re International Dairy Agreement)* [1997] 1 C.M.L.R. 281 para. 15; *Opel Austria* v. *Council* [1997] 1 C.M.L.R. 733. This is also the wording of Art. 300(7) (ex Art. 228(7)).

[68] See, for example, Macleod, Hendry and Hyett, *op. cit.* at p. 125.

[69] See above, n. 67. And see Pescatore, "The Doctrine of 'Direct Effect': An Infant Disease of Community Law" (1983) E.L.Rev. 155, who begins his discussion by suggesting that legal rules are only law if they are operative.

clearcut violation by the political institutions, for example, if there was a finding against the Community by a WTO panel.[70]

In such a case, the Court would have to clarify its position on justiciability in situations where the Community had committed an outright violation of an agreement which is clearly binding on the Community in international law and, according to the logic of its own jurisprudence and Article 300, on the institutions as a matter of Community law. The Court would find it difficult to give grounds for non-justiciability which sit comfortably with its previous assertions that the Community is required to comply with its international legal obligations. One way would be to restrict those assertions to international agreements for which it has already accepted justiciability (and where the risk of violation by the Community is in reality low). Another way would be to make otherwise non-justiciable agreements directly applicable only in so far as they directly impinge on rights of individuals or Member States that already exist in Community law. This would satisfy the finding that international agreements are binding on the institutions in international and Community law, and restrict the Court's supervision to matters that fall within its competence in Community law.

Indeed, the Court has suggested that the principle of good faith in international law is a corollary of the principle of legitimate expectations in Community law.[71] This approach could have the effect of permitting reliance on the principle of good faith, but only in cases where the principle of legitimate expectations applied.[72] This would be a self-limiting exercise of jurisdiction which would have the benefit of protecting the rule of law under the E.C. Treaty in matters that fall directly within the Treaty's purposes and objectives, while minimising the potential conflict between the Court and the political institutions over the latter's conduct of external affairs.

The principle of consistent interpretation

17.12   The Court has developed a jurisprudence concerning the interpretation of Community law in a manner which is consistent, so far as possible, with its international obligations.[73] This is apparently a consequence of the primacy of international law over secondary Community law,[74] but it is inconsistent with that principle because the qualification "so far as possible" does not include the possibility of overriding Community law. It is in fact a method of attempting to harmonise Community and international law within the scope left to the Court by the political institutions.

Examination of recent cases which indicate a practice of consistent interpretation shows that they do little more than make a passing reference to the fact that the Community legislation in question is consistent with any relevant international instruments,[75] or that, in resolving any ambiguity in the meaning of Community legislation,

---

[70] Two such panel findings have already occurred, namely *E.C.—Regime for the Importation, Sale and Distribution of Bananas* (WT/DS27) and *E.C.—Measures Affecting Meat and Meat Products (Hormones)* (WT/DS26 and WT/DS48). In each case, the E.C. has undertaken to implement the panel's recommendations and therefore the reports are unlikely to form the basis of any argument before the Court of Justice.
[71] See *Opel Austria* v. *Council* [1997] 1 C.M.L.R. 733 at para. 93.
[72] *ibid.*, at paras. 90, 93.
[73] See, for example, Case 92/71 *Interfood* v. *Hauptzollamt Hamburg* [1972] E.C.R. 231; Case C–61/94 *Commission* v. *Germany (Re International Dairy Agreement)* [1997] 1 C.M.L.R. 281 para. 52; Case C–70/94 *Werner* [1995] E.C.R. I–3189 at para. 23; Case C–83/94, *Leifer* [1995] E.C.R. I–3231 at para. 24; Case C–53/96 *Hermès* [1998] E.C.R. I–3603 para. 28.
[74] Cases 21–4/72 *International Fruit* [1972] E.C.R. 1219, [1975] 2 C.M.L.R. 1. The Court has explicitly linked primacy of international law over secondary legislation with the need to give consistent interpretation "so far as is possible", see Case C–61/94 *Commission* v. *Germany (Re International Dairy Agreement)* [1997] 1 C.M.L.R. 281.
[75] See, for example, Case C–83/94 *Leifer* [1995] E.C.R. I–3231, para. 24; Case C–177/95, *Ebony Maritime SA* v. *Prefetto della Provincia di Brindisi* [1997] 2 C.M.L.R. 24, para. 20.

the objects and purposes of a relevant international instrument should be borne in mind.[76] The Court has even designated the GATT as "relevant for the purpose of interpreting a Community instrument governing international trade"[77] and sought a co-ordinating role between its provisions and Community law.[78] This, given the Court's steadfast refusal to give the GATT direct applicability, exemplifies the gap between the primacy of international law doctrine and the practice of consistent interpretation.

However, as a rule of justiciability, this approach is unexceptionable in that the Court ought to be concerned with co-ordinating the Community's internal legal order and its external legal obligations. It fits with the Court's repeated acknowledgment that international law obligations are binding on the Community itself and that the Community, along with the Member States, is obliged to ensure compliance with them.[79] It suggests a presumption that Community acts and laws should comply with its international legal obligations, but that this presumption can be overridden by a clear intention on the part of the Community's political institutions to enact legislation which is inconsistent with those international obligations. In this way, the Court can demonstrate that it shares the objectives of the other institutions and the Community as a whole and, at the same time, remain within limits that prevent it from having to come into direct conflict with them. Any conflict which cannot be avoided because the wording of the Community measure does not allow consistent interpretation will be decided in favour of Community law. The Court is, in its consistent interpretation reasoning, effectively saying that it will avoid embarrassing the political institutions by ensuring that the Member States, and secondary legislation where ambiguous, comply with the Community's international legal obligations.

THE APPLICATION OF JUSTICIABILITY TO GATT 1947 AND THE WTO AGREEMENT

17.13   Although GATT 1947 and the WTO represent only one part of the Community's external relations, the debate over the non-applicability of the former and the potential justiciability of the latter has helped to elucidate the basic principles on which the Court might develop its case law for all types of agreements. The Community will increasingly be active in international treaties and organisations that operate in a mixture of law and overt policy. It is also likely to become party to more multilateral agreements which, by their multipolar nature, may pose particular problems in relation to justiciability in Community law. The constitutional law and practice of the Community concerning its external relations will mature just as they have in the context of domestic Community law, and the lessons drawn from the GATT case law have helped to develop and crystallise the policy issues that need to be resolved for the future.[80] With this in mind, it is proposed to look in more detail at the policy reasons for denying direct applicability to GATT 1947 and to consider what justifications might

---

[76] See, for example, Case C–84/95 *Bosphorus Hava Yollari AS* v. *Minister for Transport, Energy and Communications* [1996] 3 C.M.L.R. 257, paras. 13–14.

[77] See Case C–70/94 *Werner* [1995] E.C.R. I–3189 para. 23; Case C–83/94 *Leifer* [1995] E.C.R. I–3231 para. 24.

[78] It has applied a consistent interpretation approach to the GATT in many cases, particularly in relation to anti-dumping. See, for example, *Matsushita* v. *Council* [1992] 3 C.M.L.R. 137, Case C–179/87 *Sharp* v. *Council* [1992] 2 C.M.L.R. 415, Case C–188/88 *NMB (Deutschland)* v. *Commission* [1992] 3 C.M.L.R. 80, Case C–216/91, and Case T–162/94, *NMB France Sarl* v. *Commission* [1997] 3 C.M.L.R. 164.

[79] See above, p. 264, n. 67.

[80] For a detailed discussion of the policy issues surrounding the direct applicability of international agreements, see Jackson, "Status of Treaties in Domestic Legal Systems: A Policy Analysis" [1992] 86 A.J.I.L. 310.

be available to the Court if it also wishes to exclude the WTO from direct applicability despite its more formal legal structure.[81]

The Court's choice to exclude direct applicability can be justified by reference to a number of factors that typically underlie justiciability issues.[82] It is entitled to consider the problems of potential conflict with the political institutions and the need to avoid embarrassing them in their conduct of external trade policy.[83] Although the political institutions' acts which are taken under GATT rules can and do affect the legal position of private individuals and the Member States within the Community, the reasons for those acts may be heavily weighted by policy considerations. The decision to safeguard the interests of certain states in the legislative organisation of the Community's banana market, for example, clearly rested on important policy choices.[84] Likewise, the dispute settlement agreement concerning trade in bananas, which was reached between the Community and the complainant states after a GATT panel report found that the E.C. was in violation of its GATT obligations, was a political solution to a conflict which the Court could only have attempted to resolve in a partial and legalistic fashion.[85] The ability to settle this dispute by a negotiated agreement was possible because of the permissive nature of the GATT's enforcement provisions. It is difficult to argue that an agreed settlement, which could only be achieved by the political institutions, was an unsatisfactory alternative to a judicial settlement by the domestic court of one of the parties to the dispute.

In some cases, the Court has refused to apply the GATT because the substantive provision itself was permissive, for example, where the Community was entitled to make a decision to act "in the interests of the Community"[86] under the authority of the GATT.[87] This is a straightforward example of discretionary powers being assigned to the political institutions under the Treaty and a situation where justiciability would be clearly inappropriate.

Finally, there would be considerable practical problems in implementing a complex set of rules and principles of "foreign law", both in terms of judicial knowledge and in co-ordinating external and internal interpretations of the same provisions.[88] GATT law is complex and open-textured, requiring a degree of teleological interpretation with which the Court might be familiar but which it would be ill-equipped to employ. It is sometimes argued that authoritative statements of GATT law could be used to fill the gap in the Court's knowledge, but it is not at all clear how the Court should

---

[81] The most significant change for these purposes is the new dispute settlement procedure (Understanding on the Rules and Procedures Governing the Settlement of Disputes, WTO Agreement, Annex 2) which imposes strict time limits and does not permit panel reports to be blocked by the losing party. See, for example, Petersmann, *The GATT/WTO Dispute Settlement System: International Law, International Organizations and Dispute Settlement* (1997); Kuijper, "The New WTO Dispute Settlement System" [1995] J.W.T. 48; Jackson, "The WTO Dispute Settlement Understanding—Misunderstandings on the Nature of Legal Obligation" [1997] 91 A.J.I.L. 60.

[82] See, for example, Montaña i Mora, "A GATT with Teeth: Law Wins over Politics in the Resolution of International Trade Disputes" 31 Columbia J. Trans. L 103, at pp. 174–5.

[83] See, for example, Advocate General Gulmann's Opinion in the *Banana* case [1994] E.C.R. I–4973. See also Everling *op. cit.* at p. 97; Lee and Kennedy, *op. cit.* at pp. 87–88.

[84] Regulation 404/93 on the common organisation of the market in bananas ([1993] O.J. L47/1). This was the subject matter of a GATT panel report which found against the E.C., see above, p. 265, n. 70, and of a subsequent complaint by Germany against the Council which was decided in the *Banana* case [1994] E.C.R. I–4973.

[85] Framework Agreement on Bananas with the Republic of Costa Rica, the Republic of Colombia, the Republic of Nicaragua and the Republic of Venezuela, 1994. Challenges to the Agreement by Germany were considered by the Court in Opinion 3/94 [1995] E.C.R. I–4577, and in Case C–122/95 *Germany* v. *Council* [1998] E.C.R. I–973.

[86] Regulation 2176/84, [1984] O.J. L201/1.

[87] See, for example, Case 188/85 *Fediol* v. *Commission* [1988] E.C.R. 4193 (right of Commission to take action against foreign subsidies).

[88] See Maresceau, *op. cit.* at p. 117; Eeckhout, *op. cit.* at p. 32.

approach the question of WTO panel reports.[89] It would seem odd to make the existence of a relevant WTO panel report a condition for direct applicability where otherwise there would be none. Even if a definitive assessment of the relevant GATT rules was available in a panel report, it would still require detailed understanding on the part of the Court and an application of the report's reasoning in the context of domestic law. A direct finding of violation against the Community might be a more satisfactory trigger of justiciability, being certain in time and content, but would still entail the problems just discussed, including the problem of potentially interfering in the process of achieving a negotiated settlement.[90]

17.14   These are all common arguments for the application of a non-justiciability principle, rooted in a court's understanding of the political dynamics of the constitutional system in which it is required to operate, as well as a calculation of the feasibility of judicial supervision. As such, the Court's approach has been within the normal range of judicial function, and agreement or disagreement with the outcome is a matter of perspective or policy choice. However, one criticism of the Court's reasoning in the GATT cases is that the flexibility test used to deny the justiciability of GATT 1947 did not give a sufficiently clear and workable principle for application to other agreements.[91] This criticism might be answered by the fact that constitutions rarely place a clear line between justiciable and non-justiciable issues and by recalling that the boundary must, in the absence of clear rules in the E.C. Treaty, be determined by an interpretative intuition on the part of the Court. Lack of precision in such a test is inevitable. A more principled criticism would be that the Court had a genuine opportunity to apply the GATT and that it was therefore required by virtue of its duty to ensure the rule of law under the E.C. Treaty to extend its judicial supervision over the political institutions in all of their activities.[92] But, given the open-textured nature of the E.C. Treaty, it is difficult to say that the Court chose a "wrong" interpretation of its duty and, again, disagreement with its approach is essentially one of perspective and policy preference.[93]

It may be asked whether the Court accurately characterised GATT 1947 as essentially political. It is certainly possible to argue that the Court underplayed the legal nature of the GATT's enforcement procedures.[94] Its reasoning did not, for example, sit

---

[89] See, for example, Eeckhout, *op. cit.* at pp. 51–55. It should be noted that the Court has said that the decisions of a dispute settlement body under an international agreement bind the Community "in so far as that agreement is an integral part of the Community legal order", Op. 1/91, *supra*, note 10 at para. 39. The phrase "integral part of the Community legal order" has not been used by the Court in connection with the GATT and therefore the principle need not apply. It would have to apply to the WTO Agreement as a formally concluded treaty, but would not necessarily mean that panel reports would be accepted under a non-justiciability principle which deferred to the political institutions for the settlement of trade disputes.
[90] Kuijper, *op. cit.*
[91] See, for example, Petersmann, "The EEC as a GATT Member—Legal Conflicts Between GATT Law and European Community Law" in Hilf, Jacobs and Petersmann, *The European Community and GATT* (1986), p. 23 at pp. 58–9; Maresceau, *op. cit.* at pp. 120–121; Petersmann, "Application of GATT by the Court of Justice of the European Communities" (1983) 20 C.M.L.Rev. p. 397 at pp. 424–437; Cheyne, *op. cit.* at pp. 591–592.
[92] The Court has stated that the Community is "based on the rule of law, inasmuch as neither its Member States nor its institutions can avoid a review of the question whether the measures adopted by them are in conformity with the basic constitutional charter, the Treaty." Case 294/83 *Les Verts* v. *Parliament*, [1986] E.C.R. 1339 para. 23. See also Case C–137/92 P, *Commission* v. *BASF* [1994] E.C.R. I–2555, para. 49. And see Everling, *op. cit.* at pp. 105–106 (the Court has necessary supervisory function, but within limits); Petersmann (1983), *op. cit.* at pp. 403–404 (the Court has no explicit "political question" non-justiciability principle and it would be inappropriate in the context of the E.C. Treaty).
[93] One commentator, for example, has suggested that "approaches based on constitutional rights compete with traditions of reciprocal and balanced trade relations, decoupling national and international obligations." See Cottier, "Dispute Settlement in the World Trade Organisation: Characteristics and Structural Implications for the European Union" (1998) 35 C.M.L.Rev. 325, at 367. And see Tridimas, *op. cit.*
[94] See, for example, Petersmann (1983), *op. cit.* at pp. 424–437.

absolutely four-square with the existence of a dispute settlement procedure which, while it heavily emphasised conciliation and negotiation, was nonetheless a system predicated on the legal nature of the obligations binding on the parties. However, this is, or should be, a moot question, since the Court now has to decide how to characterise the WTO Agreement in the light of its very different characteristics.[95] Assuming it continues to be unwilling to give direct applicability to the GATT rules under the new regime, the crucial question is whether the Court will decide to justify its approach on different grounds and, if so, on what basis.[96]

Some commentators argue that the Court should continue to deny direct applicability to the GATT rules under the WTO Agreement, and many assume that it will do so.[97] The reasons for this view have been partly explained above, but a more simple reason can be outlined even though the Court has never explicitly voiced it. The key similarity that the WTO Agreement shares with GATT 1947 is that it is a genuinely multilateral agreement, in the sense that the Community has no decisive control over its implementation. It can be outvoted in questions of interpretation and implementation, and found to be in violation of its obligations in a dispute settlement procedure it cannot block. It has already been noted that the agreements given direct applicability, such as free trade and association agreements, are bilateral. Even the Yaoundé and Lomé Conventions, despite their multilateral nature, are essentially bilateral in effect.[98] Thus, in these agreements, the Community is always in a position to prevent any implementing decisions with which it disagrees and is unlikely to be faced with the prospect of unwanted legal obligations.

17.15   The problem with multilateral agreements, from the point of view of the Court and its justiciability principle, is that they increase the risk that the political institutions will be tempted to violate the Community's international legal obligations, and that they may succumb to that temptation.[99] A decision to violate a clear international legal obligation would be a political decision. To exercise justiciability over such a violation would put the Court in direct conflict with the political institutions which could only be justified if it significantly affected matters that fell directly within domestic Community law. The reasons why the Court would probably wish to continue non-justiciability of the GATT rules are therefore essentially the same as those discussed above in relation to the political nature of GATT 1947, namely the dangers inherent in coming into conflict with the political institutions, the desire to avoid embarrassment in the Community's relations with third states by giving a view at odds with that of the Community's external representatives, and the practical problems of implementing external rules and co-ordinating them with internal Community law.

Although it would be difficult for the Court to accept explicitly the position of tolerating unlawful acts by the political institutions, it can be argued that the legal significance of it would be incidental, given the fact that the legal obligation involved would be located in an external legal system over which the Court had no jurisdiction. In addition, there is a clear institutional view within the Commission and the Council that the WTO Agreement should not be given direct applicability[1] and the Advocate

---

[95] This is not to say that the Court's jurisprudence on GATT 1947 is now of purely historical interest. It provides a workable rule of non-justiciability which defines a category of agreements whose interpretation and application is inherently and systematically subject to political discretion.
[96] Discussed in more detail below.
[97] See, for example, Kuijper, *op. cit.* See also the Advocate Generals' opinions in Case C–183/95 *Affish* [1996] E.C.R. I–4315; Cases 364–365T. *Port* [1998] E.C.R. I–1023; Case C–53–96 *Hermès* [1998] E.C.R. I–3603.
[98] See above, p. 261, n. 47.
[99] Eeckhout, *op. cit.* at p. 53–55.
[1] See above, p. 264, n. 66.

Generals have so far tended to assume that the Court will wish to continue to exclude justiciability over the institutions' conduct of external trade policy.[2] In the light of this gathering consensus, the Court is unlikely to want to bring itself into direct conflict with the other institutions, particularly since the other arguments for non-justiciability discussed above would be persuasive in their own right.

One justification offered to the Court for continuing to deny direct applicability to the GATT rules is that of non-reciprocity.[3] The Commission, for example, has argued against justiciability on the grounds that the Community's major trading partners have decided that they will not permit direct applicability of the WTO Agreement by their domestic courts.[4] It is therefore argued that this would place the Community under an unnecessary disadvantage in its conduct of external trade policy. In *Hermès*,[5] Advocate General Tesauro also suggested that non-reciprocal enforcement would have significant implications that the Court should take into account, although he identified the Community traders as the group that would be disadvantaged. He, therefore, emphasised a policy which protected individual rights rather than the political discretion that the Commission was seeking. The Advocate General proposed this justification as a judicially defensible reason for continuing the Court's policy as an alternative to its original reasoning which he argued could no longer apply to the WTO.[6] However, even the Advocate General admitted that it would be a difficult principle to apply to multilateral agreements and did little more than invite the Court to use it if it saw fit.[7]

Whilst the Court has referred to the question of reciprocity, its case law on this point is not especially helpful. In terms of applying substantive provisions on a reciprocal basis, the Court has clearly indicated that this is not relevant.[8] With regards to enforcement, the Court has not conclusively indicated whether it needs to be reciprocal in order for an international agreement to be justiciable in the Community legal system. In *Kupferberg*, it said only that lack of reciprocity in enforcement was not "in itself" a reason for saying that the agreement would be implemented in a non-reciprocal manner.[9] This may indicate that the Court would be willing to take the issue into account.[10]

17.16   There are, however, some difficulties in building a principled non-justiciability principle on these grounds. One is deciding what circumstances would be sufficient to suggest that lack of reciprocal enforcement was a crucial obstacle to the implementation of an international agreement by another party. The obvious answer would be where the international agreement explicitly required that private rights be

---

[2] See Case C–183/95 *Affish* [1996] E.C.R. I–4315; Cases C–364–365 *T. Port* [1998] E.C.R. I–1023; Case C–53/96 *Hermès* [1998] E.C.R. I–3603.

[3] See, for example, Kuijper, *op. cit.* at p. 64; Eeckhout, *op. cit.* at pp. 37–39, 48–49; Lee and Kennedy, *op. cit.* at pp. 84–86; Montaña i Mora, *op. cit.* (who suggests a parallel doctrine of "equilibrium" in preference to reciprocity). For a general discussion of reciprocity in Community law, see Wils, "The Concept of Reciprocity in E.E.C. Law: An Exploration into These Realms" (1991) 28 C.M.L.Rev. 245.

[4] See, for example, Kuijper, *op. cit.* at p. 226.

[5] Case C–53/96 [1998] E.C.R. I–3603. At the time of writing, this opinion was only available in French. My thanks to Jean-François Pepin for his assistance in translating the relevant passages. Any misunderstandings of the argument are solely attributable to the author.

[6] This suggestion has also been made by academic commentators. See, for example, Montaña i Mora, *op. cit.* at pp. 52–55.

[7] Case C–53/96 [1998] E.C.R. I–3603 paras. 31–35.

[8] The Court has found that differences in the obligations between the parties does not affect the direct applicability of an international agreement. See, for example, Case 87/75, *Bresciani* [1976] E.C.R. 129 [1976] 2 C.M.L.R. 62 at paras. 22–23; Case 469/93 *Chiquita* [1995] E.C.R. I–4533 at paras. 32 and 34. It has also refused to consider the practice of other contracting parties when interpreting shared obligations under an international agreement. See, for example, Case 56/85 *Brother Industries Ltd* v. *Council* [1990] 1 C.M.L.R. 792, at para. 13; Cases 277 and 300/85 *Canon* v. *Council* [1989] 1 C.M.L.R. 915, at para. 15; Case C–150/87 *Nashua Corp.* v. *Commission and Council* [1990] 2 C.M.L.R. 6, at para. 30.

[9] Case 104/81 [1982] E.C.R. 3641, [1983] C.M.L.R. 1 para. 18.

[10] See Advocate General Tesauro's opinion in Case C–53/96 *Hermès* [1998] E.C.R. I–3603 at para. 33.

protected by access to domestic judicial process; lack of direct applicability would be prima facie evidence of failure to implement. They might also include international agreements which did not make it an explicit requirement but could not be effectively implemented without domestic judicial involvement. However, it would be difficult to suggest that the effectiveness of the WTO Agreement would be dependent upon domestic direct applicability. Another difficulty is that the Court would appear to be suggesting that, by deliberately excluding domestic direct applicability, the other contracting parties were unwilling to implement their international legal obligations. Impugning the motives of foreign states would usually be considered by national courts to constitute a breach of international comity and it is unlikely that the Court of Justice would wish to embarrass the political institutions by implying such a criticism of other parties to the WTO Agreement.[11]

The reasons discussed above for a finding of non-justiciability are essentially rooted in policy. The Court could make them explicit, but this would involve characterising a potential violation of the WTO Agreement as a purely political issue, and the Court is unlikely to be comfortable with an explicit acceptance of potential illegality, even in a different legal system. It would presumably wish to find a more judicially appropriate justification for declining to supervise the Community's conduct of external affairs.

The difficulty of finding a coherent principle of non-justiciability which is appropriate to the Community's constitutional system may be reflected in the fact that the Court has recently been invited on three occasions to rule on the issue with regard to the WTO Agreement and, on each occasion, has declined the invitation.[12] While the implications of this can be overemphasised, it does suggest that the Court is reconsidering its position on the application of the GATT and accompanying agreements in Community law. It has not immediately applied its original reasoning to the WTO, even though it has been urged to do so.[13] This might suggest that it is at least doubtful about the wisdom of using reasoning which has lost much of its force.[14]

One possibility, therefore, is that there is pressure within the Court in favour of granting direct effect on the grounds that the Court's earlier jurisprudence on the "extreme flexibility" of the GATT 1947 is simply outdated. There are, after all, policy arguments in favour of more effective enforcement of the GATT in domestic legal systems.[15] Equally, it is possible that some parts of the WTO Agreement might be considered to be eligible for direct applicability. It is likely, in any case, that the Court requires time for reflection on its approach to the WTO Agreement. The problem is probably not whether it should grant it direct effect (which, for the reasons discussed above, it will probably wish to avoid), but how to develop a workable and principled rationale for excluding the Agreement, and other comparable agreements, from the status of Community law superior to secondary acts and legislation.

The key issue which should underlie such a rationale is that the WTO, and other agreements to which the Community is party, are multilateral and the Community has no absolute right to determine how they are to be implemented. This changes the Community's role from executing Community policy, as would be the case for example in

---

[11] The political institutions could, of course, criticise other governments as a matter of policy.
[12] See above, p. 269, n. 1.
[13] See the Advocate Generals" Opinions in Case C–183/95 *Affish* [1996] E.C.R. I–4315 and Cases C–364–365 *T. Port* [1998] E.C.R. I–1023.
[14] See Advocate General Tesauro's Opinion in Case C–53/96 *Hermès* [1998] E.C.R. I–3603 and Advocate General Cosmas' Opinion in Case C–183/95 *Affish* [1996] E.C.R. I–4315. Some commentators would say that it has always been unconvincing. See, for example, Petersmann (1983), *op. cit.*
[15] *ibid.* See also Advocate Gulmann's Opinion in the *Banana* case Case C–280/93 [1994] E.C.R. I–4973; Petersmann, "Proposals for a New Constitution for the European Union: Building-Blocks for a Constitutional Theory and Constitutional Law of the EU" (1995) 32 C.M.L.Rev. 1123.

association agreements, to operating as an independent legal and political actor subject to externally determined policies. It is a valid concern of the political institutions that they have sufficient freedom to act in the international sphere and their need to do so represents a perfectly valid ground for non-justiciability. Given the difficulties in finding a legalistic justification, therefore, it would be simpler, clearer and more transparent if the Court were simply to base non-justiciability on the need to avoid unnecessary conflict with the political institutions in an area where the policy choices are so significant and the implications so diverse that it is not an area which is appropriate for judicial involvement. The justifications for doing so are established reasons for domestic courts to exclude justiciability and it is arguable that the time has come for the non-justiciability principle to "come of age" within the constitutional development of the Community legal order.

CONCLUSIONS

17.17   The discussion so far has examined two aspects of the implementation of international agreements by courts, first, the question of a rule of recognition as traditionally associated with the monist and dualist theories and, secondly, the question of justiciability as traditionally associated with domestic constitutional law and the separation of powers between government institutions. They are, in effect, two aspects of the same question; the first describes a general theory of how domestic legal systems may receive or reject international law, while the second provides a mechanism whereby an individual legal system may determine which institution is responsible for implementing it.

The Court's case law does not always clearly distinguish between these aspects and, indeed, positively blurs them in some instances. It has established a comprehensive claim to jurisdiction over international agreements concluded under and for the purposes of the E.C. Treaty. It has also repeatedly acknowledged the fact that international agreements are binding, not just on the Member States, but also on the Community institutions. However, this combined approach has not necessarily led to the Court exercising its jurisdiction and the case of GATT 1947 has long been a source of debate as to the precise ambit of the Court's judicial review. The direct applicability test applied by the Court has been consistently vague, with little reasoning to explain why some international agreements have satisfied it while the GATT did not.

Even if one accepts that the policy considerations discussed above are decisively in favour of a non-justiciability principle, there is a remaining difficulty. The powers of the institutions and, most significantly, the limits to those powers are derived from an international agreement, namely the E.C. Treaty. An analogy with national constitutions, which derive their justiciability policies from a combination of their unique political histories, constitutional law and usage, and institutionally shared policy aims, should be treated with caution. The Community's roots in an international treaty, its relatively short political history, its restricted objectives, its dynamically evolving character, and the controversy which attends much of its development, all militate against any simple assumptions about the constitutional separation of powers under the E.C. Treaty.

The dispute between those who favour strict textual interpretation of the E.C. Treaty and those who accept and support a teleological approach is well known.[16] As

---

[16]   See, for example, Hartley (1996), *op. cit.*, and see, *contra*, Arnull, *op. cit.*; Tridimas, *op. cit.*

commentators have pointed out, the open-textured style of drafting of the Treaty means that teleological interpretation is inevitable. The Treaty is of very little textual guidance in the case of judicial control over the Community institutions in external affairs, particularly in relation to acts which do not have direct consequences in the domestic legal order. The Court is effectively faced with a choice between emphasising judicial supervision over the conduct of the institutions on behalf of the Member States, or acknowledging that the institutions have independent prerogative rights to operate on the plane of international law. The Court is under increasing pressure to make that choice as the Community becomes more active in international relations and the treaty which has most challenged the Court's reasoning, namely the GATT, has been transformed into an institutional structure for which that reasoning is no longer adequate.

At present, the existing case law has not conclusively determined which choice the Court will make. It can still interpret its powers, especially those under Articles 220 and 230 (ex Articles 164 and 173), to mean that its primary judicial function is to control the institutions on behalf of the Member States.[17] This interpretation was not excluded by the judgment in the *Banana* case,[18] which was decided on the non-justiciable nature of the GATT rather than the standing of Germany to bring the action. Provided that other international agreements have clear and unconditional provisions and possess a sufficient level of legal formalism, there is no particular textual reason in the E.C. Treaty why the Court should not review the legality of the institutions' actions in international law rather than assuming that conduct of international affairs is by definition a discretionary act. At the very least, it could employ the same test of procedural guarantees, manifest error and abuse of powers that it employs for other types of exercise of discretion.

However, the policy issues discussed above are sufficiently compelling that the Court is unlikely to do more than exercise procedural judicial review. Its principal problem, therefore, is that the reasoning that it offered for excluding GATT 1947 will be difficult to apply *mutatis mutandis* to the WTO Agreement, given the latter's much greater legal formalism. The Court is therefore at a crossroads where it can lay down a clearer and more transparent principle of non-justiciability. To fail to do so would be to miss the opportunity of establishing a coherent and mature constitutional principle governing the relative powers of the Court and the political institutions in the external relations of the Community.

ADDENDUM

17.18   Since the writing of this chapter, the Court of Justice has been invited to consider the effect of WTO provisions in E.C. law in a number of cases.[19] Only one gives any further indication of the Court's approach to the questions discussed above, namely Case C–149/96, *Portugal* v. *Council*.[20]

Portugal contested a Council decision approving Memoranda of Understanding between the E.C. and Pakistan and India allowing, *inter alia*, certain concessions on the import of textiles from those countries into the E.C. Portugal claimed that the

---

[17] Individuals could not be protected under this because they could not show any rights in Community law for the purposes of Art. 234 (ex Art. 177) by definition, and no direct and individual concern for the purposes of Art. 230 (ex Art. 173).
[18] Case C–280/93 *Germany* v. *Council* [1994] E.C.R. I–4973.
[19] See, for example, Case T–48/96, *Acme Industry* v. *Council*, October 12, 1999 (unreported); Case C–104/97 P *Atlanta A.G. and others* v. *Council and Commission*, October 14, 1999 (unreported); Case T–7/99 *Medici Grimm* v. *Council*, June 29, 2000 (unreported).
[20] November 23, 1999 (unreported).

contested decision breached certain rules and fundamental principles of the WTO Agreement, and that it was entitled to rely upon those rules and principles as a matter of Community law. The Court affirmed, following *Kupferberg*,[21] that the executive institutions had the right to decide whether dispute settlement in international agreements should be a matter for domestic law[22] and, in the light of this, it determined that the WTO agreements were "not in principle" rules which could be employed by the Court in assessing the legality of the acts of Community institutions.[23]

Two main reasons were given for finding that the exercise of domestic judicial jurisdiction would be inappropriate. First, the Court found that, although there were "significant" differences between the dispute settlement procedures of GATT 1947 and the WTO Agreement, the latter continued to place "considerable importance" on negotiation even when a measure had been found to be inconsistent with an obligation contained in the WTO agreements.[24] The Court pointed out that the right to negotiate compensation was not only to provide a temporary measure when withdrawal of the offending measure was not practicable, but also if a party "fails to fulfil its obligations" to implement recommendations by the Dispute Settlement Body within a reasonable period of time.[25] Thus the Community would have considerable control over the remedy it faced as a consequence of violating its substantive obligations under any of the WTO agreements. The implication appeared to be that the nature of the WTO Agreement was not susceptible to the exercise of jurisdiction by a domestic tribunal.

This argument led naturally into the second part of the Court's reasoning, which was that the exercise of its jurisdiction in the light of the WTO Agreement would deny the Community's other institutions the freedom to negotiate a compensatory settlement.[26] More tellingly, perhaps, they would be denied the "scope for manoeuvre" enjoyed by the corresponding institutions of the Community's trading partners.[27] The Court here explicitly accepted the arguments put forward by the Commission in *Hermès*[28] and appeared to have recognised the need to exercise judicial restraint.

The outcome of this case is not unexpected, but is noteworthy because the Court of Justice has now explicitly applied its reasoning in *International Fruit*[29] to the WTO Agreement. In doing so, it has rejected any argument that the WTO is sufficiently legalistic in nature to overcome the essentially diplomatic character that it inherited from GATT 1947. The key issue was that the Community institutions retained discretion as to how disputes should finally be resolved, even in the light of a finding that it had acted in violation of its obligations under the WTO agreements. The only circumstances under which the Court could review the legality of the Community's other institutions in the light of the WTO agreements were if the relevant provisions had been incorporated as in Case 70/87 *Fediol*[30] or Case C–69/89 *Nakajima*.[31]

This reasoning extends the non-justiciability principle beyond GATT 1947, with its evident defects in legal formalism, to the WTO Agreement notwithstanding the latter's much greater procedural certainty and effect. The Court did not find the differences sufficiently strong to make it change its approach and, although some are likely to argue that it has underestimated the legalistic character of the WTO, it is at least con-

[21] Case 104/81 [1982] E.C.R. 3641.
[22] Case C–149/96, *Portugal* v. *Council* (unreported) paras. 34–35.
[23] *ibid.*, para. 47.
[24] *ibid.*, para. 36.
[25] *ibid.*, paras. 37–39.
[26] *ibid.*, paras. 40–41.
[27] *ibid.*, para. 46.
[28] Case C–53/96 [1998] E.C.R. I–3603.
[29] Cases 21–24/72 [1972] E.C.R. 1219, [1975] 2 C.M.L.R. 1.
[30] [1989] E.C.R. 1781, [1991] 2 C.M.L.R. 489.
[31] [1991] E.C.R. I–2069, para. 49.

sistent with much of its earlier case law. However, the Court did not give any further clues as to how a non-justiciability principle might be applied to other international agreements. In particular, it is not yet clear what degree of discretion on the part of the executive institutions will conclusively operate against judicial review in the light of an international agreement. Much more importantly, the Court has still not made explicit the reasoning behind the direct applicability of agreements which are bilateral or essentially bipolar in nature, and the implications of that reasoning for the direct applicability of multilateral agreements over which the Community has very little control. If the Community were to be found to be in breach of one of the latter agreements and faced with precise procedures for dispute settlement which excluded negotiation by offending parties, the Court would be required to clarify its non-justiciability principle still further.

D. EXTERNAL RELATIONS IN THE ERA OF THE AMSTERDAM TREATY

CHAPTER 18

E.C. External Relations Provision Post-Amsterdam

by

Alan Dashwood*

18.01 This chapter examines in detail the two amendments made to the E.C. Treaty by the Treaty of Amsterdam, which affected the powers of the Community in the external relations sphere. The amendments were, respectively, to Article 133 (ex Article 113) on the common commercial policy and to Article 300 (ex Article 228) on the procedures for negotiating and concluding (and now also implementing) international agreements to which the E.C. is a party. The chapter concludes with a brief evaluation of the present state of external relations provision in the Treaty.

THE NEW PARAGRAPH (5) OF ARTICLE 133 EC

18.02 The Court of Justice decided in its Opinion 1/94[1] that the exclusive competence recognised as belonging to the E.C. in matters of commercial policy did not extend to certain aspects of the international supply of services (the modes of supply identified in the GATS as involving "consumption abroad", "commercial presence" and "the presence of natural persons")[2] nor to the harmonisation of rules on the protection of intellectual property rights,[3] which was identified by the Court as the primary objective of the TRIPS.[4] Two things followed from the construction given to Article 133 in the Opinion. First, there were large parts of the WTO package of agreements in respect of which Community competence, if it existed at all, fell to be exercised on the basis of provisions other than Article 133, including Article 308 (ex Article 235) which requires the Council to act by unanimity. Secondly, those legal bases were ones under which external competence is shared between the Community and the Member States; so the latter were free, except in so far as previously enacted Community measures might be producing an *AETR* effect, to conclude the relevant parts of

---

* This chapter incorporates part of the author's article. "External Relations Provisions of the Amsterdam Treaty", which was published in (1998) 35 C.M.L.Rev. 1019. That article was reprinted in O'Keefe and Twomey, *Legal Issues of the Amsterdam Treaty* (1999, Hart), p. 201. The publication here of part of the article has received the kind permission of Kluwer Law International.
[1] [1994] E.C.R. I–5267.
[2] *ibid.*, paras. 36 to 53.
[3] *ibid.*, paras. 54 to 71.
[4] *ibid.*, para. 58, approving a submission by the French Government.

the WTO package through the collective exercise of national powers, rather than through the Community.[5]

In the event, therefore, the WTO Agreement and the texts associated with it were concluded under mixed national and Community competence, the latter based on a raft of Treaty provisions.[6] That outcome has been seen by critics of Opinion 1/94 as hampering the E.C.'s effective participation in the new institutional framework established by the Agreement.[7] It has been argued, among other things, that cross-retaliation (*e.g.* imposition of trade restrictions as a sanction for the failure by a third country adequately to protect intellectual property rights) may not, in practice, be a viable option for the Community and its Member States, where the different elements of a strategy fall to be determined under different competences.[8]

The author remains far from convinced that the alleged problems of mixity, including in the implementation of the WTO Agreement, are genuinely intractable. However, it is sufficient for present purposes that they were so perceived by the Commission and by some delegations to the Amsterdam IGC, and that strenuous efforts were made to secure an amendment to Article 133 that would undo the consequences of Opinion 1/94, at least for the purposes of action within the WTO.[9] The outcome was rather modest: the new paragraph (5) of Article 133 did not change the existing law but merely empowered the Council to do so. Acting unanimously on a proposal by the Commission, and after consulting the European Parliament, the Council may extend the application of the first four paragraphs of the Article "to international agreements and negotiations on services and intellectual property insofar as they are not covered by these paragraphs".

18.03 A Council decision taken under the new paragraph (5) would create a specific legal basis for action by the Community in matters—liberalisation of the provision of services to allow the crossing of the Community's external frontier by third country nationals and businesses—presently beyond the scope not only of the Treaty chapter on services but, perhaps, even of Article 308.[10] Such decisions effectively creating a fresh objective for the EC, ought, in an order based on the attribution of powers, to be taken at the level of primary law. That the Council should have been given

---

[5] *ibid*, paras. 78 to 105. In Case C–53/96 *Hermès International* v. *FHT Marketing Choice BV* [1998] E.C.R. I–3603, the Court said, at para. 24, that "the WTO Agreement was concluded by the Community and ratified by its Member States without any allocation between them of their respective obligations towards the other contracting parties".

[6] See Council Decision 94/800/E.C., [1994] O.J. L336/1. The legal bases were Arts. 43, 54, 57, 66, 75, 84(2), 99, 100, 100a, 113 and 235, in conjunction with the second sub-para. of Article 228(3). The text of Decision 94/800 is ambiguous as to whether the Council intended to conclude on behalf of the Community only those parts of the WTO package falling within the latter's exclusive competence.

[7] For comments (mainly critical) on the Opinion, see Bourgeois, (1995) 32 C.M.L.Rev. 763; Constantinesco, Journal du Droit International (Clunet), p.412; Emiliou, (1996) 21 E.L.Rev. 294; Hilf (1995) 6 E.J.I.L. 245; and, in a wider context, Tridimas and Eekhout, (1994) 14 Y.E.L. 143. See, also, the variety of views in Bourgeois, Dewost and Gaiffe (eds.), *Le Communauté européenne et les accords mixtes* (1997, College d'Europe, Bruges).

[8] The example would entail mixing exclusive E.C. competence in trade matters with Member State competence, moderated by the *AETR* effect, in intellectual property matters.

[9] See the proposed Art. 113a in the text, dated December 5, 1996, which was prepared for the "Dublin II" meeting of the European Council; CONF 2500/96:

[10] Opinion 1/94 confirmed that the chapter of the E.C. Treaty on services, like the one on establishment, has an exclusively internal market objective: [1994] E.C.R. I–5267 para. 81. The chapter cannot, therefore, be taken to authorise Community action, whether by way of internal legislation or the conclusion of international agreements, having as its principal aim the liberalisation of the supply of services between the Community and third countries: see chapter 8, above, and the chapter on "Implied External Competence of the E.C." contributed by the present writer to Koskenniemi (ed.) *International Law Aspects of the European Union*, (1998, Kluwer) (hereinafter cited as *Koskenniemi*), p.113, esp. pp. 120 to 122. Where competence has thus been conferred on the Community, in a specific field but for limited purposes only, it is arguable that Art. 235 cannot be used to circumvent that limitation.

this power because the IGC was evidently incapable itself of resolving the issue seems a dereliction on the part of the Union's constitution-making authority.

Be that as it may, it is necessary to be clear as to the limits imposed by the drafting of paragraph (5) on the new Community competence that may be created by the Council.

In the first place, the competence would apply only in cases not already covered by the four present paragraphs of Article 133. It would not, for instance, be needed for the cross-frontier supply of services, nor for the protection of intellectual property rights through measures applicable at border crossings, since these were held in Opinion 1/94 to fall within the common commercial policy.[11]

Secondly, the reference in paragraph (5) to "international negotiations and agreements" gives the new competence purely external application, unlike the general competence of the Community under Article 133, which is exercisable both internally and internationally. In the matters to which the paragraph relates, therefore, autonomous Community measures, even if they have an external impact, have to find their legal bases elsewhere in the Treaty. Thus, for example, the Community remains powerless to *legislate* on the international provision of services, except on matters that can be seen as incidental to the well functioning of the internal market.[12]

Thirdly, the Council has not been authorised to create a general competence for the Community to conclude international agreements on services and intellectual property, but only to extend to such agreements the application of the four existing paragraphs of Article 133, which are concerned with implementing the common commercial policy. In other words, the possibility is given of enabling the ends of the common commercial policy to be served by instruments the subject-matter of which has not fallen hitherto within the scope of an Article mainly focused on trade in goods. The sorts of agreement in question would be ones designed to remove impediments to the supply of services by, or to ensure the protection of intellectual property rights belonging to, non-nationals. On the other hand, it is submitted, a legal basis derived from Article 133 could not be used for concluding an agreement having as its essential object the harmonisation of relevant areas of the parties' internal legislation.[13]

If that analysis is right, the Community competence created pursuant to paragraph (5) would cover all four of the methods of supplying services contemplated by the GATS; but the TRIPS would mostly remain outside its ambit since, as the Court of Justice has acknowledged, the primary objective of that Agreement is "to strengthen and harmonise the protection of intellectual property on a worldwide scale".[14] Those who may have been hoping to bring within the compass of the simple procedure of Article 133 the whole range of matters contained in the WTO package for which the Community is competent, are likely, therefore, to be disappointed.

A final point is that the Council is to act by unanimity. It may not be too cynical to regard the insertion of paragraph (5) as a face-saving device, putting off any effective amendment of Article 133 until the Greek Kalends, or at all events until the next IGC. At the time of writing, there had still been no proposal put to the Council for the implementation of Article 133(5). However, it is understood that the IGC which is due to conclude its business in December 2000 has before it proposals for the amendment

---

[11] [1994] E.C.R. I–5267, at paras. 44 and 55, respectively.
[12] See above, n. 10. The possibility of including, in an internal market measure on establishment or the supply of services, ancillary provisions relating to the treatment of third country nationals in the Community, or of Community nationals in third countries, was acknowledged in Opinion 1/94 [1994] E.C.R. I–5267 paras. 90 to 94.
[13] As the Court of Justice explained in Opinion 1/94, the Community institutions may not, by concluding an agreement under Art. 133, "escape the internal constraints to which they are subject in relation to procedures and to rules as to voting": [1994] E.C.R. I–5267, para. 60.
[14] *ibid.*, para. 58.

of paragraph (5) itself, through the replacement of the unanimity rule by QMV, and/or for the insertion into the Treaty of a special protocol containing arrangements for implementing the WTO Agreement.

The changes to Article 228

18.04 The Amsterdam Treaty continued the task, begun at Maastricht, of filling out, in the light of the Council's practice, the initially somewhat meagre provisions of Article 300 on the procedure for negotiating and concluding international agreements on behalf of the Community.[15] The second sub-paragraph of paragraph (1) of the Article has been replaced, but this only entails a change of wording, consequential on amendments to paragraph (2). The new text of the latter paragraph reads as follows:

"Subject to the powers vested in the Commission in this field, the signing, which may be accompanied by a decision on provisional application before entry into force, and the conclusion of the agreements shall be decided on by the Council, acting by a qualified majority on a proposal from the Commission. The Council shall act unanimously when the agreement covers a field for which unanimity is required for the adoption of internal rules and for the agreements referred to in Article 238.

By way of derogation from the rules laid down in paragraph 3, the same procedures shall apply for a decision to suspend the application of an agreement, and for the purpose of establishing the positions to be adopted on behalf of the Community in a body set up by an agreement based on Article 238, when that body is called upon to adopt decisions having legal effects, with the exception of decisions supplementing or amending the institutional framework of the agreement.

The European Parliament shall be immediately and fully informed on any decision under this paragraph concerning the provisional application or the suspension of agreements, or the establishment of the Community position in a body set up by an agreement based on Article 238."

The first of the three sub-paragraphs reproduces the provisions of the existing paragraph (2) on the power of the Council to conclude agreements (subject to the Commission's very limited powers in this field) and on the procedure for doing so, with two additional elements.

One addition is the explicit reference to the signing of an agreement, as a distinct procedural step requiring a decision by the Council. This corresponds to the previous practice where an agreement was concluded in solemn form, which has been continued. The Council takes a decision designating the persons authorised to sign the agreement, and this is recorded in the minutes, but is not published. A formally drafted decision on the conclusion of the agreement is adopted some time later,[16] and is published together with the full text of the agreement in the "L" series of the *Official Journal*. Where appropriate, the Council may decide that an agreement is to be concluded in simplified form, merely by signature.[17] The separate reference to signing in paragraph (2) as amended should not be understood as excluding that option, which would diminish the Community's effectiveness in the international sphere.

The other addition to the text of the first sub-paragraph, and a thoroughly useful

---

[15] See the discussion of the history of Art. 300, and in particular of the pre-Maastricht practice, in chapter 8, above.
[16] This may be very much later, if the agreement is a mixed one which all the Member States have to ratify.
[17] See, Macleod, Hendry and Hyett, *The External Relations of the European Communities*, p. 93.

one, is the conferment on the Council of an express power to decide on the provisional application of an agreement between signature and entry into force. This means it is no longer necessary to enter into free-standing interim agreements, incorporating those elements of a more complex package which can be decided on pursuant to Article 133.[18]

18.05   The second subparagraph of paragraph (2) represents an advance into territory previous versions of Article 300 have left largely unoccupied. Paragraph (3) of the Article, which was added by the TEU, enables the Council to delegate to the Commission power to modify an agreement in narrowly defined circumstances, but otherwise nothing is said about the procedures applicable in the various situations that may arise in the course of implementing a concluded agreement. The assumption underlying Council practice, in more recent years, has been that implementing action must be taken in conformity with the procedural requirements laid down by the Treaty, unless derived powers exercisable under simplified procedures have been specifically provided by the act concluding the agreement in question, or by a separate Community instrument. While such derived powers have become commoner, their creation and suitability are dependent on the political winds blowing at the time of conclusion; and failure to make appropriate provision can bring serious inconvenience, at least if the letter of the law is strictly adhered to. The new sub-paragraph gives a solution at the level of the Treaty in two specific cases where, for different reasons, it was seen as appropriate for the Council to be able to act on a proposal by the Commission, with no direct involvement of the European Parliament in the decision-making.

The first case is where it is proposed to suspend the application of an agreement, for instance in the event of violation of a human rights clause by the other party.[19] Here the justification for a simplified procedure is one of urgency. Without a special provision like that contained in the new sub-paragraph, there would be no alternative to using the same procedure as for the conclusion of the agreement in question: supposing it were one of those referred to in Article 300(3), second paragraph which require the assent of the European Parliament, the political impact of a suspension might have been dissipated by the time the decision could be formally adopted.

The other case is rather more complex. An agreement may provide for the establishment of a body charged with some aspect of its implementation and endowed, for that purpose, with power to take decisions having legal effects. These are referred to hereinafter as "decision-making bodies" or "DMBs". As we have seen, the decisions of such bodies are considered by the Court of Justice to apply immediately as part of the Community order, no incorporating measure being necessary.[20] Since, in effect, that amounts to an additional way of making E.C. law, any relevant procedural requirements of the Treaty have to be satisfied at the stage of establishing the position to be put forward on behalf of the Community in the DMB concerned. The justification for a simplified procedure can be found in the frequency with which such positions may be called for. If the European Parliament had to give its assent, or even to be consulted, on every occasion, effective Community participation in DMBs would be impossible.

---

[18] *ibid*, pp. 283 to 284. For an example of a Council Decision on provisional application adopted pursuant to Art. 300(2), first sentence, see Council Decision 2000/72/E.C. concerning the Agreement with Nepal on trade in textile products: [2000] O.J. L32/1.

[19] The so-called "Bulgarian clause", which has become standard in Community agreements other than sectoral trade agreements, provides that respect for human rights "constitutes an essential element" of the relationship in question. Any serious violation of human rights may thus be considered a "material breach" for the purposes of Art. 60 of the Vienna Convention on the Law of Treaties.

[20] Case 30/88 *Greece* v. *Commission* [1989] E.C.R. 3711; Case C–192/89 *Sevince* v. *Staatssecretaris van Justitie* [1990] E.C.R. I–3461; Case C–188/91 *Deutsche Shell* v. *HZA Hamburg-Harburg* [1993] E.C.R. I–363; Case C–237/91 *Kus* v. *Landeshauptstadt Wiesbaden* [1992] E.C.R. I–6781; Case C–355/93 *Eroglu* v. *Land Baden Württemberg* [1994] E.C.R. I–5113.

An issue worth flagging for completeness, though it does not have to be resolved in this context, is how the acts of DMBs should be characterised in E.C. law. Are they international agreements in simplified form or a *sui generis* source of law? If the former, then Community positions should be established under the relevant procedure of Article 300(2) and (3); if the latter, the procedure should arguably be that of the legal basis for enacting internal legislation on the matter in question. For present purposes, it is sufficient to note that, on either analysis, the participation of the Community in DMBs might be impeded through an over-elaborate decision-making process, except where the legal basis is Article 133.

18.06 Pursuant to the new subparagraph of Article 300(2), the simplified procedure, with the Council acting on a proposal by the Commission, will be available for determining the position to be taken on behalf of the Community in DMBs set up under agreements based on Article 300 (ex Article 238). Recourse to the assent procedure, which would otherwise apply in such cases, can thus be avoided. There is an exception, however, in case of decisions supplementing or amending the institutional framework of the agreement.

The limitation of the amendment to agreements concluded under Article 310 is puzzling, since these are not the only ones under which DMBs may be set up.[21] If, as the letter of the new sub-paragraph would indicate, the simplified procedure is not to apply to Community participation in a DMB operating under an agreement based on Article 308 EC, say, there would be a legal requirement (unless the Council had had the foresight to create *ad hoc* derived powers) to consult the European Parliament each time a position fell to be determined. Such an inconvenient outcome may, perhaps, be avoidable by an argument *a fortiori*. Explicit acceptance of the simplified procedure for the purposes of the most solemn category of agreements known to the Treaty[22] may perhaps be taken to imply its acceptability in other cases where such a procedure is needed to ensure effective Community participation in DMBs.[23] Interestingly, in Council decisions on the conclusion of agreements in the post-Amsterdam period, there is no difference, in the wording of the provisions referring to such participation, as between agreements pursuant to Article 310 and ones having other legal bases.[24]

Another issue is whether the procedure provided for by the new sub-paragraph pre-empts all other ways of determining the position to be adopted on behalf of the Community under the agreements to which it applies. Will it still be permissible, for instance, to confer on the Commission derived powers to decide certain matters, as was done for the purpose of implementing the EEA Agreement?[25] Despite its mandatory language, the text should not, it is submitted, be construed in a sense liable to impair the Community's ability to function effectively in DMBs, the manifest purpose being to enhance such participation. The Amsterdam IGC surely did not intend to deprive the Council of the power it currently enjoys to tailor procedures to the specific requirements of different kinds of agreements.

---

[21] An example of an agreement setting up a DMB, and concluded, so far as concerns the E.C. Treaty, on the basis of Art. 235, was the Agreement establishing an International Science and Technology Centre, [1994] O.J. L64/1. See the elaborate set of implementing procedures in the Annex to the Council's Decision, *ibid.*
[22] Association agreements, for which Art. 238 is the legal basis, have been described by the Court of Justice as "creating special, privileged links with a non-member country which must, at least to a certain extent, take part in the Community system": Case 12/86 *Demirel* v. *Stadt Schwäbisch Gmünd* [1987] E.C.R. 3719, at 3751.
[23] That is to say, all agreements, other than ones based on Art. 133, EC, which do not establish a specific procedure for determining the Community's position.
[24] *Cf.* Art. 2 (1) of Council and Commission Decision 2000/204/E.C., ECSC, [2000] O.J. L70/1 (Euro-Mediterranean Agreement establishing an association with Morocco) and Art. 2 (1) of Council and Commission Decision 1999/602/E.C., ECSC, Euratom, [1999] O.J. L239/1 (Partnership and Cooperation Agreement with Armenia).
[25] See Regulation 2894/94, [1994] O.J. L305/6, Art. 1(2).

An unresolved question is whether, in cases where derived powers are specifically created by an act of the Council for the purposes of implementing international agreements, including through Community participation in DMBs, the provisions of the third indent of Article 202 (ex Article 145) apply. Current practice assumes they do not, since it has been the rule, rather than the exception, for the Council to reserve such powers for itself.[26] The arguments one way and the other are finely balanced: for this to be considered a case of "the implementation of rules which the Council lays down" places a severe strain on language; yet the Court of Justice has indicated that the provisions of international agreements have the quality , in E.C. law, of acts of the institution by which the agreement was concluded.[27] A clean solution would have been to insert into Article 300 a version of Article 202, third indent, suitably adjusted. Perhaps, with the new second sub-paragraph of paragraph (2), this was thought unnecessary—another good reason for interpreting the sub-paragraph widely.

The third and final sub-paragraph of paragraph (2) imposes an obligation fully and immediately to inform the European Parliament of decisions on the provisional application and the suspension of agreements, and on positions to be adopted in DMBs. The Parliament's non-involvement in the actual decision-making process need cause no democratic qualms. It enjoys a similar kind of *a posteriori* control over executive action in these matters as would be normal for parliamentary bodies in the Member States.

CURRENT EXTERNAL RELATIONS PROVISION IN THE E.C. TREATY

18.07 The changes that have been made to the Treaty through successive revisions, which have a particular bearing on the Community's external relations activity, were reviewed in chapter 8 of this volume. It was there noted that the changes have been of two main kinds. There has been, first, a tendency for newly created legal bases to be equipped with "extension provisions", making clear that the specific powers of action being conferred on the Community may be used, where appropriate, not only for the purpose of legislating internally but also in the international sphere (this in sharp contrast to the drafting style of the authors of the original E.E.C. Treaty[28]). Secondly, the procedural attribution of external relations competence has been more rigorously and systematically separated from its substantive attribution, through the transformation of Article 300 (ex Article 228) EC into a procedural code covering the essential aspects of the negotiation and conclusion of international agreements, as well as some aspects of their implementation.

In addition, it was pointed out, the "dedicated external relations provisions" of the original Treaty—Article 133 (ex Article 113) on the common commercial policy and Article 310 (ex Article 230) on association—have been supplemented by Article 181 (ex Article 130y) on international development co-operation. Nevertheless, there remain gaps in the Community's armoury of specific powers, more particularly for the

---

[26] In the words of Art. 202, third indent, "The Council may also reserve the right, *in specific cases*, to exercise directly implementing powers itself" (emphasis added). The Court of Justice has said that, if the Council does so "it must state in detail the grounds for such a decision": Case 16/88 *Commission* v. *Council* [1989] E.C.R. 3457, at p. 3485.

[27] The point was first made in Case 181/73 *Haegeman* [1974] E.C.R. 449, and has frequently been reiterated. See chapters. 2 and 17, above.

[28] *Cf.* the primordial legal bases on agriculture and transport, respectively Arts. 27 (ex Art. 43) and 71 (ex Art. 75) which are silent as to their external reach. It was, however, remarked in chapter 8 that some newly-introduced legal bases lack an extension clause, most notably those contained in Title IV of Part Three of the Treaty.

purposes of its relations with countries other than developing countries, making it necessary to fall back on Article 308 for matters such as the provision of technical assistance under the TACIS Programme, which might well be considered *ultra vires*. There is a clear need for the Community to be equipped with a complete set of "dedicated" powers in the area of external economic relations, to match the actual range of its current activities.

More generally, it is a matter for regret that the opportunity has not yet been taken of rationalising the external relations provisions of the E.C. Treaty. Under the dispensation of Amsterdam, these remain scattered, incoherent and incomplete. "Extension provisions" should, of course, stay in the Treaty Titles to which, by virtue of their subject-matter, they belong. However, the "dedicated external relations provisions", on things such as external trade, development co-operation and association, should be brought together in a separate Title of Part Three of the Treaty. Such a Title should begin with a statement of general principles, like those on the Community's international capacity and on "implied" external competence and *AETR* exclusivity, which can presently be found only in the case law.[29]

---

[29] A model Treaty Title on External Relations can be found in the *CELS (Cambridge) E.C. Treaty project* (1997) 22 E.L.Rev. 395, at pp. 504 *et seq.*

CHAPTER 19

Common Strategies and the Interface Between E.C. External Relations and the CFSP: Lessons of the Partnership Between the E.U. and Russia

by

*Christophe Hillion**

INTRODUCTION

19.01 The Treaty of Amsterdam has had a substantial impact on E.C. external relations. Not only have E.C. Articles been modified, *e.g.* Article 133, EC (ex Article 113) and Article 300 EC (ex Article 228); also, new provisions have been included in other parts of the TEU which may influence the nature and scope of the Community's external competences. The present contribution argues that the provisions establishing the Common Strategy, now included in Title V, belong to such a category. Indeed, this new instrument embodies a change in the legal connection between E.C. external relations and the Common Foreign and Security Policy (CFSP); the former being increasingly subject to the latter's objectives and instruments, due particularly to the newly decisive involvement of the European Council. The E.U. relations with Russia are illustrative of this tendency.

On June 3 and 4, 1999, the European Council meeting in Cologne decided on a "Common Strategy (CS) of the European Union on Russia" (hereinafter, the "CS").[1] It was the first time a CS was adopted and its aim was to *strengthen* the existing E.U. Partnership with Russia. The latter, established by the Partnership and Co-operation Agreement (PCA),[2] based itself on the E.C. Treaty, already constituted an original set of relations established in the framework of the TEU, as signed in Maastricht. Particularly, account was taken of the principles founding the then newly created CFSP.

Relying on two key legal instruments, elaborated according to different procedural models—E.C. Treaty (the so-called "first pillar") and CFSP (the "second pillar")—the Partnership with Russia constitutes a specific and complex formula of E.U. external

---

* A version of this chapter has been published in (2000) 37 C.M.L.Rev. The article is reprinted here with the kind permission of Kluwer Law International.
[1] [1999] O.J. L157. Another CS on Ukraine was adopted in December 1999 by the European Council meeting in Helsinki ([1999] O.J. L331), a third at the Feira European Council in June 2000 on the Mediterranean Region (*cf.* Presidency Conclusions, E.U. Bull. 6/2000).
[2] The official Title of the PCAs is "Agreement on Partnership and Co-operation establishing a partnership between the European Communities and their Member States, of one part, and the Russian Federation, of the other part".

policy illustrating a peculiar connection between the E.U. pillars on the international plane. Shedding light on the legal links between the two constituting elements of the Partnership may provide for a tentative evaluation of the consistency of the E.U. policy *vis-à-vis* Russia. It might also reveal in more general terms the interface between the CS adopted by the European Council and the Community's external competences.

The first part of this contribution will evoke the PCA as an illustration of the E.U. pillars' interpenetration. Then, the CS adopted on Russia will be considered. A final part will attempt to underline, through a brief analysis of the first implementation measures of the CS, the latter's significance from the point of view of Community's external competences.

THE PARTNERSHIP UNDER THE MAASTRICHT TREATY: AN INTERPENETRATION OF E.U. PILLARS ON THE INTERNATIONAL PLANE

19.02   The PCA constitutes the contractual instrument of the Union's relations with the former Soviet Union.[3] In contrast to the "Europe Agreement" concluded with the countries from Central and Central Europe and the "Euro-Mediterranean Agreement"; the PCA is not an Association Agreement based on Article 310 EC (ex Article 238).[4]

The E.C. Treaty does not provide for a specific legal basis for agreements such as the PCA. The Partnership agreement, similarly to the Trade and Co-operation Agreement, is a mixed agreement initially based on Articles 133 and 308 E.C. (ex Articles 113 and 235). It involves both E.C. exclusive competences relating to the common commercial policy, and shared competences between the Community and the Member States due particularly to the PCA provisions on economic co-operation.[5] The respective fields of exclusive and shared competences were clarified by the E.C.J.'s Opinion 1/94 *on the*

---

[3] Council and Commission Decision of October 30, 1997 on the conclusion of a PCA between the E.C. and their Member States, of the one part, and the Russian Federation, of the other part ([1997] O.J. L327); Council and Commission Decision of January 26, 1998 on the conclusion of the PCA between the E.C. and their Member States, of the one part, and Ukraine, of the other part ([1998] O.J. L49); Council and Commission Decision of May 28, 1998 on the conclusion of a PCA between the E.C. and their Member States, of the one part, and the Republic of Moldova, of the other part ([1998] O.J. L181); Council and Commission Decision on the conclusion of a PCA between the E.C. and their Member States, of the one part, and Armenia, of the other part ([1999] O.J. L239); Council and Commission Decision on the conclusion of a PCA between the E.C. and their Member States, of the one part, and Azerbaijan, of the other part ([1999] O.J. L246); Council and Commission Decision on the conclusion of a PCA between the E.C. and their Member States, of the one part, and Georgia, of the other part ([1999] O.J. L205); Council and Commission Decision on the conclusion of a PCA between the E.C. and their Member States, of the one part, and the Republic of Kazakhstan, of the other part ([1999] O.J. L196); Council and Commission Decision on the conclusion of a PCA between the E.C. and their Member States, of the one part, and the Kyrgyz Republic, of the other part ([1999] O.J. L196); Council and Commission Decision on the conclusion of a PCA between the E.C. and their Member States, of the one part, and Uzbekistan, of the other part ([1999] O.J. L229); see also the proposal for a Council and Commission Decision on the conclusion of the PCA between the E.C. and its Member States, on the one hand, and Belarus, on the other hand (COM(95)44); the proposal for a Council and Commission Decision on the conclusion of the PCA between the E.C. and its Member States, on the one hand, and Turkmenistan, on the other hand ([1998] O.J. C50/2).

[4] In the light of E.C.J. Decision in Case 12/86 *Demirel* v. *City of Schwäbish Gumd* [1987] ECR 3719, the PCA does not establish a "privileged link" between the "PCA-partner" and the Community nor does it allow the former to "participate, at least to a certain extent to the E.C. legal system" as in the case of the associate country.

[5] As the PCA also covers matters relating to the European Coal and Steel Community and European Atomic Energy Community, a general reference to the ECSC Treaty, particularly Art. 95, and to Art. 101 EAEC was made in the Council and Commission Decisions on the Conclusion of the PCAs.

Agreement establishing the WTO.[6] By limiting the field of the common commercial policy, the Court delineated the scope of Community's exclusive competences in the framework of the PCA. In concrete terms, the E.C. exclusive competences cover the agreement's provisions relating to trade in goods and cross-border supply of services. Concerning goods, the PCA anticipates Russia's accession to WTO and provides that trade relations shall be regulated according to the main GATT principles.[7] Outside these fields,[8] the Community shares competence with the Member States, on the basis of specific legal grounds which were arguably added to the initial legal basis of the PCA.[9] Such an inflation of legal grounds indicates that the PCA covers much more than what belongs to the common commercial policy and strengthens the mixed character of the agreement. It also underlines the Member States' decisive role not only in elaborating and concluding the PCA as a consequence of Article 308 (ex Article 235), but also in further developing the Partnership. In particular, it implies that the Member States are intimately involved in establishing the Community's positions to be defended within the Co-operation Council and the Co-operation Committee of the PCA. Article 2(1) of the Decision on the Conclusion of the PCA with Russia indicates that the position to be adopted by the Community in these two bodies shall be "determined by the Council, on a proposal from the Commission, or where appropriate by the Commission, *in each case in accordance with the relevant*

---

[6] Opinion 1/94 *WTO* [1994] E.C.R. I–5267. For comments on the opinion, see the chapters of Tridimas, Neuwahl and Burnside respectively, in this Volume, see also for instance, Tridimas and Eeckhout, "The external Competence of the Community and the Case-law of the Court of Justice: Principles versus Pragmatism"; (1994) 14 Y.E.L. 143; Simon, "La Compétence de la Communauté pour conclure l'accord OMC: l'avis 1/94 de la Cour de Justice", *Europe* (1994) Chronique 9.

[7] Among the GATT principles set out in the PCA, the Parties shall accord to one another the Most-Favoured-Nation treatment according to Art. I, paragraph 1 of the GATT. Additionally, Art. III(2) GATT introduces the principle of non-discrimination in internal taxes, charges or regulations. A reference is made to Art. V (2, 3, 4, 5) GATT to guarantee the freedom of transit, regarded as an essential condition of attaining the objectives of the Agreement. Other GATT principles on valuation for customs purposes (Article VII (1, 2, 3, 4a, 4b, 4d, 5)), on the limitation of fees and formalities connected with the importation and exportation (Art. VIII), on the marks of origin (Art. IX), on the obligation of publication and of uniform, impartial and reasonable administration of trade regulations (Art. X) are applicable *mutatis mutandis* between the Parties. In addition, the derogation to these principles is also inspired by GATT; for an analysis on GATT/WTO provisions in the PCA, see Lebullenger, "Un Accord confronté aux règles du GATT et de l'OMC" in Raux & Korovkine (eds.) *Le Partenariat entre l'Union européenne et la Fédération de Russie*, p. 199.

[8] On the basis of its exclusive competence, the Community has also concluded specific agreements. One may mention the Agreement concluded by the Community with the Russian Federation on trade in textile products ([1998] O.J. L222). An Agreement has been concluded in the form of an exchange of letters between the European Community and Ukraine establishing a double-checking system without quantitive limits in respect of the export of certain steel products covered by the EC and ECSC Treaties from the Ukraine to the Community ([1997] O.J. L210); the same agreement has been concluded with Russia ([1997] O.J. L300).

[9] In the Council and Commission Decision on the Conclusion of the PCA with Russia the following legal basis is stated: Art. 44(2) (ex Art. 54(2)), the last sentence of Art. 47(2) (ex Art. 57(2)) and Art. 55 (ex Art. 66) for the PCA provisions on services and establishment; Art. 57(3) (ex Art. 73c(3)) for the provisions on payments (connected with the movement of goods) and capitals; Art. 71 (ex Art. 75), Art. 80(2) (ex Art. 84(2)) for the provisions on transports; Art. 93 (ex Art. 99), and Art. 94 (ex Art. 100) for the provisions on direct and indirect taxation, in conjunction with the second sentence of Art. 300(2) (ex Art. 228(2)) and the second subparagraph of Art. 300(3) EC, together with Art. 95 of the Treaty establishing the European Coal and Steel Community and Art. 101 of the Treaty establishing the European Atomic Energy Community. See also the Commission Document on the amended proposal for a Council and Commission Decision on the conclusion of the PCAs with Belarus, Kazakhstan, Kirghizhstan, Moldova and Ukraine ([1995] O.J. C127/2). For an analysis on this inflation of legal basis, see Flaesch-Mougin, "Quel partenaire européen pour la Fédération de Russie: Union européenne, Communauté, Etats membres?" in Raux & Korovkine (eds.) *Le Partenariat entre l'Union européenne et la Fédération de Russie*, p. 66; See chapter by Peers, "EC Frameworks of International Relations: Co-operation, Partnership and Association" in this volume.

provisions of the Treaties establishing the European Community, the European Coal and Steel Community and the European Atomic Energy Community (emphasis added)".[10]

19.03   The role of the Member States also stems from the remarkable political dimension given to the PCA. First, the Agreement underlines the Parties' "firm" commitment to the full implementation of all principles and provisions contained in the Final document of the Conference on Security and Co-operation in Europe (CSCE), the Concluding documents of the Madrid and Vienna follow-up meetings, the document of the CSCE Bonn Conference on economic co-operation, the Charter of Paris for a New Europe and the CSCE Helsinki document 1992, "The Challenges of Change".[11] Secondly, the Parties commit themselves to promote international peace and security as well as the peaceful settlement of disputes and co-operate to this end in the framework of the United Nations and the Organisation for Security and Co-operation in Europe (OSCE; ex CSCE). Such commitments actually echo to the CFSP objectives enshrined in Article 11 TEU (ex Article J.1).

Indeed, the Preamble of the PCA underlines the "commitment of the Community and its Member States *acting in the framework of the European Union by the Treaty on European Union* (...) to strengthening the political and economic freedoms which constitute the very basis of the partnership" (emphasis added).[12] In other words, not only does the ambit of the PCA go beyond the boundaries of the E.C. common commercial policy, it also goes beyond the Community framework *stricto sensu*. Although legally based on the E.C. Treaty, the PCA also derives from the CFSP principles. The PCA illustrates that since the entry into force of the TEU and in line with the requirement of its Article 3(2) (ex Article C(2)), the Community's external relations are shaped in the light of CFSP principles. From the outset, the Partnership has been connected with the Union as a whole. It constitutes an example of a *mixed external action of the E.U.*, with a cross-pillar dimension ensured in particular by the dual nature of the Council *of the European Union*.[13]

An illustration of this specific feature is the conditionality included in the PCA. Article 2 of the Agreement states that "respect for the democratic principles and human rights as defined in the Helsinki Final Act and the Charter of Paris for the New Europe[14] underpins the internal and external policies of the Parties and constitute an *essential element* of partnership and of the Agreement". The concept of "essential element" implies that its violation by any of the Parties constitues a "case of material breach of the Agreement"[15] and in turn a "case of special urgency" which, in derogation to the rules attached to the dispute settlement mechanism established by

---

[10] See Council and Commission Decision of October 30, 1997 on the conclusion of the PCA with Russia [1997] O.J. L327. See the analysis of Flaesch-Mougin, "Quel partenaire européen pour la Fédération de Russie; Union européenne, Communauté, Etats Membres?", *op. cit.*, pp. 67–68.
[11] See the Preamble of the PCA.
[12] *ibid.*, third indent.
[13] For more on the Council's role and nature, see chapter 14, by Torrent. See also Dashwood, "The Role of the Council of the European Union" in Curtin and Huekels (eds.), *Institutional Dynamics of European Integration—Essays in Honour of Henry Schermers*, Vol. II (1994), p. 117; and "The Council of the European Union in the Era of the Amsterdam Treaty" in Heukels, Blokker and Brus (eds.), *The European Union after Amsterdam*, p. 117.
[14] Both documents are stated in Art. 11 (ex Art. J.1) TEU.
[15] A Joint Declaration to Art. 107, annexed to the PCA defines "the material breach" by reference to Art. 60(3) of the Vienna Convention on the Law of Treaties (1969) as either a repudiation of the Agreement not sanctioned by the general rules of international law or a violation of the essential elements of the Agreement.

the PCA,[16] allows the Party injured to suspend unilaterally the implementation of the Agreement.[17]

The substantive obligations covered by the concept of "essential element" are not explicitly stated in the Agreement. A Joint Declaration attached to the PCA with Russia indicates that "the reference to the respect for human rights, constituting an essential element and to the cases of special urgency, flows from the attachments of both Parties to the relevant obligations, arising in particular from the Helsinki Act and the Charter of Paris on the New Europe". Hence, the principles to be observed belong to international political documents which, by being mentioned in the core of the Agreement are given a legal value by and for the Parties. These documents were established within international political fora where the Community did not participate as such; only the Member States did, in their own capacity. Moreover, the Joint Declaration mentions that "the Community's policy in the area of human rights [is], *in conformity with the Council Declaration of 11 May 1992*,[18] requiring the inclusion of this reference in co-operation or association agreements between the Community and OSCE partners" (emphasis added). The Community's external relations are in that sense used as a legal tool to give a concrete dimension to political principles to which the Member States are committed.[19]

The actual observance of these diverse principles and control of their observance in the context of the PCA is highly dependent on the way the two Parties interpret them. Indeed, the Joint Declaration mentions "Russia's policy in the field of human rights" as one of the sources of the PCA political conditionality, increasing the risk of divergence. One may hope that some common understanding of PCA key principles might be reached within the framework for political dialogue established by the Agreement.[20] Indeed, the Agreement provides for consultations at the highest level, within the institutional framework it sets up. The Co-operation Council is, in principle, in charge of monitoring the implementation of the PCA.[21] It shall in particular handle any dispute relating to the application of the Agreement.[22] It assembles once a year the members of the Council of the E.U. and members of the Commission on the one hand and members of the Russian Government on the other hand. Additionally, the PCA with Russia provides for meetings between the President of the Council of the E.U. and the President of the Commission on one side and the President of the Russian Federation on the other side. This formula has become the so-called "E.U.-Russia Summits", the fifth of which took place on May 29,

---

[16] The PCA dispute settlement mechanism normally requires that before a Party retaliates in response to the other Party's non compliance with its obligations, the former must supply the Co-operation Council with all the relevant information required for a thorough examination of the situation with a view to seeking a solution acceptable to the Parties (Art. 101 PCA).

[17] Art. 61(1) of the Vienna Convention provides that the "material breach" by one Party allows the other Party to terminate the Agreement or suspend, partly or wholly, its implementation, in observance of the procedure set out in Art. 65 which requires three months between the notification and the suspension. The "case of special urgency" allows derogation from the obligations set out in Art. 65 of the Vienna Convention.

[18] Council Declaration of May 11, 1992, Press Release 6326/92.

[19] COM(95) 216.

[20] Art. 1, PCA.

[21] See Art. 90 PCA. A Co-operation Committee assists the Co-operation Council in performing its duties. It is composed of representatives of the members of the Council of the E.U. and members of the Commission on the one hand and representatives of the Partner's Government on the other, at senior civil servant level. Sub-committees and working parties operating under its aegis and dispossessed of the right to make recommendations assist the Committee. Finally, the dialogue also involves parliamentarians. The Parliamentary Co-operation Committee, consisting of members of the European Parliament on the one hand and of members of the partner's parliamentary body, may require information on the Agreement's implementation. It shall be informed of the recommendations adopted by the Co-operation Council, who is free to publish them, and can itself make recommendations to the latter.

[22] *e.g.* Art. 101 PCA with Russia.

2000 with the participation of the Secretary-General of the Council/High Representative for CFSP, assisting the President of the European Council.[23] Indeed, these summits have developed into a forum where difficult trade disputes and sensitive political issues between the Parties are raised; all the more so that the Co-operation Council can only adopt *recommendations* for solving disputes. The role of the Co-operation Council is therefore limited given that recommendations, in contrast to decisions adopted by the Association Council established by the association agreements, do not have binding effect.[24]

19.04   Besides the PCA multilevel institutional framework, the political dialogue can also take place on other occasions, including with the Union's troika, by mutual agreement. Moreover, the Agreement underlines that other procedures and mechanisms for political dialogue shall be set up by the Parties by establishing appropriate contacts, exchange and consultations.[25] The fact that the political dialogue takes place within or outside the PCA structures indicates a degree of flexibility of the Partnership. This is indeed necessary considering the limits of the dispute settlement mechanism. Yet, it also reflects the dual institutional logic existing within the Union.

At the first meeting of the Co-operation Council with Russia, the Parties acknowledged that "implementing the PCA would ensure greater coherence between the various aspects of their relations, such as the political dialogue on foreign policy issues of mutual interest; co-operation in the fight against crime; trade relations and economic co-operation including the creation of the necessary conditions for the future establishment of a free trade area".[26] Nonetheless, in the course of their proceedings, the Parties "adopted" three documents among which were a "joint work programme for 1998" and "Conclusions on foreign policy subjects".[27] The separation of the two documents indicates that foreign policy issues, although a matter explicitly covered by the political dialogue established by the PCA, do not belong to the PCA work as such. Indeed, the official press release of the Co-operation Council mentions that the "Parties" discussed a "Joint PCA Work Programme" while "*Ministers*" had an exchange of views "on foreign policy issues *over dinner*" (italics added).[28] Thus, the substantive distinction is coupled with an institutional division of tasks. The meeting of the Co-operation Council offers an occasion for its members to discuss political matters but outside the room and with another mandate and a different loyalty. Such distinction would seem legitimate given the prima facie compartmentalised structure of the Union. Yet, it does not seem to be systematic, given that the item "Justice and Home Affairs" was included in the PCA work programme.[29]

Therefore, the PCA embodies a variety of procedural formula *ratione materiae*, fol-

---

[23] See Joint Statement E.U.-Russia Summit, May 29, 2000, Press Rlease 8976/00.
[24] Art. 101(3) PCA.
[25] Art. 8 PCA.
[26] Press Release 05273/98 of the first Co-operation Council between the E.U. and the Russian Federation.
[27] Document "Conclusions on Foreign Policy Subjects by the E.U./Russia Co-operation Council on January 27".
[28] The press releases of the Co-operation Council meetings with Russia and Ukraine respectively mention that "Ministers had a exchange of view on Foreign policy issues *over dinner*" (italics added). Dinners and lunches should not be underestimated. See in that respect the *Bangladesh* joined cases C–181/91 & C248–/91 *EP* v. *Council and Commission* [1993] E.C.R. 3685.
[29] "[On the vasis of Art. 84 PCA] both sides will seek to give new impetus to co-operation in tackling organised crime including drug trafficking and illegal activities in the sphere of economics. They will explore in particular the possibilities for enhancing practical law enforcement co-operation", point 17 of "Joint PCA work programme for 1998", Annex 1 to the Press Release of the first Co-operation Council between the E.U. and the Russian Federation, *op. cit.* Indeed the Press Release states that the "Co-operation Council welcomed the commitment of the *Parties* to step up their fight against organised crime in its various manifestations" (italics added).

lowing the evolving internal institutional arrangements of the E.U. The Secretary-
General/High Representative for the CFSP attended the third meeting of the Co-
operation Council with Russia. He also participated in the E.U./Russia Summit in
Moscow on May 29, 2000, assisting the President of the European Council.[30] A more
systematic presence of the High Representative for the CFSP in the PCA institutional
framework, which remains to be confirmed,[31] would emphasise a further institutionalisation of the CFSP's influence on the PCA development and consequently a growing
interpenetration of the different EU pillars within the Partnership. Depending on one's
view, it could also illustrate a growing CFSP *interference* in Community work after the
Amsterdam Treaty.[32]

THE EU PARTNERSHIP WITH RUSSIA UNDER THE AMSTERDAM TREATY: THE COEXISTENCE OF EU PILLARS

19.05   The reform of the TEU introduced the Common Strategy (CS) as a new
CFSP instrument.[33] The establishment of the CS directly involves the European Council as a decision-taking institution and deeply influences the Union's activities. Used for
the first time in relation to Russia, it represents a potential for strengthening the Partnership, provided it develops consistently with the existing instruments, *inter alia*, the
PCA. More generally, the CS shall be adopted and implemented in accordance with the
requirement of consistency, consolidated by the Treaty of Amsterdam.

The new decisive role of the European Council

19.06   Contrary to the PCA, the CS has a specific legal basis in the TEU, which
presents it as an instrument of external policy. Article 13 (ex Article J.3) included in
Title V on CFSP provides that:

> "The European Council shall *decide on common strategies* to be implemented
> by the Union in areas where the Member States have important interests in com-
> mon" (italics added).

The Council of the E.U. shall recommend the CS to the European Council[34] following the principles and general guidelines previously defined by the latter.[35] Anticipating
the entry into force of the Amsterdam Treaty, the Vienna European Council already
invited the Council, following the latter's recommendations,[36] to prepare CSs on Russia, Ukraine, the Mediterranean region, as well as on the Western Balkans, on the
understanding that the first CS would be on Russia.[37] The recommendations made by
the Council underlined that the first CSs "should focus on the neighbouring regions of
the E.U. Not least in the context of enlargement and the development of the *acquis*; it is

---

[30] See the Joint Statement following the Russia-E.U. Summit, Press Release 8976/00.
[31] *N.B.*, the High Representative did not attend a later meeting of the Co-operation Council with Ukraine, see Press Release nr. 8741/00 following the third meeting of the Co-operation Council on May 23, 2000.
[32] This development might not necessarily be appreciated on the side of the Commission, particularly the Commissioner in charge of external relations.
[33] For a deeper analysis of this new instrument, see Dashwood, "External relations provisions of the Amsterdam Treaty", (1998) 35 C.M.L.Rev. 1019–1045; and Pierre des Nerviens, "Les relations exté-rieures", (1997) 33 R.T.D. eur. 801–812.
[34] Art. 13(3.1) TEU.
[35] Art. 13(1) TEU.
[36] Document submitted to the Vienna European Council, December 11–12, 1998, Press Release 13643/98.
[37] See point 74, Conclusions of the Presidency, Vienna European Council, December 11–12, 1998, EU Bull. 12/98 p. 8.

there that the E.U. has the greatest long term common interests and the greatest need for coherence and effectiveness".[38]

Although there is no EU obligation to discuss the CS with its addressee, it was nonetheless presented to Russian officials during the second EU-Russia Summit on February 18, 1999. The draft CS was then introduced in the agenda of the General Affairs Council meeting on May 17, 1999 for approbation, after consensus had finally emerged at the level of both the Committee of the Permanent Representatives (COREPER) and the Political Committee.[39] The same day, the E.U. briefed Russian authorities on the CS within the Co-operation Council, *i.e.* within the institutional framework established by the PCA.[40] The European Council meeting in Cologne eventually endorsed the CS on Russia in June 1999.[41]

19.07   Besides the Council and the European Council, the European Commission is entitled by the TEU to be "fully associated" with the work carried out in the CFSP. The Commission prepared, already before Amsterdam, the draft of a "Common Position on European Union-Russia relations" included in a Communication "on the future relations between the European Union and Russia".[42] Indeed, the CS with Russia clearly recalls that the Commission shall be "fully associated"[43] in accordance with Articles 18 and 27 of the TEU.[44] Hence, one may assume that the Commission is entitled to take part both in the definition and the implementation of the CS.[45] Also, the European Commission participates in the adoption of the CS by the European Council given that, on the basis of Article 4(2) TEU (ex Article D(2)), its President is one of its members. This element has been seen as a veto power given to the Commission in the adoption of CSs,[46] although it seems unlikely that the Commission would go against a consensus reached by the Member States. In any case it provides the Commission with a tool to make its views considered.

The European Parliament (EP) may equally make recommendations to the Council and it shall also be consulted by the Presidency of the Union on *the main aspects and the basic choices of the CFSP* and in principle its views shall be duly taken into consideration.[47] Indeed, the EP adopted several resolutions concerning EU-Russia relations,[48] one of which preceded the adoption by the European Council of the CS on Russia. However, the EP does not participate in the CS adoption. Complaining about the lack of consideration accorded to its work, the EP asked in its recommendation to the Council to be *formally* consulted on CSs, arguing that they constitue "a basic

---

[38] Document submitted to the Vienna European Council, December 11–12, 1998, *op. cit.*
[39] *Europe* nr. 7465, May 15, 1999, p. 8.
[40] See Press Release 99/152 of the second meeting of the Co-operation Council between the E.U. and Russia. Brussels, May 17, 1999.
[41] See point 78, Presidency Conclusions, Cologne European Council, June 3–4, 1999; EU Bull. 6/99; p. 7.
[42] COM(95)223.
[43] See Part on "Instruments and Means".
[44] Art. 18(4) TEU indicates that the Commission is "fully associated in the tasks referred to in paragraphs 1 and 2", that is, *inter alia*, implementation of decisions taken under the CFSP. Art. 27, TEU provides that the Commission is "fully associated with the work carried out in the common foreign and security policy field".
[45] Art. 22 TEU (ex Art. J.12).
[46] See Dashwood, "External relations provisions of the Amsterdam Treaty", *op. cit.*, at p. 1031.
[47] Art. 21 TEU (ex Art. J.11).
[48] See for instance Report of February 12, 1998 on the Commission Communication "The future of relations between the European Union and Russia" and the Action Plan "The European Union and Russia— the future relationship" (A4-0060/98); Report of February 11, 1998 on the Communication from the Commission to the Council on an Action Plan for Ukraine (A4-0059/98).

choice of the CFSP".[49] It also called for such consultation on CSs to be made "the subject of an inter-institutional agreement which spells out the respective responsibilities and commitment of Parliament, the Commission and the Council (in particular of its Presidency and High Representative for the CFSP)".[50]

Be it as it may, the CS was adopted for an initial duration of four years with the possibility of being prolonged, reviewed and if necessary adapted by the European Council, on the recommendation of the Council. Hence, as a corollary to the European Council and Council's crucial role in establishing the Strategy, the two bodies also keep discretion in further developing it. The impact of such powers is all the more substantial as the CS is granted a dominating role with respect to existing Community instruments in the context of EU-Russia relations, *viz.* the PCA.

The supremacy of the Common Strategy

19.08   The CS is conceived by the E.U. as means to strengthen the "strategic partnership" with its partner.[51] It sets out the E.U.'s "strategic goals" with respect to Russia and consequently determines the E.U.'s "vision of the partnership". In other words, the CS strengthens the political aspect of the EU's relation to Russia, based on the PCA.

Just as important as the "vision of the partnership" is the idea that the CS represents a single framework designed to foster the co-ordination of all policies and instruments elaborated by the Community and its Member States with respect to Russia. Indeed, the CS states that "the E.U. and its Member States will develop the co-ordination, coherence and complementarity of all aspects of their policy towards Russia. The Union, the Community and its Member States will also work together with and within regional and other organisations and with like-minded partners to meet the objectives set out in this Common Strategy. The positions taken by the Member States in all relevant forums will *conform* to this [CS]" (emphasis added).[52]

In order to give a concrete dimension to the "strategic goals", the CS provides for priority areas generating "specific initiatives" on which the E.U. and its Member States shall focus. Although not necessarily dealt with in similar terms in the CS and in the PCA, some fields of co-operation are dealt with by both instruments,[53] raising the question of how the risks of duplication will be avoided. Solving this issue is actually the guarantee that the CS brings an added value to the Partnership.

A way to avoid duplication is to grant the CS precedence over other E.U. measures. Although recognising that "the core of the relationship between the Union and Russia

---

[49] The EP claims that "the provisions of Art. J.11 (new Art. 21 TEU), already in the Maastricht Treaty, *have never been applied*, despite repeated calls by Parliament, notably during the annual debate on the CFSP" (emphasis added). See Report containing a proposal for a European Parliament recommendation to the Council on the common strategy towards the Russian Federation (A4-0219/99).

[50] *ibid.*

[51] The E.U. wants a "stable, open and pluralistic democracy in Russia, governed by the rule of law and underpinning a prosperous market economy benefiting alike all the people of Russia and of the E.U."; in addition, the E.U. wishes "to maintain European stability promoting global security and responding to the common challenges of the continent through intensified co-operation with Russia". See para. 4 of Part I ("Vision of the EU for its Partnership with Russia") CS; see also point 78, Presidency Conclusions, Cologne European Council, June 3–4, 1999, *op. cit.*

[52] See fifth para. of Part I. *N.B.*, the CS on Ukraine contains the same provisions except that in addition to the "objectives of the CS", it also refers to "the objectives of the PCA": "the EU and its Member States will develop the co-ordination, coherence and complementarity of all aspects of their policy towards Ukraine. The Union, the Community and its Member States will also work together with and within regional and other organisations and with like-minded partners to meet the objectives set out *in the PCA* and in this Common Strategy" (emphasis added) [Para. 8 of Part I of the CS on Ukraine].

[53] Para. 4 of Part II indicates that "the *EU* will, in particular, cooperate with Russia, in energy and nuclear safety, environment and health" while "Co-operation in the field of Environment, Energy and nuclear safety" is also covered by the co-operation established by the PCA.

remains the PCA",[54] the CS calls on the Council, the Commission and the Member States to *review*, according to their powers and capacities, *existing* actions, programmes, instruments and policies to *ensure their consistency* with the CS.[55] They shall also make full and appropriate use of existing instruments and means, *in particular the PCA, to implement the CS.*[56]

Therefore, by adopting a CS, the European Council mobilises *all* existing and future E.U. instruments—in a very wide sense—and institutions to achieve the objectives set out in the Strategy. The CS becomes a vehicle for consistency of the E.U's external policy *vis-à-vis* Russia by being established as hierarchically superior to any other instruments adopted in the framework of the E.U., E.C. external relations included. Indeed, according to the wording of the CS, the PCA becomes an instrument that shall give effect to the Strategy. Once again, Community measures are determined by and employed to give concrete dimension to common political commitments of the Member States, meeting here within the European Council.

According to the TEU, the CS sets out its objectives, duration and means to be made available by the Union and the Member States.[57] Thus, the CS establishes a framework to be followed by additional measures. A brief analysis of the latter, looking particularly at the way they are combined with existing instruments, may indicate to what extent the CS actually "strengthens" the Partnership.

Implementation of the Common Strategy through all the Union's means

19.09   The CS is "implemented by the Union" in accordance with Article 13 TEU. The Treaty adds that the Council takes the decisions necessary for implementing the CS[58] through instruments such as joint actions and common positions.[59]

However, the provisions of the CS state that it shall be implemented in accordance with the applicable procedures of the *Treaties*. A Declaration of the European Council attached to the Strategy clarifies the procedural aspects of the implementation.[60] It underlines that the Council acts by qualified majority when adopting joint actions, common positions or any other decisions within the scope of Title V of the TEU, on the basis of the CS. In addition, "*acts adopted outside the scope of Title V* of the TEU shall continue to be adopted according to the appropriate decision-making procedures provided by *the relevant provisions of the Treaties, including the Treaty establishing the European Community and Title VI of the Treaty on European Union*" (emphasis added).[61]

Therefore, although established on the basis of Title V as a CFSP measure, the CS is implemented through instruments other than those available in the framework of CFSP, such as joint actions and common positions. The E.C. Treaty and Title VI on Police and Judicial Co-operation in Criminal Matters can be employed to give effect to the CS, in accordance with their respective procedural requirements. In that sense, the

---

[54] Para. 5, Part I.
[55] See point 2 of "Instruments and Means" of the CS on Russia. *N.B.*, the CS on Ukraine requires the positions taken by *the Community* and its Member States in all relevant fora to conform to the CS, see point 8 of Part I of the CS on Ukraine. In that sense, it goes further than the CS on Russia which obliges only the Member States to conform their positions to the CS, not the Community; see para. 5 of Part I.
[56] *ibid.*
[57] Art. 13(2) TEU.
[58] Art. 13(3) TEU.
[59] Art. 23(2) TEU.
[60] "European Council Declaration on the Common Strategy on Russia".
[61] See para. 2 of the Declaration, *op. cit.*

CS strengthens the "cross-pillar" dimension[62] of the Partnership but, formally introducing the different pillars' procedural frameworks in its development.[63] Through the CS, the *E.U.*, as described in Article 1(3) TEU (ex Article A), emerges as an international actor *vis-à-vis* Russia. Two measures, falling in principle under the scope of the two "inter-governmental" pillars, have been taken to implement the CS.

The first measure is a Council Joint Action (JA) adopted in December 1999, *establishing an EU co-operation programme for non-proliferation and disarmament in the Russian Federation.*[64] It is grounded on Article 14 TEU (ex Article J.4) which is the legal basis for the adoption of joint actions, and Article 23(2) TEU (ex Article J.13(2)) allowing the use of qualified majority voting within the Council when adopting joint actions on the basis of a CS.[65] The JA also clearly states in its Preamble that it derives from the CS on Russia. The Programme it establishes aims at supporting Russia in its efforts towards arms control and disarmament, in line with the "strategic goals" and the "specific initiatives" set out by the CS. In addition, the Preamble states that the JA also corresponds to the objectives of the PCA, as it promotes "*inter alia* an increasing convergence of Parties' positions on international issues of mutual concern thus increasing security and stability".

19.10   The combination of PCA and CS references indicates the Council's awareness of the *dual* nature of the subject. Indeed, the Preamble of the JA stresses that the activities covered by the programme will take place *in parallel* with activities carried out by the E.C. and the Member States implying co-ordination to the greatest extent possible to avoid unnecessary duplication. Thus, one presumes that the Council is willing to ensure coherence in the E.U.'s policy in the framework of the Partnership. Indeed, the provisions of the JA underline that the latter is subject to bilateral consultations, with Russia and other partners *within the framework of existing political meetings, i.e.* within the institutional framework established by the PCA. It also recalls the Council and Commission's general obligation to ensure co-ordination between the programme, Community assistance and the bilateral assistance provided by the Member States. Hence, overall, the JA appears to show that the implementation of the CS is done in co-ordination with existing frameworks in order not to impede the Partnership.

The E.U. Action Plan (AP) *on Common Action for the Russian Federation on combating organised crime* adopted by the Council[66] is the second measure taken "in fulfilment of the E.U. Common Strategy on Russia as adopted by the European Council in Cologne". The specificity of the AP is that in principle, it touches upon all three pillars of the Union and as a consequence should embody a high level of co-ordination. It is a

[62] The Finnish Presidency's Progress Report on the Implementation of the Common Strategy of the E.U. on Russia and the Presidency Work Plan, submitted to the Helsinki European Council, clearly recognised the "cross-pillar" feature of the CS; see Press Release nr. 13860/99.
[63] In its Report on the CS towards the Russian Federation, the EP considers that "the purpose of the common strategy should be both to add value to the existing partnership and to ensure the coherence and consistency of the E.U.'s relationship with the Russian Federation, *both within and between each of the pillars of the E.U.'s activities* ("cross-pillar approach") (emphasis added)"; Report by the Committee on Foreign Affairs, Security and Defence Policy, on the common strategy towards the Russian Federation (A4-0219/99.
[64] Council Joint Action 1999/878/CFSP of December 17, 1999 establishing an E.U. co-operation programme for non-proliferation and disarmament in the Russian Federation. [1999] O.J. L331/11.
[65] Art. 23, TEU provides that, by derogation from the rule applying in the field of CFSP, namely decisions being taken by unanimity at the Council, "the Council shall act by qualified majority when adopting joint actions, common positions or taking any other decision on the basis of a common strategy".
[66] [2000] O.J. C106/5.

measure implementing the CS on Russia adopted on the basis of Title V (CFSP),[67] it concerns criminal matters referred to in Article 29 TEU (Title VI, on Police and Judicial Co-operation in Criminal Matters)[68] but also covers issues such as *money laundering* dealt with in the E.C. framework. Some E.C. legislation has been adopted on the basis of Article 47(2) EC (ex Article 57(2)) included in the Title on free movement of persons, services and capital on the one hand and Article 95 EC (ex Article 100a) on the other, relating to the internal market.[69]

The AP deals with a subject covered by the fields of co-operation included in the PCA. Although the Agreement does not explicitly mention the concept of "organised crime", it does however contain provisions on the prevention of illegal activities (Title VIII), drug trafficking (Article 82) and money laundering (Article 81) which are also issues covered by the Judicial Co-operation in Criminal Matters mentioned in Article 29(2), TEU (ex Article K.1), and as stated above, also by the CS. Moreover, the field of Justice and Home Affairs was included from the outset in the PCA work programme approved by the Parties.[70] Indeed, the AP mentions the PCA. Its Preamble "*takes into account*" the fact that it "*entered into force*".[71] It also recalls the PCA's "*reference*" to co-operation against illegal activities including money laundering and drug trafficking and acknowledges the "*work on organised crime undertaken by the relevant sub-committee established under the PCA*".[72]

This being said, the AP is not an instrument promoting such a co-operation on the basis and in the framework of the PCA. It clearly provides for a specific co-operation based on the third pillar of the TEU, as defined by the Amsterdam Treaty. Moreover, it follows the commitment of the Cologne European Council to set a *durable and effective* co-operation with Russia in the area of Justice and Home Affairs.[73] Also, the AP is conceived as an E.U. external action contributing to the establishment of an area of freedom, security and justice in the E.U.[74] Finally, the General Principles (Part III) of the Plan mention that "account should be taken of related work already pursued by

---

[67] Point 4 of the "Areas of Action" in the CS on Russia provides that the E.U. will co-operate with Russia in *inter alia*, the fight against organised crime, money laundering and illicit traffic in human beings. Moreover, the "Specific Initiatives" include provisions on the fight against organised crime whereby the Union is "proposing to set up a plan focused on common action with Russia to fight against organised crime, including actions to fight corruption, money laundering, trafficking in drugs, human beings and illegal immigration".

[68] Art. 29 TEU (ex Art. K.1), para. 2 states that the objective linked to the police and judicial co-operation in criminal matters shall be achieved by "preventing and combating crime, organised or otherwise, in particular terrorism, trafficking in persons and offences against children, illicit drug trafficking and illicit arms trafficking, corruption and fraud".

[69] Council Directive 91/308/EEC of June 10, 1991 on prevention of the use of the financial system for the purpose of money laundering; [1991] O.J. L166/77. A new proposal has been prepared by the Commission for a EP and Council Directive amending Council Directive 91/308/EEC; see COM(1999)352.

[70] See above.

[71] See fifth indent, Preamble of the AP.

[72] In the CS, the "Specific Initiative" (Part III) on "Fight against organised crime" provides that Discussion with Russia *within the PCA framework* and an ongoing dialogue between the competent Russian bodies and European Union Member States liaison officers based in Moscow will make it possible to analyse Russia's requirements in this area more precisely (emphasis added). The Presidency also underlines that concerning co-operation in Justice and Home Affairs, the "PCA Sub-Committee 6 (dealing, *inter alia*, with fight against crime) is a central common institution for dialogue in this area" [*cf.* Presidency's Progress Report on the Implementation of the Common Strategy of the European Union on Russia and the Presidency's Work Plan; Press Release 13860/99.]

[73] Before any mention to the PCA, the Preamble of the AP refers to the Common Strategy on Russia endorsed by the 1999 Cologne European Council and to Russia's "Medium-term strategy for development of relations between the Russian Federation and the E.U. (2000 to 2010)", then to the Union's Action Plan on organised crime approved by the Amsterdam European Council in 1997 and to the E.U. drug strategy (2000–2004) endorsed by the Helsinki European Council in 1999.

[74] The AP refers to para. 56 of the Conclusions of the Tampere European Council, requiring "all competences and instruments, particularly external relations to be used in an *integrated and consistent way* to build an area of freedom, security and justice" (emphasis added).

individual Member States or carried out in other international forums and of the possible need for co-ordination in that regard" (emphasis added).

Therefore, the AP introduces a new development in the EU-Russia relations by establishing a specific framework for co-operation in a given field of Justice and Home Affairs. It does so by disconnecting the issue from the PCA. Part D of the AP dealing with the "implementation of the Action Plan" states the E.U.'s will to "urgently consider the question of developing an agreement under Article 38 TEU with the Russian Federation for the purpose of implementing this Action Plan".[75] Article 38, TEU, which is the only clear reference the AP makes to the Treaty and more precisely to Title VI, provides for the possibility to conclude "Union's agreements", with one or more states or international organisations in the framework of Title VI, by reference to the new procedure set out in Article 24 (Title V) TEU.

19.11 Although initially covered by the PCA work programme,[76] the issue shall now be dealt with in a separate agreement, on the basis of Title VI of the TEU. Legally, one may argue that the choice is in line with the procedural requirement of the TEU's architecture, as indeed underlined in the European Council Declaration attached to the CS. Then, why was Justice and Home Affairs included in the PCA work programme in the first place? One could suppose that the lack of mechanisms under the Maastricht Treaty to establish E.U. external agreements with Russia on non-Community issues, had the effect of making the Member States rely on the mixed character of the PCA. The introduction in the Amsterdam Treaty of Article 24/38 TEU establishes such a mechanism. As illustrated by the AP, it affects the scope of the PCA. More generally, this new mechanism may have an effect on the scope of Community's mixed agreements.

Article 24 TEU allows the Council, acting unanimously, to ask the Presidency, assisted by the Commission as appropriate, to open negotiations with a third state of international organisation. The Presidency recommends the negotiated agreement to the Council that can conclude it, acting unanimously. Such a procedure is heavy and the outcome rather unpredictable given that in order to conclude such an "E.U. international agreement" with Russia, a double unanimity is required within the Council. It should be noted that one of the side-effects of the European Council Declaration attached to the CS is in fact to reintroduce unanimity for implementing the CS whose essential feature was to allow qualified majority in the field of CFSP. The "more *effective* co-operation between the E.U. and Russia", which was the main objective of the AP and a commitment of the Cologne European Council, might eventually be a difficult exercise, just as the development of the PCA itself.[77]

---

[75] The overall approach follows the "Action Plan of the Council and the Commission on how best to implement the provisions of the Treaty of Amsterdam on an area of freedom, security and justice" adopted by the Justice and Home Affairs Council of December 3, 1998. Part E of the Plan's introductory part states that "the advances introduced by the Amsterdam Treaty will also enhance the Union's role as a player and partner on the international stage ..., this external aspect of the Union's action can be expected to take on a new and more demanding dimension. Full use will need to be made of new instruments available under the Treaty .... In those subjects which remain in Title VI of the TEU, the Union can also make use of the possibility for the Council to conclude international agreements in matters relating to Title VI of the Treaty, as well as for the Presidency, assisted by the General Secretariat of the Council and in full association with the Commission, to represent the Union in these areas"; [1999] O.J. C19.

[76] See developments above.

[77] The development of the co-operation covered by the PCA is a complex venture given the lack of binding effect attached to the recommendations of the Co-operation Council. Any further measure to develop the PCA implies the negotiation, the conclusion and the ratification of an additional agreement between the Parties in accordance with their respective procedures. Art. 3 of the PCA with Russia provides that: "The Parties undertake to consider development of the relevant titles of this Agreement .... The Co-operation Council may make recommendations on such developments. ... Such development shall only be put into effect by virtue of an Agreement between the parties in accordance with their respective procedures".

The complex implementation procedure introduced by the AP clearly illustrates that following the Amsterdam Treaty and as a result of the CS, the E.U. complex structure and logic penetrate the E.U's relations with Russia.[78] Although such a development might create a new momentum for widening the ambit of the Partnership, it might remain limited in effect if the various procedural frameworks involved work too independently from one another. Duplication and risks of contradiction might appear in the E.U.'s position *vis-à-vis* its Partner.[79]

In that regard, the TEU insists on the Commission and Council's responsibility to ensure the consistency of the Union's "external activities as a whole".[80] Indeed, the Treaty of Amsterdam introduced an *obligation* for the two institutions to co-operate to this end. However, it might turn out to be a difficult exercise considering the different logic according to which each of the two institutions work. Moreover, the Treaty is itself equivocal. The provisions concerning the CS only refer to the *Council* for ensuring "unity, consistency and effectiveness of action by the Union".[81] Indeed, the Council's report that was submitted to the Vienna European Council is informative on the Council's role.[82] It explicitly states that the General Affairs Council will be responsible for ensuring coherence in the Common Strategies *on all aspects of the E.U. external relations*, by making full use of all means and instruments available to the E.U.

Hence, the adoption of the CS strengthens the position of the European Council and the Council in the field of external relations. At the internal level, tensions could arise between institutions as the EP's reaction stated above underlines. It might be so particularly with respect to the choice of legal basis for adopting acts supposed to implement the CS.[83] The Council Report on Common Strategy,[84] insists on the respect of the decision-making procedures foreseen by the Treaties and on the observance of Article 47 TEU (ex Article M). In other words, the establishment of the CS shall respect the respective powers of the institutions and make sure that the CS does not affect the Treaties establishing the European Communities and subsequent Treaties and Acts modifying or supplementing them. This reference is of great interest. It means that judicial procedures are possible given that Article 46 TEU (ex Article L) recognises the E.C.J.'s jurisdiction to guarantee the due observance of Article 47 TEU. Indeed, in a decision of May 12, 1998, the E.C.J. acknowledged its jurisdiction to review the content of a Council's Act adopted on the basis of Title VI, in the light of former Article 100c of the E.C. Treaty. The Court did so "in order to ascertain whether *the Act affects the powers of the Community under that provision* and to annul the act if it appears that it should have been based on Article 100c of the E.C. Treaty".[85] The

---

[78] In a speech given on May 29, 2000 at Maly Manege in Moscow, Romano Prodi, President of the Commission, explained why the CS had been adopted: "It was essential to bring our partnership into line with the new emerging dimensions of the EU - the introduction of the Euro and the significant headway made in the fields of Justice and Home Affairs and of our Common Foreign and Security Policy. Russia was the obvious choice for our very first Common Strategy, which is a new foreign policy tool under the Amsterdam Treaty".
[79] For instance the provisions on the establishment of a free trade area with Ukraine are different in the PCA and in the CS. The former provides in Art. 3 that the Parties "shall examine together in the year 1998 whether circumstances allow the beginning of negotiations on the establishment of a free trade area". The latter provides that the Union will examine the circumstances which might, *in addition to the WTO accession*, allow for the future establishment of an E.U.-Ukraine free trade area.
[80] Art. 3 TEU (ex Art. C).
[81] Art. 13(3) TEU, last indent.
[82] Document submitted to the Vienna European Council, December 11–12, 1998, Press release 13643/98.
[83] As mentioned earlier, the EP called for the "consultation of the European Parliament on CSs to be made the subject of an interinstitutional agreement which [would] spell out the respective responsibilities and commitments of Parliament, the Commission and the Council (and in particular of its Presidency and High Representative for the CFSP), so that the CS constitutes an instrument which is both democratic and effective"; *op. cit.*, p. 5.
[84] *op. cit.*
[85] See Case 170/96 *Commission v. Council* [1998] E.C.R. I–2763; annotation by Simon, *Europe*, 220, July 1998, pp. 6–7.

question is whether the Court would adopt the same approach should a conflict of legal basis arise, involving a CFSP measure implementing the CS which would affect the powers of the Community. This would give the Court an occasion, to draw a line in the spirit of Opinion 1/94, between the Community's external competences, exclusive or shared, and non-Community's competences, belonging to the other pillars or even to the Member States in their own rights.

CONCLUDING REMARKS

19.12   From the outset the Partnership between the E.U. and Russia has had a cross-pillar dimension. Through its mixed nature, the PCA on which the Partnership has developed, allowed an *interpenetration* of the different E.U. pillars within a single institutional framework established by the Agreement.

This feature has now been modified by the Amsterdam Treaty, in particular after the adoption of the CS. As a consequence of the latter, the various aspects of the increasingly multi-faceted Partnership have referred to the different legal frameworks and procedures established by the TEU, without necessarily connecting them. Although the CS states that the PCA remains the core of the relationship, some fields of co-operation covered by the Agreement might be dealt with outside the latter's framework, reducing its scope accordingly.

In other words, the CS introduces the *co-existence* of different pillars within the Partnership, corresponding to the pillar structure of the Treaty. This could reflect a more general tendency whereby certain fields covered by Community's mixed agreements by default, may be dealt with through other mechanisms such as Articles 24 and 38, TEU. This development makes the requirement for consistency in E.U.'s external action more meaningful than ever.

Paradoxically, it was in the name of ensuring the coherence of the Partnership that the European Council adopted the CS. By setting up a framework whereby the activities of the various institutions are determined, it has become a crucial actor in E.U.-Russia relations. More generally, the enhanced role of the European Council in deciding on CSs also affects the institutional functioning of the Community and the Union as a whole. In particular, it may generate the development of a hierarchy of acts in the Union's external policy. As a consequence, the sophisticated construction of EC external relations, as extensively explored in this volume, might be profoundly affected.

INDEX

abortion
  freedom to provide services, 5.08
  population policies, 7.04
action plans, 14.04, 19.10, 19.11
AETR, 1.02–08
  capacity and competence, 1.05–06
  case, 1.02
  common rules, 12.05
    effect on, 12.10
  complementarity, 8.20
  effet utile, 1.07–08, 8.03
  implicit external competence, 8.03, 8.14,
    8.20
  principle, 1.03–04, 1.18, 1.19, 8.13,
    8.19
  true construction principle, 8.22
Agreement on Technical Barriers to Trade,
  10.06, 10.09
agriculture
  development treaties, 7.07
  international agreements, 8.06
  WTO Agreement, 4.06, 10.04
AIDS, 7.02
  development treaties, 7.09
  discrimination, 7.04
Albania, 11.13
  co-operation agreement, 11.16
  partnership agreement, 11.07
Amsterdam Treaty, 14.09–13
  co-operation, 19.11
  common commercial policy, 7.06
  common strategies, 19.12
  effect on trade agreements, 11.08
  external relations provisions, 18.01–07
    extension of external competence,
      10.11, 15.01–07, 19.01
    procedure, 8.09, 8.10, 18.02–03
  fundamental rights, 5.13–16
  mixed agreements, 19.11
  negotiations, 14.12
  partnership with Russia, 19.05–11
  women's role, 7.09
Andean states, co-operation agreements,
  11.05
Ankara Agreement, 2.11, 2.14
anti-dumping regulations, 2.16, 8.04
Argentina
  co-operation agreement, 11.05
  free trade agreement, 11.04
  soya trade, 2.13

Armenia, partnership agreement, 11.07,
  19.02[n3]
ASEAN states, co-operation agreements,
  11.05
Association Agreement Council, 2.15
association agreements, 2.11, 11.01, 11.06
  aid, 11.11
  co-operation and trade, 11.05
  contents, 11.03
  Cyprus, 11.03, 11.11
  developing countries, 11.12
  direct applicability, 17.06
  EC Treaty, 12.02
  EEA, 11.06, 11.11
  express external powers, 11.03
  future membership, 11.03
  Greece, 11.03, 11.04, 11.11
  human rights clauses, 11.09
  immigration clauses, 11.08[n44]
  legality, 11.11–12, 11.18
  Malta, 11.03, 11.11
  mixed agreements, interpretation, 13.09
  Morocco, 11.03
  non-reciprocity, 11.11
  procedure, 8.05, 8.09
    Treaty of Amsterdam, 8.10
  southern Mediterranean states, 11.04
  Tunisia, 11.03
  Turkey, 11.03, 11.04, 11.11
  Yaoundé Convention, 11.03
asylum, 5.14, 8.08
Athens Agreement
  direct applicability, 2.04, 2.07
  purpose, 2.07
attribution of external competence,
  8.01–23
  alternative principle of attribution,
    8.21–23
  development, 8.03
  EC Treaty, 8.01
    amendments, 8.07
    extension provisions, 8.08
    original provisions, 8.04
  implicit powers *see* **implicit external
    competence**
  principles, 8.01, 8.02
  procedural and substantive attribution,
    8.06, 8.09–11
Azerbaijan, partnership agreement, 11.07,
  19.02[n3]

Balkan countries, common strategies, 19.06
Baltic states, free trade agreements, 11.06, 11.07
banana market, conflict with GATT, 2.18
  policy choice, 17.13
  taxation, 2.20
Bangladesh
  bilateral agreement, 13.13
  free trade agreement, 11.04
Bangladesh case, 3.01, 3.02
Belarus, partnership and co-operation agreement, 11.06, 19.02[n3]
bilateral agreements, 13.05
  concurrent competences, 13.12
  recent agreements, 13.13
branches, 10.07
Brazil
  co-operation agreement, 11.05
  free trade agreement, 11.04
Brussels Agreement
  derogation powers, 2.10
  direct applicability, 2.08, 2.10
Bulgaria, co-operation agreement, 11.05

Cambodia, bilateral agreement, 13.13
Canada, action plans, 14.04
Central America, co-operation agreements, 11.05
Central Europe, 11.13
  association agreements, 11.06
Charter of Paris for the New Europe, 19.03
chemicals, safety, 1.16
Chile
  development agreement, 7.10, 11.13
  partnership agreement, 11.07
China
  co-operation agreement, 11.05
  free trade agreement, 11.04
co-operation
  agreements, 11.01, 11.05
    developing countries, 11.06
    direct applicability, 17.06
    Euro-Mediterranean agreements, 11.12
    human rights clauses, 11.10
    legality, 11.16, 11.18
  EC Treaty, 8.05, 8.08
  Maastricht Treaty, 8.07
  national and EC authorities *see* duty of co-operation
  Single European Act, 8.07
  Treaty of Amsterdam, 19.11
Co-operation Council with Russia, 19.03, 19.04
commodity funds, 7.02
common commercial policy, 4.03–06
  Amsterdam Treaty, 18.02–03
  ancillary provisions, 13.04
  and OECD national treatment rule, 4.10
  EC Treaty, 8.04, 12.02, 12.04

common commercial policy—*cont.*
  express external powers, 11.03
  post 1994 developments, 10.11
  scope, 4.13, 8.13
    after Opinion 1/94, 10.01–11
    agriculture, 10.04
    autonomous measures, 10.05
    ECJ approach, 10.02–09
    goods, 10.03, 11.14
    intellectual property, 10.09, 11.08
    services, 9.01, 10.07, 11.08
    transport, 10.08
    Treaty of Amsterdam, 7.06
Common Fisheries Policy, 6.02, 12.04
Common Foreign and Security Policy, 13.01, 14.02
  Commission participation, 19.07
  common strategies *see* common strategies
  European Parliament participation, 19.07
  jurisdiction over decisions, 3.01
  principles, PCA with Russia, 19.01, 19.03
  respect for fundamental rights, 5.03
common rules
  contradiction with proposed agreements, 12.10
  doctrine, 12.05–14
  effect on, 12.10
  non exhaustive, shared competence, 12.20
  source of exclusive external competence, 4.08, 4.11, 8.20
    repeal of rules, 12.11
common strategies
  Amsterdam Treaty, 19.12
  implementation, 19.09–11
  preparation, 19.06
  supremacy, 19.08
  TEU provision, 19.06
  with Russia, 19.01
    introduction, 19.05
    non-proliferation and disarmament, 19.09
    supremacy, 19.08
competence *see* external competence
competition
  clauses
    interim agreements, 11.17
    partnership agreements, 11.15
  international agreements, 8.06
complementary principle, 8.13
  AETR, 8.20
  alternative principle, 8.21–23
  ECJ approach, 8.17, 8.18, 8.19
  internal provisions, 8.16, 8.17
  Kramer, 1.09–11, 8.02
  open provisions, 8.16
  Opinion 1/76, 1.12–15
  Opinion 2/91, 1.17
  versus parallelism, 8.13–16

Conference on Security and Co-operation
    in Europe, 19.03
constitutionality
    actions of EC institutions, 3.01–06
    Community powers, 8.01
Convention against Torture, 5.11[n72]
Convention No 170, 1.16
    Community competence, 1.16, 8.13
    mixed agreement, 13.05
Convention of Luxembourg, 1.15
Convention of Mannheim, 1.15
COREPER, 6.03, 6.05, 6.06, 6.07
    constitutional position, 6.08, 6.13
    mixed agreement procedure, 15.08
    reviewability of actions, 6.08
Council of Europe, EC Treaty obligations,
    8.05
Council of Ministers
    negotiation of international agreements,
        8.09
        voting rules, 8.09
    role, 14.06–07
counterfeit goods, 10.09
credit institutions, authorisation, 8.15
crime prevention
    Common Action for Russian Federation,
        19.09
    PCA with Russia, 19.04[n30]
criminal procedure, preliminary rulings,
    5.15
culture
    external competence, 12.02
    Maastricht Treaty, 8.07
Cyprus, association agreement, 11.03,
    11.11
Czechoslovakia
    co-operation agreement, 11.05
    trade agreement, 11.05

decision-making bodies, 18.05, 18.06
Declaration on Democracy, 5.03
Demirel, 2.11–12, 2.15, 11.09
    application of test, 2.16
    contents of association agreements,
        11.11
    justiciability of international agreements,
        17.06
democracy, 5.14
    and development agreements, 7.10
    Declaration on Democracy, 5.03
    PCA with Russia, 19.03
developing countries
    association agreements, 11.12
    co-operation agreements, 11.06
    definition, 11.13
development agreements, 7.01–11
    agriculture, 7.07
    commodity funds, 7.02
    Community competence, 7.01
    concurrent competences, 13.14
    democracy, 7.10
    double taxation, 7.09

development agreements—*cont.*
    environment, 7.07
    fishing, 7.07
    foreign policy, 7.10, 11.10
    gender issues, 7.02, 7.08, 7.09
    health, 7.09
    human rights
        Mexico, 7.05
        suspension clauses, 7.03, 7.04, 11.09
    India *see* **India**
    investment policies, 7.09
    mining, 7.07
    Mongolia, 11.06[n30]
    population policies, 7.09
    public administration, 7.10
    scientific and technical matters, 7.07
    shared competence, 7.02, 11.13, 12.17,
        12.18–19
    tariff reductions, 7.02
    training, 7.09
    transport, 7.07
development aid, 3.01–06
    EU competence, 3.04, 3.05
development policies
    Community approach, 7.11
    concurrent powers, 11.13
    external competence, 12.02
        general law-making provisions, 12.15
    legality, 11.13
    Maastricht Treaty, 7.02, 8.07, 11.06,
        12.18
    monetary policy, 7.09
    procedure, 8.10
    refugees, 7.10
    role of women, 7.02, 7.08, 7.09
    validity of legislation, 7.03
    whether reviewable, 7.04
discrimination, Treaty of Amsterdam, 5.13
dispute resolution
    GATS, 13.09
    PCA with Russia, 19.03
    TRIPS, 13.09
    WTO agreement, 4.02, 13.08
double taxation, development agreements,
    7.09
drugs
    abuse, development policies, 7.07
    trafficking, PCA with Russia, 19.04[n30],
        19.09
duty of co-operation, 16.01–07
    art 10, 1.08
    ECJ approach, 9.06
    FAO Opinion, 6.11, 6.14
    flexibility, 16.01
        individual international organisations,
            16.06
        most suitable models, 16.03–04
    implementation of international
        agreements, 4.01
    law and policy, 16.01
    mixed agreements, 13.14, 16.02
    mutual co-operation, 16.04

duty of co-operation—*cont.*
  nature of obligation, 15.02, 15.03–06
  obligation of loyalty, 6.12
  partial exclusivity, 1.21
  procedure, 15.07–09
    treaty changes, 16.05
  WTO
    code of conduct, 15.10
    Opinion, 4.12, 12.21, 16.03
    procedure, 16.06

Eastern Europe, association agreements,
    11.06
EC Treaty
  conferment of powers, 8.01
  exclusive competence provisions, 12.04
  external competence provisions, 8.04,
    8.05, 12.02
    after Treaty of Amsterdam, 18.07
    extension provisions, 8.08
    fragmentation, 8.07
    procedural and substantive, 8.06
  international co-operation, 8.05
  interpretation, 17.17
  separation of powers, 17.17
education, external competence, 12.02
effet utile, 8.20
  AETR, 1.07–08, 8.03
  Kramer, 1.10, 8.02
  Opinion 1/76, 1.13
EFTA
  association agreements, 11.06
  free trade agreements, 11.04, 11.17
embargoes, 10.08, 13.13
emergency humanitarian funding, 7.02
environment
  concurrent competences, 13.14
  development treaties, 7.07
  external competence, 12.02
    general law-making provisions, 12.15
  international co-operation, 8.07, 8.08,
    8.10
establishment, 10.07
estoppel, international law, 6.09[n53]
EU Charter of Fundamental Rights, 5.16
EU Commission
  absolutist approach, 9.02
  actions outside treaty powers, 3.03
  challenges by European Parliament, 3.05
  differences with Council, mixed
    agreements, 13.13
  negotiation of international agreements,
    8.05, 8.09
  participation in CFSP, 19.07
  reviewability of actions, 3.04
EU institutions, constitutional position,
    6.13
EU law, supremacy, 8.19, 8.20
  exclusive external competence, 12.05,
    12.10
Euratom products
  common commercial policy, 10.03
  trade, 9.03

Euro-Mediterranean Agreements, 11.06,
    11.12
Europe Agreements, 11.06, 11.11, 11.12
European Bank for Reconstruction and
    Reconstruction, 13.03
European Coal and Steel Community
  demise of Treaty, 10.03
  products, 10.09, 10.10
    common commercial policy, 10.03
    trade, 9.03
European Convention on Human Rights
  compatibility with EC Treaty, 5.05
  compliance, 5.02
  EU accession, 5.01–16
    competence, 5.06, 11.09
    constitutional reasoning, 5.10–12
    lack of consensus, 5.13, 5.16
    Opinion, 5.05–06
  protocols, 5.04
European Court of Justice
  jurisdiction
    Association Agreement Council, 2.15
    constitutionality of actions of EC
      institutions, 3.05
    effect of international agreements,
      2.02, 2.11
    FAO voting rights, 6.07–09
    GATT protocols, 2.11
    international agreements, 2.02, 2.12,
      2.24, 17.02–04, 17.09
    member state/Community powers,
      4.09
    OECD Opinion, 4.09
    Title IV, 5.14
    Title VI, 5.15
    TRIPs Agreement, 2.22
    WTO Agreement, 4.02
  recognition of fundamental rights, 5.02,
    5.07
  references *see* **preliminary rulings**
European Development Fund, 3.01, 3.05
  establishment, 3.05
  member states competence, 14.04
  policy, 7.02
European Economic Area
  Agreement
    direct applicability, 2.21
    Opinion, 5.05
  association agreements, 11.06, 11.11,
    11.12
European Parliament
  challenges of Commission actions, 3.05
  consent to WTO agreement, 15.08
  infringement of powers, 3.02, 3.03, 3.05
  international agreements
    consent, 11.18
    consultation, 8.09
    information, 18.04, 18.06
  recommendations on CFSP, 19.07
  role enhancement, 8.10
  seat, 16.04

European Union
Maastricht Treaty *see* **Treaty on European Union**
pillars, 14.01
pre-accession strategy with CCEE, 14.04
exclusive Community competence
AETR, 1.02–08
ancillary provisions, 13.12
ECJ reluctance, 1.16
effect, 12.16
establishment, 1.04
extension, Amsterdam Treaty, 14.10
fisheries conservation, 1.18, 6.01, 12.04
FAO agreement, 6.07, 6.10
GATS, 4.03–06, 8.14, 9.02, 9.06
grounds, 1.21
justification, 1.15
minimum standards, 12.08
Opinion 1/76, 1.15
Opinion 1/94, 8.17
Opinion 2/91, 1.16, 1.18–19
pre-emptive exclusivity, 1.21, 9.02, 9.05
restriction, 12.02
rules, 4.11
sources, 12.03–16
common rules, 4.08, 4.11, 8.20, 12.05
express internal provisions, 12.12
general law-making provisions, 12.15
internal Community measures, 1.18, 12.05–14
loyalty principle, 12.05, 12.09
naturally arising, 1.10, 1.11, 6.01, 8.17
necessity, 4.13, 8.17, 9.02, 9.05, 12.13, 12.14
treaty provisions, 1.18, 12.04
test, 12.07
TRIPS, 4.03–06, 9.02, 9.05, 9.06
WTO Opinion *see* **WTO agreements**
exclusive economic zones, 6.01
external competence
AETR, 1.03–08, 9.03
Amsterdam Treaty provisions, 18.01–07
ancillary to internal competence, 1.14
and capacity, 1.05–06
and exclusive competence, 1.09
attribution *see* **attribution of external competence**
complementary principle *see* **complementary principle**
concurrent competence *see* **shared competence**
EC Treaty, 8.04, 8.05
after Treaty of Amsterdam, 18.07
procedural and substantive provisions, 8.06
European Convention on Human Rights, accession, 5.05, 5.06
exclusivity *see* **exclusive Community competence**
express and implicit authorisation, 1.20
FAO membership rights, 6.04–13

external competence—*cont.*
general basis, 1.14, 1.20
grounds, 1.20, 8.01
implied *see* **implicit external competence**
incomplete Treaty provisions, 8.01
Kramer, 1.09–11
necessity, 1.17, 8.02, 8.17–18
negotiations by Commission, 8.05
Opinion 1/76 *see* **Opinion 1/76**
potential powers, 9.01
preliminary rulings, competence, 1.16
restrictions, ECJ approach, 9.06
rules, 4.11, 5.10
shared competence *see* **shared competence**
sources, 12.02
implied competence *see* **implicit external competence**
internal competence, 8.17, 9.03
legal basis, 9.07–09
uncertainty, 9.05
WTO Opinion *see* **WTO Opinion**
external trade
Agreement on Technical Barriers to Trade, 10.06, 10.09
exclusive Community competence, 1.18, 4.05, 10.03
export restrictions, 10.11
liberalisation, 9.04, 11.13
negotiating procedure, 8.05, 8.09
practices of third countries, 2.13
WTO agreement, 4.02

FAO
agreement on high sea fishing, 6.01–14
binding commitments, 6.10–12
mixed agreement, 13.08
agreement on the Flagging of Vessels, 6.01, 6.02
exercise of voting rights, 6.01–14
alternatively, 6.04
competence, 6.04
reviewability, 6.07–09
rules, 15.07
purpose of agreement, 12.19
fisheries conservation, 1.09
Common Fisheries Policy, 6.02, 12.04
Community powers, 1.10, 6.10
development treaties, 7.07
exclusive Community competence, 1.18, 6.01, 12.04
FAO agreement, 6.07, 6.10
necessity, 8.17
flags of convenience, 6.01, 6.02, 9.04
high seas, 6.01, 9.04
external competence, 6.10
FAO agreement, 6.05
international agreements, 8.06
straddling fish stocks agreement, 13.03, 13.11
food aid, 7.02
Maastricht Treaty, 8.07

foreign exchange, external competence, 12.02
foreign policy
development agreements, 7.10, 11.10
export restrictions, 10.11
free movement of goods
applicability, 4.05
exclusive Community competence, 9.06
free movement of persons, 5.14, 9.02
association agreement with Turkey, 13.09
free movement of workers, 9.02
free trade agreements, 11.04
direct applicability, 17.06
freedom of establishment, 1.17, 9.02
EC Treaty provisions, 8.14
implicit external competence, 4.07, 8.13, 8.14, 8.15
internal provisions, 8.16
no international dimension, 9.03
freedom of expression, 5.08
freedom to provide services, 1.17, 9.02
abortion, 5.08
EC Treaty provisions, 8.14
implicit external competence, 4.07, 8.13, 8.14, 8.15
internal provisions, 8.16
no international dimensions, 9.03
scope, 10.07
fundamental rights *see* human rights

GATS
categorisation of services, 10.07
dispute settlement, 13.09
implicit external competence, 8.12
international transport, 8.14
objectives, 14.10
whether exclusive Community competence, 4.03–06, 8.14
Commission's approach, 9.02
ECJ approach, 9.06
GATT
Anti-Dumping Code, 2.16
banana market, 2.18, 2.20
direct applicability, 2.01, 2.02, 2.03, 2.11, 17.14
banana market, 2.19
flexibility, 2.14
implementation, 2.05
integration into EU law, 2.05
justiciability, 2.18, 17.13–16
non-reciprocity, 17.15
permissive provisions, 17.13
political instrument, 17.14
principles, PCA with Russia, 19.02
reliance by member states, 2.18
rights of individuals, 2.13
supremacy over EU law, 2.02
Tariff protocols, 2.11
whether exclusive Community competence, 10.01
Gaza, 7.09

gender issues, development agreements, 7.02, 7.08, 7.09
General System of Preferences, 11.04, 11.13
Georgia, partnership agreement, 11.07, 19.02[n3]
good faith principle, 2.21
international law, 17.11
Greece, association agreement, 11.03, 11.04, 11.11
Gulf Co-operation Council, 11.05

Haegeman, 2.04–06, 2.09, 2.12, 2.24
jurisdiction of ECJ, 2.12, 17.03, 17.04, 17.10
health and safety at work, 8.17, 12.08
health, development agreements, 7.09
human rights, 5.02–04 *see also* European Convention on Human Rights; individual rights
breaches
suspension of agreements, 11.09, 18.05
suspension of member states, 5.14
clauses, 7.03–05, 11.09, 13.12, 13.13
interim trade agreements, 11.10
suspension of agreements, 18.05
Community list, 5.12
development policies, 7.03
Mexico, 7.05
subject to human right protection, 7.04
suspension clauses, 7.03
EU Charter of Fundamental Rights, 5.16
EU recognition, 5.06
failure to observe, challengeability of decisions, 7.04
interpretation of Community provisions, 5.03
PCA with Russia, 19.03
political commitment, 5.03
population policies, 7.04
protection in Community, 5.07
objective, 5.10
recognition by ECJ, 5.02, 5.07
scope of Community powers, 5.10
Treaty of Amsterdam, 5.13–16
western concept, 7.05
humanitarian aid, 7.02, 7.04
association agreements, 11.11
concurrent competence, 12.18–19
legality, 11.13
Maastricht Treaty, 8.07
Hungary, co-operation agreement, 11.05

ILO
conventions, 1.19
chemicals at work, 1.16
no Community membership, 13.08
IMF, 14.09

immigration, 5.14, 8.08
clauses, association agreements, 11.08[n44]
implicit external competence, 1.10,
1.12–15, 1.21, 8.12–20
AETR case, 8.03
complementarity *see* **complementarity
principle**
doctrine, 1.20, 8.02
ECJ approach, 9.03
ECJ development, 8.01
scope, 8.08
sources, 8.19–20, 12.02
express powers, 8.03
internal provisions, 8.16
necessity, 12.13
open provisions, 8.16
WTO Opinion, 4.07–08, 9.01–10
India
development agreement, 7.01, 11.05,
11.15
Community competence, 13.13
drug abuse provisions, 7.07
fundamental rights, 7.03, 11.09
intellectual property rights, 7.06
free trade agreement, 11.04
indirect taxation, harmonisation, 8.06
industrial designs, 4.11
inland waterways, 1.12, 4.07
intellectual property rights
concurrent competences, 13.14
India development agreement, 7.06
jurisdiction, 2.22
scope of common commercial policy,
10.01, 10.09, 11.08
Amsterdam Treaty, 18.02
WTO agreement *see* **TRIPS**
interim trade agreements, 11.06
human rights clauses, 11.10
legality, 11.17
internal market, 8.08
implicit external competence, 8.16
internal security, 5.14
international agreements
applicability in EU law, 2.01
binding EU, 2.08, 17.17
Community powers *see* **external
competence**
compliance obligations, 2.13
conflict with EU secondary legislation,
2.24
consistent interpretation, 17.12
credit institutions, authorisation, 8.15
development *see* **development
agreements**
direct applicability, 17.06–07
Ankara Agreement, 2.11, 2.14
Athens Agreement, 2.04, 2.07
Brussels Agreement, 2.08, 2.10
criteria, 2.10
EEC-Morocco Cooperation
Agreement, 2.16
European Economic Area Agreement,
2.21

international agreements—*cont.*
direct applicability—*cont.*
flexibility, 2.10, 2.11, 2.22, 17.07,
17.14, 17.16
GATT, 2.03, 2.11, 2.13, 2.18, 17.07,
17.11, 17.13–16
Anti-Dumping Code, 2.16
banana market, 2.19, 2.20
good faith principle, 2.21, 17.11
lack of legal formalism, 2.10, 2.11,
17.07
legal certainty, 2.12, 2.14, 2.20
Lomé Convention, 2.18, 2.20, 17.07
nature and purpose, 2.24[n153], 17.06
pre-emption, 2.09, 2.19, 17.10
precision and clarity, 17.05, 17.07
reciprocity, 2.23
test, 2.11, 2.12
WTO Agreement, 2.22–23, 17.13–16
Yaoundé Convention, 2.06, 17.07
ECJ jurisdiction, 2.02, 2.12, 2.24,
17.02–04, 17.09
FAO *see* **FAO**
implementation, 17.01–18
integration into EU law, 2.04, 2.08,
2.14, 2.15
legislative acts, 17.10
rights of individuals, 2.13, 2.17
rights of states and individuals, 2.09
judicial applicability, 2.03
jurisdiction
and justiciability, 17.08–12
reception into Community law, 17.03
justiciability *see* **justiciability**
primacy over secondary EU legislation,
2.01, 2.02, 17.03, 17.12
procedure, 8.05, 8.09
Treaty of Amsterdam, 18.04–06
provisional application, 18.04
purpose, 5.05
recognition *see* **recognition of
international agreements**
signing, 18.04
suspension, 8.10, 18.05
breach of human rights, 11.09, 18.05
types of agreements, 11.01
international co-operation *see* **co-operation**
**International Covenant on Economic,
Social and Cultural Rights,** 5.11[n72]
International Fruit, 2.02–04, 2.10, 2.11,
17.03, 17.18
international organisations
EC relations with, 8.05
joint participation of EC/member states,
15.01–11
interpretation
compliance with fundamental rights,
5.03
consistency with international
obligations, 17.12
investigation powers, 5.07, 5.08

investment
multilateral agreement on investment,
14.03, 14.08
policies, development treaties, 7.09
Israel
association agreement, 11.04, 11.17
Euro-Mediterranean Agreement, 11.06
mixed protocol, 11.04

Jordan, Euro-Mediterranean Agreement,
11.06
judicial review
international law grounds, 17.03
protection of fundamental rights, 5.07
reviewable decisions, 6.08
development policies, 7.04
EC Commission actions, 3.04
exercise of external relations, 2.01,
2.09, 2.12, 2.24
failure to observe human rights, 7.04
international agreements, 17.10
legal effects, 6.07–09
precondition, 6.09
substance of decisions, 7.04
justiciability
GATT provisions, 2.14, 2.18, 17.13–16
international agreements, 2.10, 2.12,
17.01
application into Community law,
17.05–07
clarity and precision, 17.05
consistent interpretation, 17.12
direct applicability, 17.06, 17.07
good faith, 17.11
jurisdiction and justiciability,
17.08–12
justifications, 17.16
law and policy, 17.13, 17.15, 17.16
purpose of agreements, 17.06
test, 2.24, 17.06
legal certainty, 2.12, 2.14, 2.15, 2.20,
2.24
multilateral agreements, 17.15
WTO agreements, 17.13–16, 17.18

**Kazakhstan, partnership and co-operation
agreement,** 11.06, 19.02n3
Korea, partnership agreement, 11.07,
11.15
Kramer, 1.09–11
complementary principle, 8.02
necessity, 8.17
effect utile, 1.10, 8.02
**Kyrgystan, partnership and co-operation
agreement,** 11.06, 19.02n3

Laos, bilateral agreement, 13.13
**Lebanon, reservation from UN Convention
on Drugs,** 13.07
legal capacity, Community, 1.05
international law, 8.01n2, 8.22

legal personality, Community, 1.05, 8.22
international law, 8.01n2
legitimate expectations, 2.21, 17.11
liberty, 5.14
Lomé Conventions, 11.11, 14.04
direct applicability, 2.18, 2.20, 17.07
First Convention, 11.04
Fourth Convention, suspension clause,
13.07
obligations, 3.05
loyalty
obligation, 15.02
duty of co-operation, 6.12
source of exclusive external competence,
12.05, 12.09

Maastricht Treaty *see* **Treaty on European
Union**
Macedonia
bilateral agreement, 13.13
partnership agreement, 11.07
Madrid Agreement, 13.03
Maghreb, association agreements, 11.04,
11.12
Malta, association agreement, 11.03,
11.11
Mediterranean agreements, 11.04, 11.06
aid, 11.12
member states
competence
development aid, 3.06
European Development Fund, 14.04
exercise, 14.08
GATS and TRIPS, 4.03
human rights clauses, 11.09
compliance with international
agreements, 2.08, 17.09
concurrent competence *see* **shared
competence**
exercise of non-exclusive competence,
15.01
WTO agreements, 16.03
hidden agendas, 9.01
joint participation in international
organisations, 15.01–11
shared competence *see* **shared
competence**
suspension for breach of fundamental
rights, 5.14
transfer of sovereignty, 12.02, 12.15
transitional competence, 1.11
treaty-making powers, 1.03
Mercosur, partnership agreements, 11.06,
11.13, 13.13
Mexico
free trade agreement, 11.04
interim agreement, 11.13, 11.17
partnership agreement, 11.07, 11.09,
11.14
transport, 11.15
mining, development treaties, 7.07

mixed agreements, 1.21, 9.01, 9.02
  Amsterdam Treaty, 19.11
  application, 13.08–11
  association agreements, 11.03
    southern Mediterranean states, 11.04
  bilateral and multilateral, 13.05
  cases, 13.02
  classification, 13.03–05
  co-existence competence, 13.03, 13.11
  commencement, 13.06
  concept, 13.01
  conclusion, 13.06
  concurrent competence, 13.03, 13.04,
    13.11
  Council's role, 14.07
  development, 7.02
  differences between Commission and
    Council, 13.13
  direct effect, 13.10
  duty of co-operation *see* **duty of co-**
    operation
  Euro-Mediterranean Agreements, 11.06
  forms of mixity, 15.02
    classic/real mixity, 15.02
    facultative mixity, 13.04
    false mixity, 13.04, 15.02
    obligatory mixity, 13.04
    quasi mixity, 15.02
  horizontal distribution of competences,
    13.03
  implementation, 13.08–11
  judicial control, 13.09
  Lomé Convention, 11.04
  PCA with Russia, 19.02
  problems, 13.06–11, 13.14, 18.02
  procedure, 16.05
  relevance, 13.02
    increasing numbers, 13.02
  reservations, 13.07
  suspension, 13.06, 13.07
  termination, 13.06
  vertical distribution of competences,
    13.03
  withdrawals, 13.06
  WTO agreements, 9.07
    dispute settlement, 13.08
Moldova, partnership and co-operation
  agreement, 11.06, 19.02[n3]
monetary policy
  development agreements, 7.09
  external competence, 12.02, 14.02
  Maastricht Treaty, 8.07
  shared competence, 12.17
money laundering, 7.07
  PCA with Russia, 19.09
Mongolia, development agreement,
  11.06[n30]
Morocco
  association agreement, 11.03
  Cooperation Agreement, 2.16
  Euro-Mediterranean Agreement, 11.06

most favoured nation status, 11.04
  development agreements, 11.13
  partnership agreements, 11.14
  Russia, 11.16
multilateral agreement on investment,
  14.03, 14.08
multilateral agreements, 13.05
  justiciability, 17.15, 17.16

NGOs, 7.02
  challenges of development policies, 7.04
North-East Atlantic Fisheries Convention,
  1.09
  competence of member states, 1.11

OECD
  duty of cooperation, procedure, 16.06
  multilateral agreement on investment,
    14.03, 14.08
  no Community membership, 13.08
OECD Opinion, 4.09–12, 12.06
  national treatment rule, 4.09
  necessity, 12.14
Opinion 1/76, 1.12–15, 4.07, 4.13
  effect utile, 1.13
  external competence, 9.04
    complementarity principle, 8.13, 8.19
    necessity, 8.17, 9.04, 12.13
  parallel competence, 12.13
Opinion 1/94, 4.01–08, 6.14
  complementary principle, 8.15, 8.16
  harmonisation of Community rules,
    12.07
  implicit external competence, 8.12, 8.16
    common rules, 12.06
    exclusivity, 8.17, 8.18
  parallelism, 8.13, 8.14
  scope of common commercial policy,
    10.01–11
  shared competence, 16.02
Opinion 2/91, 1.16–19
  complementarity principle, 8.13, 8.17
  minimum standards, 12.08
  obligation of loyalty, 12.09
  parallelism, 8.13
  social policy, 12.07
Opinion 2/92 *see* **OECD Opinion**
Opinion 2/94, 5.01–16, 7.05
  complementarity principle, 8.13, 8.18
  human rights competence, 11.09
  implicit external competence, 8.12
  parallelism, 8.14
  principles of attribution of external
    competence, 8.01
Organisation for Security and Co-
  operation in Europe, 19.03

Pakistan
  bilateral agreement, 13.13
  co-operation agreement, 11.05
  free trade agreement, 11.04

parallel competence, 1.14
  and shared competence, 13.03, 13.04
  Opinion 1/76, 12.13
  responsibility for implementation, 13.10
  versus complementary principle,
    8.13–16
  WTO agreements, 9.02, 9.03
partnership agreements, 11.01, 11.06
  ex-Soviet republics, 14.03
  human rights clauses, 11.09
  legality, 11.14–15, 11.18
partnership and co-operation agreements,
  11.06
  ex-Soviet states, 11.15, 11.16, 19.02[n3]
  Russia, 19.01–04
patents, 4.11
PLO
  agreement, 7.09, 11.13
  bilateral agreement, 13.13
Poland, co-operation agreement, 11.05
population policies, 7.02
  conditions, 7.04
  in development agreements, 7.09
  role of women, 7.09
Portugal v Council, 7.01–11, 11.09, 11.13,
  17.18
  shared competence, development policy,
    12.18
  two-step test, 11.14
Portugal, mixed protocol, 11.04, 11.12
preliminary rulings
  accession to European Convention on
    Human Rights, 5.04
    admissibility of request, 5.05, 5.09
  competence, 1.16
  consideration of international
    agreements, 17.09
  fishing quotas, 1.09
  function, 5.09
  inland waterways vessels, 1.12
  interpretation of mixed agreement,
    13.02
    association agreements, 13.09
  interpretation of Title IV, 5.14
  interpretation of Title VI, 5.15
  procedure, 5.09
  safety of chemicals, 1.16
  WTO Opinion *see* WTO Opinion
Proba 20, 15.07
Prodi, Romano, 19.11[n79]
public health
  external competence, 12.02
  Maastricht Treaty, 8.07
  prohibition of imports, 2.22

qualified majority voting, 10.09
  development agreements, 11.13
  mixed agreements, 16.05

recognition of international agreements,
  17.01, 17.02
  art 234, 17.04
  ECJ rules, 17.03
    uncertainty, 17.04
  monism and dualism, 17.03
  rules, 17.03
  without legislative acts, 17.04
refugees, development policies, 7.10
research
  external competence, 12.02
  international co-operation, 8.07, 8.10
right to fair trial, 5.08
right to respect for private and family life,
  5.07
right to silence, 5.08
Romania
  co-operation agreement, 11.16
  trade agreement, 11.05
rule of law, 5.14
Russia
  Action Plan, 19.10, 19.11
  Common Strategy, 19.01
    implementation, 19.09
    introduction, 19.05
    non-proliferation and disarmament,
      19.09
    supremacy, 19.08
  human rights policy, 19.03
  Partnership and Co-operation
    Agreement, 11.06, 11.07, 19.01–04
    CFSP principles, 19.03
    dispute settlement, 19.03
    flexibility, 19.04
    provisional application, 13.06
  partnership with EU, 19.01–12
    under Amsterdam Treaty, 19.05–11

San Marino
  co-operation agreement, 11.16
    commencement, 13.06
    enlargement protocol, 13.06
    ratification, 13.06
  trade agreement, 11.07
search powers, 5.07
self-incrimination, 5.08
separation of powers
  justiciability of international agreements,
    17.05, 17.17
  under EC Treaty, 17.17
services *see also* GATS
  liberalisation, 18.03
  modes of supply, 4.04, 10.07
  scope of common commercial policy,
    10.01, 10.07, 11.08
    Amsterdam Treaty, 18.02, 18.03
  WTO agreement, 4.02, 4.04–06, 9.01
    external Community powers, 9.02

shared competence, 1.16, 6.10, 9.01,
    12.02, 12.17–21 *see also* mixed
    agreements
  Amsterdam Treaty, 14.09–13
  and parallel competence, 13.03
  co-existent competences, 13.03, 13.04
  concurrent competences, 13.04, 13.14
  development agreements, 7.02, 11.13,
    12.17, 12.18–19
  duty of co-operation *see* duty of co-
    operation
  ECJ jurisdiction, 4.09
  effect, 12.21
  examples, 12.20
  exclusion, 1.08, 1.15
  exercise by Community, 14.08
  FAO agreement, 6.10
  forms, 15.02
  humanitarian aid, 12.18–19
  intellectual property, 7.06
  investment policies, 7.09
  joint actions, 12.19
  meaning, 12.03
  monetary policy, 12.17
  non exhaustive common rules, 12.20
  OECD Opinion, 4.10
  Opinion 2/91, 1.18
  organising joint participation, 15.01–11
  standards, 6.14
Singapore, 11.13
Single European Act
  extension provisions, 8.06
  international co-operation, 8.07
  recognition of fundamental rights, 5.03
Slovenia, partnership agreement, 11.08
SMEs, social protection of workers, 8.16
Social Charter, 5.11[n72]
social dumping, 1.17
social policy, 8.08
  external competence, 8.13, 8.16
  legislative competence, 8.16
  Opinion 2/91, 12.07
social security, 8.16
soft law, 7.09, 13.12
South Africa, trade agreement, 13.14
Soviet Union, co-operation agreement,
    11.05
Spaak, Paul Henry, 15.01, 15.11
Spain, free trade agreement, 11.04
Sri Lanka, free trade agreement, 11.04
standard interim agreements, 11.06
statehood, 6.01
status, international status, 6.01, 6.14
subordinate legislation, 12.07
subsidiarity, 9.09
supremacy of Community law, 8.19, 8.20
  exclusive external competence, 12.05,
    12.10

tariff reductions, 11.04
  development agreements, 7.02

technical aid, 7.02
TEU *see* Treaty on European Union
trade *see* external trade
trade agreements, 11.01–18
  classification, 11.01, 11.18
  Community practice, 11.02–07
    legality, 11.09–17
  effect of Amsterdam Treaty, 11.08
  human rights clauses, 11.09, 11.10
trade embargoes, 10.08, 13.13
trade marks, 4.11
  interpretation of TRIPS, 13.10
  Madrid Agreement, 13.03
training
  development agreements, 7.09
  external competence, 12.02
  Maastricht Treaty, 8.07
transport
  common policy, 1.08, 1.12, 8.14, 10.08
  development treaties, 7.07
  external competence, 1.02, 8.14
    ECJ approach, 9.03
    exclusivity, 1.08, 4.06, 4.07, 4.08
    necessity, 8.18
  GATS provisions, 8.14
  international agreements, 8.06
  partnership agreements, 11.15
  road transport, 1.02
trapping standards, 8.11
treaties *see* international agreements
Treaty on European Union, 14.01–15
  development co-operation, 7.02, 8.07,
    11.06, 12.18
  Fourth Pillar, 14.01–04
    Council's role, 14.06–07
    legal framework, 14.05–08
  international competence provisions,
    8.07, 8.11, 14.03
  procedure, 8.09
  monetary policy, 8.07
  pillars, 14.01, 14.03, 14.15
  preference for Community competence,
    13.13
  recognition of fundamental rights, 5.03
TRIPS, 4.02
  and common commercial policy, 10.09
  and Treaty of Amsterdam, 18.03
  counterfeit goods, 10.09
  dispute settlement, 13.09
  ECJ jurisdiction, 2.22
  implicit external competence, 8.12
  interpretation, 13.10
  objectives, 4.06, 10.09, 14.10
  whether exclusive Community
    competence, 4.03–06
    Commission's approach, 9.02
    ECJ approach, 9.05, 9.06
Tunisia
  association agreement, 11.03
  Euro-Mediterranean Agreement, 11.06

Turkey, association agreement, 11.03, 11.04, 11.11
interpretation, 13.09
Turkmenistan, partnership agreement, 11.07

Ukraine
common strategies, 19.06, 19.11[n80]
partnership and co-operation agreement, 11.06, 19.02[n3], 19.11[n80]
provisional application, 13.06
UN Conferences on the Law of the Sea, 6.02[n12]
mixed agreement, 13.03
United States
action plans, 14.04
government procurement agreement, 15.01
Uruguay Round, 4.02, 9.01, 9.02
co-operation procedure, 16.06
legal basis for external competence, 9.07–09
Uruguay, free trade agreement, 11.04
Uzbekistan, 19.02[n3]
partnership agreement, 11.07

Vietnam, bilateral agreement, 13.13
visas, 5.14, 8.08
voting rights, exercise in FAO, 6.01–13

West Bank, 7.09
women
population policies, 7.09
role in development policies, 7.02, 7.08, 7.09

WTO agreements, 1.17, 4.02
agriculture, 10.04
common commercial policy, 4.04–06, 10.01–11
consent of European Parliament, 15.08
direct applicability, 2.22–23
dispute settlement, 4.02, 13.08
duty of cooperation, 4.12, 12.21
code of conduct, 15.10
procedure, 16.06
implicit Community powers, 4.07–08, 9.01–10
issues, 4.03
justiciability, 17.13–16, 17.18
mixed agreements, 9.07
services, 4.04–06
SPS Agreement, 2.22
whether exclusive Community competence, 4.02, 4.03, 4.05, 4.06, 8.12
necessity, 8.17, 8.18
WTO Opinion, 4.01–08
approach of the Court, 9.03–06
background, 4.02
Commission's approach, 9.02
duty of co-operation, 16.03
implicit Community powers, 9.01–10

Yaoundé Convention, 2.06, 14.04
direct applicability, 2.06, 17.07
provisions, 11.03
Yemen
bilateral agreement, 13.13
co-operation agreement, 11.05
Yugoslavia
association agreement, 11.12
external competence, 14.02
free trade agreement, 11.04